crafting
modernism

Midcentury American Art and Design

Jeannine Falino

GENERAL EDITOR

Jeannine Falino with Jennifer Scanlan

CURATORS

crafting modernism

Midcentury American Art and Design

WITH ESSAYS BY

GLENN ADAMSON

DONALD ALBRECHT

ELISSA AUTHER

DAVID L. BARQUIST

ULYSSES GRANT DIETZ

PATRICIA FAILING

JEANNINE FALINO

CAROLINE M. HANNAH

URSULA ILSE-NEUMAN

BRUCE METCALF

JENNIFER SCANLAN

LOWERY STOKES SIMS

ABRAMS, NEW YORK

IN ASSOCIATION WITH

museum of arts and design

THIS BOOK IS PUBLISHED ON THE OCCASION OF THE EXHIBITION

Crafting Modernism: Midcentury American Art and Design
VOLUME 4 OF THE HISTORY OF TWENTIETH-CENTURY AMERICAN CRAFT

MUSEUM OF ARTS AND DESIGN, NEW YORK, NEW YORK
OCTOBER 11, 2011–JANUARY 15, 2012

MEMORIAL ART GALLERY, ROCHESTER, NEW YORK
FEBRUARY 27–MAY 21, 2012

Crafting Modernism: Midcentury American Art and Design is made possible
in part through the generosity of the National Endowment for the Arts;
the Henry Luce Foundation; and the Center for Craft, Creativity and
Design. Major support for the exhibition catalogue has been provided by
the Windgate Charitable Foundation.

ART WORKS.
arts.gov

FRONTISPIECE, CAT. 1
**Irving Harper, designer for
George Nelson and Associates
Schiffer Prints Division; Mil-Art
Co., Inc., manufacturer, *China
Shop*, c. 1953. Printed cotton.
62½ x 52½ in. (158.8 x 133.4
cm). Metropolitan Museum of
Art, New York, Gift of Geoffrey
N. Bradfield, 1995; 1995.355.**

RIGHT
**John Mason working on *Blue
Wall* in the Glendale studio,
1959. Courtesy of John Mason.**

FRONT COVER
See page 83 (cat. 62)

BACK COVER
See page 69 (cat. 43)

ABRAMS HARDCOVER EDITION
**BINDING CASE: (Front) see page
72 (cat. 49); (back) see page
222 (cat. 172). ENDPAPERS:
Exhibition catalogue covers from
the last several decades, which
were produced by the Museum
of Contemporary Crafts (MCC)
and/or the American Craftsman's
Council (ACC).**

CONTENTS

Works of art in this exhibition are numerically ordered
in this catalogue and are listed in boldface in the index.
Regarding dimensions, height precedes width and depth, or
diameter, wherever possible. A Reader's Guide, providing
abbreviations (some of which are used in the essay endnotes)
and a list of shortened references, is located on page 266.

CONTRIBUTORS

GLENN ADAMSON is deputy head of research and head of graduate studies at the Victoria and Albert Museum, London (V&A). He leads a graduate program in the history of design, collaboratively offered by the V&A and the Royal College of Art. Dr. Adamson is co-editor (with Tanya Harrod and Edward S. Cooke Jr.) of the triannual *Journal of Modern Craft.* He is a frequent contributor to museum catalogues and to such journals as *Crafts* and *American Craft.* His other publications include *Thinking Through Craft* (2007), *The Craft Reader* (2010), *Industrial Strength Design: How Brooks Stevens Shaped Your World* (2003), and, with Gary Michael Dault, David Dorenbaum, and Gord Peteran, *Gord Peteran: Furniture Meets Its Maker* (2008). Adamson also maintains a blog titled "From Sketch to Product" on the V&A website and is presently curating an exhibition of postmodernism, to be held at the V&A in 2011.

DONALD ALBRECHT is Curator of Architecture and Design at the Museum of the City of New York (MCNY) and an independent curator. He has been curator and catalogue author, *The Mythic City: Photographs of New York by Samuel H. Gottscho, 1925–1940* (MCNY, 2005) and *The High Style of Dorothy Draper* (MCNY, 2006); co-curator and co-author, *Cars, Culture and the City* (MCNY, 2010); curator and catalogue editor, *Paris/NewYork: Design Fashion Culture, 1925–1940* (MCNY, 2008) and *The Work of Charles and Ray Eames* (Library of Congress and Vitra Design Museum, 1997); and curator and catalogue co-editor, *Eero Saarinen: Shaping the Future* (Finnish Cultural Institute, the Museum of Finnish Architecture, National Building Museum, with support of Yale University School of Architecture, 2006).

ELISSA AUTHER is associate professor of contemporary art at the University of Colorado at Colorado Springs. Her book, *String, Felt, Thread: The Hierarchy of Art and Craft in American Art* (2010), focuses on the broad use of fiber in American art of the 1960s and '70s and the changing hierarchical relationship between art and craft expressed by the medium's new visibility. She has also written on a range of subjects: the art criticism of Clement Greenberg, the history of "the decorative," the use of yarn and other types of fiber in feminist antiwar activism, artist-produced wallpapers, and the contemporary film installations of Isaac Julien. In addition, she co-directs Feminism & Co.: Art, Sex, Politics, a public program at the Museum of Contemporary Art Denver that focuses on issues of women and gender through creative practice. She is currently at work on *The Countercultural Experiment: Consciousness and Encounters at the Edge of Art,* an exhibition and catalogue scheduled for 2011, which investigates the diverse visual and material culture of the American counterculture of the 1960s and '70s.

DAVID L. BARQUIST is the H. Richard Dietrich, Jr., Curator of American Decorative Arts at the Philadelphia Museum of Art. He served for twenty-three years as assistant, associate, and acting curator of American decorative arts at the Yale University Art Gallery. His 1992 publication *American Tables and Looking Glasses in the Mabel Brady Garvan and Other Collections at Yale University* received the 1993 Charles F. Montgomery Prize from the Decorative Arts Society for "the most distinguished contribution to the study of American decorative arts." Barquist is the author of *Myer Myers: Jewish Silversmith in Colonial New York* (2001), which accompanied a traveling exhibition of the same title. With Carol Borchert Cadou, he co-curated another traveling exhibition, *Setting the President's Table: American Presidential China from the Robert L. McNeil, Jr., Collection at the Philadelphia Museum of Art* (2008–9), and contributed "Presidents and Porcelain: 'To Fix the Taste of Our Country Properly'" to a parallel publication titled *American Presidential China: The Robert L. McNeil, Jr., Collection at the Philadelphia Museum of Art* (2008).

ULYSSES GRANT DIETZ has been the curator of decorative arts at the Newark Museum since 1980, responsible for more than one hundred exhibitions. He conducted a major study of the Newark Museum's 1885 Ballantine House (a twenty-seven-room brick mansion), which reinterpreted this building that was restored as the centerpiece of the decorative arts department in 1994 with the installation "House & Home." Dietz was project director for *The Glitter & The Gold: Fashioning America's Jewelry* (1997), an exhibition and book on Newark's once-vast jewelry industry. He also curated *Great Pots: Contemporary Ceramics from Function to Fantasy* (2003) and *Masterpieces of Art Pottery, 1880–1930* (2008) and wrote the accompanying catalogues. Dietz is co-author of *Dream House: The White House as an American Home* (2009).

PATRICIA FAILING is a visual arts writer and professor of art history at the University of Washington, Seattle, where she teaches modern and contemporary art and art criticism. Other research areas include legal and ethical issues in the visual arts and the sculpture of Edgar Degas. She has written many articles for *Art News, American Craft, Sculpture Review* and *Journal of Aesthetics and Art Criticism,* among others, and is the author of *Howard Kottler: Face to Face* (1995).

JEANNINE FALINO, Museum of Arts and Design (MAD) curator, was formerly the Carolyn and Peter Lynch Curator of Decorative Arts and Sculpture, Art of the Americas, Museum of Fine Arts, Boston. She has lectured and written extensively on American decorative arts from the colonial period to the present, with a focus on the colonial period, the Arts and Crafts era, and twentieth-century craft and design. She recently served as co-editor and lead author of *Silver of the Americas, Museum of Fine Arts, Boston,* vol. 3 (2008); guest co-curator, *Artistic Luxury: Fabergé—Tiffany—Lalique* (Cleveland Museum of Art, 2008); curator, *Edge of the Sublime: Enamels by Jamie Bennett* (Fuller Craft Museum, Brockton, MA, 2008); co-editor, *American Luxury: Jewels from the House of Tiffany* (2008); and contributor, *Craft in America: Celebrating Two Centuries of Artists and Objects* (2007). She is also the author of *Shaped by the Revolution: Portraits of a Boston Family—Speakman, Rowe, Inman, Linzee, Coffin, and Amory* (2005).

CAROLINE M. HANNAH is a design historian and writer, and a PhD candidate at the Bard Graduate Center: Decorative Arts, Design History, Material Culture. Her dissertation "Henry Varnum Poor: Crow House, Craft, and Design" has received support from The Metropolitan Museum of Art, New York (Jane and Morgan Whitney Predoctoral Fellow); the Smithsonian Institution, Washington, DC (James R. Renwick Predoctoral Fellow in American Craft); the Center for Craft, Creativity, and Design, Hendersonville, NC (Craft Research Fund grant); and the Bard Graduate Center (academic and writing fellowships). She has also served as acting assistant curator of American decorative arts at the Yale University Art Gallery.

URSULA ILSE-NEUMAN joined the Museum of Arts and Design (MAD) in 1992 and is presently curator of jewelry. She has curated more than thirty exhibitions in all media and has written extensively on jewelry in the museum's collection: *Inspired Jewelry* (2009), *Glass Wear: Glass in Contemporary Jewelry* (2007), and *Zero Karat: Jewelry from the Donna Schneier Collection* (2002). She was co-author for *Corporal Identity: Body Language, 9th Triennial for Form and Content, USA and Germany* (2003), held in collaboration with the Museum of Applied Arts in Frankfurt, Germany. Her forthcoming exhibitions at MAD are *Light, Space, Structure: The Jewelry of Margaret De Patta* (2012) and *Multiple Exposures: Jewelry and Photography* (2013). She has lectured widely in the U.S., Europe, and Asia and is curator of the American section of *Abhushan: Design Dialogues in Jewelry* (2011), organized by the World Crafts Council in New Delhi, India.

BRUCE METCALF is a studio jeweler and writer from the Philadelphia area. He received a BFA from Syracuse University in 1971 and an MFA from Tyler School of Art in 1977. Since then he has taught at Kent State University, the University of the Arts in Philadelphia, and several other schools. He has written extensively about issues in contemporary craft in numerous domestic and foreign publications, and is co-author with Janet Koplos of *Makers: A History of American Studio Craft* (2010). Metcalf's own jewelry designs, sculpture, and drawings have also been widely seen in national and international exhibitions over the past forty years. A retrospective exhibition, *The Miniature Worlds of Bruce Metcalf* (Palo Alto Cultural Center, 2008), toured the U.S. (2008–10).

JENNIFER SCANLAN is associate curator at the Museum of Arts and Design (MAD), where she has organized many exhibitions, including *Eat Drink Art Design* (2010); *Cheers! A MAD Collection of Goblets* (2008); *Why? 25 Case Studies* (2006); and *Paul Stankard: A Floating World—Forty Years of an American Master in Glass* (2004). Recent publications include "Joseph Cavalieri" in *Neues Glas/New Glass* (2010). She was also co-author of the exhibition catalogue *Radical Lace and Subversive Knitting* (2006); and contributed "Paul Stankard: An American Master in Glass" to *SOFA NY* (2004) and "Illuminating Vision: Light in Abstract Glass Sculpture" to *Dual Vision* (2005). Scanlan has lectured internationally at the Conference of the International Committee of Design History and Design Studies (Brussels, Belgium, 2010); Taiwan Craft Research and Development Institute (Taichung, Taiwan, 2009); Association for the Study of Jewelry and Related Arts (New York, 2007); and the Glass Art Society Conference (Adelaide, Australia, 2005). She has a BA in art history and Italian from Vassar College, Poughkeepsie, New York, and an MA in the history of decorative arts, design, and culture from the Bard Graduate Center, New York. She has also taught at the Courtauld Institute of Art Summer School in London, England, and is an instructor in the Historic Preservation Program at Drew University, Madison, New Jersey.

LOWERY STOKES SIMS is the Charles Bronfman International Curator at the Museum of Arts and Design. Sims co-curated the inaugural exhibition, *Second Lives*, for MAD's 2008 reopening at New York's Columbus Circle. In 2010 she organized the museum's venue for the traveling exhibition *Bigger Better More: The Art of Viola Frey*, co-curated *Dead or Alive,* and curated *The Global Africa Project.* A specialist in modern and contemporary art, Sims is known for her expertise in the work of African, Latino, Native, and Asian American artists. She served as executive director, president, and adjunct curator for the permanent collection at the Studio Museum in Harlem (2000–2007). While on the education and curatorial staff of The Metropolitan Museum of Art (1972–99), she organized many exhibitions, including retrospectives of the work of Stuart Davis (1991) and Richard Pousette-Dart

(1997). Sims has lectured and guest-curated exhibitions nationally and internationally. She was a fellow at the Clark Art Institute (spring 2007); visiting professor at Queens College and Hunter College in New York City (2005–7); and visiting scholar in the department of art at the University of Minnesota, Twin Cities (fall 2007). Sims is on the board of ArtTable, Inc., the Tiffany Foundation, and Art Matters, Inc.

TARA LEIGH TAPPERT is an independent scholar, an archivist, and American art consultant. Through Tappert and Associates, she provides research, writing, and collections management services to arts and cultural organizations as well as private clients. Her scholarly focus is on late nineteenth- and early twentieth-century American art and culture and twentieth-century American craft history. She is the author of "Out of the Background: Cecilia Beaux and the Art of Portraiture" (1994; published online, 2009) and has written the Resource Lists, containing biographies and institutional histories, for MAD's three previous volumes on the history of twentieth-century American craft. She is currently investigating the ways in which the U.S. military embraced arts and crafts—in World War I as rehabilitation for healing and vocational training and in World War II as recreation to promote well-being and efficacy—with funding from the Center for Craft, Creativity & Design, Hendersonville, NC.

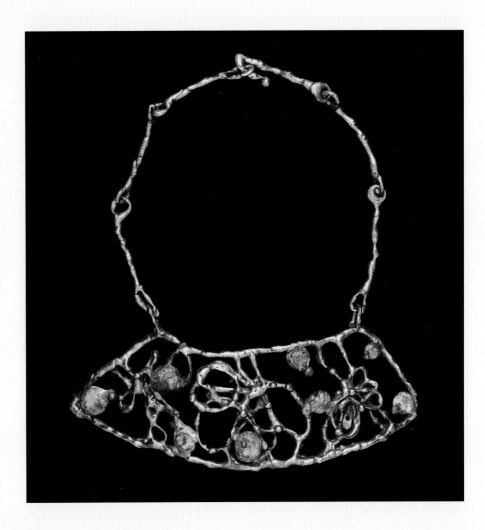

CAT. 2
Ibram Lassaw, *Untitled (Necklace)***, c. 1950. Bronze. 6⅛ x 1¹⁵⁄₁₆ in. (15.5 x 5 cm). Collection of Ernestine Lassaw, East Hampton, New York.**

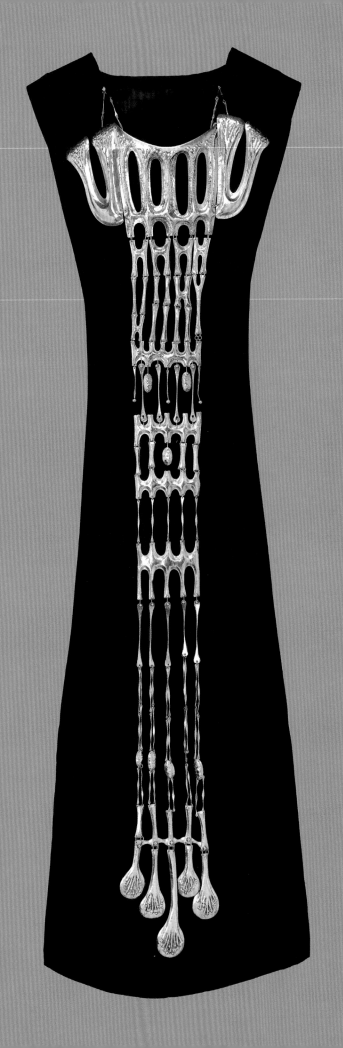

Museum of Arts and Design
BOARD OF TRUSTEES

3
ARLINE M. FISCH
Body Ornament, 1966
STERLING SILVER, SYNTHETIC CREPE, AND SILK
FRONT: 45 X 12¼ IN. (114.3 X 31.1 CM);
BACK: 41 X 4½ IN. (104.1 X 11.4 CM);
VESTMENT: 53 X 15½ IN. (134.6 X 39.4 CM)
MUSEUM OF ARTS AND DESIGN,
GIFT OF THE JOHNSON WAX COMPANY, THROUGH
THE AMERICAN CRAFT COUNCIL, 1977

ACKNOWLEDGMENTS

Crafting Modernism: Midcentury American Art and Design is the fourth in a series of exhibitions, catalogues, and conferences titled the Centenary Project. Originally funded by the National Endowment for the Arts, Rockefeller Foundation, and Lila Wallace–Reader's Digest Fund, the Centenary Project was conceived by Janet Kardon, former director of the Museum, as the first in-depth examination of twentieth-century American craft. The first three acclaimed exhibitions—*The Ideal Home*; *Revivals! Diverse Traditions*; and *Craft in the Machine Age*—took place between 1993 and 1995. Plans for a fourth exhibition, focusing on the important post–World War II era, were suspended when scholars agreed that more time and perspective were needed before the topic was ready for presentation. The project was renewed in 2008, allowing us to present this important exhibition at our new location at 2 Columbus Circle. The 2011 exhibition has benefited from the guidance, support, and thoughtful contributions of an exceptional number of people.

In difficult economic times, we are profoundly grateful to the institutions, foundations, and individuals whose financial support made this project possible. The Centenary Project, including *Crafting Modernism*, was made possible at the outset by a major grant from the Lila Wallace–Readers' Digest Fund. Additional support for *Crafting Modernism* was provided by National Endowment for the Arts, the Henry Luce Foundation, and the Center for Craft, Creativity and Design. Major support for the exhibition catalogue was provided by the Windgate Charitable Foundation.

At the Museum, Director Holly Hotchner and Chief Curator David McFadden provided essential leadership for this project at the institutional level. Their dedication to the project over a number of years and their willingness to commit institutional resources to develop a major scholarly exhibition have ensured a legacy for the Museum as the first to present a comprehensive review of midcentury studio craft and design. We are also grateful for the support of MAD's board of trustees, many of whom are passionately committed to the importance of the project and this exhibition in particular.

For insight into such a wide-ranging topic, we called on a group of scholars whose diverse perspectives were particularly helpful in establishing a broad and balanced approach. Advisors who generously offered their time and feedback at various stages of the project included: Glenn Adamson; Donald Albrecht; Garth Clark and Mark Del Vecchio, Clark + Del Vecchio; Edward S. Cooke, Yale University; Arthur Danto, Columbia University; Diane Douglas, Seattle City Club; Janet Kardon; Pat Kirkham and Catherine Whalen, Bard Graduate Center: Decorative Arts, Design History, Material Culture; Gerhardt Knodel; Mark Leach, Southeastern Center for Contemporary Art; Bruce Metcalf; Jane Milosch, Smithsonian Institution; Michael Monroe; Derek Ostergard; Suzanne Ramljak, *Metalsmith* magazine; and Tara Tappert.

The catalogue is greatly enriched by the knowledgeable contributions of our essayists: Glenn Adamson; Donald Albrecht; Elissa Author; David Barquist; Ulysses Grant Dietz; Patricia Failing; Caroline Hannah; Ursula Ilse-Neuman; Bruce Metcalf, and Lowery Stokes Sims; Tara Tappert was lead author for the Artist Resource List. Our wise editor, Martina D'Alton, handled our lengthy manuscript with good humor, grace, and wit. We would also like to thank our publisher, Harry N. Abrams, Inc., for support of the catalogue from the beginning, and especially Senior Editor Andrea Danese, Managing Editor David Blatty, Designer Sarah Gifford, and Editorial Assistant Caitlin Kenney, for their dedication to creating a beautiful and lasting publication.

An exhibition and catalogue of this scope calls for a project manager of exceptional organizational talents. Assistant Curator Nurit Einik not only capably managed administrative and myriad other details, but she contributed her wide-ranging skills in everything from spreadsheets to graphic design, enhancing the project at every level. During the course of the project, we were fortunate to have the talented staff of the Museum of Arts and Design, including: John D'Ambrosio, Marisa Bartolucci, Dorothy Globus, Ellen Holdorf, Willow Holdorf, Judith Kamien, Cathleen Lewis, Josh Lucas-Falk, Brian McElhose, Molly McFadden, Brian MacFarland, Jane Ro, Robert Salemo, and Jake Yuzna. Keelin Burrows and Osanna Urbay were involved in early stages of this project. We would also like to single out Ursula Ilse-Neuman and Derek Ostergard, along with Ursula's assistants Jessica Nicewarner and Sarah Archer, whose early work on the exhibition laid fundamental groundwork. Wendy Evans Joseph, designer, and Chris Good, project manager, of Cooper Joseph Studio, created a rich and handsome setting for the varied objects in this exhibition.

To those private collectors who generously opened their doors to us, many of whom wish to remain anonymous, we are especially grateful for the opportunity to examine rare treasures. And to the museum curators, registrars, and collections managers at sister institutions around the country who kindly set aside time in their schedules to discuss and share their collections, guide us in our search, and lend their prized works, we offer heartfelt thanks. Among the many who assisted in our efforts, we wish to recognize David Barquist, Elizabeth Agro, Kathryn Hiesinger, and Shanon Schuler, Philadelphia Museum of Art; Margaret Bullock, Tacoma Art Museum; Timothy Anglin Burgard, Elizabeth Cornu, and Stephen Correll, Fine Arts Museums of San Francisco; Ashley Callahan, Georgia Museum of Fine Art; Christina Burke, Philbrook Museum of Art; Simona and Jerry Chazen; David Park Curry and Brittany Emens, Baltimore Museum of Art; Cheri Falkenstien-Doyle, Wheelwright Museum of the American Indian; Jamie Franklin, Bennington Museum; Catherine Futter, Nelson-Atkins Museum; Mary Douglas, Kamm Teapot Foundation; Barbara Haskell and Sasha Nicholas, Whitney Museum of American Art; Helen A. Harrison, Pollock-Krasner House and Study Center; Stephen Harrison, Cleveland Museum of Art; Rebecca R. Hart, The Detroit Institute of Arts; Barry Harwood, Brooklyn Museum; Eunice Haugen, Goldstein Museum of Design, University of Minnesota; Peter Held, Ceramics Research Center, Arizona State University; Sandford Hirsch and Nancy Litwin, The Adolph & Esther Gottlieb Foundation, Inc.; Patricia Kane and John Stuart Gordon, Yale University Art Gallery; Susan Kowalczyk, Schein-Joseph International Museum of Ceramic Art; Juliet Kinchin, Aidan O'Connor, and Paul Galloway, Museum of Modern Art; Matthew Kirsch, The Noguchi Museum; Kelly L'Ecuyer, Lauren Whitley and Emily Zilber, Museum of Fine Arts, Boston; Leah Levy, the Jay deFeo Estate; Kristin Makholm, Minnesota Museum of American Art; Mary McNaughton and Kirk Delman, Ruth Chandler Williamson Gallery, Scripps College; Forrest L. Merrill; Julie Muñiz, Oakland Museum of California; Tina Oldknow, Corning Museum of Glass; Diana Pardue, The Heard Museum; Sue Ann Robinson, Long Beach Museum; Debora Ryan, Everson Museum of Art; Judy Sourakli, Henry Art Gallery, University of Washington; Bobbye Tigerman, Los Angeles County Museum of Art; Rebecca Tilghman, Metropolitan Museum of Art; Kevin Tucker, Dallas Museum of Art; Jill A. Wiltse and H. Kirk Brown III; John Zarobell, San Francisco Museum of Modern Art.

Additionally we are exceptionally grateful to a number of people who offered valuable assistance, resources, and counsel, greatly benefiting both the exhibition and catalogue. These included: Soomi Hahn Amagasu, George Nakashima Woodworker, S.A.; Mary Barringer, editor, *Studio Potter*; Dick Boak, C.F. Martin & Co; Judith Burton, Columbia University Teachers College; Jan Brooks and Lane Coulter; Ralph Caplan; Tripp Carpenter; Margaret Carney, The Blair Museum of Lithophanes; Dane Cloutier; Harry Cooper, National Gallery of Art; Barbara Cowles; Helen Drutt; Kathryn Dudley, Yale University; Anna Fariello, Western Carolina University; Grant Feichtmeir; David Fine; Judith Hoos Fox, curatorsquared; Suzanne Frantz; Andrea Gill, John Gill, and Mary McInnes, New York State College of Ceramics, Alfred University; Jenny M. Gill; Andrew Glasgow; Dale Gluckman; Deborah Goldberg; Toni Greenbaum; David Hanks; Mary Hu and

Patty Warashina, Washington University; Bernard Jazzar; Christy Johnson, American Museum of Ceramic Art; Stuart Kestenbaum, Haystack Mountain School of Craft; Eric King; Shelly Langdale, Philadelphia Museum of Art; Jo Lauria; Stanley Lechtzin, Tyler School of Art, Temple University; Melissa Leventon, Curatrix Group; Barbara Lovenheim, NYCityWoman.com; Tom Loeser, University of Wisconsin–Madison; Kate Lydon, Society for Contemporary Craft, Pittsburgh; Patricia Malarcher and Willy Malarcher; Rod McCormick, Sharon Church, William P. Daley, Jim Makins, and Warren Seelig, University of the Arts, Philadelphia; Lucia de Respinis, Nicholas Fasciano, Irving Harper, Hilda Longinotti, Tomoko Miho, Lance Wyman, and Tony Zamora, George Nelson & Associates; Hal Nelson, The Huntington Library; Judith Nicolaidis; Arthur Ollman and Todd Partridge, San Diego State University; Kevin Pearson, The Prairie School; Dianne Pierce, Manitoga, The Russel Wright Design Center; Rago Arts and Auction Center; Bryna Pomp; Ramona Sakiestewa; Alan Rosenberg; Sidney Rosoff; Beverly Sanders, *American Craft Magazine*; Jewel Stern; Kenneth Trapp; Wendy van Deusen, LongHouse Reserve; Namita Gupta Wiggers, Museum of Contemporary Craft, Portland; Karen Zukowski and David Diamond.

In the marketplace, we have been guided by seasoned dealers with specialties in midcentury furnishings, jewelry, and fine art, and we extend our gratitude to Robert Aibel, Moderne Gallery; Bif Brigman; Stephen Cadwalader, Jason McCoy, Inc.; Julie Schafler Dale, Julie's Artisans Gallery; Kenneth Dukoff, The Dukoff Collection; James Elkind, Lost City Arts; Steve Elmore, Steve Elmore Indian Art; Jed Faust, Shiprock Gallery; Andrea Fisher, Andrea Fisher Gallery; Titi Halle, Cora Ginsberg; David Hampton, Objects USA; Mike Holmes and Elizabeth Shypertt, Velvet da Vinci; halley k harrisburg and Michael Rosenfeld, Michael Rosenfeld Gallery; Emily-Jane Kirwan and Ken Fernandez, Pace Gallery; Peter and Shannon Loughrey, Los Angeles Modern Auctions; David Martin, Martin-Zambito Fine Art; Gerard O'Brien, Reform Gallery; Jane Sauer, Jane Sauer Gallery; Marcie Burns, Marcie Burns American Indian Arts; Marbeth Schon, M. Schon Modern; Anita Shapolsky, Anita Shapolsky Gallery; Jeffrey Spahn; Shannon Trimble, Braunstein/Quay Gallery; Larry Weinberg, Weinberg Modern; Matt Umanov, Matt Umanov Guitars; Richard Wright, Wright Auctions, and James Zemaitis, Sotheby's.

Research for the exhibition has been graciously aided by librarians and archivists at a host of institutions. We owe a great debt of thanks to the staff at the Archives of American Art, Smithsonian Institution, and to the artists and interviewers who took part in the oral histories supported by Nanette Laitman, the Museum's former president of the board of trustees, who provided critical funding for the Nanette L. Laitman Documentation Project for Craft and Decorative Arts in America at the Smithsonian. The interviews, now available online, have provided key primary source material for this exhibition. We offer special thanks to Gail Bardhan, Rakow Library, Corning Museum of Glass; Terri Boesel, SC Johnson; Elizabeth Broman, Cooper-Hewitt National Design Library; Elizabeth Cameron,

Paley Studios, Ltd; Tara Cuthbert, Brooklyn Museum; Elizabeth Gulacsy, New York State College of Ceramics at Alfred University; Marga Hirsch, Park Avenue Synagogue, New York; David Shuford, American Craft Council; and Tricia Tinling, Wendell Castle Studio, for their valuable research assistance.

For the many artists and their families who have opened their hearts and homes to us, in person, and via telephone and email, we have the deepest gratitude. These artists include Ruth Asawa, Bernard Bernstein, Jim Blashfield, Fong Chow, Domenic Di Mare, Michael Jerry, Vladimir Kagan, John Kapel, Brent Kington, Bonnie MacLean, Rex Mason, merry renk, John Paul Miller, Eudorah Moore, Jack and Kathryn Risley, Jens Risom, Dick Seeger, June Schwarcz, Ruth Strick, Rick Turner, and Kore Yoors. Those artists, collectors, and curators who agreed to be interviewed for this catalogue showed great patience in bringing their oral history to the printed page: Wendell Castle, Betty Cooke, Willis "Bing" Davis, Jack Lenor Larsen, Forrest L. Merrill, Joel Philip Myers, Kay Sekimachi, and Paul Smith. In the course of preparing for this exhibition, we have lost five artists: Margret Craver, Sam Maloof, Paul Soldner, Toshiko Takaezu, and Susan Peterson, all of whom devoted their lives to their chosen endeavors—the first two were early pioneers in their respective fields of metal and wood, and the latter were exemplary ceramists.

Paul Smith, Director Emeritus of the Museum of Arts and Design, deserves special recognition for his contributions to this volume. As an employee of the Museum from its beginnings, and director from 1963 until 1987, Paul possesses unsurpassed knowledge of the craft world in the timeframe covered by this exhibition. His careful attention to detail, vast archives, dedication to accuracy, and commitment to recording the important history of this period was absolutely essential to both the exhibition and the catalogue.

We are always grateful to our interns and volunteers, who give freely of their time and contribute their wide-ranging skills with energy and enthusiasm. Many helped with research and organization, including: Genevieve Cortinovis, Fenna Mandalong, Maxine Ferencz, Elaine Harris, Kimberly Kelly, Shane Kline, Randy Mauer, Ann Peel, Paulette Pitman, Katie Positerry, Katherine Reis, Jennifer Shaifer, Kaitlin Shinnick, Olivia Sholler, Alex Smith, Stephanie Strass, Nava Sutter, Randi Teague, and Gayle Weiss. Others conducted research and provided entries for the Resource List in this volume, including Natalie Balthrop, Louisa Bann, Sarah Froelich, Jeanne Gardner, Carolyn Kelly, Monique Long, Bella Neyman, Maile Pingel, Jane Port, Lindsey Rossi, Michele Sala, and Catherine Zusy.

Exhibitions of this size and scope are years in the making, and we are indebted to a vast network of individuals around the country who have offered assistance in ways both large and small. On the home front, however, where exhibition demands supplanted dinner hours and relaxing weekends, we are indebted to the unstinting

support of our loved ones, David Heath, Morgan Heath, and Brandon Seekins.

Finally, we would like to dedicate this exhibition and catalogue to Aileen Osborn Webb, whose vision and unflagging support led to the founding of the Museum of Arts and Design, and in no small measure to the birth of the studio craft movement itself. Her dedication nurtured generations of artists and designers who chose to work with craft materials, and infused countless lives with an appreciation of the creative spirit.

Jeannine Falino and Jennifer Scanlan

IT IS WITH GREAT PRIDE THAT WE PRESENT *CRAFTING Modernism: Midcentury American Art and Design,* an exhibition that has been long in the making. It represents the fourth installment in a series of exhibitions we have called the History of Twentieth-Century American Craft: The Centenary Project, initiated by my predecessor Janet Kardon. *Crafting Modernism* covers the period from 1945 to 1969, an especially meaningful time for our own Museum, which was founded in 1956 and played an active role in advancing the importance of the handmade object in the postwar era.

In planning this exhibition, it became clear that the Museum's mission today is still closely linked to the early years of our history. The Museum—first named the Museum of Contemporary Crafts (MCC) and later the American Craft Museum (ACM)—became the Museum of Arts and Design in 2002, a name chosen to reflect new definitions of "craft" as now encompassing a range of practices and disciplines, some of the most interesting of these defying strict categorization. *Craftsmanship in a Changing World* (1956), the first exhibition shown at the newly founded MCC, demonstrated this ecumenical vision by featuring a range of works that incorporated craftsmanship, from the mass produced to the unique object, from a cocktail shaker by Paul Evans to printed fabrics by Eszter Haraszty for Knoll and sculpture by Harry Bertoia.

Craftsmanship in a Changing World fell right in the middle of the period covered in *Crafting Modernism,* when the world of craft, art, and design certainly was changing. In the period immediately after World War II, the crafted object, and the process of making things by hand, became an invigorating counterbalance to wartime experiences and privations, the homogeneity of mass-production, and the creeping alienation of suburban and corporate life. Early in the period, these objects were strictly functional, made in independent studio settings as well as integrated into the factory, with designer-craftsmen serving as a bridge between the hand and machine.

As the movement began to define itself, through the founding of organizations, school programs, publications, and especially the establishment of the American Craft Council and the MCC, the interest in craft broadened. Students and professors in craft programs at art schools began to experiment with the artistic potential of craft materials. Concurrent with an interest in materiality and new materials in the modern art world, the focus of the craft movement shifted toward making unique works of art, as demonstrated in the MCC's groundbreaking exhibition, *Objects: USA* (1969–70), which closes the era covered by *Crafting Modernism.* While functional objects, particularly furniture and jewelry, were among the works featured in that exhibition, many artists chose craft materials to create sculptural works. These developments had the effect of blurring the boundaries between craft, design, and the so-called fine arts, which the Museum has sought to investigate ever since.

The crafted object has a renewed resonance in today's global society. In our technological age, the handmade has once again become an important expression of individuality. Global communities are finding ways to revive traditional handcrafts in new designs, providing economic support as well as creative outlets to developing countries. Human beings are still fascinated by the process of making, and at the Museum of Arts and Design, we continue to celebrate their creativity in our galleries, artists studios, programs, and website. As a museum focused on the contemporary expression of art, we are certain that the future will move in unexpected ways, and we look forward to documenting the innovations of the next generations. At the same time, we welcome the opportunity to look carefully at the past, and build upon the passion and commitment of those who have gone before.

CAT. 4
Alexander Calder, *Hanging Spider*, c. 1940. Painted sheet metal and wire. Overall: 49½ x 35½ in. (125.7 x 90.2 cm). Whitney Museum of American Art, Mrs. John B. Putnam Bequest, 84.41.

Holly Hotchner
Nanette L. Laitman Director
Museum of Arts and Design

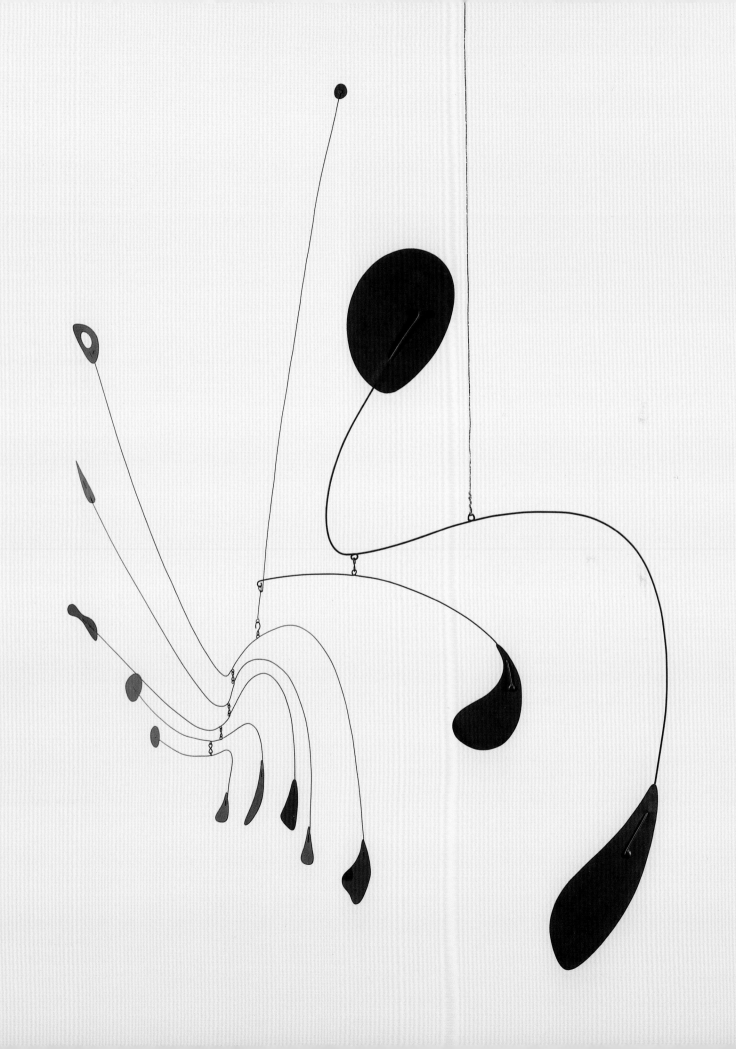

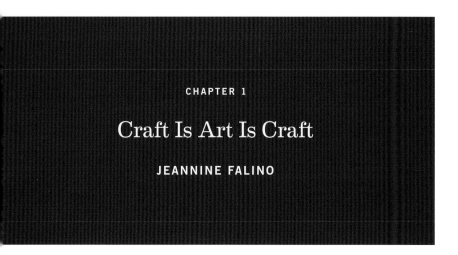

CHAPTER 1

Craft Is Art Is Craft

JEANNINE FALINO

CRAFTING MODERNISM: MIDCENTURY AMERICAN ART and Design is the first exhibition to trace the rise of the handcrafted object in the postwar era, defined here as 1945 to 1969, which had wide-ranging ramifications in the fields of fine art and design.

The most significant development explored in this exhibition is the arrival of the crafted object as an aspect of modern art. Long subservient to an artificial hierarchy of the arts that had been established in the Renaissance, the handmade object underwent a paradigm shift in the postwar period to become an assertive form of artistic expression. Artists working in craft media found affirmation in the creations of Alexander Calder and Isamu Noguchi, who roamed freely across media and disciplines without regard for superficial divisions. The new status of craft was not widely acknowledged by the fine arts world, a situation still true today, but the altered relationship was nevertheless made plain by those artists who appropriated craft-based materials and techniques into aspects of postwar art, and by craftspeople whose work addressed process, form, and content.[1]

Today the studio craft movement is a vital aspect of the world art scene, supported by innumerable galleries, periodicals, conferences, fairs, and collectors—a far cry from its scattered, isolated origins in the postwar era. Its emergence is indebted to the developments sketched out in this exhibition and catalogue: the artists who took their materials and techniques to new frontiers, the entrepreneurs who opened the first galleries, and the individuals who collectively worked, discussed, educated, and

organized their field into a regional, national, and ultimately international presence.

Several factors contributed to these developments. The chief catalyst for change was Aileen Osborn Webb, a philanthropist of great vision and energy. Webb was responsible for conceiving and setting in motion a range of organizational "firsts" that supported craftspeople and promoted the crafted object. She began taking steps as early as 1940, when she opened America House, the first gallery to showcase contemporary handcrafted work made in this country, and founded the American Craft Council to serve artists working in craft media. She established the School for American Craftsmen, the first modern educational facility in this country dedicated to the field. Webb also created *Craft Horizons* magazine (today's *American Craft*) as a means of sharing new work by artists in America and around the globe and founded the Museum of Contemporary Crafts (later American Craft Museum and today the Museum of Arts and Design), the first museum in the United States to feature craft media by living artists. Webb's last great contribution was the World Crafts Council, an idealistic organization formed in 1964 whose mission was to provide support for indigenous craftspeople around the world. In less than twenty-five years of sustained effort, Webb's many-faceted enterprises spawned countless related activities at the state and local level, as well as national organizations that formed to support specific craft media—the Society of North American Goldsmiths being just one example.

Webb's School for American Craftsmen, originally founded to educate returning veterans, was among the many schools of higher education fueled by the Servicemen's Readjustment Act of 1944, better known as the GI Bill, which assured a college education for American servicemen. The GI Bill set a high-water mark in the history of higher education, bringing a rising tide of students to American universities. It caused the rapid creation or expansion of craft-based programs which shifted craft from its factory- and apprentice-based origins into the academic realm where students encountered contemporary artistic trends and theories.[2] The GI Bill also provided veterans with stipends that enabled them to choose their educational path independent of parental support.[3]

Greater numbers of students meant an increase in educators as well. The arts benefited from the experience of recent émigrés from Europe, such as ceramists

Frans and Marguerite Wildenhain and the painter Josef Albers and his wife, weaver Anni Albers. They brought a modernist perspective shaped by the Bauhaus, the avantgarde German school whose objective was to unify art, craft, and industry. Other teachers came with traditional training, among them School for American Craftsmen professors John Prip and Tage Frid of Denmark, highly skilled journeymen in their respective areas of metalsmithing and woodworking.

The GI Bill had further advantages as white-collar work became a reality for many graduates, who were often the first in their family to receive a college degree. Education brought middle-class life within reach for many Americans, along with home ownership, spurring the growth of suburban developments throughout the United States and the commensurate furnishings they required, both manufactured and handmade.

The end of the war and the returning servicemen meant a restoration to normalcy. The myriad wartime fears and privations that had weighed upon many Americans began to recede. Peace brought with it a newfound freedom of spirit which sometimes crystallized in a countercultural critique of the establishment and a search for purpose in a world that was increasingly dominated by the bureaucratic machinations of business and government. Some resisted the need to conform, whether in a material sense as homeowners in modern suburbia, or in the standardized behavior and dress expected of corporate employees. These topics were addressed in books like Sloan Wilson's *Man in the Gray Flannel Suit* and David Riesman's *Lonely Crowd*.[4] It was a world that was focused on the efficient management of workers to the detriment of the individual's creativity and the increasing, if empty, consumption of factory products.

The choice of a crafts lifestyle was attractive to many who were concerned with these societal issues. Some chose self-employment, seeing small-scale production work as a means to a self-sufficient lifestyle. Phillip Lloyd Powell and Paul Evans were two such craftsmen who worked independently and often collaboratively, first fashioning simple wood and pewter accessories and eventually producing complex furniture installations and sculpture as their clientele grew. Other craftspeople chose teaching careers as schools continued to swell in size throughout the 1960s. A further option was to team with industry, where the term *designer-craftsman* was coined to describe artists who created objects with mass-

CAT. 5

Isamu Noguchi, designer; Ozeki Lanterns Co. Ltd., manufacturer, *Akari 820 lamp*, 1951–52. Mino washi paper, bamboo, metal, and electric cord. 23 x 17 in. (58.4 x 43.2 cm). Noguchi Museum, New York.

production capabilities. In most cases, the career choices were less a romanticized rejection of industrial society than a determination to direct their own lives through such choices. As ceramist Robert Turner recalled, "Many . . . saw this [the life of a craftsperson] as a simple, humbler approach to finding a life which had meaning," and according to ceramist James McKinnell, a "sense of control over one's destiny."[5]

Industrial design had emerged as a separate profession earlier in the century, and in the 1950s many designers employed a reductive and spare approach to furnishings to match the international style then prevalent in architecture. Nonetheless, the popularity of the craft aesthetic prompted some to employ it as a defining feature of manufactured goods, thereby providing a humanized

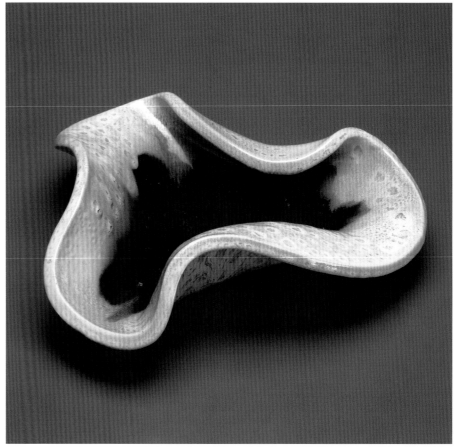

modernism more attractive to consumers. Ceramics and textiles yielded particularly effective results from this approach, as seen in Russel Wright's thickly glazed Bauer ceramics and Jack Lenor Larsen's textiles that softened the geometry of corporate interiors. In furniture, Ray Eames borrowed from the sculptural aspects of African art to create her jaunty stool for the lobby of the Time-Life Building, and Ed Wormley incorporated ceramics by Otto and Gertrud Natzler into the dressers and tables he designed for Dunbar. *An Exhibition for Modern Living* (1949) held at the Detroit Institute of Arts, MoMA's Good Design series, and the *Designer Craftsmen U.S.A. 1953* exhibition held at the Brooklyn Museum are the best-known of the many shows that demonstrated the fluidity between the two fields, as functional works made by hand and by machine were shown side by side.[6]

The potential of new materials and techniques became a powerful attraction for some artists. Glass, the last of the traditional craft media to receive renewed attention in this period, burst upon the scene in the early 1960s with the concerted efforts of Dominick Labino and Harvey Littleton. Many others, such as Dale Chihuly, followed, energized by the possibilities of hot glass and soon putting it to new and experimental ends. Meanwhile,

FIG. 1.1
Dick Seeger, Wall divider, 1968. From *Monsanto Magazine* (March 1968), cover image. Courtesy Monsanto Corp.

CAT. 6
Russel Wright, designer; Bauer Pottery Company, manufacturer, *Centerpiece Bowl*, 1946. Porcelain. 4½ x 14 in. (11.4 x 35.6 cm). Collection of Dennis Mykytyn.

Tom Lynn tackled aluminum casting, and Ruth and Toza Radakovich, Ted Hallman, Jan de Swart, and Dick Seeger embraced the promise of plastics **(FIG. 1.1)**. Others mined historic techniques to modern ends, as in the case of Margret Craver, who adapted a sixteenth-century enameling technique called *en résille* for her own purposes, and John Paul Miller, who adorned his enameled jewelry with the first examples of granulation made in this country after a long hiatus.

The 1950s and '60s offered myriad opportunities for cultural and technical growth, fostered by the new convenience of air travel. The Fulbright International Exchange Program allowed artists to study abroad. Jeweler Arline Fisch, for example, attended the Kunsthaandvaerkerskolen in Denmark to further her studies in metalsmithing, and Robert Sowers went to the United Kingdom to work in stained glass, while Ross Littell and Niels Diffrient traveled to Italy and Douglas Kelley to Germany for work in industrial design. Fiber artists Ed Rossbach and his wife Katherine Westphal were among the many academics who scheduled international travel during summers and sabbaticals. Independent studio artists also expanded their work through travel. The peripatetic young Sheila Hicks was powerfully influenced by her early experiments in fiber while in Mexico, Peru, and India **(FIG. 1.2)**. Ceramists Warren and Alix MacKenzie spent several years in England apprenticing with Bernard Leach and later arranged for his tour of the United States with Japanese ceramist Shoji Hamada and Japanese *mingei* (folk art) advocate Soetsu Yanagi. Travel for the World Crafts Council, formed in New York in 1964, created another wave of Americans who went abroad, many of them for the first time, to conferences in Montreaux, Switzerland (1966), and Lima, Peru (1968).

The outside world also came to the United States through publications and exhibitions. *Craft Horizons* featured the work of folk craftspeople and internationally ranked artists from abroad and reviewed exhibitions at MoMA of Japanese ceramics by Kitaoji Rosanjin and liturgical vestments by Henri Matisse, while foreign magazines such as *Domus, Abitare,* and *Graphis* brought the latest thinking on European architecture and design to American doorsteps. The widespread influence of

FIG. 1.2

Sheila Hicks weaving on back-strap loom in Oaxaca, Mexico, 1960. Photograph collection of Faith Stern.

CAT. 7

Gertrud Natzler, ceramist; Otto Natzler, ceramist; Edward Wormley, designer; Dunbar Furniture Company, manufacturer, *Table*, c. 1957. Wood and glazed ceramic tile. 23¾ x 11¼ x 11¼ in. (60.3 x 28.6 x 28.6 cm). Forrest L. Merrill Collection.

Scandinavian design had begun in the 1920s when the Danish silversmithing firm Georg Jensen opened its first New York showroom. By midcentury, New York galleries were devoted to the genre, and exhibitions such as *Design in Scandinavia* circulated in 1954 by the Societies of Arts and Crafts and Industrial Design of Denmark, Finland, Norway and Sweden, to twenty-two museums in the United States, and *The Arts of Denmark: Viking to Modern* (The Metropolitan Museum of Art, 1960) only increased its visibility. The Long Island–based firm Dansk traded on the American attraction to the organic design and truth-to-materials characteristic of Nordic crafts with a successful line of household products that was entirely Danish in origin.

At home, Native American artists began to make their own unique contributions to the field. Alaskan Inupiat Ron Senungetuk and Hopi artists Charles and Otellie Loloma attended the School for American Craftsmen, blending their cultural perspectives with a newly acquired modernist sensibility **(CAT. 8)**. Lloyd

Kiva New, of Cherokee and Scottish/Irish heritage and a graduate of the Art Institute of Chicago, moved from textile design to early leadership in the southwestern crafts movement (CAT. 9). New established the Institute for American Indian Arts to enable young Native American artists to create truly modern art based upon their tribal roots.

American advancements in craft had an effect beyond the nation's borders. Americans began to participate in international exhibitions, such as the Milan Triennale, the Lausanne International Tapestry Biennale, and ceramics exhibitions held in various locations by the International Academy of Ceramics. A special installation of craft, which included a modernist beverage server by Arthur Pulos, was shown in the American Pavilion of the 1958 Brussels International Exhibition (FIG. 1.3).

Other Americans traveled abroad to make their contributions in craft. Cranbrook graduate Robert Stearns worked at Venini Glass in Murano in 1960, thanks to a fellowship from the Italian government and a Fulbright grant. His designs, carried out by Venini glassblowers, briefly received the Gold Medal for Glass in the Venice Biennale of 1962, until it was learned he was American.[7] Glass artist Sam Herman, a student of Harvey Littleton, traveled to the Edinburgh College of Art on a Fulbright in 1966. Herman stayed in Scotland and spent much of his career teaching in the United Kingdom, establishing its first independent glass workshop; he is credited with single-handedly introducing hot-glass

CAT. 8

Charles Loloma, *Untitled (Bracelet)*, 1968. Sterling silver, turquoise, ivory, ebony, and coral. 1½ x 2⅝ x 2 in. (3.8 x 6.7 x 5.1 cm). Museum of Arts and Design, Gift of the Johnson Wax Company, through the American Craft Council, 1977.

FIG. 1.3

Arthur Pulos, *Beverage Server and Cover*, 1956. Silver and ebony. 9½ x 5½ x 7½ in. (24.1 x 14.0 x 19.1 cm). Art Institute of Chicago, Restricted gift of Marilyn and Thomas L. Karsten in honor of her parents, Gertrude and Perry S. Herst; 1985.513.

techniques to students there.[8] Sheila Hicks moved to Paris in 1967 and began to fulfill large corporate commissions that introduced new concepts in fiber arts to a wide audience. This rich combination of talented artists, educational programs, international art forums, and a large, diverse student body set the stage for a profusion of activity across all craft media.

In the two decades following World War II, abstract expressionism, surrealism, and pop art proved particularly attractive art movements for craft artists who began to explore the purely formal properties of production. Abstract expressionist approaches to painting were adapted to ceramics by Peter Voulkos, who was the first ceramist to cut ties with functionalism by making vessels of unprecedented scale and vitality, revealing a commitment to process. He took risks, and his work embodied energy. The seeds of Voulkos's improvisational approach to clay were sown during a 1953 visit to the East Coast, first at Black Mountain College, where he briefly taught that summer, and later in New York City, where he encountered potter and poet M. C. Richards, painters Robert Rauschenberg and Franz Kline, dancer Merce Cunningham, and composer John Cage, among others. All were conversant with the notion of gestalt therapy that encouraged action and process-based behavior, revealing the interaction between the artist and his medium, concepts that soon emerged with great vigor in Voulkos's work and that of many who followed in his wake.[9]

This was a two-way street. Just as Voulkos drew from abstract expressionism, craft media were appropriated by fine arts practitioners. Lucas Samaras, Jasper Johns, Claes Oldenburg, and Rauschenberg, among others, unreservedly wove ceramic, fiber, wood, found objects, and other materials into their work. In so doing, they upended time-honored conventions of painting and sculpture and opened the door to further experimentation. They also followed in the footsteps of Calder and Noguchi, who continuously worked across the functional/nonfunctional divide, blurring concepts of art, craft, and design. These rich examples of artistic cross-fertilization are a special part of *Crafting Modernism*.

As the Civil Rights movement, the Vietnam War, and women's liberation introduced sweeping changes to American society, crafts practitioners began to express cultural identity, artistic innovation, and social commentary in their work. Robert Arneson led the "California Funk" movement, which thumbed its collective nose at the status quo using political and often bawdy humor. Many others were choosing personal expression and the crafts lifestyle as a means of personal rebellion against the homogeneity and mass-production prevalent in American society. Aspiring craftspeople could turn to the *Whole Earth Catalog*, Stewart Brand's manual for independent living, for guidance in making virtually anything.[10] Lastly, with the advent of the late-sixties psychedelic culture, artists turned to fashioning such countercultural goods as pipes for smoking banned substances and otherwise adorning themselves and the objects around them with the melting, curvilinear designs characteristic of poster art from the period.

The creations of these artists, craftspeople, and designers entered the public realm through museum exhibitions and publications, many of them first brought to public attention by the Museum of Contemporary Crafts.

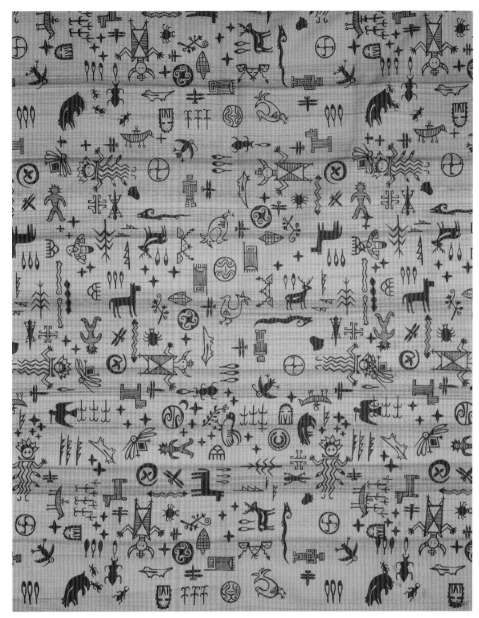

CAT. 9

Lloyd Kiva New, *Dress Fabric*, c. 1960. Hand-screened silk. 35½ x 27¾ in. (90.2 x 70.5 cm). Heard Museum Collection, Phoenix, Arizona, 4422-2.

These new works added to the ongoing dialogue on meaning in American art and life that was shared with poetry, literature, dance, music, and theater. Its continued growth today, combined at last with a rising body of critical literature, is a measure of how far we have come.

Author's Note: Portions of this essay appeared in *Crafting Modernism: Midcentury American Art and Design* by Jeannine Falino and Jennifer Scanlan, SOFA New York 2011 (Chicago: The Art Fair Company, 2011), 18–23.

1   This hierarchical approach continued well into the twentieth century, led by Clement Greenberg's career-long invective against "the decorative." For a fine analysis of Greenberg and others, see Elissa Auther, "The Decorative, Abstraction, and the Hierarchy of Art and Craft in the Art Criticism of Clement Greenberg," *Oxford Art Journal* 27 (December 2004), 339–64.

2   Total college enrollments increased by nearly 21 percent between 1950 and 1960 and nearly 167 percent from 1960 to 1970. Adolph Reed, "A GI Bill for Everybody," *Dissent* 48 (fall 2001), 53–58. Beverly Sanders, "The G.I. Bill and the American Studio Craft Movement," *American Craft* 67 (August/September 2007), 54–62. Further scholarship is needed to quantify the schools and students in craft that benefited from this historic bill.

3   Veterans' stipends were the equivalent of $15,900 in 2009. Reed, 53.

4   Sloan Wilson, *The Man in the Gray Flannel* Suit (New York: Simon and Schuster, 1955); David Riesman, *The Lonely Crowd: A Study of the Changing American Character* (New Haven: Yale University Press, 1950). See also Paul Goodman, *Growing Up Absurd: Problems of Youth in the Organized Society* (New York: Vintage Books, 1960), who lamented that efficiency was held in higher regard than creativity.

5   Vicki Halpert and Diane Douglas, eds., *Choosing Craft,* *The Artist's Viewpoint* (Chapel Hill, NC: UNC Press, 2009), 14–15.

6   See the Selected Bibliography in this volume for a survey of exhibitions during this period.

7   Thomas Stearns, "The Facades of Venice: Recollections of My Residency in Venice, 1960–1962," in William Warmus, *The Venetians, Modern Glass 1919–1990* (New York: Muriel Karasik Gallery, 1989), 63–68.

8   Tanya Harrod, *The Crafts in Britain in the 20th Century* (New Haven: Published for the Bard Graduate Center for Studies in the Decorative Arts by Yale University Press, 1999).

9   See Daniel Belgrad, *The Culture of Spontaneity, Improvisation and the Arts in Postwar America* (Chicago and London: University of Chicago Press, 1998), 145–75. M. C. Richards, *Centering in Pottery, Poetry, and the Person* (1962; rev. ed., Middletown, CT: Wesleyan University Press, 1989); this remains an influential book on being an artist and the physical and psychological process of working in a chosen medium.

10 Early issues of the *Whole Earth Catalog* included a chapter devoted to "Industry and Craft."

10

PAUL EVANS

Screen, 1969

STEEL AND COLORED PIGMENTS

72 X 36 X 5 IN. (182.9 X 91.4 X 12.7 CM)

COLLECTION OF DORSEY READING

11

RAMONA SOLBERG

Shaman's Necklace, 1968

STERLING SILVER, ALASKAN IVORY, FOUND OBJECTS

10⅜ X 5⅜ X ¾ IN. (26.4 X 13.7 X 1.9 CM)

MUSEUM OF ARTS AND DESIGN,

GIFT OF THE JOHNSON WAX COMPANY, THROUGH

THE AMERICAN CRAFT COUNCIL, 1977

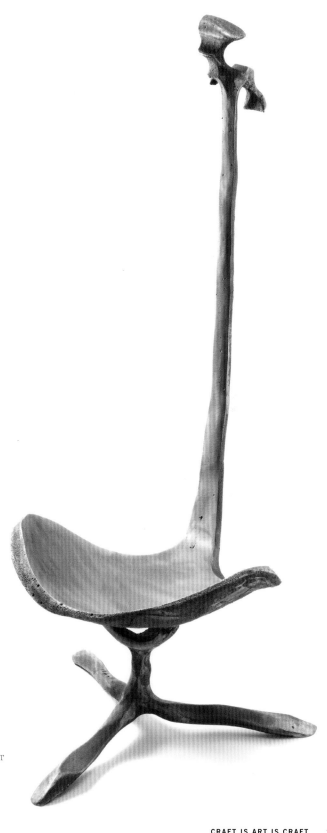

12

THOMAS LYNN

Chair with Back, 1968

ALUMINUM

H. 56½ X 24 X 34 IN. (143.5 X 61 X 86.4 CM)

MINNESOTA MUSEUM OF AMERICAN ART

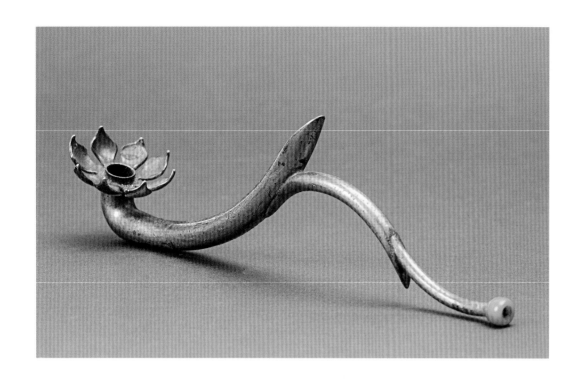

15

ROBERT TURNER

Jar, 1966

STONEWARE

H. 12½ IN. (31.8 CM), DIAM. 12 IN. (30.5 CM)

MUSEUM OF ARTS AND DESIGN, GIFT OF THE ARTIST,
THROUGH THE AMERICAN CRAFT COUNCIL, 1967

16

MARGRET CRAVER

Hair Ornament, 1959

YELLOW GOLD, EN RÉSILLE ENAMEL, AND GOLD FOIL

5¾ X 2⅜ X ⅞ IN. (14.6 X 6 X 2.2 CM)

MUSEUM OF ARTS AND DESIGN, COMMISSIONED BY
THE AMERICAN CRAFT COUNCIL, 1959

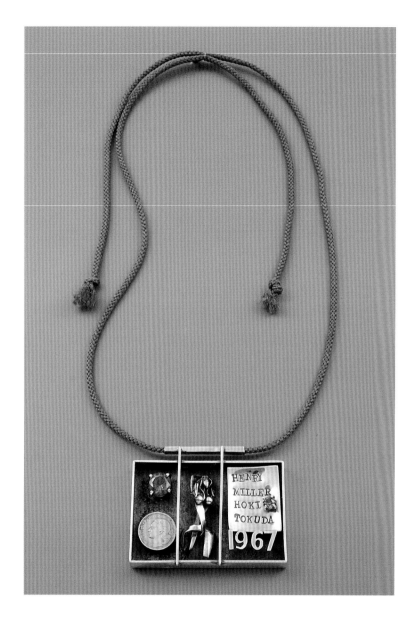

17
DONALD PAUL TOMPKINS
Henry Miller, Hoki Tokuda
(Commemorative Medal Pendant), 1967
STERLING SILVER, COIN, AND SYNTHETIC GEMS
2⅛ X 3⅛ X ⅜ IN. (5.4 X 7.9 X 1 CM)
TACOMA ART MUSEUM, GIFT OF
RUSSELL AND MARJORIE DAY, 2003.52

18
DAVID GILHOOLY
Nero Frog Watching Rome Burn, c. 1968
GLAZED EARTHENWARE
11 IN. (27.9 CM); DIAM. 11¾ IN. (29.8 CM)
MUSEUM OF ARTS AND DESIGN, GIFT OF THE ARTIST,
THROUGH THE AMERICAN CRAFT COUNCIL, 1968

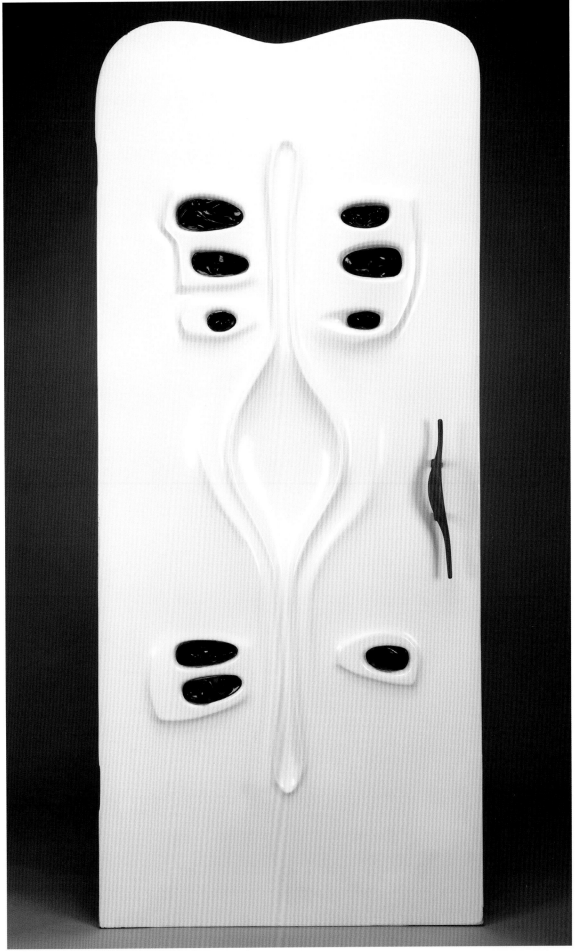

19

RUTH RADAKOVICH

Door, 1969

FIBERGLASS, RESIN, LENSES, AND WOOD

84 X 36 IN. (213.4 X 91.4 CM)

COLLECTION OF THE PRAIRIE SCHOOL,

RACINE, WISCONSIN

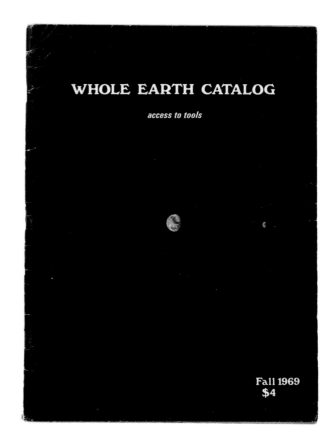

22

ROBERT ARNESON

Self-Portrait of the Artist Losing His Marbles, 1965

EARTHENWARE, LUSTER GLAZE, MARBLES, AND PIGMENTS

31 X 17½ X 9½ IN. (78.7 X 44.5 X 24.1 CM)

MUSEUM OF ARTS AND DESIGN, GIFT OF THE JOHNSON WAX COMPANY,

THROUGH THE AMERICAN CRAFT COUNCIL, 1977

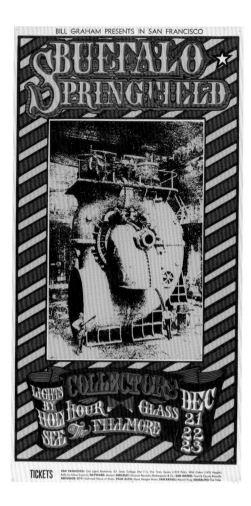

23, 24, 25

TOP ROW, FROM LEFT TO RIGHT

ALTON KELLEY

STANLEY MOUSE

Bill Graham Presents:

Buffalo Springfield, December 21–23, 1967

OFFSET LITHOGRAPH POSTER

21⅛ X 11 IN. (53.7 X 27.9 CM)

THE GLOBUS COLLECTION

JIM BLASHFIELD

Bill Graham Presents:

Jefferson Airplane, September 25, 1967

OFFSET LITHOGRAPH POSTER

21⅜ X 14 IN. (54.3 X 35.6 CM)

THE GLOBUS COLLECTION

WES WILSON

Bill Graham Presents:

Butterfield Blues Band, October 7–8, 1966

OFFSET LITHOGRAPH POSTER

24¼ X 11⅞ IN. (61.6 X 30.2 CM)

THE GLOBUS COLLECTION

26, 27, 28

BOTTOM ROW, FROM LEFT TO RIGHT

WES WILSON

Bill Graham Presents:

Jefferson Airplane, February 3–5, 1967

OFFSET LITHOGRAPH POSTER

23¼ X 13¾ IN. (59.1 X 34.9 CM)

THE GLOBUS COLLECTION

BONNIE MacLEAN

Bill Graham Presents:

Butterfield Blues Band, July 11–16, 1967

OFFSET LITHOGRAPH POSTER

21 X 14 IN. (53.3 X 35.6 CM)

THE GLOBUS COLLECTION

JIM BLASHFIELD

Bill Graham Presents:

Count Basie, Chuck Berry, et al.,

August 15–21, 1967

OFFSET LITHOGRAPH POSTER

21 X 14 IN. (53.3 X 35.6 CM)

THE GLOBUS COLLECTION

CHAPTER 2

Gatherings: Creating the Studio Craft Movement

GLENN ADAMSON

FOR THE AMERICAN CRAFT MOVEMENT, THE YEARS from 1945 to 1969 were the golden age. The country's greatest modern craft artists were in their prime, and in their hands a relatively confined set of ideas about craftsmanship—rooted in good design, functionality, and skill—splintered into countless artistic directions: expressionist, satirical, narrative, political, conceptual. While a national council grew to maturity, smaller craft groups advanced the cause in nearly every major American city. A museum devoted to the movement opened in New York, and each year hundreds of exhibitions presented craft to the public there and at other venues across the country. By any measure, these organizational efforts were resoundingly successful. By 1970 craft was in fashion as it had never been before, the stylistic identity of the counterculture. Most important, craftspeople themselves flourished in universities and small-scale businesses nationwide. They rediscovered old techniques and forged new links to one another.

As with any creative movement, studio craft's early days were exciting and undefined. With success came stability and coherence, but also, gradually, a degree of inflexibility. In the period after 1970, studio craft would become a known quantity: a reliable arena of commodity production increasingly set in its ways. The history of the movement's institutionalization, therefore, serves as both an inspiration and a cautionary tale. Key moments in this process shed light on the means by which the craft movement gathered itself. This story is intriguing on its own terms, for it is populated with individuals of extraordinary

energy, vision, and commitment. It also affords an opportunity to ask what was gained, and lost, when craft was constituted as a single "field." Today, craft seems most attractive because it is difficult to pin down; it is implicated in a wide range of practices that may have nothing else in common. Back then, however, the whole point was to get together.

AGAINST CONFORMITY: CRAFT AND INDIVIDUALISM

In a way, it is surprising a craft movement flourished most successfully in America rather than elsewhere in the wake of World War II. Many countries, such as Italy and Japan, had no choice but to focus on craft production because their industrial sectors had been demolished and they were desperate to rebuild. America was obviously not in this situation. Craft was not an economic activity of last resort. Perhaps this is precisely why the United States had a craft movement instead of a craft industry. While artisans elsewhere were subject to the dictates of economic development, the American movement was expressly intended to safeguard individualism. This might seem contradictory—the movement was, after all, a process of centralization and definition—but in the early 1950s, few could have foreseen any conflict between the diverse interests of individual craft artists and the mandate of a single organization. Put simply, there was a sense of crisis about the future of the handmade. Those involved in the initial stages of the movement followed a line of thinking that had begun in the Arts and Crafts movement at the end of the nineteenth century: They believed in craft as a moral imperative. They feared that if they failed, something fundamental would disappear from the modern world.

Parallel to this conviction was a sense that individuals required help in order to resist the tide of conformity that was thought to typify postwar America. Books such as David Potter's *People of Plenty: Economic Abundance and the American Character* (1954), Sloan Wilson's *Man in the Gray Flannel Suit* (1955; made into a film with Gregory Peck the following year), and William Whyte's *Organization Man* (1957) criticized corporate culture as endemically conformist. David Riesman's *Lonely Crowd* (1950) took a sociological angle, describing the postwar generation in general as "other-directed." Riesman saw Americans as obsessed with peer approval and out of touch with the self-defined goals that had made the nation's nineteenth-century expansion possible. Craft was emblematic of this disappearing spirit of individualism, which had seemingly been lost in the comfortable but homogenous tracts of suburbia. As academics anxiously postulated that Americans had lost their "instinct of workmanship," self-help literature counseled men and women to take up a craft in the hope of finding their true personalities.[1]

This overriding concern with individualism permeated the bewilderingly diverse range of American craft during the postwar years, from production design to expressionist sculpture, from high-tech textiles to hippie pottery. The individual was at the heart of the School for American Craftsmen (founded as a "program for individual opportunities through manual industry and the hand arts") and of the "designer-craftsmen" organizations of the early 1950s, which were dedicated to carving out a space for the creative, independent artisan in industry.[2] The notion that broader frameworks were necessary to nurture individuality remained crucial even in the counterculture. As Charles Reich wrote in *The Greening of America* (1970), "the search for self cannot take place in isolation; that self must be realized in a community."[3] But within this story of continuity, a debate was gradually forming. What did individual craftspeople really need? How should they be best supported? What was the cultural importance of their work? These were difficult questions to answer, and given the increasing diversity of the movement, they only became more challenging over time.

ORGANIZATION WOMAN:
AILEEN OSBORN WEBB

Existing narratives of the postwar craft movement often emphasize the war itself. Most historians have treated 1945 as the start of a new chapter—with good reason. Many people came to craft because of the war, or rather because of the Servicemen's Readjustment Act of 1944 (usually called the GI Bill). This legislation made it possible for many veterans to attend college after demobilization, dramatically increasing the student population and giving them access to newly established craft courses. Meanwhile, others had already become craftspeople during the war. Bob Stocksdale made his first lathe-turned bowl at a conscientious objectors' camp in Michigan, while George Nakashima learned the rudiments of carpentry from a fellow resident at a Japanese internment camp.[4] Others picked up woodworking or other skills while employed by the military. Many leading craftspeople found their way to America after fleeing their

homes in Central Europe, among them textile artist Anni Albers, enamelist Karl Drerup, and ceramist Marguerite Wildenhain. Nevertheless it is also easy to overestimate the impact of the war, especially when considering the process by which an institutional basis for the studio craft movement was created. If anything, the outbreak of hostilities was an interruption to this effort.

The postwar craft movement had deep roots in the infrastructure laid down by regional groups since the turn of the century, such as the League of New Hampshire Craftsmen, the Boston Society of Arts and Crafts, and the Southern Highland Handicraft Guild. Depression-era government projects like the Civil Works Administration aided and supplemented these organizations, all of which sought to develop local craft production as a way of maintaining heritage and boosting tourism. It was in this context that Aileen Osborn Webb, unquestionably the most important figure in American craft history, got her start (FIG. 2.1). Born into a wealthy New York political family,

Webb never had a full-time job and never went to college, yet she accomplished more, and more intelligently, than any craft advocate before or since. Her grandfather William Henry Osborn had made his fortune in the railroad business. Her father was a lawyer who was active in charitable organizations, such as the Children's Aid Society, and in the arts as president of The Metropolitan Museum of Art. Young Aileen Osborn also led a life of charity work.[5] By the time of the Depression, as a member of the Women's Democratic Committee of Putnam County, just north of New York City in the Hudson River Valley, she became involved in welfare for the unemployed of the region. This led her to start Putnam County Products, funded through the Public Works of Art Project under the umbrella of the Civil Works Administration. "We would market anything that anybody in the County could either grow or make," Webb later recalled. "I thought of it more as string beans and eggs. But actually within two months it was things which people made by hand."[6] Soon the organization had opened a store in Carmel, New York, for the sale of local crafts (there was also one in New York City, albeit briefly). It was through Putnam County Products that Webb acquired the networking and retailing skills that were so important in later years. She also became dedicated to helping craftspeople make a good living.

Meanwhile in Manhattan, another group of well-connected men and women were considering the formation of a national craft organization: the American Handicraft Council (AHC). Though it is little known today, this forerunner to the American Craft Council (ACC) was critical to establishing the objectives and the social network of the postwar movement. It was instigated by Webb's friend, another well-to-do woman, Anne Morgan—daughter of the magnate J. P. Morgan—and led by a group of men and women with ties to museums, craft organizations, charitable foundations, retailing, and business.[7] In 1938 the group had laid plans for an economic study of American craft and a major exhibition at Rockefeller Center to accompany the New York World's Fair the following year. The Rockefeller Center exhibition never materialized, but the report was completed with funding from the Carnegie Corporation.[8] More important, the AHC established principles that would remain central to the craft movement in its immediate postwar incarnation: a suspicion of amateurs and an emphasis on collaboration between the crafts and mass production. Board member Richard F. Bach put this succinctly in a 1938 summary of the group's philosophy: "It will be wise to separate handicraft, which is in the nature of business, wherever or however practiced, from homecraft, which is primarily time-filling. . . . The whole undertaking must be seen as a form of industrial art, subject to all the handicaps and limitations which other types of industrial art products must meet."[9]

Webb first corresponded with the AHC about joining forces in June 1939. Characteristically, despite the modest scale of her achievements in Putnam County, she already had big plans and suggested creating a single umbrella organization that could coordinate regional efforts throughout the country.[10] This was to be the Handcraft Cooperative League of America (HCLA), an affiliation of regional craft groups organized by Webb. When in 1942 the AHC merged with the HCLA, becoming the American Craftsmen's Cooperative Council, Inc. (ACCC), the result was that "the patrician directors of the former were somewhat balanced by the grassroots organizations comprising the League."[11] Even before this, however, in 1940, Webb had founded America House in Manhattan under the auspices of the HCLA. Until the founding of the Museum of Contemporary Crafts (the original name of the Museum of Arts and Design) in 1956, this would be the most innovative venue for craft in the country, despite its status as a small retail outlet. The program encompassed "every aspect of the hand arts from jewelry and the art of the lapidary to the decoration of Easter eggs and decoupage."[12] This breadth was partly due to the fact that, like Putnam County Products, America House was a group effort. The operation of the shop was overseen by Frances Wright Caroë, a daughter of Frank Lloyd Wright; further support came from a trio of extraordinary women, whom Webb described as "a galaxy of Dorothys."[13] Dorothy Liebes was the ideal "designer-craftsman," a handweaver who created textiles for mass production; Dorothy Draper was a glamorous interior decorator who, among her other grand projects, designed the restaurant at the Metropolitan Museum (in certain circles, it acquired the nickname "the Dorotheum"); and Dorothy Shaver was rising through the ranks at Lord & Taylor—in 1945 she became the company's president, one of the first women to head a New York corporate board.[14] All three acted as board members of America House and helped to publicize the early activities of the council.

America House quickly gave rise to a series of further ventures. First came the magazine *Craft Horizons*, which started in 1941 as "a one-page mimeographed information sheet for the people who were selling through America House."[15] Webb herself took on editorial duties, though she would be succeeded by Mary Lyon, Belle Krasne (briefly, in 1955), Conrad Brown, and the formidable Rose Slivka. The ACCC was renamed the American Craftsmen's Educational Council (ACEC) in 1943 when it was officially incorporated, with support from the League of New Hampshire Craftsmen under the directorship of architect David Campbell.[16] In 1944 the School for American Craftsmen (SAC) opened at Dartmouth College in Hanover, New Hampshire. (Webb recalled that its first student was a fifty-year-old wounded Seabee, who didn't last long at the school.)[17] The school was set up along principles similar to those pioneered at the Bauhaus, which was just then being transplanted to Chicago: "A master craftsman will direct each department.... An understanding of the basic principles of Design will be taught and where creative aptitude is found it will be encouraged and developed.... It is planned that individuals, before they have finished their training, will be working on craft objects which are actually being sold."[18]

As this short summary suggests, the craft establishment that existed in 1945 was very much the creation of independently wealthy men and women whose perspectives were formed prior to the war. While the GI Bill was important to the formation of the movement, more critical were institutions that had originated in the Arts and Crafts era, as well as the more recent lessons learned during the Depression. It is also important to note that of the key movers in wartime craft, none had any significant connection to fine art, while many were involved in various aspects of economic development, design, and retailing. None was a professional craftsperson. It was this formula—a patrician prescription for financial viability, combined with grassroots networking—that would shape the craft movement's first steps in the postwar period.

EXPERIMENTING FOR INDUSTRY:
DESIGNER-CRAFTSMEN IN THE 1950s

It is a measure of the quality of Webb's contacts, but also of the close relationship between craft and design, that the ACEC looked to the Museum of Modern Art (MoMA) as one model for their programming during this period. The two organizations, located on the same block in Manhattan, had a strong connection through Webb's personal friendship with MoMA director René d'Harnoncourt, who

FIG. 2.2
Designer Craftsman U.S.A., installation view, Brooklyn venue (October 22, 1953–January 23, 1954). Records of the Department of Photography, Brooklyn Museum Archives.

served on the council's board of trustees. Together, the institutions conducted a national survey on art education in 1951,[19] and in 1952 a State Department–sponsored craft exhibition traveled abroad, designed by MoMA's circulating department curator, Carlus Dyer.[20] Greta Daniel, a German-born curator of design at MoMA, wrote frequently for *Craft Horizons*. The museum's outward-looking education department under Victor d'Amico was also an inspiration for the Museum of Contemporary Crafts.[21] Most important, the council's programming was influenced by the ethos forwarded at MoMA under curators Edgar J. Kaufmann Jr. and Bernard Rudofsky in a series of Good Design exhibitions from 1950 to 1955. Like the Walker Art Center's Everyday Art Gallery in Minneapolis, or the California Design series in Pasadena, America House followed MoMA's emphasis on affordable design, or *Good Home Design on a Limited Budget* (as the title of one 1951 America House exhibition had it).[22]

MoMA's Good Design ideal strongly influenced the first national display of craft objects, an exhibition titled *Designer Craftsmen U.S.A.,* which opened at the Brooklyn Museum of Art in 1953 and subsequently traveled to the Art Institute of Chicago and the San Francisco Museum of Art **(FIG. 2.2)**. The 243 pieces in the exhibition, by 203 craftspeople, had been subjected to an extensive process of jurying, organized by ten regional institutions.[23] (In addition to a "technical panel," including furniture maker Tage Frid and silversmith/designer Arthur Pulos, among the final judges were Hugh Lawson, formerly of the Chicago department store Carson Pirie Scott, and the industrial designer John Van Koert.) There had been important regional craft shows before this—the May Show in Cleveland and the Ceramic Nationals in Syracuse, for example—and the postwar period had also seen the inception of new exhibition series in Wichita and St. Paul. But *Designer Craftsmen U.S.A.* was different: It was an exhibition with a thesis. Every aspect of the project stressed the happy marriage of craft with industry, with the proviso that such collaboration must always respect the individual maker's unforced creativity. The designer-craftsman was positioned both as an aid to manufacturing and a corrective to its dehumanizing effects, a message that drew equally from the legacies of the Bauhaus and the Arts and Crafts movement. This argument was carried through from the exhibition's title to the awards, which were funded by companies such as Abraham and Straus, Kittinger, and Bergdorf Goodman. Awards were given not only to production-friendly pieces such as H. Lee DuSell's aluminum table **(FIG. 2.3)**, but also to a hand-thrown and sgraffito-decorated bowl by Ed and Mary Scheier. The catalogue featured a nuanced essay by Dorothy Giles,

FIG. 2.3
H. Lee DuSell, *Dining Table***, 1952. Birch, cast aluminum legs. 28 x 83½ x 34¾ in. (71.1 x 212.1 x 88.3 cm). Museum of Fine Arts, Boston; Museum purchase with funds donated by The Seminarians, 2005.567.**

who argued that "a society in which direction is inspired by artists and by designer craftsmen is a healthier, richer and more productive society than one which leaves it to industry and business to point the way and set the pace."[24]

The designer-craftsman ideal was not monolithic. Its most extreme advocates could make craft sound like an elaborate prototyping system, a research-and-development phase of mass production. But insofar as the movement's true purpose was to preserve the viability of craft, a more important goal still was to encourage craftspeople to learn from professional designers, simply in order to make their products more salable. If these two objectives were not necessarily identical—one was essentially about the reform of style, and the other about preserving individualism—they were at least consonant. *Designer Craftsmen U.S.A.* was buttressed by a number of projects that conveyed this message. America House staged *Planned for Craftsmen: A Visual Definition of the Elements of Design* to coincide with the exhibition when it opened in Brooklyn. *Craft Horizons* published a series of articles on the relation between craft and design, inaugurated by Walker Art Center director Dan Defenbacher in 1951. And the most comprehensive document of the

moment was *Shaping America's Products* (1956), by flatware and furniture designer Don Wallance. Sponsored by the ACEC and the Walker Art Center, the book departed from the Brooklyn show—which followed the rigid materials-based structure that was fast becoming the norm in craft exhibitions and publications—and was instead organized according to different approaches to manufacturing. Wallance was not opposed to large industry, but he was concerned that "individual creativity and genius are less important today than they were in the past. They are being absorbed into working relationships which are increasingly collective in nature."[25] He praised examples of small shop practice ranging from craftspeople who designed for industry, such as George Nakashima, to designers who treated craft as a form of research, such as Charles and Ray Eames, and small-scale manufacturers such as the swimwear firm Jantzen, who developed new production techniques as a way of gaining distinction in the marketplace. Wallance projected an ecumenical image of craft as a pervasive concern in the productive economy, an issue

that every manufacturer could and should consider.

The breadth of vision seen in *Shaping America's Products* was also reflected at the national conference of craftspeople held at Asilomar, California, in 1957 **(FIG. 2.4)**. This was the first major gathering of American craftspeople since the war, and it was a life-changing experience for those who attended. They were thrilled by a sense of discovery: of techniques, of ideas, but most of all, of one another.[26] Like the Brooklyn show, the Asilomar conference was expressly designed to promote the relation between crafts and industry, and the roster of speakers reflected that fact. Prominent designers such as Charles Eames, Jay Doblin, and Lawrence Peabody were invited to attend, and an honored role was accorded to Asger Fischer, the director of Danish design association Den Permanente. (Many in America felt that Scandinavian design was the most compelling model for integrating craft with mass production.) Most of the makers who spoke at the conference were exemplary artists: Marguerite Wildenhain and Anni Albers of Bauhaus fame; the weaver Jack Lenor

Larsen; and the British designer Michael Higgins, who with his wife, Frances, operated a small-scale glass manufactory in Chicago.

On the whole, therefore, audiences at Asilomar heard ideas that were compatible with the designer-craftsman ideal. According to Albers, it was only in the industrial field that "the craftsman can regain his status as a pioneer: as experimenting outpost for an industry that itself has come to experiment,"[27] while Eames pronounced, "In our world and in our time, we are deeply in need of the values which come under the head of 'craftsmanship.' I would venture to say that society today is more in need of these values than of any other thing."[28] A panel on woodwork declined even to distinguish between batch production and studio craft, with Sam Maloof commenting, "If I make fifty chairs, that may not be mass production but it is production in quantity," and woodturner Jake May stating his respect for factory hands: "It's amazing the amount each worker in the furniture factory knows. These men are still craftsmen."[29] The group concurred that craftsmanship could exist in any type of production—it was a matter of quality, not quantity. *Craft Horizons* dedicated an issue to Asilomar, and the editors underlined the message: "The craftsman's unfettered activity (compared to the industrial designer) often constitutes 'pure research'—as important as anything happening now within the whole area of contemporary design."[30]

There were also, however, moments of dissent. For Michael Higgins, the real need was for artisans without artistic pretensions: "We discovered early in our existence that we needed craftsmen very badly and that they are completely unobtainable. Designer-craftsmen we needed like a hole in the head though, because once we were seriously in production we only got about eight hours a year to design ourselves and what there was of designing we wanted to have for us."[31] More potentially explosive was the implication that the designer-craftsperson idea was effectively selling out the integrity of the nascent movement. For a few attendees, craft as an individualistic pursuit was inherently *opposed* to the mechanisms of capital. Harvey Littleton described his decision to become a craftsman as a rejection of the corporate life: "I did not like the people I met in industrial design or in business. Unfortunately pottery has led me back into business again; but this time a business that I like. . . . I find this a tremendously rewarding experience and ample justification for leading the kind of life I want to live instead of hunting

the almighty dollar."[32] He framed craft as an alternative to what he called "consumer councils" like Denmark's Den Permanente.[33] Peter Voulkos was even more infuriated by the general run of conversation at Asilomar. In a heated exchange, he rejected a Code of Ethics drafted by the Midwest Designer-Craftsmen, arguing that any institutionalization of the craft culture was inimical to personal expression: "It seems to me we work the way we like to work. This brings to mind why I try to avoid most organizations. You start getting all kinds of rules and regulations. The only reason I do what I do is that I like to do it."[34]

In the context of the Asilomar conference, Voulkos might have seemed an eccentric figure, but he spoke for a large number of the young people who were entering the craft scene in the late 1950s. This generation had been educated in the new university programs, and they had different expectations from those who were oriented to design for industry. Already at the council's next national conference, held in 1958, Jack Lenor Larsen was voicing alarm at a rising tide of purely expressive individualism, which he described as "directionless irresponsibility—ideal soil for that kind of parasitic, fruitless individualism that impedes our cause. Masquerading as guileless self-expression is a self-projection more insidious than is 'Commercial Art.'"[35] In retrospect, it is amazing how quickly the opposition between commercial and expressive impulses developed. Only six years separate the mild observation, made in 1955, that a potter should "think more of the values he receives from the doing and the expression itself than the price which might be set upon the object in the market place" and Rose Slivka's barnstorming, benchmark essay "The New Ceramic Presence" (1961).[36] Slivka's assessment of the West Coast scene conceded the importance of the machine to American culture, noting "its power, its speed, its strength, its force, its energy, its productivity, its violence," but she reserved her greatest praise for craft that embodied American individualism: "the action of men—ruggedly individual and vernacular men (the pioneer, the cowboy) with a genius for improvisation."[37] After taking over sole editorship of *Craft Horizons* in 1959, Slivka gradually steered the publication away from its orientation to design and toward an art-based model derived from the uncompromising stance of abstract expressionism. For a time in the 1950s, seemingly every issue of the magazine had featured a handweaver designing for a large mill in the Dorothy Liebes mode, including such now-forgotten figures as Lore Kadden,

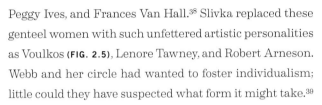

Peggy Ives, and Frances Van Hall.[38] Slivka replaced these genteel women with such unfettered artistic personalities as Voulkos (FIG. 2.5), Lenore Tawney, and Robert Arneson. Webb and her circle had wanted to foster individualism; little could they have suspected what form it might take.[39]

A GREAT INDIVIDUALIZING EXPERIENCE: THE WORLD CRAFTS COUNCIL, 1964

If Webb's ideals were tested by the emergence of an American avant-garde, she faced a challenge of an entirely different order when she brought her vision of humanizing craft revival into contact with the wider world. The first World Crafts Council conference, held at Columbia University in 1964, was an event of breathtaking ambition (FIG. 2.6). Planning had started in 1959, when Webb's friend Margaret M. Patch had approached her with a modest proposal: What if she were to take an investigative trip around the world on behalf of the council? The following year, Patch set off for Japan and over the ensuing months traveled throughout Southeast Asia, India, Pakistan, Communist Eastern Europe, and North Africa. Everywhere she went, despite the barriers of language and politics, she managed to make contact with local craft leaders.[40] Many of these figures were featured guests at the 1964 conference, which dramatically exceeded

FIG. 2.5
Peter Voulkos giving a pottery demonstration, location unknown, 1976. Photograph courtesy of ACC.

FIG. 2.6
Aileen Osborn Webb and members of the World Crafts Council, Columbia University, New York City, 1964. Photograph courtsey of ACC.

expectations by drawing 500 Americans and 250 delegates from around the world (Webb had optimistically hoped that 50 might attend).[41] Presentations were commissioned from a diversity of speakers, including international craft leaders Kamaladevi Chattopadhyay from India and Mohammed Alaoui from Morocco. American luminaries—d'Harnoncourt, novelist Ralph Ellison, architect Louis Kahn, and art theorist Rudolf Arnheim, among others—also attended. Harvey Littleton and Dominick Labino set up a glassblowing demonstration, one of the first public displays of this newly revived studio craft, and the conferees were taken to the New York World's Fair by bus.[42]

Despite the diversity of the event, the World Crafts Council was focused on exporting the message of American individualism abroad. Thus it was structured around a principle of universality: "Though the social and economic position of the contemporary craftsman varies from country to country—whether he be a village artisan in a cottage industry or an urbanized designer-craftsman working for a sophisticated public—he shares problems common to all."[43] As at Asilomar, this core conviction received general acceptance at the conference, but also a degree of resistance. Americans and Europeans were most likely to uphold a vision of craft as humanistic and self-directed. Slivka, as usual, put it best, arguing that "internationalizing is not a leveling experience. On the contrary, it is a great individualizing experience."[44] D'Arcy Hayman, the French head of arts and cultural development for UNESCO (United Nations Educational,

Scientific and Cultural Organization), which would take on the World Crafts Council as a member organization the following year, sounded an anxious variation on this theme, observing that "when we find difficulty in guessing whether a painting, teapot, tapestry, or book binding was made in Italy, Venezuela, Sweden or Japan, it is wonderful in one sense, and sad in another. Wonderful in that the whole world is becoming a community of man in which equal respect and appreciation [are] growing for the art forms of all peoples, and sad in that the great and endless variety of art forms and traditions [is] being lost in the clean sweep of the new technology and intercultural influence."[45] But speakers from other parts of the world were less apt to concern themselves with the preoccupations of individual craftspeople. Craft's role in supporting tourism and economic development was of greater concern. Assessments varied, from Alaoui's rosy view of craft production in Morocco, where government planning had succeeded in improving workplace conditions and quality of output, to R. Vanjah Richards's statement that "in Africa, or some parts of it, the tradition of our art has suffered terribly. Why? Because of the tourists." Pakistani delegate Abbasi S. Akhtar voiced outright despair: "Even the traditional producers of excellent handmade objects prefer cheap machine-made designs in their zeal to be modern. Whatever crafts like pottery, basketry, or folk arts persist, they do so not because the craftsmen take pride in their work but because the profession has been forced on them by the necessities of livelihood."[46]

In future conferences of the World Crafts Council—at Montreux, Switzerland, in 1966; Lima, Peru, in 1968; and many other sites in the ensuing decade—the underlying conflict between an individualist, art-based model and the desire to develop tourist markets became increasingly obvious. The metalsmith Arline Fisch, who attended World Crafts Council events from 1964 into the 1980s, recalled a disagreement about a proposal for an organizational seal of approval. This was seen as a potentially valuable aid for craft producers, but Webb and her American colleagues argued that it would be impossible to maintain standards within such a program, and they did not want to see the organization become a marketing board.[47] Another question was whether to attempt to preserve traditional crafts in places like India and Africa, or to accept their gradual decline and look forward to a revival on the American model. Patwant Singh had identified this issue in New York in 1964, predicting that craft would be valued in India only once it met "virtual extinction as a result of technological change."[48] While Fisch does not remember these issues as being particularly divisive, Harvey Littleton has described an increasingly dysfunctional situation: "[Webb] didn't really understand the difference between the indigenous craftsmen and the artist-craftsmen. So those World Crafts Council meetings became a division that was unbelievable. . . . There were two concepts of conservation."[49] Littleton may have underestimated Webb's comprehension of the international situation. In 1965 she had already accurately predicted that "the crafts of India (and other Eastern lands) will be produced in large plants or 'open sheds' rather than in the home."[50] She was both knowledgeable about and sympathetic toward crafts producers elsewhere in the world. But it is certainly true that exposure to the global experience showed how very American the American craft movement was.

"AN OLYMPIAN HOAX":
THE ARTIST-CRAFTSMEN TAKE CHARGE

As Webb was turning her attention to the project of geographical expansion, American craft was approaching its most exciting and controversial years at home. Having largely abandoned the project of allying itself with modernist design, the craft movement became more firmly embedded in the only framework that could support it: academia. There was essentially no market for avant-garde craft in the 1960s. The only sales venues were craft shops and local fairs. But at universities, artistically adventurous makers were becoming, if not the norm, then certainly commonplace. At the same time, the academic logic of medium-based departments helped to set craft's identity within a set repertoire of materials—the now-familiar catechism of clay, fiber, glass, metal, and wood. This had both advantages and disadvantages. On the downside, more flexible conceptions of craft, which might have included a broader range of practices (from auto repair to architecture) and people (from factory workers to hobbyists) fell by the wayside. Furthermore, the identification of craft with specific materials soon became a liability for artist-craftsmen, as conceptualism and associated developments made dedication to a single medium seem suspect, or at least unduly constraining. On the other hand, material specificity was almost certainly necessary in a craft community that was building its skills and infrastructure. Universities were only willing to invest in expensive kilns and glass furnaces, woodshops and weaving studios, because they served the cause of developing medium-based expertise.

Another direct result of the academic enfranchisement of craft was that museum exhibitions became crucial. This was the only way for those without regular gallery representation to show their work. One of the most important supporters in this regard was Paul Smith, who became director of the Museum of Contemporary Crafts in 1963. Smith was not, perhaps, an obvious choice for the job. While Slivka had already been an experienced writer and editor when she joined *Craft Horizons*, Smith had been primarily a woodworker and jewelry maker (he had trained at the School for American Craftsmen in Rochester). His most relevant experience in display before joining the council was in a department store in Buffalo, New York. But he had impressive organizational experience, having been president of the Buffalo Craftsmen and a key figure in the York State Craftsmen, alongside such eminent potters as Fong Chow and Robert Turner. He also brought with him a strikingly open mind. He continued the museum's tradition of reporting on commercial applications of the crafts (in, for example, his exhibition, *Designed for Production: The Craftsman's Approach* in 1964) as well as on miscellaneous subjects such as baking, haute couture, and plastics, as Webb had done at America House. Yet, like Slivka, Smith also charted new territory. He organized a series of groundbreaking one-person retrospectives, very much along the lines of art museum exhibitions, and brought the feeling of the sixties "be-in" culture to the museum with such shows as *Mind Extenders* (1969) and *Contemplation Environments* (1970). Smith's approach to the crafts was varied, and he felt that his central objective was always to report what was going on, rather than to prescribe a particular direction for the movement. But there is no question that, like Slivka, he was alive to the reorientation of craft away from design and toward gallery-based art.

Elsewhere in America, that shift was still more dramatic. The long-running series of California Design exhibitions in Pasadena, under the leadership of Eudorah Moore, took a left turn in 1968. Previously it had been very much a West Coast version of the Good Design imperative emanating from New York, with a mix of handmade and manufactured goods and little that could be described as experimental. Now, influenced by the countercultural mood that was sweeping the state, the jury introduced a spate of aggressively experimental craft, including expressionist clay sculptures, body jewelry, and crudely humorous Funk ceramics and glass. Helen Giambruni, who reviewed the show for *Craft Horizons*, noted with approval its forays into the "new and challenging," in contrast to what she saw as the "overrefinement" of earlier installments in the series, and added, "the improvement may no doubt be attributed not to a change of scene, for there was surely as much good work three years ago as today, but to a more progressive jury for crafts."[51]

But the most vivid conflict between the two generations—designer-craftsmen versus artist-craftsmen—came about in the most established of the national craft exhibitions, the Ceramic Nationals in Syracuse, New York. From its inception in the 1930s, the series had showcased individual potters' ties to industry. Syracuse was a center for the commercial manufacture of china, and the Ceramic Nationals were backed by manufacturers who provided funding and offered prizes to artists who submitted designs suitable for mass production. Because of this history, the series had retained a conservative cast throughout the early postwar period and did little to document the rising tide of avant-garde work in the medium. As late as 1960, the museum's director wrote, "With the present critical variance over current expressions in the fine arts, it is reassuring to find one's self involved in the relative calm of an art form disciplined by considerations of craftsmanship."[52] Though the Ceramic Nationals catalogues of the early 1960s noted—with some perplexity—the increasing scale and "bizarre forms, color and decoration which quite definitely find parallels in contemporary painting and sculpture,"[53] the exhibitions continued to be dominated by straightforward functional wares. The 1966 show was juried by eight potters, most of whom expressed dissatisfaction with the "self-conscious" quality of the entries. As juror Warren MacKenzie put it: "I want to make pots that relate to the home life of people. Not for exhibitions."[54]

The twenty-fifth Ceramic National in 1968, which was shown in the Everson Museum of Art's new building by architect I. M. Pei, marked an abrupt turnaround from this state of affairs. The catalogue proclaimed that "it is really a sculpture show; utilitarian pottery as such is barely represented. . . . The media, the fact that they are ceramic, seems incidental."[55] As if in reply to the previous group of jurors, Dextra Frankel (who had also contributed to the California Design exhibition of the same year) wrote: "How to separate from the traditional means of application seems to me to be the most important point of departure; how to break with the rigid confines of the process, to break these limitations and create a vital, meaningful statement by means of concept, form and content."[56] Similarly, while the *Craft Horizons* reviewer of the 1966 exhibition had dismissed the sculptural inclusions as "uneven in quality" and "frequently obstreperous,"[57] in 1968 the magazine's reviewer was positively stunned: "It must be seen to be believed. The material is clay, the prospectus demands it, the catalog proclaims it, but where have all the potters gone? There is sculpture aplenty."[58] Not everyone was pleased. Oregon potter Lotte Streisinger sent a grief-stricken letter to the editor: "If the craftsman does not uphold the enduring values of humanity and the works of the human hand, who will? And if nobody does, we are lost, lost, lost."[59]

In 1972 the uneasy peace in Syracuse was shattered. This time the three jurors were Voulkos, Jeff Schlanger, and Robert Turner, all leading ceramists. Faced with what they saw as an uninspiring slate of entries, they canceled the juried exhibition, rejecting 4,500 slides, and implemented an invitational instead.[60] The resulting furor put an end to the Nationals entirely (they would not be revived until 1987). Many potters felt that the jury had sent a loud, clear message: the elite of the ceramics world were no longer inclined to show alongside their inferiors. Though the jurors claimed that the cancellation was due to the impossibility of reviewing work from slides, *Craft Horizons* probably represented public sentiment accurately in writing that the affair seemed like an "Olympian hoax, perpetrated by larger-than-life ceramic figures pointing a collective finger."[61] As if to underline this perception, the Everson's next director, Ronald Kuchta, replaced the next Ceramic National with a show titled *New Works in Clay by Painters and Sculptors*. Curated by Margie Hughto, the exhibition featured experimental works by prominent painters and sculptors (including Helen Frankenthaler, Larry Poons, Jules Olitski, and Anthony Caro) who were invited to create works in clay.[62]

Other crafts media were not as established in museums as ceramics, and perhaps for this reason did not experience a traumatic confrontation like the one that occurred at the Everson in Syracuse. Similar shifts, however, can be detected elsewhere in the crafts: Wendell Castle's impatience to move his furniture into the realm of sculpture, for example, or the embrace of radical ideas in jewelry that were being pioneered in Germany and the Netherlands. Perhaps the most public attention was garnered by the fiber art movement, which was featured in such exhibitions as the tendentiously titled *Beyond Craft: The Art Fabric* at the Museum of Modern Art in 1972 (curated by Jack Lenor Larsen and Mildred Constantine) and a remarkable installation of work by Polish artist Magdalena Abakanowicz at the Oakland Museum (curated by Eudorah Moore). The latter prompted macramé authority Mary Jane Leland to rhapsodic praise in *Craft Horizons*: "Treating them as infinite forms, she established a new environment by relating the works to themselves, to the floor, and to the space, to affirm their infinite pliability."[63] The shift from designer-craftspeople to artist-craftspeople was complete.

DEFINITIONS LATER—OBJECTS: USA, 1969

The conflict over the Ceramic Nationals was indicative of a fundamental shift in the movement, but it was a mere tempest in a teapot compared to the response to *Objects: USA* (FIG. 2.7). This massive exhibition of more than three hundred works traveled to twenty-one American and ten European venues, breaking attendance records at many stops and setting a standard for craft exhibitions that has been emulated (if never quite equaled) in future exhibitions.[64] In the process, the show upended the formula that had been set by *Designer Craftsmen U.S.A.* Comparison of the titles alone is instructive. People have been replaced with "objects," and the relational tone set by the term *designer-craftsman* has been replaced, too, by a note of final certainty. As weaver and basket maker Ed Rossbach put it, the exhibition "seemed to formalize the past, chronicle it into a permanent bound volume, the authorized version. Modifications and corrections would be accomplished only with great difficulty."[65]

If *Designer Craftsmen U.S.A.* was Webb's brainchild, then *Objects: USA* owed its existence to New York City art dealer Lee Nordness. A decade earlier, he had organized a large exhibition of painting, sculpture, and other media at the Coliseum, in New York, titled *Art: USA: 59*. The selection included a group of crafts under the rubric of "Fine Art in Living."[66] Nordness was then tapped by the Johnson Wax Company of Racine, Wisconsin, to curate *Art: USA: Now* (1962), a touring exhibition of color-field and late abstract expressionist paintings.[67] When he returned to Samuel Johnson of Johnson Wax for sponsorship, this time with the idea of a show featuring contemporary crafts, he was able to secure full funding for an enormous exhibition. Insofar as Nordness acted as the spokesman for the titanic project, his feeling that craft should be promoted as a full-fledged member of the fine art world was tremendously influential. But he did not curate *Objects: USA* alone; he was paired with Paul Smith of the Museum of Contemporary Crafts. The two were an odd couple to be sure: one an upmarket art dealer, and the other a veteran of the craft movement's grassroots trenches. Yet they were an ideal combination, too. Nordness had the flair, Smith the in-depth knowledge. While Smith took little credit for the show (he was not, for example, listed as an author of the catalogue), he was vital to its success due to the breadth of his connections in the field.[68] Indeed, even with the benefit of hindsight, it is difficult to think of any area of the crafts of the late 1960s that is not well represented in *Objects: USA*. From established designer-craftsmen to cutting-edge potters and jewelers, from back-to-the-land rural furniture makers to those experimenting with plastics and neon, all of the factions of the craft scene were

FIG. 2.7
Objects: USA, **installation view with Maloof cradle in rear center (see CAT. 183), Washington venue (October 3–November 6, 1969). Photograph courtesy private collection.**

present. As a result of the exhibition's international tour, it also set a benchmark in the reputation of American craft abroad. Although a display of American craft had been shown at the World's Fair in Brussels in 1958, Europeans had never had a chance to see such a diversity of work from the United States.

Yet, when *Objects: USA* was presented to the American public, few noted its rich internal variety. Following the lead of Nordness's press releases, newspapers treated it rather simplistically, as evidence that the craft world had come into its own as a contemporary art movement. As the *Detroit Sunday News* had it, "*Objects: USA* crashes through a wall of prejudice to demolish the snobbish distinction between so-called fine arts and the crafts."[69] The *Minneapolis Star* proclaimed, "If proof were still needed, the *Objects: USA* exhibition finally tramples the neat picket fences between 'crafts' and 'fine arts.' That is the major purpose of the show and it succeeds magnificently."[70] *Woman's Day* explained, "The creations

of many of the new breed of craftsmen are not necessarily functional, but intended purely for the owners to contemplate and enjoy as works of art—which is why the generic term used for the exhibition is 'objects.'"[71] The exhibition was also featured on television, but even as the project was promoted far and wide, its ramifications were not always accepted, and perhaps not very well understood. A Washington, DC, critic neatly summarized the problem: "The crafts, in many places and in many ways, [are] turning themselves into art (definitions later)."[72]

When Nordness first started showing craft objects in his gallery in 1960, he had actually insisted that they be functional, presumably because he thought of them merely as a contrasting accent to the painting and sculpture that were his mainstay. But by the mid-1960s, as he put it, "I saw a pot so meaningful to me that, hold water or not, I had to have it. The craftsmen . . . forced me to reorient my thinking."[73] At this point, Nordness was carrying a fairly conservative roster of formalist sculptors, color-field painters, and latter-day abstract expressionists in his gallery, many of whom had been included in *Art: USA: Now*.[74] Judging from these commitments to fine art, it seems likely that at this point Nordness began to see craft as an arena in which modernist artistic values might be preserved and extended. His taste in craft quickly grew more progressive, however, and in 1968 he staged his first one-craftsperson show, for Wendell Castle. By the time *Objects: USA* opened a year later, about half of the Nordness Gallery stable was made up of exhibitors from the exhibition, and Nordness had exclusive rights not only to Castle's furniture, but also to the work of ceramist Howard Kottler, metalsmith Stanley Lechtzin, glass artist Harvey Littleton, and fiber artists Ed Rossbach and Katherine Westphal, among others. He also was one of the first dealers to show glass artists Dale Chihuly, Marvin Lipofsky, and Joel Philip Myers.[75] Thanks to *Objects: USA*, Nordness was in a unique position to establish the reputations of a select group, and he performed that task well.

To his frustration, however, Nordness found it difficult to convince the art world that studio craftspeople were playing on their side. In a 1971 talk he ruefully admitted, "I am having one hell of a time selling anything but paintings and bronzes in New York because the critics will not endorse the craft-media work."[76] True to form, the only New York art critic of any stature to review *Objects: USA* panned it. Writing in *New York Magazine*, Barbara Rose pronounced the exhibition to be "a disaster for the crafts," and further explained:

> The individual, divorced from a community of artisans, taking from fine art the license of self-expression, amusement, and occasional formal interest, is not capable of participating in a genuine craft tradition. *Objects: USA*, consequently, is a collection of absurdist fantasies produced by individual egos striving for self-expression, as unwilling to assume any role of social responsibility as the fine artist.[77]

For Rose, craft was appealing precisely because it was functional, and therefore bound to the social landscape in a way that individualistic art could not be. *Objects: USA* seemed to her a rejection of this connection to the everyday.

A similar critique came from craft's socially activist flank. *Studio Potter* editor Gerry Williams, for example, found the exhibition "academically oriented, gallery oriented, and museum oriented" and, despite the inclusion of his own work, saw it as divorced from the ethical orientation of craft.[78] David Zack, a partisan of the California Funk ceramics movement, vented his frustration in a vigorous critique of *Objects: USA* published in *ARTnews*. Committed to an ideal of the rebellious craftsman, Zack bristled at the show's emphasis on "the artists' personal worthiness, hardworking qualities and essentially harmless conformity," and sarcastically objected to Nordness's goal of creating a wider and better market: "Did the stagers of the 'Object' [*sic*] show have any idea what lay behind what they rather pretentiously labeled the new art movement? All indications suggest they were mainly out to help sell the objects in galleries after publicizing them through museums."[79] In presenting a multivalent picture of the craft movement, the exhibition managed to both inspire and infuriate onlookers on all sides.

The most ironic fact about *Objects: USA*, though, was that it owed its success—and perhaps even its existence—to just the type of craft that it was dedicated to transcending through art. Samuel Johnson's reasons for getting involved as the project's Medici had something to do with his personal connection to Nordness and with his leadership as a corporate patron of the arts, but his main affinity to craft lay in his own hobbies. Johnson was a keen amateur woodworker. A *New York Times* profile, published shortly after *Objects: USA* opened, included an image prominently showcasing one of his mosaic-topped coffee tables. He was also interested in cutting and polishing figured stones. After seeing the exhibition, his wife, Imogene Powers Johnson, commented, "I suppose it's fair to say that we like the crafts a bit better than the arts. When we saw this Johnson craft exhibit it was especially interesting because of the things we've done in our own workshop. I think a lot of other people will feel the same way. Crafts are something most people understand."[80] This genuine enthusiasm for hobby craft could hardly have been espoused by Nordness the art dealer, nor even by the relatively open-minded Paul Smith, who frequently bemoaned the amateurish look of objects on sale at the fairs and shops of the day. But Mrs. Johnson's words point to a basic truth about craft's public. Earlier in the decade, the always pragmatic David Campbell, then director of the Museum of Contemporary Crafts, had predicted as much: "Amateurs have developed the imagination which allows them to appreciate the perfected skill of professionals, even though they are denied the ability to produce creative work of their own. . . . Avocational artists and craftsmen [have] become an appreciative audience for the artist without which he would find it difficult to survive."[81]

How many of the people in *Objects: USA*'s record-breaking crowds came because they were interested in crafts as a progressive art form, and how many came because they saw a connection to things they'd done (or would have liked to do) at home? No audience surveys survive to tell us, but an answer was strongly implied in the press reaction to *Objects: USA*, which identified crafts-as-art as an alternative to the increasingly incomprehensible excesses of contemporary art. A Cincinnati writer, for example, recognized that "the general public is far more receptive to this kind of work than they are to the more exclusively fine arts media." It was a point pithily echoed by journalist Sarah Booth Conroy, who not only wrote the *New York Times* profile of the Johnsons, but also noted in her own review of *Objects: USA* that "when art can be a stuffed goat or a laser beam . . . people who like their art straight may find it easier today to accept crafts as art."[82]

⌗

The story of *Objects: USA* suggests that if the craft movement was at its height in 1970, it was also at a crossroads. After three decades of intense professionalization, the

movement nonetheless owed its success partly to a wave of popular and amateur craft. This was an area of activity that the American Handicraft Council (soon to be renamed the American Craft Council, as it remains today) had actively tried to hold at bay in the first years of its history. Now, though, there was a meeting of the minds. Looking back, Paul Smith recalled that "it was all about individualism. People suddenly said, forget the past, we want to do our thing. . . . There were two things going on. There was a larger group of people learning to bake and grow sunflowers or whatever, and there was another group of people doing more sophisticated work. But in the air there was something going on that linked them, and nurtured ideas."[83] The craft movement now covered a huge swathe of artistic idioms—from functional to Funk and back again—and had found a firm footing in the countercultural spirit of the day. The national council, based in New York, achieved undoubted preeminence, and it developed a successful program oriented to regional activity. In 1960 it initiated a research service supported by a grant from the Rockefeller Foundation and dedicated to preserving the archive of the movement. The council's focus on academically trained professionals, mostly confined to a few media, however, may have limited the movement's reach. The 1970s would see a turn away from the undisciplined edges of craft and toward higher-end markets. Craftspeople became increasingly concerned with commercial success and less involved with political conviction and avant-garde exploration.[84] Meanwhile, in a broader geographical context, the World Crafts Council had brought together an international group of makers and advocates seeking common ground, but participants discovered that geographical difference was even more forbidding, and more fascinating, than they had expected.

Most important, *Objects: USA* brought the logic of individualism that had propelled the movement to its predictable conclusion. After the war, the fear had been that corporate and institutional forces would erode the American character. Webb and her allies managed to construct a framework so encouraging of individual creativity that its own institutional imperatives came to seem suspect. As the maverick studio furniture maker Art Espenet Carpenter explained, "I have a fundamental belief: the more independent people there are, who are not connected with any organization, the better society is."[85] The organizational infrastructure of craft today is incomparably superior to that enjoyed by the movement's pioneers.

But—perhaps for that very reason—the sense that studio craft is an urgent project united by fragile ideals is long gone. In the 1970s and '80s, the movement gradually lost the cultural relevance it once seemed to possess. Certain caricatures—macramé, brown pots, hand-dyed clothing—became emblems of unfashionability for a time. It could even be argued that for all the vibrancy of the craft scene in the past forty years, there have been no creative break-throughs that quite match the drama and impact of the 1950s and '60s: radical ceramics, off-loom weaving, found-object jewelry, sculptural furniture, and the emergence of studio glass.

Meanwhile, today's young DIY (do-it-yourself) "crafters," who are the inheritors of the studio craft movement's anxieties about individual expression, have actually inverted its logic. Most are well versed in contemporary art, but only some have been trained in academic craft programs (and those who are often seek to move into other fields, such as video or installation art, rather than dedicate themselves to a particular medium). While the postwar generation fought courageously to be taken seriously as professionals and artists, the new craft subculture presents itself as a community of amateurs and small business owners. Rather than building national and international organizations, they are content to band together in small groups, which interact through the new virtual and viral tools afforded by the Internet. Contemporary artists, designers, and institutions are even more suspicious of the craft brand, maintaining a studied distance from the "c" word even as they apply artisanal thinking in new and thrilling ways.

But in so many respects, craft's multifarious present was made possible by the innovations of those in the past. Without the legacy of Webb's financial support and organizational genius, or Slivka's critical acuity, or Smith's showcasing of craft's many guises, or Nordness's sheer ambition, our sense of the possibilities would be greatly diminished. Perhaps the real gift of the postwar generation has been the opportunity to take craft for granted. In 1945 it seemed a real possibility that handmade things might disappear from the earth and that only concerted and coordinated effort could preserve their place in American culture. Today, the reverse is true. Handmade is here to stay, but organizations struggle to find a role in the increasingly fragmented craftscape. Much of what was built in the 1940s, '50s, and '60s is being disassembled in the name of post-disciplinary progress. At such a

moment, it is worth revisiting the postwar decades, if only to be reminded of what was gained, as well as lost, when these individuals banded together.

I would like to thank Edward S. Cooke, Jr., Jeannine Falino, Arline Fisch, Lois Moran, and Paul Smith for their generous comments regarding preliminary drafts of this essay. —GA

1 Don Martindale, "Timidity, Conformity, and the Search for Personal Identity," *Annals of the American Academy of Political and Social Science* 378 (July 1968), 86; Irene Taviss Thomson, "From Conflict to Embedment: The Individual-Society Relationship, 1920–1991," *Sociological Forum* 12 (December 1997), 631–58.

2 "Bulletin No. 1 on the Program for Individual Opportunities Through Manual Industry and the Hand Arts," [c. 1943], Boston Society of Arts and Crafts papers, AAA, SI.

3 Charles Reich, *The Greening of America* (New York: Random House, 1970), 384.

4 Bob Stocksdale, oral history interview by Signe Mayfield, February 16–March 21, 2001, AAA, SI; Mira Nakashima, *Nature, Form and Spirit: The Life and Legacy of George Nakashima* (New York: Harry N. Abrams, 2003).

5 Between 1920 and 1922, for example, she was president of New York City's Junior League. "Mrs. Webb Given Members' Award of Junior League," *New York Times*, April 30, 1963, 24.

6 Aileen Osborn Webb, oral history interview by Paul Cummings, May 7, 1970, AAA, SI.

7 Among the board members were Richard F. Bach, curator and director of industrial relations for The Metropolitan Museum of Art, New York; Louise Bonney, executive secretary for a committee of the New York World's Fair; Holger Cahill, director of the Federal Art Project of the Works Progress Administration; R. Guy Cowan, ceramic designer; Horace Jayne, director of the University of Pennsylvania Art Museum; Humphrey J. Emery, head of the Boston Society of Arts and Crafts; and Alfred Auerbach, the editor of *Retailing* magazine; see Executive Meeting minutes, June 21 1939, and "Tentative Agreement with the Rockefeller Center," [c. 1939]. American Handicraft Council papers, AAA, SI.

8 The report was conducted by Robert L. Hurley, a recent graduate of the Harvard Business School, in conjunction with Humphrey Emery. Research began in New England in 1939 and broadened to New York, the Southern Highlands, Ohio, and Michigan in 1940. In addition questionnaires were sent to makers and companies, including Porter Blanchard in California, Maurice Heaton in New York, Samuel Yellin in Philadelphia, and the glass firm W. H. Blenko in West Virginia. A preliminary report on New England, also extant, had been prepared by William Drown Phelps in 1938; see American Handicraft Council papers, AAA, SI.

9 Richard F. Bach, "Crafts, Handicrafts and Homecrafts," 1938, American Handicraft Council papers, AAA, SI.

10 Webb had by this point already held an exploratory meeting of twelve craft organizations from around the country in

Shelburne, Vermont. Webb, "Almost a Century," typescript, 1977, 70, Aileen Osborn Webb papers, AAA, SI. The AHC's minutes record the following response to her invitation: "It seems that Mrs. Webb desires to bring together ten craft organizations in the east, with headquarters and a salesroom in New York . . . This seemed unlikely for the Council has no intention, at the moment, of covering the whole field of handicrafts and Mrs. Webb's group would doubtless be one of the last to be absorbed" (Executive Meeting minutes, June 21, 1939. American Handicraft Council papers, AAA, SI).

11 Lois Moran, letter to the author, March 31, 2009. Webb recalled in her autobiography that she and Morgan "met and talked over our problem, for it seemed ridiculous for us both to have duplicate organizations with almost the same name. . . . Both groups had the same aims, and that was the deciding factor for the amalgamation of the two boards" (Webb, "Almost a Century," 73–74, and 90–91).

12 ACEC: The Record of Ten Years, 1943–1953, pamphlet (New York: American Craftsmen's Educational Council, 1953), n.p.

13 Webb, "Almost a Century," 71–72, 83.

14 Carleton Varney, The Draper Touch (New York: Simon and Schuster, 1988); "Fifth Avenue's First Lady," Time Magazine (December 31, 1945). America House would close in 1971, but for a time it had successful branches in Sun Valley, Idaho; Seattle; and Bloomfield Hills, Michigan (Webb, "Almost a Century," 75–76).

15 Webb, oral history interview.

16 Campbell became director of

the League of New Hampshire Craftsmen in 1938 (at the age of thirty-one) and went on to be one of Webb's closest advisers, a president of the council, and director of the Museum of Contemporary Crafts.

17 Webb, oral history interview. Frances Wright Caroë was again instrumental in the planning and founding of the SAC; according to Webb, she "had an idée fixe that it should not be turned into an 'arty' school, but should train people for life" (Webb, "Almost a Century," 113).

18 "Bulletin No. 1 on the Program for Individual Opportunities." The SAC soon moved to Alfred University in upstate New York, and then to the Rochester Institute of Technology, where it remains today.

19 "Survey of Craft Education," CH 11 (summer 1951), 42.

20 Carlus Dyer, "Craftsmanship in Display," CH 13 (January/February 1953), 35–40.

21 Paul Smith, interview with the author, March 10, 2009. Smith emphasized that while Rudolfsky and d'Amico were particularly important influences for him, "there wasn't really a big love affair" between the institutions despite their proximity, and direct collaborations were limited.

22 "Exhibitions," CH 11 (summer 1951), 43. On the MoMA Good Design exhibitions and their influence, see Terence Riley and Edward Eigen, "Between the Museum and the Marketplace: Selling Good Design," in John Szarkowski et al., The Museum of Modern Art at Mid-Century: At Home and Abroad (New York: Museum of Modern Art and Harry N. Abrams, 1995), 151–77.

23 These were the Art Institute of Chicago, Brooklyn Museum of Art, City Art Museum of St.

Louis, Cleveland Museum of Art, Currier Gallery of Art, Denver Art Museum, Detroit Institute of Arts, San Francisco Museum of Art, Virginia Museum of Fine Arts, and Wadsworth Atheneum, Hartford. Some of these museums staged exhibitions in advance of the national show.

24 Dorothy Giles, "The Craftsman in America," in Designer Craftsmen U.S.A., exh. cat. (Brooklyn: Brooklyn Museum and the American Craftsmen's Educational Council, 1953), 13.

25 Don Wallance, Shaping America's Products (New York: Reinhold, 1956).

26 The Asilomar conference was the first in a series of four national conferences; the others were held at Lake Geneva, Wisconsin (1958); Lake George, New York (1959); and the University of Washington in Seattle (1961). The series was revived in 1968 for the council's twenty-fifth anniversary. Lois Moran notes that there was also a precedent in a small conference held in San Francisco in 1955, dedicated to discussing "the program of services to American craftsmen" (Moran, letter).

27 ACC, Asilomar: First Annual Conference of American Craftsmen, proceedings (New York: ACC, 1957), 63.

28 Ibid.

29 Ibid., 39–40.

30 Philip McConnell, "The Significance of a Pavilion and the Case for Merchandising," CH 17 (July/August 1957), 67.

31 "Asilomar: An On-the-Scene Report from the First National Conference of American Craftsmen," CH 17 (July/August 1957), 17–32.

32 Asilomar, 138.

33 Ibid., 139.

34 Ibid., 142.

35 Jack Lenor Larsen, remarks at the 1958 American Craftsmen's Educational Conference in Lake Geneva, as quoted in Diane Douglas and Vicki Halper, Choosing Craft: The Artist's Viewpoint (Chapel Hill: University of North Carolina Press, 2009), 197.

36 Scripps College, introduction to The Enjoyment of Ceramic Art, exh. cat. (Claremont: Scripps College, 1955), n.p.; Rose Slivka, "The New Ceramic Presence," CH 21 (July/August 1961), 30–37.

37 Ibid., 32.

38 Dorothy Liebes, "Designing Textiles for Industry," CH 12 (May–June 1952), 19–21; Lore Kadden, "Designing for the Fashion Market," CH 13 (March/April 1953), 38–39; Peggy Ives, "Handweaver Prospers with the Haute Couture," CH 13 (July/August 1953), 39–41; Frances Van Hall, "Cottons Designed on a Hand Loom," CH 13 (September/October 1953), 35–37.

39 While this new generation of artist-craftspeople was not necessarily to Webb's liking, she was broad-minded enough to accept their innovative spirit. In commenting on Funk ceramics, for example, she noted that "it has been difficult for me to bear at times when Paul Smith has shown a ceramic purse that imitates leather, or a toilet of even more doubtful beauty. He has felt it was incumbent upon him [to] show the passing scene and he is right, but I have found it hard sometimes to accept" (Webb, "Almost a Century," 128). Smith concurs: "There were things she just couldn't stand, like [Robert] Arneson for example. She just would say, 'I don't like it.' . . . I would say,

'Mrs. Webb, this is what is happening.' [But] she would never take anything out of a show, or cancel a show. . . . She didn't relate to it, but she didn't stop it" (Smith, interview, March 10, 2009).

40 "The Craftsman," prepared as a report to the ACC, 1961, typescript, Folder 39, Box 5, Margaret Merwin Patch Papers, AAA, SI.

41 Margaret Merwin Patch, "Beginning of the World Crafts Council," typescript, 1982, Folder 12, Box 7, Margaret Merwin Patch Papers, AAA, SI; Rita Reif, "Craftsmen of 52 Nations Meet Today," New York Times, June 8, 1964, 24.

42 Arline Fisch, interview with the author, February 9, 2009.

43 World Crafts Council Conference, pamphlet, 1964, Folder 1, Box 7, Margaret Merwin Patch Papers, AAA, SI.

44 The First World Conference of Craftsmen, proceedings (New York: ACC, 1965), 79.

45 Ibid., 12.

46 Ibid., 47, 38, 66.

47 Fisch, interview.

48 First World Conference of Craftsmen, 74.

49 Harvey K. Littleton, oral history interview by Joan Falconer Byrd, March 15, 2001, AAA, SI. Lois Moran echoes this perspective: "WCC delegates, particularly those from Asia, Africa and South America, pressed for the organization to be proactive in marketing, but this desire was never effectively realized within the WCC structure. It is interesting to note that the former WCC Secretary General, James Plaut, achieved more in the marketing arena by founding Aid to Artisans, which today enjoys considerable success" (Moran, letter).

50 "World Crafts to be Aided by

UNESCO," *New York Times*, March 17, 1965, 40. Webb would remain the president of the WCC through 1974.

51 Helen Giambruni, "California Design X," *CH* 28 (March/April 1968), 11, 54–56. The jurors were Bernard Kester, Paul Mills, and Frank Laury. Kester, a weaver and potter who also designed several of the California Design installations, would go on to organize the seminal fiber survey exhibition *Deliberate Entanglements* for the UCLA art gallery in 1972. He is still active as an exhibition designer at the Los Angeles County Museum of Art.

52 William Hull, foreword to *XXI Ceramic National* (Syracuse: Everson Museum of Art, 1960), 5.

53 Max W. Sullivan, introduction to *24th Ceramic National Exhibition* (Syracuse: Everson Museum of Art, 1966), 9.

54 Warren MacKenzie, juror's statement in ibid., 10–11.

55 Max W. Sullivan, 7.

56 Dextra Frankel, juror's statement in ibid., 11. Other jurors included Rudy Autio, Paul Soldner, the Funk potter Joseph Pugliese, and Ka-Kwong Hui, a New York City potter who was involved with pop art as the maker of Roy Lichtenstein's ceramics.

57 Donald McKinley, "24th Ceramic National," *CH* 26 (November/December 1966), 59, 60.

58 Jean Deluis, "25th Ceramic National," *CH* 29 1 (January/February 1969), 31.

59 Lotte Streisinger, letter to the editor, *CH* 29 (May/June 1969), 9.

60 Donna Nicholas, "The XXVII Ceramic National at Syracuse," *CH* 32 (December 1972), 27. See also Garth Clark,

"Ceramics Since 1950," in Barbara Perry, ed., *American Ceramics: The Collection of the Everson Museum of Art* (New York: Rizzoli, 1989), 203; and Garth Clark and Margie Hughto, *A Century of Ceramics in the United States 1878–1978* (New York: E. P. Dutton and Everson Museum of Art, 1979), 196–97.

61 Nicholas, XXVII Ceramic National, 31.

62 On this project, see Margie Hughto, *New Works in Clay by Contemporary Painters and Sculptors* (Syracuse: Everson Museum of Art, 1976); "Museum Clay at the Everson," *CH* 36 (April 1976), 26–29; and Kenneth Moffett, "Ceramics and the Avant-Garde Since World War II," in Moffett and Jonathan Fairbanks, *Directions in Contemporary American Ceramics* (Boston: Museum of Fine Arts, 1984).

63 Mary Jane Leland, "Entanglements," *CH* 32 (February 1972), 54. On this transformative moment in fiber see Elissa Auther, "Fiber Art and the Hierarchy of Art and Craft, 1960–1980," *The Journal of Modern Craft* 1 (March 2008), 13–34.

64 Nordness, *Objects: USA*. "*Objects: USA* here Nov. 17, has drawn 533,120 visitors," press release prepared by Carl Byoir and Associates, 1971, ACC Archive, M. 80/9. The extensive itinerary included Washington, Boston, Rochester, Bloomfield Hills (Cranbrook), Indianapolis, Cincinnati, St. Paul, Iowa City, Little Rock, Seattle, Portland, Los Angeles, Oakland, Phoenix, Lincoln, Milwaukee, Chattanooga, Pittsburgh, Columbia (SC), Atlanta, New York City, Madrid, Milan, Zurich, Cologne, Hamburg, Stockholm, Helsinki, Edinburgh, Birmingham, and

Brussels. See "Crafts Exhibit Itinerary Is From Coast to Coast," *AIA Journal* 52 (November 1969), 15–16.

65 Ed Rossbach, "Objects: USA Revisited," *CH* 32 (August 1972), 38–39.

66 American Art Expositions, *Art: USA: 59: A Force, a Language, a Frontier*, exh. cat. (New York: American Art Expositions, 1959); see also Jeremy Adamson, *The Furniture of Sam Maloof* (Washington, DC: Smithsonian American Art Museum; New York: W. W. Norton & Company, 2001), 92.

67 Lee Nordness, ed., *Art: USA: Now*, text by Allen S. Weller, exh. cat. (Lucerne: C. J. Bucher; New York: Viking Press, 1962).

68 The work was selected on the basis of visits to schools and studios; Smith proposed a list of craftspeople to Nordness, and the two traveled the country together. Paul Smith, interview by the author, December 14, 1998. Smith also was able to acquire more than a third of the work from the exhibition, which became a core of the Museum of Contemporary Crafts' collection; other work was distributed to venues that had participated in the American tour.

69 Joy Hakanson, "Art World: Lo, an Angel," *Detroit Sunday News*, February 22, 1970, clipping, *Objects: USA* file, ACC Archive.

70 Don Morrison, quoted in "*Objects: USA* on Tour, a Sampling of Critical Comments," Museum of Contemporary Crafts press package, M. 80/10, ACC Archive.

71 "*Objects: USA*, Tomorrow's Heirlooms from Today's American Craftsmen," *Women's Day* (August 1969), 46.

72 Frank Getlein, "New Things

Are Happening in Some Old Media," *Sunday Star,* October 5, 1969, clipping, *Objects: USA* file, ACC Archive.

73 Lee Nordness, lecture, [c. 1967], Box 10, Lee Nordness papers, AAA, SI.

74 "Permanent Roster: partial listing," c. 1969, Box 112, Lee Nordness papers, AAA, SI.

75 Ibid.; Louise Bruner, "Proper Recognition for Artist-Craftsmen Is in the Offing," [Toledo] *Blade*, December 29, 1968, clipping, *Objects: USA* file, ACC Archive; "Exclusivity as of June 17, 1969," Box 106, Lee Nordness papers, AAA, SI; various gallery records, Boxes 106, 112, 435, Lee Nordness Papers, AAA, SI.

76 Lee Nordness and Margaret Phillips, performance lecture, 1971, 20–21. AAA, SI, Lee Nordness Papers. Box 10, pp. 20–21. Paul Smith emphasizes the limitations of Nordness's space, located in a basement on Seventy-fifth Street: "It was not a 57th Street or Madison Avenue gallery. I don't want to degrade it. He was very enterprising and had lots of social contacts, but he wouldn't have been getting reviewers from the *Times* there. He wasn't in that arena, especially in the sixties when there was so much going on" (Smith, interview, March 10, 2009).

77 Barbara Rose, "Crafts Ain't What They Used to Be," *New York Magazine* (June 19, 1972), 72–73.

78 Gerry Williams, interview by author, February 15, 1999.

79 David Zack, "Nut Art in Quake Time," *ARTnews* 69 (March 1970), 38–40, 77.

80 Sarah Booth Conroy, "At Home With Johnson (Wax)

Family: Decor Shows What They Enjoy Doing," *New York Times*, October 19, 1969, 82.

81 David R. Campbell, "Decorative Arts and Crafts," Voice of America broadcast script, [c. 1959–62], microfilm1518, David C. Campbell papers, AAA, SI.

82 Owen Findsen, "The New Object," *Cincinnati Enquirer*, April 26, 1970; and Sarah Booth Conroy, "Crafts Steal March on the Arts," *Washington Daily News*, October 7, 1969, *Objects: USA* file, ACC Archive.

83 Smith, interview, March 10, 2009.

84 Perhaps the best instance of this shift is in glass, where counterculture experiment gave way to sophisticated commercial enterprise. The story is well told in Tina Oldknow, *Pilchuck: A Glass School* (Seattle: Washington University Press, 1996). See also Edward S. Cooke Jr., "Wood in the 1980s: Expansion or Commodification?" in Davira Taragin et al., *Contemporary Crafts and the Saxe Collection* (New York: Hudson Hills, 1993).

85 Quoted in Rick Mastelli, "Art Carpenter: The Independent Spirit of the Baulines Craftsmen's Guild," *Fine Woodworking* 37 (December 1982), 65; reprinted in Douglas and Halper, *Choosing Craft*, p. 21.

29

MARY SCHEIER
EDWIN SCHEIER
Bowl with Abstract
Figure Design, 1957
EARTHENWARE
16⅛ X 11⅛ X 11⅛ IN.
(41 X 28.3 X 28.3 CM)
MUSEUM OF ARTS AND DESIGN,
PURCHASED BY THE
AMERICAN CRAFT COUNCIL, 1958

30

ALBERT PALEY

Fibula Brooch, 1969

STERLING SILVER, 14-KARAT GOLD,
PEARLS, AND LABRADORITE

6 X 3½ X 1 IN. (15.2 X 8.9 X 2.5 CM)

MUSEUM OF FINE ARTS, HOUSTON,
PROMISED GIFT OF HELEN WILLIAMS

DRUTT ENGLISH TR 1065-2006

32

WILLIAM CLARKE

Police State Badge, 1969

STERLING SILVER AND 14-KARAT GOLD

2⅞ X 2¹⁵⁄₁₆ X 3¹⁵⁄₁₆ IN. (7.3 X 7.5 X 10 CM)

COURTESY OF VELVET DA VINCI GALLERY,

SAN FRANCISCO, CA

31

RONALD SENUNGETUK

Pin, 1969

STERLING SILVER

2⅜ X 1⅝ X ¼ IN. (6 X 4.1 X 0.6 CM)

MUSEUM OF ARTS AND DESIGN,

GIFT OF THE JOHNSON WAX COMPANY, THROUGH

THE AMERICAN CRAFT COUNCIL, 1977

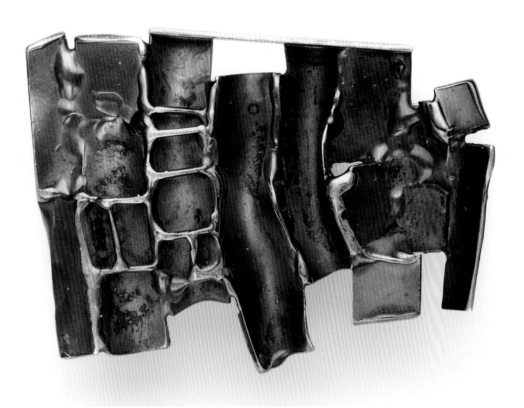

33

RICHARD SHAW

Couch and Chair with Landscape and Cows, 1966–67

EARTHENWARE, ACRYLIC PAINT, WOOD, AND LEATHER

CHAIR, 9 X 10 X 5¾ IN. (22.9 X 25.4 X 14.6 CM);

COUCH, 9¾ X 18½ X 10 IN. (24.8 X 47 X 25.4 CM)

MUSEUM OF ARTS AND DESIGN, GIFT OF THE JOHNSON WAX COMPANY,

THROUGH THE AMERICAN CRAFT COUNCIL, 1977

34

KA KWONG HUI

Form, 1968

EARTHENWARE

20 IN. (50.8 CM); DIAM. 19 IN. (48.3 CM)

MUSEUM OF ARTS AND DESIGN,

GIFT OF THE JOHNSON WAX COMPANY, THROUGH

THE AMERICAN CRAFT COUNCIL, 1977

36

ROBERT SPERRY

Totem Crying for Lost Memory, 1962

STONEWARE

48 X 17 X 10 IN. (121.9 X 43.2 X 25.4 CM)

TACOMA ART MUSEUM, GIFT OF

GENE AND LIZ BRANDZEL, 2000.37.2

35

CLAYTON BAILEY

Untitled, c. 1970

CERAMIC AND FOUND SUITCASE WITH VELVET LINING

OPEN: 8¼ X 30½ X 25¼ IN. (21 X 77.5 X 64.1 CM)

MUSEUM OF ARTS AND DESIGN,

GIFT OF FLORENCE RUBENFELD, 2001

37

JOEL EDWARDS

Lidded Vessel, c. 1966

STONEWARE

16¾ IN. (42.5 CM);

DIAM. 11¾ IN. (29.8 CM)

FORREST L. MERRILL

COLLECTION

38

WILLIAM WYMAN
*Homage
to Robert Frost*, 1962
STONEWARE
27 X 16 X 3½ IN.
(68.6 X 40.6 X 8.9 CM)
EVERSON MUSEUM OF ART,
SYRACUSE, MUSEUM PURCHASE
PRIZE GIVEN BY SYRACUSE
CHINA CORPORATION,
22ND CERAMIC NATIONAL,
1962–64; 62.40

CHAPTER 3

Rothko and the Four Seasons Commission: A Parable of Art and Design at the Mid-Twentieth Century

LOWERY STOKES SIMS

IN THE 2010 BROADWAY PRODUCTION *RED*—WHICH provided entrée to the studio of the abstract expressionist painter Mark Rothko—a secondary plot development by playwright John Logan provides the thematic focus of this essay. The play is set in the 1950s when Rothko and his contemporaries had gained more recognition in the art world and society at large. In the midst of agonizing over his current position and stature in the art world, Rothko obsesses about his decision to accept a commission from architects Philip Johnson and Ludwig Mies van der Rohe to create a series of paintings for the new Four Seasons Restaurant in the Seagram Building **(FIG. 3.1)**. Rothko worries that by accepting this commission he has allowed his work to become mere decor—the backdrop for mealtime conversations—or worse, subordinate to architecture **(FIG. 3.2)**.

This plot twist—well documented by contemporary sources[1]—demonstrates how the creative sector would prove to be a central player in the emergence of the United States as a world power after World War II. At that moment the ranks of those involved in craft and design were bolstered by an influx of students—many of them returning GIs—and practitioners who were poised to meet the demand for innovative and exciting interior treatments for the burgeoning home market created by GIs and their families. Abstract expressionism was being promoted as the preeminent art movement in the United States as this country assumed center stage in the global art scene. No longer would the United States be a backwater locale. And the arenas of design and craft, in addition to art, would figure in the perception of American society as fully modern and progressive.

But what also occurred between 1945 and 1969 was a solidification of the lines of demarcation between "art" and "craft" or "art" and "design" in critical and theoretic circles, particularly the most advanced modernist ones. This despite the fact that avant-garde movements of the earlier twentieth century in Russia, Germany, and the Netherlands recruited from all three creative arenas to create visions of modern utopian societies unfettered by the social, political, and economic concerns of the past. So despite the egalitarian aspirations of early modernism, the phenomenon of mass production in the midst of a more pervasive prosperity in postwar America was anathema to "critics committed to preserving the sanctity of high-art modernism."[2]

One commentator who "devoted his critical project to the defense of high-art modernism"—and certainly the most influential—was Clement Greenberg. Along with social critics Bernard Rosenberg and David Manning White, Greenberg shared the opinion that vigilance was required against "the encroachment of middle-class culture—what he, borrowing the term from [William H.] White, called 'the middlebrow.'"[3] Greenberg had outlined his critical perspective in "The Avant-Garde and Kitsch" (1939).[4] He established an evolutionary track for modernist art—specifically painting—disparaging all forms of artistic endeavor related to sentiment or functionality. His essay was a pointed attack on content in art, a position that Greenberg saw as a safeguard against the possible deleterious influence of propaganda or polemical art. As Rosenberg also warned, "At its worst, mass culture threatens not merely to cretinize our taste but to brutalize our senses while paving the way to totalitarianism."[5] Given the intractability of these positions, it is no wonder that for Greenberg only painting, particularly abstract painting, could represent the epitome of the new era of American cultural expression. He disregarded the achievements of designers such as Ray and Charles Eames, Jack Lenor Larsen, and Dorothy Liebes, or of craftsmen like Peter Voulkos—who created objects meant to function and possibly elicit sentiment.

Despite this critical divide, however, during the 1940s, '50s, and '60s, there were many "fine" artists who were involved in making work that would be designated as "craft" or "design" or contributing elements to interior design in residential, business, and religious contexts. This

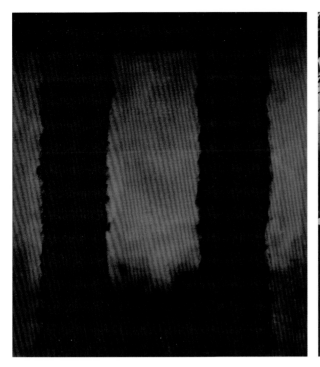

demonstrates the presence and influence of European immigrants who had been involved in early European modernism in the United States starting around World War II. Anni and Josef Albers, for example, shaped their careers exploring the interconnectedness of textiles and paintings and transplanted this sensibility based on their experiences in the German Bauhaus to a new generation of creators, first at Black Mountain College in North Carolina and later at Yale University. At Black Mountain, the Albers' students included painter and collagist Robert Rauschenberg and his future wife, sculptor Susan Weil. Similarly Hungarian-born constructivist sculptor László Moholy-Nagy established an American version of the Bauhaus in Chicago, where his philosophy was key to the development of jeweler Margaret De Patta, textile artist Lenore Tawney, and many others.

Tawney also studied at the Penland School of Crafts in North Carolina but found her signature medium of fiber while working in a studio on Coenties Slip in New York City, where painters Rauschenberg, Ellsworth Kelly, Agnes Martin, and Jasper Johns were her neighbors. Tawney's presentation of simple centralized shapes paralleled such iconic elements populating the canvases of Kelly and Adolph Gottlieb, and her open-weave technique paralleled the spare grid-line themes in Martin's paintings. Tawney's career evolution highlights the contradictory, even schizophrenic situation as craft and art maneuvered to establish their positions in art discourse. Tawney developed a mode of working characterized by

FIG. 3.1
Mark Rothko, *Red on Maroon* (Seagram Building series), 1959. Oil on canvas. 105 x 94 in. (266.7 x 238.8 cm). Courtesy of Tate, London.

FIG. 3.2
Waiters serving tables at the Four Seasons restaurant, c. 1959.

what art critic Holland Cotter described as a "distinctive open-warp technique that was basically like drawing or painting with individual floating threads," leaving "much of the fabric unwoven and transparent."[6] Traditional weaving circles found Tawney's work "heretical," while the art world designated it as too "craftsy."[7] But Tawney found a supportive colleague in Martin, who recognized "that Tawney's weavings were extraordinary."[8] She wrote in the brochure of Tawney's first major exhibition, held at the Staten Island Museum, that "to see new and original expression in a very old medium, and not just one new form but a complete new form in each piece of work, is wholly unlooked for, and is a wonderful and gratifying experience."[9]

Even a mainstream art star such as Rauschenberg could not escape the materialist approach of craft in his work. His appropriations of actual (or "found") objects—such as his own bed (FIG. 3.3), a taxidermied sheep and rubber tire (*Monogram*, 1955–56), and more modestly in the collaged imagery of *Signs* (1970) (CAT. 85)—are characteristic of trends in assemblage associated with Californian crafts. At the same time, the work of individuals firmly anchored in the craft world, such as Peter Voulkos, John Mason, and Jim Melchert, also breached the art/craft divide. Their sculptural ceramics were beyond all functional concern, and—in Melchert's case—interfaced with performance art and Happenings. Indeed many of the works to be found in *Crafting Modernism* demonstrate this blurred zone among the genres, which

was not critically recognized as such at the time. In myriad ways individuals on both sides of craft and art crossed the boundary. They engaged in a rich and multifarious dialogue, encompassing the traditionally divided concerns of art, craft, and design, between the end of World War II and the late 1960s.

Within this chronological span, the objects presented bridge several identified stylistic tendencies that have become canonical benchmarks in the history of twentieth-century American art: the formal fracturing and spontaneity of abstract expressionism, the insouciant parody of pop art, the simplicity and serial (pattern) instincts of color-field painting and minimalism, and the then-burgeoning psychedelic expressions. And while there were "craftspeople" who challenged notions of utility and functionality in their formal exercises comparable to what was going on in painting and sculpture, there were also "artists" creating in the "craft" categories and those who found a new path moving from art to craft media and vice versa.

Attitudes about craft in the art world percolated to the surface in the art commentary of the time. The paintings of Robert Barrell (a lesser-known contemporary of the abstract expressionists), for example, were dismissed as "too craftsmanlike" because they resembled "well woven mosaics." This alone, notes art historian Ann Gibson, would have been "deadly in Abstract Expressionist circles."[10] But while the evocation of mosaic could have been a pejorative in the case of Barrell, its adoption in artistic practice in contemporary art (along with stained glass) speaks to the exploration of the relationship of art to architecture in general and interiors specifically. Alone among her contemporaries, Jeanne Reynal worked exclusively in mosaic (FIG. 3.4), but devising a more free-form approach in which the individual tesserae were seemingly tossed at random into the concrete or binding medium. A more canonical adaptation of the mosaic technique can be seen in the 1947 table by painter Lee Krasner (CAT. 49). Set within the metal rim of a wagon wheel, it features sections of colored glass as well as "such trivia as keys and coins" in the concrete, creating "a varied pattern."[11]

The Krasner table was included in *The Modern House Comes Alive*, a 1948–49 exhibition organized by the Bertha Schaefer Gallery in New York. This project brought together the work of architects, interior designers, and artists in installations that demonstrated "the interplay of fabrics, sculpture, paintings and furniture in a room scheme." These were to represent "parts of houses, also displayed in miniature, to be built near New York."[12] The house for which Krasner created her table was designed by architect Edward Durell Stone, and according to the prospectus in the exhibition, it was "planned for a site bounded by three brooks . . . [with] . . . expanses of glass to make the most of the view. One of the few areas of solid wall in the living room has been decorated by a mural, *which exemplifies one way in which artists and architects can work together* [emphasis added]."

Such inter-genre marriages as those made in the Schaefer Gallery were part and parcel of a number of strategies to make modern art more accessible to a general audience. In 1934, for example, the pioneering gallerist Edith Halpert organized the exhibition *Practical Manifestation in American Art* at her Downtown Gallery in New York City to demonstrate how modern art could be applied to commercial design. The noted abstract artist Stuart Davis was among those who participated, exhibiting one of his paintings and designs for dress fabrics.[13] The following year the exhibition *Modern American Art in Modern Room Settings* was organized at the Modernage Furniture Company showrooms in New York.[14]

Krasner continued to work with mosaics, and in the late 1950s she and Ronald Stein collaborated on a mosaic mural eighty-six feet long and twelve feet high for a new office building at 2 Broadway built by Uris Brothers, real estate developers, and designed by the architectural firm of Emery Roth & Sons. Consisting of "irregular shapes of multi-colored glass . . . set in brown cement,"[15] the murals were created in a manner similar to the Krasner coffee table by breaking down "circular plates of glass . . . into irregular sizes for setting into the cement."[16] Krasner and Stein were also commissioned by Uris Brothers to do another mural for the Broad Street side of the building.[17]

The vogue for mosaic murals as architectural features also led to two designs by Krasner's teacher and abstract expressionist predecessor Hans Hofmann. In 1956 he created a lobby and elevator tower treatment for the William Kaufmann Building at 711 Third Avenue **(FIG. 3.5)**. This mural features a numbers of abstract motifs including Hofmann's signature rectangular spaces which articulated his theoretical mantra of "push-pull," a means to suggest space through the manipulation of the saturation of color and the position in the composition relative to other shapes. Having such a contemporary visual statement in this context would indeed expose modern art

FIG. 3.3 (OPPOSITE)
Robert Rauschenberg, *Bed*, 1955. Combine painting: oil and pencil on pillow, quilt and sheet on wood supports. 75¼ x 31½ x 8 in. (191 x 80 x 20.3 cm). Collection of The Museum of Modern Art, Gift of Leo Castelli in honor of Alfred H. Barr, Jr.

FIG. 3.4
Jeanne Reynal, *Sphere*, c. 1950. Cement, mixed media. 29 in. (73.6 cm). Courtesy of Anita Shapolsky Gallery, New York.

to a larger audience, which might then become intrigued by this new visual vocabulary. Two years later Hofmann created another mosaic mural for the facade of the High School of Graphic Communication Arts on Forty-ninth Street between Ninth and Tenth avenues **(FIG. 3.6)**. As if to reflect the curricular focus of the school, Hofmann dispersed various polygons and rectangles across a white field that was divided by a large yellow area.

Writing about Hofmann's work as a muralist, Frederick Stallknecht Wight observes that the artist's success in mosaic may be attributed to the fact that in his painting he "often achieves a lapidary effect with his heavy, coruscant pigment."[18] Furthermore Wight suggests that "there is a rightness" about the scale of these projects which is not only germane to Hofmann's own artistic development, but certainly would also reflect the scale of ambition that has been noted as a characteristic of abstract expressionist painting: "The adaptation of abstract expressionist painting to architecture seems so natural that we must remind ourselves that is not more

natural than anything else in art."[19] Wight further positions these projects as harbingers of later collaborations between artists and architects which would certainly affect what was described earlier as the "notoriously antipathetical" interaction between the two constituencies.[20]

In addition to mosaic, New York School artists engaged in a number of other craft and design techniques during this period. While many of the abstract expressionists contemplated religious contexts for their work and entertained notions of creating such structures, only Gottlieb and Rothko actually executed such pieces. Rothko's chapel adjacent to the Menil Foundation in Houston provides a nondenominational space for meditation and contemplation. Gottlieb's collaborations were in the context of canonical religious service—stained-glass windows and religious paraphernalia for synagogues in the New York–New Jersey area—and his challenge was to "create a visual language without specific literal meaning."[21]

Gottlieb became known in the 1940s for his pictographic visual vocabulary that set simply scribed images within irregularly drawn grids. The symbols—"eyes, pointing fingers, biting teeth, crowns and palaces"—came as much from various tribal sources as from Jungian notions of collective consciousness.[22] The *Untitled* stained-glass window from 1954 [also titled *Pictograph*] was fabricated in the shop of Heinigke & Smith in New York City from a full-sized drawing provided by the artist. This example from his studio is not connected with an

FIG. 3.5

Hans Hofmann, mosaic mural, 711 Third Avenue, New York, 1956. Courtesy of S. L. Green Realty Corp., 2011.

FIG. 3.6

Hans Hofmann, mosaic mural, High School of Graphic Communication Arts, 1958. Courtesy of Ameringer McEnery, Yohe, New York, 2011.

architectural project but demonstrates techniques similar to those "employed in the very earliest Byzantine windows."[23] It also shows how Gottlieb adapted his pictographic style of the 1940s to stained glass in an intriguing design of interlocking geometric shapes, even after he had moved on in his painting to the presentation of disks of color hovering over chaotic forms. In a review of a 1953 exhibition titled *New Work in Stain Glass by Contemporary Americans* at the Borgenicht Gallery in New York City, critic Sidney Geist suggested that Gottlieb's "pictographic design fits snugly into the leaded structure of stain glass."[24]

Gottlieb's stained-glass designs for synagogues in the metropolitan New York area included those for the Park Avenue Synagogue in Manhattan and the Kingsway Jewish Center in Brooklyn. Often these projects involved the design of Torah ark curtains, such as one originally made for Congregation B'nai Israel in Milburn, New Jersey, and now in the Jewish Museum in New York City (**FIG. 3.7**).[25] This aspect of Gottlieb's art has not yet received the attention it warrants. In addition to demonstrating a viable crossover between art and craft, Gottlieb's involvement in religious genres also reveals the often hidden contribution of women to such projects. Gottlieb's wife, Esther, was a key collaborator and was instrumental in recruiting women in the various congregations to execute Gottlieb's designs in textiles.

Perhaps the most versatile genre-shifter was Isamu Noguchi, who from the 1940s onward worked simultaneously in sculpture, furniture, lighting, and stage design, bringing his signature biomorphic language to all these disciplines. His easy transition from one to another belied the conventional wisdom—probably over-considered—that craft and design were at best an amusing sideline in the career of a "real" artist and at worst mutually exclusive. Mosuke Yoshitake, writing about Noguchi's work in *Industrial Art News* in 1950, summarized the special place that Noguchi established for himself in the worlds of art and design. Noting that "Noguchi's specialty is in art not industrial design," Yoshitake emphasized his "meticulous care for the elements of the sculpture being assembled—for its composition and the finish selected specifically for the material—and his consideration of the final installation environment all emphasize an adaptable and perceptive nature that is far from yesterday's sculptural philosophy."[26] For Yoshitake, Noguchi's "abstractionism" in his sculpture led to his creations in furniture, stage costumes, and set designs.[27]

In addition to this focus on making/process and form, art historian Dore Ashton attributed Noguchi's genre versatility to his convictions about "the larger implications of art and its important function in social communication."[28] In this Noguchi agreed with Stuart Davis who believed that art was inherently socially engaged because the artist's "whole life is socially determined."[29] Noguchi's convictions were also influenced by his friendship with the architect–engineer–theorist R. Buckminster Fuller, as well as his sojourn in Japan during the 1930s, where perhaps "he had begun to think about the nature of the manifold work of art in which sculptures, paintings, buildings, and gardens are conceived as a single entity, governed by an articulated intention to shape an environment."[30]

If architecture was one way that art engaged with design and craft, another was through jewelry or portable forms designated as sculptures. Many jewelers of the time also worked in other media, including painting, fiber, and clay.[31] The West Coast abstractionist Claire Falkenstein translated the metal skeins of her sculptures into her glass and metal jewelry, while her New York counterpart sculptor Ibram Lassaw adapted the open boxlike lattices of his sculpture to jewelry forms (CAT. 2, 42, 48, 51, 52). This became a lucrative sideline by which he could support himself and his family. Obliquely associated with abstract expressionism, Lassaw's sculptural translations of the "drip" and the "gesture" resulted in their seeming to have been suspended in space. Neckpieces by Lassaw from the 1950s and 1960s demonstrate an

FIG. 3.7

Adolph Gottlieb, *Torah Ark Curtain*, 1950–51. Velvet: appliqué, embroidered metallic thread. Upper section: 112 ¾ x 80 ½ in. (286.4 x 204.5 cm); lower section: 121¾ x 81½ in. (309.2 x 207 cm). Collection of The Jewish Museum, Gift of Congregation B'nai Israel, Millburn, New Jersey; 1987.23a,b.

interest in "free form" that was shared by jewelers Irena Brynner, Orville Chatt, and Lynda Watson among others in this exhibition.

Given the presumptions of exclusivity claimed by art aficionados such as Greenberg, it is interesting that a later commentator, Toni Greenbaum, who specializes in metalwork and jewelry, noted that "studio jewelry was made for the liberal, intellectual fringe of the American middle class—the young free-spirited champions of modern art."[32] Additionally this population "needed the individuality of adornment that handmade jewelry offered."[33] In contrast to the virtuoso mimicry or "matched" formality of traditional jewelry, these makers focused on organic and/or anatomical forms, natural materials, decidedly un-precious elements (such as bits of hardware), and asymmetrical arrangements often with mobile parts. Native American and African styles became important influences on this group of creators, paralleling developments in contemporary painting and sculpture. The objects and work created by abstract expressionist painter Richard Pousette-Dart exemplify this trend.

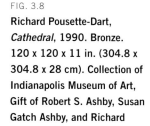

FIG. 3.8

Richard Pousette-Dart, *Cathedral*, 1990. Bronze. 120 x 120 x 11 in. (304.8 x 304.8 x 28 cm). Collection of Indianapolis Museum of Art, Gift of Robert S. Ashby, Susan Gatch Ashby, and Richard Pousette-Dart.

As seen in *Forms Transcendental* of 1950, Pousette-Dart's work starting in the late 1930s featured symbolic shapes that established his unique visual language. Based in his interest in Native American and African art early on, he began translating hybrids of birds, fish, and animals into small three-dimensional brass forms.[34] At once figural and amphibian, these pieces have simple geometric shapes that resemble Northwest Coast Indian art, which had a strong influence on abstract expressionism. Barnett Newman, in particular, elegized the work of "the Kwakiutl" (Kwakwaka'wakw) artist, whose "plastic language" of "abstract shapes . . . was directed by a ritualistic will towards metaphysical understanding" and served as "a vehicle for an abstract thought-complex."[35] While the critical positioning of abstract expressionism would eventually purge the aspect of meaning from art, Pousette-Dart maintained a sense of "metaphysical understanding" in his own work. He translated his characteristic symbolic language into the bronze gate/screen, *Cathedral* **(FIG. 3.8)**, which had been commissioned by the Indianapolis Museum of Art in 1990.

Perhaps the one artist most closely associated with developments in modern jewelry was sculptor Alexander Calder. He was more comfortable than Rothko in lending his talents to vernacular creative endeavors. In 1975 he even accepted a commission from the French race car driver Hervé Poulain to decorate Poulain's BMW for a race in Le Mans. The result was the BMW art car phenomenon.[36] Calder's influence and versatility are evident in several media. His invention of freely moving suspended forms, which he dubbed "mobiles" when they were suspended and "stabiles" when they were settled on the ground, is captured in the *Untitled* gouache from 1956 and translated into the economical squiggle of his *Brooch* of about 1945 **(CAT. 4, 161–62)**. The cantilevered hanging elements in Calder's work proved to be effective formal strategies in jewelry design. Betty Cooke's *Neckpiece* **(CAT. 96)** features a series of interlocking and suspended ovoid forms. Bay Area painter Jay DeFeo's small "sculptures," whose shapes suggest earring and pendants, also combine these formal elements; and Ramona Solberg's *Shaman's Necklace* **(CAT. 11)**, speaks to the era's fascination with totemic imagery and meaning, suspending several found, fabricated, and assembled elements from the neckpiece.

Since the mid-1940s an East Coast/West Coast divide has assigned certain notions of intellectual rigor, material

integrity, and market viability to the East Coast and a more idiosyncratic creativity to the West Coast. Assemblage, for example, has long been considered a particularly West Coast phenomenon. It served to interject narrative and commentary into art when formalism prevailed in critical circles on the East Coast. This predicated the work of Robert Arneson, Howard Kottler, Viola Frey, Clayton Bailey, and David Gilhooly. Within a strain of assemblage dubbed Funk, these artists animated the functionally bound ceramic medium.[37] They demonstrated how a focus on objects from everyday life—whether rescued or created—allowed for a certain ease in shifting between what was considered art and what was considered craft.

However, this coastal divide does not hold when we consider the contemporaneous phenomena of Happenings on the East Coast. Here the distaff side of decor played a role in the pre–pop art installations staged in New York in the late 1960s such as *The Store* (1961), the mock retail venture of Claes Oldenburg whereby he "circumvented" the gallery system to sell his work in a storefront he rented on Manhattan's Lower East Side. The offering included "sculptures of undergarments and slices of blueberry pie and other pastries made out of painted plaster."[38] *Giant BLT (Bacon, Lettuce and Tomato Sandwich)* of 1963 is typical of his work **(CAT. 59)**. These objects flirted with the art/craft distinction and were literally crafted out of vinyl, kapok fibers, and painted and plain wood. Other Oldenburg objects of this period—a vinyl telephone and fan, a gigantic hamburger—were constructed in collaboration with his first wife, Patricia, thus implicating art in the domestic realm so often associated with craft and design during this period. Greenberg especially disparaged pop art for its engagement of the "sentimental, the romantic," "kitsch."[39]

Among those who moved from craft to art were Harry Bertoia and Richard Artschwager. Working first as a designer and then a sculptor, Bertoia was involved in jewelry mostly in the late 1930s and '40s when he was teaching at the Cranbrook Academy of Art.[40] Greenbaum notes that Bertoia "worked in a manner similar to Calder and even exhibited with him on several occasions."[41] Bertoia's *Tree Branch* **(CAT. 14)** brooch has an organic, even quasi-fractal quality which represents the "repetition of slightly varied units or modules, similar to the appearance of the cellular structures seen under a microscope."[42]

Bertoia is probably best known for his "sounding sculptures," which feature multiple rods with auditory qualities, and for his densely crenulated "bush" compositions, which consist of fused forged elements.[43] His design work also included the *"Bird" Lounge Chair and Ottoman* **(CAT. 71)**, created after 1952 for Knoll International, and the paneled, "multiplane" constructions that exploit the textural effect resulting from the brazed treatment of the surface. Bertoia clarified the interconnectedness of the various strains of his creativity by noting: "In the sculpture I am concerned primarily with space, form and the characteristics of metal. In the chairs many functional problems have to be established first . . . but when you get right down to it, the chairs are studies in space, form and metal."[44] He points out that as the sculptures are built up from "a lot of little units," it is "the same with the chairs" which each having "a lot of little diamond shapes in its wire cage and they all add up to one very large diamond shape. . . . It is really an organic principle, like a cellular structure."[45]

During the 1950s Richard Artschwager designed and made furniture in New York, turning to sculpture in 1958 after a fire destroyed his workshop. *Description of a Table* **(CAT. 41)** from 1964 indicates how Artschwager found an "art" voice and became a poster child for the blurring of lines between furniture and sculpture.[46] This work, which creates the visual effect of a brown square table covered by a white tablecloth, is indeed a concept of a table. Artschwager has created a minimalist cube by reducing the incidental details to schematics on the surface of that cube. His mimetic approach results not in an actual object but rather a representation of an object, and the viewer has the option of accepting the work as a cube or as an allusion to a table.

Artschwager's conceptual transformation of material and process is comparable to Robert Morris's *Box with the Sound of Its Own Making*, originally conceived in 1961. The sounds of the box being made emanate from a recording played on a device concealed within the simple enclosed box. Again Morris represents the process of making without evidencing the palpable results of that making. The focus is on the conceptual aspect of the box: the relationship of the auditory experience to the perception of the physical object and the presumptions about its use and accompanying characteristics.

Similar ideas have predicated sculptor H. C. Westermann's *Secrets* of 1964 **(CAT. 40)** in which a closed hinged box (undoubtedly crafted by the artist) is presented for contemplation and Lucas Samaras's schizophrenically appointed *Chair Transformation Number 10 A* **(CAT. 60)** which marries a craftlike looping of wool elements with an unadorned modernist chair. These works seem to function by frustrating our expected experience of a familiar object: While the outsized proportions of the Samaras chair nullify function, the completely closed Wester-mann box denies access to what is inside. In this nexus, idea is privileged over execution, a distinction that became the hallmark of the difference between art and craft.

The critical strategies that ossified the positioning of art and craft in the modernist pantheon, predicated on a shedding of meaning, were seen as protecting modern art from its conservative critics. But the emergence of these strategies may also be related to what art historian Jeffrey L. Meikle described as the ambivalence that accompanied the "domestication" (acceptance) of modernism in the United States. He enumerates "three modes of domesticating modernity during the inter-war years," and of these, "the first . . . situated modernity in a historical continuum linking past, present and future. . . . The second . . . involved limiting modernity in space to a discrete zone—the modern city. . . . A third . . . [involved] . . . directly appropriating and incorporating icons of the modern into one's own personal environment."[47]

In a sense—as craft and the handmade came to represent a more "rural" alternative to the mass-produced and impersonal represented by the city—this also served to create a fissure between the genres. In truth these pat associations overlook the many craftspeople who worked in cities and the artists who retreated to the countryside. As sculptor Martin Puryear—whose exquisitely wrought sculptures in wood lead him to be perceived within the craft context—has described, the "art/craft division in American culture" in fact centered more on a "class issue," that pits "thought" against "manual work," or "concept" against "execution."[48]

The stringency of that differentiation did not play out in absolute terms in the 1945–69 period; the overlaps, tangencies, and convergences during this period point to developments that can be discerned in the global art market today. Indeed at this moment, at the start of the second decade of the twenty-first century—as the market for and interest in midcentury art, craft, and design is on the rise—these different genres are increasingly seen as interconnected. In this context, perhaps Mark Rothko would have found collaborating with architects to be more satisfying than he suspected, perhaps he would have agonized less over the perception and placement of his paintings in a restaurant. Most important, generations of diners would have had access to a space enhanced by his art, open to the public, for a special dining experience. In the end Rothko canceled the Four Seasons commission and returned the money. Just before his suicide in 1970, he donated nine of his Four Seasons paintings to the Tate Gallery in London.[49] These works are currently on permanent view in a gallery known as the Rothko Room.[50] Art and interior are united, fulfilling the promise from the inception of Rothko's Four Seasons commission.

1 See John Lahr, "Escape Artist," *The New Yorker* (April 12, 2010), 81. See also Ronald Alley, *Catalogue of the Tate Gallery's Collection of Modern Art Other Than Works by British Artists*, Tate Gallery and Sotheby Parke-Bernet, London 1981), 657, online at Tate Collection, http://www.tate.org.uk/servlet/ViewWork?workid=12965&searchid=17769&tabview=text.

2 Cécile Whiting, *A Taste for Pop: Pop Art, Gender, and Consumer Culture* (Cambridge, England, New York and Melbourne: Cambridge University Press, 1997), 60.

3 Ibid., 61. See also Maria Elena Buszek, *The Ordinary Made Extra/Ordinary: Craft and Contemporary Art*, (Durham, NC and London: Duke University, 2011), 3–5.

4 Clement Greenberg, "The Avant-Garde and Kitsch," *Partisan Review* 6, no. 5 (1939), 34–49; reprinted in Greenberg, *Art and Culture: Critical Essays* (Boston: Beacon Press, 1961), 3–21.

5 Quoted in Whiting, *A Taste for Pop*, 61.

6 Holland Cotter, George Emerl, and Lenore Tawney, *Lenore Tawney: Signs on the Wind, Postcard Collages* (Petaluma, CA: Pomegranate Communications, 2002), 7.

7 Ibid., 7.

8 Ibid., 8.

9 Ibid.

10 Judith Kaye Reed, "From Law to Art," *Art Digest* 19 (May 15, 1945); referenced in Ann Eden Gibson, *Issues in Abstract Expressionism: The Artist-Run Periodicals* (Ann Arbor and London: U.M.I. Research Press, 1990), 12.

11 See "House that 'Lives' Theme of Exhibit," *New York Times*, September 20, 1948, 22.

12 Ibid.

13 See Lowery Stokes Sims, "Stuart Davis in the 1930s: A Search for Social Relevance in Abstract Art," in Sims, *Stuart Davis, American Painter*, exh. cat. (New York: The Metropolitan Museum of Art, 1991), 67.

14 See *Modern American Art in Modern Room Settings*, exh. cat. (New York: Modernage Furniture Company, 1935).

15 "Skyscraper Gets Mural in Mosaic," *New York Times*, August 16, 1959, R 5.

16 Ibid.

17 Ibid.

18 Frederick Stallknecht Wight, *Hans Hofmann* (Berkeley: University of California Press, 1957), 59.

19 Ibid.

20 Alice B. Louchheim, "Gallery, Decorator and Work of Art," *New York Times*, September 26, 1948, X9.

21 Samuel D. Gruber, "Paned Expressions," *Tablet Magazine* (October 14, 2009), http://www.tabletmag.com/arts-and-culture/18271/paned-express-sions/print/.

22 Stephen Polcari, "Gottlieb and Kline," *Art Journal* (spring 1996), 87–92.

23 Letter from Heinigke & Smith to the American Federation of Arts, New York, in response to an inquiry, dated July 20, 1953, Archives of the Gottlieb Foundation, New York City.

24 Sidney Geist, "Platitudes in Stain Glass Attitudes," *Art Digest* (September 1953), 17.

25 See Samuel D. Gruber, "Paned Expressions," *Tablet Magazine* (October 14, 2009), http://222.tabletmag.com/arts-and-culture/18271/paned-expressions/print/.

26 Mosuke Yoshitake, "The Work of Sculptor Isamu Noguchi," *Industrial Art News* 18 (October 1950), 24–25; reprinted in Bonnie Rychlak et al., *Design: Isamu Noguchi and Isamu Kenmochi*, exh. cat. (New York: Five Ties Publishing, Inc. in association with The Isamu Noguchi Foundation and Garden Museum, 2007), 134–35.

27 Ibid.

28 Dore Ashton, *Noguchi: East and West* (New York: Alfred A. Knopf, 1992), 50.

29 Stuart Davis Papers, September 20, 1937, Harvard University Art Museums, Fogg Art Museum, Cambridge, Massachusetts, cited in Sims, "Stuart Davis in the 1930s," 58.

30 Ashton, *Noguchi,* 50.

31 Toni Greenbaum, "Messengers of Modernism," in Martin Eidelberg, ed., *Messengers of Modernism: American Studio Jewelry, 1940–1960*, exh. cat. (Montreal: Montreal Museum of Decorative Arts in associa-tion with Flammarion, Paris, 1996), 18.

32 Ibid., 20.

33 Ibid.

34 See Lowery Stokes Sims, "Ciphering and Deciphering: The Art and Writings of Richard Pousette-Dart," in Lowery Stokes Sims and Stephen Polcari, *Richard Pousette-Dart (1916–1992)*, exh. cat. (New York: The Metropolitan Museum of Art, 1997), 12.

35 Barnet Newman, *The Ideographic Picture*, Betty Parsons Gallery, January 20–February 8, 1947, excerpted in Barbara Rose, ed., *Readings in American Art Since 1900: A Documentary Survey* (New York and Wash-ington: Frederick A. Praeger, Publishers, 1968), 145.

36 See "BMW Art Cars: Symbiosis Between BMW Cars and Art," at BMWDrives, http://www.bmwdrives.com/bmw-artcars.php.

37 See Peter Plagens, *Sunshine Muse: Art on the West Coast, 1945–1970* (Berkeley, Los Angeles and London, England: University of California Press, 1999), 86–69.

38 *The Store* was announced in the following poster: Claes Oldenburg, *The Store,* 1961. Letterpress, composition: $26^5/_8$ x $20^7/_{16}$ in. (67.6 x 51.9 cm); sheet: $28^3/_8$ x $22^1/_8$ in. (72.1 x 56.2 cm). The Museum of Modern Art; Mary Ellen Meehan Fund, 56.1999 © 2011 Claes Oldenburg.

39 Whiting, *A Taste for Pop*, 135.

40 Greenbaum, "Messengers of Modernism," 30.

41 Ibid.

42 Ibid.

43 Toni Lesser Wolf, "Introduction," in *Masterworks of Contemporary American Jewelry: Sources and Concepts*, exh. cat. (London: Victoria and Albert Museum, 1985), 9.

44 *Chairs in Motion*, exh. cat. (Fullerton, CA: Art Gallery, California State University, 1974).

45 Ibid.

46 See for example, Suzanne Slesin, "Blurring the Boundaries Between Art and Furniture," *New York Times*, February 12, 1981, C1; "The Object: Still Life," *CH* (September/October, 1963), 28–30, 54.

47 Jeffrey L. Meikle, "Domesticating Modernity: Ambivalence and Appropri-ation, 1920–40," in Wendy Kaplan, ed., *Designing Modernity: The Arts of Reform and Persuasion, 1885–1945: Selections from the Wolfsonian* (New York: Thames and Hudson, Inc., 1995), 143–44.

48 See Robert Hughes, "Martin Puryear," http://www.time.com/time/magazine/article/0,9171,1000284,00.html?iid=chix-sphere.

49 Rothko's Seagram murals were dispersed, primarily among three locations: London's Tate Britain, Japan's Kawamura Memorial Museum, and the National Gallery of Art in Washington, DC. See also Jeffrey Weiss, *Mark Rothko* (Washington DC: National Gallery of Art; New Haven: Yale University Press, 1998). See also Jeffrey S. Weiss et al., *Mark Rothko* (Washington, D.C.: National Gallery of Art; New Haven: Yale University Press, 1998).

50 See Jonathan Jones, "Feeding Fury," [London] *Guardian*, December, 7, 2002, online at http://www.guardian.co.uk/culture/2002/dec/07/artsfeatures.

39

HOWARD KOTTLER

Guilt Feeler, 1967

STONEWARE AND FUR

16 IN. (40.6 CM); DIAM. 9½ IN. (24.1 CM)

MUSEUM OF ARTS AND DESIGN, GIFT OF

HOWARD KOTTLER TESTAMENTARY TRUST, 1991

40

H. C. WESTERMANN

Secrets, 1964

AMERICAN WALNUT AND BRASS

6¾ X 11 X 8½ IN. (17.1 X 27.9 X 21.6 CM)

SAN FRANCISCO MUSEUM OF MODERN ART,

MUSEUM PURCHASE, 77.193

41

RICHARD ARTSCHWAGER

Description of Table, 1964

MELAMINE LAMINATE, AND PLYWOOD

26⅛ X 31⅞ X 31⅞ IN. (66.4 X 81 X 81 CM)

WHITNEY MUSEUM OF AMERICAN ART,

NEW YORK, GIFT OF THE HOWARD

AND JEAN LIPMAN FOUNDATION INC., 66.48

42

CLAIRE FALKENSTEIN
Element, 1965
COPPER TUBING AND GLASS
8¾ X 16¾ X 15 IN. (22.2 X 42.5 X 38.1 CM)
LONG BEACH MUSEUM OF ART,
GIFT OF THE ARTIST, 95.53

43

ALEXANDER CALDER

Mountain Range, 1965

GOUACHE ON PAPER

29 X 42 IN. (73.7 X 106.7 CM)

THE SIMONA AND JEROME CHAZEN COLLECTION

44

WAYNE THIEBAUD

Big Suckers, 1971

COLOR AQUATINT

22 1/16 X 29 3/4 IN. (56 X 75.6 CM.)

MEMORIAL ART GALLERY, UNIVERSITY OF
ROCHESTER, GIFT OF ROBERT AND ANNE-
MARIE LOGAN

45

JAY DEFEO

Untitled, c. 1954

IRON WIRE, BRASS WIRE, SILVER, CLEAR PLASTIC,
BRASS BEADS, AND GLASS BEADS
2³⁄₈ X 1⁵⁄₈ X ¾ IN. (6 X 4.1 X 1.9 CM)
THE JAY DEFEO TRUST, E3109

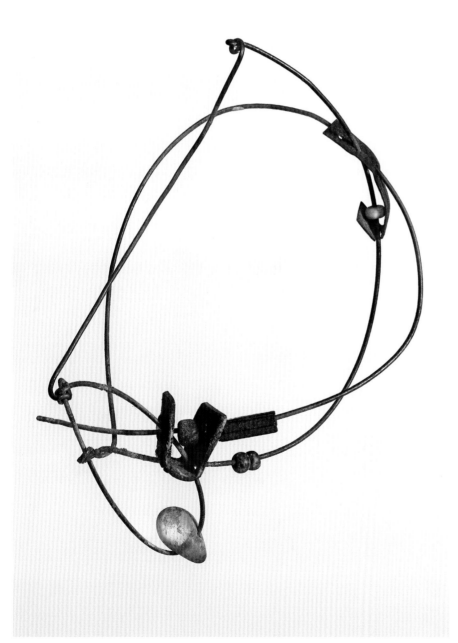

46

JAY DEFEO

Untitled, c. 1954

SILVER WIRE
2¾ X 1⁵⁄₈ X ¾ IN. (7 X 4.1 X 1.9 CM)
THE JAY DEFEO TRUST, E3094

47

DOMINIC L. Di MARE

Boat, c. 1967

WOOD, STRING, PLANT MATERIALS, AND CLAY

23 X 22 X 10 IN. (58.4 X 55.9 X 25.4 CM)

COLLECTION OF DANIEL AND HILARY GOLDSTINE

48

CLAIRE FALKENSTEIN

Pendant, 1961

GLASS AND IRON

4¾ X 4¼ X ½ IN. (12.1 X 10.8 X 1.3 CM)

THE DUKOFF COLLECTION

49

LEE KRASNER

Mosaic Table, 1947

MIXED MEDIA INCLUDING BROKEN GLASS, KEYS, COINS,
CERAMIC, PEBBLES, CEMENT, IRON WAGON-WHEEL, AND STEEL
H. 21¾ IN. (55.2 CM), DIAM. 46¾ IN. (118.7 CM)
COURTESY OF THE MICHAEL ROSENFELD GALLERY,
NEW YORK, NEW YORK

50

HOWARD KOTTLER

Peacemakers, 1967

PORCELAIN

H. 1 IN. (2.5 CM), DIAM. 10¼ IN. (26 CM)

MUSEUM OF ARTS AND DESIGN,

GIFT OF MAREN MONSEN, 1996

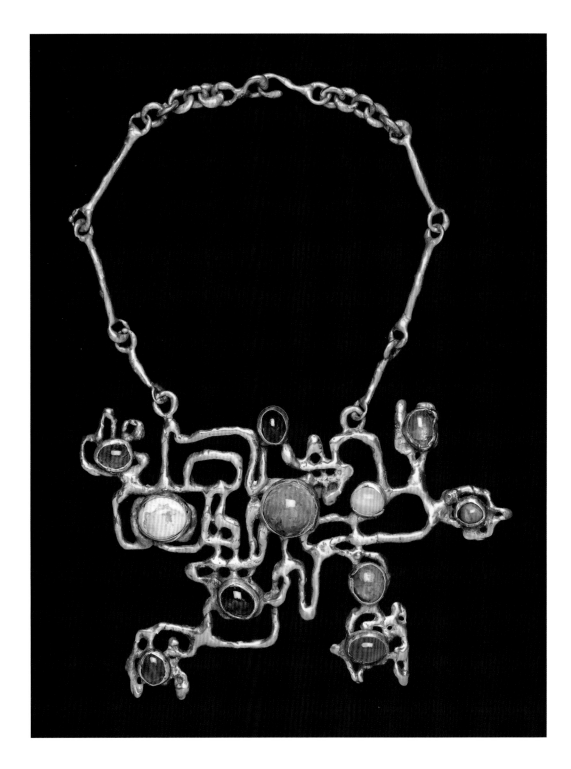

51

IBRAM LASSAW

Untitled (Necklace), 1960

BRONZE, LAPIS, AMETHYST, TOPAZ, OPAL, CARNELIAN,
ROSE QUARTZ, MALACHITE, AND AMAZONITE

4⁷⁄₁₆ X 6⁵⁄₁₆ IN. (11.3 X 16 CM)

COLLECTION OF DENISE LASSAW, EAST HAMPTON, NEW YORK

52

IBRAM LASSAW

Sirius, 1951

BRONZE OVER GALVANIZED WIRE

21½ X 22 X 17 IN. (54.6 X 55.9 X 43.2 CM)

PRIVATE COLLECTION, NEW YORK

53

REX MASON

Untitled Vessel, 1954

STONEWARE

H. 10⅞ (27.6 CM), DIAM. 8 IN. (20.3 CM)

FORREST L. MERRILL COLLECTION

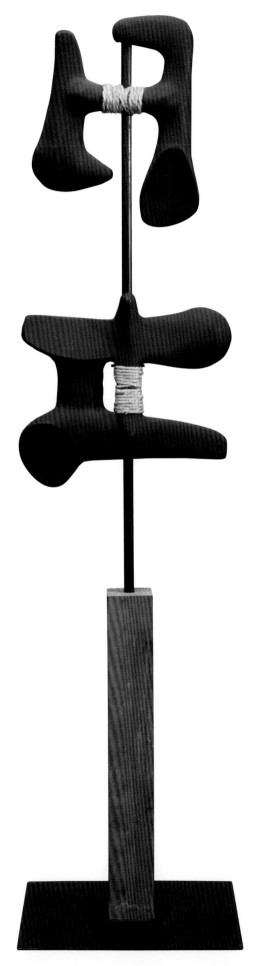

54

ISAMU NOGUCHI
Calligraphics, 1957
IRON, WOOD, AND ROPE
70⅝ X 18 X 3⅝ IN. (179.4 X 45.7 X 9.2 CM)
ROCHESTER MEMORIAL ART GALLERY,
R.T. MILLER BEQUEST, 60.2

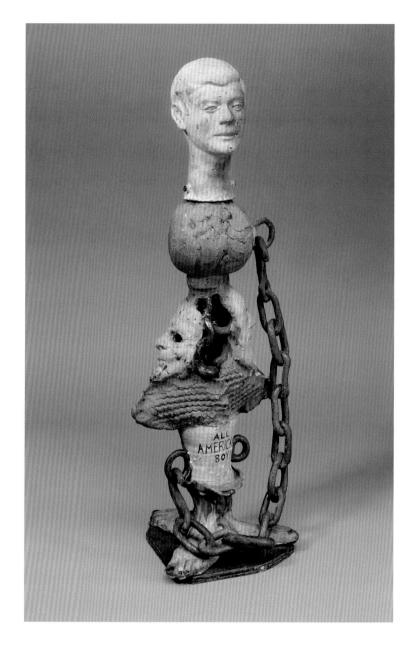

55

JOHN MASON
Sculptural Form, 1961
STONEWARE
64 X 13 X 13 IN. (162.6 X 33 X 33 CM)
MUSEUM OF ARTS AND DESIGN, PURCHASED BY
THE AMERICAN CRAFT COUNCIL, 1967

56

JAMES LEEDY
All-American Boy Trophy, 1968
EARTHENWARE
42 X 14½ X 12½ IN. (106.7 X 36.8 X 31.8 CM)
MUSEUM OF ARTS AND DESIGN, GIFT OF
THE JOHNSON WAX COMPANY, THROUGH THE
AMERICAN CRAFT COUNCIL, 1977

57

RICHARD POUSETTE-DART
Forms: Transcendental, 1950
GOUACHE ON PANEL
24 X 19½ IN. (61 X 49.5 CM)
THE SIMONA AND JEROME CHAZEN COLLECTION

R.R.

RAUSCHENBERG 22/50 70

58

ROBERT RAUSCHENBERG

Signs, 1970

SCREENPRINT

SHEET: 43 X 34 IN. (109.2 X 86.4 CM);

COMPOSITION: 35³⁄₁₆ X 26¾ IN. (89.4 X 67.9 CM)

MUSEUM OF MODERN ART, GIFT OF
LEO AND JEAN-CHRISTOPHE CASTELLI
IN MEMORY OF TONY CASTELLI, 369.1988

59

CLAES OLDENBURG

*Giant BLT (Bacon, Lettuce, and
Tomato Sandwich)*, 1963

VINYL, KAPOK FIBERS, PAINTED WOOD, AND WOOD

32 X 39 X 29 IN. (81.3 X 99.1 X 73.7 CM)

WHITNEY MUSEUM OF AMERICAN ART, NEW YORK;
GIFT OF THE AMERICAN CONTEMPORARY
ART FOUNDATION INC., LEONARD A. LAUDER,
PRESIDENT 2002.255A-S

60

LUCAS SAMARAS

*Chair Transformation
Number 10A*, 1969–70

MELAMINE LAMINATE, WOOD, AND WOOL

96¹³⁄₁₆ X 50¹³⁄₁₆ X 45¹¹⁄₁₆ IN. (245.9 X 129 X 116.1 CM)

WHITNEY MUSEUM OF AMERICAN ART, NEW YORK;
PURCHASE WITH FUNDS FROM THE HOWARD
AND JEAN LIPMAN FOUNDATION INC., 70.1572

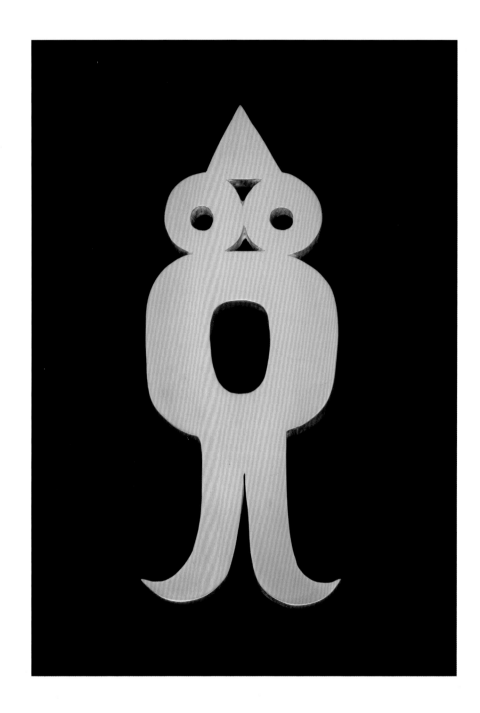

61

RICHARD POUSETTE-DART

Untitled, c. 1945

BRASS

4½ X 2 X ¼ IN. (11.4 X 5.1 X 0.6 CM)

THE ESTATE OF RICHARD POUSETTE-DART

62

JAN YOORS, DESIGNER

ANNABERT VAN WETTUM, WEAVER

MARIANNE CITROEN, WEAVER

Lop Noor, 1966

COTTON, PERSIAN WOOL

60 X 84 IN. (15A2.4 X 213.4 CM)

COLLECTION OF THE RORIMER FAMILY

CHAPTER 4

The Hand That Helped the Machine

DONALD ALBRECHT

IN 1944 NEW YORK'S MUSEUM OF MODERN ART (MoMA) presented *Art in Progress*, an exhibition marking the museum's fifteenth anniversary and surveying the course of modernism over the previous half-century. In the accompanying catalogue, Serge Chermayeff and René d'Harnoncourt—co-curators of the industrial design section of the exhibition—looked back on the 1930s and concluded that the "enthusiasm created by the discovery of 'machine art' led in some cases to an uncritical dismissal of manual work as obsolete, but we are now beginning to realize that there are specific values in the direct contacts between man and material that call for a re-evaluation of craftsmanship in the light of the demands of the modern world."[1]

Writing near the end of World War II, Chermayeff and d'Harnoncourt had witnessed the democratization of modern architecture and design. During the war, thousands of new armament factories and mass-produced houses for defense workers were being built across the country. Their functionalist aesthetic came to embody the architecture of an optimistic *pax Americana*. But modernism's victory was hardly unanimous. For many designers and critics, the modern style that had taken firm hold in postwar America was too cold and impersonal. Their recommended antidote to the high tech of the machine was the soft touch of craft.

Following the war, Americans were eager to understand the changing nature of their society. More than fifteen years of economic depression and war had caused fiscal and psychological dislocation; military victory brought power and prosperity, thrusting Americans into an international spotlight. Postwar commentators, historians, and sociologists helped the nation understand the character of modern America.[2] As part of this campaign to define the nation's contemporary identity, design professionals guided American taste into the postwar period.

Elizabeth Gordon, editor of *House Beautiful* magazine, was an advocate of craft as a means of humanizing the new architecture. Like most shelter magazines of the period, *House Beautiful* targeted a middle class that was leaving the cities for the unfamiliar suburbs in unprecedented numbers. For these new homeowners, the magazine proposed a "station wagon way of life" in 1950—informal, outdoorsy, easy to maintain, and full of vibrantly colored and textured objects that were often made by hand.[3] The station-wagoners no longer needed Europe as a design source. Gordon's hero, Frank Lloyd Wright, had proved the supremacy of native talent. Readers were encouraged to choose contemporary American furnishings, which they could combine with an eclectic array of decorative objects and craft products.

In the June 1952 issue, *House Beautiful* illustrated this new, ostensibly carefree lifestyle with a house designed by California architect Cliff May, whose modest ranch-style homes were vernacular versions of high-style Arts and Crafts residences by California architects Greene and Greene at the turn of the twentieth century. Exposed beams in the house's sloped ceiling, natural cork flooring, and rag carpeting provided warm relief to floor-to-ceiling windows, which were softened by sheer curtains of hand-woven wool **(FIG. 4.1)**. *House Beautiful* also focused on the kind of interior design its readers could easily afford: practical household articles. The dining room table in the May house, for example, was set with pottery plates, wooden holders for geraniums, and textured napkins. Selecting and arranging such domestic objects was a primary way that homeowners could define their own individual sense of style. By transferring Cold War rhetoric to the field of interior design, the magazine suggested that the American homeowner's ability to mix objects that were modern and old, craft-produced and machine-made, represented American democracy in contrast to the authoritarian state style of the Soviet Union.

House Beautiful also published interiors that it considered exemplary of this "peculiarly American brand of democracy."[4] A series of rooms designed by T. H. Robsjohn-Gibbings in 1950 for the Widdicomb Furniture

FIG 4.1

Living room for a ranch house designed by Cliff May, Borrego Springs, California c. 1951. Furniture designed by Paul Frankl.

Company in Grand Rapids, Michigan, featured wood and upholstered furniture of his own design. These svelte, polished pieces were simplified versions of the old, hand-made American sawbuck table, slat-back chair, spindle bed, and rocking chair, set within a practical yet elegant interior of clay-tile floors and whitewashed brick walls. Interiors that mixed objects of various cultures were also praised. Designer Paul Frankl's renovated California Spanish home blended contemporary furniture, bamboo window shades, and a diverse collection of Chinese bowls, Mexican Tarascan pottery, and tin candelabras.[5]

Favoring the comfortable modernism of Frankl, Robsjohn-Gibbings, and May, *House Beautiful* condemned the "well-established movement in modern architecture . . . which is promoting the mystical idea that 'less is more.'"[6] According to Gordon, Ludwig Mies van der Rohe's famous dictum promoted an anticonsumerist and un-American way of life, and the insistent purity of Mies's Farnsworth House (1950) outside Chicago was an overt "threat to the next America."[7]

Charles and Ray Eames, leaders in postwar American furniture and interior design, struck a balance between Mies's severity and Gordon's gemütlichkeit, or informality. They used craft in two ways: to create handmade foils to the hard edges of their industrial interiors and to draw upon the fundamental precepts of craft in the design of their mass-produced furniture. The Eameses' own house in Los Angeles is indicative of their strategy to humanize architecture with craft objects **(FIG. 4.2)**. The exterior has a kit-of-parts quality: a large-scale Erector set by way of Piet Mondrian. (Eames had collaborated with architect Eero Saarinen on an initial, unbuilt version of the house.) The final version of the Eameses' house was constructed of ordinary, off-the-shelf parts and materials that virtually anyone could buy. Initially, simple furnishings and floor pillows decorated the interior, but over time—certainly by the late 1950s—stark austerity evolved into elaborately staged domestic tableaus: a Thonet bentwood chair among modern Eames furniture, a Piero Fornasetti plate in a cluster of seashells, dime-store trinkets with Indian kites

and Mexican pots, and other exotic objects that warmed the building's cool, industrial modernism. Expressing the Eameses' collagist aesthetic, the effect was one of studied contrasts between old and new, rich and humble, foreign and familiar.

The Eameses' house was one of thirty-six experimental residences designed as part of the Case Study House Program sponsored by the avant-garde Los Angeles magazine *Art & Architecture*. The houses were designed and the majority constructed between 1945 and 1966. The program was a socially conscious crusade to bring "the good life" to the general public, integrating high and low art forms, craft, and design. While one-of-a-kind objects such as ceramics by Gertrud and Otto Natzler were featured, the program emphasized mass-produced architecture, furnishings, and accessories as the ideal way to spread low-cost, high-quality modern design.

FIG 4.2

Designer house by Charles Eames, August 1950. Design elements included a 17-foot ceiling height, exposed steel-truss construction, and clamp-on lighting, *Life Magazine* **29 (September 11, 1950) 149.**

The Case Study House Program was only one of the Eameses' efforts to promote modern design. *An Exhibition for Modern Living*, held at the Detroit Institute of Art in 1949, included an Eames-designed demonstration room featuring their own furniture. Included were molded-plywood chairs and a full-scale mockup of the molded, plastic-reinforced fiberglass *La Chaise* that had been submitted to MoMA's 1948 *Low-Cost Furniture Competition*. Although the Eameses believed that the machine had replaced the hand as an appropriate method of manufacture for the egalitarian mass market of the twentieth century, their furniture retained the organic quality of the handmade and adhered to the Ruskinian precepts of traditional craftsmanship, such as truth to materials and honestly expressed methods of construction. Producing prototypes by hand remained an essential aspect of the Eameses' design process, and they were often photographed molding, shaping, and bending new materials into various experimental forms. Fabricated of modern industrial materials, their chairs of molded plywood and fiberglass were soft to the touch, shaped to the body. With the *Chaise* prototype they effectively pushed the expressive limits of its new material as forcefully as did any craft artist working in traditional clay, wood, or metal.

In addition to the Eameses' chairs, the Detroit exhibition's demonstration room featured an artfully random arrangement of a kite, a Mexican mask, a pot of paper flowers, and a Charles Eames photograph of bark, all hung from a rectangular grid of pegs. Such grids allowed contemporary designers to position "natural" or handmade objects within the framework of a man-made modernity. The Eameses' *ESU* storage unit, making its public debut here, was a miniature version of the couple's house. Its off-the-shelf materials and modular design contrasted dramatically with displays of straw baskets, clay pots, stones, and starfish.

The Eameses also took part in MoMA's influential Good Design program. Begun in 1950 and directed by Edgar J. Kaufmann Jr. (whose father had commissioned Frank Lloyd Wright's Fallingwater, in Mill Run, Pennsylvania, in 1934), the Good Design program was a five-year series of exhibitions of home furnishings, organized by the museum and the Merchandise Mart in Chicago and shown each year at both venues. Like the Case Study House Program, Good Design sought to promote modern design to the middle-class homeowner. Contemporary furniture, appliances, flatware, tools, textiles, and carpets were selected from thousands of entries submitted by manufacturers and distributors. The museum appointed the selection committees, which over the years included curators, retailers, designers, architects, and manufacturers. The submissions criteria were broadly democratic. Open to consideration was any object—"home made or foreign, machine made or handcraft"[8]—that could be purchased in the United States, was new to the market, and did not attempt to imitate the past. Over the years, the Good Design exhibitions introduced average Americans to the full range of postwar plenty, from Eames chairs to Venini glass vases, handwoven and hand-painted linen textiles by Jack Lenor Larsen, Baccarat highball glass, Scandinavian ceramics, and Gray-N-Ware plastic mixing bowls.

In its comprehensive approach, Good Design signaled a shift from MoMA's "machine art" position of the early 1930s. Other efforts were launched in the same direction. In 1944 the museum started a Department of Manual Industry under the direction of René d'Harnoncourt that sought to assure the survival of craft traditions in the face of rapid industrialization. ("Hands Will Help Machines After War," the *Dallas Times Herald* proclaimed at the time.[9]) MoMA also assisted the U.S. government's postwar efforts to increase trade between the United States and underdeveloped nations by stimulating foreign craft industries and importing handmade goods. In 1947 it published *The Manual Industries of Peru* by Truman E. Bailey that reported on a project of the Inter-American Development Commission and detailed the rehabilitation of high-quality Peruvian handcrafts and the establishment of a handcraft center in Lima for commercial production and export. A representative of Lord & Taylor, the Fifth Avenue department store, and a merchandise editor from Fairchild Publications visited the center in Lima. Their report concluded, however, that local demand for goods from Peruvians and foreign residents far exceeded capacity and as a result production had not yet reached the proportions necessary for export.[10]

MoMA's efforts to reach a broad public extended to the design of its installations, which often blurred the line between art gallery and store display. The "housewife's corner" that was part of the Eameses' installation design for the first Good Design exhibition featured a Thonet bentwood rocker against a checkerboard wall of perforated acoustical panels from which a variety of beautiful but utilitarian gadgets were hung from golf tees. The 1955 exhibition, *Textiles and Ornamental Arts of India,* took the form of an imaginary bazaar or marketplace filled with Indian arts and crafts.

The museum also stressed the value of making things with one's own hands, especially as a shared activity for busy postwar families. *Art for the Family*, a 1954 book written by MoMA's education staff, encouraged readers to work with clay and papier-mâché. While decorating magazines and books promoted do-it-yourself activities from mosaic-making to copper enameling to Japanese paper folding, *Art for the Family*, juxtaposed craft and fine art, including an ancient Egyptian faience hippopotamus, a metal mobile by Alexander Calder, and a sculpture of wood, glass, wire, and string by Alberto Giacometti. "This is art," the book said of everyday craft. "You don't have to be an artist. . . . Everyone can do it."[11]

Promoting the role of craft in modern life was not solely the province of MoMA. Hollywood cameras offered moviegoers the chance to move among the bric-a-brac of contemporary interiors. The film industry's widespread adoption of color cinematography and film stocks with higher resolution after the war increasingly brought rich color and textured surfaces to the set designers' repertoires. The value of working with one's hands was underscored in director Douglas Sirk's 1955 melodrama *All That Heaven Allows*. A widow (Jane Wyman) narrowly escapes the cold, conformist country-club world of her late husband by marrying a young gardener (Rock Hudson), who is converting a barn into a unique home outfitted with craft objects and whose friends are craftspeople. The film dramatized what many Americans had begun to fear: that the uniformity of the postwar landscape, of mass-produced Levittowns and trailer parks, steel-and-glass offices, fast-food restaurants, and chain motels, all indistinguishable, turned people into automatons. In the catalogue for the 1957 exhibition *Designer-Craftsmen of the Mississippi Basin*, a writer claimed that because of the machine, "the American home has become the most efficient, the most sanitary, and the most sterile home in the world."[12] In the catalogue to *Designer Craftsmen U.S.A.*, a national exhibition of craft objects initiated by the American Craftsmen's Educational Council, Dorothy Giles concurred: "We have become a land of mechanized and servantless homes."[13] The products of both the "craftsman" who produces one-of-a-kind objects by hand, without regard for the machine, and the "designer-craftsman" who works for industry would be needed to counteract the dehumanizing effect of postwar modern life.

In addition to exhibitions devoted to craft, in 1940 the Handcraft Cooperative League of America established a retail outlet in New York—America House—to promote and sell American crafts for the home. America House relocated in 1943 and again in 1959, the year it became an independent entity, to a renovated brownstone on West Fifty-third Street designed by David R. Campbell, an architect who also created the 1956 interiors of the Museum of Contemporary Crafts.[14] Campbell's America House featured a mezzanine floating between walls of exposed brick and an open-air trellised courtyard in the rear, just the kind of tactile environment that seemed ideally suited to its merchandise.

A retailing trendsetter, the original America House inspired many other retail stores selling stylish but modestly priced objects for the home, often including craft pieces.[15] None was more aesthetically daring than Alexander Girard's Textiles and Objects, a shop on East Fifty-third Street, a division of Michigan-based furniture-maker Herman Miller that sold textiles and objects designed or selected by Girard.

Designer of fabrics, furniture, exhibitions, and interiors, Girard mixed the modern, historical, exotic, and home-grown with élan. His house in Grosse Pointe, Michigan, was chronicled in a twenty-one-page *House*

Beautiful essay titled "How Homemaking Can Be an Art." Author Joseph A. Barry quoted Emerson, Carlyle, Santayana, and Blake to praise Girard's "free taste" in arranging modern furniture, decorative accessories, and table settings.[16] One such setting was Girard's aesthetic in miniature: a pair of Swedish plywood trays with mats of Philippine pineapple fiber, a Navajo basket used to hold fruit, Victorian egg cups, a contemporary metal Thermos flask, and hand-embroidered Italian napkins. "Art is only art," Girard said, "when it is applied to living."[17] Girard moved to Santa Fe in 1953, where he renovated a historic adobe house adding low platforms supporting cushioned pillows and decorative objects. The Santa Fe house reveals Girard less as an architect than an art director for theatrical settings. His Textiles and Objects shop opened in 1961, offering not only Girard-designed fabrics, but also toys and craft objects acquired by him during his world travels **(FIG. 4.3)**. The hanging fabric panels that modulated the tiny, white space created a colorful and playful "hide-and-seek" environment for the materials displayed. The overall effect was theatrical, psychedelic, and a ready-to-take-off anticipation of op art.

Even more scenographic was La Fonda del Sol, a restaurant completed the same year **(FIG. 4.4)**. Tucked behind the austere steel-and-glass facade of New York's

Such efforts to humanize modern design were not confined to the East Coast. In the San Francisco area, the "Bay Region School" that emerged after the war combined modern devices—the free-form plan, the steel frame, the flat cantilevered roof—with Arts and Crafts influences and local building traditions and materials. While the California architects Irving Gill and Rudolph Schindler had used similar themes earlier in the century, it was only after the war that these ideas became a kind of suburban vernacular in the residential work of such West Coast architects as William Wurster. The regional focus of these houses challenged the dominance of the International Style by making a modern architecture that responded to the local climate, site conditions, and an outdoorsy California way of life.

Even more influential was the Cranbrook Academy of Art, in Bloomfield Hills, Michigan, not far from Detroit. Many of the postwar period's great designer-craftsmen were graduates. Drawing upon abstract painting and sculpture, they designed furniture, metalwork, bookbindings, textiles, and ceramics that elevated craft to new artistic levels. Cranbrook designers also often collaborated with architects such as Eero Saarinen, one of the most important postwar architects. The son of Finnish-born architect Eliel Saarinen, president of Cranbrook Academy from 1932 to 1946, Eero truly launched his postwar career with the design of the General Motors Technical Center in Warren, Michigan (1956), a twenty-five-building corporate center of assembly-line precision and the template for innumerable campus-like headquarters built in the American suburbs over the following two decades. For the center's gridded metal-and-glass exterior, Saarinen drew largely upon the cool Platonic logic of Mies van der Rohe. The interiors, however, were the collaborative effort of designers Saarinen knew from Cranbrook. Metalsmith-jeweler Harry Bertoia fabricated a delicate metal screen, thirty-six feet in length, for the entrance to the staff cafeteria, and weaver Marianne Strengell designed hand-woven carpets and fabrics for use throughout the complex.

The Cranbrook circle—including Charles and Ray Eames, Jack Lenor Larsen, and Pipsan Saarinen (Eliel's daughter and Eero's sister)—would come to define the look of elite corporate modernism in 1950s America. Strengell, for example, created rugs, curtain fabrics, and murals for the various architectural projects of Skidmore, Owings & Merrill and Edward Durell Stone, for industrial concerns such as the Aluminum Company of America (Alcoa),

new Time-Life Building, the Latin American–inspired La Fonda was a revolutionary experiment in design: part Walt Disney, part Mies van der Rohe. Its theme was all-encompassing—down to the buttons on the waiters' jackets, the menus, and the matchbooks. Virtually every idea was Girard's, from the Spanish American concepts to the tiled cook's grill (visible to restaurant patrons), imported dishware, evocative menus, and the articulated brass sun that was the restaurant's logo. The restaurant mixed a modern ceiling lighting grid with a bar enclosed in an adobe hut, its walls pierced with openings containing beautiful craft and folk art treasures. The windows were screened with golden layers of tautly stretched ribbons made of multiple materials from natural jute to synthetic Lurex. An article in *Interiors* magazine proclaimed: "There is up-to-date industrial design on every hand, but nothing of the cold feel, rigidity, or sharp edges that alert human flesh against machine products."[18]

FIG 4.4
La Fonda del Sol restaurant, designed by Alexander Girard, New York, 1961. *Life Magazine* 50 (April 7, 1961), 64.

Owens Corning Fiberglas, and virtually every major American automobile company. Florence Knoll Bassett, a close friend of the Saarinen family, created distinctive interiors for numerous corporate clients as head of the Knoll Company's Planning Unit. Far more spare and less witty than the aesthetic of the Eameses or Alexander Girard, the "Knoll look" for Saarinen's CBS Building in New York or Skidmore's 1952 Connecticut General Life Insurance Company in Hartford, Connecticut, combined economical office layouts, modular furniture, and richly textured draperies, carpets, and upholstery. Knoll's bywords were luxury, poise, and balance. Their repertoire included walls of beige cashmere and French walnut, delicate geometric sculptured screens by Bertoia, and bold abstract fabrics by outstanding designers and weavers, including Strengell, Evelyn Hill, Anni Albers, Eszter Haraszty, and Suzanne Huguenin.

FIG 4.5
Sculptural screen by Harry Bertoia in the Manufacturers Trust building at 510 Fifth Avenue, New York, 1954. Architect: Skidmore, Owings & Merrill.

Two New York City interiors—completed in 1954 and located within blocks of each other—illustrate the range of such collaborations between architects and craftspeople. In the banking hall of Skidmore's Manufacturers Trust Company at the corner of Fifth Avenue and Forty-third Street, a rigorous Cartesian geometry frames its primary decorative element, Bertoia's seventy-foot-long screen of eight hundred bronze- and gold-metal panels set in a matrix of interlocking wires (**FIG. 4.5**). Architecture critic Ada Louise Huxtable said that Bertoia added "a note of Byzantine splendor in an otherwise austerely elegant interior."[19]

In contrast to this interior—which had kept the handcrafted in check—the new store for the Italian business machine-manufacturer Olivetti at 584 Fifth Avenue, between Forty-seventh and Forty-eighth streets, gave the hand free-range. This weighty and sensuous interior was dominated by *Hospitality*, a cast-sand sculptural mural, seventy feet in length, by Costantino Nivola. Smooth marble "stalagmites" rose from the green marble floor supporting an array of typewriters, illuminated by brightly colored Venetian-glass pendant lights. "We wished to give a sense of natural richness and interpenetration,"[20] said lead architect, Enrico Peressutti. Even the way the interior was designed suggested an organic process; Peressutti would often arrive at the site to make ad-hoc changes, which he would sketch on a section of bare wall.

The use of highly textured, planar screens or murals was one method modern architects used to imprint a handcrafted feeling onto contemporary designs. The panels of the metal balustrade designed by Philip Johnson for the lobby of the New York State Theater at the Lincoln Center for the Performing Arts (1959–64) suggest the highly modeled bronze sculptures of Alberto Giacometti. Eero Saarinen's Samuel F. B. Morse and Ezra Stiles Colleges (1962) in New Haven, Connecticut, evokes the rough-hewn surfaces and irregular piazzas of Italian hill towns, with sculptures by Nivola (**FIGS. 4.6, 4.7**), while architects

FIG 4.6
Sculpture by Costantino Nivola incorporated into the façade of the Samuel F. B. Morse and Ezra Stiles Colleges, Yale University, New Haven, Connecticut, 1962. Architect: Eero Saarinen.

FIG 4.7
Costantino Nivola working on his sculpture in New Haven, c. 1962.

Wallace Harrison and Max Abramowitz created a faceted aluminum skin for the corporate headquarters in Pittsburgh for Alcoa in 1953. A similar quality informs Paul Rudolph's Mary Cooper Jewett Arts Center (1958) at Wellesley College in Massachusetts. Rudolph employed projecting porcelain-enameled aluminum screens to relate, in their delicate texture, to the campus's Gothic-revival buildings.

The aesthetic of Rudolph's Jewett Arts Center stands midway between the sleekness of the architect's early career and the ruggedness to come. In fact, when in 1944 Chermayeff and d'Harnoncourt sought to reevaluate craftsmanship and encourage "direct contact between man and material," they could hardly have envisioned Rudolph's Art and Architecture Building (1963) for Yale. In designing the building, Rudolph specified that narrow gaps be left between the wood boards of the structure's concrete formwork. The concrete, when poured, oozed out through the spaces and was later chiseled by hand to create an effect of highly jagged corduroy. Far from simply "helping the machine," the hand in Rudolph's case had come to mask it.

This essay was written in 1996 when an earlier version of this exhibition was planned but not mounted. In the intervening years, parts of the current text have been published elsewhere. —DA

1 Serge Chermayeff and René d'Harnoncourt, "Design for Use," in *Art in Progress: A Survey Prepared for the Fifteenth Anniversary of the Museum of Modern Art* (New York: Museum of Modern Art, 1944), 191. At this time René d'Harnoncourt was director of the newly created Department of Manual Industries and vice president in charge of foreign activities; Chermayeff was then an adjunct curator of design.

2 Defining the American character was the subject of many contemporary books; see Henry Steele Commager, *The American Mind: An Interpretation of American Thought and Character Since the 1880s* (New Haven: Yale University Press, 1950); David Riesman with Nathan Glazer and Reuel Denny, *The Lonely Crowd: A Study of the Changing American Character* (New Haven: Yale University Press, 1950); and David Potter, *People of Plenty: Economic Abundance and the American Character* (Chicago: University of Chicago Press, 1954).

3 Frances Heard, "What Is the Station Wagon Way of Life?" *House Beautiful* 94 (June 1952), 104–9. This term was coined by *House Beautiful* about 1950 in previous articles on this subject.

4 Mary Roche, "The American Ideal of Leveling Up," *House Beautiful* 93 (May 1950), 128–33, 199–200.

5 Frances Heard, "American Taste Has an Unmistakable Flavor," *House Beautiful* 94 (May 1952), 140–43.

6 Elizabeth Gordon, "The Threat to the Next America," *House Beautiful* 95 (April 1953), 126–31, 250–51.

7 Ibid.

8 Unpaginated brochure from the Museum of Modern Art file on *Good Design* exhibition, September–November 1953.

9 *Dallas Times Herald,* February 24, 1944, clipping file, Department of Manual Industry, archive of the Museum of Modern Art, New York.

10 In the book's foreword, d'Harnoncourt described Bailey as a well-known designer who had studied the native crafts of China, Polynesia, Mexico, Guatemala, Peru, and Chile. Between 1934 and 1940, Bailey headed a project for a group of American retailers to create an American market for indigenous handcrafts of the Pacific area. By the time the book was published, the Inter-American Development Commission had transferred its rights and interests to an institute mandated by the Peruvian government.

11 Victor D'Amico, Moreen Maser, and Frances Wilson, *Art for the Family* (New York: Museum of Modern Art, 1954), 9.

12 Roy Ginstrom, "By the Work of Our Hands . . . ," in *Midwest Designer-Craftsmen: Exhibition of Works by Designer-Craftsmen of the Mississippi Basin* (Chicago: Art Institute of Chicago and Midwest Designer-Craftsmen, 1957), n.p.

13 Dorothy Giles, "The Craftsman in America," in *Designer Craftsmen U.S.A.* (New York: American Craftsmen's Educational Council, 1953), 25. This exhibition was shown at the Brooklyn Museum (October 16, 1953–January 4, 1954), Art Institute of Chicago (March 15–April 26, 1954), and San Francisco Museum of Art (June 17–August 15, 1954).

14 Among his many craft-related activities, Campbell was a trustee of the council since the time of its founding and its president from 1958. He died in 1963.

15 Manhattan examples include Georg Jensen in 1946; New Design, Inc., in 1948; Bonniers in 1949; Wilburt's in 1960; and D/R International [Design Research] in 1963.

16 Joseph A. Barry, "How Homemaking Can Be an Art," *House Beautiful* 95 (February 1953), 67–89.

17 Ibid.

18 Olga Gueft, "The Inn of the Sun," *Interiors* 120 (February 1961), 88–89.

19 Ada Louise Huxtable, "Bankers' Showcase," *Arts Digest* 29 (December 1, 1954), 12–13.

20 Enrico Peressutti quoted in "The Talk of the Town: Natural," *New Yorker* 30 (June 5, 1954), 21–22.

63

JOHN NEUHART, DESIGNER
HERMAN MILLER FURNITURE
COMPANY, MANUFACTURER
Textiles and Objects Announcement, 1961
27 X 11 IN. (68.6 X 27.9 CM)
LITHOGRAPH POSTER
COLLECTION OF HILDA LONGINOTTI

64

ALEXANDER GIRARD,
DESIGNER
HERMAN MILLER
FURNITURE COMPANY,
MANUFACTURER
Objects Selected
by Alexander Girard
for Herman Miller,
Inc., c. 1961
37 X 25½ IN. (94 X 64.8 CM)
LITHOGRAPH POSTER
COLLECTION OF HILDA
LONGINOTTI

Objects selected by Alexander Girard for Herman Miller, Inc.

65

ALEXANDER GIRARD, DESIGNER

HERMAN MILLER FURNITURE

COMPANY, MANUFACTURER

"Old Sun" Panel, 1971

PRINTED COTTON

46 X 46 IN. (116.8 X 116.8 CM)

COLLECTION OF HILDA LONGINOTTI

66

ARIETO (HARRY) BERTOIA
Untitled (Sculpture), c. 1958
BRASS AND COPPER
49 X 29 X 13 IN. (124.5 X 73.7 X 33 CM)
COURTESY OF JAMES ELKIND, LOST CITY ARTS

67

RAY EAMES, DESIGNER

CHARLES EAMES, DESIGNER

HERMAN MILLER FURNITURE

COMPANY, MANUFACTURER

Stool, 1960

WALNUT

15 IN. (38.1 CM); DIAM. 13 IN. (33 CM)

PRIVATE COLLECTION

68

RICHARD SCHULTZ, DESIGNER

KNOLL ASSOCIATES, MANUFACTURER

Petal Table, 1960

TEAK, POWDER-COATED STAINLESS STEEL, AND ALUMINUM

H. 19⅛ IN. (48.6 CM); DIAM. 16⅛ IN. (41 CM)

COLLECTION OF PETER SCHULTZ

69

CHARLES EAMES, DESIGNER

RAY EAMES, DESIGNER

HERMAN MILLER FURNITURE COMPANY, MANUFACTURER

Lounge Chair and Ottoman, designed 1956

ROSEWOOD, LEATHER, AND ALUMINUM

CHAIR: 33½ X 33 X 32 IN. (85.1 X 83.8 X 81.3 CM)

OTTOMAN: 16½ X 26 X 21 IN. (41.9 X 66 X 53.3 CM)

PHILADELPHIA MUSEUM OF ART, PURCHASED WITH FUNDS

CONTRIBUTED BY MR. AND MRS. ADOLPH G. ROSENGARTEN JR.,

IN MEMORY OF CALVIN HATHAWAY, 1976

CHAPTER 5

Handmade Modernism: Craft in Industry in the Postwar Period

JENNIFER SCANLAN

AFTER WORLD WAR II, MEMBERS OF THE BURGEONING craft movement sought to define the role of the craftsperson in a society moving increasingly toward industrialization. A 1947 article in *Craft Horizons* suggested three ways in which craftspeople could work with industry: They could serve as designers, as technicians making prototypes for industry, or as "mere" artisans who hand-finished machine-made pieces.[1] The reality was much more complex. After the war, modern design, as defined by style arbiters such as museums and publications, began to include aspects of craft. Unique handmade articles could serve as decorative accents in interiors, and features of the handmade, such as natural materials or irregularity in form, might be incorporated into mass-produced goods. Craft increasingly intersected with the world of production. The craftsperson as industrial designer was one model, particularly successful in the textile industry, while in the furniture industry especially, new styles helped to maintain and perpetuate existing craft traditions. In many cases, the renewed interest in incorporating craft into the modern interior created a market for small craft-based businesses. Craft and industry, far from presenting opposing forces, were in fact often closely allied in the early years of the craft movement.

※

At the end of World War II, as manufacturers shifted gears for peacetime production, the goods appearing on the market reflected a new direction in modern design. In 1946 designer Eva Zeisel wrote with pleasure that "lines and forms have become communicative once more. They express the designer's moods and his sense of humor. The change is taking place in the design of useful objects; these are the most indicative of progress in design."[2] That same year the Museum of Modern Art, New York (MoMA), staged *Modern Rooms of the Last Fifty Years,* and in the exhibition catalogue they noted the recent move away from the "strictness and purity of the great modern work of the 20s and early 30s." They partly attributed this change to the renewed connection between modern design and craft, tracing it to modern design coming from Scandinavia in the 1930s, where

> by 1935 a satisfactory synthesis of both tendencies was noticeable, especially in furniture from Finland by Alvar and Aino Aalto, and from Sweden by Bruno Mathsson. Since then modern design and modern rooms have shown a consistent trend, blending craft with industry, free curves with stricter shapes, still guided by the same principles that have prevailed ever since the earliest modern efforts—honesty of means, simplicity, clarity, lightness, unity.[3]

This new form of modernism valued many of the elements associated with craft: natural materials and textures (wood, ceramics, metal, fiber, and glass); curving "sculpted" shapes that often gave the appearance of being hand-formed; traditional techniques (weaving, carving, metalsmithing, glassblowing); and perhaps most importantly, evidence of the individual—the maker's hand—through irregularity in pattern and form, and in one-of-a-kind works. In direct contrast to the machine-made modernism of the previous era, this was a handmade modernism.

Objects in this category encompassed a wide array of production methods, from the unique object by one maker to industrially designed pieces that included some of the stylistic characteristics of the handmade. This range was evident in works displayed in museum exhibitions defining "good design." In 1946 the Walker Art Center in Minneapolis inaugurated its Everyday Art Gallery, stating: "the new Gallery is devoted to selecting and displaying the best ideas concerning the home and the many articles that go into it, from factory-made

coffee pots to handwoven fabrics."[4] In 1949 Alexander Girard, then a Detroit architect, organized *An Exhibition for Modern Living* at the Detroit Institute of Arts, which included more than two thousand examples of "good design," both mass-produced and handmade. Perhaps most famously, Edgar Kaufmann Jr., the director of the department of industrial design at MoMA, organized the museum's series of Good Design exhibitions from 1950 to 1955. Hugely influential, these exhibitions gave visibility, along with a MoMA "Good Design" stamp of approval, to a series of objects, which consistently ranged from mass-produced to completely handmade.

While handmade versus machine-made was presented as a dichotomy, in reality there was often overlap between the two. In 1946 Kaufmann noted that "few issues have been more discussed and misunderstood than the differences in quality and in beauty between an object made by hand and one made by machine. In truth, very few machine made objects in common use are entirely exempt from direct human forming during their production. And very few handmade things do not employ some

process or implement evolved by the machine technology of our time."[5]

In some cases, visual cues hinted at the handmade: Firms such as George Nelson and Knoll Associates that designed integrated modern interiors would use designs with natural materials such as wood and ceramic in furnishings that were industrially produced. In other cases, mass-produced goods only made reference to the handmade. The pattern on Eszter Haraszty's *Fibra* fabric was produced from a photograph of the heddles of a loom, and George Nelson's *China Shop* featured the irregular ceramic forms popular in the period **(CAT. 73, 1)**.[6] For many firms, however, handcrafting techniques were an important part of the manufacturing process, in degrees which varied widely.

This intersection between the handmade and the machine-made was particularly relevant during the immediate postwar period as a group of individuals and companies took advantage of a growing market for domestic goods in the handcrafted modern style. Not surprisingly, many of the first designers to exploit this

industrial designer Don Wallance cited Gustavsberg as an outstanding example: a large-scale ceramics factory with thousands of workers which invited "artist-craftsmen" to live there and create relatively free of production concerns.[8]

One designer who successfully brought the Scandinavian model to the United States was John Prip, who was Danish American. When his family moved back to Copenhagen in 1933, Prip's father returned to the family silversmithing factory, and John apprenticed with a nearby silversmithing firm four years later. In 1948 Prip became head of the department of jewelry and silversmithing at the School for American Craftsmen in Alfred, New York. In 1957 he entered into an agreement with silver manufacturing firm Reed & Barton to become a designer-in-residence or, as he titled himself, "Artist-Craftsman-In-Residence." Prip was free to develop prototypes by hand, sculpting models out of plaster and working with the sales staff and workers to develop them into profitable production designs.

Prip's childhood experiences in his father's factory made his relationship with Reed & Barton especially fruitful. He remembered playing "in silver factories since I could walk, so it was nothing new and frightening to me, although I still can't completely understand certain things."[9] Reed & Barton's president, Roger Hallowell, also fully supported Prip's role at the factory, saying later that he believed "firmly that the craftsman has a place in industry, and that place is one of leadership. I believe that the craftsman can, because he is an individual, lead the mass producer to finer things."[10] Prip worked full-time at Reed & Barton for a few years and continued to design for them on a part-time basis after 1960, along with teaching and creating his own work.

Another Scandinavian who successfully transplanted handmade modernism to the United States was Danish-born designer Jens Risom. Soon after coming to the United States in 1939, he met Hans Knoll, and he designed Knoll's first line of furniture in 1942. Risom found creative design solutions to wartime restrictions, using non-priority wood and surplus Army webbing for chairs reminiscent of the work of Scandinavian designers such as Mathsson.[11] Risom later set up his own firm, Jens Risom Design Inc., and marketed his furniture to decorators through a showroom on Fifth Avenue in New York, as well as at upscale stores such as Georg Jensen.[12]

Risom, who was not a furniture maker himself, worked with craftspeople on designs that highlighted

connection were from northern Europe—Scandinavia and Germany—where links between craftsmanship and modern design had been forged before World War II.

Hallmarks of Scandinavian design included smooth, biomorphic shapes, primarily natural materials, curved warm surfaces that seemed inviting to the touch, and frequent references to traditional patterns. While the lines were clean, they were not rigidly geometric and regular, tending instead toward ovals and S-curves. Ceramics often had deliberately naive or whimsical surface decorations and irregular glazes. Wooden utensils were beautifully carved, and furniture solidly made and well finished. References to craftsmanship and the human touch were everywhere.

Scandinavia was often cited as a model for relationships between craft and industry. In 1964 Just Lunning, president of the New York retail branch of the Danish company Georg Jensen, Inc., ascribed this to a closeness between industrialists and craftsmen-designers that had begun in Scandinavia in the 1920s.[7] New York

CAT. 70

Marianne Strengell, designer; Chatham Manufacturing Co., manufacturer, *1959 Lincoln Continental Panel*, 1959. Fiber and plastic. 58¾ x 33 in. (149.2 x 83.8 cm). Museum of Arts and Design, Gift of the artist, through the American Craft Council, 1984.

natural materials and craft techniques. When his designs were included in *An Exhibition for Modern Living*, the catalogue emphasized his connection to Scandinavian crafts traditions: "The designer's emphasis on personal expression is shown in the furniture which, although designed for today's workmanship and machinery, was produced in small cuttings, thereby assuring a proper craftsmanlike treatment of materials."[13] He incorporated such hallmarks of Danish furniture making as hand-rubbed finishes and elegant joinery, and like other designers working in the handmade modern style, he used handwoven upholstery fabrics.

Furniture designer Vladimir Kagan came from a family of European cabinetmakers. They immigrated to New York in 1937, and, while at the High School of Industrial Arts, Kagan studied ceramics, which would later influence his furniture designs. He remembered

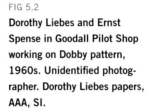

FIG 5.2

Dorothy Liebes and Ernst Spense in Goodall Pilot Shop working on Dobby pattern, 1960s. Unidentified photographer. Dorothy Liebes papers, AAA, SI.

being "drawn to clay modeling and sculpture, the sensuousness of clay in your hands is hard to describe.... These experiences inspired my fascination with organic shapes, which became the free-form expressions of my furniture."[14] He learned the furniture trade in his father's workshop and was taught to "honor the handcraft" from the German craftspeople that his father employed.[15] His design style was inspired by the Bauhaus and Danish modern furniture, but also included decorative embellishments, such as Venetian glass tiles and metalwork. When he opened his own shop, he included both furniture and other kinds of home furnishings, with an emphasis on the handmade. Kagan's early signature style was the "sculptured look" as evidenced in a 1952 tripod end table whose base, according to the *New York Times*, had been carved by hand.[16] By 1958, another version of this "sculptured" base showed up in metal, demonstrating Kagan's willingness to experiment with new materials and not rely solely on the handmade modernist style.

Ed Wormley became interested in modern design after traveling to Europe before the war. At the Dunbar Furniture Manufacturing Co., which operated in Berne, Indiana, Wormley designed furniture lines that were modern in style, but evoked traditional craftsmanship in construction and finish, use of fine materials, and such visual cues as the incorporation of crafted elements into the ornamentation. By the postwar period, his designs for Dunbar were exclusively in the modern style, though one that was more palatable to consumers through references to tradition, such as the use of caning and American walnut.[17] Wormley's version of modernism incorporated what a contemporary article called his "love affair with the beauty of wood and fine craftsmanship," with clean lines and practical, multiuse pieces which proved immensely popular.[18] The firm remained midsized throughout the postwar period: In the late 1950s, Dunbar had three hundred employees and sales of less than three million dollars.[19] Craft production methods included hand-stitched upholstery, dovetailed corners, and hand-rubbed finishes.[20] Dunbar collaborated with other artists and designers associated with handmade modernism—Dorothy Liebes (upholstery) and Gertrud and Otto Natzler (ceramic tiles).

John Kapel worked both with industrial processes and as an independent craftsman, designing for furniture companies, most notably Glenn of California for twenty years, as well as creating one-of-a-kind pieces and

commissions. After graduating from Cranbrook in 1950 and spending a year in Prague on a Carnegie Fellowship, he went to work with George Nelson, who was then the chief designer for the Herman Miller Furniture Company in New York. After two years, Kapel left to pursue a more independent life in California, inspired by the example of Sam Maloof. His knowledge of craftsmanship was instrumental in his success: He later noted that other designers unfamiliar with furniture-making techniques would design in ways that were inefficient or difficult to put into production.[21] His personal interest in handmade works led to a sensitivity to form and materials. His candlesticks of 1955 feature some of his signature elements: expressive use of woods and elegant curves, along with metal elements cleverly repurposed from furniture feet (CAT. 82).

While the postwar furniture industry still incorporated craftsmanship as part of the manufacturing process, textiles had been completely industrialized since the nineteenth century. Handmade modernism, if not present in the process, was present in the aesthetics of woven and printed textiles. In 1949 the *New York Times* announced that "the newest look in upholstery fabrics this fall is the hand-loomed look, which is about the best evidence there is that the individual hand-weaver is no arts-and-craftsy eccentric, but an important contributor to the march of industry. Fabric manufactures (along with the makers of dinnerware and decorative accessories) are turning more and more for new ideas to the men and women who create with their hands rather than a pencil."[22]

This "hand-loomed look" was characterized by texture, irregular nubs in the fiber, and a design that reinforced and revealed the two-dimensionality of the weave structure. Because handwoven samples were reproducible by machine on a large scale, textiles represented one of the most successful integrations of the handmade and machine-made, with a number of handweavers designing for industry. They were also widely accessible: In 1949, you could set your table with place mats designed by Anni Albers, Marianne Strengell, or Lenore Tawney.[23]

Dorothy Liebes was perhaps the best-known and most influential of these textile designers. A self-taught weaver who began by designing custom textiles in San Francisco, Liebes was singled out in 1940 by the *New York Times* for her "versatility and ingenuity in creating new textiles," which noted particularly her bold use of colors, combining purple, blue, and green in one example.[24] Soon after, she began working with large-scale textile manufacturers,

signing a contract with Goodall Fabrics and later with Dobeckmun Co., to work largely with Lurex, a glittery metallic fiber that became one of her style signatures (FIG. 5.2).[25] She went on to design for a number of large companies, most notably DuPont, focusing on their synthetic fabrics. In addition to synthetics, Liebes used a number of unusual natural materials, including grasses, reeds, bamboo, and metal. In a 1950 article for *Craft Horizons*, she recommended incorporating regional materials, saying that for handweavers "it is of prime importance . . . to draw upon their immediate surroundings and to develop and combine materials that may be lying unnoticed at hand."[26]

Marianne Strengell was another handweaver who achieved great success designing for industry. After studying weaving in her native Finland, she came to the United States and eventually became the head of the weaving department at Cranbrook, where she combined her work as an influential teacher with a career designing custom fabrics for architects and design firms. She worked with many notable architects and designers—Skidmore, Owings & Merrill, Eero Saarinen, Edward Durell Stone, Raymond Loewy, Russel Wright, and Knoll Associates. She created handmade prototypes for industry with a modernist emphasis on two-dimensional structure but also incorporating an irregular texture which warmed International Style architectural interiors. Her designs for the auto industry added glamour and comfort to the 1959 Lincoln Continental by Ford, among other auto makers (CAT. 70).

Strengell's student Jack Lenor Larsen similarly blended an interest in the handcrafting process, an eye for interesting combinations of fiber and color, and a facility for designing for mass production. In his long career Larsen has not only produced a broad range of designs but also has developed a number of handcrafted weaving and printing techniques suitable for larger-scale production, working primarily with power looms. In 1964, however, he noted that his firm's output still did not qualify as mass production: "The limited kind of production that I do has nothing to do with the J. P. Stevens Company . . . . The power looming that my plant does—the turning out of 100 yards of this and that—simply is not production to them. It is using power tools but almost in a handcraft tradition. Mass production is for one man to watch sixty looms all going at once, all weaving the same thing without flaws."[27]

In addition to working with industry, both Larsen and Liebes were very active in the crafts community, writing for *Craft Horizons* and serving on the board of the American Craft Council (ACC). Liebes's identity as a handweaver was an important part of the marketing of her designs, with advertisements often showing her working at a loom.[28] Larsen retained an interest in the craft object as artwork, collecting one-of-a-kind craft objects which he often donated later to museums and co-curating *Wall Hangings* at MoMA with Mildred Constantine in 1969.

In 1949 another trend in upholstery fabrics was noted—hand-printed designs.[29] Silkscreening was a relatively new process at the time, which allowed for textiles to be printed with inexpensive equipment and in small batches. It gave small producers more opportunity to be creative and experimental with their designs. Screenprinting also produced a slight irregularity to the tone and around the edge of the printed pattern that gave the fabrics a handmade look.

Elenhank Designers, Inc., a small Chicago firm, used hand-printing to create their modern textile designs. Formed by the husband-and-wife team of Eleanor and Henry Kluck, Elenhank sold block-printed and silkscreened fabrics through architects and interior designers on a custom-order basis. In 1951 they introduced "random prints" which allowed customers to specify the placement of the design motifs.[30] Despite the popularity of their designs, the firm remained small, with a staff that had expanded by only seven additional people by 1961. The screenprinting was contracted out to a company in Rhode Island.[31] By 1970, the Klucks were producing large flat panels in op art prints that could be hung like paintings.[32] They successfully incorporated changes in modern design aesthetics while also capitalizing on the growing consideration of textiles as works of art.

Laverne Originals was another husband-and-wife team, Erwine and Estelle Laverne, producing modern silkscreened textiles. Established in 1934, in the postwar period, it became well-known for textiles and wallpaper in contemporary and traditional patterns.[33] The Lavernes used their own designs and also commissioned graphic designers such as Ray Komai and Alvin Lustig to create patterns that had a hand-drawn look. Alexander Calder made two designs for them after fashioning a mobile for their home, a showcase of their hand-screened designs.[34]

FIG 5.3

Edith Heath, ca. 1949. Seagull Portrait Studios, photographer. Miscellaneous photograph collection, AAA, SI.

Ceramics were both decorative and functional in the handmade modern aesthetic. Their use as accents in a modern room was promoted by an exhibition of the New York Society of Ceramic Arts in 1953. Designers incorporated ceramics sculptures and vessels into a series of interiors for the exhibition. In one, gallery owner Bertha Schaefer displayed a textbook example of the handmade modern interior, combining texture, exotic accents (in the colorful silks and irregular shelves, probably inspired by Japanese examples), and artwork that included both paintings and craft media. The *New York Times* singled it out in a review, noting the many textiles: "Grey flannel and an amber and maroon silk cover the walls, a tweed-like fabric appears on the couches, a shaggy rug covers the floor. Textured contemporary embroideries and colorful abstract paintings decorate the walls, while the many ceramics, subdued in coloring, appear in a cabinet with an irregular shelf arrangement and on the several tables in the room."[35]

In 1946, *Everyday Art Quarterly* surveyed the range of contemporary ceramic production. Factory ware was defined as "pieces produced in quantities by casting, jiggering, or molding processes." Eva Zeisel's design for MoMA, which was manufactured by the large, high-end company Castleton China, included her trademark gentle curves, the only organic element in the otherwise pristine machine-made service. Russel Wright's vessels made in collaboration with the smaller California-based Bauer Pottery Company, while mass-produced, featured "textured glazes, the result of eight months of research," which gave the forms the appearance of the handmade. A section of "hand made pottery and porcelain," defined as "individually made pieces thrown on the potter's wheel," included works by the Edwin and Mary Scheier, Beatrice Wood, and Gertrud and Otto Natzler.[36]

Glidden Pottery represented yet another type of ceramic manufacture. The company used modern production methods of slip casting or RAM pressing, but each piece was glazed and decorated by hand.[37] The firm was located in Alfred, New York, where owner Glidden Parker and his wife, Harriet Hamill Parker, had studied ceramics. Glidden giftware proved to be immensely popular, and the firm grew from one or two employees in 1940 to fifty-five in 1946, decreasing to thirty-three in 1950.[38] While Parker designed many of the pieces himself, he also hired Alfred graduates, notably Fong Chow, who joined Glidden in 1953. Chow developed forms and glazes, often featuring brilliantly colored patterns such as in his *Gulfstream Blue* series (CAT. 83).[39]

David Gil also opened a pottery after graduating from Alfred University. The company, eventually known as Bennington Potters, grew in fits and starts, as Gil worked to develop a line that would sell on a national scale. Gil began to achieve recognition as a designer, winning first prize in 1951 in the National Ceramic Show at the Everson Museum in Syracuse, New York. His work was also included in the MoMA Good Design exhibitions. Eventually Bennington Potters was distributed by Raymor, which allowed the company to expand, and by 1964, the pottery employed thirty-five people. Like the Glidden Pottery, Bennington Potters used slip casting and RAM pressing to create works based on plaster models. The pieces were then trimmed or "fettled" and glazed by hand.[40] Gil designed most of the Bennington

pieces with simple forms and subtly irregular glazes. A 1961 article reported that Gil also employed an artist-in-residence, by which "a trained ceramist is invited to use the facilities of their shop for a year while working freely on his or her own work." The artist-in-residence also helped with custom orders and large-scale contract designs for restaurants.[41]

During the war Gump's department store in San Francisco featured a number of local craftspeople to support the community but also because of wartime restrictions on imports.[42] Edith Heath, a ceramics teacher in San Francisco, was among those selected for her dinnerware. She soon began to sell all over the country through a distributor, and had about ten employees working for her. The ceramics were created on a "jigger wheel," in which a mold shaped the piece on the rotating wheel (FIG 5.3). While this method did allow for rapid production with less variance in the output, as Heath later noted, "jiggering, while it seems like practically any fool can do it, it does require a good deal of skill."[43] Her designs were characterized by simple, sturdy forms and subtle matte glazes which she developed herself. They had the irregularity of hand-finished pieces, and often the slight texture of the clay body showed through. Understated and elegant, made in quantity with visual evidence of the craft traditions behind them, Heathware pieces soon became icons of handmade modernism, and examples were acquired by MoMA in 1948.

Handmade modern glass was elegant and spare in form. Its connection to the handmade modern came through its reliance on craft traditions, especially those of Italy and Scandinavia. The Blenko Glass Company of West Virginia emphasized this connection and began to hire designers in the mid-1940s. Joel Philip Myers joined the firm in 1963, seeing it as an opportunity to learn traditional glass skills, as no institutions taught glassblowing at that time. In a 1964 article, Myers confirmed that the relatively small factory of 160 workers relied entirely on handcrafting methods to create the decorative glass that was its signature product.[44]

Myers's collaboration with Blenko reflected the Scandinavian model, and he was encouraged to experiment in the studio. The head of the company, William Blenko Sr., commented in 1964 that "The designer should be given complete freedom. One cannot expect creativity without giving free rein. We believe proper environment produces better things. We don't tell the designer what we want."[45] Despite this environment, Myers found it difficult to move the company beyond more conventional design.

Michael and Frances Higgins chose a more independent route. Frances had been experimenting with "slumped" glass, melted in a kiln, and after their marriage in 1948, the Higginses began working on the designs together in their apartment. They created a line of decorative glassware that they sold to high-end department stores such as Marshall Field, Bloomingdales, Georg Jensen, and Gump's.[46] Plates, ashtrays, and tiles were decorated with layers of colored glass and enamel in multi-hued, irregular designs.

In 1957 they began a short-lived collaboration with the Dearborn Glass Company, which produced glass for industrial purposes. Dearborn decided to diversify by bringing in the Higginses to make decorative glassware in large quantities. The pair set up a studio in the Dearborn factory and began to adapt their lamination and decoration methods to a much larger scale of production. The experiment proved difficult. The machinery, marketing, and distribution were not easily shifted from industrial products to decorative goods.[47] While the collaboration produced many beautiful pieces—including a series of gray glass ashtrays made from cast-offs of Dearborn's production of television screens—the collaboration ended in 1964, and the Higginses soon went back to working on a smaller scale.

In 1964 the Museum of Contemporary Crafts mounted *Designed for Production: The Craftsman's Approach,* an exhibition that included most of the designers and craftspeople mentioned in this essay. A companion issue of *Craft Horizons* devoted many articles to the collaboration of craftspeople with industry. By that time, however, a shift was already underway. Designers such as Vladimir Kagan and the Klucks at Elenhank were already moving away from handmade modern to a style more related to op art and the space age. In the world of craft, craftspeople who had been educated in art schools were less interested in partnering with industry. For the 1960 *Designer Craftsmen U.S.A.* exhibition, jurors noted with dismay that "It was evident in this show that few craftsmen concerned themselves with the subtitle 'Designed and Handcrafted for Use.' . . . The three of us agreed that the special function of craftsmanship 'for use' was to design objects which might serve as pilot models for industry or objects which could not be appropriately made by machine."[48] They were disappointed with the results that year.

Indicative of this new direction was *The American Craftsman,* an exhibition in 1964 following *Designed for Production* at the Museum of Contemporary Crafts. It was dedicated to the "artist-craftsman" and featured one-of-a-kind, primarily nonfunctional work. By 1969, only a few of the objects included in the *Objects: USA* exhibition had been part of any production series. One of the rare examples, flatware by Robert King, had been designed fourteen years earlier **(CAT. 86).** While Heath Ceramics and Bennington Potters continued operating, they were no longer connected to the craft movement, which began to align itself more with the fine arts.

⁂

For a nation recovering from war, and faced with the specter of an impersonal world filled with mass-produced objects, handmade modernism offered a comforting return to more traditional values and natural materials, as well as a more human-centered approach to design. It also offered opportunities for people to make a living using their hands and creative skills. Still, as the crafts movement grew and flourished, people working in craft materials eventually lost interest in collaborating with industry as a means of survival. Schools, museums, and even galleries provided new contexts for their work. Examination of the early connections between craft and industry, however, provides a more nuanced and varied view of the postwar birth of the studio craft movement and demonstrates the many ways in which craft became an important part of everyday life in the postwar period and beyond.

1 "Craftsmen and Industry," *CH* 6 (February 1947), 16.

2 Eva Zeisel, "Registering a New Trend," *Everyday Art Quarterly* 2 (Autumn 1946), 1.

3 *Modern Rooms of the Last Fifty Years*, exh. cat. (New York: Museum of Modern Art, 1946), 11.

4 *Everyday Art Quarterly* 1 (summer 1946), 2.

5 Edgar Kaufmann Jr., "Hand-made and Machine-made Art," *Everyday Art Quarterly* 1 (summer 1946), 3.

6 Christine W. Laidlaw, "Eszter Haraszty," in *Design 1935–1965: What Modern Was* (New York: Harry N. Abrams, Inc., 1991), 224.

7 Jan McDevitt, "The Craftsman in Production: A Frank Discussion of the Rewards and Pitfalls," *CH* 24 (March/April 1964), 13.

8 Ibid.

9 John Prip, "John Prip and Reed & Barton," *CH* 24 (March/April 1964), 40.

10 Quoted in McDevitt, "Craftsman in Production," 10.

11 Arthur Pulos, *The American Design Adventure, 1940–1975* (Cambridge, MA: MIT Press, 1988), 83.

12 Steven Rouland and Linda Rouland, *Knoll Furniture, 1938–1960* (Atglen, PA: Schiffer Publishing Ltd., 1999), 28.

13 *An Exhibition for Modern Living*, exh. cat. Edited by A. H. Girard and W. D. Laurie Jr. (Detroit: Detroit Institute of Arts, 1949), 74.

14 Vladimir Kagan, *The Complete Kagan* (New York: Pointed Leaf Press, 2004), 26.

15 Ibid., 50.

16 "Sculptured Look Predominates in New Table Designs," *New York Times,* April 30, 1952, 30.

17 Cynthia Kellogg, "Modern Furniture is an Old Story to Designer," *New York Times*, January 4, 1957, 24.

18 J. W., "Wormley's Way," *Interiors* 123 (November 1963), 112.

19 Judith Guru, "History of Dunbar," *Ed Wormley: The Other Face of Modernism* (New York: DESIGNbase/ Lin-Weinberg Gallery, 1997), 15.

20 Ibid.

21 John Kapel, discussion with author, October 2009.

22 Mary Roche, "The Hand-Loomed Look," *New York Times,* September 4, 1949, 106.

23 Hilde Reiss, "Fresh, Contemporary Designs for the Dining-Room Table," *New York Times,* September 25, 1949, XX15.

24 Walter Rendell Storey, "Home Decoration: Modernity in a More Gracious Pattern," *New York Times*, December 29, 1940, D9.

25 Regina Lee Blaszczyk, "Designing Synthetics, Promoting Brands: Dorothy Liebes, DuPont Fibres and Post-war American Interiors," *Journal of Design History* 21 (2008), 81.

26 Dorothy Liebes, "All is grist . . . to our mill," *CH* 10 (spring 1950), 16.

27 Quoted in McDevitt, "Craftsman in Production," 12.

28 For a selection of Liebes advertisements and promotional photos, see Blaszczyk, "Designing Synthetics," 82, 91.

29 Roche, "Hand-Loomed Look," 106.

30 Christa C. Mayer Thurman, *Rooted in Chicago: Fifty Years of Textile Design Traditions, Museum Studies* 23, no. 1 (Chicago: Art Institute of Chicago, 1997), 44.

31 Ibid., 44, 47.

32 [Advertisement for W.& J. Sloane], *New York Times,* April 19, 1970, 10.

33 A 1948 article in the *New York Times* noted that "designers Erwine and Estelle Laverne divide their loyalty about equally between abstract designs and a type of whimsy with the flavor of the Pennsylvania Dutch." Mary Roche, "Abstract Designs, Plus Whimsy, Featured in New Spring Slipcover Fabric Prints," *New York Times,* March 15, 1948, 20.

34 Elaine Mayers Salkaln, "The Invisibles," *New York Times,* April 18, 2004, C50.

35 Cynthia Kellogg, "Use of Ceramics in Home is Shown," *New York Times,* February 4, 1953, 30.

36 All quotations from "Contemporary American Ceramics," *Everyday Art Quarterly* 2 (autumn 1946), 3–9.

37 Margaret Carney, "The History of Glidden Pottery," *Studio Potter* 30 (December 2001), 80.

38 Ibid., 81.

39 Fong Chow, oral history interview by Margaret Carney, February 6, 2002, AAA, SI.

40 Jane McCullough Thompson, "The Bennington Potters," *Vermont Life* 16 (winter 1961), 43ff.

41 Ibid., 46.

42 Edith Heath, *Tableware and Tile for the World, Heath Ceramics, 1944–1994.* Oral history conducted by Rosalie Ross, 1990–1992, 1994. Edited by Julie Gordon Shearer and Germaine LaBerge. California Craft Artists Oral History Series, University of California, Berkeley, CA, 115–19.

43 Ibid., 145.

44 Joel Myers, "Joel Myers and Blenko Glass," *CH* 24 (March/April 1964), 25.

45 McDevitt, "Craftsman in Production," 11.

46 Donald-Brian Johnson and Leslie Piña, *Higgins: Adventures in Glass* (Atglen, PA: Schiffer Publishing Company, 1997), 9.

47 Ibid., 18.

48 David Campbell, "Designer Craftsmen U.S.A. 1960," *CH* 20 (July/August 1960), 17. Campbell was then president of the American Craft Council and director of the Museum of Contemporary Crafts.

71

ARIETO (HARRY) BERTOIA, DESIGNER
KNOLL INTERNATIONAL, MANUFACTURER
"Bird" Lounge Chair and Ottoman, after 1952
STEEL AND UPHOLSTERY
40¼ X 38½ X 33 IN. (102.2 X 97.8 X 83.8 CM)
PRIVATE COLLECTION

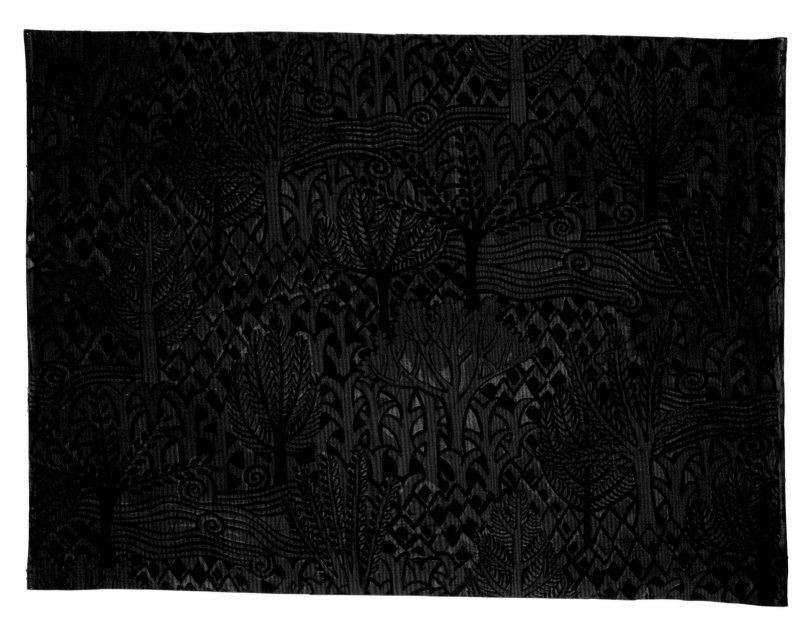

72

JACK LENOR LARSEN, DESIGNER

LARSEN DESIGN STUDIO, MANUFACTURER

Bas Relief, 1968

COTTON VELVET, RESIST-DYED,

INDIGO-DYED, PRINTED, HANDBLOCKED

36 X 50 IN. (91.4 X 127 CM)

MUSEUM OF ARTS AND DESIGN,

GIFT OF JACK LENOR LARSEN, 2001

73

ESZTER HARASZTY,
DESIGNER
KNOLL ASSOCIATES,
MANUFACTURER
Fibra, c. 1950
LINEN
54 X 24¾ IN. (135.89 X 63.5 CM)
COLLECTION OF JILL A. WILTSE
AND H. KIRK BROWN III,
DENVER, COLORADO

74

EERO SAARINEN, DESIGNER
KNOLL ASSOCIATES, MANUFACTURER
"Grasshopper" Chair, 1946–65
LAMINATED BIRCH AND FABRIC
36 X 28 X 34 IN. (91.4 X 71.1 X 86.4 CM)
PHILADELPHIA MUSEUM OF ART,
GIFT OF MR. AND MRS. FRED FELDKAMP, 1978

75

ISAMU NOGUCHI

My Mu (Watashi no mu), 1950

SHIGARAKI CERAMIC

13½ X 9½ X 6⅝ IN. (34.3 X 24.1 X 16.8 CM)

NOGUCHI MUSEUM, NEW YORK

76

GEORGE NELSON, DESIGNER

HERMAN MILLER FURNITURE

COMPANY, MANUFACTURER

Bench, designed 1946, produced 1946–67

PRIMAVERA, BIRCH, AND PAINT

14 X 18½ X 60 IN. (35.6 X 4/ X 152.4 CM)

COLLECTION OF HILDA LONGINOTTI

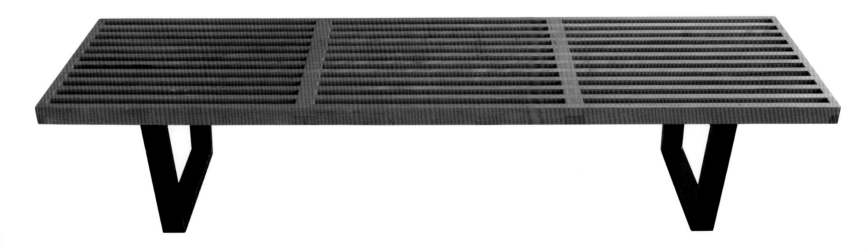

77

VLADIMIR KAGAN

Mosaic Tile Table on Cube Base, before 1957

WALNUT AND ITALIAN GLASS TILES

11¾ X 66½ X 16½ IN. (29.8 X 168.9 X 41.9 CM)

COLLECTION OF VLADIMIR KAGAN

79

JENS RISOM, DESIGNER
KNOLL ASSOCIATES, MANUFACTURER
Chair, Model 666 WSP, c. 1948
BIRCH AND COTTON WEBBING
30½ X 17½ X 21 IN. (77.5 X 44.5 X 53.3 CM)
COLLECTION OF LARRY WEINBERG

78

IRVING HARPER, DESIGNER FOR
GEORGE NELSON AND ASSOCIATES
HYALYN PORCELAIN INC., MANUFACTURER,
AND HOWARD MILLER CLOCK
COMPANY, MANUFACTURER
Ceramic Clock Prototype,
No. 2206-2212, 1953
PORCELAIN, MECHANICAL ELEMENTS
9 X 6 IN. (22.9 X 15.2 CM)
COLLECTION OF HILDA LONGINOTTI

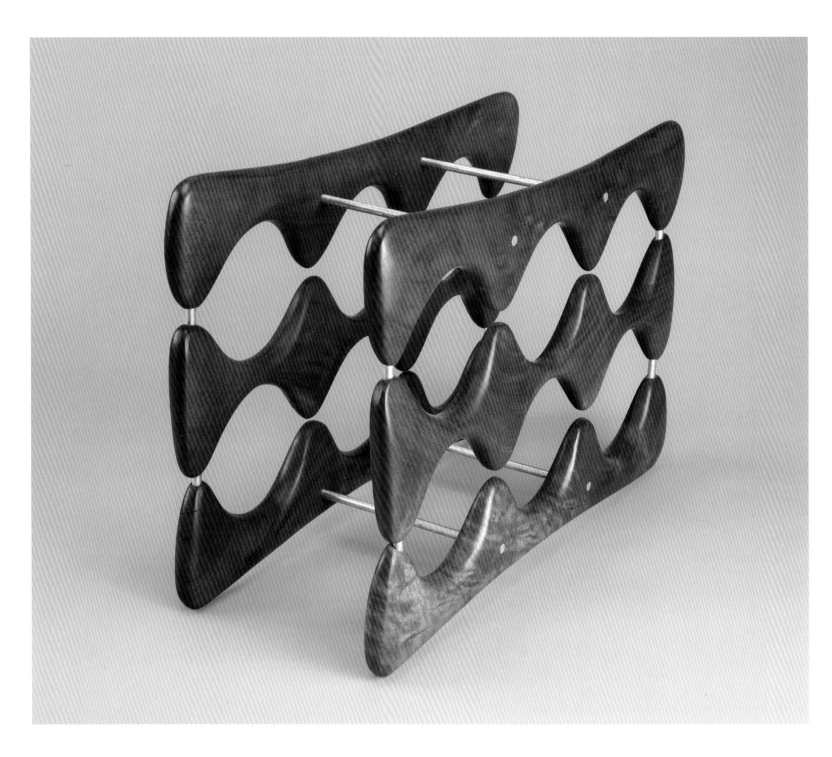

80

ARTHUR ESPENET CARPENTER

Wine Rack, 1968

WALNUT AND STEEL

11 X 16½ X 7 IN. (27.9 X 41.9 X 17.8 CM)

MUSEUM OF ARTS AND DESIGN, GIFT OF THE JOHNSON WAX

COMPANY, THROUGH THE AMERICAN CRAFT COUNCIL, 1977

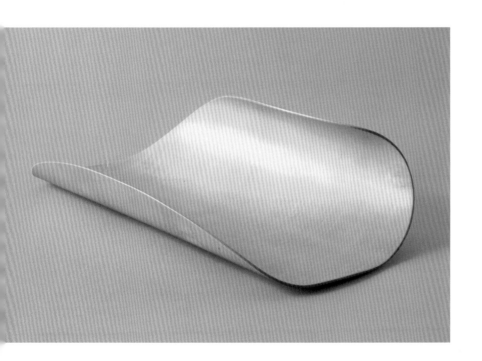

81

JAMES PRESTINI

Bent Plywood Bowl, 1954

PLYWOOD

8¼ X 17 X 4¼ IN. (21 X 43.2 X 10.8 CM)

LENT BY MICHAEL AND SUSAN RICH

82

JOHN KAPEL

Pair of Candlesticks, 1955

CHERRY, WALNUT, AND BRASS

EACH: 14 X 6¾ X 6 IN. (35.6 X 17.1 X 15.2 CM)

LONG BEACH MUSEUM OF ART, GIFT OF THE ARTIST, 58.9.6

83

FONG CHOW, DESIGNER
GLIDDEN POTTERY, MANUFACTURER
Gulfstream Blue Artware, 1956
STONEWARE
FROM LEFT TO RIGHT
VASE: 9½ IN. (24.1 CM); DIAM. 2½ IN. (6.4 CM);
VESSEL: 10¼ IN. (26 CM); DIAM. 3¼ IN. (8.3 3 CM);
CANDELABRA: 9½ X 7½ X 3½ IN. (24.1 X 19.1 X 8.9 CM)
MUSEUM OF ARTS AND DESIGN, GIFT OF FONG CHOW
IN MEMORY OF AILEEN OSBORN WEBB, 2010

84

LUCIA N. DeRESPINIS, DESIGNER FOR

GEORGE NELSON AND ASSOCIATES

BENNINGTON POTTERS, MANUFACTURER

Set of Three Beverage Servers, 1960

STONEWARE

CREAMER: 3¾ X 2¼ X 9 IN. (9.5 X 5.7 X 22.9 CM);

COVERED BOWL WITH LID: H. 3½ IN. (8.9 CM), DIAM. 8 IN. (20.3 CM);

TALL COVERED BOWL WITH LID: H. 4¾ IN. (12.1 CM), DIAM. 3½ IN. (8.9 CM)

COLLECTION OF HILDA LONGINOTTI

85

EDITH HEATH, DESIGNER

HEATH CERAMICS, MANUFACTURER

Sauceboat, c. 1960

EARTHENWARE

4 X 6 IN. (10.2 X 15.2 CM)

COLLECTION OF LAGUNA POTTERY,

SEATTLE, WASHINGTON

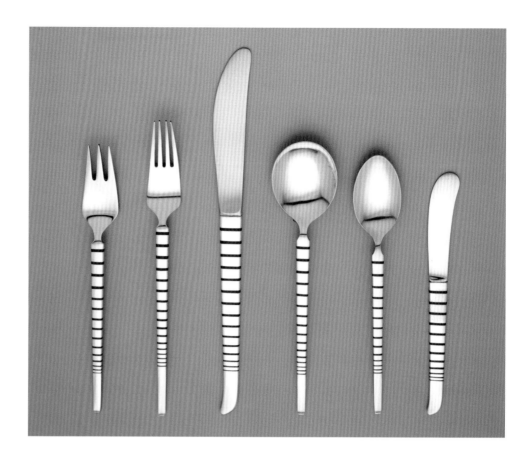

86

ROBERT J. KING

Flatware, 1955

STERLING SILVER WITH CHAMPLEVÉ ENAMEL

AVERAGE MEASUREMENT 2 X 7 IN. (5.1 X 17.8 CM)

DALLAS MUSEUM OF ART,

GIFT OF THE ARTIST, 2005.86.1-6

87

JOHN PRIP, DESIGNER

REED & BARTON, MANUFACTURER

HALL CHINA COMPANY, MANUFACTURER

Connoisseur Casserole, designed 1963

SILVERPLATE AND CERAMIC

6¼ X 10½ X 7½ IN. (15.9 X 26.7 X 19.1 CM)

MUSEUM OF ARTS AND DESIGN,

GIFT OF JEWEL STERN, 2011

88

MICHAEL HIGGINS

FRANCES HIGGINS

Cake Stand, ca. 1962

GLASS AND BRASS

H. 6 IN. (15.2 CM); DIAM. 12½ IN. (31.8 CM)

COLLECTION OF AUDREY KING LIPTON

89

DOROTHY LIEBES

Textile Samples, 1948–68

WOOL, SYNTHETIC FIBERS, AND REEDS

VARIOUS DIMENSIONS

MUSEUM OF ARTS AND DESIGN,

GIFT OF DOROTHY LIEBES DESIGN,

THROUGH THE AMERICAN CRAFT COUNCIL, 1973

CHAPTER 6

An "Exploding Craft Market," 1945–1969

CAROLINE M. HANNAH

PARALLEL TO THE EMERGENCE OF A "MOVEMENT" IN the twenty-five years following the end of World War II, a market for studio craft began to take shape in the United States. In this dynamic period, the general prewar concept of craft as local, amateur, handmade functional goods, often informed by a longing for a preindustrial era, made room for a new perception of craft as sophisticated, unique, handmade design objects that were aesthetically attuned to the contemporary tastes of a national, urban/suburban market. Middle- and upper-middle-class consumers came to accept craft objects as an appropriate and desirable component of modern domestic (and often corporate) spaces, because they provided "psychic compensation" for a world inundated by what were considered bland, lifeless products of the industrial era.[1] By the end of this period, consumers increasingly regarded craft objects as "fine art" as well. Simultaneously the center of gravity in the marketplace began to shift from seasonal country fairs and shops selling gifts and housewares to art galleries, where more experimental expressions in craft media were gaining traction by the late 1960s. Between these two poles existed a web of possible retail venues—women's exchanges, gift shops, department stores with gallerylike settings, cooperative ventures, craft sales and fairs, design shops, and the artist-designer-craftsman's own studio—varying greatly depending on the region and the individual, but all suggesting that that interior decoration, gift-giving, commissions, and increasingly, collecting lay at the core of craft's profitability.[2]

If the "craftsman's market," as one marketing expert put it, "consists of people with extra money to spend," the actual profit base of most craftspeople was far more complicated, as few could support themselves through sales alone.[3] Many enhanced their bottom lines by plying their trade in the related fields of design, industry, fine art, and academia. In order to understand the ways in which individuals navigated the rapidly expanding marketplace in the early decades of the studio craft movement, six makers, one collector, and a former museum director shared their stories for this publication (their names appear in **BOLDFACE** in this essay).[4] Excerpts from the transcribed narratives follow this essay, which provides contextualization of these extraordinary, personal accounts.

Most craft artists of this period received their training in academic settings and learned on their own how to market themselves through developing networks, participating in craft fairs and museum exhibitions, and courting the media. Traditional routes into professional craft practice, through family or apprenticeship, all but disappeared in the post–World War II era as many of these trades had become obsolete.[5] When they did occur, as with Vladimir Kagan and Evert Sodergren, both sons of furniture makers, they were usually governed by personal choice.[6] Success at making a living during this era depended more often on being part of a network that included educational institutions and organizations. University programs did little to prepare those working in craft media for careers outside of teaching, but they did provide contacts that often opened doors, as **JACK LENOR LARSEN** found when he moved to New York City after graduating from Cranbrook Academy of Art in 1951. Art Smith, an African American jeweler trained at the Cooper Union, tapped into the bohemian scene of Greenwich Village, where he actively supported early black modern dance groups as well as black and gay civil rights.[7] This sense of community helped Smith deflect discrimination when he first opened a shop on Cornelia Street in 1946, and it provided a base of support when he moved to nearby West Fourth Street where his business thrived for more than three decades.[8] Fashion photography and "pictorial coverage in both *Vogue* and *Harper's Bazaar*" in the early 1950s helped launch Smith's jewelry beyond the Village (**FIG. 6.1**).[9]

For the majority of craftspeople, local and regional organizations served their economic needs by generating public awareness while fostering retail opportunities. Established organizations, such as the Southern Highland

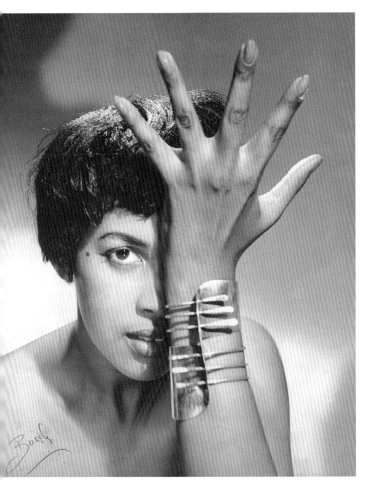

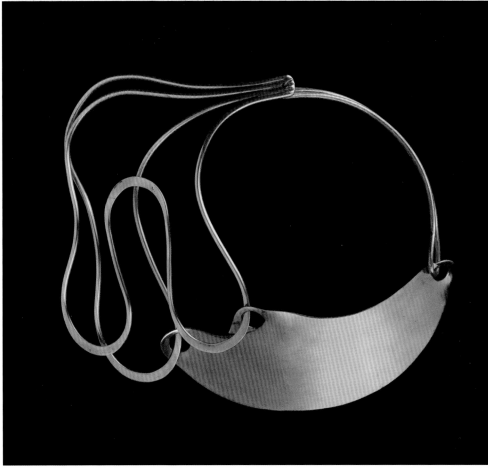

Handicraft Guild, chartered in 1930 in Asheville, North Carolina, and the League of New Hampshire Craftsmen, founded in 1932, operated successful year-round shops, respectively, on the Blue Ridge Parkway and at various locations in the Granite State. A novel if looser approach can be found in the Arizona Designer-Craftsmen, which was established in 1959 by Lloyd Kiva New and provided studio space to enterprising craftspeople in the Scottsdale area, attracting both resort visitors and architects inclined to commission work.[10]

Most visibly, craft fairs organized by such organizations served the greatest number of makers. Fairs could "publicize the work of American Craftsmen and [provide] them with growing outlets for their wares [as well as raising] the standard of all craft work through congregation and competition."[11] They gave makers not only a chance to sell their work but also to meet buyers face-to-face and develop a clientele. Many grew into multimedia events in every sense, such as the York State Craft Fair held every summer in Ithaca, New York, and the Sidewalk Art Shows that gained momentum in the early 1950s in Berkeley, California.[12] The first northeast craft fair, part of the Crafts and Craftsmen Confrontation organized by

a regional arm of the ACC and held in Stowe, Vermont, in August 1966 took on the atmosphere of a medieval fair with its peer-juried Court of Honor and roasted ox on a spit (FIGS. 6.2, 6.3). Seventy-seven exhibiting artists sold upward of $17,000 gross retail over the long weekend; by 1969 when the fair was held in Bennington, Vermont, those figures had grown to almost three times as many vendors and more than six times the gross sales.[13] In addition to the general public, these early annual fairs attracted scores of buyers and shopkeepers from throughout the region and as far away as Florida and Michigan. In 1968 ninety-six buyers came to Mt. Snow, Vermont, site of the second and third craft fairs.[14] These promising if modest beginnings morphed into American Craft Enterprises, which operates the American Craft Council's fairs today.

On a national level, Aileen Osborn Webb, founder of the American Craft Council (ACC), sought to connect such pockets of enterprise with marketing initiatives from the beginning.[15] Webb got her first taste of marketing craft in the 1930s via Putnam County Products, which she founded, an experience that ultimately led to the realization that stimulating rural economies through the revival of handcraft required a dedicated retail outlet in a major metropolitan center. When Webb opened America House in midtown Manhattan in 1940 with executive director Frances Wright Caroë, daughter of the most famous architect in America, the "two crafty women" not only championed the best craft available to consumers but also seized the opportunity to demonstrate to craftspeople how the market might work for them.[16] *Craft Horizons*, the national magazine that Webb started in 1941 "as a mimeographed newsletter for those who sold work at America House," provided a convenient soapbox.[17] By the late 1940s, articles such as "What Makes a Successful Craftsman?," "Where Does Your Money Go?," "This Is What Decorators Want," and "The Visual Aspects of Selling" appeared regularly in an effort to professionalize the craft force. Caroë's prescriptive "Prevailing Winds" columns attempted to demystify retail, wholesale, and styling, "solely for the practicing craftsmen whose incomes are in whole or part derived from their hand work."[18] For both makers and the buying public, the magazine rewarded good design and workmanship in regular roundups of modern handmade objects available at America House and seen at such stylish shops as Georg Jensen and Bonniers, both of which specialized in Scandinavian craft and design (and

influenced a generation of artist-designer-craftsmen), and department stores such as Nieman-Marcus, which regularly carried both domestic and imported craft and design (**FIG. 6.4**).[19]

By 1960 America House had moved into a chic new home at 44 West 53rd Street, designed by David Campbell, president of the ACC. The new space boasted a total of 2,100 square feet divided between three levels with a teak staircase leading to a mezzanine with display "islands" to merchandise specific areas such as liturgical craft and fashion, and larger home furnishings on the floor above (**FIG. 6.5**).[20] Endeavoring to "sell quality work for the craftsmen of the U.S.A. at a price that will pay expenses," the management of America House launched a multipronged strategy that included selling craft work at a 50-percent markup and phasing out consignments.[21] It also offered trade discounts, special orders, referral fees, distribution to other stores, a mail-order catalogue service, and architectural and interior design services. Promotion received particular emphasis via advertising, editorial placement, store displays, demonstrations, and a specially designed product tag with information about the artist. A "collector's room" showcased higher end one-of-a-kind work.

FIG. 6.2

Poster designed by Erik Erikson for *Crafts and Craftsmen Confrontation Craft Fair*, 1966.

FIG. 6.3

Toshiko Takaezu and Robert Turner at the *Crafts and Craftsmen Confrontation Craft Fair*, Stowe, Vermont, 1966.

FIG. 6.4

The Peter Voulkos exhibition at Bonniers, New York, 1957.

The ACC's first conference, held in Asilomar, California, in 1957, took on the business of craft in a forum of makers for the first time, with two days devoted to the "socio-economic outlook" and "professional practices." Most of the assembled craftspeople recognized that the success of their medium was due to the fulfillment of a basic human need for personal expression—theirs and the buying public's—and voiced concerns over their future in an increasingly technological society. While the session on business practices focused on individual experiences, including those of glass designer Michael Higgins (who astutely called for a market for craftspeople as well as craft product), silversmith Allan Adler, and ceramics designers Harold and Trudi Sitterle, the other daylong session surveyed a range of makers who spoke out on broader socio-economic issues.[22] Enamelists groused about the poor design quality of cheap enamels in the marketplace and the need for freer experimentation with scale and new forms.[23] Arthur Pulos, a designer for industry, called for intense devotion to craft, in order to reach the status it held in Scandinavia, while others cautioned against aping Europe for fear it would dispel individual character. Sam Maloof, already a successful furniture maker, and designer Charles Eames parsed the distinction between production and mass production in relation to furniture. Daniel Rhodes urged fellow potters to adapt to "modern realities" by developing a more expressive, spiritual ceramic tradition and ceding to industry "the task of furnishing inexpensive wares for daily use."[24] Weavers felt this most acutely, "in a world of no-iron, wipe-clean, drip-dry fabrics" where even "the 'handwoven look' can be bought for $2.98 a yard."[25] Potter Marguerite Wildenhain exposed a widening rift between university teachers who collected salaries and received studio space and independent makers like herself who competed outside of the system.[26]

While many makers relied on teaching for all or part of their income, dividing makers into two distinct camps does not credit the flexible, pluralistic approaches artist-designer-craftsmen took to fashioning their careers. Particularly during the early part of this period, when

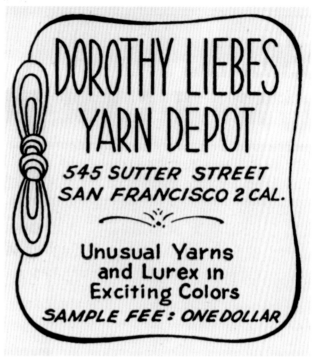

divisions between art, craft, and design had not quite solidified, makers showed a general willingness to explore any lucrative route that did not infringe upon their values. Peter Voulkos, before making pierced and punched ceramic sculpture, expertly turned out functional ware and even sold lamps at America House.[27] Dorothy Liebes, already a renowned weaver and designer, opened the Yarn Depot in San Francisco in 1949 and sold it four years later to "ten weaver-craftsmen" who ran it on a cooperative basis (**FIG. 6.6**).[28] By 1970 it included a nationwide mail-order business, exhibition space, and a thirty-loom studio/classroom offering an impressive array of intensive courses employing local and visiting textile artists such as Ted Hallman, Glen Kaufman, and Malin Selander.[29] In 1964 and 1965 Susan Peterson, a potter and influential educator, developed and hosted an instructional television

FIG. 6.5
America House, 44 West 53rd Street, c. 1959. Architect: David Campbell.

FIG. 6.6
Advertisement for Dorothy Liebes's Yarn Depot, 1952. From *CH* **12 (January 1952), 48.**

series, *Wheels, Kilns and Clay*, broadcast live from KNXT Los Angeles, then an affiliate of CBS, and transmitted to eleven other western states. As she also taught at the University of Southern California, it remains unclear whether she was paid for her television work, but it most certainly elevated her profile.[30]

Others looked outside the areas for which they would become known. The Berkeley weaver **KAY SEKIMACHI** created a cottage industry in the early 1950s with her sister Kazuko, silk-screening greeting cards that were carried in select shops nationwide.[31] The Baltimore jeweler **BETTY COOKE**, with her husband, William O. Steinmetz, developed a successful business designing commercial interiors, most notably for a national chain of bowling lanes. At the same time, Cooke taught at the Maryland Institute College of Art (MICA) and ran a successful retail shop, which she opened in the late 1940s and still operates today as The Store, Ltd., a name it was given in 1965 when it relocated to an upscale Maryland shopping center.

Many makers found themselves working for industry at one point or another. "By selling his services or some of his designs to industry," as Dorothy Giles optimistically advised in *Designer Craftsmen U.S.A.*, "the contemporary craftsman widens his sphere of influence on contemporary styles, and at the same time greatly increases his earnings from his craft."[32] John Prip, a fourth-generation metalsmith, would fit Giles's profile. In 1957 he was hired as artist-in-residence to silversmith manufacturer Reed & Barton, where many of his organic designs for silver plate were produced and he maintained a long-term arrangement as a design consultant.[33] **JACK LENOR LARSEN** initially intended to consult for the textiles industry, but instead found himself incorporating his own firm and producing textiles with craft appeal on power looms. **JOEL PHILIP MYERS**, buoyed by degrees from Parsons School of Design in New York, Copenhagen's Kunsthaandvaerkerskolen, and Alfred University, as well as design experience in the office of Donald Deskey and others, moved to Milton, West Virginia, in 1963 to become chief designer for the Blenko Glass Company—though glass was a medium he had yet to learn. While both Larsen and Myers benefited from relationships with industry, they recognized that some level of artistic compromise was generally required in order to meet the commercial needs of America's large industries.

Like Larsen, Edith Heath formed her own company, Heath Ceramics, and turned to semi-mass-production methods to meet consumer demand. What began in 1944 as a wheel-throwing operation for Gump's (when the war in the Pacific curtailed Asian imports) expanded into a small factory in nearby Sausalito, initially financed by a legal partnership.[34] For Heath, the potter's wheel remained her "sketch pad," but some viewed her tableware as lying outside the craft movement.[35] Small-scale production also thrived at Bennington Potters in Vermont, established in 1948 as Cooperative Design, and at Glidden Pottery (1940–57), in Alfred, New York—both of which were started by New York State College of Ceramics alumni, David Gil at Bennington and Glidden Parker at the pottery bearing his name (**FIG. 6.7**).[36] MoMA's Good Design shows, which from 1944 to 1956 sought to shape consumer taste, exhibited stoneware from all three potteries, thereby contributing to their wider appeal (and making them attractive to collectors today). Such well-designed, durable, and reasonably priced home goods found ready markets, particularly in the design shops that sprang up in university towns and select urban centers, such as Fraser's in Berkeley, Shop One in Rochester, Chiku-Rin (later known as Hanamura's) in Detroit and Birmingham (Michigan), the Signature Shop in Atlanta, and Design Research in Cambridge (**FIG. 6.8**).[37]

Despite these achievements, in the 1960s many designer-craftsmen seemed to lament the state of craft's role in American industry. The Scandinavian model—based on a closer alliance between artist-designer-craftsmen and the craft-based industries, embodied by Prip and also

Den Permanente, the ongoing art-craft-design showcase in Copenhagen established by the Danish Society of Arts and Crafts and Industrial Design and described by Asger Fischer at Asilomar—for the most part had not materialized.[38] In 1964 a special issue of *Craft Horizons* appeared with **JOEL PHILIP MYERS**'s richly hued glass designed for Blenko on the cover.[39] Based on the exhibition *Designed for Production: The Craftsman's Approach*, at the Museum of Contemporary Crafts (MCC), the magazine's contents exposed some of these limitations as well as the successes of the craftsperson working in industry.

For the increasing numbers intent on working as artists in this period, industry held no appeal. For them, two things were required to achieve financial independence: exposure and, more often than not, a patron. Exposure came increasingly through media coverage, local newspapers, and magazines with national circulation. Rose Slivka, promoted to editor of *Craft Horizons* in 1959, championed craft as art and featured the work of many who were exploiting the sculptural possibilities of their media. She increasingly ran profiles of individuals such as Lenore Tawney, whose textiles dissolved the distinctions. In this way, the magazine became an invaluable resource not only for craftspeople but also for collectors.

Museums—particularly MCC but also other venues such as the Pasadena Art Museum, home base of the California Design exhibitions from 1955 to 1976—provided visibility and also validation.[40] The Young Americans exhibitions, held first at America House in 1951 and then

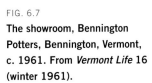

FIG. 6.7

The showroom, Bennington Potters, Bennington, Vermont, c. 1961. From *Vermont Life* 16 (winter 1961).

at MCC, gave early exposure to many craft artists. Other MCC shows, both thematic and solo under the direction of **PAUL J. SMITH** from 1963, improved craft artists' chances of finding a gallery, individual sales, commissions, or even jobs in teaching or industry. Although the museum could not effectively be a patron itself, it could and did acknowledge patronage as with the exhibition *The Patron Church*, which demonstrated fruitful collaborations between architects and makers, such as abstract painter Adolph Gottlieb, who designed Torah curtains and stained glass.[41] The museum could also connect artists and makers to industry, institutions, and individuals. Lancaster attorney Bob Pfannebecker acknowledges "the Museum [MCC] and Paul's shows as absolutely essential," with *Craftsmen '66* proving "instrumental" to his development as a collector.[42] Few artists could claim a patron in the traditional sense as could Jun Kaneko, who upon arrival in this country in 1963 found himself deposited at the Los Angeles home of Fred and Mary Marer.[43] Their early support and awe-inspiring collection of American studio pottery eased the Japanese immigrant's acculturation and altered his artistic direction forever.[44] For **FORREST MERRILL**, another early collector, personal friendships with makers strengthened his emotional response to their work.

In the early years, craft collectors, like galleries, were few, leaving the role of patron to be filled by academia, as **PAUL SMITH** has suggested.[45] Abundant teaching positions provided the surest route to unfettered creative

FIG. 6.8
Ronald Pearson and Jack Prip, two of the founders of Shop One in Rochester, c. 1950s.

FIG. 6.9
Quay Gallery, Tiburon, California, 1961.

expression. Artists such as Robert Arneson, who taught in the sanctuary of the University of California, Davis, could create challenging works without worrying whether they would sell.[46] Time in the classroom, however, meant less time in the studio, restricting output as **WILLIS "BING" DAVIS** recalled.[47] Nonetheless, this situation frequently suited the freewheeling and often politically motivated work produced at the end of this era.

By the late 1960s, established gallery owners such as Marian Willard, who had been operating in Manhattan since 1936, and newcomers like Lee Nordness, who opened his eponymous New York gallery in 1958 (and showed sculptural furniture by **WENDELL CASTLE** among others), and Ruth Braunstein, who opened Quay Gallery in the Bay Area in 1961, embraced the sculptural potential and increasingly edgier content of the new craft culture **(FIG. 6.9)**.[48] By 1969, however, although more galleries exhibited craft (continuing a trend begun in the 1920s when, for example, the erstwhile Montross Gallery in Manhattan first displayed pottery by Henry Varnum Poor), they still represented only a fraction of the retail opportunities available to artists in today's market.[49] Acknowledging the booming national marketplace, in 1967 the ACC began publishing an annual guide to the hundreds of shops, galleries, and studio-workshops selling craft nationwide, and the council redoubled efforts to turn free-spirited craftspeople into pragmatic businessmen.[50] Paradoxically, in December 1970, in the midst of the gift-giving season, Webb announced that America House would close.[51] Her ambition of creating a craft market had been reached, with the ACC remaining the "driving force in building the national market" to the benefit of many makers nationwide.[52] While there was no clear-cut route to earning a living, apart from perhaps teaching, there was a market for studio craft, which reveals a complexity apace with both the varied works produced and the richly layered lives of the makers during this twenty-five-year period of explosive growth and change.

I wish to thank, in addition to those whose names appear in the general acknowledgments, Wendell Castle and Tricia Tining, Betty Cooke, Veronica Conkling, Willis "Bing" Davis, Ellen Denker, Nurit Einik, Jeannine Falino, Robert Hanamura, Barry Harwood, Liza Kirwin, Jack Lenor Larsen, David McFadden, Spice Maybee, Mark Masyga, Forrest Merrill, Joel Philip Myers, Bob Pfannebecker, Jennifer Scanlan, Kay Sekimachi, Paul Smith, and Catherine Whalen. —CMH

1 Rose Krevit citing Norbert Nelson in "ACC Forum: By and for Members of the American Craftsmen's Council, Enameling: 'Communication of our best right ideas,'" *CH* 21 (January/February 1961), 50–51. Norbert's phrase "exploding craft market" is cited by Krevit and has been adapted for the title of this article.

2 Gloria Hickey, "Craft Within a Consuming Society," in *The Culture of Craft: Status and Future*, ed. Peter Dormer (Manchester and New York: Manchester University Press, 1997), 83–100; April Laskey Aerni, "The Economics of the Crafts Industry," PhD diss., University of Cincinnati, 1987; *Economic Study of Handicrafts in U.S.*, 1940, ACC Archives.

3 Norbert Nelson, "A Look into the Growing Crafts Market," *CH* 10 (March–April 1960), 25–27.

4 Their comments derive from oral history interviews by the author: Wendell Castle (April 14, 2009), Betty Cooke (April 10, 2009), Willis "Bing" Davis (April 18, 2009), Jack Lenor Larsen (April 28, 2009), Forrest Merrill (May 4, 2009), Joel Philip Myers (April 10, 2009), Kay Sekimachi (April 10, 2009), and Paul Smith (May 1, 2009), with some follow-up in 2010. Some of these individuals also appear in the Oral History Interviews with Craft Artists, an ongoing project of the Smithsonian Institution's Archives of American Art, many of which were made possible by a generous gift in 2000 from Nannette L. Laitman, former president of the board of trustees at the Museum of Arts and Design. They form part of the AAA's Nanette L. Laitman Documentation Project for Craft and Decorative Arts in America. These interviews proved instrumental in preparing the author's own inquiry, as did the essays and narratives compiled in Vicki Halper and Diane Douglas, eds., *Choosing Craft: The Artist's Viewpoint* (Chapel Hill: University of North Carolina Press, 2009).

5 Halper and Douglas, *Choosing Craft*, 28.

6 Edward S. Cooke, Jr., Gerald W. R. Ward, and Kelly H. L'Ecuyer, *The Maker's Hand: American Studio Furniture, 1940–1990* (Boston: MFA Publications, 2003), 126, 138.

7 See Barry R. Harwood, *From the Village to Vogue: Modernist Jewelry of Art Smith* (Brooklyn: Brooklyn Museum, 2009). A collection of Art Smith's silver and gold jewelry, other objects, and papers is at the Brooklyn Museum.

8 Art Smith, "Jewelry Making Is my Craft," *Opportunity: Journal of Negro Life* (winter 1948), 14; Art Smith Papers [SC03]: Magazines, Brooklyn Museum Archives.

9 Harwood, *From the Village to Vogue*, 6.

10 "The Environment for Sales: Scottsdale, Arizona, Where Craftsmen are their own Retailers," *CH* 17 (July/August 1957), 14–16.

11 "The Craftsman Markets His Wares," *CH* 10 (August 1950), 44–45.

12 The York State Craft Fair was sponsored by the New York State Craftsmen and along with areas devoted to the selling of various craft media, held special exhibits, lectures, and demonstrations. See "Fifth Annual York State Craft Fair Will Be Held Aug. 21–23 at Ithaca College," *Schenectady Gazette*, August 15, 1958, 24. Likewise, the Sidewalk Art Shows in Berkeley included "music, dancers, art demonstrations, strolling players and outdoor cafes" along with a variety of visual displays. See "Local Participant Enters Berkeley Sidewalk Show," *Modesto Bee*, June 28, 1957, 5.

13 N. E. Craft Fairs Data gathered by L. Moran, November 1977, ACC Archives.

14 "List of Buyers Attending Mt. Snow Fair, 1968," ACC Archives.

15 See Resource List in this volume for a biography of Webb and the history of American Craft Council.

16 Aileen O. Webb, oral history interview by Paul Cummings, May 7–June 9, 1970, AAA, SI, quoted in Spice Maybee, "Forming the Studio Craft Movement: *Craft Horizons*, 1941–1959," MA thesis, Bard Graduate Center for Studies in the Decorative Arts, Design History, and Culture, 2009, 67.

17 Aileen Osborn Webb, quoted in *CH* 26, 25th anniversary issue (June 1966), 3.

18 Frances Wright Caroë, "Prevailing Winds," *CH* 8 (November 1947), 28–30.

19 "Craft Countercues" later "Countercues" appeared in *Craft Horizons* in the 1950s and 1960s.

20 Charles Burwell, "The New America House and Its Policies, Part One," *CH* 20 (September/October 1960), 50–51.

21 Ibid.; Burwell, "The New America House and Its Policies, Part Two" *CH* 20 (November/December 1960), 56–57. Selling on consignment was barred altogether in "The Code of *Business Ethics* and Practices" established by the *Midwest Designer Craftsmen*, under the chairmanship of Harvey Littleton. Copies were distributed at the ACC conference at Asilomar in 1957.

22 See "Professional Practices" presentations and discussion recorded in ACC, *Asilomar: First Annual Conference of American Craftsmen*, proceedings (New York: American Craftsmen's Council, 1957), 111–61; "Socio-Economic Outlook" presentations and discussions, ibid., 7–42.

23 Ibid., 23–28.

24 Ibid., 11–12.

25 Ibid., 35.

26 Ibid., 17–18.

27 Paul Smith, interviewed by the author, May 1, 2009.

28 "The Yarn Depot," *CH* 3 (May/June 1970), 30. The Yarn Depot, formerly Dorothy Liebes's Yarn Depot, started as a means of importing the yarns Liebes needed for her studio, according to Alexa Winton Griffith, author of the forthcoming biography of the designer. Liebes owned the shop even after relocating to New York, where she had settled by 1949.

29 Ibid.

30 Jennifer Sorkin, "Susan Peterson: The 'Julia Child of Ceramics,' 1964–1972," a talk derived from Sorkin, "Live Form: Gender and the Performance of Craft, 1940–1970," PhD diss., Yale University, 2010. Sorkin's talk was delivered at the Museum of Arts and Design on April 7, 2010, as part of "Then, Now, and Next: Studio Pottery in the Early 21st Century," a panel discussion sponsored by Greenwich House Pottery, New York.

31 "Sather-Made Handprints Known throughout Nation," *Berkeley Daily Press*, clipping c. 1955, courtesy of Kay Sekimachi.

32 Dorothy Giles, "The Craftsman in America" in *Designer-Craftsmen: U.S.A.*, exh. cat. (Brooklyn: Brooklyn Museum and the American Craftsmen's Educational Council, 1953), 19.

33 It appears to be a common misperception that Prip's designs remain in production. However, a representative of Reed & Barton confirmed via e-mail (June 4, 2010) that they are not. Prip also enjoyed a distinguished career as an educator (School for American

Craftsmen, Alfred and Rochester, New York; the School of the Museum of Fine Arts, Boston; Rhode Island School of Design, Providence) and was a co-owner of Shop One. See Jeannine Falino, "Restless Dane: The Evolving Metalwork of John Prip," *Metalsmith* 30 (2010), 44–51.

34 Edith Heath, "A Small Business in Ceramics," in ACC, *Asilomar*, 124–27.

35 For example, Frances Caroë dropped Heath Ceramics from America House. See Edith Heath, *Tableware and Tile for the World, 1944–1994*. Oral history conducted by Rosalie Ross, 1990–1992, 1994. Edited by Julie Gordon Shearer and Germaine La Berge. California Craft Artists Oral History Series, University of California, Berkeley, CA, 138–39.

36 Caroline Hannah, "Tradition, Innovation, and Good Design: The Ceramics of David Gil," *The Magazine Antiques* (April 9, 2009) www.themagazine antiques.com. For Glidden see Margaret Carney et al., *Glidden Pottery* (Alfred, NY: Schein-Joseph International Museum of Ceramic Art, 2001).

37 For discussion of Fraser's, see Heath *Tableware and Tile*, 140. Prip, Ronald Pearson, and Tage Frid opened Shop One in Rochester in 1953 "as an outlet for high-level work" for craftspeople affiliated with the School for American Craftsmen. Barbara Lovenheim, *Breaking Ground: A Century of Craft in Western New York* (Rochester: Institute of Technology, 2010), 35–36. Bob Hanamura's store Chiku-Rin ("bamboo forest"), opened in Detroit in 1951 and moved to nearby Birmingham two years later. It served as a showroom for Knoll and Herman-Miller with work by Eero Saarinen, Ray and

Charles Eames, as well as other Cranbrook affiliates such as Jack Lenor Larsen and Toshiko Takaezu. Robert Hanamura, interviewed by the author, April 15, 2010. I thank Paul Smith for alerting me to the Signature Shop in Atlanta, which was founded in 1962 by Blanche Reeves as an interior design business dealing in Scandinavian and other design accessories; Carr McCuiston (present owner), e-mail communications with the author, June 28 and 29, 2010. Many of these stores supplied modern architects with stylish goods and some were started by architects, as was the case with Design Research, to serve this need. Both Design Research and the Pottery Barn sent buyers to some of the early Northeast Craft fairs. See Jane Thompson and Amanda Lange, *Design Research:The Store That Brought Modern Living to American Homes* (San Francisco: Chronicle Books, 2010).

38 ACC, *Asilomar*, 111–18; Kane Roberts, "Danish Mart: Scandinavian Shopping Centers are Modernized," *New York Times* (May 15, 1955), X41.

39 See *CH* (March 1964).

40 See Glenn Adamson, introduction to Eudorah Moore, "The Craftsman Lifestyle: The Gentle Revolution," in *The Craft Reader*, ed. Adamson (Oxford and New York: Berg, 2010), 214.

41 "The Jewish Museum—Modern Art, Sacred Space: Motherwell, Ferber and Gottlieb, Adolph Gottlieb: Torah Ark Curtain," n.d., www.thejewishmuseum .org/millburngottlieb; Samuel D. Gruber, "Paned Expressions," *Tablet Magazine: A New Read on Jewish Life*, October 14, 2009, www.tabletmag.com/ arts-and-culture/18271/ paned-expressions/.

42 Robert L. Pfannebecker, interviewed by the author, April 14, 2010.

43 Jun Kaneko, oral history interview by Mary Drach McInnis, May 23–24, 2005, AAA, SI.

44 Martha Drexler Lynn, "Contemporary Ceramics in Marer Collection, 1960–1990," in Mary Davis MacNaughton et al., *Revolution in Clay: The Marer Collection of Contemporary Ceramics* (Claremont, CA: Ruth Chandler Williamson Gallery, Scripps College, in association with University of Washington Press, 1994), 110.

45 Paul Smith, interview.

46 See Hilarie Faberman, *Fired at Davis: Figurative Ceramic Sculpture by Robert Arneson, Visiting Professors, and Students at the University of California at Davis, the Paula and Ross Turk Collection* (Stanford, CA: Iris & B. Gerald Cantor Center for Visual Arts at Stanford University, 2005).

47 Willis "Bing" Davis, interviewed by the author, April 18, 2009.

48 The Willard Gallery, as it was called from c. 1945, showed Lenore Tawney's hanging fiber sculpture in 1967 and represented the jewelry of Alexander Calder in the early 1940s. Lee Nordness purchased Wendell Castle's "chest of drawers with many legs" from MCC's *Fantasy Furniture* exhibition. Nordness sought to commission furniture from Castle before representing him in the Nordness Gallery. Lee Nordness to Wendell Castle, Rochester, NY, November 4, 1966, Wendell Castle papers, 1965–1975, AAA, SI.

49 As addressed by the author in a talk, "Making Clay Modern: The Decorated Pottery of Henry Varnum Poor" at the Greenwich House Pottery, New York,

November 12, 2009, and in her "Henry Varnum Poor: Crow House, Craft, and Design," PhD diss., Bard College, forthcoming.

50 This is evidenced through the publication of *Taxes and the Craftsmen Prepared Expressly for Members of the American Craftsmen's Council by Sydney Prerau* (1964) and *Craftsmen in Business: A Guide to Financial Management and Matters* (1975) and, most visibly today, through the establishment of American Craft Enterprises, the marketing subsidiary of the ACC that runs its major craft fairs.

51 Aileen Osborn Webb open letter to craftspeople, December 17, 1970, ACC Archives.

52 Ellen Paul Denker, "Aileen Osborn Webb and the Infrastructure of Contemporary Craft," typescript (2008), 1; I am grateful to the author for sharing an early version of this article, which is in preparation for publication in the *Journal of Modern Craft*.

91

STAN DANN

Fantasia, 1964

CALIFORNIA WALNUT AND PAINT

21¾ X 20¼ X 1¾ IN. (55.2 X 51.4 X 4.4 CM)

FORREST L. MERRILL COLLECTION

92

TOSHIKO TAKAEZU

Platter, 1964

STONEWARE

1¾ X 16½ X 16¼ IN. (4.4 X 41.9 X 41.3 CM)

MUSEUM OF ARTS AND DESIGN, GIFT OF THE ARTIST,

THROUGH THE AMERICAN CRAFT COUNCIL, 1964

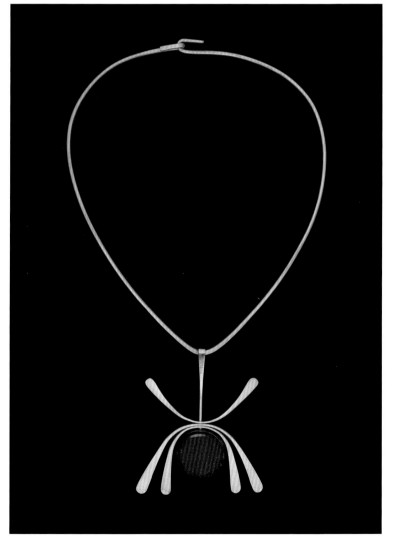

93

ELSA FREUND

Neckpiece, 1961

STERLING SILVER, EARTHENWARE,

AND FUSED GLASS

8½ X 5 X¾ IN. (21.6 X 12.7 X 1.9 CM)

MUSEUM OF ARTS AND DESIGN,

GIFT OF JANE HERSHEY, 1991

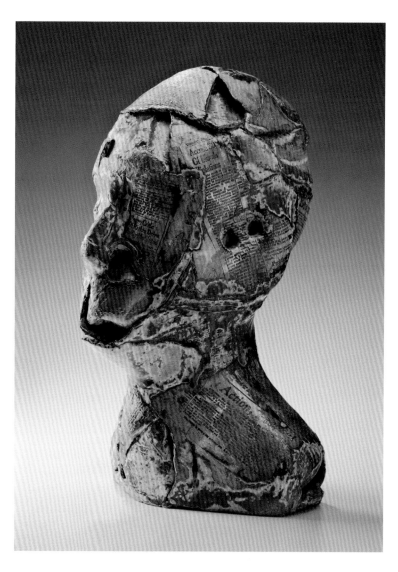

95

JOHN STEPHENSON

The Man, 1965

STONEWARE

19¼ X 12⅜ X 12⅜ IN. (48.9 X 31.4 X 31.4 CM)

FORREST L. MERRILL COLLECTION

94

CARL JENNINGS

Lamp, c. 1964

METAL, PARCHMENT, AND ELECTRICAL COMPONENTS

28½ X 14⅜ X 9 IN. (72.4 X 36.5 X 22.9 CM)

FORREST L. MERRILL COLLECTION

to Rochester [School for American Craftsmen at the Rochester Institute of Technology] that my bargain with myself was that as soon as I can make as much money on my work as I'm making teaching, I'm leaving teaching. And that happened in like sixty-four when I got a huge commission to do a whole bunch of stuff. So one commission was enough, more than my salary.

And so, well, then I thought maybe I won't quit teaching. Maybe I'll just hire somebody now so there will be somebody in the studio when I'm not there. So I hired my first assistant then, full-time. There were some part-time people a little bit before that. And so I taught there until 1969. And then I took a job offer to teach sculpture at the State University of New York that paid more, and I only had to teach two days a week instead of three. I taught there for about ten years and then quit teaching.

The Memorial Art Gallery in Rochester had a juried art show, which was open to everything, really. At that time, the top prizewinner gets a one-man show in the gallery, and they buy a piece. And I won that in sixty-four. Then in sixty-five I had the show, which worked out very well. That's how they ended up with one of the pieces they have. Then I was in some other juried things. Not too much. I started to get invited to things. By the late sixties I was getting invited. By sixty-eight I had a New York City gallery. Lee Nordness started representing me around then—maybe a little earlier? I think it was earlier, actually, because he started the gallery where he began to show craft work in sixty-eight or sixty-nine.

I didn't really expect to sell much. And I really felt that it would be bad to sell very much because then I wouldn't have anything to exhibit. And then I took a strategy, I don't know why I did, but I've kept it to this day. That I'd enter something in a show, and some things are for sale, and if it didn't sell before I entered it into the next show, I'd raise the price. So I had some pieces that never sold. Well, not for a long time. That chair that I made in college—that sculptural one—had as a pricetag when it was in a show in Kansas City for three hundred dollars. That was 1960. And about ten years ago, maybe less, no, maybe five years ago, a dealer—not my dealer but another dealer—was visiting me and he wanted to see things. And back in a corner was this piece. I never sold it. And he said, "What is that?" And I told him. And he said, "Well, I know somebody who might like to buy that." And he said, "How much do you want for it?" And I thought, "Gee, I don't know," catching me

WENDELL CASTLE

One of the first pieces I made was a music stand, which is in the collection—or one of them; there're twelve—of this museum, and Jack Lenor Larsen liked it a lot and borrowed one **(FIG 6.10; CAT. 185).** He was curating or organizing the *Triennale* in Italy in sixty-four. And he put one in. And it got a huge amount of press. So all of a sudden I got a huge amount of press.

I sold the music stands—a few of those. First for a hundred and fifty dollars, and then I realized that I was losing money and raised the price to three hundred dollars. I sold a few. But I said to myself when I went

FIG. 6.10
Wendell Castle at work, *Life* **61 (July 29, 1966), 35.**

without thinking much about it. So I just blurted out, "A hundred thousand dollars." And he said, "Well, I think he'll be interested," and he calls this guy. He was down in Florida. And he says the guy will fly up next week in his private plane. So we set a date. Well, that date came and he called and said he can't come, something's come up, but he'll take it anyway. So I knew I'd underpriced it.

BETTY COOKE

I suppose I really didn't think of what I was going to do. I just knew that in some way I had to make a living. It was part of my upbringing: you should have a degree and make your own living. This was in the 1940s while I was at the Maryland Institute and Johns Hopkins University studying art and education . . . I was to become a teacher. And I did for a short time but realized that I didn't want to teach high school. I went on to teach at Maryland Institute for twenty years.

At that time, I was always making jewelry and objects of metal, leather, wood. I participated in every exhib-

ition and competition that came up. Not that there was that much then, but what was there was exciting . . . and it was rewarding be it painting, crafts, design. I never did any fairs. I used to go to them. I went to the first ACC fair up in Rhinebeck, and the Los Angeles County Fair—but not as an exhibitor. I wanted to see all that was happening.

While teaching at this time, in 1946, there was a block of slum houses that were being fixed up by an artist, a museum director and architect, house by house. I was intrigued and ended up buying one of these slum houses. For three thousand dollars. It became my shop-studio-home. It was all of fifteen feet wide and twenty feet deep, with two floors. It remained a slum area for a couple of years. Eventually this place—903 Tyson Street—became a very important example of restoring old houses in Baltimore. It drew a lot of attention. So my clientele started to grow—I suddenly had some wonderful people who understood what I was doing because it was very fresh and simple.

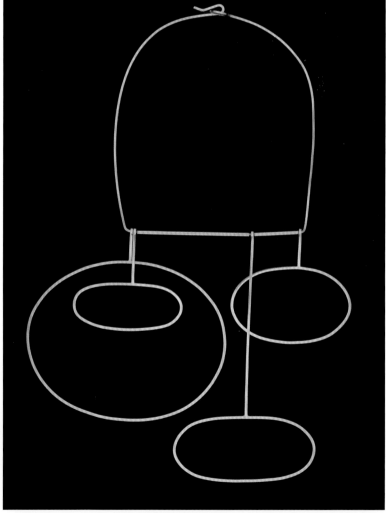

Well, this little shop was pretty interesting. The entire front of the showroom was only ten by fifteen feet with a fireplace and winding, pie-shaped stairs—a very interesting little antique house. The word *showroom* might be deceiving, because I had torn most of the plaster off the walls and there were brick walls, wainscoting, the fireplace, and big wooden panels. It was very simple. It had to be simple, for a small place reflecting my style. But people found it exciting. Exciting as the studio space with benches, motors, soldering, and lots of work in process.

At that time, people would come with their drivers and their very nice cars, chauffeured, and stop at my "Shop" and "Studio" signs. It was that kind of area. We were near an antique district, so it attracted people with a great deal of taste. And, of course, a lot of architects came by. It was also near a medical center and offices. So most of my customers were doctors, architects, lawyers, professional people, and interesting, sophisticated shoppers.

A friend of mine and I—we were like Girl Scouts and we made an interesting trip out west in an old car—we were campers. We had our sleeping bags, gear, jeans, and so forth. I had taken a skirt and blouse because I also carried my jewelry in a fine walnut box along with a list of all the stores in the country that I thought I'd like to see and like to be in. They were mainly design stores. First I stopped by the Walker Art Center in Minneapolis, where they were in process of hanging this exhibition, design under fifty dollars [*Modern Jewelry Under Fifty Dollars: The 2nd Annual Exhibition of Contemporary Jewelry*, Walker Art Center, March 1948], and I go in with my little box of jewelry and a skirt and a blouse, got all dressed up [laughs]! And they took some pieces for the exhibit, which was quite exciting and nice. I went on my way to find good outlets for my jewelry. [According to the WAC's archivist, two works by Cooke indeed were included in the 1948 show, although Cooke's name does not appear in the exhibition's checklist, which had already been printed.]

I was married in 1955 to William O. Steinmetz, a former student and then fellow instructor at MICA. We lived in the little Tyson Street house for a while, but when the house next door came up for rent, we rented it, broke a door through, and set up a design office. We designed commercial interiors, restaurants, showrooms, and exhibits. We just worked from the house–home–shop–studio and now office, too. Our clients grew from our location, exhibitions, and word of mouth.

I remember one day a gentleman called us and said he was fond of the restaurant we had designed. And he'd like to know if we'd be interested in working on some bowling "lanes." Smoky, cruddy spaces with . . . oh, they were a mess. So our first job, which we were to do with little budget, was to revitalize their five old existing bowling alleys. We did it. We painted the gray, drab furniture—all the bowling equipment was gray at the time—and we painted it orange, yellow, and blue. We designed bold wall treatments. That led to designing a new chain of Fairlane's Bowling Lanes. Of course that was a big, big thing. It became a family recreation place, which was just fantastic. We designed babysitting areas and child's play areas, meeting rooms, cafés, and everything safe for families. We brought in new Eames, Knoll, and Herman Miller furniture and made it a new, colorful environment. We worked on fifty of these centers all over the country.

And my jewelry continued on and on, giving pleasure.

We called it a design revolution. There it all was and here we were, in Baltimore. . . . It was an exciting time for a young person to be starting out.

WILLIS "BING" DAVIS

I was the fourth of six children raised by my mother. From the first grade on, she was a single parent—but

FIG. 6.12
**Willis "Bing" Davis,
Dayton, Ohio, 1968.**

CAT. 97
Willis "Bing" Davis, *Ghetto Voice in Orange*, 1967. Stoneware. 10 x 5 x 5 in. (25.4 x 12.7 x 12.7 cm) National Afro-American Museum and Cultural Center.

she still encouraged all of us to follow our dreams and our vision. So she knew I was interested in the arts, and she nourished it as best she could. She didn't view herself a craftsperson or an artist but as a maker of quilts. So I had that exposure growing up and seeing her working on those quilts and piecing them together, even assisting her in pinning on the paper patterns to the cloth. It seemed very natural to me in the small community where I grew up that art was OK. As a teenager and as a young adult, I felt some of that pressure from people saying, "Well, you are not really working unless you are using big muscles and you sweat. It's fun to do art but what are you going to do for real?" But as I look back, I was one of those fortunate ones who just knew that somehow I was going to eke out an existence for myself as an artist.

For me and many of my colleagues, I went into teaching art. Teaching has always been a source of joy and pleasure for me. I became a high school teacher fresh out of college at twenty-one. I knew I also wanted to develop my craft besides just teaching, because you could get hung up in the act of teaching and let go of your own personal artistic growth. What I did was take

a compass and make a five-hundred-mile circle around Dayton, my hometown and where I began my teaching career, and that circle meant that I could go to craft fairs and malls and enter competitions within that five-hundred-mile circle on weekends and still make it back for my eight-o'clock class in the high school on Monday morning. I set that as my goal, and I began to search for opportunities. I said I would enter at least four to five competitions a year and try to have at least one show a year, and to go to free lectures and workshops and read publications and go to the libraries. I just had that personal commitment that somehow I was going to make this work for me.

Richard Peeler was a production potter who was part of the nucleus that started NCECA [National Council on Education for the Ceramic Arts]. He was a highly skilled, highly educated, highly motivating potter who built his rammed-earth home/studio near DePauw University. He and his wife, Marj, were shipping to craft shops and museums around the country while he was teaching. So I had him as a teacher, and he was my advisor and my mentor. I saw how he handled the tasks of packing and shipping and contacting and invoicing. That was part of the education. He took us often to his home/studio so we heard his conversations on art, teaching, and life as young seventeen- or eighteen-year-old college students. He went way beyond the curriculum and the textbook and continually shared his thoughts on what it was really like being a professional craftsman. We stayed close friends until his death in 1998. All he gave us we modeled. We idolized him and just sucked up all he had to offer like a sponge. And he was also bringing in his colleagues like Aaron Bohrod (University of Wisconsin–Madison), Dick Hay (Indiana State University), and Professor Marsch (Indiana University). We didn't realize at the time how important this was, having these visiting scholars and artists coming on to the campus, watching the slide presentations, bringing in the judges, and interacting with the judges when they came in to see various shows. And I was just looking and learning and absorbing all that I could because I wanted to be a part of that life of making a living by creating, as part of my whole life. The main thing that I got from my teacher and his friends was the need to find my own "artistic voice."

JACK LENOR LARSEN

In the summer of 1947 when I traveled from Seattle to Southern California, then a hotbed of modern weaving, I stopped in San Francisco to meet the great weaver Dorothy Liebes. Was her life one I wanted? Although I later enrolled in architecture at the University of Southern California, my spare time was spent at Handcraft House, where I taught design and color while learning more about weaving. [Weaver Dorothea Hulse operated Handcraft House, a Los Angeles workshop for weaving and pottery.]

Finally, I returned to the University of Washington, where I became graduate assistant to Ed Rossbach, who had just come from Cranbrook. There he had converted—from a painter and a potter—to become a weaver. As I learned from him and his example, there I was—about twenty years old—teaching modern design and color to handweavers at the Seattle Art Museum. I also began to receive commissions.

The thing was, modern fabrics didn't exist. There were no showrooms for them as we have today. If someone built a modern house, they needed to find a weaver. So, I

FIG. 6.13

Jack Lenor Larsen. Photograph courtesy of Longhouse Reserve.

got into that with some help from students in Rossbach's classes. My studio was in a professional building near the campus, where painters Mark Tobey and Morris Graves had small studios. That's where I worked and lived. I even wove fabrics for the president of Boeing Aircraft, which in Seattle was about as good as you could get. I was bothered by having as much joy in a sale as in what I thought a breakthrough. That people wanted to pay for what I was doing was new. Was this good?

I needed academic credits, which I could now select as an upperclassman. As I enjoyed academia, the thought came of being a professor . . . and that's why I took my master's at Cranbrook. Marianne Strengell, our master [weaver] there, was a designer for Knoll and Saarinen, with what seemed a glamorous life. Then, on spring break a carful of students was going to New York, so I went along, with portfolio. I had lived in Los Angeles, I knew Chicago and San Francisco, but New York seemed a foreign city: So many people were foreign-born, and it hadn't yet modernized like California. I loved it! And decided here is where I would like to be.

I received job offers to teach at large universities, but that didn't seem at all interesting. So, with no fiscal reason, I came to New York, which was the best option because this was the epicenter of the modern movement. MoMA then was the Design Vatican—internationally. Europe was still asleep, and the press was here. And I was lucky, even achieving commissions.

My Cranbrook connection opened doors: "I'm from Cranbrook." "Then, come in." Then they would send me on to someone else. The school's reputation was magical because of graduates Eames and Saarinen, Bertoia and Knoll. Soon I was asked to do the prestigious lobby fabrics for Lever House, the first corporate tower, and exhibited in all the Good Design shows—with more designs than most. I met the judges and was soon swept up into their wonderful world. I loved it.

I found a four-room top floor on Seventy-third Street near Fifth Avenue. It was a walk-up and needed some fixing up, but what I could afford. As there was a fine design showroom downstairs appealing to the best designers, a number of them walked upstairs to see what was going on.

All through the fifties, we kept our handweaving studio busy with custom work, but it wasn't that gratifying as too often we were supporting a client's ego and not those of the better architects. Finally, our accountant asked, "Do you realize how much we're losing on the hand-weaving studio?" That was a big shock, as I thought that this work at all hours was contributing income. So, we closed the handweaving studio and converted to a design studio, putting more energy into things we would produce in our New Jersey mill or abroad, where we had access to handspun yarns. About that same time, in the mid-fifties, we started silkscreen printing.

There came a day when I knew I should design for the marketplace, but I had no such ability. Not knowing how to follow, I led. What I excelled in was doing something new and then finding a following for it. In advising younger people like Chihuly, that is what I advised: "Do it first! Produce a little magic and people will want it. That's the way to go! Not following the market because . . . well, first of all, it's fickle and not foolproof!"

FORREST L. MERRILL

My first art purchase was in 1950. I was among a group of high school art students visiting a clay and glass show at the Pasadena Art Institute in Southern California. Some things were for sale. I bought a five-piece slumped-glass salad set made by Glen Lukens. The price was forty dollars. I had saved the money from cutting neighbors' lawns the previous summer. Hoover High School in Glendale had great art classes. My design teacher, Gladys Merrick, had studied ceramics with Lukens at the University of Southern California in Los Angeles, so my purchase did not just happen in a vacuum. It reflected what high school art education can encourage. The fact that I discovered mid-twentieth-century aesthetics during the 1950s, and not in the 1980s, has always been important to me.

During graduate work in Sweden at the University of Stockholm, I purchased a number of Scandinavian pots. I returned to Northern California and later visited the Pond Farm workshop of Marguerite Wildenhain in Guerneville. She was a Bauhaus-trained potter, and I found her ideas about teaching a craft very interesting. Many visits later—and after some purchases—she invited me to observe her teaching at her summer workshops. She had an intense way of working with her students and refining their ability "to look and to see." In my own way, I tried to learn.

At first I focused my collecting on clay because that was my interest in high school. I liked vessels, vessels that you can put in the palm of your two hands. That's where I began. My resources were limited. There was a wonderful art community in the San Francisco Bay Area,

FIG. 6.14

Forrest L. Merrill, c. 2011. Photograph by Bill Schwob.

and I focused on collecting the works of artists who were nearby. I've joked with my friends that it helps to be near the kiln so that you can be the first to see the newest work.

For a collector there were a number of great publications available at the time. My favorite was a magazine called *Craft Horizons* [now *American Craft*]. It makes my heart skip a beat when I look at some of those old issues and see page after page of information and illustrations of work by artists who became icons. It's a learning experience to look at similar publications today and try to select the artists who will become icons of the future.

Another way I informed myself was by listening to artists and absorbing their point of view, their reaction to different objects. One really needs an aesthetic mentor as a guide regarding form, texture, color, and economy of material. Reading something in a book is one way to learn; having someone teach you is another. I remember going to a gallery with an architect friend to see a show in San Francisco in the late sixties. I paid attention to what he paused to look at, and his comments about each piece. My response was, "That's interesting. I didn't see that object in quite the same way." Later I noticed that when I visited other places on my own, I was seeing things in part through his eyes. I think such a process as that can be very instructive.

I went to the original art gallery at Gump's in San Francisco. They had marvelous Natzler pots for sale. Gump's is where I got the idea of collecting an artist's work in depth. I also visited Dalzell Hatfield Gallery in Los Angeles, which sold pots of the Natzlers, along with works by Harrison McIntosh, Glen Lukens, and others. I related to the three-dimensional art the gallery sold more than their French impressionist paintings. About that same time, I started collecting the wood bowls of Bob Stocksdale, which were sold at the home furnishing store Fraser's in Berkeley. Bob and his wife, Kay Sekimachi, were nearby neighbors, and we became close friends. Kay is an amazing fiber artist, and I have since collected her work as well. Bob encouraged me to visit enamel artist June Schwarcz, whom he described as "a housewife in Sausalito who works in enamel." Since my first visit to her studio, I have now collected more than a hundred of her enamel vessels.

My artist friends have greatly enriched my life. The work they create is stimulating to live with, and my friendships with them are treasures in themselves. My collection represents my life's work. I take great pleasure in lending pieces to museum shows, thereby giving them a public life.

JOEL PHILIP MYERS

My intention was to become a teacher of ceramics. In 1959 I returned from Denmark, where I'd studied ceramics and where I'd met and married my wife, Birthe Noer, and we both continued our studies at Alfred University College of Ceramics. In 1963, after completing my first graduate year, I was offered the position of design director for Blenko Glass at the recommendation of Ted Randall, head of the art department at Alfred. Our first child was born in 1961, and number two was on the way in 1963. The reality of being a father certainly caused me to feel under some pressure to provide. I was more or less forced to consider a position I had never even imagined.

It's rather ironic that in 1962 I had been invited to participate in Harvey Littleton's first glass workshop at the Toledo Museum of Art, but I couldn't afford to go. However, subsequent articles in *Craft Horizons* showed me the possibilities of a studio-based approach to glass-making. With this germ of an idea lodged in my head, I went rather reluctantly to Milton, West Virginia, to see the Blenko factory. My first reaction, when I saw the factory

floor with the blazing furnaces and the workers milling about and working the glass was, *wow*, what drama!

I realized that since everything was made by hand, I'd be able to learn how to blow glass in the factory. I visualized a potential future as an individual artist-craftsman working in the medium of glass. But I wasn't hired to learn how to blow glass; I was hired solely as a designer of glass, just as my two predecessors, both Alfred graduates, had been.

In 1964 I read in *Craft Horizons* about a forthcoming exhibition titled *Designed for Production: The Craftsman's Approach*. And I thought, who other than me could possibly qualify in the field of glass. So I wrote to Paul Smith, the organizer of the exhibition, and Paul actually traveled to Milton to see what I was up to. I must have impressed him, because he invited me to participate. My designs were chosen for the cover of *Craft Horizons* in 1964, and as a result of this exposure, I was invited to participate in the First World Congress of Craftsmen at Columbia University in the summer of 1964, where, for the first time, I met Harvey and his students and the participating international glass designers.

I have always been aware of how luck and coincidence play a part in life. This "break" gave me immediate visibility and some degree of recognition. I also had the luck to have a group of unique, one-off Blenko designs fill

FIG. 6.15
Joel Philip Myers, Skive, Denmark, 1972.

the entire front window of America House during the conference. I wish I had a photo of that!

In 1965 I developed a line—a special signature line—of heavy, cased, multicolored pieces. These pieces sold very well, but since they required special technical expertise, they took more time to make than pieces in our regular line of inventory. As a result, pieces from this line of heavy, cased pieces were often removed from an order to expedite completion of the order. Since we were very, very busy, Blenko chose to ship an order as soon as possible. This policy finally led to the end of the special line. I was asked by Gump's of San Francisco to design a special decanter for them, which I did and which I was very proud of. They even sent me a photo of a group of them in their window display. The decanter was illustrated in the 1967–77 issue of *Decorative Art in Modern Design*, a British publication.

I believe in 1965 or '66 the Mint Museum in North Carolina had an invitational [Fourth Annual Piedmont Exhibition, 1966]. I entered it and won best of show with

CAT. 98

Joel Philip Myers, designer; Blenko Glass Co., Inc., manufacturer, *Vessel #6710*, 1967. Glass. 9¾ x 5¾ in. (24.8 x 14.6 cm). Museum of Arts and Design, Gift of Karen Birthe Eriksen Noer Myers.

a piece that was the beginning of a series I really felt very good about. . . . They were rather unique glass forms imploded: a series of interior forms within a sphere. Winning at the Mint was a real boost, and it was probably important to glass, since a number of other museums, like the Toledo Museum of Art, the Louisville Museum of Art, et cetera, staged shows in which glass was featured. You have to realize that up to this point people had little exposure to glass made by studio artists, and they were not impressed with what they saw.

After the Mint came the Toledo shows, the Cleveland Nationals, and that's when it began to . . . feel that there was somewhere you could exhibit your work. Having lived in Denmark for almost two years, I knew that almost all glass manufacturers employed designers, and that they almost universally promoted their designers. I thought that perhaps we could do the same thing at Blenko. I told Mr. Blenko that I would be willing to blow pieces for the firm, to create an exhibition of my work to be sold by Blenko at a number of their finer department stores. We tried it at Frost Brothers, San Antonio, and somewhere else I can't remember. I ended up not selling a single piece, but I signed a great number of two-dollar ashtrays. I guess I forgot Blenko wasn't Orrefors.

In twenty-seven years of teaching, I never encouraged any of my students to think about working in the glass industry. [Myers left Blenko to start the glassblowing program at Illinois State University at Normal, where he taught until 1997, when he retired from teaching.] The reason for that is, in order to work for industry, you must realize that as a designer you are always in the position of justifying your designs from the standpoint of marketability. In that role you are put in more of an adversarial position with the sales representative and management. Glass industry today . . . there is no glass industry today. Do you know what the American glass industry is today? The hundreds of small glass studios scattered throughout the U.S.

KAY SEKIMACHI

I started out by apprenticing myself to Dorothy Ahrens at her studio. All I did was make warps and thread looms for a very small amount of money. I could see that this wasn't going to be enough. So at the same time my younger sister, Kazuko, and I—both of us had taken silk-screening and design at CCAC [California College of Arts and Crafts, now the California College of the Arts, Oakland]—well,

we started a little business of silkscreening Christmas cards and that kind of grew into all-occasion cards. And so we managed to make enough money to live on, but we lived on very little at that time. This was early 1950s. And I think we lived on about two thousand dollars a year.

We got our inspiration for the cards from looking at children's books and cards that were already on the market. Actually, our cards were really very well accepted. We started selling just locally, like at a shop here in Berkeley called Fraser's and a few shops in San Francisco—a very nice little shop called Local Color—then we found ourselves expanding across the country. We even had some outlets in Detroit—I remember the Chiku-Rin Gallery—and one in New York. I cannot remember exactly where, but I know that we did have some outlets there. But anyway, that went on for a few years . . . all in the early fifties. [Chiku-Rin was Bob Hanamura's first gallery, started in about 1951 in Detroit but relocated in 1953 to nearby Birmingham to better show work of the craftsmen and designers associated with the Cranbrook Academy of Art in Bloomfield Hills: Jack Lenor Larsen, Toshiko Takaezu, Ray and Charles Eames, and Eero Saarinen, among others.]

We had a little cottage industry going. We had a line of cards, and of course we had to stock so many cards of each design because we didn't know how many orders we would be getting, and they had to be packaged and then sent off. And one day a relative came by and saw us

FIG. 6.16
Kay Sekimachi at the loom, 1950, unidentified photographer. Bob Stocksdale and Kay Sekimachi papers, 1937–2004, AAA, SI.

FIG. 6.17
Kay Sekimachi, "Sekimachi Handprints" packing label, c. 1952.

doing all this work, and he said, "Why don't you hire some high school kids to do the packing for you?"

I think all the local craftsmen participated in the California State Fair, the SF Art Festival, and then, in Richmond, California, at the Arts Center, where every year they had a craft exhibition. It was something that we all wanted to get into. Fortunately, I got into a number of them. I think this is when my interest turned to weaving from the silkscreening. I do remember, though, way way back in 1949, there was a show at the Rotunda Gallery at the City of Paris in San Francisco. I did have some silkscreened textiles in that exhibition, and I think I even got an award.

I know that I showed the monofilament hangings all over the place. They just caught on. A lot of the weavers were doing three-dimensional things, too. I think one of the first museum shows was at the Museum of Modern Art in New York, the one that Jack Larsen and Mildred Constantine organized [*Wall Hangings*, MoMA, 1969]. Shows like that went all over the place, even to New Zealand. Hall's, the department store in Kansas City, had an exhibition gallery, and I was in a show curated by Ruth Kaufman [*Fibre Art*, March 15–April 21, 1973; Hall's was a subsidiary of the Hallmark Corporation, and Kaufman was the owner of the Ruth Kaufman Gallery in New York]. I know my hangings went all over the place, but I don't remember selling many. If I did, like with the cards, I think I sold them much too reasonably . . . by not having any business sense or listening to other people, either!

PAUL J. SMITH

For those pursuing a career in the crafts during the early post–World War II period, there were two main areas. The dominant one was academia, which was rapidly expanding as a result of the GI Bill that offered free tuition to returning soldiers. This had a profound effect in creating a vast growth of educational arts programs throughout the country.

Earning a living as a teacher was an ideal arrangement that provided an annual salary with benefits, often a schedule with free days and sabbaticals that allowed artists to have time to develop their own art. While teaching could be a rewarding experience, it also provided an ideal support environment for creating new work. I characterize this period as schools being the patrons of the "studio craft movement."

The other dominant career path in the 1940s and '50s was maintaining an independent studio at a time when there was a very limited market. I should point out that

FIG. 6.18

Paul J. Smith, at his desk at the Museum of Contemporary Crafts, October 1963.

a few designed for the home furnishings industry, such as Dorothy Liebes, and some . . . did commission works for public buildings and religious centers.

For the independent craftsman it was a challenge to sell and earn a living from the studio and required motivation and innovation to reach potential customers. Wharton Esherick, a pioneer furniture maker who started in the 1920s, developed a friendship with his clientele, resulting in continuing support for commissioned work. This personal approach with clients was central to the success of many of the early studio artists, including potter Karen Karnes, who was part of an art colony in Stony Point, New York.

To create selling opportunities, several annual craft fairs were initiated by organizations like the League of New Hampshire Craftsmen, who also established year-round marketing outlets in the state. The Southern Highland Handicraft Guild also developed an important marketing program. Both of these organizations began in the early 1930s during the Depression. Other local and regional programs and events provided outlets and gave visibility to work—the Cleveland Museum of Art's annual May Show, the Ceramic Nationals at the Everson in Syracuse, and a few specialized high-end gifts shops like Gump's in San Francisco that sold ceramics by the Natzlers, Peter Voulkos, and selected other makers from the area.

Each medium had its specialized marketing venues. As there was always a need for custom jewelry and wedding rings, several metal craftsmen maintained selling outlets or created a market from their home studio. Important were the Greenwich Village jewelers in New York City—including Art Smith, Ed Wiener, and Sam Kramer, who cultivated a successful market by making one-of-a-kind and limited editions of modernist jewelry that was affordable. Irena Brynner had a very small store on West Fifty-fourth Street. There were others around the country, including Nanny Benderson's shop called Nanny's in San Francisco.

One of the early national outlets was America House that opened in 1940 in New York City. America House presented a broad range of work by both established and emerging talent. In August 1966 the American Craftsmen's Council pioneered a new marketing concept when its Northeast Regional Assembly held a conference and craft fair in Stowe, Vermont. About eighty craftsmen exhibited, and the gross weekend event was close to eighteen thousand dollars, a great sum for its time. The success of this first fair resulted in an expanded ACC marketing program that today conducts four fairs per year around the country.

Several schools with a focused craft program spawned early marketing outlets, such as Shop One in Rochester that featured work by faculty and students at RIT's School for American Craftsmen. Cranbrook Academy of Arts in Bloomfield Hills, Michigan, also nurtured outlets in the community. Graduates often remained in the area and opened studios. This was characteristic of other schools that had important craft educational programs.

During the late 1950s and '60s there was a very gradual expansion of marketing venues, including a few galleries that featured work in the craft media. The New York Willard Gallery exhibited the innovative work of Lenore Tawney, and in Los Angeles several of the students and faculty at Otis Art Institute—including Peter Voulkos and John Mason—were featured in group or one-person

shows at galleries on La Cienega Boulevard, a lively art center. But it wasn't until the 1970s that galleries around the country began to focus on artists working in glass, clay, and other specialized media.

Serious collecting was also very limited in the 1950s and '60s. The word *collector* was seldom associated with the few individuals who were acquiring work. Their primary motivation was to buy work they liked and to develop a friendship with the maker. Robert Pfannebecker was one of the early pioneers who bought through an artist and school network, and often on an installment plan. He would go to graduating student shows at Alfred and acquire emerging work, resulting in a unique collection documenting activity in all media from that early period. Another pioneer collector was Fred Marer, who became attracted to ceramic activity at the Otis Art Institute and began to purchase work on his limited faculty salary. John Mason remembered Fred coming to the clay studio frequently to see new work, and Peter Voulkos said one

FIG. 6.19
Paul J. Smith, in the *Plastic as Plastic* installation, 1968.

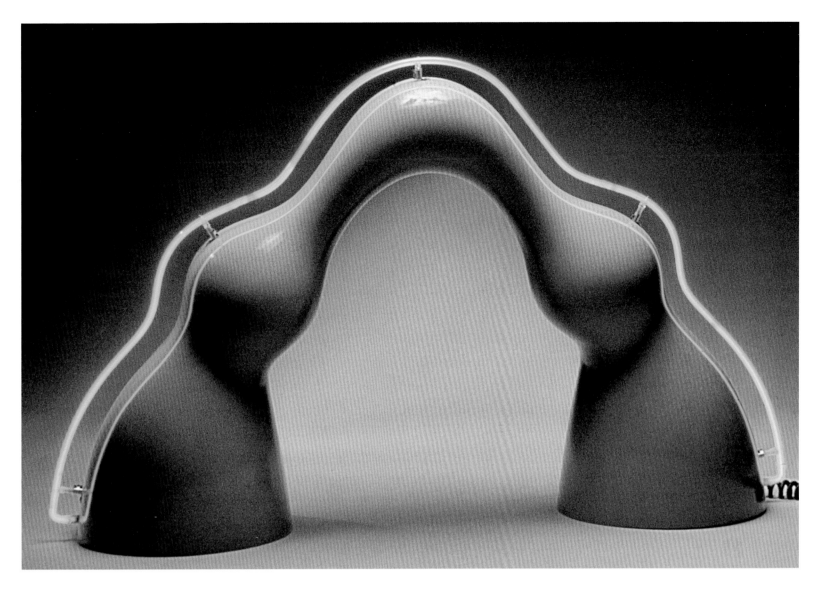

CAT. 99

Wendell Castle, *Benny Lamp*, 1969. Fiberglass and neon. 34¾ x 57¼ x 16½ in. (88.3 x 145.4 x 41.9 cm). Courtesy of the artist.

day, "Here comes Mr. What's New" [Mason, oral history interview by Paul Smith, 2006, AAA, SI]. He was very supportive of artists. When Jun Kaneko arrived from Japan as a student, Fred gave him a place to stay, and I know he helped many others by buying work to support their continuing as a student. Another ceramic collector was Joseph Monson in Seattle, who was acquiring the new ceramic expressions mainly from the West Coast and assembled an important collection. While there were a few others who acquired a lot of work, the collecting focus of today did not exist at the time.

In looking back at the mid-twentieth-century activity, I see it as a time of a vast amount of new and innovative work in every discipline of the arts that broke from tradition. An important influence at the time was the changing cultural environment that took place in America—the "back-to-the-earth" movement, rebellion against the past, and an attitude that anything was possible. Most of the new experimental work took place in academia, where faculty was not dependent on selling. Exploring new concepts and exhibiting work were confirmations of being a good teacher and also good for the résumé. Another factor was the sharing of technical discoveries with students, resulting in a dialogue between faculty and students who inspired each other. This important period gradually led to more public awareness of innovative work, the desire to seriously collect, and a development of a vast national and international marketing network that today can be referred to as the "market as patron."

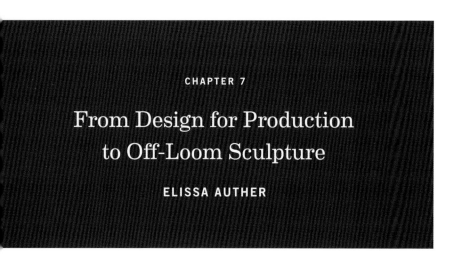

CHAPTER 7

From Design for Production to Off-Loom Sculpture

ELISSA AUTHER

BETWEEN 1945 AND 1969 FIBER ARTS EXPERIENCED dramatic growth and diversification, resulting in a new visibility for a medium long dismissed in the United States and elsewhere as irrelevant to art. The direction of the field examined in this essay—its movement from an amateur pursuit to professional spheres of practice in textile design and the fine arts—was ignited by a range of social, historical, and aesthetic forces in the postwar period. These included the ascendency of modernism in art and architecture, the expansion of university art departments, the counterculture of the 1960s, the revitalization of tapestry weaving in Europe, and the avant-garde's broad experimentation with new media.

The major turning point occurred in the late 1950s and early 1960s with the emergence of a studio practice characterized by individual experimentation and freedom from the commercial textile market. By the time of its flowering in the mid-1960s, this new practice eclipsed the earlier established ideal of the weaver-designer dedicated to collaborating with architects and industry in the production of functional textiles. For the weaver-designer, the handwoven textile was more or less accepted as a utilitarian component of interior design. The emergence of a group of weavers with the desire to explore the potential of fiber as art rather than a product to be subordinated in an architectural scheme created a new context for challenging fiber's presumed place in the design world and its historical marginalization as decoration, women's work, or mere craft.

THE 1940s

Handweaving, a "preparatory step to machine production."[1]
Four handweavers—Anni Albers, Mary Meigs Atwater, Dorothy Liebes, and Marianne Strengell—dominated the textile scene in the 1940s. Their careers, their aesthetic philosophies, and the contexts in which they worked provide an excellent starting point for considering the professional identities available to weavers under modernism, as well as the eventual emergence of nonutilitarian weaving as a legitimate art form.[2]

Albers, Atwater, Liebes, and Strengell never came together as a group or formed a movement, yet each confronted in common the place of handweaving in an industrialized society. For Liebes and Strengell, both of whom embraced a weaver-designer role, handweaving was an essential part of the process of designing for production. For Atwater, preserving handweaving as a craft was paramount, and for Albers, handweaving—while a "preparatory step to machine production"—also had potential as art.

Dorothy Liebes opened her first studio in San Francisco in 1930, and within a decade she had built a reputation for herself as a weaver of unorthodox fabrics featuring brilliant color combinations and textured elements. Her earliest work for industry dates to 1940, and over the course of her career, she held contracts with most of the major textile companies, often experimenting with new synthetic or metallic yarns. To Liebes, the textile was "a dependent expression,"[3] meaning it found its role as a furnishing, necessarily subordinated to a larger interior or architectural scheme.

Other professional weavers shared Liebes's perspective. Marianne Strengell, for example, similarly sought success in the world of design and architecture.[4] Strengell embraced handweaving as a laboratory for industrial production, a relationship between craft and industry promoted by the Bauhaus at Dessau, Germany, in the 1920s and recognized throughout textile centers in Europe. This approach was adopted in the United States from the teaching and example of European émigrés, including Strengell, in the late 1930s and early 1940s. Like Liebes, Strengell conceived of textiles as functional elements of architecture, whether to divide rooms, soften surfaces, or control light, but her work, which eschewed pattern or figuration in favor of subdued color and subtle texture effects, represented a counterpoint to Liebes's electric design sensibility.

industries known as the Southern Highland Handicraft Guild, included the promotion of the region's distinctive tradition of overshot coverlet weaving.[5] Albers viewed this revival as backward because it depended on "traditional formulas, which once proved successful."[6] Her reaction throws into relief the gulf that existed between professional weaver-designers and other handweavers in the 1940s. For the weaver-designer, working with architects and designers carved out a place for weaving—however subordinate—in the modern world of industrial production. For Albers, reviving and preserving historic forms of weaving out-of-step with the modern world of design posed a threat to handweaving's relevance, if not its existence in contemporary culture.

The opposite view was held by Mary Meigs Atwater. The leader of American handweavers who founded the Shuttle Craft Guild in 1920, Atwater adhered to a belief in weaving as a traditional leisure-time or therapeutic activity and a humble craft. In 1923, after settling in Cambridge, Massachusetts, she undertook an extensive study of American colonial weaving, resulting in a facsimile edition of patterns from the period. In addition, she published a number of popular how-to guides for handweavers. Her down-to-earth approach to the craft of weaving, emphasis on reproducing historical patterns, and uncomplicated acceptance of the practice as a pleasurable diversion were at odds with the professional aspirations of the weaver-designer. An exchange between Albers and Atwater over the value of handweaving in the pages of one of the day's leading periodicals in the field, the *Weaver*, illuminates the stakes of these opposing tendencies in the 1940s.

Regarding the practice of weavers reproducing historical examples, Albers argued that "such work, is often no more than a romantic attempt to recall a *temps perdu*" and that the field of American handweaving required a reconceptualization that would allow for work to "take responsible part in a new development."[7] Atwater responded to Albers's criticism with an article titled "It's Pretty—But Is It Art?"[8] She reasserted her belief in the primary value of handweaving as an "escape from the distresses or the hum-drum detail of our daily lives."[9] Atwater wielded immense influence over the amateur handweaving community in the 1940s, but it was Albers's view of fiber as capable of serving both utilitarian and artistic functions that presaged the future direction of the field.

FIG. 7.1

Imogen Cunningham, *Ruth Asawa, Sculptor*, 1956. Image courtesy of the Imogen Cunningham Trust.

The weaver-designer's adherence to the notion of woven textiles as utilitarian products subordinated to interior design or architecture was tested and eventually abandoned by the Bauhaus-trained weaver Anni Albers. In 1933 Albers immigrated to the United States for a teaching post at the experimental liberal arts school, Black Mountain College, outside Asheville, North Carolina. There she implemented a curriculum that approached handweaving through preliminary exercises in color, texture, and structure, reflecting her Bauhaus training as well as the color investigations of her husband, the painter Josef Albers. The move to Asheville took place during the Appalachian craft revival. This revival, advanced by a coalition of independent craft

Although Albers adhered to the weaver-designer model throughout the 1930s and into the 1940s, the sensitive color relationships and self-referential structure of her weaves—an aspect of her practice influenced by modernist abstraction and her study of ancient Andean weaving—led to her work being noticed in the art world.[10] Such recognition was unique among her peers. In 1949 Albers was given a solo exhibition, *Anni Albers Textiles*, at the Museum of Modern Art (MoMA)—a first for textiles—curated by Philip Johnson and Edgar J. Kaufmann of MoMA's department of architecture and design. It featured her utilitarian textiles as well as her earliest "pictorial weaves," nonutilitarian wall hangings inspired by her firsthand encounter with the ancient monuments of Mexico. Albers continued to draw from the architecture and visual culture of the ancient Americas for her woven works of art throughout the 1950s and '60s. In 1959 she summarized her expanded vision for fiber as an art form with the declaration: "Let threads be articulate . . . and find a form for themselves to no other end than their own orchestration, not to be sat on, walked on, only to be looked at."[11]

THE 1950s

That whole phase of [handweaving as a preparatory step to production], you wonder what in the world all that was [about].

—ED ROSSBACH[12]

In 1949 the Alberses resettled in New Haven, Connecticut. For the next decade and beyond Anni Albers continued to pursue weaving as an art form, a project encouraged by the steady acquisition of her nonutilitarian, pictorial weaves by museums and private collectors.

In the same period, Albers's weaver-designer peers continued to design for industrial adaptation, which remained a viable career for weavers throughout the 1950s. One weaver new to the scene in the 1950s was Jack Lenor Larsen, whose extraordinary success as a weaver-designer, author, and entrepreneur ran parallel to the ascendency of modern architecture. Larsen received his MFA in textile design under Strengell at the Cranbrook Academy of Art in Bloomfield Hills, Michigan, in 1951, and soon landed his first major commission for the draperies of the lobby of Lever House, Manhattan's first International Style office high-rise. Known for his innovative use of pattern and combinations of unorthodox materials—often inspired by indigenous textile traditions from around the world—the Larsen Design Studio developed

over three thousand fabrics in the course of nearly fifty years of the company's existence.[13]

Although handweavers continued to design for industry throughout the 1950s, the blind veneration of the weaver-designer model began to wane in this period.[14] Beyond the Larsen Design Studio's work for industry or the yards of handwoven upholstery, casement cloth, and fabric for clothing that appeared in many juried textile shows in the 1950s, unique hangings in tapestry, stitchery, and fabric collage also began to appear, indicating a gradual openness to the idea of nonutilitarian weaving—or fiber in general—as a medium of art. A 1957 exhibition at the Museum of Contemporary Crafts, *Wall Hangings and Rugs*, is representative of this nascent formation. The exhibition included unique tapestries, needlework hangings, and hand-knotted, hand-hooked, and hand-woven rugs by a number of prominent figures of the field in the 1950s situated across the country, including Trude Guermonprez, Mariska Karasz, Eve Peri, and Lenore Tawney. About the work in the show, a reviewer noted the shift toward individualized expressions in fiber as representative of a "strong movement among weavers for the artistic entity in textiles. . . . In outlook, technique and application, modern weavers have made it a new and vital art."[15]

In the area of contemporary embroidery, appliqué, or "stitchery," as needlework creations were often called in the 1950s, Mariska Karasz and Eve Peri produced the best-known work. Probably more than any other factor, Karasz's publications, including *Adventures in Stitches* (1949; revised 1959), and her series of articles, "Creative Arts of the Needle," for *House Beautiful* from 1952 to 1953, were responsible for the revival and popularization of needlework in the United States in the period. Her own work, which was exhibited widely in the 1950s, ranged from compositions inspired by the landscape of Westchester County to folk art–inspired abstractions. Peri, a textile designer by trade, began producing what she called "fabstracts" in the 1930s. These works, which she continued to produce through the 1960s, consisted of appliqué, fabric collage, and embroidery, combined with a language of abstract form in common with modernist painters such as Matisse, Hans Arp, and Stuart Davis, among others.

In handweaving, Trude Guermonprez played a role in the transition away from the industrial applications of woven textiles. Guermonprez was an established weaver-designer based in Holland before coming to the States in

1947 to teach at Black Mountain College during Albers's sabbatical. Although Guermonprez would continue to design for industry into the 1960s, she began to expand her work to include unique wall hangings while in residence at Black Mountain. One small tapestry on a painted warp, *Leaf Study* (1948), remains from this period of experimentation and was the basis for an extended series of nonutilitarian weaves that Guermonprez would eventually refer to as "Textile Graphics." By the early 1960s, this group of works included three-dimensional woven hangings.

In 1949 Guermonprez accepted an invitation from ceramist Marguerite Wildenhain to join the new artist community, Pond Farm, in Guerneville, California, as the resident weaver. For three years at Pond Farm, Guermonprez conducted weaving workshops, building a reputation for herself as a gifted teacher. In 1954 she joined the faculty of the California College of Arts and Crafts, transforming weaving from a single course into a viable undergraduate program and, in 1967, introducing a graduate degree in fibers. Regarding her impact on the field on the West Coast, fiber artist and former student Kay Sekimachi recalled that when Guermonprez arrived, "all the weavers around here [were] interested only in making pretty placemats and glittery fabrics."[16]

Guermonprez's recognition in the 1950s of the legitimacy of nonutilitarian weaving marks a turning point in the field. The days of the close professional affiliation with industry and architecture were coming to an end. However, it would take the next generation of weavers, who may have been trained under the model of designing for industry but had little interest in exclusively pursuing such a career path, to completely sever this relationship, propelling the field into new territory. This group included, among others, Ed Rossbach, Mary Balzer Buskirk, Ted Hallman, Alice Kagawa Parrott, Katherine Westphal, Mildred Fischer, Lenore Tawney, Franklin Colvin, Thelma Becherer, and Kay Sekimachi. In the mid- to late 1950s, these fiber artists began to produce work that departed from the applied textile tradition in which they were educated.

Exploration of historic techniques and a more free-form approach to composition, often carried out directly upon the loom, were characteristic of the nonutilitarian weaving practiced by the group in this period. Tawney's use of the open warp, Hallman's incorporation of dyed resin elements, Rossbach's adoption of hand-manipulated forms in a variety of ancient techniques, and Becherer's

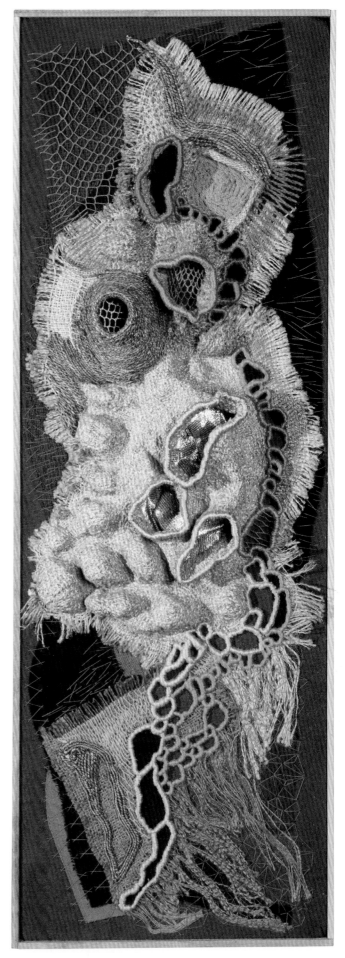

FIG. 7.2

Evelyn Svec Ward, *Cadena De Oro*, 1968. Cotton and miscellaneous threads. 28½ x 10¼ in. (72.4 x 26 cm). Philadelphia Museum of Art, Gift of William E. Ward; 1995-21-1.

integration of natural materials such as dried cattails all stand out as representative of the new desire to explore "what was possible and wonderful" with fiber once freed from the demands of industry.[17]

The San Francisco–based sculptor Ruth Asawa, another pioneer, used the off-loom technique of crochet in the 1950s (FIG. 7.1). Between 1946 and 1949, she had attended Black Mountain College where she studied with Josef Albers. His Bauhaus-oriented pedagogical method, which stressed experimentation with materials, color, and texture, fostered in Asawa an unusual openness toward artistic practices like fiber craft that were dismissed by most mainstream artists at the time as "nonart." Asawa learned to crochet in 1947 on a summer trip to Mexico, where a stop in the town of Toluca, a site known for its folkloric and art histories, introduced her to the technique's wide variety of applications. Upon her return home, she began to experiment with what would become her signature style—crocheted three-dimensional hanging forms in wire—contributing to the Bay Area fiber scene's larger investigation of the artistic potential of fiber and other flexible media as pursued by Rossbach, Sekimachi, Westphal, and others.[18]

In the 1950s the fledgling support system for unique works in fiber in the form of museum exhibitions, galleries, and periodicals was largely centered in New York City. Between 1953 and 1957, in addition to exhibitions organized by the Museum of Contemporary Crafts, shows

FIG. 7.3 & 7.4

Wall Hangings, **installation view, The Museum of Modern Art, New York (February 25, 1969– May 4, 1969).**

of Scandinavian craft, textiles included, drawn from the Milan Design Triennials, were mounted at the Georg Jensen showroom on Madison Avenue. Finnish rugs in the traditional *rya* technique exhibited at the showroom in this period fueled the rage for designer-made, long-pile rugs and wall hangings in the United States that extended well into the 1960s. The interior designer Bertha Schaefer opened the Bertha Schaefer Gallery of Contemporary Art in 1944, and throughout the 1950s she regularly exhibited rugs and unique wall hangings in a room set aside for craft and domestic furnishings. MoMA's Good Design program, sponsored by the Merchandise Mart in Chicago, also exhibited both utilitarian and nonutilitarian work in fiber from 1950 to 1955. Additional notable exhibitions of the 1950s include *Textiles USA* (1956) at MoMA, which included nonutilitarian wall hangings by Franklin Colvin and Thelma Becherer.[19]

THE 1960s

During the last ten years, developments in weaving have caused us to revise our concepts of this craft and to view the work within the confines of twentieth-century art.

—MILDRED CONSTANTINE AND JACK LENOR LARSEN[20]

The idea that an object constructed of fiber was credible as a work of art drove much of the activity of the field in the 1960s, resulting in new genres and a considerably expanded audience for fiber-based work. *The American Craftsman,* a 1964 exhibition held at the Museum of Contemporary

Crafts, presented a broad survey of non-utilitarian work in fiber. It provides a useful point of departure for considering the rise of one such new genre—autonomous fiber sculpture—as well as the continued expansion of previously established genres such as "stitchery," "wall hangings," and "tapestry."[21] In the exhibition, stitchery featured Elizabeth Jennerjahn, Marie Kelly, Marilyn Pappas, Lillian Elliott, Alma Lesch, Nik Krevitsky, and Evelyn Svec Ward (FIG. 7.2), all of whom used a variety of needlework techniques and appliqué to create two and three-dimensional collage-like constructions. Kelly built hanging fabric and crochet constructions around armatures, and Pappas and Lesch used cast-off clothing. These three shared affinities with assemblage sculpture of the period. Svec Ward's heavily textured, surreal landscapes of irregularly shaped growths that were built up through netting and couching (an embroidery technique) contributed to the vast range of non-woven or off-loom techniques adopted by artists in constructing two- and three-dimensional forms in fiber. In the early 1960s, Rossbach, Walter Nottingham, Mary Walker Phillips, Spencer Depas, and Virginia Harvey, among many others, were focused on recovering off-loom, everyday techniques such as crochet, knitting, netting, and various forms of knotting as viable techniques for art.[22] In their hands, the negative cultural associations of these techniques as domestic, decorative, or superficial were dismissed in favor of an exploration that highlighted the ancient historical sources of these practices, their structural capacity, and their abstract complexities.

The wall hangings and tapestry coverage in *The American Craftsman* featured two-dimensional work by a host of familiar and new names, including Lili Blumenau, Lenore Tawney, Claire Zeisler, Dorian Zachai, Alice Adams, Sheila Hicks, Else Regensteiner, Ed Rossbach, Kay Sekimachi, Glen Kaufman, Luella Williams, and Mary Walker Phillips. The modest scale of this work was standard fare for even the most forward-looking exhibitions in the early 1960s, such as the groundbreaking 1963 show *Woven Forms* at the Museum of Contemporary Crafts.[23] It included the work of five of these artists: Adams, Hicks, Tawney, Zeisler, and Zachai. Although the show was a landmark for its inclusion of woven work incorporating free-hanging elements, found objects, and some off-loom techniques, the most innovative work was still a far cry from the outsized, free-standing, three-dimensional forms that would begin to appear a few years later.

FIG. 7.5

Ted Hallman, *Meditation Environment*, 1969. Cotton, acrylic, and steel. 74⅛ x 74 x 84 in. (188.3 x 188 x 213.4 cm). Museum of Arts and Design, Gift of the artist through the American Craft Council, 1987; 1987.12.a-aa.

Several factors played a role in pushing the field beyond the two-dimensional, small-scale wall hangings shown in *The American Craftsman* and *Woven Forms* toward the more imposing fiber-based sculpture that would come to be called "fiber art" by the early 1970s. Of particular importance to this development were exhibitions such as the Lausanne Tapestry Biennials in Switzerland, which exposed American artists to the more advanced work of their peers in Europe in the mid-1960s.[24] The Centre Internationale de la Tapisserie Ancienne et Moderne inaugurated the Lausanne Biennale in 1962 to promote the production of tapestry weaving. By 1967, however, the biennial had become a hotbed for large-scale, unorthodox woven and off-loom work. These exhibitions were documented in the American fiber art press, and by the late 1960s, many American fiber artists attended, then returned to their studios inspired to work large, wild, and woolly. On the heels of the 1967 Lausanne Biennale was MoMA's *Wall Hangings* of 1969 (FIGS. 7.3 AND 7.4). Curated by Mildred Constantine and Jack Lenor Larsen, this groundbreaking international survey of non-

utilitarian woven and off-loom sculpture further encouraged American artists working in fiber to think beyond the dictates of the loom.

Despite the innovative contemporary work exhibited in *Wall Hangings*, its reception outside the fiber world remained cool. While Constantine and Larsen believed in the work as art with a capital "A," others, such as the artist Louise Bourgeois, who reviewed the show for *Craft Horizons*, declared the work to be "decorative" and thus lacking the intellectual and aesthetic demands of painting and sculpture. Such equivocations about the status of

Françoise Grossen, *Five Rivers*, 1969. Manila rope. 108 x 96 in. (274.3 x 243.8 cm). Private collection.

work in fiber represented nothing new in the field's history; they continued to be based on presumptions about fiber or craft's connections to the feminine realm of the home, hobby art, the commercial world of design, and other forms of practice dismissed as "nonart" that had long plagued the field's identity.

It was against this backdrop—fiber's historical and cultural associations with the "low"—that many of the artists featured in *Wall Hangings* worked. Their efforts to transform cultural perceptions about the field resulted in some of the most radical work ever created in fiber. Works included in the show—such as Magdalena Abakanowicz's large-scale shaped weavings with added off-loom elements, or Sheila Hicks's repetitive, stacked skeins of vibrantly colored linen and silk—posed significant challenges to aesthetic boundaries that subordinated fiber to the realm of "craft." At the same time, the desire for art world legitimacy drove critical supporters such as Constantine and Larsen to avoid the politics of the art world that marginalized fiber as a lesser medium in the first place and instead to directly elevate select work to the category of "high art." What was most fascinating about this work—the way it upended assumptions about what could count as "art" through innovation in "craft," a practice generally dismissed as an irrelevant force in the art world—was left unexamined, although this oversight was understandable, given the art world's rigid orthodoxies in the 1960s.

The Lausanne Bienniales and MoMA's *Wall Hangings* were catalysts for a number of additional influential exhibitions opening in the early 1970s, which, although slightly outside the time frame of this essay, played a role in constituting the field of fiber art. They include *Sculpture in Fiber* (1973) at the Museum of Contemporary Crafts, *Forms in Fiber* (1970) at the Art Institute of Chicago, and a flurry of exhibitions in the Los Angeles area in 1971 and 1972, culminating in *Deliberate Entanglements*, which was curated by Bernard Kester for the UCLA Art Gallery. The Sidney Janis Gallery's *String and Rope* (1970) isolated the use of fiber, primarily string and rope but also felt and other fabric, in the work of artists Eva Hesse, Barry Flanagan, and others associated with process art, a movement that focused on the means used in creating an artwork. The exhibition included an earlier generation of avant-garde artists such as Marcel Duchamp and Hans Arp, but also highlighted the new interest in fiber in the art of Robert Rauschenberg, Claes Oldenburg, and others.

In addition to these exhibitions, the publication of Ruth Kaufmann's *New American Tapestry* (1969) and Mildred Constantine and Jack Lenor Larsen's *Beyond Craft* (1972) documented and fostered the tremendous expansion of fiber art in the United States.[25]

Works from the late 1960s and early 1970s, such as Debra Rapoport's *Knitted Environment* (1970), Ted Hallman's *Meditation Environment* (FIG. 7.5), and Alexandra Jacopetti's *Macramé Park* in Bolinas, California (1974), among others, illustrate that the counterculture of the late 1960s and the popular revival of fiber crafts it fostered also influenced the development of American fiber art, especially on the West Coast. Rossbach, who had a front-row seat to the cultural radicalism centered in the San Francisco Bay Area, remarked upon "the wonderful Hippie clothes to be seen everywhere in Berkeley. The visual quality of the Berkeley scene [is] endlessly enchanting and stimulating, [and] a constant textile experience."[26] Katherine Westphal's *Peruvian Monkeys* (1967) (CAT. 115), which combined quilting, embroidery, batik, and block printing, and Lillian Elliott's distressed woven hanging *Campaign Promises* (1968), provide additional examples of how artists working in fiber drew upon the rich forms of countercultural visual expression and the political climate from which it emerged in the late 1960s.

By the late 1960s and early 1970s, the fiber scene in the United States was dominated by the off-loom work of a host of artists—Françoise Grossen (FIG. 7.6), Barbara Shawcroft, Neda Al-Hilali, Dominic Di Mare, Ron King, Ferne Jacobs, Jon Wahling, Jean Stamsta, Lillian Elliott, Glen Kaufman, and Joan Michaels Paque, as well as many of those already discussed, including Zeisler, Hicks (FIG. 7.7), Hallman, Nottingham, and Rossbach. To Rose Slivka, the influential editor of *Craft Horizons*, these artists were "the revolutionaries of rope [who reject] orthodox textile construction in which the thread is buried in fabric as the final two-dimensional limp skin. They think thread. They want thread to be about itself—to rib and wrap, knot, twist, loop into itself so that it builds strength purely out of its own material technology and even becomes self-supporting."[27] Slivka and others, who characterized the loom as an impotent instrument, equated off-loom fiber sculpture with the power and virility of modern art. While positive for off-loom artists who sought a legitimate place in the world of high art, this construct nearly eclipsed attention to weaving. Yet weavers in this period such as Kay Sekimachi, Helena Hernmarck, Jan

FIG. 7.7

Sheila Hicks, *Les os s'amusent*, 1965. Cotton and synthetic fill. 7⅞ x 6¼ in. (20.1 x 16 cm). Private collection.

Janeiro, Candace Crockett, Adela Akers, Cynthia Shira, Lia Cook, Arturo Alonzo Sandoval, and Laurie Herrick were also busy testing materials and techniques. In addition, artists such as Gerhardt Knodel, who worked with woven textile in a variety of forms, were innovating ways of integrating it into architectural space. Works such as Hernmarck's *Talking Trudeau-Nixon* (CAT. 116) in her photorealist style of the period demonstrates how weavers sought to reinvent the possibilities of weaving in the late 1960s and early 1970s.

From the late 1940s to the late 1960s, the field of fiber underwent a sea change. Old and new spheres of practice shifted dramatically. Weaving, stitchery, fabric collage wall hangings, and fiber sculpture as well as other methods reinvented in the mid-1970s such as basketry and quiltmaking, continue to constitute what is now called the fiber arts movement. The diversity of this movement, its multitudinous connections to the realms of art, industry, and material culture, and the challenges it faced in legitimating itself in the art world, underscore its distinctiveness in the history of the American studio movement.

1 Anni Albers, "Handweaving Today: Textile Work at Black Mountain College," *Weaver* 6 (January/February 1941), 3.

2 The work, writing, and teaching of Lili Blumenau and Marli Ehrman also played a role in the development of the field in this period. For Blumenau, see the Resource List in this volume. Marli Ehrman trained at the Bauhaus and arrived in the United States in 1938. From 1939 to 1947 she directed the textile department of the New Bauhaus (School of Design), Chicago, and taught evening courses in weaving at Hull House.

3 Liebes quoted in Ed Rossbach, "Fiber in the Forties," *AC* 42 (October/November 1982), 18. I have drawn on the writing and interviews of Ed Rossbach, whose career as a fiber artist spanned the period surveyed. His thoughtful and often humorous observations regarding the evolution of the fiber field are invaluable to any history of the period. See also Ed Rossbach, *Ed Rossbach: Artist, Professor, Mentor, Writer*, oral history interview by Harriet Nathan, 1983, intro. by Jack Lenor Larson, Fiber Arts Oral History Series (Berkeley: University of California, 1987); Ed Rossbach, oral history interview by Carole Austin, August 27–29, 2002, AAA, SI.

4 Marianne Strengell, born and raised in Helsinki, Finland, joined the faculty of the Cranbrook Academy of Art, Bloomfield Hills, Michigan, in 1937 as a weaving instructor. In 1942 she became director of the department of weaving and textile design, a post she held until 1961.

5 Janet Kardon, ed., *Revivals! Diverse Traditions, 1920–1945* (New York: Harry N. Abrams, in association with the American Craft Museum, 1994).

Appalachian handweavers in the 1930s and '40s also created fabrics for clothing, linens, and towels.

6 Albers, "Hand Weaving Today," 3.

7 Ibid.

8 Mary Atwater, "It's Pretty—But Is It Art?" *Weaver* 6 (1941), 13–14, 26.

9 Ibid., 13.

10 On Andean textiles, see Virginia Gardner Troy, *Anni Albers and Ancient American Textiles: From Bauhaus to Black Mountain* (Burlington, VT: Ashgate, 2002).

11 Anni Albers, *Pictorial Weaves* (Cambridge, MA: MIT Press, 1959), 5.

12 Rossbach, *Ed Rossbach*, 57.

13 Denise Guerin and Stephanie Watson, eds., *Interplay: Perspectives on the Design Legacy of Jack Lenor Larsen*, exh. cat. (Minneapolis: Goldstein Museum of Design, 2002).

14 For a good snapshot of the range of handwoven fabrics, room dividers, and wall hangings, see Virginia Nagle, "American Weaving," *Design Quarterly* nos. 48/49 (1960), 1, 3–53. Some of those included, such as Ed Rossbach, Kay Sekimachi, and Lenore Tawney, would soon lead the field away from utilitarian practice.

15 "Wall Hangings and Rugs: Museum of Contemporary Crafts Exhibit," *CH* 17 (May/June 1957), 20.

16 Kay Sekimachi Stocksdale, "Trude Remembered," in *The Tapestries of Trude Guermonprez*, exh. cat. (Oakland: Oakland Museum, 1982), 22.

17 Rossbach, "Marianne Strengell," *AC* 44 (April/May 1984), 10.

18 See Daniell Cornell et al., *The Sculpture of Ruth Asawa: Contours in the Air*, exh. cat. (San Francisco: Fine Arts Museums of San Francisco; Berkeley: University of California Press, 2006).

19 Thank you to New York–based weaver-designer Nell Znamierowski for her recollections of the fiber scene in New York City in the 1950s. On the West Coast in the 1950s, established venues for viewing contemporary fiber art were very limited, consisting of annual juried craft shows and the occasional university gallery exhibition.

20 Mildred Constantine and Jack Lenor Larsen, *Wall Hangings*, exh. cat. (New York: Museum of Modern Art, 1969), n.p.

21 See Rose Slivka, "The American Craftsman/1964," *CH* 24 (May/June 1964), 12–31.

22 Spencer Depas, who was Haitian by birth, came to the United States on a scholarship to Cranbrook Academy in the mid-1950s. In the late 1960s he taught at the Lili Blumenau Studio, where Tawney, Zeisler, and Shawcroft, among many others, sought out his instruction in knotting or macramé.

23 *Woven Forms* (New York: Museum of Contemporary Crafts, 1963).

24 Dianne Taylor, "The First Through the Tenth Biennales Internationales des la Tapisserie," PhD diss., Ohio State University, 1983.

25 From 1969 until its closing in 1979, the Ruth Kaufmann Gallery in New York created visibility for fiber artists by catering to architects who sought large-scale weavings and fiber sculpture. In 1973 artist Gyöngy Laky established Fiberworks, Center for Textile Arts in Berkeley, California, which greatly increased the visibility of contemporary fiber art in the region and contributed to the growth of the fiber art movement in the 1970s and '80s. The Allrich Gallery, established in San Francisco by Louise Allrich in 1975, exhibited the work of numerous contemporary fiber artists, providing additional support and visibility. See Gyöngy Laky, "Fiber Art: Visual Thinking and the Intelligent Handartist," interviewed by Harriet Nathan, 2003, transcript, Regional Oral History Office, Bancroft Library, University of California, Berkeley. For Anneberg Gallery, see Resource List.

26 Rossbach, quoted in Mildred Constantine and Jack Lenor Larsen, *Beyond Craft: The Art Fabric* (New York: Van Nostrand Reinhold Company, 1972), 220. On counterculture fiber craft, see Alexandra Jacopetti, *Native Funk & Flash* (San Francisco: Scrimshaw Press, 1974).

27 Rose Slivka, "Hard String," *CH* 32 (April 1972), 17.

100

ANNI ALBERS

Sheep May Safely Graze, 1959

COTTON AND SYNTHETIC FIBER

14½ X 23½ IN. (36.8 X 59.7 CM)

MUSEUM OF ARTS AND DESIGN,

GIFT OF KAREN JOHNSON BOYD, THROUGH

THE AMERICAN CRAFT COUNCIL, 1977

102

CLAIRE ZEISLER

Red Wednesday, 1967

JUTE AND WOOL

68 X 40 X 40 IN. (172.7 X 101.6 X 101.6 CM)

MUSEUM OF ARTS AND DESIGN,

GIFT OF THE DREYFUS CORPORATION, THROUGH

THE AMERICAN CRAFT COUNCIL, 1989

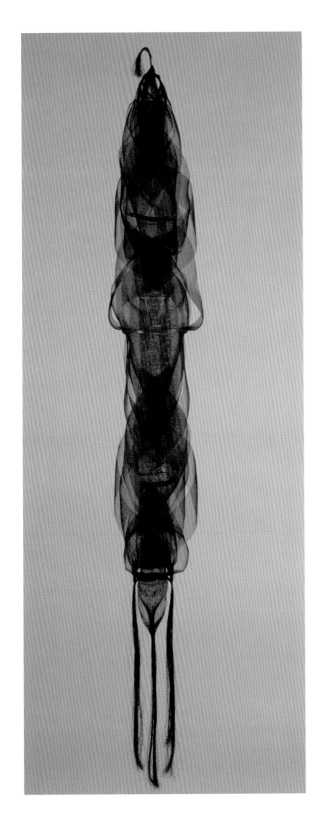

103

KAY SEKIMACHI

Nagare III, 1968

NYLON MONOFILAMENT

87 X 10 X 11 IN. (221 X 25.4 X 27.9 CM)

MUSEUM OF ARTS AND DESIGN,

GIFT OF THE JOHNSON WAX COMPANY, THROUGH THE

AMERICAN CRAFT COUNCIL, 1977

104

MARILYN R. PAPPAS

Opera Coat, 1968

SATIN, LINEN, FUR, YARN, AND SYNTHETIC FABRICS

63 X 46 X 5 IN. (160 X 116.8 X 12.7 CM)

MUSEUM OF ARTS AND DESIGN, GIFT OF THE JOHNSON WAX

COMPANY, THROUGH THE AMERICAN CRAFT COUNCIL, 1977

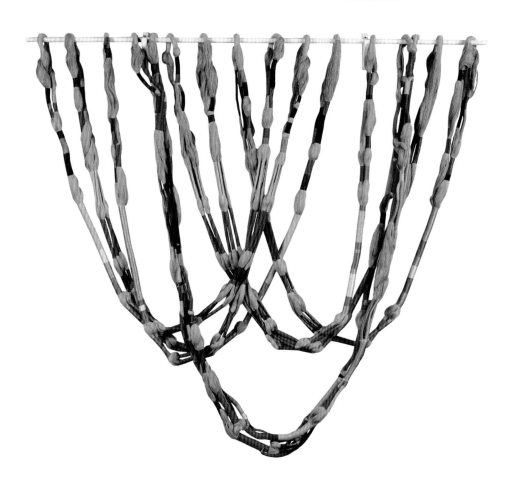

107

TED HALLMAN

Water Lily Pads, 1964

LINEN, WOVEN STRUCTURE, AND DYED ACRYLIC INCLUSIONS

77 X 34 IN. (195.6 X 86.4 CM)

THE HELEN WILLIAMS DRUTT ENGLISH COLLECTION

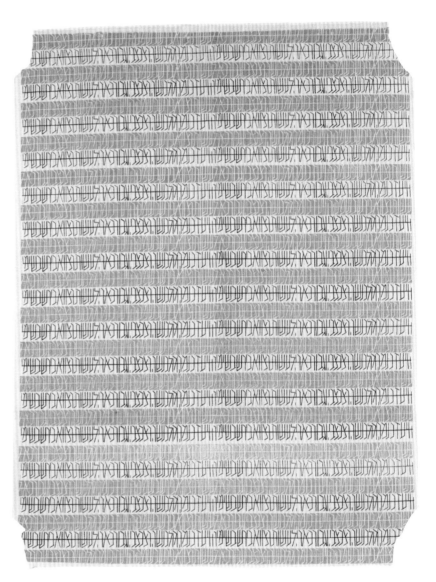

108

LUDWIG YEHUDA WOLPERT, DESIGNER

Wall Hanging, 1959

SCREEN PRINT ON FIBERGLASS

64 X 48½ IN. (162.6 X 123.2 CM)

THE JEWISH MUSEUM, NEW YORK, GIFT OF

BETTY WOLPERT, WIDOW OF THE ARTIST, 1992-158

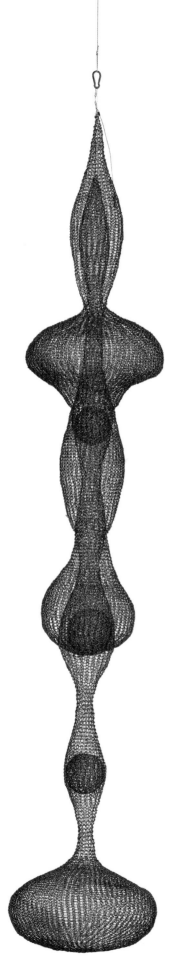

109

RUTH ASAWA

Untitled, c. 1968

COPPER AND BRASS WIRE

H. 123 IN. (312.4 CM), DIAM. 16 IN. (40.6 CM)

FINE ARTS MUSEUMS OF SAN FRANCISCO,

GIFT OF JACQUELINE HOEFER, 2006.76.2

110

ADELA AKERS

Shield of a New Standard, 1968

WOOL, COW HAIR, AND LINEN

76 X 52 IN. (193 X 132.1 CM)

MUSEUM OF ARTS AND DESIGN,

GIFT OF THE JOHNSON WAX COMPANY, THROUGH

THE AMERICAN CRAFT COUNCIL, 1977

111

LILI BLUMENAU

Casement Cloth, 1955

FIBER

76 X 38½ IN. (193 X 97.8 CM)

MUSEUM OF ARTS AND DESIGN, PURCHASED BY

THE AMERICAN CRAFT COUNCIL, 1959

112

MARY ADRIENNE DUMAS

Wall Hanging, 1952

SILK BATIK

122¾ X 36½ IN. (311.8 X 92.7 CM)

OAKLAND MUSEUM OF CALIFORNIA;

GIFT OF MRS. M.V. SUTTON

113

LENORE TAWNEY
Jupiter, 1959
SILK, WOOL, AND WOOD
53 X 41 IN. (134.6 X 104.1 CM)
MUSEUM OF ARTS AND DESIGN,
GIFT OF THE JOHNSON WAX
COMPANY, THROUGH THE
AMERICAN CRAFT COUNCIL, 1977

115

KATHERINE WESTPHAL

Peruvian Monkeys, 1967

COTTON

19¼ X 19¾ IN. (48.9 X 50.2 CM)

MUSEUM OF FINE ARTS, BOSTON,

THE DAPHNE FARAGO COLLECTION 2004.2138

114

GEORGE WELLS

Embers No. 2, 1963

WOOL

120 X 96 IN. (304.8 X 243.8 CM)

MUSEUM OF ARTS AND DESIGN,

GIFT OF THE JOHNSON WAX COMPANY, THROUGH

THE AMERICAN CRAFT COUNCIL, 1977

116

HELENA HERNMARCK

Talking Trudeau-Nixon

[PART 1: Tapestry Triptych (left section)], 1969

WOOL, NYLON, AND LINEN

51 X 42 IN. (129.5 X 106.7 CM)

MUSEUM OF ARTS AND DESIGN, GIFT OF THE ARTIST, 1990

117

MARY ANN SCHILDKNECHT

Blouse and Skirt, 1969

BED SHEET AND SILK EMBROIDERY THREAD

BLOUSE, 21 X 17 IN. (53.3 X 43.18 CM);

SKIRT, 33 X 32 IN. (83.82 X 81.28CM)

THE ARTIST, PHOTOGRAPHED c. 1970

COURTESY OF MARY ANN SCHILDKNECHT

118
ED ROSSBACH
Homage to
John Glenn, 1962
COTTON
48¼ X 29½ IN. (122.6 X 74.9 CM)
MUSEUM OF FINE ARTS, BOSTON,
THE DAPHNE FARAGO
COLLECTION, 2004 2004.2099

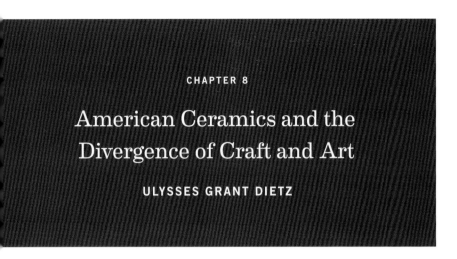

American Ceramics and the Divergence of Craft and Art

ULYSSES GRANT DIETZ

CERAMICS HAD DEEP ROOTS IN AMERICA'S CRAFT traditions and a complex legacy to uphold as the field underwent the seismic upheavals of the postwar years. Grounded in pottery traditions stretching back to colonial times, the craft of ceramics had already been pushed in new directions by the art pottery movement of the early twentieth century. By the end of World War II, however, art pottery no longer seemed relevant and change was in the air.

In 1945 the first Scripps College invitational ceramics exhibition was organized by ceramist William Manker in Claremont, California. This show would evolve into an important annual survey of developments in American ceramic art.[1] The next year, the Detroit Institute of Arts began sponsoring exhibitions of Michigan artist-craftsmen and in the process encouraged students at Cranbrook Academy of Art in nearby Bloomfield Hills to pursue ceramics under the enlightened teaching of Maija Grotell. Meanwhile, in Syracuse, New York, the Ceramic National exhibitions, which had been established in 1932 as a memorial to Adelaide Robineau, a pioneering studio potter of the 1910s and '20s, resumed at the Syracuse Museum of Fine Arts after a wartime hiatus.[2] These venues for the display of modern ceramics—a college art gallery in Southern California, a large urban museum in America's industrial heartland, and a small-town museum in upstate New York—represent the beginnings of a remarkable artistic phenomenon in the United States: the postwar emergence of a vast national network of potters who exhibited together in all their stylistic and technical diversity.

By the early 1960s this network began to split into two distinct, ideologically divided camps that have largely persisted to the present day, each with its own legacy. One camp had no single geographic center. It included studio potters—such as Maija Grotell in Michigan, Marguerite Wildenhain in California, Alix and Warren MacKenzie in Minnesota, and Otto and Gertrud Natzler in California—who clung to ceramic tradition and were less anxious to cast off the domestic and folk-art roots of their craft than were their counterparts. It was quiet, rather conservative, and very persistent. The other camp, which centered on the West Coast, was replete with macho energy and a nonconformist spirit. It included avant-garde potter-artists led by Peter Voulkos, who collectively helped launch the midcentury ceramic revolution. Most of them owed a debt to artists and sculptors, such as David Smith, Joseph Cornell, Louise Nevelson, Helen Frankenthaler, and Alexander Calder, who were participating in the extraordinary changes taking place in the world of fine art. Techniques employed in the arts, such as assemblage, fabrication, and the use of found objects were among the new ideas embraced by some ceramic artists. In the late 1940s abstract expressionism had a particular appeal to potters like Voulkos, because this movement not only represented a startling new direction, but also had originated in America, rather than Europe.[3] Ceramists in both camps defined themselves as artists, revolutionaries, and counterrevolutionaries in equal measure.

These two camps came into being against the wider backdrop of the changes occurring in the teaching of art and craft, which were manifested in the gradual blurring of old boundaries. The early postwar years saw significant shifts, both in the range of available courses at the college level and in the ways these courses were taught. The GI Bill led to a surge in college attendance and a corresponding influx of students in ceramics programs across the country. Nonacademic craft courses proliferated as well. After 1945 the teaching of ceramics gradually moved from the treatment of pottery as a manual skill to presenting it as an art discipline akin to painting or sculpture. This shift had begun in the late 1930s, when potters such as Glen Lukens at the University of Southern California, Los Angeles, emerged as role models and teachers. Lukens encouraged his students—including Carlton Ball, Vivika Heino, and Beatrice Wood—to approach clay intuitively and expressively.[4]

Like Lukens, Marguerite Friedlander Wildenhain, also in California, and Maija Grotell in Michigan saw themselves as artists and professionals. French-born Wildenhain, who made cool minimalist vessels that later gave way to a style more akin to folk art, established the Pond Farm workshop in Guerneville, California, in 1942, where her summer ceramics program drew students from around the world.[5] Her Bauhaus training and her adherence to its premise that there is no distinction between art and craft inspired her students. In forums such as *Craft Horizons* and the first American Craftsmen's Council (ACC) conference, held in 1957 at Asilomar, California, however, Wildenhain remained a conservative voice, proselytizing for traditional craft values.

Grotell, a Finnish-born potter, became head of the ceramics department at the Cranbrook Academy of Art in 1938. There, she brought her vision of artistic individualism based on the vessel to a generation of studio potters, including Toshiko Takaezu, John Glick, and Richard DeVore.[6] Both Wildenhain and Grotell introduced European modernist ideas to American ceramics in the decade before World War II. With teachers such as Lukens, Wildenhain, and Grotell, it was inevitable that the new generation of potters would emerge from their studies with a perspective skewed toward art rather than craft.

Another important event was the tour made by several foreign potters through the United States after the war, bringing the cumulative weight of international ceramic traditions to postwar America. Ironically they played equally important roles in both camps, as inspiring to one as to the other. English potter Bernard Leach was steeped in the traditions of English and Japanese folk pottery. He first brought his Zen ideas to the United States in late 1949 with a hugely popular national lecture tour.[7] When he returned to the States in 1952, he brought Japanese potter Shoji Hamada and philosopher Soetsu Yanagi with him on an even more successful tour organized by Minnesota potter Alix MacKenzie.[8] Yanagi and Hamada had founded the Japanese *mingei* movement in 1926—an art movement that revered folk-art traditions, and ceramics in particular, which were being threatened by Japan's rapid modernization. As they hopscotched the country, the trio met and was seen by a broad range of potters, many of whom would establish themselves as leading lights in the ceramics world. Of particular interest was a meeting between the visiting Japanese and English ceramists and the legendary Pueblo potter

Maria Martinez in New Mexico, an occasion touted as a historical meeting of the great ceramic traditions of three continents **(FIG. 8.1)**.[9]

These visiting potters introduced a distinctly nineteenth-century, folk-based perspective on ceramics to their American audiences in the early 1950s. Their aesthetic sparked a revolution but was actually closely allied to the English Arts and Crafts movement of the 1870s. The quaintly noncommercial approach shared by Leach, Hamada, and Yanagi was rooted in William Morris's belief that art should be available to everyone and should not be the basis for profit.[10] This appealed to idealistic young American potters yearning to be artists and not mere makers of objects. Most important, the trio imparted to their audiences a deep love and respect for clay as an artistic medium. Hamada and Yanagi brought with them the Japanese lack of distinction between "fine" and "applied" art. In the West, the dichotomy between the arts had been momentarily bridged during the Renaissance and again during the Aesthetic Reform movement of the late nineteenth century, but with the rise of modern art in the twentieth century, painting and sculpture had reasserted their dominance and once again had forced handcraft into a secondary status.

FUNCTION AND QUIET BEAUTY

Like Grotell and Wildenhain, many American potters at midcentury had developed their craft before World War II

FIG. 8.1

Pottery demonstration at the Museum of International Folk Art, Santa Fe, New Mexico, December 1952. From left: Bernard Leach, Shoji Hamada, and Warren Gilbertson; in the audience are Maria Martinez and Georgia O'Keeffe. Laura Gilpin Papers © 1979 Amon Carter Museum of American Art Archives, Fort Worth, Texas; 2007.069.133.125.

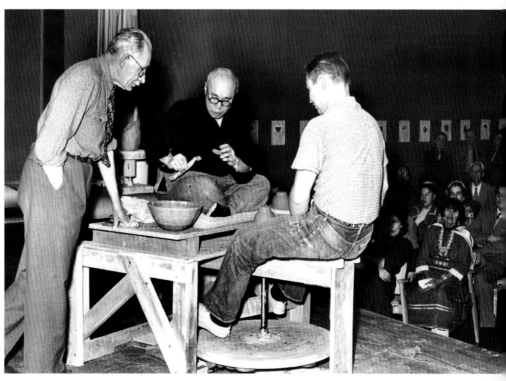

FIG. 8.2

Edwin and Mary Scheier in the ceramic studio, Hewitt Hall, University of New Hampshire, Durham, 1956. Milne Special Collections and Archives, University of New Hampshire, Durham.

and retained a deep connection to functional pottery, to making objects of beauty for everyday use. Many of these potters were also teachers, often serving as role models for the next generation. Edwin and Mary Scheier had learned their craft from rural potters in the South in the 1930s and set out to revive and interpret Appalachian folk pottery traditions in their own work (FIG. 8.2).[11] In 1940 they were hired together to develop a ceramics program at the University of New Hampshire, and there they established a model for the academic artist-potter that would be reiterated in colleges across the country in the coming decades.

At the New York State College of Ceramics at Alfred University, Daniel Rhodes experimented with clays and glazes and published his findings.[12] His investigations of form breathed new energy into the august old ceramics program, moving it past the looming influence of Charles Binns, who had established the school in 1900 on a foundation of technical perfection and conservative aesthetics.

Although analysis of West Coast ceramic art largely focuses on the explosion of energy surrounding the potter-artists who developed in the 1960s, there were several early influential functional potters. Laura Andreson (FIG. 8.3), for example, was a California-born artist whose technical refinement as a potter and austere modernist aesthetic had been influenced by the vessels of Gertrud Natzler,

with whom she had studied.[13] Andreson's achievements were soon recognized and as early as 1944 the Baltimore Museum of Art added her work to its collection, as did MoMA in 1946.[14] A charismatic teacher, she was innovative in her use of clays, introducing newly discovered local sources into California ceramics in 1948 and working with porcelain beginning in 1957.[15]

Gertrud and Otto Natzler, who settled in Los Angeles in 1938, taught only briefly. Their influence rested on the work they created. Gertrud had an unmatched mastery of throwing, and Otto was unparalleled as a glaze chemist. Their work, which embodied a profound respect for technique, set a high bar for formal standards in pottery. Gertrud's philosophical approach to her vessels was based on the dictum that "in pottery, form is content."[16]

Founded in 1933 as an experiment in art education, Black Mountain College in Asheville, North Carolina, had a powerful influence on ceramists—and artists working in other disciplines—throughout its history. In 1948 the summer session included artists Robert Rauschenberg and Kenneth Noland, and the filmmaker Arthur Penn, while among the teaching staff were composer John Cage, choreographer Merce Cunningham, and painter Willem de Kooning.[17] Black Mountain became a platform for many important ceramists, starting with Alfred graduate Robert Turner, who established the ceramics program there between 1949 and 1951.[18] Karen Karnes, who had also studied at Alfred, and her husband David Weinrib, followed Turner as potters-in-residence at Black Mountain between 1952 and 1954. They introduced Leach, Hamada, and Yanagi to their students, as well as Wildenhain. Karnes had experimented with biomorphic forms early in her career (a direction she returned to around 1990), while in the late 1960s Turner began to explore the vessel as a sculptural form.[19]

Among other influential ceramists who hewed to the traditions of beautifully made utilitarian ware were Katherine Choy and Henry Okamoto, who founded the Clay Art Center in Port Chester, New York, in 1957. Choy's work combined a reverence for Asian antecedents with experiments in gestural form and glaze that were avant-garde for their time. Aileen Osborn Webb, founder of the American Craft Council and an amateur potter herself, was an early patron of the Clay Art Center.

An underappreciated figure in the ceramic revolution is Montana potter Frances Senska, who studied with László Moholy-Nagy at the Chicago Institute, with Grotell at Cranbrook, and with Wildenhain at the Pond Farm. She made quiet pots in the modernist tradition. As a teacher at Montana State College in Bozeman, she influenced some extraordinary students, including Peter Voulkos and Rudy Autio. Both studied with Senska under the GI Bill, learning to make functional ware.[20] Senska introduced her students to a wider world of ceramic exploration by bringing to remote Montana such nationally known ceramists as the Natzlers and another of her former teachers, the California ceramist and industrial designer Edith Heath, who had founded Heath Ceramics.

Carlton Ball was another influential, peripatetic teacher who had studied with Lukens and then, like a Johnny Appleseed of clay, sowed the seeds of his craft at several West Coast schools. Although Ball remained true to the functional form, by the 1960s, like the most muscular California ceramists, he had greatly increased the scale and surface appearance of his vessels. Susan Peterson, one of Ball's students, also had a long and impressive teaching career.[21] As a teacher at Chouinard she became a follower of Leach and Hamada during their epic cross-country trip in 1952. She established a summer ceramics program at the university's Idyllwild School in the San Jacinto Mountains of Southern California, and in the 1960s filmed her pottery classes for local television. Although a potter and teacher all her life, it was as a writer on ceramic process and history, and especially as an advocate for the Pueblo potters of the Southwest, that Peterson became best known.[22]

Alix and Warren MacKenzie, who had apprenticed with Leach and were steeped in his philosophy, championed the folk-art ideal in their work and contributed greatly to the aesthetic sensibility and philosophy of a generation of potters. In 1952 they set up their own studio in Stillwater, Minnesota, which would initiate two generations of potters into the Japanese folk-inspired traditionalist ceramics.[23] The MacKenzies deliberately sought a rural Minnesota setting for their studio, and they maintained a self-consciously modest, utilitarian focus. Their work and philosophy through the postwar years constituted a strong link with the folk roots of ceramics that is still in play in the twenty-first century.

In the spring of 1964, the Museum of Contemporary Crafts in New York presented *The American Craftsman*, a large survey exhibition. The ceramics on view ranged from classic vessels by the Natzlers to sculptures by John Mason to the vessel transformed by Toshiko Takaezu.[24]

This exhibition and the next one—*New Ceramic Forms* held at the museum in the same year—made it clear that nonfunctional pottery was elbowing its way onto the stage, and the exhilarating opening act of the artist-potter was underway.

PUSHING THE FORM: ARTIST-POTTERS

In 1961 a cultural tremor was felt when Rose Slivka, editor of *Craft Horizons*, published an article titled "The New Ceramic Presence."[25] Her essay focused on the seismic changes underway in California's ceramic art world. Slivka knew Peter Voulkos and his students and had introduced them to New York painters such as De Kooning. Her essay approached ceramics from an art critic's point of view, which was something entirely new, and if Slivka did not entirely grasp the ceramic history of the 1950s and how it had affected Voulkos and his peers, she still connected with the dramatic new spontaneity and gesture—which she likened to contemporary jazz—that had infused contemporary ceramic art. Slivka's article made it clear that, if the 1950s had been the decade of the vessel as art, then the 1960s would be the decade of ceramic sculpture. It was an awakening.

Emblematic of the experimentation among this generation of ceramic artists was James Leedy, a professor at the Kansas City Art Institute, who joined Ken Ferguson there in 1966. Leedy was producing ceramic work in 1953

FIG. 8.3
Laura Andreson at the kiln, University of California, Los Angeles, c. 1962. Laura Andreson Papers, 1902–1991. AAA, SI.

and 1954 that prefigured Voulkos and Autio's embrace of abstract expressionism later in the 1950s. Inspired by artists such as De Kooning and Franz Kline, whom he had known during his years in New York, Leedy also drew inspiration for his ceramic art from such diverse vessel forms as Shang bronzes, raku stoneware, and Tang sculptures.[26]

Another early explorer in breaking the tyranny of the vessel was Hawaiian-born Toshiko Takaezu who developed a distinctive vocabulary of painterly non-vessel forms. In her Quakertown, New Jersey, studio in the 1960s, she quietly destroyed functionality by simply closing the openings of her large forms and shaping them into the Zen sculptures for which she has become known.

In 1951 a Montana brickmaker named Archie Bray set up an experimental artist-in-residence program for ceramic art that became the Archie Bray Foundation for the Ceramic Arts, one of the most influential and visionary ceramic art centers in the country. Voulkos, Autio, their teacher Senska, and another potter, Kelly Wong, built the Bray's kilns and were, so to speak, present at the birth of the Bray.[27] Autio's work in the 1950s and '60s paralleled that of Voulkos, with strong gestural earth-colored vessels treated with painterly sweeps of glaze and physical alterations that gave his art an abstracted anthropomorphism. His later, more figurative and colorful ceramics would evolve from these early sculptural vessels.

In 1952 Voulkos and Autio were present when Leach, Hamada, and Yanagi arrived to give a workshop in December 1952 **(FIG. 8.4)**. During the visit Hamada galvanized Voulkos and Autio with his love of clay and its expressive potential.[28] Hamada handled the clay very freely, in a way not seen by American potters. These foreign potters exhibited an energy and "willingness to allow the material to express its inherent characteristics."[29]

It was this spirit that Voulkos brought with him to the Los Angeles County Art Institute (renamed the Otis Art Institute of Los Angeles County in 1961) when he joined the faculty in the fall of 1954 and helped to make Los Angeles the red-hot center of the ceramic revolution.[30] Although his work of the early 1950s was masterful in its craftsmanship and in line with the dominant vessel tradition up to that time, by the mid-1950s he had begun to create outsized, nonfunctional pots that were splashed with glaze and altered to destroy the perfection of traditional thrown vessels. By the 1960s he began to produce his massive slashed and altered plates and his

FIG. 8.4

Workshop at the Archie Bray Foundation, 1952. From left: Soetsu Yanagi, Bernard Leach, Rudy Autio, Peter Voulkos, and Shoji Hamada. William P. Daley papers, AAA, SI.

iconic stacked pots. Although he achieved success with bronze sculpture in the 1960s, his sculptural vessels became his greatest legacy.[31]

The emergence of the "Otis Group" in the mid-1960s under Voulkos was a seminal event in the ceramic world. This was the core of West Coast ceramics and signaled the rise of the potter as artist. Voulkos's fiery persona was influenced by the Zen of Japanese pottery, the gestural power of abstract expressionist painting, and the constructivist freedom of contemporary sculpture.[32]

One of Voulkos's first students was Paul Soldner, who was followed by a cadre of energetic and passionate artists including Ken Price, John Mason **(FIG. TK)**, Jerry Rothman, and Jim Melchert. Their explorations of scale and gestural techniques produced sculptural pots the likes of which had never been seen before. Soldner began teaching at Scripps in 1956, where he launched an exploration of the Japanese raku techniques he had only read about, adapting it for his own use.[33] Soldner's raku process, along with Don Reitz's work with salt glazes at Alfred, became central elements in American ceramic art during the 1960s.[34]

In 1963 the Kaiser Center in Oakland hosted *California Sculpture*, an exhibition including Voulkos, Mason, and Robert Arneson, who had studied ceramics at Mills College, Oakland. Arneson, who was a keen admirer of Voulkos and Mason, submitted *Toilet*, which featured a colorful, nonfunctional bathroom toilet. The statement was bold, but the piece was ultimately rejected by the organizers and removed from the exhibition after one day (**FIG. 8.5**).[35] His embrace of lurid glazes and a white clay body developed by San Francisco artists Ron Nagle and Jim Melchert, along with his scatological iconography, had pushed the envelope beyond accepted norms of the California art establishment.

Meanwhile, traditional high-fired stoneware also came under attack elsewhere, as Howard Kottler at the University of Washington, Seattle, was one of the group of West Coast ceramic artists—including Nagle, Patti Warashina and Fred Bauer in Seattle, and Ken Price in Los Angeles—who chose low-fire china paints for their juicy colors and slick surfaces—something that would have been all but blasphemous in serious ceramic art circles (**CAT. 119**). Nagle had also been inspired by Price's use of small forms, and the two became known for their fetishistic, small-scale precious objects in bright low-fire glaze colors on white earthenware (**FIG. 8.6**). Kottler went even further, applying store-bought decal graphics to commercial ceramic bodies, producing work that was ironic and politically charged but highly finished.[36] By abandoning Japanese-influenced stoneware with its traditional earthy palette, these Westerners opened up a path to an entirely new adventure in ceramic art.[37] Another artist-potter to use material other than stoneware was Rudolf Staffel, whose work emphasized the luminosity of the unglazed porcelain. It was as radical in its quiet, small-scale, nonfunctional way as anything that came out of California in the Voulkos years.[38]

GETTING THE WORD OUT

Throughout the immediate postwar period, ceramics education continued to expand in academic and nonacademic venues. For newly minted potters hungry for news of developments in the field, *Ceramics Monthly* magazine (founded 1953), provided technical information and news about exhibitions. It would be nearly twenty years before the first issue of *Studio Potter*, another important forum for potters, was published, with *American Ceramics* joining the ranks in 1982.

By the early 1950s, craft exhibitions had begun to proliferate, and some were dedicated to ceramics. In Washington, DC, the Kiln Club (founded in 1946) mounted the first *Exhibition of Ceramic Art* in 1950 at the National Collection of Fine Arts (now the Smithsonian American Art Museum) (**FIG. 8.7**). The organizers invited American artists such as the Scheiers, Russell Aitken, Thelma Frazier Winter, Henry Varnum Poor, Arthur Baggs, and Charles Binns, to show their work alongside British artists Leach, Michael Cardew, and Samuel Haile. International in scope, it included additional loan

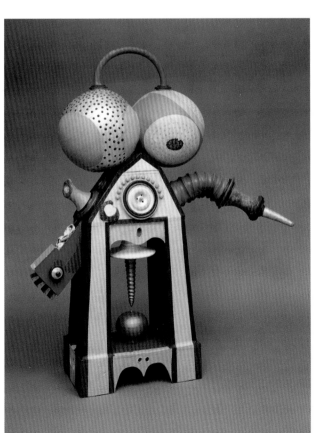

CAT. 119
Fred Bauer, Steam Drill-slot Pump, 1967. Earthenware and acrylic paint. 56 x 46 x 14 in. (142.2 x 116.8 x 35.6 cm). Museum of Arts and Design. Gift of the Johnson Wax Company, through the American Craft Council, 1977.

FIG. 8.5
Robert Arneson, *John With Art*, 1964. Glazed stoneware. 34½ x 18 x 25½ in. (87.63 x 45.72 x 64.77 cm). Seattle Art Museum, Gift of Manual Neri; 82.82. *John With Art* was made in 1964, a year after the original *Toilet* of 1963 by Arneson for the Kaiser Center.

objects of works by Maria Martinez from the Indian Arts and Crafts Board, Belleek from the ambassador of Ireland, Dutch ceramics from the Netherlands embassy, and ceramics from the Norwegian embassy.[39]

In 1952, the year Leach, Hamada, and Yanagi were making their national tour, the Henry Museum at the University of Washington in Seattle, in concert with the Seattle Clay Club, mounted the *Seattle Centennial Ceramic Exhibition*, setting the stage for that city's role in the ceramic revolution of the 1960s.[40] It laid the groundwork for future shows held by the Northwest Craftsmen Designers, another regional organization, which initiated annual exhibitions in all media beginning in 1956.

The Ceramic Nationals, which had been put on hold during the war years, resumed in 1946 in Syracuse, New York. The seventeenth Ceramic National reflected a flourishing, vibrant craft—still focused on traditional functional ware, but with a division for ceramic sculpture. Coverage in the *New York Times* the day of the National's opening (November 9, 1952) included illustrations of work by Carlton Ball, Frans Wildenhain, and Ka Kwong Hui.[41] Other reviewers emphasized the ways that ceramics were "useful" and "harmonious" in the modern home but rarely singled out individual potters or discussed them as artists. The craft–art dichotomy continued to hold sway.[42]

The National Council on Education in Ceramic Arts (NCECA) was developed by "forward-thinking ceramic artists" as a way of supporting ceramics teachers and artists and providing them with both a forum to promote their work and a professional organization to give them a sense

Ron Nagle, *Cup*, 1968. Glazed clay, plastic, wood, brass, and Plexiglas. Box: 2½ x 16⅝ x 8 in. (6.4 x 42.2 x 20.3 cm); cup: 3 x 4½ x 3¼ in. (7.6 x 11.4 x 8.3 cm). Museum of Arts and Design, Gift of the Johnson Wax Company, through the American Craft Council, 1977.

FIG. 8.7
Kiln Club exhibition, installation view, Washington, DC, 1956. Smithsonian Archives, History Division, SI.

of identity. Originally affiliated with the Ceramics Education Council of the American Ceramic Society, NCECA started out in 1961 with just seventeen ceramics educators and became an independent organization in 1966, virtually the first national organization devoted to a single medium.[43]

A national venue for ceramic art, unprejudiced by fine arts biases, was established in 1956, with the opening of the Museum of Contemporary Crafts in New York, its first acquisition being a bowl by Edwin and Mary Scheier **(CAT. 29)**.[44] The same year the museum hosted the Syracuse Ceramic National.[45] Over the next two decades, the museum featured many exhibitions of ceramics, including several solo shows—Beatrice Wood and David Weinrib in 1958, Fong Chow in 1960, Toshiko Takaezu in 1962, and the Natzlers in 1964, to name but a few.[46]

By the 1960s other museums began to expand boundaries by encompassing some of the new expressions in the medium. In 1960 Voulkos was given a solo show of paintings and ceramics at the Museum of Modern Art in New York, organized by MoMA's curator of painting and sculpture, Peter Selz, as part of the museum's New Talent series.[47] The exhibition marked the beginning of a newfound respect for ceramics on the part of the fine arts world.

By 1965 functional pottery was no longer the primary focus of avant-garde ceramics exhibitions. That year the Museum of Contemporary Crafts mounted *New Ceramic Forms* and reported that pop art and a hard-edge aesthetic had replaced abstract expressionism in ceramics. The organizers also lauded Voulkos as the show's most important influence, as all of the (male-only) artists with work

shown represented "the most ingenious regional adaptation of . . . Abstract Expressionism" that had yet appeared on the American art scene. The exhibition took the ceramic revolution public, cast a bright light on the Otis artists as its leaders, and legitimized ceramic art in the art world.[49]

Another 1967 show shed a very different light on new developments in California ceramics. *Funk Art*, which opened at the University Art Museum in Berkeley, came out of a loose art movement in the San Francisco Bay Area that was breaking away from the tenets of abstract expressionism. Funk was "hot not cool," influenced by Dada and surrealism, and defiant in its rejection of traditional aesthetics and techniques.[50] Peter Selz, the show's curator, saw Voulkos's pots as Funk because they were useless.[51] Arneson was represented by *No Return* **(FIG. 8.8)**, a ceramic bottle from 1961 that prefigured Andy Warhol's silk-screened Coke bottles of 1962. David Gilhooly's frog-filled work and Arneson's china-painted sculpture were clearly Funk, but Price's hard-edged, brightly colored work was part of the highly crafted Los Angeles "fetish-finish" look. Melchert's expressionistic vessels had evolved into increasingly conceptual sculptural clay objects and installations.[52] Like *Abstract Expressionist Ceramics*, however, *Funk Art* positioned ceramics in mainstream art and proclaimed ceramists to be artists.[53]

In 1969 *Objects: USA* featured some of the most important ceramics objects of the decade, including Melchert's *Leg Pot #1* **(CAT. 122)** and Autio's *Button Pot*.[54] The selection was not meant to represent American ceramics as a whole but to focus on the "newest directions and inventions of the creative leaders" in the ceramics world.[55] With the end of the 1960s in sight, the ceramic revolution was not over. The radical innovators who had emerged in the 1950s had stepped into a national spotlight and had dramatically shifted the parameters for both teaching and imagining ceramic art in America. These revolutionary figures—with Peter Voulkos enshrined as their George Washington—had made strides toward achieving recognition as artists rather than as craftsmen, never questioning the assumption that being an artist was superior in some way to being a craftsman. For all their glamour and showmanship, however, the radicals were still far outnumbered nationwide by America's counterrevolutionary ceramists: the traditionalists, for whom vessels, as well as the age-old techniques of the studio potter, were still sacred. As the *Craft Horizons* reviewer of *Objects: USA* noted: "Tradition works, and it has its reasons."[56]

on view were either his students or students of his students. By now the inhibiting, old-fashioned restrictions on the use of clay had been "destroyed" by Voulkos and others. The rejection of traditional ceramics techniques, such as throwing on the wheel and even slab-building in favor of sculpting, was hailed. China paints used as surface color on a whiteware body for brilliance were central to much of the work. Pop culture influences—from car culture to photography, seen in the use of auto paint and photoscreen transfers—were heralded as signs of the "superiority of the artist's idea over any considerations of the propriety of the materials." These works were presented by the museum as "representative of the best traditions of craftsmanship."[48] Voulkos, Nagle, Melchert, Arneson, and the rest of the iconoclasts of the ceramic tradition had overthrown the domestic inclination of the potter's art and had instead discovered an exciting and fertile medium through which to explore modern artistic expression.

The pursuit of art in ceramics continued throughout the decade. The 1967 exhibition *Abstract Expressionist Ceramics*, organized by art critic John Coplans at the University of California, Irvine, was a watershed moment in modern ceramic history. Coplans declared that the work

1 Garth Clark, *American Ceramics 1876 to the Present* (New York: Abbeville Press, 1987), 141.

2 Elaine Levin, *The History of American Ceramics: 1607 to the Present: From Pipkins and Bean Pots to Contemporary Forms* (New York: Harry N. Abrams, Inc., 1988), 193.

3 Clark, *American Ceramics*, 102.

4 Ibid., 84. See also Martha Drexler Lynn, *Clay Today: Contemporary Ceramists and Their Work* (Los Angeles, Los Angeles County Museum of Art, 1990), 96. Lukens, like other ceramists born during Queen Victoria's reign, including Carl Walters and Henry Varnum Poor, witnessed the rise of art pottery firsthand, as well as that of modernism in design and art in the early twentieth century; see Janet Kardon, ed., *Craft in the Machine Age 1920–1945: The History of Twentieth-Century American Craft* (New York: American Craft Museum and Harry N. Abrams, 1995).

5 Clark, *American Ceramics*, 308.

6 In 1967 Cranbrook gave Grotell a retrospective exhibition that traveled to the Museum of Contemporary Crafts in New York, where it was titled *Maija Grotell—Objects* (June 21–September 8, 1968); *Maija Grotell,* exh. cat. (Bloomfield Hills, MI: Cranbrook Academy of Art, 1967).

7 Clark, *American Ceramics*, 100. Bernard Leach, U.S. itinerary, 1950: the New York State Ceramic Society; the School at the Museum of Fine Arts, Boston; the New York State College of Ceramics at Alfred University; the Toledo Museum, Ohio State University; Detroit Institute of Art; University of Michigan in Ann Arbor; Wichita Art Association; and the American Ceramic Society, where he received the Charles Fergus Binns Medal (itinerary courtesy of the New York State College of Ceramics, College Archives, Alfred, NY). He also traveled to California, Seattle, and Washington, DC, that year. For further information on these momentous voyages, see Emmanuel Cooper, *Bernard Leach: Life and Work* (New Haven: Published for the Paul Mellon Centre for Studies in British Art by Yale University Press, 2003); and Bernard Leach, *Beyond East and West: Memoirs, Portraits, and Essays* (New York: Watson-Guptill Publications, 1978).

8 Leach, Hamada, and Yanagi gave seminars at Black Mountain College; the St. Paul Gallery in Minnesota; the Chouinard Gallery in Los Angeles; Mills College in Oakland, CA; the University of Hawaii, as well as demonstrations at the Archie Bray Foundation in Montana. The group gave lectures and presentations at the Corcoran Gallery and the Potters Guild in Washington, DC; New York University; the Worcester Art Museum, the University of Michigan; the Museum of International Folk Art in Santa Fe; the Los Angeles County Museum; San Francisco Museum of Fine Art; University of California (whether USC or UCLA is not clear); as well as to groups of Japanese living in America, Buddhist groups and "tea lovers"; see "The American Journey with Yanagi and Hamada: October 7, 1952–February 17, 1953," Bernard Leach's personal diary of his 1952–53 travels in the United States, n.p., Charles M. Harder Papers, MC 8, Courtesy of the New York State College of Ceramics Archives, Alfred, NY. Another Japanese artist, Kitaoji Rosanjin, a legendary restaurant owner turned potter, toured the country on his own in 1954, lecturing and exhibiting, including participation in the New York exhibition, *Japanese Pottery* (MoMA Exh. #557, April 29–May 21, 1954).

9 See the December 14, 1952, issue of the *New Mexican* (Santa Fe), B3, with photographs by Laura Gilpin documenting the visit. Bernard Leach described the occasion in his diary: "We have driven hundreds of miles on Indian Pueblos, San Domingo, Taos and at San Ildefonso [and] were lucky enough to arrive just when Maria Martinez (the famous potter) was about to rake out of the ash heap a batch of 2 doz pots. Black & shining from under horse dung ash, adobe wall behind & the arid 'pinole' dotted landscape behind that again. She was friendly and later came in to the International Museum of Crafts to our demonstrations and lectures dressed in her Indian best blankets, necklaces of coral, jet, silver & turquoise. I went and talked to her whilst Hamada was throwing & found her lit up and all barriers down. Her son Popovi Da came & called next morning and we only wished that we had more time to visit"; Bernard Leach, diary of his 1952–53 travels in the United States, n.p., Charles M. Harder Papers.

10 William Morris, *News from Nowhere* (Boston: Roberts Brothers, 1890). Morris was a man of contradictions as a socialist intellectual born into money, who decorated for the wealthy. See Doreen Bolger Burke et al., *In Pursuit of Beauty: Americans and the Aesthetic Movement*, (New York: Metropolitan Museum of Art and Rizzoli International Publications, 1987), 455–57.

11 Levin, *History of American Ceramics*, 181. See Michael Komanecky, *American Potters: Mary and Edwin Scheier* (Manchester, NH: Currier Gallery of Art, 1993).

12 Rhodes's books on technical aspects of pottery were groundbreaking: *Clay and Glazes for the Potter* (Philadelphia: Chilton Book Co., 1957) is now in its 3rd ed. (revised by Robin Hopper); Rhodes also helped to demystify the firing process in *Kilns: Design, Construction and Operation* (Philadelphia: Chilton Book Co., 1968).

13 Levin, *History of American Ceramics*, 175.

14 Clark, *American Ceramics*, 73. Although association with MoMA added prestige to a ceramic artist's résumé, it is the author's position that the Ceramic Nationals were more important in the development of ceramics after World War II than either The Metropolitan Museum of Art or the Museum of Modern Art.

15 Clark, *American Ceramics*, 251.

16 Levin, *History of American Ceramics*, 177.

17 Mary Emma Harris, *The Arts at Black Mountain College* (Cambridge, MA: The MIT Press, 2002).

18 Martha Drexler Lynn, *Clay Today—Contemporary Ceramicists and Their Work: A Catalogue of the Howard and Gwen Laurie Smits Collection at the Los Angeles County Museum of Art* (Los Angeles: Los Angeles County Museum of Art; San Francisco: Chronicle Books, 1990), 152.

19 Ibid., 89.

20 Levin, *History of American Ceramics*, 188.

21 Claire Noland, obituary of Susan Peterson, *Los Angeles Times*, April 12, 2009.

22 Peterson wrote the first biography of Shoji Hamada in 1974 as well as important books on Native American women potters. See Susan Peterson, *Shoji Hamada: A Potter's Way and Work* (Tokyo: Kodansha International, 1974); Peterson, *The Living Tradition of Maria Martinez* (Tokyo: Kodansha International; distributed through Harper and Row, New York, 1977); Noland, obituary.

23 Levin, *History of American Ceramics*, 199; "American Ceramics Since 1950," in Barbara Perry, ed., *American Ceramics: The Collection of Everson Museum of Art* (New York: Rizzoli International Publications, 1989), 201.

24 Exhibition brochure, MAD archives. An exhibition of Native American potters was held simultaneously—among the artists were Lucy Lewis (Acoma), Maria Martinez (San Ildefonso), and Sadie Adams (Hopi).

25 Rose Slivka, "The New Ceramic Presence," *CH* 21 (July/August 1961), 30-37.

26 Matthew Kangas and Jim Leedy, *Jim Leedy: Artist Across Boundaries* (Kansas City, MO: Kansas City Art Institute, 2000), 40–41.

27 "The Bray at 50," *AC* 61 (April/May 2001), 56–61.

28 Ibid., 61.

29 Levin, *History of American Ceramics*, 201.

30 Ibid.

31 Clark, *American Ceramics*, 305. See also Betty Freudenheim, "Voulkos's Ceramic Pots: Total Involvement in Clay," *New York Times*, April 17, 1986, C7.

32 Clark, *American Ceramics*, 99.

33 Soldner first read about Japanese raku in Bernard Leach, *A Potter's Book*

(London: Faber and Faber limited, 1940).

34 Levin, *History of American Ceramics*, 216, 217.

35 Clark, *American Ceramics*, 120–21.

36 Ibid., 129.

37 Levin, *History of American Ceramics*, 214.

38 Clark, *American Ceramics*, 300.

39 The first exhibition: *Exhibition of Ceramic Art: The Kiln Club of Washington* (Washington, DC: National Collection of Fine Arts, 1950). The Kiln Club continues to hold juried exhibitions at the Scope Gallery in Alexandria, Virginia.

40 "Exhibit to Be First of Its Kind in N.W.," *Seattle Times*, February 17, 1952; "Club Exhibit Spotlights Ceramic Talent," *Seattle Times*, March 23, 1952, 92.

41 Betty Pepis, "Character in Clay," *New York Times*, November 9, 1952, SM46.

42 See also Cynthia Kellogg, "Use of Ceramics in Home Is Shown," which referred to a "Renaissance" in ceramic art (*New York Times*, February 4, 1953, 30); see also Kellogg, "Whimsy Marks Ceramics Showings, with Some Bowls Resembling Birds," *New York Times*, May 18, 1953, 24; Kellogg, "New Vases Suited to be Decoration," *New York Times*, June 16, 1953, 22. The latter mentioned the Natzlers as well as Pablo Picasso's pottery and that of Fong Chow, who was listed as a "student at Alfred University." These articles promoted retail outlets such as Bonniers, but also the New York Society of Ceramic Arts, which sponsored an exhibition at the American Museum of Natural History.

43 NCECA website, http://nceca .net/static/about.php.

44 *Forty Years*, 15.

45 Ibid., 19.

46 "Exhibitions 1956–1982," *American Craft Museum 25* (New York: American Craft Council, 1981), n.p.

47 Clark, *American Ceramics*, 305. *New Talent*, February 2–March 13, 1960, Museum of Modern Art, New York.

48 Quotations from exhibition brochure, *New Ceramic Forms*, MAD files.

49 Clark, *American Ceramics*, 118.

50 Peter Selz, "Notes on Funk," in *Funk* (Berkeley, California: University Art Museum, University of California, Berkeley, 1967), 3. The term *funk* has its roots in African American popular music of the 1960s. Selz may not have coined the term in relation to art, but he appears to have been the first to use it in print in connection to ceramics.

51 Selz, "Notes on Funk," 3–6.

52 Clark, *American Ceramics*, 283.

53 Ibid., 118.

54 Ibid., 129.

55 Robert Hilton Simmons, "Objects: USA, The Johnson Wax Collection of Contemporary Crafts," *CH 29* (November/December, 1969), 25–27, 66; Clark, *American Ceramics*, 129.

56 "Objects: USA," 66.

120

MICHAEL FRIMKESS
Things Ain't What They Used To Be, 1965
STONEWARE AND CHINA PAINT
37¾ IN. (95.9 CM); DIAM. 13 IN. (33 CM)
MUSEUM OF ARTS AND DESIGN,
GIFT OF THE JOHNSON WAX COMPANY, THROUGH
THE AMERICAN CRAFT COUNCIL, 1977

121

DANIEL RHODES

Vessel, 1967

STONEWARE

42½ X 21 X 17½ IN. (108 X 53.3 X 44.5 CM)

MUSEUM OF ARTS AND DESIGN, GIFT OF THE JOHNSON WAX
COMPANY, THROUGH THE AMERICAN CRAFT COUNCIL, 1977

122

JAMES MELCHERT

Leg Pot I, 1962

STONEWARE, LEAD, AND CLOTH INLAY

11 X 32 X 13 IN. (27.9 X 81.3 X 33 CM)

MUSEUM OF ARTS AND DESIGN, GIFT OF THE JOHNSON WAX
COMPANY, THROUGH THE AMERICAN CRAFT COUNCIL, 1977

123
F. CARLTON BALL
Untitled, c. 1965
STONEWARE
13 X 13¾ X 8¾ IN. (33 X 34.9 X 22.2 CM)
FORREST L. MERRILL COLLECTION

124
LEZA McVEY
Ceramic Form No. 33, 34, 1951
STONEWARE
LEFT, 10⅛ X 7 X 5 IN. (25.7 X 17.8 X 12.7 CM);
RIGHT, 16 X 6 X 5 IN. (40.6 X 15.2 X 12.7 CM)
EVERSON MUSEUM OF ART, SYRACUSE, PURCHASE
PRIZE, 16TH CERAMIC NATIONAL 1951, GIFT OF HARSHAW
CHEMICAL COMPANY, 52.635.1-2

125, 126

WARREN MacKENZIE

ALIX MacKENZIE

Two Vases, 1959

STONEWARE

LEFT: H. 8½ IN. (21 CM), DIAM. 3½ IN. (8.9 CM)

RIGHT: H. 7 IN. (17.8 CM), DIAM. 5½ IN. (14 CM)

MINNESOTA MUSEUM OF AMERICAN ART

127

KATHERINE CHOY

Bowl, 1958

STONEWARE

4¼ X 15 X 14¾ IN. (10.8 X 38.1 X 37.5 CM)

MUSEUM OF ARTS AND DESIGN, GIFT OF AILEEN OSBORN WEBB,

THROUGH THE AMERICAN CRAFT COUNCIL, 1958

128
MARIA MARTINEZ
POPOVI DA
Bowl with Feather Design, 1968
TERRACOTTA
H. 2½ IN. (6.4 CM); DIAM. 12¼ IN. (31.1 CM)
MUSEUM OF ARTS AND DESIGN,
GIFT OF THE JOHNSON WAX COMPANY, THROUGH
THE AMERICAN CRAFT COUNCIL, 1977

129
KAREN KARNES
Double Vase, 1951
EARTHENWARE
9½ X 13⅞ IN. (24.1 X 35.2 CM)
EVERSON MUSEUM OF ART, PURCHASE
PRIZE GIVEN BY LORD & TAYLOR,
16TH CERAMIC NATIONAL, 1951, 52.624.2

130

MARGUERITE WILDENHAIN
Square and Textured Vase, 1966
STONEWARE
10⅞ X 8 X 8 IN. (27.6 X 20.3 X 20.3 CM)
MUSEUM OF ARTS AND DESIGN,
GIFT OF THE JOHNSON WAX COMPANY, THROUGH
THE AMERICAN CRAFT COUNCIL, 1977

131

GERTRUD NATZLER

OTTO NATZLER
Large Bowl (H331), 1956
EARTHENWARE
H. 13¾ (34.9CM); DIAM. 17¾ IN. (45.1CM)
MUSEUM OF ARTS AND DESIGN,
GIFT OF THE JOHNSON WAX COMPANY, THROUGH
THE AMERICAN CRAFT COUNCIL, 1977

132

JERRY ROTHMAN

Sky Pot, 1960

STONEWARE

28½ X 25 X 9 IN. (72.4 X 63.5 X 22.86 CM)

SCRIPPS COLLEGE, CLAREMONT, CA.

GIFT OF MR. AND MRS. FRED MARER

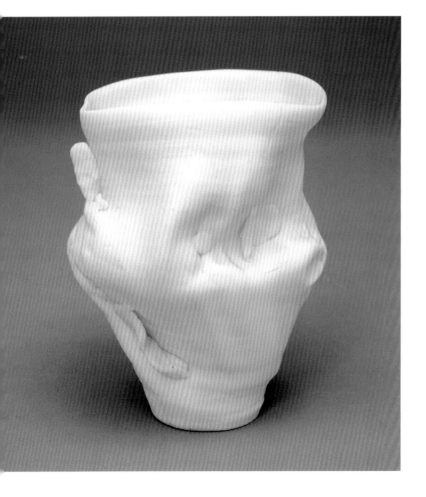

133

RUDOLF STAFFEL

Vase, 1968

PORCELAIN

7⅛ X 5½ X 6¼ IN. (18.1 X 14 X 15.9 CM)

MUSEUM OF ARTS AND DESIGN,

GIFT OF THE JOHNSON WAX COMPANY, THROUGH

THE AMERICAN CRAFT COUNCIL, 1977

134

HENRY TADAKI TAKEMOTO

First Kumu, 1959

STONEWARE

H. 21¾ IN. (55.2 CM), DIAM. 22 IN. (55.9 CM)

SCRIPPS COLLEGE, CLAREMONT, CA.

GIFT OF MR. AND MRS. FRED MARER

135

WIN NG

Branch Vase, 1961

EARTHENWARE

30½ X 17 X 6 IN. (77.5 X 43.2 X 15.2 CM)

MUSEUM OF ARTS AND DESIGN,

GIFT OF MR. AND MRS. JACKSON BURKE, THROUGH

THE AMERICAN CRAFT COUNCIL, 1961

136

JUN KANEKO

Tegata, 1966

STONEWARE

19 X 20 X 5 IN. (48.3 X 50.8 X 12.7 CM)

EVERSON MUSEUM OF ART, PURCHASE PRIZE
GIVEN BY ARCADIAN LANDSCAPING COMPANY,
24TH CERAMIC NATIONAL, 1966, 68.29

137

PAUL SOLDNER

Vase, c. 1964

STONEWARE

H. 8¾ (22.2 CM); DIAM. 8½ IN. (21.6 CM)

MUSEUM OF ARTS AND DESIGN, GIFT OF THE
N.Y. STATE COUNCIL TRAVELING EXHIBITION, THROUGH
THE AMERICAN CRAFT COUNCIL, 1981

138

PETER VOULKOS
Vee, 1958
STONEWARE, SAND, IRON AND
COBALT BRUSH DRAWING
89½ X 57³⁄₁₆ X 39⅜ IN. (227.3 X 145.3 X 100.1 CM)
FINE ARTS MUSEUMS OF SAN FRANCISCO,
GIFT FROM THE ESTATE OF
JOHN LOWELL JONES AND CHARLOTTE
JOHNSON JONES 2004.36.1

CHAPTER 9

Accommodating Modernism: Midcentury Silversmithing and Enameling

BRUCE METCALF

POSTWAR SILVERSMITHING AND JEWELRY MAKING followed very different trajectories. Even though most American metalsmiths knew how to make both jewelry and hollowware, the two fields had sharply divided contexts. The segregation was even more acute for enameling, an entirely separate craft that was regarded as being more closely related to painting or ceramics.[1]

The techniques necessary to make a vessel in metal are more difficult to master than the basic skills needed to make jewelry. The barrier to entry into this field is higher; the aspiring silversmith must practice for years before achieving a high degree of control. Compared to a beginning jeweler, who might use a few simple tools, the silversmith must have a wide variety of stakes and hammers, requiring a substantial capital expenditure. In addition, a single piece of hollowware demands a significant investment of planning and time: the solo silversmith needs several weeks—sometimes more—to complete a single teapot. The functionalist credo of the times, the substantial investment in technique and tools, and the limited volume of work that a single smith could produce made silversmiths conservative and less willing to experiment. Failure was costly, and therefore a casual approach was uncommon. Until the late 1960s, smiths were less willing to innovate than jewelers.

Silversmiths could not afford to follow the trends that jewelers embraced. The fusing technique employed by Sam Kramer, Ibram Lassaw, and many others could not generate a useful hollow form. Alexander Calder's favorite process, forging, could be used to make flatware, but it is difficult to forge a hollow form bigger than a ladle. Nor were silversmiths quite as adventurous in applying non-traditional materials such as plastics and found objects. As a result, works by silversmiths rarely showed the influences of surrealism, expressionism, and primitivism that were so common in 1940s ands '50s studio jewelry.

In the 1940s good information and training in metalworking was difficult to access. A few vocational-education manuals contained rudimentary descriptions, but they were laughably incomplete, and only a few skilled smiths were teaching immediately after the war. Arthur Neville Kirk taught at Wayne State College, Detroit, about 1946; Peter Müller-Munk taught industrial design at Carnegie Institute of Technology (now Carnegie Mellon University), and both Laurits Christian Eichner and Adda Husted-Anderson taught at the Craft Students League in New York City. It is not clear whether any of them actually gave instruction in silver-smithing, but there were some small silversmithing shops still in operation after the war. The Kalo Shop in Chicago stayed open until 1970, and Allan Adler took over his father-in-law Porter Blanchard's shop in Hollywood in 1941. Alphonse LaPaglia worked for the Georg Jensen store in New York City during the war years.[2] The craft had declined by this time, however, as a larger number of smiths either died or closed their shops during the 1930s and '40s.[3]

The American silver industry had been decimated by the Depression and further diminished during the war, but what remained was a repository of craft knowledge. For the budding silversmith before the war, the only way to learn trade knowledge was to work in a silverware factory over an extended period of time, submitting to the values of the employer. The industry tended to be conservative, favoring styles from the American colonial period. Some silver companies, such as Reed & Barton, embraced modern design in the 1950s when the success of Scandinavian design became increasingly difficult to ignore. The new generation of studio metalworkers after the war usually rejected historicism, and many avoided the commercial world. As a result, the postwar generation of aspiring silversmiths rarely looked to the trade for knowledge and skills.

At the end of the war, studio silversmiths faced an entirely different set of problems than jewelers. Silversmithing is closely tied to utility. The names of most hollow metal forms denote their function: teapots, coffeepots, creamers, sugars, pitchers, chalices, and so on.

In the modernist ethos that came to dominate much thinking about craft in the 1940s and '50s, physical function was thought to determine the basic form. Ornament, when used, was expected to enhance the form and never interfere with the function. In 1957 metalsmith and industrial designer Arthur Pulos explained this position: "In hollow ware and flatware . . . only after functional needs have been imaginatively and effectively met should the piece be refined in form and detail. . . . Although good form can be its own ornament, additional enrichment if felt necessary must enhance rather than destroy."[4] In essence, Pulos was articulating the credo of "good design."

"Good design" was tied to the Museum of Modern Art's messianic promotion of an abstract, useful, and apolitical design style. The icon of postwar functionalism was the molded plywood LCW chair by Charles and Ray Eames. It was comfortable and undecorated, its material clearly exposed and its form almost as abstract as biomorphic sculpture. Not surprisingly, early postwar silversmithing followed this model: useful, undecorated, and organic in form, with the silver itself front-and-center.

The influence of Scandinavian silversmithing was also very strong, although some smiths would deny it. Margret Craver recounts how, when she returned from training with Swedish smith Baron Erik Fleming, her work was described as looking Scandinavian. She responded by saying that it was only contemporary.[5] Still, a distinctive Scandinavian style had appeared by 1935, characterized by smooth, rounded forms, polished surfaces, almost total absence of decoration, and parts that flowed into one another. Applied molding (to strengthen edges) was seen as backward—better to thicken the metal edge by hammering it. And asymmetry was highly valued, in large part because such irregular forms were difficult to achieve by machine. The leader of the Danish silver industry was the Georg Jensen company, particularly in the brilliant designs of Henning Koppel.

After an initial flirtation with contemporary English silversmithing, American studio smiths enthusiastically accepted the Scandinavian style.[6] Other modes of hollowware design—the rigid geometric solids and angular asymmetries of the Bauhaus, the blocky forms of French art deco, and the stepped edges and linear "speed whiskers" of geometric modernism—never found much favor after the war.

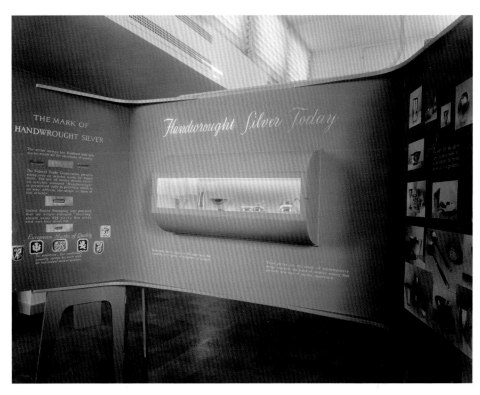

FIG. 9.1
Form in Handwrought Silver, installation view, the Metropolitan Museum of Art, New York (December 16, 1949–January 29, 1950). Courtesy of The Metropolitan Museum of Art, New York.

There are three basic metal-forming techniques: sinking (hammering thin sheet metal into a shallow depression), raising (hammering thin metal over a series of specially shaped anvils, called "stakes"), and stretching (hammering thick metal until it balloons outward). Each technique requires training. By 1945 most American jewelry teachers had very limited experience making hollowware, and those who wanted to learn silversmithing had few options in the United States.

Into this picture stepped Margret Craver, who almost single-handedly jump-started American studio silversmithing.[7] Craver had studied with a number of individual silversmiths in the 1930s, including Arthur Stone in Gardner, Massachusetts, and Baron Erik Fleming in Stockholm. In 1944, underwritten by the New York metal-refining company Handy & Harman, she set up the Hospital Service Program, which used metalworking as a therapy for wounded soldiers. (Ironically, she could not use brass and copper because of wartime shortages, but silver was readily available.) After the war, she organized a series of five summer workshops to reintroduce silversmithing techniques to American educators. The Handy & Harman workshops offered hands-on instruction and solid information to would-be silversmiths. In doing so, they changed the course of the craft.

The hollowware made during the Handy & Harman workshops tended to be simple and perhaps a bit timid, befitting the educational nature of the experience.

A small silver bowl, designed by Craver and made by British metalsmith William Ernest Bennett in 1947, is perfectly symmetrical, with plain decorative molding applied to the foot and rim (CAT. 155). Handy & Harman, under Craver's direction, filmed the making of this bowl, called *Handwrought Silver*, and distributed it to schools nationwide. An exhibition was held at The Metropolitan Museum of Art, New York (FIG. 9.1), and instructional booklets were published.[8] Very quickly, as American smiths gained experience, they also gained confidence. Robert J. King's *Carafe* from 1952, made only five years after the first Handy & Harman workshop, is far different from Craver's bowl (FIG. 9.2). King's

piece has a pronounced asymmetry and narrow neck, both difficult technical feats to achieve.

There were other lineages as well.[9] Richard Thomas picked up silversmithing at the Cranbrook Academy of Art during a brief study with the German-trained Hermann Gurfinkel. Later, as head of Cranbrook's department of metalsmithing, Thomas taught some of the country's most talented students in the 1950s and '60s.

Other smiths taught themselves. Impatient with the modest abilities of his instructors at the Cleveland School of Art (now the Cleveland Institute of Art) in the 1930s, Hudson Roysher learned the raising technique for himself and became a very skilled smith. Philip Fike was also self-taught in this area. When he was offered a teaching job in 1953, he used one of the Handy & Harman brochures to learn raising.

Although a few Americans had studied with Europeans, it was not until after the war that European expertise became more widely available to American silversmiths.[10] Two skilled Danish-trained silversmiths made important contributions: John Prip and Hans Christensen. Prip arrived from Copenhagen in 1948 (on the same boat as woodworker Tage Frid) to teach at the School for American Craftsmen (SAC), then in Alfred, New York.[11] While he had been born in New York to a family of Danish silversmiths, he had been trained in Copenhagen. At first Prip hewed to the functionalist line. His "onion" teapot, a prototype later named *Dimension* by Reed & Barton (FIG. 9.3), shows how closely he paralleled developments in Denmark: a Henning Koppel design for Georg Jensen from the same year is remarkably similar.[12]

Prip left SAC in 1954, determined to work with industry. He designed for the Hickok Jewelry Manufacturing Company in Rochester, New York, along with Ron Pearson, and later worked as a craftsman-designer for Reed & Barton in Taunton, Massachusetts. The primary market for the silver industry was not hollowware, but flatware—place settings and serving implements. The Scandinavian style eliminated the decorative flourishes on the handles of sterling flatware and focused instead on plain handles, streamlined forms for bowls of spoons and knife blades, and elegant transitions between the two. Essentially, these were created by forging. A skilled smith could generate a prototype that was better resolved than a design on paper, simply because he was working directly in the material. Silversmiths designed some of the best flatware of the 1950s

FIG. 9.2

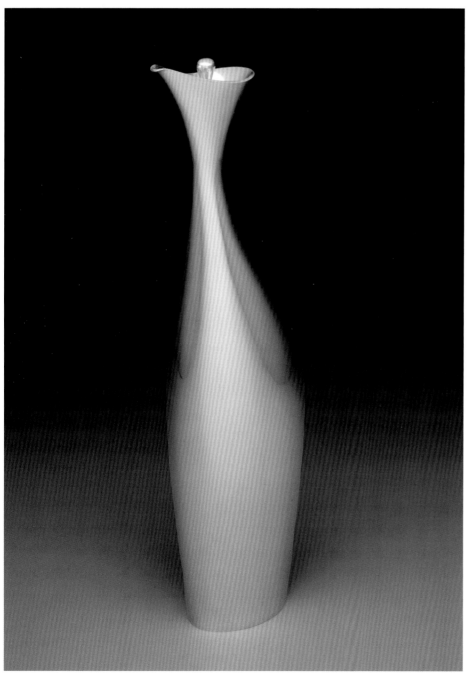

Robert J. King, *Carafe*, 1952–53. Sterling silver. 14½ x 5 x 3½ in. (36.83 x 12.7 x 8.89 cm) overall. Dallas Museum of Art, the Jewel Stern American Silver Collection, Gift of Jewel Stern in honor of Robert J. King; 2002.29.101.A-B. This hand-raised prototype was exhibited at the 1964 New York World's Fair but never put into production.

FIG. 9.3

John Prip, "Onion" teapot (prototype, later named *Dimension*), 1954. Sterling silver, ebony, and rattan. 6¼ x 10⅞ x 7¼ in. (15.8 x 27.5 x 18.5 cm). Museum of Fine Arts, Boston, Gift of Stephen and Betty Jane Andrus, 1995; 1995.137.

FIG. 9.4

Fred Miller at the bench, c. 1950. Photograph courtesy John Paul Miller.

and '60s, among them *Dimension* (1960) and *Tapestry* (1964) by Prip for Reed & Barton, and *Contour* (1950) by Robert King for Towle.[13] Prip did not confine himself to designing elegant functional silver, however. He credits ceramist Frans Wildenhain with proving that a craft could be more than a trade, that it could be invested with a personal vision. From the mid-1950s, Prip was the most inventive and wide-ranging of all American silversmiths. In *Shield with Horns* (CAT. 149), for example, he used metalsmithing techniques to make a radically new sculpture. He also experimented with a series of delightful boxes and tea strainers, and worked in materials as diverse as cast pewter and carved stone.

The other Danish silversmith, Hans Christensen,[14] replaced Prip at SAC in 1954 and taught there until his death in 1983. Christensen was extraordinarily skillful, having executed prototypes for Georg Jensen's designers in Copenhagen. Many Jensen designs were spun on a lathe, and Christensen could justify hand-production only if there was an element of asymmetry. In his design for *Coffee Pot* of 1958 (CAT. 140), he had begun to move away from the familiar Danish style. While sculpted, asymmetrical, and fully functional, it also has an unconventional handle emerging from the top. Christensen was a rigorous teacher, and many of the best young American silversmiths learned their craft from him, including Bernard Bernstein, Michael Jerry, Ronald

Senungetuk, Olaf Skoogfors, and Joe Reyes Apodaca Jr. As a teacher he was less open-minded than Prip and was reluctant to allow his students to enamel on silver. He also discouraged casting as a technique because the work was done in wax, not metal.

Frederick Miller had attended the second Handy & Harman workshop, at which Baron Erik Fleming demonstrated stretching.[15] The great advantage of stretching metal is that it is comparatively easy to make an irregular shape, avoiding a form that could be made by machine. Stretching is a process of thinning the middle of a thick sheet of metal, which then bellies out. The edge is not thinned, so it retains its original outline. If the outline is irregular at the outset, it remains so at the end. Miller specialized in asymmetry, as demonstrated by his *Bottle* (CAT. 148), which shows an organic irregularity in all views.

Miller departed from pure Scandinavian modern style in several ways. He decorated his silver with engraved lines that were emphatically not functional. The transitional elements that separate the feet from the body on some of his forms are engraved with simple repeated lines. Later, Miller would occasionally run deeply engraved lines across his stretched forms, accenting the form itself and defining the surface. Miller also had a quiet sense of humor about his materials. Traditionally, insulating materials such as wood and ivory were used to make handles and sometimes feet for teapots and coffeepots. Wood

insulates from heat, so the pots could be lifted without fear of scalding or could be set on tables without damage to the surface. But in many of Miller's free-form vessels, where there is no need to protect tables or hands from the contents of the bowl, the feet are nonetheless capped with carved ebony. Such a sly substitution would have been unthinkable in Danish silver at the time.

Miller taught at the Cleveland Institute of Art from 1947 until his retirement in 1975, and many generations of students learned the stretching process from him **(FIG. 9.4)**. His most notable student was John Marshall, who carried the asymmetrical stretched form to almost baroque extremes.

As the fifties ended, the Scandinavian modern approach was increasingly criticized. In 1958 a disgruntled young craftsman remarked that much craft from that decade "could have been made by rather clever robots."[16] Ronald Pearson, writing in 1962 about the work in the American Craft Museum's *Young Americans* exhibition,

FIG. 9.5
Michael Jerry, *Coffee Service*, c. 1959. Pewter, cane. Coffee pot with lid: 12¼ x 5¼ x 2⅜ in. (31.0 x 13.3 x 6.2 cm); sugar bowl with lid: 3⅝ x 6⅛ x 5¾ in. (9.2 x 15.4 x 14.6 cm); creamer with lid: 4⅝ x 4¼ x 2⅜ in. (11.7 x 10.8 x 6 cm); spoon ¼ x 6⅛ x 1½ in. (0.6 x 15.4 x 3.8 cm). Brooklyn Museum of Art, Modernism Benefit Fund; 1993 158.1-4.

suggested that, "perhaps the Scandinavian influence now tends to be a restraining influence on American craftsmen. Whatever the reasons, silver design today seems inhibited and unimpressive when compared with creative work in other fields."[17] There was a note of dissatisfaction with "good design," and a simultaneous ambition to make more expressive objects.

By the late 1950s, the flowing organic forms of Henning Koppel no longer dominated Scandinavian silver design. Michael Jerry's pewter coffee set **(FIG. 9.5)** shows how American designers began to reject the doctrine of pure usefulness and to search for idiosyncratic forms that did more than efficiently answer a need. Forced by economic necessity to move from limited-production luxury objects to mass manufacturing, Scandinavian silver became more accommodating to machine processes. Forms became more elongated, more geometric, with straight lines and creases. Americans followed suit.

One of the venues in which these stylistic changes were most visible was the Sterling Today Competition, an annual contest sponsored by a trade group, the Sterling Silversmiths' Guild of America. Initially open to professionals and students alike, it was later limited just to students. To stimulate entries and perhaps to foster a spirit of experimentation, the guild refunded every student for the value of the silver in their entry. The guild also sent glossy black-and-white prints of the winners' designs to every school that competed, creating great buzz for students about to enter the job market. Making elaborate silver objects for the Sterling Competition became an annual rite of spring for metalsmithing students.

The first competition was held in 1957. Over the years, designs became increasingly removed from the dictates of functionality and more concerned with visual drama. Coffeepots and teapots were elevated on stems, a form perhaps more appropriate for chalices. Teapots also grew unnaturally tall. Sharp edges appeared. Simplicity became the exception, not the rule. Val Link's 1967 award-winning teapot typifies the silver design of the era **(FIG. 9.6)**. The craftsmanship is excellent, the surface flawless. The body is held aloft by a conical foot, giving the design both lightness and high drama. A single hard edge flows from spout to handle. The lid is placed off-center, and it tilts toward the spout. The handle is positioned for maximum visual impact, not ease of use. Like many other Sterling Silver Design prizewinners, it is more beautiful than practical.

By the late 1960s, dozens of art schools and universities offered sound training in silversmithing techniques, and during those early years, an MFA in the field was a virtual guarantee of employment. Many silversmiths became teachers at the new jewelry and metalsmithing programs throughout the country. Some went to work for the industry, becoming designers for Oneida, Gorham, Wallace, and other manufacturers. A few taught and ran silversmithing businesses at the same time. Kurt Matzdorf, for instance, began his long teaching career at the State University of New York, New Paltz, in 1957, all the while producing Jewish ceremonial silver for clients throughout the Hudson River Valley. Similarly, Vincent Ferrini spent much of his career teaching at Boston University while maintaining an independent studio practice.[18] All in all, the period from 1955 to 1965 represents the heyday of American silversmithing.

However, it was not to last. Americans no longer desired domestic silver the way previous generations had. Few households could afford servants to polish sterling silverware, and in a culture that valued convenience, the inevitable tarnish on silver seemed an annoyance. Newly informal lifestyles made the rituals that required silverware, like teas and large formal dinners, seem old-fashioned. The demand for custom-made silver, already modest, continued to decline. As for American silver manufacturers, they could not match the low labor costs of overseas factories. In desperation, the industry abandoned

contemporary design and tried to retrench with colonial revival styles. The strategy failed, and by the late 1980s, the industry had collapsed.

Young silversmiths, perhaps anticipating the drastic changes to come, proposed a new approach in the late 1960s. The idea of repudiating function in favor of sculptural form had already been embraced in ceramics, textiles, and furniture making. Alma Eikerman, who had been a student at the 1948 Handy & Harman workshop, encouraged her students to think of hollowware in formal terms, as arrangements of mass and void in space. When Eikerman received a grant from the Carnegie Foundation in 1968 to buy sheets of brass, copper, and silver for her students, her classes put her teaching into practice.[19] Some created raised asymmetrical vessels, while the more daring constructed their work out of shaped pieces. Marjorie Schick's *Open Pot Form* (FIG. 9.7) aroused considerable comment because she did not solder a bottom on the form. Schick had opened the door to nonfunctional hollow forms—objects that laid claim to being both craft and sculpture.[20]

ENAMELING

Studio enameling in America first flowered in the Boston area under the influence of Massachusetts-born Laurin Hovey Martin, who studied at the Birmingham School of Art in England, as well as with English Arts and Crafts enamelist Alexander Fisher. Upon his return,

FIG. 9.6
Val Link, *Teapot*, 1967. Silver, ebony. Dim.: 9 x 11 in. (22.9 x 27.9 cm). Private collection.

FIG. 9.7
Marjorie Schick, *Open Pot Form*, 1968. Sterling silver. Approximately 8½ x 8½ x 8½ in. (21.6 x 21.6 x 21.6 cm).

Martin taught for almost forty years at the Massachusetts College of Art and briefly at the Rhode Island School of Design. His students gradually filtered out into the rest of the country.[21]

Before World War II, enameling was not a clearly defined field. Typically, Arts and Crafts enamels were set as small medallions on silver or copper boxes. Most Arts and Crafts enameling was done in the Limoges technique, using the medium as if it were paint. Enameling did not truly have its own identity, and for decades, enamels were exhibited in ceramics shows. The logic was that enamel was fused glass applied to a substrate of another material, just as glaze is applied to a ceramic pot.

By the late 1920s two of Martin's students, Mildred Watkins and Kenneth Bates, were teaching at the Cleveland School of Art. Watkins incorporated enameling as a component of the regular jewelry classes she had been teaching since about 1918. Bates, who graduated from the Massachusetts College of Art in 1927, was immediately hired to teach design in Cleveland. His enameled butterfly, set in the lid of a covered copper bowl, dates from that year.[22] It won first prize in the May Show of 1927 at the Cleveland Museum of Art—in the category of "Metal Work Other Than Silver."[23] Motivated by his success, Bates went on to research the craft extensively, eventually becoming the foremost U.S. authority on enameling technique. Thousands of enamelists learned the craft from his book, *Enameling: Principles and Practice* (1951), including June Schwarcz **(CAT. 156)** and the author of this essay.

Bates traveled to Europe in 1928 and 1931 and regarded the experience as transformative. He was exposed not only to Byzantine and medieval enamels, but to contemporary French painting. Thereafter he considered himself a progressive artist. While his work often recalled historical enameling, he also composed his designs with a fractured cubist space and a bright Fauve palette. He occasionally ventured into pure abstraction, but always a decorative, highly patterned abstraction, never a gestural or painterly one. He favored floral or undersea imagery. By the 1940s most of his work was done on round copper blanks with rolled edges (for stiffness), with the design pressing out to the limits of the surface. The reference to plates assured a comfortable domesticity, while the bold designs were associated with contemporary painting.

Another Cleveland enamelist, Edward Winter, was instrumental in expanding the scale of the enameled

Edward Winter, *Burning Bush*, 1963. Enamel on steel. 31½ x 20½ in. (80 x 50.8 cm). Western Reserve Historical Society.

object. When he graduated from the Cleveland School of Art in 1931, he felt no great affinity for enameling. At the suggestion of one of his design teachers, Julius Mihalik, however, he studied it in Vienna during a scholarship year abroad. Upon returning to Cleveland, Winter produced a series of abstract rondels that won immediate critical approval. In about 1935 he arranged with Ferro Enamel Corporation to use the company's enormous furnaces at night. Built for making industrial enamels on steel, Ferro's kilns allowed Winter to fire plaques up to six feet in size.

The drastic increase in scale forced Winter to try industrial technologies, especially spraying enamel. Not surprisingly, many of Winter's panels from the 1940s resemble period airbrush illustration, with their combination of hard stenciled edges and feathered colors. He also experimented with other ways to work large and fast, including sgraffito, combing, squirting liquid enamel directly onto his panels, and applying high-fire white enamel over low-fire backgrounds to create vivid crackled surfaces. This craquelure became one of his signature effects.

Edward Winter and his wife, Thelma Frazier Winter, ran a successful business supplying enameled objects to design and department stores nationwide, where their enamels were often purchased as gifts. Winter enamels were easy to make and inexpensive, exhibiting the splashy techniques Winter had developed for his panels. Their bowls, platters, and trays with craquelure and lumps of colored frit became icons of contemporary decoration, and the Winters profited accordingly. Winter continued to produce large panels, and in the 1960s experimented with effects such as pouring and dripping (FIG. 9.8).[24]

The artist who gave American enameling a painterly inflection was German expatriate Karl Drerup, who had studied painting and printmaking in the 1920s in Münster and Berlin. Although he was familiar with the Bauhaus and other cutting-edge movements, he favored a painterly, pictorial approach to art. He may have seen exhibits of paintings by Paul Klee and Pablo Picasso,[25] and his sympathies clearly lay with the School of Paris style that dominated European painting in the 1930s. This style married a formulaic cubism with randomly fractured space, simple figures in conventional motifs, and a bright palette.

Drerup and his wife immigrated to the United States in 1937 to escape the fascist anti-Semitism that was spreading across Europe. Within a few years, after achieving some success in ceramics, Drerup discovered enameling. With the help of a friend who ran an enameled-sign shop, Drerup developed a variation of the Limoges technique. He treated his enamels as if they were small easel paintings. His typical format was a rectangle that rarely exceeded fifteen inches, the size being determined by the dimensions of his kiln. He built up layers of transparent enamels, analogous to glazing in oil painting.

Enamel, however, is not paint. It usually has a granular texture that remains visible even after firing. Accepting this quality, Drerup focused on the strength of the material: brilliant colors and rich deep transparencies. To look at a Drerup enamel closely is to lose yourself in contrasts of transparent and opaque enamels, and the balanced color. Drerup's painterly enamels were popular throughout the late 1940s and '50s, and he was regarded by many as the equal of Kenneth Bates. The School of Paris style aged poorly, however, and when the seminal *Objects: USA* exhibition was organized in the late 1960s, Drerup was not even invited.

Many other postwar American enamelists started out as painters, including Jean and Arthur Ames, Ellamarie Wooley, and Virginia Dudley.[26] Not surprisingly, much of their enamel work resembles painting from the preceding decade or two, often a compromise between representation and pure abstraction that was called "abstractionist" at the time. Curtis Tann's plaque *Untitled (Urban Scene)* (FIG. 9.9) divides space with a network of lines and fragments of words, rather like synthetic cubism. At the same time, the figures of children at play allowed Tann to pursue his goal of dignify-ing African Americans by depicting their everyday life.[27] It was common to assert that enameling was more closely connected to painting than any other craft, but it could also be said that "contemporary design is more easily and widely accepted in enamel than in painting."[28]

Still, the potency of abstract expressionist painting was hard to deny, and throughout the 1950s and '60s enamelists embraced complete abstraction. One of the immediate problems concerned size: how could enamelists expand the scale of the enameled object to compete with the enormous scale of abstract expressionist canvases? Another problem was technical: how could enamel be applied so that it had the same gestural qualities as paint?

FIG. 9.9

Curtis Tann, *Untitled (Urban Scene)*, 1958. Enamel on copper. 12 x 8¾ in. (30.5 x 22.2 cm). Long Beach Museum of Art, Gift of Annemarie Davidson; 2002.13.

The scale problem could be solved by cutting the enamel into parts that could be fired in small kilns and then pieced together in large compositions. This was the solution that Jackson and Ellamarie Wooley used to create their large-scale architectural murals. The same approach can be seen in Earl Pardon's *Suspended Forms* (CAT. 173), a grouping of enameled segments that total an impressive fifty-four inches in width.

For enamelists with access to large kilns, the challenge was to get enamel to imitate the fluidity of paint. Paul Hultberg sifted enamel over a sticky gum solution that he applied with large brushes, replicating Franz Kline's legendary brushstrokes.[29] Dorothy Sturm fired sheets of glass directly onto her copper panels. Fred Ball developed a technique of firing thin copper sheets with a hand-held torch that allowed him to build up the enamel surface in the process of firing. For a time, abstract enameling was received with enthusiasm. Hultberg, Ball, and the Wooleys all received major architectural commissions, and the Museum of Modern Art purchased an enamel panel by the English painter Stefan Knapp.[30]

In the end, however, abstract enamelists suffered the same fate as many second- and third-generation New York School painters. Their work was deemed derivative. As abstract painting began to wane, pop art and minimalism grabbed the art world's attention. Whatever the cause, the moment of large-scale painterly enameling soon passed, and much of the work is now neglected or in storage.

Enameling may have been tainted by its association with craft as hobby. Kenneth Bates helped design the first hobbyist enameling kiln for the Craftint Company in Cleveland about 1950. This was followed shortly by the Trinkit kiln. Both were sold as kits, with a selection of powdered enamels and lumps of frit, and they were wildly successful. As *Craft Horizons* observed in 1957, the popularity of enameling "put serious enamellists under the obligation to raise the level of taste in this field which is too often garish and poorly executed."[31]

Enameling eventually regained its footing not as a branch of painting, but as a contemporary decorative art. The enamelist who led the field in that direction was June Schwarcz.[32] She studied industrial design at Pratt Institute but learned to enamel from Bates's book. She began to etch her copper blanks before applying enamel, hoping to emphasize a graphic quality. In the process she had rediscovered *basse-taille*, a low-relief technique, and it

became her first signature technique. Treating the copper like an etching plate, Schwarcz created complex textures on the metal and then accentuated them with layers of transparent enamel. While she made a number of panels, she also remained dedicated to bowls and vessels.

Schwarcz started enameling in about 1954 and was recognized almost immediately. Her work was included in the inaugural exhibition of the Museum of Contemporary Crafts in 1956, and in 1959 the museum commissioned her to make a piece for their first major survey of contemporary enameling. *Bowl (332)* was the result. Richly textured and colored, it is also restrained and completely abstract. Instead of trying to overwhelm with "heroic" scale, Schwarcz's bowl invites viewers to linger and explore. Only eleven inches long, it can be handled, rotated, turned over. This kind of tactile, bodily experience has always been one of the strengths of the decorative arts.

Schwarcz went on to develop a brilliant series of enameled vessels made of copper foil and electroformed for rigidity. Like her bowls, they are unassumingly small but compellingly rich. Her enamels did not use the medium to ape painting, but to be more fully itself. Her emphasis on the innate properties of the material would profoundly influence the next generation of enamelists.

✻

The midcentury was a period of complementary—and competing—modernisms. American silversmiths looked to the organic functionalism of the Scandinavian modern style. The designer-craftsman ideal inspired metalsmiths like John Prip and Ronald Pearson to collaborate with industry. At the same time, enamelists looked to School of Paris painting for inspiration and viewed enameling as a branch of that medium, rendering the demands of utility and mass-production irrelevant.

If there was a single tendency in the crafts throughout the 1950s and '60s, it was to move away from functionalism and toward artistic experimentation. The heroes of craft in 1947 were designers Charles and Ray Eames, but by 1960 that role had been assumed by ceramist Peter Voulkos. The constraints of "good design" were increasingly ignored, replaced by a growing sense of freedom. In silver this trajectory is visible in the distance between Margret Craver's simple bowl of 1947 and Marjorie Schick's complex sculptural construction of 1968. The change was enormous—and irreversible.

1 Enamelist Jackson Wooley, for example, "agreed that enamels was the craft most closely connected to painting, although the technical demands of enamels are greater" ("Asilomar: An On-the-Scene Report from the First National Conference of American Craftsmen," *CH* 17 [July/August 1957], 23). For the purposes of this essay, silversmithing and enameling are treated as distinct fields.

2 See Alan Rosenberg, "Modern American Silver," *Modernism* 4 (Fall 2001), 30.

3 Arthur J. Stone died in 1938; Robert Jarvie in 1941; Peer Smed in 1943. William Waldo Dodge closed his shop in 1941.

4 Pulos, quoted in "Asilomar: An On-the-Scene Report," 23.

5 Margret Craver, interview with the author, February 1996.

6 Annalies Krekel-Aalberse, *Art Nouveau and Art Deco Silver* (London: Thames and Hudson Ltd., 1989), 104–5.

7 Star Miller-Sacks, "Master Metalsmith: Margret Craver," *Metalsmith* 2 (winter 1981–82), 6–10; Lisa Hammel, "On Her Mettle: Margret Craver," *American Craft* 51 (June/July 1991), 54–60; Jeannine Falino and Yvonne Markowitz, "Margret Craver, Jeweler, Educator, Visionary," *Journal of the American Society of Jewelry Historians* 1 (spring 1997), 9–23.

8 Margret Craver, *Handwrought Silver* (New York: Handy & Harman, 1947); Handy & Harman Craft Service Department, *Contemporary Silversmithing . . . The Stretching Method* (New York: Handy & Harman, 1952). The Metropolitan Museum of Art exhibition *Form in Handwrought Silver* took place from December 16,

1949 to January 29, 1950, as cited in "List of Exhibitions," *Metropolitan Museum of Art Bulletin*, New Series, 10 (summer 1951), 40.

9 J. David Farmer, "Metalwork and Bookbinding," in Robert Judson Clark et al., *Design in America: The Cranbrook Vision, 1925–1950* (Detroit: Detroit Institute of Art; New York: Metropolitan Museum of Art, in association with Harry N. Abrams, 1993), 144–71; Jeannine Falino, "Metalsmithing at Mid-century," in *Sculptural Concerns: Contemporary American Metal Working*, exh. cat. (Cincinnati: Contemporary Arts Center; Fort Wayne, IN: Museum of Art, 1993), 10–27.

10 For a summary of European smiths who immigrated to the United States before 1940, see Jewel Stern, "Striking the Modern Note in Metal," in Janet Kardon, ed., *Craft in the Machine Age, 1920–1945* (New York: Harry N. Abrams and the American Craft Museum, 1995), 122–34.

11 For Prip, see Tim McCreight, "Master Metalsmith: John Prip," *Metalsmith* 3 (fall 1983), 6–11; Madeleine Vanderpoel et al., "John Prip: Arrangements of Changeable Form," *Metalsmith* 8 (fall 1988), 14–21.

12 Jeannine Falino and Gerald W. R. Ward, eds., *Silver of the Americas, 1600–2000: American Silver in the Museum of Fine Arts, Boston* (Boston: MFA Publications, 2008), 436–37, cat. no. 354.

13 Jewel Stern, Kevin W. Tucker, and Charles L. Venable, *Modernism in American Silver: 20th-Century Design* (Dallas: Dallas Museum of Art, 2005), 197, 250, 282.

14 Mary LaPrade, ed., "Biography and Conversations of Hans

Christensen," *Goldsmiths Journal* 15, vol. 3, no. 6 (December 1977), 36–37.

15 "Fred Miller Makes a Silver Bowl," *CH* 16 (December 1956), 37–39; William Baran-Mickle, "Frederick A. Miller: A Precarious Balance," *Metalsmith* 13 (spring 1993), 34–39.

16 English potter John Chappell, who spent the previous two years living in Sweden, quoted in Conrad Brown, "Scandinavia's Young Dissenters," *CH* 18, insert (March/April 1958), n.p.

17 Ronald Pearson, "Jewelry," *CH* 22 (July/August, 1962), 13.

18 "Campus Loses Kurt Matzdorf, Pioneer of College's Metal Program," *News Pulse, State University of New York at New Paltz*, December 22, 2008, http://newspulse.newpaltz.edu/tag/kurt-matzdorf/.

19 Helen Shirk, "Initiation," in Marjorie Schick et al., *Sculpture to Wear: The Jewelry of Marjorie Schick* (Stuttgart: Arnoldsche, 2007), 25.

20 Schick commented, "I guess it caused lots of discussion at IU as to whether it was really a pot. Obviously, it didn't worry me. I was just trying for the best form and I considered it a pot whether it had a bottom or not. I don't think it was odd at all. It was a very exciting time when metalsmithing was just beginning to expand its traditional definitions"; Marjorie Schick, e-mail to the author, January 3, 2007.

21 Unfortunately, Martin's enamels are scarce, and scholarship on his career is sparse. For Martin, see Jeannine Falino's biography of him in Marilee Boyd Meyer, ed., *Inspiring Reform: Boston's Arts and Crafts Movement* (Wellesley, MA:

Davis Museum and Cultural Center, 1997), 222–23.

22 It was executed in Martin's enameling style, which suggests that Bates had studied enameling under Martin, although Bates later claimed only to have received "first inspirations" from Martin, not specifically instruction in the craft; see Kenneth Bates, *Enameling: Principles and Practice* (New York: Funk & Wagnalls, 1951), 18. Much later, Bates recalled that "one of [Martin's] classroom techniques was to slowly unwrap from tissue one of his beautiful little trays or match box covers which was done in 'opalescent' enamel, a method which is little known today. He was a craftsman par excellence and has never left my memory or my gratitude"; Bates, letter to Jeannine Falino, March 30, 1993.

23 "Review of the Exhibition," *Bulletin of the Cleveland Museum of Art* 5 (May 1927), 95, illus. The covered bowl is in the Cleveland Museum of Art, 1991.132a,b.

24 For Winter, see Bernard N. Jazzar and Harold B. Nelson, *Painting with Fire* (Long Beach, CA: Long Beach Museum of Art, 2007), 54–67.

25 Ibid., 70. For more on Drerup, see Jane L. Port, *Karl Drerup (1904–2000) Enchanted Gardens: Enamels by an American Master* (Plymouth, NH: Karl Drerup Gallery, Plymouth State University, 2007), 11–26.

26 For Ellamarie and Jackson Wooley, see Janice Keaffaber, "The Wooleys: Pioneers in Enamel," *Metalsmith* 13 (winter 1993), 28–37. For Virginia Dudley, see J. Spenser Moran, "Rising Faun Enamels," *CH* 14 (January/February 1954), 26–31.

27 Jazzar and Nelson, *Painting with Fire*, 275.

28 Jackson Wooley, quoted in "Asilomar: An On-the-Scene Report," 23.

29 M. C. Richards, "Paul Hultberg: The Enamel as Mural," *CH* 20 (March/April 1960), 25–28.

30 Rose Slivka, "Stefan Knapp: Painter Enamelist," *CH* 18 (May/June 1958), 22–28.

31 "Asilomar: An On-the-Scene Report," 23.

32 For Schwarcz, see Yoshiko Uchida, "June Schwarcz," *CH* 19 (September/October 1959), 26–30; Jazzar and Nelson, *Painting with Fire*, 208–21; Carole Austin, *June Schwarcz: Forty Years/Forty Pieces* (San Francisco: San Francisco Craft & Folk Art Museum, 1998).

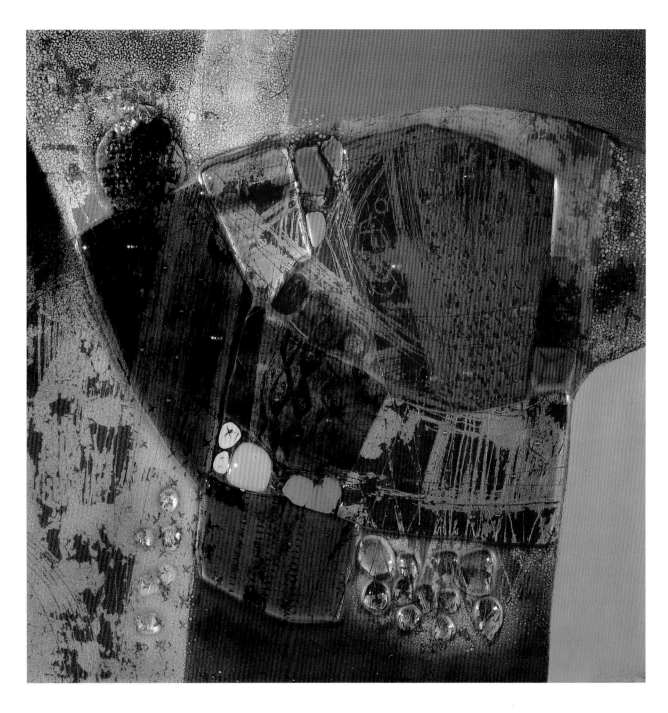

139

DOROTHY STURM

Untitled, c. 1968

ENAMEL, COPPER

12 X 12 IN. (30.5 X 30.5 CM)

COLLECTION OF JIMMY LEWIS AND SARLA NICHOLS

140

HANS CHRISTENSEN

Coffeepot, c. 1960

STERLING SILVER AND ROSEWOOD

H. 9⅝ IN. (24.5 CM)

YALE UNIVERSITY ART GALLERY,

AMERICAN ARTS PURCHASE FUND, 1978.90

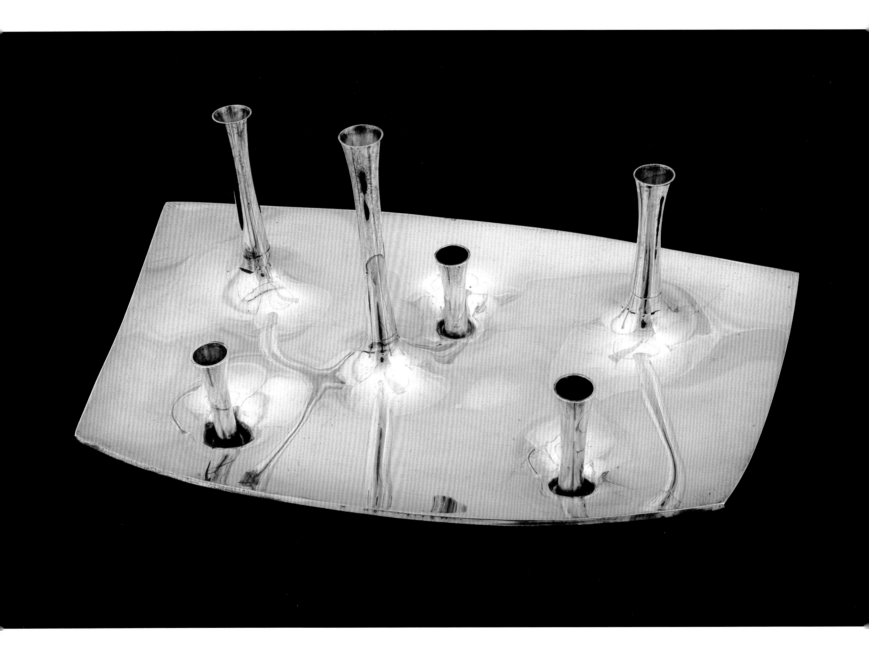

141

JOE REYES APODACA JR.

Candelabrum, 1966

STERLING SILVER

5½ X 11½ X 6¼ IN. (14 X 29.2 X 15.9 CM)

SMITHSONIAN AMERICAN ART MUSEUM,

GIFT OF S.C.JOHNSON & SON, INC. 1977.118.6

142

OLAF SKOOGFORS

Candelabrum, 1957

STERLING SILVER

H. 5¹³⁄₁₆ IN. (14.8 CM); DIAM. 8½ IN. (21.6 CM)

PHILADELPHIA MUSEUM OF ART,

GIFT OF JUDY SKOOGFORS, 1986-102-1

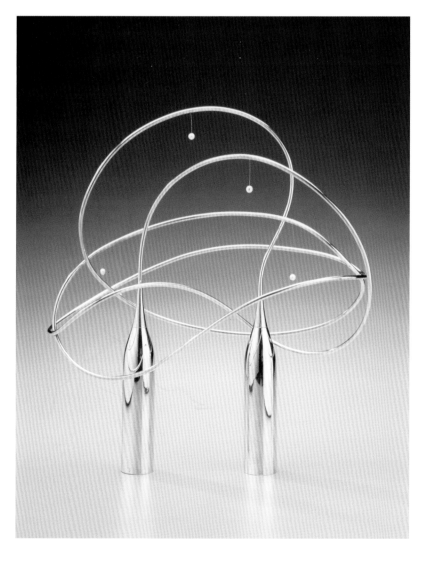

143

MOSHE ZABARI

Torah Crown, 1969

STERLING SILVER, PEARLS

13½ IN. (34.3 CM) X DIAM. 15⅜ IN. (39 CM)

THE JEWISH MUSEUM, NEW YORK, GIFT OF THE

ALBERT A. LIST FAMILY, JM 85-69

144

LORNA PEARSON

Pitcher, 1948

STERLING SILVER

6⅝ X 5⅜ X 8¹³⁄₁₆ IN. (16.8 X 13.7 X 22.4 CM)

YALE UNIVERSITY ART GALLERY, THE JANET
AND SIMEON BRAGUIN FUND, 2000.72.1

145

L. BRENT KINGTON

Dragster, 1969

STERLING SILVER

12 X 4 X 3 IN. (30.5 X 10.2 X 7.6 CM)

MUSEUM OF ARTS AND DESIGN, GIFT OF THE ARTIST,

THROUGH THE AMERICAN CRAFT COUNCIL, 1969

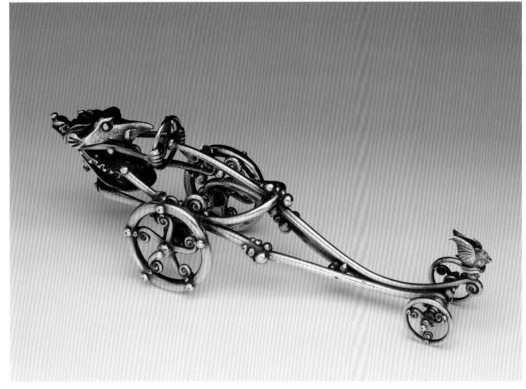

146

VINCENT FERRINI

Pair of Candlesticks, c. 1960

STERLING SILVER

LEFT: H. 7⅛ IN. (18 CM), DIAM. 8½ IN. (21.6 CM);

RIGHT: H. 9 IN. (22.86 CM), DIAM. 8½ IN. (21.6 CM)

COLLECTION OF THE ARTIST

147

JOHN C. MARSHALL
Chalice, 1967
SILVER GILT AND RUBIES
13½ X 6 X 6½ IN. (34.3 X 15.2 X 16.5 CM)
MUSEUM OF ARTS AND DESIGN, GIFT OF THE JOHNSON WAX
COMPANY, THROUGH THE AMERICAN CRAFT COUNCIL, 1977

148

FREDERICK MILLER
Bottle, 1969
STERLING SILVER AND 23-KARAT GOLD
7½ X 5½ X 4½ IN. (19.05 X 13.97 X 11.43 CM)
COURTESY OF S.C. JOHNSON, INC.

149

JOHN PRIP

Horn Shield, 1963

39 X 25 X 17 IN. (99.1 X 63.5 X 43.2 CM)

BRONZE, GRANITE

COLLECTION OF PETER PRIP

150, 151, 152

JOHN PRIP

Vessel, Decanter, Sculpture, 1968

PEWTER

FROM LEFT: VESSEL 10 X 15 IN. (25.4 X 38.1 CM);

DECANTER 9½ X 6 X 4¼ IN. (24.1 X 15.2 X 10.8 CM);

SCULPTURE 8½ X 25 X 17 IN. (99.1 X 63.5 X 43.2 CM)

MINNESOTA MUSEUM OF AMERICAN ART, L2006.62.37

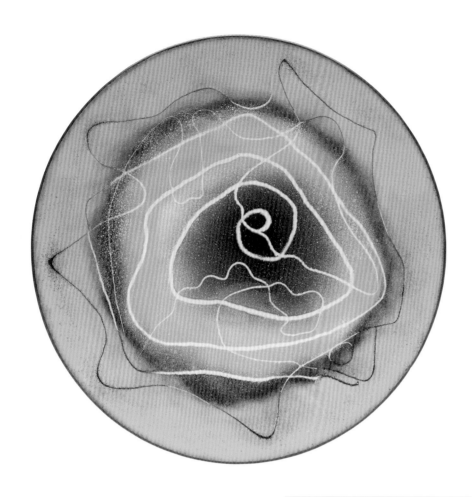

153

KENNETH BATES

Plate, 1950

ENAMEL, COPPER

DIAM. 11 IN. (27.9 CM)

MUSEUM OF ARTS AND DESIGN,

GIFT OF ANDREW GLASGOW, 2011

154

KARL DRERUP

Plaque, 1954

ENAMELED STEEL

13⅞ X 13⅞ X 1⅝ IN. (35.2 X 35.2 X 4.1 CM)

MUSEUM OF ARTS AND DESIGN, PURCHASED

BY THE AMERICAN CRAFT COUNCIL, 1958

155

MARGRET CRAVER, DESIGNER

WILLIAM ERNEST BENNETT, SILVERSMITH

Bowl for the Movie
"Handwrought Silver," 1947

STERLING SILVER

H. 3⁹⁄₁₆ IN. (9 CM), DIAM. 5⁹⁄₁₆ IN. (14.1 CM)

YALE UNIVERSITY ART GALLERY,

GIFT OF THE ASSOCIATES IN FINE ARTS,

BY EXCHANGE 1994.2.1

156

JUNE SCHWARCZ

Bowl (544), 1969

ENAMEL, COPPER, AND IRON

4⅜ X 8 X 7 IN. (11.1 X 20.3 X 17.8 CM)

OAKLAND MUSEUM OF CALIFORNIA; BEQUEST

OF MRS. DOROTHEA ADAMS MCCOY, 1969.79

CHAPTER 10

A Community Emerges:
The American Studio
Jewelry Movement, 1945–1969

URSULA ILSE-NEUMAN

IN 1946 VISITORS TO NEW YORK'S MUSEUM OF
Modern Art were startled to see a necklace fashioned
from a drain sieve, paper clips, and a beaded chain **(FIG.
10.1)**. Created by Anni Albers and Alex Reed, it was a
major attraction at the exhibition *Modern Handmade
Jewelry* demonstrating that a wearable art object could be
made out of common materials. Although unheralded at
the time, the exhibition is now acknowledged as a landmark that presented jewelry as an art form for the first
time. The event brought together the "artist as jeweler,"
featuring ornaments for the body by painters and sculptors including Richard Pousette-Dart, José De Rivera,
Jacques Lipchitz, and Alexander Calder, and the "jeweler
as artist," premiering new work by then lesser-known
artists Harry Bertoia, Margaret De Patta, Paul Lobel,
Adda Husted-Andersen, and Sam Kramer.

In the twenty-five-year period following World War
II, the evolution of American jewelry both anticipated
and followed far-reaching changes then taking place
in American society. The pioneering jewelers of the
1940s and early 1950s turned away from the dehumanizing effects of war and industrialization and challenged
the anonymity and uniformity of industrial production. These groundbreaking artists made one-of-a-kind
pieces and limited-production items that stood apart
from the luxury and low-cost mass-produced jewelry of
the day, much of which was still fashioned in Victorian
and art deco styles. This new avant-garde jewelry con-
ferred status on its makers and wearers, but not through
the market value of its materials or its suggestions of

wealth. In the words of art historian Blanche Brown,
"Diamonds were the badge of the philistine."[1]

Prior to the 1960s the development of the studio jewelry movement was both hindered but also enlivened by
the lack of formal metalwork training programs available in America. While innovative jewelers seeking to
acquire basic metalworking skills had few choices, they
were also unencumbered by the constraints of traditional
conventions. Unlike European goldsmiths, who required
years of training and apprenticeship before they were
deemed masters, American jewelers were free to experiment and invent.

It was in the first fifteen years after World War II that
jewelry making in America underwent an extraordinary
transformation. This period marked the establishment
of jewelry and metalworking programs in colleges and
universities across the country and through industry-
sponsored workshops. These university- and workshop-
trained jewelers of the 1950s and early 1960s then established individual studios and seized control of the work
process from start to finish. They incorporated nontraditional materials into artistically inspired designs, creating
pieces that celebrated conceptual brilliance and the mark
of the hand. By the mid-1960s, students were responding
to the social and cultural revolutions of the decade, producing content-based work that reflected the influences
of pop art and Funk and boldly addressed issues of the day.

An emerging professionalization across the larger
craft world during this period also benefited jewelers and
the work they produced. Jewelry began to be included in
media-diverse museum exhibitions, and jewelry-focused
shows were assembled. Markets began to develop—some
jewelers participated in craft fairs and others found gallery representation. Soon, it became useful to establish a
professional organization, and in 1968, the Society of North
American Goldsmiths was formed.[2] By the late 1960s the
American studio jewelry movement was in full flower.

GATHERING FORCES: PRE–WORLD WAR II

When America entered World War II in 1941, appreciation
for the handmade had diminished to the extent that, when
traveling in the United States, French writer Simone de
Beauvoir stated, "'Craftsmanship' does not exist in the
States."[3] Indeed, with regard to jewelry making, there
were not many places in the country where metalworking
skills were taught. Nevertheless, during the war a handful
of American schools offered classes in metalworking and

jewelry making, including Cranbrook Academy of Art in Bloomfield Hills, Michigan; the California College of Arts and Crafts (now California College of the Arts) in Oakland; the Philadelphia Museum School of Industrial Arts (now the University of the Arts); and the School of Design in Chicago (renamed the Institute of Design in 1945), to cite just a few.[4] But even in these institutions, instruction was disrupted as students and teachers alike were called into military service and wartime requirements made metals scarce and expensive.

At Cranbrook, noted artist and designer Harry Bertoia established and headed the metalworking studio from 1939 until 1943, when it was closed due to wartime restrictions on materials.[5] Despite Bertoia's short career as a jewelry artist, the delicate and fanciful pieces he created at Cranbrook left a mark on the field. Other American jewelry artists who laid the foundation for future developments included Ruth Penington in Seattle; Francisco Rebajes in New York; Margaret De Patta in San Francisco; and, most prominently, the artist generally considered a seminal figure for American jewelry, Alexander Calder, in Roxbury, Connecticut.

During his lifetime Calder produced more than eighteen hundred pieces of jewelry, primarily in brass and silver and often embellished with found objects such as beach glass, ceramic shards, and wood. While other renowned painters and sculptors, such as Pablo Picasso, Jean Arp, and Jacques Lipchitz, began designing jewelry in the 1930s, their later designs of the 1960s, generally in gold, were executed by highly accomplished artisans or goldsmiths. Calder, by contrast, fabricated his own jewelry, using few tools and precious materials, demonstrating that jewelry need not depend upon gold and gemstones.

Calder's jewelry was first widely exhibited in the 1940s, and his work became an inspiration to many self-taught studio jewelers.[6] New York jewelry artist Ed Wiener noted, "As I began to see more of Calder's wire jewelry, I recognized a craft so specific in its limitation as to appear crude and anti-craft, yet visually very sophisticated. Joined with hammered rivets, polished with a hammer face, the result was a thin, textured surface tension, bursting with energy, ready to ring if struck."[7]

PROFESSIONAL TRAINING: POST-WORLD WAR II

After the war the craft of jewelry making appealed to both artists and amateurs alike. Regarded as a medium that did not involve a great deal of specialized technical knowledge, training, or space, it was seen as a viable way to make an independent living. As Calder demonstrated, hammering wire (forging) or fusing metals are simple, intuitive processes requiring few tools. In addition, jewelry pieces are relatively small, quickly fabricated, and can be easily replicated. Objects such as brooches or pendants could be any shape and did not need to serve a utilitarian function, as did hollowware or a ceramic vessel.

Such a straightforward approach to jewelry making was fine until the need to realize more sophisticated concepts became apparent. By the late 1940s professionally trained goldsmiths and metalworkers—initially European artisans who had the knowledge and experience—were being hired for industry-sponsored workshops and for college and university programs. Margret Craver, an exceptional silversmith and jeweler, was the first to recognize that American metalsmiths needed to acquire greater working knowledge of materials and techniques in order to rise to new levels of creative expression. For five years, beginning in 1947, Craver organized the National Silversmithing Workshop Conferences, and many of their nationally selected participants went on to become prominent jewelers and professors.

Cleveland native John Paul Miller was among the major jewelers to emerge from Craver's workshops. Known as a master of the ancient art of granulation, a

FIG. 10.1

Anni Albers and Alex Reed, *Brooch*, 1946. Aluminum strainer, paper clips, and safety pin. 4¼ x 3⅛ x ⅜ in. (10.8 x 7.9 x 1 cm). Museum of Fine Arts, Boston, The Daphne Farago Collection; 2006.44.

FIG. 10.2
Robert von Neumann, *Daphne* **pendant, c. 1968. Silver. 2¾ x 1½ x ¼ in. (7 x 3.8 x 0.6 cm). Collection Alice von Neumann.**

In 1961 Neumann published *The Design and Creation of Jewelry*, still a standard reference for jewelry makers at all skill levels. His *Daphne* pendant (**FIG. 10.2**) illustrates his figurative style, which he described as translations in metal of his two-dimensional sketchbook designs.[9]

One of the most far-reaching metalsmithing programs was at the School for American Craftsmen (SAC) in Rochester, New York. Here students were not only trained to become craftsmen but were also prepared to compete in the marketplace as industrial designers or as studio jewelers. One of the school's first instructors was Philip Morton, a self-trained jeweler who taught at the school from 1944 to 1947 when it was located in Alfred, New York. Although he later published a key reference work, *Contemporary Jewelry: A Studio Handbook* (1970), his purely aesthetic approach did not fit with the school's practical philosophy.[10] His most notable student was Ronald Hayes Pearson, who did not graduate but nevertheless became a successful independent jeweler.[11] Pearson produced a large body of work that is notable for its Scandinavian influence, featuring unembellished shapes, a lack of figuration, and smooth, polished surfaces.

Under the tutelage of John Prip and Danish-born Hans Christensen, a number of SAC students flourished. Ruth Clark Radakovich attended in 1950–51, by which time the school had relocated to Rochester, and later taught at the Rochester Memorial Art Gallery with her fellow student, Yugoslavia-born husband and jeweler, Svetozar (Toza) Radakovich. In 1959 the couple moved to California, where Ruth used forging and casting techniques to create elaborate and imaginative sculptural works. Swedish-born Olaf Skoogfors, a prominent studio jeweler, produced one-of-a-kind and production jewelry using the lost-wax casting process, a technique he learned from the Radakoviches while a student at SAC. Skoogfors joined the faculty at the Philadelphia College of Art in 1959, where he created both one-of-a-kind jewelry—many wax-cast in silver and then gilded—and a production jewelry line noted for its modern, sleek lines, and typically described as "Scando-organic."[12]

EXUBERANT PIONEERS IN GREENWICH VILLAGE

The distinction between studio jewelry and jewelry produced solely for commercial purposes was made clear in postwar New York City, then home to one of the largest concentrations of studio jewelers in the United

technique developed by the ancient Etruscans (seventh–sixth century B.C.E.), in which minute grains or balls of gold are applied to a gold surface, Miller had been inspired by photographs he came across in a German magazine while a student at the Cleveland School of Art (now the Cleveland Institute of Art) in 1940. As he explained, "I was confounded by . . . how you could do something as minute and elegant as that without seeing any signs of soldering."[8] His early mastery of and virtuosity in this technique and his close observation of nature are a hallmark of his entire career.

Another graduate was painter and sculptor Earl Pardon, who taught enameling and jewelry making in a long and distinguished career at Skidmore College in Saratoga Springs, New York. Regarded as a master of cloisonné enameling, Pardon also worked with free-form shapes that resonate with the spontaneity of a Jackson Pollock abstract expressionist "drip" painting, exemplifying his painterly approach to the medium.

In the decade following the war, increasing numbers of universities and colleges offered jewelry-making courses, as did older art schools such as the California College of Arts and Crafts and the Cleveland Institute of Art. In the Midwest a new center for jewelry emerged at the Urbana-Champaign campus of the University of Illinois, under German-born Robert von Neumann.

States.[13] Even before the war, the vibrant Greenwich Village café scene had been the epicenter of an extraordinary community of avant-garde artists, writers, musicians, and filmmakers. Studio jewelers, energized by the creativity that surrounded them, fashioned modernist works reflecting such twentieth-century art movements as cubism, Dadaism, primitivism, surrealism, constructivism, and abstract expressionism. Rejecting traditional jewelry forms and a dependence on precious metals and stones, they opened shops as small galleries and sold their unique creations at moderate prices.

Dominican American Francisco Rebajes opened his first jewelry shop on West Fourth Street in Greenwich Village in the mid-1930s.[14] By the mid-1940s he had an elegant store on Fifth Avenue **(FIG. 10.3)**, with more than one hundred artisans hand-assembling his bracelets, necklaces, brooches, and earrings. Although Rebajes's jewelry was produced in multiples, hammer marks were employed to impart the desired handcrafted effect.[15]

Sam Kramer was the most eccentric of the Greenwich Village jewelers. After taking a jewelry-making class in 1936 at the University of Southern California with ceramist Glen Lukens, he settled in New York City and

FIG. 10.3
Frank Rebajes's Fifth Avenue store, early 1950s. Photograph collection of Patricia Riveron Lee.

found his inspiration in surrealist imagery. He opened his shop on West Eighth Street in 1939. Self-taught from that point on, Kramer developed a technique of "controlled melting," working with a simple blow torch to form splattered droplets of molten silver. These drops—perhaps inspired by Lukens's dripped and pooled ceramic glazes—became an iconic characteristic of Kramer's work, imparting a random quality to his compositions and confirming their handmade creation **(CAT. 157)**.[16] The artist intended his work to be shocking, and he was delighted when his jewelry disturbed visitors.

Ed Wiener, active in Greenwich Village and Provincetown, Massachusetts, was never formally trained. After buying a pair of earrings from Sam Kramer for $1.50,[17] he taught himself how to make jewelry using plumbers' and carpenters' tools. In contrast to the surrealistic fantasies by Kramer, Wiener's jewelry was unembellished. His *Dancer* is an abstracted form, inspired by a photograph of choreographer Martha Graham, who was a client.

New York native Paul A. Lobel made a name for himself as an industrial designer before turning to jewelry. He opened a shop in 1944 after concluding that there was

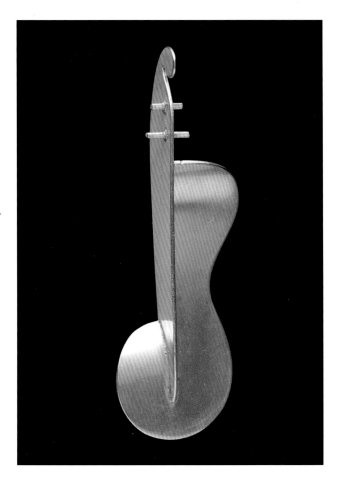

"too much trash in costume jewelry.... [Women] are receptive to simple forms executed of good material."[18] Lobel fashioned imaginative and graceful three-dimensional forms from flat sheet metal, abstracting lyrical compositions from familiar objects such as the violin (**FIG. 10.4**).

Art Smith set up his jewelry workshop in Greenwich Village in 1946. An African American, Smith was a devotee of black modern dance groups. His dramatic jewelry designs were fully realized when worn and had a particular appeal to dancers. His extravagant neckpieces and bracelets recall Calder's aesthetic with their mark of the hand and extensive use of brass, but they were lighter in weight and more wearable than Calder's work. As a result, Smith's pieces created a greater awareness of the body as a living armature. To Smith, the question was "not how do bracelets go, but what can be done with an arm?"[19] Combining biomorphic forms with sensitivity to the colors and textures of materials, Smith's hand-hammered metals are elegantly contoured and exemplify his sensuous approach to jewelry.

EXPLORERS ON THE WEST COAST

The wild and "irrational" Dadaist style exemplified by Sam Kramer had its opposite pole on the West Coast in the sophisticated, controlled compositions of Margaret De Patta, who was the outstanding voice for rational structure and spatial control in jewelry. Trained as a painter, she began her jewelry career in the 1930s and became one of the most influential jewelers of the post-war era. An important turning point for her occurred when she attended the School of Design in Chicago in 1940 and '41 and adopted the constructivist ideas of former Bauhaus master László Moholy-Nagy.

De Patta became particularly fascinated with concepts of transparency and movement in space, arguing that "problems common to sculpture and architecture are inherent in jewelry design—i.e., space, form, tension, organic structure, scale, texture, interpenetration, super-imposition and economy of means."[20] Her pieces, conceived as "wearable miniature sculptures," often include biomorphic elements and movable parts that soften constructivism's mechanical tendencies.

De Patta's most striking compositions feature rutilated quartz with "opticuts," her term for the innovative cuts she used to produce dazzling optical effects.[21] In 1946 her husband, designer Eugene Bielawski, encouraged her to focus on high-quality limited production for a wider audience. Although they eventually established a profitable business, after twelve years of production work the details of running the business proved too time consuming, and De Patta returned to experimental work.[22]

Another West Coast artist who took a sculptural approach to jewelry was Claire Falkenstein. During the early 1930s, she attended a master class at Mills College in Oakland with Russian-born sculptor Alexander Archipenko and started making jewelry in 1946 as part of her experimentation with metal welding. "I began to explore ideas and shape and form and so on through metal, which I'd never done before. And then I got really serious about it [jewelry] around 1951."[23] Falkenstein was also influenced by Alexander Calder's jewelry, often using dense wire formations, as he did, to enclose space.[24]

In contrast to the many New York artists who sold their jewelry in small, artist-owned shops, most jewelry artists in the San Francisco Bay Area found outlets for their work in craft galleries and department stores and through the annual outdoor art festivals in San Francisco that led to the establishment of the San Francisco Metal Arts Guild in 1951.[25] The self-taught Peter Macchiarini was a founding member who combined constructivism with elements inspired by African tribal artifacts (FIG. 10.5).

Another Bay Area artist, Byron Wilson, was recognized for his sculptural forms and innovative use of materials and tools to fabricate pieces that incorporated tribal imagery. Wilson taught at the California College

of Arts and Crafts in Oakland alongside Bob Winston, whose influential book *Cast Away* (1970) helped revive the ancient practice of lost-wax casting. Winston employed this technique to create highly sculptural and textured jewelry.

Irena Brynner, who studied with Winston and apprenticed with jewelers Carolyn Rosine and Franz Bergman in 1949, turned from sculpture to jewelry in 1950 after seeing a piece of jewelry by Falkenstein. Brynner explained, "Somebody had a band, a silver band, and here hung a completely free ... mobile. And I thought, my God, but that is sculpture! I don't have to go away from sculpture, I just will change the size and approach, and it has to be in relation to the human body! That was a revelation to me."[26] Brynner's early works demonstrate the influence of constructivist concepts as well as the memories of images from her youth in China (FIG. 10.6).

Entirely self-taught as a jeweler, merry renk (as she prefers her name to be styled) came to the medium after studying with Moholy-Nagy, as Margaret De Patta had before her, at the Institute of Design in Chicago in 1946 and 1947. She then moved to San Francisco and was a founding member of the Metal Arts Guild.[27] Following Bauhaus design principles and working in the constructivist spirit, she made brilliant use of interlocking forms to create three-dimensional structures.

Farther down the coast, among the pioneering jewelers in Southern California was Ernest Ziegfeld, who

FIG. 10.5
Peter Macchiarini, *Bracelet*, c. 1948. Silver, copper. 2½ x 2½ x ¾ in. (6.4 x 6.4 x 1.9 cm) overall. Collection of Susan Grant Lewin.

FIG. 10.6
Irena Brynner, *Earrings*, c. 1951. Silver, gold. 2½ x 1½ x ⅛ in. (6.1 x 4.2 x 2.1 cm). The Montreal Museum of Fine Arts, Liliane and David M. Stewart Collection, Gift of Paul Leblanc; D94.215.1.

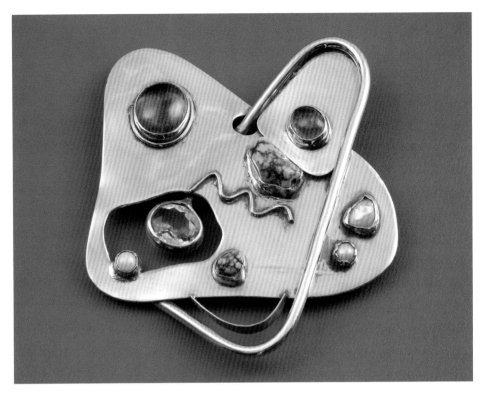

led the jewelry program at California State University in Long Beach in the 1950s. Ziegfeld, who obtained a doctorate in art education from Columbia University's Teachers College, gained attention for his necklaces and hair ornaments, many decorated with eccentric fringes.[28]

The Pacific Northwest was another important center for studio jewelry, and it benefited for more than forty years from the leadership of Ruth Penington. A founding member of Northwest Designer Craftsmen and Friends of the Craft in Seattle, Penington taught at the University of Washington from 1928 to 1970, retiring as head of the metals department. Like Ziegfeld, Penington studied art education at Columbia's Teachers College, she studied in Asia, and she also completed an apprenticeship in silversmithing in Copenhagen in 1952.[29] Penington's work was "either richly encrusted" and of "great delicacy," or was large scale and "rendered architecturally."[30] Her jewelry and more utilitarian pieces married clean geometric lines—often associated with Scandinavian design—and a "sense of the archaic," drawn from Byzantine, Viking, and pre-Columbian cultures **(FIG. 10.7)**.[31]

SUNDRY MESSENGERS: THE 1960s

By the 1960s the pioneering studio jewelers of the 1930s and '40s had been working for more than twenty years and were at the height of their artistic powers. In recognition of their talents the Museum of Contemporary Crafts presented many solo exhibitions honoring the accomplishments of these trailblazers.[32] Yet predictably, as older pioneers continued to work in the styles that brought them recognition, what was once avant-garde became mainstream and what had once been innovative turned to repetition and imitation in the hands of lesser artists. Fortunately, however, this situation was about to change dramatically!

An important and unique characteristic of American jewelry programs was their presence in colleges and universities. It was in this more encompassing intellectual setting, where avenues of humanist inquiry were opened beyond the mere mastery of jewelry techniques and materials, that a younger generation of artists trained by the now established masters began to realize their own startling visions.

The 1960s generation of jewelry makers is known for the introduction of explicit content into their work. The turbulent and dramatic events of the decade combined with unprecedented freedoms resulted in a body of bold, brazen, and controversial work. Pop art and its West Coast relative, Funk, replaced the modernist idioms of the 1940s and '50s. Contemporary imagery was introduced, along with a wide range of nontraditional jewelry materials and techniques.[33]

One of the first to use jewelry for political and social commentary was Minnesota artist Christian Schmidt. His *Medal of Honor* **(CAT. 158)** was a subversive form of protest against the lack of consistent judging criteria at the St. Paul Gallery and School of Art's *Fiber, Clay and Metal* exhibition in 1964. To Schmidt's consternation, the inclusion of the sheriff's metallic badge with its sardonic title, was taken literally and enthusiastically welcomed as a pungent antiwar pop art expression.[34]

That same year J. Fred Woell, on a visit to New York City, was appalled at the widespread availability of inexpensive Scandinavian silver jewelry at the expense of American work. In protest to the monetary value of materials dictating a jewel's success, he decided to utilize materials that had no value whatsoever, such as the paint-encrusted wood and staples in *The Good Guys* pendant **(CAT. 172)**. By elevating the popular cartoon characters rendered in his work into sacred icons, Woell not only challenged the material composition of jewelry, but also questioned the American value system and the country's choice of heroic figures.

Robert Ebendorf earned a fine arts degree in his native Kansas in the 1960s and then pursued a rigorous

Scandinavian aesthetic before establishing himself as an important innovator, incorporating found objects as central elements in his work. Starting in the late 1960s, Ebendorf gained a new perspective by using the artifacts of daily life, reversing the idea of preciousness, and involving the viewer/wearer in the evocation of past associations and memories.

In the Northwest, Ken Cory used the Funk idiom in small-scale brooches that carried a sharp antiestablishment message. Often coupled with bawdy humor and irreverence, his groundbreaking assemblages influenced many younger jewelers and helped create a new role for jewelry as a messenger of subversive ideas. Conveyed in eye-catching works of impeccable craftsmanship, Cory's concepts skillfully trod the line between the beautiful and the perverse.

INTERSECTING WEBS:
MARKETS AND EXHIBITIONS

Although the establishment of metalsmithing programs was crucial to the field, studio jewelry would not have become a national movement without its other major catalyst—the emergence of a burgeoning market for American craft spurred by sales outlets and exhibitions. As studio jewelry widened its appeal, it outstripped existing marketing structures. With few gallery outlets available at that time, many craftsmen and jewelry artists turned increasingly to craft fairs, which drew thousands of visitors and became an important outlet for up-and-coming jewelers. While jewelers at craft fairs were taking the bottom-up approach to establishing a name for themselves, museum and gallery exhibitions were creating a top-down awareness of the new jewelry.

Beginning in the early 1940s, studio jewelry was regularly featured at America House in New York, including work by such artists as Margaret De Patta, Robert von Neumann, Bob Winston, and John Paul Miller.[35] The 1946 MoMA exhibition, *Modern Handmade Jewelry,* however, is widely regarded as the first major show to acknowledge "wearable art as a movement in America." Two years later *Modern Jewelry Under Fifty Dollars* opened at the Walker Art Center in Minneapolis, making it the next key event to showcase American studio jewelry.[36] Featuring thirty-two prominent artists, the exhibition traveled for two years, introducing Americans to the work of some of the nation's leading studio jewelers.

In 1955 the Huntington Galleries in West Virginia juried *American Jewelry and Related Objects, 1955: First National Exhibition,* a show that was later circulated by the Smithsonian Institution Traveling Exhibition Service. The success of this effort was quickly followed in 1956 by *American Jewelry and Related Objects, 1956: Second National Exhibition,* this time sponsored by the Memorial Art Gallery at the University of Rochester and again toured by the Smithsonian.

While these exhibitions were the most prominent, they were not isolated examples. Studio jewelry was also being promoted through exhibitions and competitions throughout the country. Many of these were annual events, notably the Wichita Art Association's annual *Decorative Art and Ceramics Exhibition,* which began in 1946,[37] and the *Fiber, Clay, and Metal* juried exhibitions initiated by the St. Paul Gallery and Art School in 1952. Such expositions attracted outstanding craftsmen from around the country.

The revolutionary changes in contemporary American jewelry soon became part of wider and more international developments. In 1961 the *First International Exhibition of Modern Jewelry,* curated by Graham Hughes and held in Goldsmiths' Hall, London, included a number of former outlier American artists—Irena Brynner, Alexander Calder, Claire Falkenstein, Mary Kretsinger, Stanley Lechtzin, and Margaret De Patta, among them—marking a defining moment in the international recognition of jewelry as an art form. When Hughes updated his study of modern jewelry in 1968, other American jewelers, such as Margret Craver, Fred Farr, Esther Hartshorn, Arthur King, Ibram Lassaw, John Paul Miller, and Ilya Schor were added to the international pantheon.[38]

IN FULL FLOWER

The diversity and vitality of international contemporary jewelry can trace its roots to the innovations of the American studio movement that flowered between 1945 and 1970. From the modernist idioms of the 1940s to the pop and Funk art of the 1960s, American jewelry makers transformed the world of ideas into wearable forms, uniting art, craft, and design to create the most intimate of artistic expressions. Drawing inspiration from a wide range of art movements and contemporary culture, American postwar jewelry artists took the field in new directions, employing innovative technologies and incorporating nontraditional materials in the highly inventive pieces they produced. The revolutionary movement that Americans set in motion between 1945 and 1970 was informed by European jewelry practices. In turn, they introduced ideas that have transformed international contemporary jewelry into a vibrant art form that continues to evolve and reflect a dynamically changing society and cultural landscape.

1 Milton W. Brown, Blanche R. Brown, Ed Wiener, *Jewelry by Ed Wiener: A Retrospective Exhibition*, exh. cat. (New York: Fifty/50 Gallery, 1988), 13.

2 The Society of North American Goldsmiths (SNAG) was formed in 1968.

3 Simone de Beauvoir, *America Day by Day* (New York: Grove Press, 1953), 331.

4 For art schools offering metalsmithing and jewelry classes in the mid-twentieth century, see Jeannine Falino, "Metalsmithing at Midcentury," in exh. cat., *Sculptural Concerns: Contemporary American Metal Working* (Cincinnati, OH: The Contemporary Arts Center, and Fort Wayne, IN: Fort Wayne Museum of Art, 1993) and W. Scott Braznell, "The Early Career of Ronald Hayes Pearson and the Post–World War II Revival of American Silversmithing and Jewelry-making," *Winterthur Portfolio* 34 (winter 1999), 189.

5 In 1943 Bertoia left for California to work with Charles and Ray Eames. After 1950 he concentrated on furniture design and sculpture.

6 Willard Gallery, New York, showed Calder's jewelry in the 1940s, and it was included in the 1943 MoMA exhibition *Alexander Calder: Sculptures and Constructions*.

7 Brown, Brown, and Wiener, *Jewelry by Ed Wiener*, 33. Ironically, Calder's inventive if not always wearable jewelry became a status symbol for wealthy individuals who wanted to be associated with the artistic avant-garde. Jane Adlin, "Calder and Adornment," in Alexander S. C. Rower and Holton Rower, eds., *Calder Jewelry* (New York: Calder Foundation, 2007), 173. John Paul Miller, oral history interview by Jan Yager, August 22–23, 2004, AAA, SI.

8 John Paul Miller, oral history interview.

9 Meg Torbert, ed., *Design Quarterly*, nos. 45/46, *American Jewelry* (1959), 63.

10 Philip Morton, *Contemporary Jewelry: A Studio Handbook* (New York: Holt, Rinehart and Winston, 1970). Morton went on to have a successful jewelrymaking and teaching career, after which he became a Jungian psychotherapist.

11 Ronald H. Pearson, oral history interview by Robert Brown, May 31, 1979 and November 23, 1981, AAA, SI.

12 Elisabeth R. Agro, "A Resonant Silence: The Unfinished Work of Olaf Skoogfors," *Metalsmith* 29 (winter 2009), 40–49.

13 Francisco Rebajes opened his studio/retail shop in the mid-1930s, followed by Sam Kramer in 1939, Paul Lobel in 1944, and Art Smith in 1946. Uptown shops were opened in the 1940s by Adda Husted-Anderson, Ed Weiner, and Henry Steig. Irena Brynner came to New York from the West Coast in 1957. Other studio jewelers working in and close to Greenwich Village in the 1940s and early 1950s included Bob and Esta Blood, Arthur King, Idella La Vista, Ed Levin, Frank Miraglia, Bill Tendler, Paul Voltaire, and Armand Winfield. Marbeth Schon, *Form and Function: American Modernist Jewelry, 1940–1970* (Aglen, Pennsylvania: Schiffer Publishing, 2008), 47.

14 Toni Greenbaum, *Messengers of Modernism: American Studio Jewelry 1940–1960*, exh. cat. (New York: The Montreal Museum of Decorative Arts in association with Flammarion, 1996), 22.

15 For a brief biography of Rebajes, see Rosemarie Haag Bletter, "The Myth of Modernism," in Janet Kardon, ed., *Craft in the Machine Age 1920–1945: The History of Twentieth-Century American Craft* (New York: Harry N. Abrams, 1995), 243. See also Toni Greenbaum, "The Double Life of Frank Rebajes," *Modernism Magazine* 5 (winter 2002), 62–69.

16 Greenbaum, *Messengers*, 74–76.

17 Ibid., 140.

18 From "These Two Hands: A Greenwich Villager Makes Many Objects from Many Materials," newspaper clipping, New York, June 1944, Paul Lobel papers, AAA, SI, quoted in Greenbaum, *Messengers*, 98.

19 *Art Smith: Jewelry*, exh. cat. (New York: Museum of Contemporary Crafts, 1969), 13.

20 "Jewelry Designers: Bertoia, De Patta, Kramer, Morton, and Winston," *Design Quarterly*, no. 33, *American Jewelry Designers and Their Work* (1955), 6.

21 Margaret De Patta, "From the Inside," *Palette* 32 (Spring 1952), 16–17. Rutilated quartz is a form of the mineral that contains needlelike crystal inclusions.

22 Yoshiko Uchida, "Margaret De Patta," in *The Jewelry of Margaret De Patta: A Retrospective Exhibition*, exh. cat. (Oakland: The Oakland Museum, 1976), 18.

23 Claire Falkenstein, oral history interview by Marjorie Rogers, September 16, 23, 1976; October 10, 28, 1976; November 7, 18, 1976; December 2, 18, 1976; January 20, 22, 1977, Center for Oral History Research, UCLA Library, University of California, Los Angeles.

24 According to De Patta, "Falkenstein got everything from Calder, hook, line and sinker"; quoted in *The Modernist Jewelry of Claire Falkenstein*, exh. cat. (Long Beach, CA: Long Beach Museum of Art, 2004), n.p.

25 The founding members included Peter Macchiarini, merry renk, Byron Wilson, Bob Winston, Florence Resnikoff, and Irena Brynner.

26 Irena Brynner, oral history interview by Arline M. Fisch, April 26–27, 2001, AAA, SI.

27 "We exchanged names of customers, we exchanged names of sources, we exchanged names of classes. We were able to just be as open with each other that no guild that we have heard of the past had. And we had exhibits that the group was invited to, or the organization accumulated cases and equipment that we could show [at] an open fair; the art festival was one. To me it was amazing"; merry renk, oral history interview by Arline M. Fisch, January 18–19, 2001, AAA, SI.

28 For more on this region, see Toni Greenbaum, "California Dreamin': Modernist Jewelers in Los Angeles, 1940–1970," *Metalsmith* 22 (winter, 2002), 40–47.

29 Ruth Penington, oral history interview by LaMar Harrington, February 10–11, 1983, AAA, SI.

30 Carole Beers, "Ruth Penington Brought Activism to Her Art Career," *Seattle Times* (March 15, 1998).

31 Ibid.

32 Irena Brynner (1957), Stanley Lechtzin (1965), John Paul Miller (1969), Art Smith (1969), and Margaret De Patta (1965).

33 For an excellent discussion of the craftsmen of this era, see "The Challenge of Freewheeling Artist-Craftsmen: Tradition and Innovation in the 1960s," in Edward S. Cooke, Jr., Gerald W. R. Ward, and Kelly H. L'Ecuyer, *The Maker's Hand: American Studio Furniture, 1940–1990*, exh. cat. (Boston: MFA Publications, 2003), 38–53.

34 Reid Hastie and Christian Schmidt, *Encounter with Art* (New York: McGraw Hill, 1969), 25–26.

35 "Jewelry Designs Shown by Five Artists," *New York Times* (April 2, 1954), 20.

36 Participating artists with pieces priced under fifty dollars included Margaret De Patta, Sam Kramer, Paul Lobel, Art Smith, Harry Bertoia, Claire Falkenstein, Philip Morton, and Bob Winston. The exhibition traveled across the country over a two-year period and was followed by additional exhibitions and print catalogues in 1955 and 1959.

37 In 1960 Rose Slivka noted that "it has been a heavy exhibition season. . . . The number of competitive group shows, local, regional and national were overwhelming," as quoted in Nordness, *Objects: USA*, 13.

38 Graham Hughes, *Modern Jewelry: An International Survey, 1890–1967* (London: Studio Vista, 1968).

159

IRENA BRYNNER

Earrings, 1967

18-KARAT GOLD

EACH: 3⅜ X 3 X ½ IN. (8.6 X 7.6 X 1.3 CM)

MUSEUM OF ARTS AND DESIGN, GIFT OF

THE JOHNSON WAX COMPANY, THROUGH THE

AMERICAN CRAFT COUNCIL, 1978

158

CHRISTIAN SCHMIDT

Medal of Honor, 1964

METALS, SEMIPRECIOUS STONES, CAMEO, FIBER, AND CLAY

L. (CLOSED) 9¼ IN. (23.5 CM)

MINNESOTA MUSEUM OF AMERICAN ART

160

RUTH RADAKOVICH

Cocktail Ring, 1969

14-KARAT GOLD AND TITANIUM RUTILE

2¾ X 1⅝ X 1⅝ IN. (7 X 4.1 X 4.1 CM)

MUSEUM OF ARTS AND DESIGN,

GIFT OF THE JOHNSON WAX COMPANY, THROUGH

THE AMERICAN CRAFT COUNCIL, 1977

161

ALEXANDER CALDER

Brooch, c. 1945

GOLD, STEEL WIRE

5¾ X 2⅛ IN. (14.6 X 5.6 CM)

COLLECTION OF PATRICIA PASTOR

162

ALEXANDER CALDER

Untitled, 1956

GOUACHE ON PAPER

35¼ X 43¼ IN. (89.5 X 109.9 CM)

COLLECTION OF PATRICIA PASTOR

AND BARRY FRIEDMAN

163

ERNEST ZIEGFELD

Necklace, c. 1958

STERLING SILVER

H. 6½ IN. (16.5 CM); DIAM. 4¾ IN. (12.1 CM)

LONG BEACH MUSEUM OF ART 58-9-1,

GIFT OF THE ARTIST

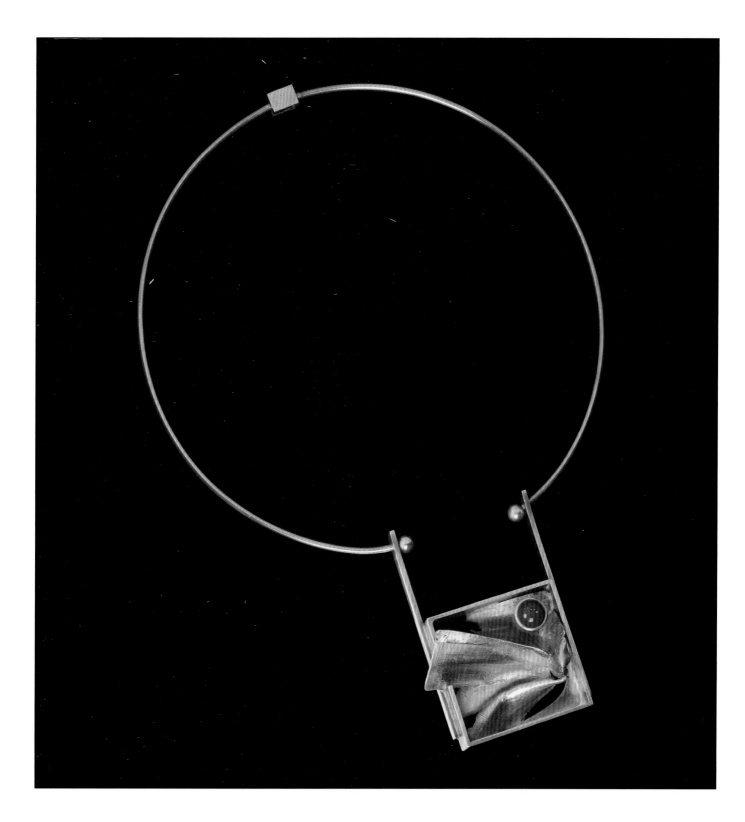

164

OLAF SKOOGFORS

Untitled (Necklace), 1967

STERLING SILVER, SILVER GILT, AND LAPIS LAZULI

8¼ X 5¾ X¾ IN. (21 X 14.6 X 1.9 CM)

MUSEUM OF ARTS AND DESIGN, GIFT OF FRIENDS

AND STUDENTS OF THE ARTIST, THROUGH

THE AMERICAN CRAFT COUNCIL, 1968

RONALD HAYES PEARSON
Untitled (Necklace), c. 1959
STERLING SILVER
5¼ X 5 X½ IN. (13.3 X 12.7 X 1.3 CM)
MUSEUM OF ARTS AND DESIGN, PURCHASED
BY THE AMERICAN CRAFT COUNCIL, 1959

165

JOHN PAUL MILLER
Necklace, 1953
GOLD
NECKLACE, L. 17 IN. (43.2 CM);
PENDANT, 2¾ X 1¾ IN. (7 X 4.6 CM)
CLEVELAND MUSEUM OF ART,
SILVER JUBILEE TREASURE FUND 1953.181

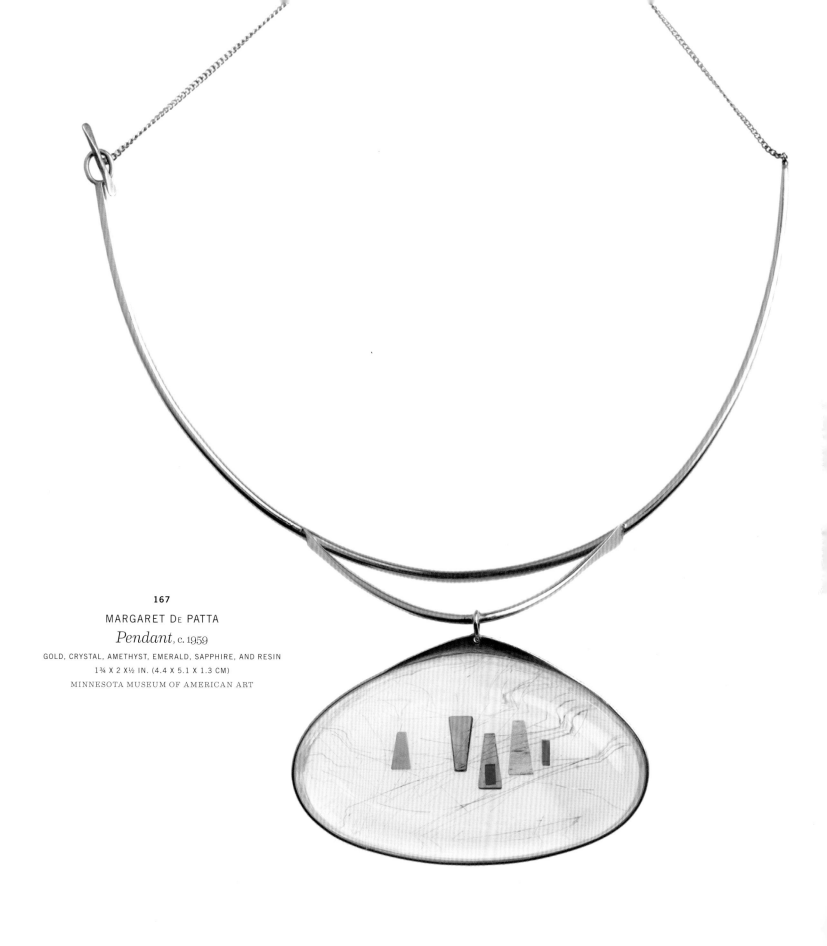

167

MARGARET De PATTA

Pendant, c. 1959

GOLD, CRYSTAL, AMETHYST, EMERALD, SAPPHIRE, AND RESIN

1¾ X 2 X½ IN. (4.4 X 5.1 X 1.3 CM)

MINNESOTA MUSEUM OF AMERICAN ART

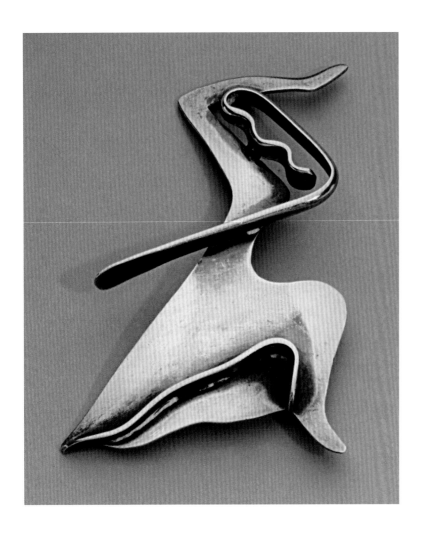

168

ED WIENER

Brooch, 1955

STERLING SILVER

3⅛ X 2 IN. (7.9 X 5.1 CM)

COLLECTION OF THE NEWARK MUSEUM, GIFT OF
BARBARA AND MICHAEL PRESS, 1998

169

KEN CORY

Tongue, 1967

STERLING SILVER, AMBER, AND LEATHER

2 X 1⁹⁄₁₆ X ½ IN. (5.1 X 4 X 1.3 CM)

TACOMA ART MUSEUM, GIFT OF THE
ESTATE OF KEN CORY, 1998.29.4

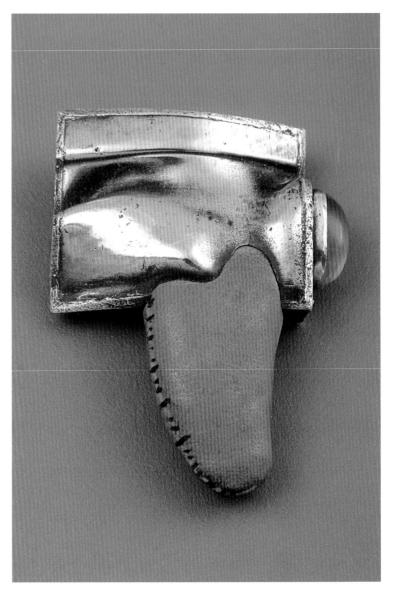

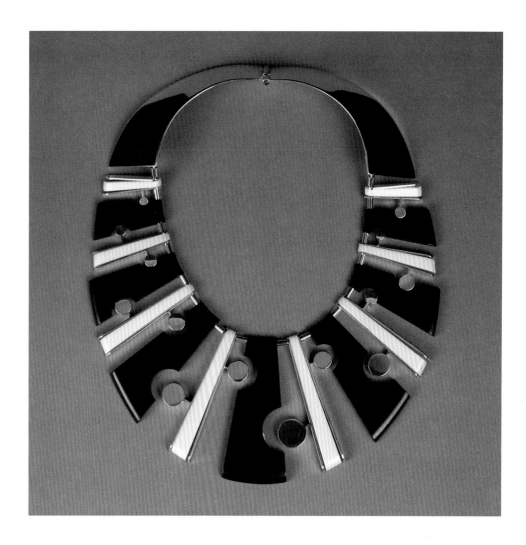

171

BYRON WILSON

Necklace, c. 1958

STERLING SILVER, EBONY, AND IVORY

14 X 2⅝ IN. (35.6 X 6.7 CM)

ROCHESTER MEMORIAL ART GALLERY 58.144

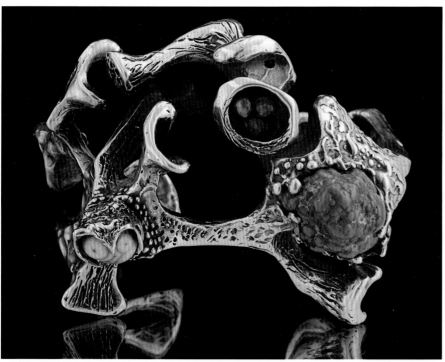

170

BOB WINSTON

Bracelet with Nest, Three Eggs,
and Large Turquoise, 1948

STERLING SILVER, TURQUOISE, AND BRASS

2½ X 3½ X 4 IN. (6.4 X 8.9 X 10.2 CM)

SMITHSONIAN AMERICAN ART MUSEUM, GIFT
OF BOB AND JANEDARE WINSTON 2002.61.1

172

J. FRED WOELL

The Good Guys, 1966

WALNUT, STEEL, COPPER, PLASTIC,
STERLING SILVER, AND GOLD LEAF
4 X ½ IN. (10.2 X 1.3 CM)
MUSEUM OF ARTS AND DESIGN, GIFT OF
THE JOHNSON WAX COMPANY, THROUGH THE
AMERICAN CRAFT COUNCIL, 1977

173

EARL PARDON

Suspended Forms, 1959

ENAMEL, COPPER, PINE, AND BRASS
20⅛ X 54½ X 6 IN. (51.1 X 138.4 X 15.2 CM)
MUSEUM OF ARTS AND DESIGN, COMMISSIONED
BY THE AMERICAN CRAFT COUNCIL, 1959

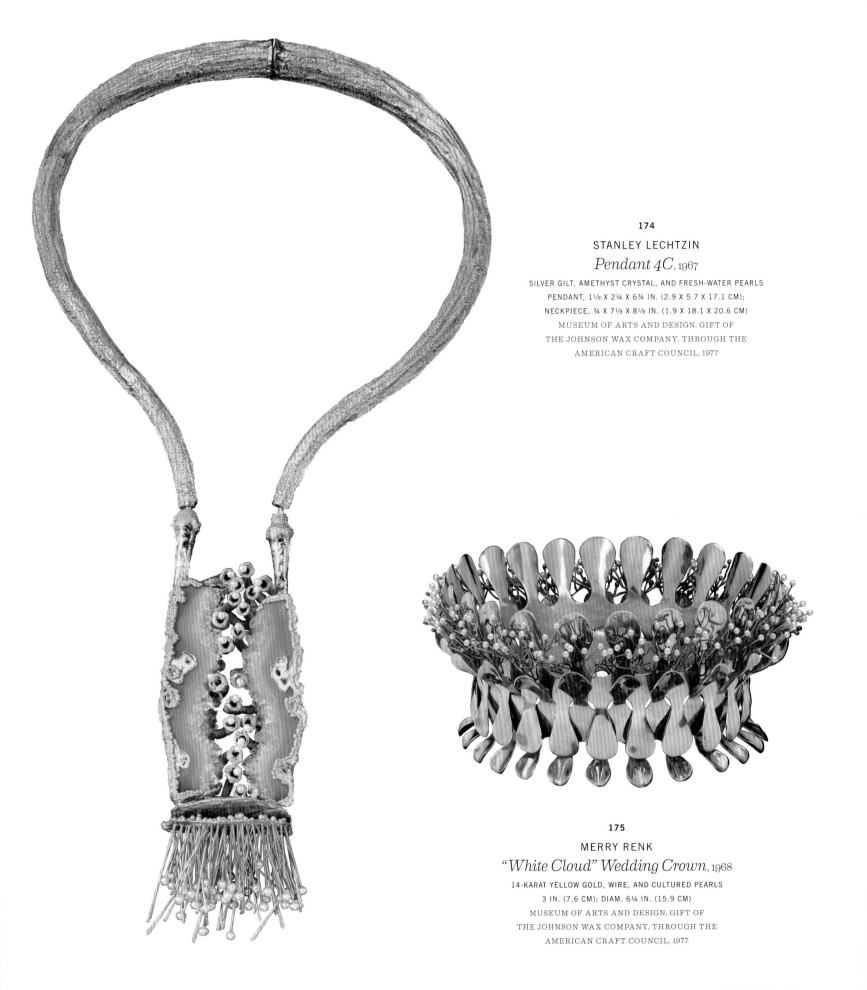

174

STANLEY LECHTZIN
Pendant 4C, 1967
SILVER GILT, AMETHYST CRYSTAL, AND FRESH-WATER PEARLS
PENDANT, 1⅛ X 2¼ X 6¾ IN. (2.9 X 5.7 X 17.1 CM);
NECKPIECE, ¾ X 7⅛ X 8⅛ IN. (1.9 X 18.1 X 20.6 CM)
MUSEUM OF ARTS AND DESIGN, GIFT OF
THE JOHNSON WAX COMPANY, THROUGH THE
AMERICAN CRAFT COUNCIL, 1977

175

MERRY RENK
"White Cloud" Wedding Crown, 1968
14-KARAT YELLOW GOLD, WIRE, AND CULTURED PEARLS
3 IN. (7.6 CM); DIAM. 6¼ IN. (15.9 CM)
MUSEUM OF ARTS AND DESIGN, GIFT OF
THE JOHNSON WAX COMPANY, THROUGH THE
AMERICAN CRAFT COUNCIL, 1977

176

ORVILLE CHATT

Untitled (Necklace), c. 1965

STERLING SILVER, JADE, AND PEARLS

14½ X 6½ IN. (36.8 X 16.5 CM)

TACOMA ART MUSEUM,

GIFT OF THE ARTIST, 2004.14.2

177

LYNDA WATSON

*Landscape
(Neckpiece),* 1968

STERLING SILVER AND ENAMEL

11 X 9¼ IN. (27.9 X 23.5 CM)

MUSEUM OF ARTS AND DESIGN,

GIFT OF THE JOHNSON WAX

COMPANY THROUGH THE

AMERICAN CRAFT COUNCIL, 1977

CHAPTER 11

Druids and Dropouts: Working Wood, 1945–1969

DAVID L. BARQUIST

THE QUARTER CENTURY BETWEEN 1945 AND 1970 was one of the seminal periods for woodworking in the United States. During the Great Depression, metal, glass, and other industrial materials had triumphed as the ultimate in modernity and sophistication. The postwar generation, seeking an alternative to the austerity of the Depression and war years, embraced wood as a more natural and traditional medium. A dazzling sequence of iconic landmarks in the history of American craft followed, beginning with Rude Osolnik's irregular wood turnings of about 1945 and George Nakashima's natural-edge, slab-top coffee table of 1946, through the elegant lines of Sam Maloof's trademark rocking chair of 1963 and Wendell Castle's music stand of 1964. There were the bold forms of Art Carpenter's *Wishbone Chair* and of Tommy Simpson's *Man Balancing a Feather on His Knows*, both from 1968, as well as Jere Osgood's *Chest of Drawers* of 1969 **(FIG. 11.1)**.[1]

These craftsmen celebrated wood with a passion that became the identifying characteristic of makers of handmade furniture and turnings in the decades after the war. Artists as different as Nakashima and J. B. Blunk shared a similar devotion to their medium. Nakashima was renowned for his spiritual response, laboring not to impose designs on the material but to bring out what he called "the soul of the tree"; as he explained, "We work with boards from these trees, to fulfill their yearning for a second life, to release their richness and beauty . . . to fulfill the tree's destiny and ours."[2] Blunk, who carefully chose exceptional root forms, was also looking for "the soul of the piece."[3]

As an organic material, wood, unlike most other mediums, imparted an individual identity to each object, reinforcing the uniqueness of the finished work. "Wood is a living material and I am fascinated with its use as such," Osgood observed in 1970. "Each wood has an inherent structure—a color, texture, and workability—a feeling that will suggest the mass or shape of a piece of furniture."[4] Furniture designer Edward Wormley extolled this aspect of wood in 1953:

> Wood, so palpably a living thing marked with the idiosyncrasies of its will to grow, cannot fail to spark the imagination of the artist in ways in which impersonal metal or dead clay cannot do. . . . For every individual board of every species of wood, like the human face, has its own unique markings and in selecting it the designer exercises his utmost sensitivity. With his experience and skill he knows that his shaping of the elements of his design must take advantage of the wood figure, and the true sculptor in this raw material will find it impossible to ignore the complement of this natural pattern to the form he has imagined.[5]

Not all woodworkers, however, approached their medium with the same reverence. Carpenter observed, "With wood, what do you have to know? The stuff grows and you just cut it down and make something."[6]

From an appreciation of wood's inherent uniqueness, it followed that the maker's role was less to design a given object than to respond sympathetically to the specific piece of wood chosen for that project. The finished work united the material's individual character with the maker's unique vision. "I don't know where my shapes come from, they just grow as I turn," Bob Stocksdale reported.[7] Nakashima stated, "Design should sing more to the hum of four blades turning at 4,000 r.p.m., or to the soft rustle of long curled shavings from a keen edge, and less to the scratch of a pencil over a drafting board."[8] Philip Lloyd Powell similarly saw designing and crafting as complementary processes: "I continue remodeling, add or cut to create an entire finished whole piece. It's a gradual process."[9]

This notion of responding to individual pieces of wood resulted in one of the signature aspects of objects made by American woodworkers during this period—the retention of natural irregularities that previously would have been cut away, sanded down, or otherwise refined.

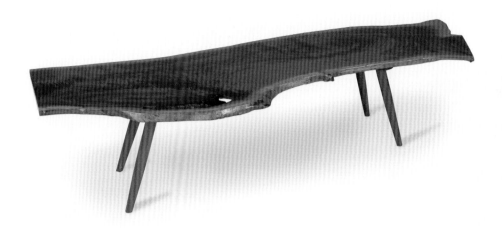

Nakashima's 1946 coffee table for the Stanley Brogren House in Pittsburgh, whose plank top had contours following the tree's original silhouette, was one of the earliest American objects to feature what he called a "free edge" **(FIG. 11.2)**.[10] He also chose to leave unfilled any holes present in the board. "There may be a large hole where decay has started and the tree has healed itself," Nakashima declared, "a positive statement of life which makes an extraordinary design expression."[11] Another pioneer in retaining features of individual pieces of wood was Rude Osolnik, who chose to turn tree spurs, projections from roots or trunks, resulting in shapes he called "free-form." "I could not wait to put it on the lathe to see the beauty of each piece," Osolnik recalled. "The more knotty, craggy, and gnarly the piece, the more it excited me."[12]

In part this renewed interest in wood reflected the economic prosperity and industrial progress of postwar America. As the United States became a world superpower, products from all over the globe became available domestically, including kinds of wood that previous generations would have found costly and difficult to procure. Stocksdale was renowned for spending as much time seeking exotic woods as he did turning in his studio.[13]

Nakashima sought out woods from all over the world, insisting on supervising the cutting of logs, "like cutting a diamond."[14] The wartime development of new epoxies opened the way for new methods of joining and laminating wood. "What I'm doing now wouldn't have been possible years ago," Osgood observed. "All of the good glues were developed after or during World War II time, so these lamination processes that I use just wouldn't have existed prior to 1942."[15] Plywood, in fact, had been the medium used by Eero Saarinen and Charles Eames for their landmark molded furniture shown at the Museum of Modern Art (MoMA) in New York in 1941.

The overwhelming majority of these woodworkers were either self-taught or had minimal training, Osgood being the notable exception. Although World War II had a profound impact on their lives, their beginnings as craftsmen were almost inadvertent results of the war. Almost none of them attended any of the craft schools that sprang up after the war, although the GI Bill did allow veterans such as Carpenter to purchase tools and begin work. Most had been trained in other professions: Edgar Anderson, Nakashima, and Osgood studied architecture; Jerry Glaser, Philip Lloyd Powell, and James Prestini were engineers; Wendell Castle, Jack Rogers Hopkins, and Tommy Simpson studied painting, sculpture, and photography; Blunk focused on ceramics, and Richard Artschwager trained as a bacteriological chemist. Several makers proudly claimed that their furniture making was the result of personal trial and error. "You figure somehow

Arthur Espenet Carpenter, *Wishbone Chair*, **1970. Walnut and leather. 31 x 21¼ x 21½ in. (78.7 x 54 x 54.6 cm). Yale University Art Gallery; 1999.70.**

traditional cabinetmaking. By favoring personal expression over financial security, with limited production that was not always economically viable, these craftsmen challenged the prevailing culture of conformity and prosperity. "I do not want to be in the *business* [emphasis added] of making furniture," Powell stated. "When I had eight employees, I realized I was in the business. As a dropout I did not want to be just a designer."[19] In other words, Powell wanted to keep his hand in, to make furniture for himself, not just design and delegate to others. A similar ethos was shared by many of his contemporaries, including Edgar and Joyce Anderson: "We have the capacity to make a lot more money, but we choose what we want to do and live accordingly."[20] Osgood also recalled, "In the sixties . . . we were going strong. . . . You could go out in the bushes and start weaving, and be a success and sleep under a rock, and like it."[21]

Wharton Esherick pioneered the archetype of the self-taught woodworker producing innovative designs in rural isolation, beginning in the 1920s. Trained as a painter, Esherick gradually transitioned into a full-time designer and sculptor, relying on assistants who were trained cabinetmakers to fabricate his furniture. Much like his successors, Esherick had a quasi-spiritual relationship with wood: "Trees were the very life of Wharton," architect Louis I. Kahn observed. "He had a love affair with them; a sense of oneness with the very wood itself."[22]

Esherick's furniture and fittings, especially the dramatic staircase for George Howe's "Pennsylvania Hill House" interior at the 1939 New York World's Fair, brought him national attention, and his work was featured in virtually every article on and exhibition of handmade furniture in the postwar period. Critics and historians credited him with "almost singlehandedly establish[ing] the twentieth-century style of American woodworking."[23] The studio woodworkers, particularly those of the younger generation, acknowledged him as a major inspiration. "When I saw his work, what it was, was permission to do what I wanted to do in the way of furniture forms," Jere Osgood declared.[24] In 1958 the recently graduated Wendell Castle traveled to Paoli, Pennsylvania, to meet the reclusive Esherick but was unsuccessful. Nevertheless, he later observed, "Esherick taught me that the making of furniture could be a form of sculpture."[25]

In the quarter century between 1945 and 1970, two distinct phases of work emerged. The first phase, from 1945 until the early 1960s, consisted primarily of fine

you can make a table, and you use beautiful materials," Artschwager observed. "You tell people 'I'll build you anything,' and you hope it holds together."[16] Similarly, when asked about the origin of his *Wishbone Chair* (FIG. 11.3), Carpenter noted, "[It] took me a year or two to figure out. I mean, I was a very slow learner. . . . I had to do probably ten years before I got to this chair."[17]

These woodworkers adhered to the model of the solitary craftsman, working in a natural setting, creating unique objects. They were perceived as such by industrial designers such as Charles Eames, who in an interview questioned "how one was to bring the juices of craftsmanship into the joints of a piece of furniture when the handcraftsmen were off somewhere making pots."[18] The postwar woodworkers were comfortable working alone in a studio as opposed to the cooperative workshop of furniture and turned vessels made by a generation of craftsmen born before 1930, including Nakashima, Maloof, Osolnik, Stocksdale, and Carpenter, whose adult lives and careers were affected directly by World War II. The furniture and objects they made during this period were primarily traditional, functional forms: chairs, stools, tables, cabinets, chests of drawers, open bowls, and wooden vessels. Turned elements were tapered and attenuated, frequently joined to other members at an angle. Attempts were made to lighten the mass of individual pieces by reducing the size of the frame elements, often by carving away sections not needed as points of attachment, so that chair seats and backs and the tops of tables and cabinets appeared to float. Some woodworkers eliminated seat frames altogether, using plank seats with other elements doweled in place.

One aspect of this style was characterized by the *New York Times* as "the popular 'sculptured look.'"[26] Wooden elements were curved or shaped to soften their rectilinearity, and surface carving, paint, and other applied decoration were almost completely absent. Walnut was a particularly favorite wood. Philip Lloyd Powell, for example, preferred it because it was easier to shape with his favorite tool, a spoke shave, "which requires a sculptor's skill."[27] Evert Sodergren made this same connection, naming a 1953 design *Sculptured Chair*.[28] The frequently noted "California roundover" style, typified by Art Carpenter's work, seems part of this same preference for smooth, sculpted surfaces, rather than being a distinctly regional phenomenon.[29]

Another important stylistic feature of furniture from this period was having different parts of a piece flow together, accomplished with dynamic curved lines instead of right angles or parabolic openings in turned vessels. Edgar Anderson observed that "to be successful, a piece must have a continuum from one design element to another."[30] Other designers sought to combine legs, arms, and seat frame into a single sculptural entity, as in Sodergren's *Sculptured Chair* and Carpenter's *Wishbone Chair*.

European furniture design was an important influence on these American craftsmen. Jean Prouvé, Charlotte Perriand, Carlo Mollino, and Gio Ponti created furniture in the 1940s and '50s with marked similarities to many contemporary American works. For example, Nakashima's "free edge" may have been inspired by Perriand's table with a top cut out of a tree root, which was exhibited in 1941 at the Takashimaya store in Tokyo.[31]

For the postwar generation of Americans, however, Danish furniture designers of the 1940s were the most influential. Architect Finn Juhl's chairs with floating seats and attenuated members were featured in a 1948 article by Edgar Kaufmann Jr., and in 1951 Juhl designed a group for Baker Furniture.[32] His *Chieftan Armchair* was included in the traveling exhibition *Design in Scandinavia* (1954–57) **(FIG. 11.4)**, as was Hans Wegner's *Round Armchair* of 1949, which was marketed in both New York and San Francisco.[33] By the early 1950s the United States accounted for a high percentage of the export market for Danish furniture, primarily of high-end production, such as chairs by Wegner and Juhl.[34] In addition, Danish craftsmen and designers, most notably Tage Frid and Jens Risom, respectively, worked in the United States. As the founding faculty member for woodworking at the School for American Craftsmen, which was then located at Alfred University but moved to the Rochester Institute of Technology a few years later, Frid taught many younger woodworkers, including Jere Osgood.[35]

FIG. 11.4

Finn Juhl, *"Chieftan" Armchair*, designed 1949 (original model made by Niels Vodder). Teak and leather. 37 x 41 x 37 in. (94 x 104.1 x 94 cm). Museum of Art & Design Denmark; 5/1983.

FIG. 11.5
Russel Wright, *Armchair with adjustable back*, 1932. Mahogany, leather, and pony fur. 31½ x 29 x 27 in. (80 x 73.7 x 68.6 cm). The Museum of Modern Art, New York, NY, Purchase Fund 150.1958.

These design elements, sympathetic to the studio woodworker's tendency to follow the natural, organic form of the wood, were echoed in pieces by contemporary craftsmen. In his interior for the 1939 "Pennsylvania Hill House" installation, Esherick combined angular, cubist forms that he had been exploring since the late 1920s with organic, curved shapes (most notably the spiral staircase) that presaged his work of the 1940s into the 1960s.

Much like the Danish imports that inspired them, the furniture produced by these postwar American craftsmen was well received. Beginning in the late 1940s, Maloof and Nakashima received extensive press coverage in *House Beautiful*, *Life*, *Look*, and *Newsweek*, as well as in *Craft Horizons* and other art and architecture periodicals.[38] Two exhibitions—*Designer Craftsmen U.S.A.*, which traveled in 1953–54 and was organized by the Brooklyn Museum, and *Furniture by Craftsmen* (1957), shown at the Museum of Contemporary Crafts—focused on American furniture and objects influenced by Scandinavian models. Several craftsmen sought to capitalize on this attention by broadening their markets. Nakashima designed four pieces of furniture for mass production by Knoll Associates (1946–54), and he created a larger Origins line for Widdicomb-Mueller (1957–61; **FIG. 11.6**).[39] Paul Evans designed for Directional Industries beginning in the early 1960s.

As popularity increased demand, the concomitant pressure to increase production raised issues of technology and technique. Much of the rhetoric of postwar woodworking paralleled the Arts and Crafts movement of the early twentieth century, which idealized wood as a natural material that a solitary artist could work (and in some cases, even harvest) by himself, using relatively simple technology, in ways that highlighted the material's unique qualities. Like their Arts and Crafts predecessors, the craftsmen working after World War II also had to confront the reality of furniture visually embodying their aesthetics being made with modern machines and a division of labor in order to be affordable.[40] Both Nakashima and Maloof had technology and shop practices in place, including the use of assistants, that allowed them to expand their production. Nakashima declared in 1953, "We must adapt to our experiences and our technology. To accomplish this, as I see it, a whole new environment has to be created, an environment not based on the sentiments of the spinning wheel, but also not based on the sentiments and tyrannies of the production line. Rather an environment which provides a synthesis of what is

Traditional American furniture was another important source. Eighteenth-century Windsor chairs and nineteenth-century Shaker furniture were recognized as major influences by designers and commentators as diverse as T. H. Robsjohn-Gibbings and Elizabeth Tower Halsey.[36] Organic or biomorphic designs from the preceding decades were equally significant. As early as 1932, Russel Wright had created an armchair with sculpted, curvilinear elements of primavera wood that responded to the form of a human sitter **(FIG. 11.5)**. Although a unique object made for his own use, the chair was included in *Art of Our Time*, a 1939 exhibition at MoMA, and at the end of the same year, examples of his naturalistic Oceana line of wood table accessories were featured in the exhibition *Useful Objects of American Design Under $10.00*, also at MoMA.[37] Biomorphic elements, flat-sawn from plywood, appeared on chairs designed in 1939 by Walter Gropius and Marcel Breuer for the Frank House in Pittsburgh, and on Frederick Kiesler's furniture in 1942 for Peggy Guggenheim's Art of this Century Gallery in New York.

good for us as human beings, who are in control of their environment, not victims of it."[41] Carpenter put it more succinctly: "I did not care how I made it, provided it came out right."[42]

Nakashima and Maloof's acceptance of electrical power, machine tools, and shop assistants ran counter to the image they cultivated of a solitary artisan crafting unique objects. Subsequent analyses of their work have focused on this contradiction. On the one hand, furniture that was handmade in small quantities was necessarily more expensive than factory-produced objects, so the work was seen as elitist.[43] On the other hand, artists such as Nakashima and to a lesser extent Maloof, who were successful in marketing their work on a larger scale, were seen as operating quasi-factories. As part of this emphasis on production, their designs showed only subtle changes over time. In fact, Nakashima's Origins line for Widdicomb-Mueller was marketed as "timeless" design. One critic noted that "once a prototype is perfected, Maloof will work from it indefinitely because he believes that trends and fashion are transient, but classic design and good craftsmanship will endure over time."[44] In a period of fifty years, Sodergren estimated that he made over two hundred replicas of his *Sculptured Chair*.[45]

These tensions and contradictions in the woodworking community increasingly became a point of contention for a younger generation of artists, critics, and consumers. By the early 1960s the work of the previous fifteen years began to seem uninspired. It was criticized for what was characterized as its derivative style; furniture designer Tony Chastain-Chapman sarcastically noted that "the Early Craft Revival Style (squared off Scandinavian Modern cum Shaker with exposed joinery) was becoming a bore."[46] The quasi-religious veneration of wood by Nakashima and others was ridiculed by woodworker William Keyser as "searching for God in a knothole," and John Kelsey of *Fine Woodworking* magazine derisively referred to such craftsmen as "Druids."[47]

Beginning in the early 1960s, a generation of woodworkers born after 1930 came of age, including Blunk, Castle, Dan Jackson, Melvin Lindquist, Osgood, and Tommy Simpson. Although most were raised during wartime, their careers began in the postwar period, and their priorities were very different from their immediate forebears'. A primary difference was their rejection of the preciousness of wood. Artschwager commented, "It was Formica which touched it off. Formica, the great ugly material, the horror

of the age, which I came to like suddenly because I was sick of looking at all this beautiful wood."[48] The careful choice of woods for individual pieces was replaced by the use of inferior woods whose surfaces would be painted over or by laminated blocks that offered new opportunities for fabrication as well as increases in scale.

Part of this devaluation of wood lay in the younger craftsmen's use of it as a means for realizing their own artistic self-expression. Whereas older artists had used wood to guide the outcome of their work, the younger artists relied on their vision. Castle, who became perhaps the best known of this generation, summed up their attitude in 1970: "It is important not to be subservient to a material. The significant thing about my work is not what it is made of but what it is."[49] Powell similarly observed, "My imagination runs over itself. It far exceeded what I could make."[50] This approach rendered traditional cabinetmaking skills less useful, and several makers turned to such nontraditional tools as the chain saw. Blunk was extolled for exploring "the sublime qualities of shape and

FIG. 11.6
George Nakashima,
Origins Chair #257, 1960.
Manufacturer: Widdicomb-Mueller. Walnut and upholstery fabric. Courtesy of George Nakashima Woodworker S.A.

color in an abstract way, avoiding the generic and reductive methods of carpentry."[51]

The act of creation, therefore, was not to be predetermined by patterns or material, but became an opportunity for the craftsman to tap into and express his innermost self. Blunk described his method of working: "Since I principally use a chain saw to do this, it is a process that moves quickly. . . . At times the cutting away and forming happen so fast it is almost unconscious."[52] Simpson similarly observed, "The act of making brings to me an awareness of my body, my heart and my mind. When I start to work, I can let go of everything, the everyday world is released from my consciousness. The most intimate me flows open, unobstructed, infusing itself with the work at hand."[53] These statements echoed the ideology of abstract expressionist artists from the late 1940s and early 1950s, for whom a painting stood as a record of the act of its creation. As Robert Motherwell famously stated, "The process of painting then is conceived of as an adventure, without preconceived ideas on the part of persons of intelligence, sensibility and passion. Fidelity to what occurs between oneself and the canvas, no matter how unexpected, becomes central."[54]

It followed that the resulting objects would reveal much more of the individual artist than the furniture

and turnings made by the previous generation of craftsmen. Instead of uniformly smooth, sculptured surfaces, objects showed the irregularities of the artist's hand. Both *Blunk's Hunk*, a public seating sculpture made in 1968 for the University of California at Santa Cruz, and *Planet*, made by Blunk in 1969 for the Oakland Museum **(FIG. 11.7)**, had a variety of surface treatments, both rough and smooth, that were associated with Blunk's desire to avoid "the type of perfection that made a piece too precious for use."[55] Jerry Glaser's bowl of 1963 had a carved edge, surface, and feet that were very different from the precision of work by Prestini or Osolnik.[56] The covered vessel made by Frank E. Cummings III featured not only carved and hand-shaped passages, but applied decorations that made explicit references to African prototypes and Cummings's own African heritage. It logically followed that objects could become almost a double of their maker. Speaking of furniture by Dan Jackson, his student Alphonse Mattia observed, "Dan always looked like he was doing an impression of a piece of his own furniture. Cowboy hat and boots, backbent swag—sometimes he looked like a perfect illustration of the springy stick 'S curve' he taught us so well."[57]

The objects produced by these craftsmen looked very different from those of their immediate predecessors.

FIG. 11.7

J. B. Blunk, *Planet*, 1969. Redwood burl. 36 x 144 x 144 in. (91.4 x 365.8 x 365.8 cm). Oakland Museum of California, Founders Fund.

Whereas traditional vessels and furniture forms had dominated the output of the previous generation, objects now appeared in shapes that seemingly defied functionality. Cabinets took on bulbous or anthropomorphic forms; tables and chairs were fused into single elements. Dramatic designs and surprising or witty elements underscored this unconventional quality. Craftsmen repeatedly stated their desire to be freed from the traditional furniture forms. "I'm not interested in reassembling dead furniture makers' body parts," Osgood stated.[58] Castle was equally succinct: "I was interested in . . . getting the base out from under the table and making the whole thing a piece of sculpture."[59] Paul Evans, a metalworker who collaborated with Philip Lloyd Powell, saw the elegant lines and silhouettes of earlier furniture as better suited to mass production: "Mr. Evans is of the opinion that handmade products should show the hand. Good line is not enough because that can be produced industrially."[60]

The two most important influences on these younger woodworkers were Esherick and Isamu Noguchi. Esherick's approach to woodworking had from the beginning been that of an artist: "I begin to shape [wood] as I go along. The piece just grows beneath my hands. I treat furniture as though it were a piece of sculpture. I dig up what I do out of my soul."[61] The abstract forms and voids of Noguchi's furniture, such as his laminated and carved table of about 1941, were the same as those found in his contemporaneous wood sculpture (**FIG. 11.8**). Much like Nakashima, Noguchi was inspired by Eastern metaphysics and preferred wood as a medium because of the expressive potential of its figure.[62] Osgood cited Noguchi as an important influence, praising his "pure forms that doesn't [sic] refer to other furniture forms."[63] Blunk's career was largely determined by Noguchi, who befriended him in Japan, and Blunk's work similarly shows an interest in bold, abstract forms and varied textures. Interestingly, a number of postwar sculptors who used wood as their medium, including H. C. Westermann and George Sugarman, produced work that offered striking parallels in technique and intent to the furniture of second-generation studio furniture makers; in fact, Castle cited Sugarman's sculpture as an important influence on his work (**FIG. 11.9**).[64]

The focus on objects as a vehicle for self-expression beyond function and the blurring of boundaries between functional furniture and art were characteristic of the 1960s. Pop artists in particular took ordinary objects as

FIG. 11.8
Isamu Noguchi, *Table*, c. 1941. Avodire. 30 x 41 x 16 in. (76.2 x 104.1 x 40.16 cm). Museum of Modern Art, New York, The Philip L. Goodwin Collection, Gift of James L. Goodwin, Henry Sage Goodwin, and Richmond L. Brown; 107.1958.

subjects for art. "Furniture in its largest sense is an object which celebrates something that people do—or sanctifies it," Artschwager observed. "I'm making objects for non-use. . . . By killing off the use part, non-use aspects are allowed living space, breathing space."[65] His *Cradle* of 1967 evoked ideas of enclosure and security, but in monolithic shapes veneered in a dark, wood-patterned Formica that were at once menacing and ironic.[66] Tommy Simpson's *Man Balancing a Feather on His Knows* of 1968 offered less function than commentary. Describing this object, Simpson said, "I approach the problem through the abstraction of the space, composition, line, etc. of furniture and the meaning of furniture. I desire my furniture to depict storage as an adjective as well as a noun. I see an object which is for the safekeeping of goods take on its meaning as the depository of hopes, loves, sorrows as well as for books, foodstuffs, and underwear."[67] His words are strikingly similar to Claes Oldenburg's statement concerning his vinyl objects in 1965: "What I want to do is create an independent object which has its existence in a world outside of both the real world as we know it and

FIG. 11.9
George Sugarman, *Yellow Top*, 1960. Wood and paint. 89 x 46 x 34 in. (226.1 x 116.8 x 86.4 cm). Walker Art Center, Minneapolis, Minnesota, Gift of the T.B. Walker Foundation, 1966; 1966.19.

the world of art. It's an independent thing which has its own power, just to sit there and remain something of a mystery."[68] One critic has also linked Simpson's work to Funk artists: "combining whimsy with images from the world of dreams, these artists seek to charm and transport rather than to offend or provoke.... Theirs is an art of recognizable content, far removed from the nonreferential forms of abstraction."[69]

Artschwager was perhaps the best known of a number of woodworkers from the earlier generation who moved from making traditional furniture to creating sculpture. Osgood later mused, "Maybe the earlier furniture looked more like furniture. And people do say now that my work does look more like sculpture; its influence is more from sculpture."[70] In the 1970s Edgar and Joyce Anderson similarly moved away from Scandinavian-influenced forms to more witty designs, such as a Chest of Drawers series shaped like female torsos.[71]

Not surprisingly, the work of the younger generation found less universal acclaim than the furniture made by their predecessors, appealing instead to an elite audience. If *Designer Craftsmen U.S.A.* and *Furniture by Craftsmen* were the seminal exhibitions for promoting the work of earlier woodworkers, so *Fantasy Furniture* at the Museum

of Contemporary Crafts and the traveling exhibition *Objects: USA* of 1969 promoted the work of wood artists who "refuse to accept the tradition of functionalism."[72] Their self-consciously expressive, artistic works met with much criticism, often from fellow craftsmen with a different outlook. "It is all too easy to conceive of a piece that could be executed in theory, but that in practice would be simply too hard to handle," Osgood observed. "Being able to build a piece of furniture that bulges wildly in all directions at once is not a good enough reason for doing so."[73] Carpenter similarly remained skeptical of pieces that lacked a function. "If you put utility on one side and art on the other side, I think most of them [independent craftsmen] were surviving close to the art side rather than the utility side.... The schools, in particular, push the art aspect. I suppose they figure that IKEA can do all of the utility."[74] The outspoken critic of the younger generation was woodworker James Krenov, who dismissed Castle as having forsaken the "integrity and humility of his craft to achieve commercial success by overplaying the 'art' of novel forms."[75]

Despite these differences, woodworkers in the period between 1945 and 1970 shared several important accomplishments. Collectively they restored wood as a primary medium for artistic achievement after about two decades of modernist celebration of new materials. They affirmed the archetype of the studio woodworker that Esherick had pioneered. In the next decade, the field would expand and professionalize rapidly: instead of isolated dropouts working in natural settings, woodworkers sought education in specialized programs and exhibited their work in specialized galleries. Seminal events such as the 1972 exhibition *Woodenworks* at the Renwick Gallery in Washington, DC, or the first Wood Turning Symposium at the George School in Newtown, Pennsylvania, in 1976 brought woodworking to a national audience. By the end of the decade, the traveling exhibition *New Handmade Furniture* illustrated how the new directions of the late 1940s and '50s and the radical experiments of the 1960s had generated a major phenomenon. The spectacular objects made during the postwar years remain as an impressive legacy of their makers and time.

1 For an in-depth survey of American handmade furniture from this period, see Edward S. Cooke Jr., Gerald W. R. Ward, and Kelly H. L'Ecuyer, *The Maker's Hand: American Studio Furniture, 1940–1990* (Boston: MFA Publications, 2003), esp. 18–53; for an in-depth survey of wood turning of the same period, see Edward S. Cooke Jr., "From Manual Training to Freewheeling Craft: The Transformation of Wood Turning, 1900–76," in *Wood Turning in North America since 1930* (Philadelphia: Wood Turning Center; New Haven: Yale University Art Gallery, 2001), 12–63.

2 George Nakashima, *The Soul of a Tree: A Woodworker's Reflections* (Tokyo, New York, and San Francisco: Kodansha International, 1981), xxi.

3 Quoted in Todd Merrill and Julie Iovine, eds., *Modern Americana: Studio Furniture from High Craft to High Glam* (New York: Rizzoli, 2007), 35.

4 Lee Nordness, *Objects: USA—Works by Artist-Craftsmen in Ceramic, Enamel, Glass, Metal, Plastic, Mosaic, Wood, and Fiber* (New York: Viking Press/Studio Books, 1970), 265.

5 Edward J. Wormley, "Wood," in *Designer Craftsmen U.S.A.* (New York: Brooklyn Museum and the American Craftsmen's Educational Council, 1953), 52, 54.

6 Kathleen Hannah and Arthur Espenet Carpenter, "A Straightforward Desire for Utility: An Interview with Furniture Maker Arthur Espenet Carpenter," *Archives of American Art Journal* 43, nos. 1 and 2 (2003), 32.

7 Quoted in Michael A. Stone, *Contemporary American Woodworkers* (Salt Lake City: Gibbs Smith, 1986), 35.

8 Mira Nakashima, *Nature, Form, and Spirit: The Life and Legacy of George Nakashima* (New York: Harry N. Abrams, 2003), 77, quoting Bernard Rudofsky, "Modern Doesn't Pay or Does It?" *Interiors* 105 (March 1946), 66–75.

9 Edith Skiba Lamonica, "Behind the Eye: Philip Lloyd Powell," 2005, www.artsbridgeonline.com/behindtheeye/powell.shtml.

10 G. Nakashima, *Soul of a Tree*, 38; see also Derek Ostergard, *George Nakashima: Full Circle* (New York: American Craft Museum, 1989), 117, illus.

11 G. Nakashima, *Soul of a Tree*, 112.

12 Jane Kessler and Dick Burrows, *Rude Osolnik: A Life Turning Wood* (Louisville, Kentucky: Crescent Hill Books, 1997), 15.

13 Julie Hall, *Tradition and Change: The New American Craftsman* (New York: E. P. Dutton, 1977), 30; Bob Stocksdale, *Bob Stocksdale: Pioneer Wood-Lathe Artist, and Master Creator of Bowls from Fine and Rare Woods*, interviews conducted by Harriet Nathan, Regional Oral History Office, Fiber Arts Oral History Series (Berkeley, CA: University of California, 1998), 39–43.

14 Quoted in Renwick Gallery, *Woodenworks: Furniture Objects by Five Contemporary Craftsmen*, exh. cat. (Washington, DC: Renwick Gallery of the National Collection of Fine Arts, 1972), 4; Hall, *Tradition and Change*, 1977, 37.

15 Jere Osgood, oral history interview by Donna Gold, September 19–October 8, 2001, AAA, SI.

16 Douglas C. McGill, "He Furnishes Objects to Fit a World Gone Awry," *New York Times*, January 17, 1988, H31.

17 Hannah and Carpenter, "Straightforward Desire," 33.

18 Charles Eames, interviewed by Mildred S. Friedman, 1974, n.p., quoted in Esther McCoy, "The Rationalist Period," David A. Hanks, et al., *High Styles: Twentieth-Century American Design*, exh. cat. (New York: Whitney Museum of American Art and Summit Books, 1985), 130.

19 Lamonica, "Behind the Eye."

20 Quoted in Patricia Malarcher, "Can Aesthetics Live Happily with Economics?" *New York Times*, September 20, 1981, NJ2.

21 Osgood, oral history interview.

22 Quoted in Stone, *Contemporary American Woodworkers*, 4.

23 Hall, *Tradition and Change*, 54.

24 Osgood, oral history interview.

25 Quoted in Renwick Gallery, *Woodenworks*, 38.

26 "Furniture Group Has Fluid Look," *New York Times*, December 17, 1952, 46; "New Tables Offer Sculptured Look," ibid., April 30, 1952, 30.

27 Lamonica, "Behind the Eye."

28 Oscar P. Fitzgerald, *Studio Furniture of the Renwick Gallery, Smithsonian American Art Museum* (Washington, DC: Smithsonian American Art Museum, 2008), 176–77.

29 In the late 1960s John Kelsey first coined the term *roundover* (Hannah and Carpenter, "Straightforward Desire," 34); for further discussion, see Cooke, Ward, and L'Ecuyer, *Maker's Hand*, 44.

30 Quoted in Malarcher, "Can Aesthetics Live," 2.

31 Steven Beyer and Matilda McQuaid, *George Nakashima and the Modernist Moment* (Doylestown, PA: James A. Michener Art Museum, 2001), 11.

32 Esbjørn Hiort, *Finn Juhl: Furniture, Architecture, Applied Art: A Biography* (Copenhagen: Danish Architectural Press, 1990), 30–36; Edgar Kaufmann Jr., "Finn Juhl of Copenhagen," *Interiors*, 108 (November 1948): 96–99.

33 Kevin Davies, "Markets, Marketing, and Design: The Danish Furniture Industry, c. 1947–65," *Scandinavian Journal of Design History* 9 (1999), 58, 60; Arne Remlov, ed., *Design in Scandinavia: An Exhibition of Objects for the Home* (New York: American Federation of Arts, 1954), 94–95, 100.

34 Davies, "Markets," 58.

35 Osgood later observed, "He was a big influence. . . . Tage Frid was terribly important to me." Osgood, oral history interview.

36 T. H. Robsjohn-Gibbings, *Homes of the Brave* (New York: Alfred A. Knopf, 1954), 56–57; Elizabeth Tower Halsey, *Ladies' Home Journal Book of Interior Decoration* (Philadelphia: Curtis Publishing Company, 1954), 45. For references to Shaker or Windsor furniture as sources of contemporary work, see, among many others, Mary Roche, "Useful Then, Useful Now," *New York Times Magazine*, December 12, 1948, 48–49; Kate Ellen Rogers, *The Modern House U.S.A.: Its Design and Decoration* (New York and Evanston: Harper and Row, 1962), 215.

37 Rosemarie Haag Bletter, "The World of Tomorrow: The Future with a Past," in Hanks, *High Styles*, 113–14; William J. Hennessey, *Russel Wright: American Designer* (Hamilton, New York: Gallery Association of New York State, 1983), 28;

Donald Albrecht, Robert Schonfeld, and Lindsay Stamm Shapiro, *Russel Wright: Creating American Lifestyle* (New York: Harry N. Abrams, 2001), 94–95. The latter two sources date the chair to 1932; Bletter dates it to 1934. Edgar Kaufmann Jr., "Hand-Made and Machine-Made Art," *Everyday Art Quarterly*, no. 1 (Summer 1946), 4. For overviews of biomorphic design in the United States, see Bletter, "World of Tomorrow," 112–20; Brooke Kamin Rappaport, "The Greater Mystery of Things: Aspects of Vital Forms in American Art," in Brooke Kamin Rappaport and Kevin L. Stayton, eds., *Vital Forms: American Art and Design in the Atomic Age, 1940–1960*, exh. cat. (New York: Brooklyn Museum of Art and Harry N. Abrams, 2001), 78–119; and Martin Filler, "Building Organic Form: Architecture, Ceramics, Glass, and Metal in the 1940s and 1950s," in ibid., 122–61.

38 For a bibliography for Maloof, see Jeremy Adamson, *The Furniture of Sam Maloof*, exh. cat. (Washington, DC: Smithsonian American Art Museum; New York: W. W. Norton, 2001), 262; for Nakashima, see Ostergard, *George Nakashima*, 188–92.

39 M. Nakashima, *Nature, Form*, 73–77, 162–64; Beyer and McQuaid, *George Nakashima*, 24–30.

40 Edward S. Cooke, Jr., "Arts and Crafts Furniture: Process or Product?" Janet Kardon, ed., *The Ideal Home,1900–1920* (New York: Harry N. Abrams, 1993), 64–76; Edward S. Cooke Jr., "The Long Shadow of William Morris: Paradigmatic Problems of Twentieth-Century Furniture," *American Furniture* (2003), 225–29.

41 Quoted in Beyer and McQuaid, *George Nakashima*, 24.

42 Hannah and Carpenter, "Straightforward Desire," 27.

43 McCoy 1985, p. 152.

44 Hall, *Tradition and Change*, 27.

45 Fitzgerald 2008, p. 177.

46 Stone, *Contemporary American Woodworkers*, xv.

47 Ibid., 19.

48 "The Object: Still Life," *CH* 25 (September/October 1965), 54.

49 Nordness, *Objects: USA*, 257.

50 Lamonica, "Behind the Eye."

51 Quoted in Merrill and Iovine, *Modern Americana*, 35.

52 Quoted in ibid., 36.

53 Quoted in Pam Koob, "Marked by Joy," in Tommy Simpson, *Two Looks to Home: The Art of Tommy Simpson* (Boston: Little, Brown and Company, 1999), 7.

54 Quoted in Irving Sandler, *The Triumph of American Painting: A History of Abstract Expressionism* (New York: Praeger, 1970), 96.

55 Merrill and Iovine, *Modern Americana*, 39.

56 Glazer's bowl is illustrated in *Wood Turning in North America since 1930*, (Philadelphia, Woodturning Center; New Haven, Yale University Art Gallery, 2001), 35, cat. 23.

57 Nancy A. Corwin, "Vital Connections: The Furniture of Daniel Jackson," *AC* 50 (June/July 1990), 52.

58 Osgood, oral history interview.

59 Quoted in Renwick Gallery, *Woodenworks*, 38.

60 "Craftsman Shows His Hand," *New York Times*, October 11, 1961, 55.

61 Quoted in Stone, *Contemporary American Woodworkers*, 11.

62 Bert Winther-Tamaki, "The Asian Dimensions of Postwar Abstract Art: Calligraphy and Metaphysics," in Alexandra Munroe, *The Third Mind: American Artists Contemplate Asia, 1860–1989,* exh. cat. (New York: Guggenheim Museum, 2009), 150–51, pl. 67.

63 Osgood, oral history interview.

64 Davira S. Taragin, Edward S. Cooke Jr., and Joseph Giovannini, *Furniture by Wendell Castle* (New York: Hudson Hills Press, 1989), 30. For a survey of American sculptors of this period working in wood, including Sugarman, see Dona Z. Meilach, *Contemporary Art with Wood: Creative Techniques and Appreciation* (New York: Crown Publishers, 1968).

65 "The Object: Still Life," 29–30.

66 Artschwager's *Cradle* is illustrated in Richard Armstrong, *Artschwager, Richard* (New York: Whitney Museum of American Art, 1988), 85, cat. 42.

67 Nordness, *Objects: USA*, 269.

68 "The Object: Still Life," 31.

69 Hall, *Tradition and Change*, 19, 118.

70 Osgood, oral history interview.

71 See Patricia Malarcher, "State Museum: Works in Wood," *New York Times*, June 23, 1985, New Jersey section, NJ2.

72 ACC/Museum of Contemporary Crafts, *Fantasy Furniture* (New York: MCC, 1966), n.p.

73 Jere Osgood, artist's statement, in Tanya Barter, John Dunnigan, and Seth Stem, *Bentwood*, exh. cat. (Providence: Museum of Art, Rhode Island School of Design, 1984), 42.

74 Quoted in Hannah and Carpenter, "Straightforward Desire," 29.

75 Quoted in Stone, *Contemporary American Woodworkers*, 103; Carpenter has expressed his admiration for Krenov's point of view (Hannah and Carpenter, "Straightforward Desire," 31).

178

WHARTON ESHERICK
Chest-table, 1969
WALNUT, METAL, AND PAINT
29½ X 31 X 21¾ IN. (74.9 X 78.7 X 55.2 CM)
MUSEUM OF ARTS AND DESIGN, GIFT OF
THE JOHNSON WAX COMPANY, THROUGH THE
AMERICAN CRAFT COUNCIL, 1977

179

J. B. BLUNK

Scrap Chair, 1968

CYPRESS
39½ X 49¼ X 26 IN. (100.3 X 125.1 X 66 CM)
COURTESY OF THE J.B. BLUNK ESTATE

180

EVERT SODERGREN

Sculptured Chair, 1953

WALNUT AND LEATHER

28½ X 26¾ X 23 IN. (72.4 X 67.9 X 58.4 CM)

COLLECTION OF MARGARET MINNICK

181

RUDE OSOLNIK

Turned Bowl, c. 1940

WALNUT

2¼ X 19 X 18⅜ IN. (5.7 X 48.3 X 46.7 CM)

MUSEUM OF ARTS AND DESIGN,

GIFT OF THE ARTIST AND FAMILY, 1995

182

JACK ROGERS HOPKINS

Edition Chair, 1970

FINNISH PLYWOOD

28 X 54 X 28 IN. (71.1 X 137.2 X 71.1 CM)

COLLECTION OF ANN HOPKINS BEGLEY

184

SAM MALOOF

Rocking Chair, 1957

WALNUT AND UPHOLSTERY FABRIC

45¾ X 27½ X 42 IN. (116.2 X 69.9 X 106.7 CM)

MUSEUM OF ARTS AND DESIGN, GIFT OF THE ARTIST,

THROUGH THE AMERICAN CRAFT COUNCIL, 1967

183

SAM MALOOF

Cradle Cabinet, 1968

WALNUT AND BRASS

68½ X 47¾ X 18 IN. (174 X 121.3 X 45.7 CM)

MUSEUM OF ARTS AND DESIGN, GIFT OF

THE JOHNSON WAX COMPANY, THROUGH THE

AMERICAN CRAFT COUNCIL, 1977

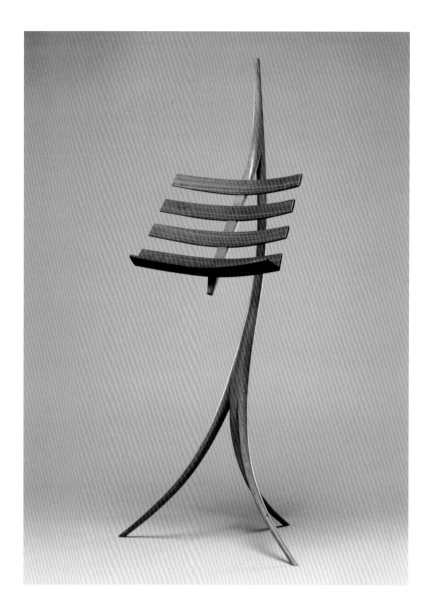

185

WENDELL CASTLE

Music Rack, 1964

OAK AND ROSEWOOD

55½ X 25 X 20 IN. (141 X 63.5 X 50.8 CM)

MUSEUM OF ARTS AND DESIGN, PURCHASED
BY THE AMERICAN CRAFT COUNCIL, 1964

186

JAN DE SWART

Blanket Chest, c. 1965

JELUTONG

15 X 32 X 17¼ IN. (38.1 X 81.3 X 43.8 CM)

COLLECTION OF MARK McDONALD

187

BOB STOCKSDALE

Plate, c. 1953

ENGLISH HAREWOOD

H. ⅞ IN. (2.2 CM); DIAM. 13⅝ IN. (34.6 CM)

YALE UNIVERSITY ART GALLERY, MABEL BRADY
GARVAN COLLECTION, BY EXCHANGE, AND A GIFT
FROM STEPHEN S. LASH, B.A. 1962, IN HONOR
OF RUTH AND DAVID WATERBURY, B.A. 1958 2002.23.1

188

GEORGE NAKASHIMA

Small Table, c. 1960

WALNUT

51½ X 28¾ X 13 IN. (130.8 X 73 X 33 CM)

COURTESY OF THE COLLECTION OF DAVID BAROWICH
WITH THE ASSISTANCE OF BOB AIBEL
AND THE MODERNE GALLERY

189

PHILIP LLOYD POWELL

Door, 1964

WALNUT, STEEL, 23-KARAT GOLD LEAF

94 X 40 IN. (238.8 X 101.6 CM)

COLLECTION OF DORSEY READING AND JOHN SOLLO

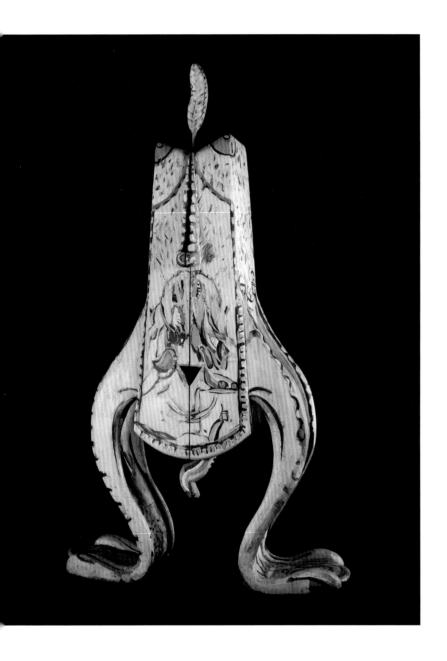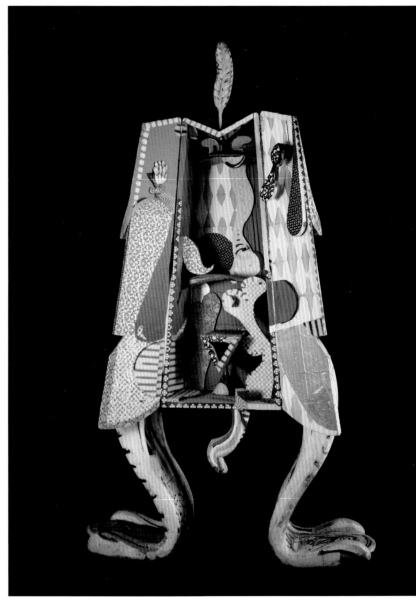

190

TOMMY SIMPSON

*Man Balancing a Feather
on His Knows*, 1968

CLOSED (LEFT); OPEN (RIGHT)

PINEWOOD, ACRYLIC, RICE PAPER, GLUE, AND STEEL

74½ X 45 X 13½ IN. (189.2 X 114.3 X 34.3 CM)

MUSEUM OF ARTS AND DESIGN, GIFT OF

THE JOHNSON WAX COMPANY, THROUGH THE

AMERICAN CRAFT COUNCIL, 1979

191

FRANK E. CUMMINGS III

Vessel, c. 1960

EAST INDIAN ROSEWOOD, BUFFALO FUR,
GOAT HAIR, AND HORSEHAIR
11⅜ X 7½ DIAM. IN. (28.9 X 19.1CM)
COLLECTION OF HARLAND AND
ELIZABETH GOLDWATER

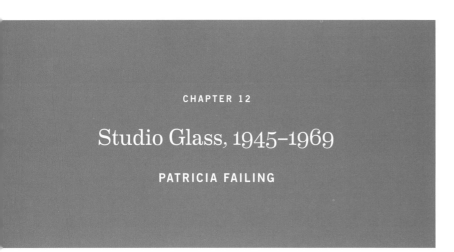

CHAPTER 12

Studio Glass, 1945–1969

PATRICIA FAILING

IN 1960 PAUL PERROT, THE DIRECTOR OF CORNING
Glass, announced that "the rise of the artist-craftsman
in glass has been one of the surprising developments of
the post-war years. Even more astonishing is the fact
that this is a unique American phenomenon and that
one searches in vain for a similar movement abroad."[1]
Until recently, this "surprising development" was
largely unexamined in histories of modern studio glass.
Dominick Labino's *Visual Art in Glass* (1968), one of the
first survey books by an American glass artist, records
some of the perceptions that obscured the accomplishments of the 1950s. Labino briefly acknowledged several
American artist-craftsmen who produced glass independently in the United States during that decade. These
artists, he explained, designed or worked in glass "in its
cold state, either by casting, lamp working, laminating
or enameling."[2] Labino then credits a "strong resurgence
of interest in glass as a medium of creative expression"
not to their precedent, but to more recent work in hot
glass, especially "the impact of creative glassblowing"
associated with artists such as Harvey Littleton, Marvin
Lipofsky, and Labino himself.[3] Hot replaced cold in the
1960s, diverting attention from the "unique American
phenomenon" of the previous decade.[4] As the accomplishments of the small band of adventurers who developed
the postwar movement in studio glass are reinscribed in
craft history, however, it becomes clear that their ingenuity and dedication provided the essential groundwork
for the reemergence of glass as a viable medium for individual expression during the next decade.

"At a time when glass has become so universally
accepted and so consummately practiced . . . it is easy to
forget there was a time when virtually no one believed it
could be done by individual artists," Perrot observed in
1982. "It is to those who did that the rich inheritance we
have today is in major part due."[5] The occasion for this
reflection was a fifty-year retrospective of the work of
Edris Eckhardt, a successful ceramist and teacher based
in Cleveland, Ohio, who had reached a crisis point in her
career in the early 1950s. Together with John Burton,
Earl McCutchen, and Frances and Michael Higgins,
Eckhardt was one of the country's leading studio glass
artists in the 1950s. Yet as she recalled, "When the cult of
the big and empty, and sometimes ugly, struck ceramic
sculpture in the early 1950s, I was dismayed by the effect
size and color (or lack of it) had on juries of that time. I
realized how cults, fashions and brainwashing prevailed
in the art field. . . . In such a frame of mind I visited The
Metropolitan Museum of Art in 1953. I quite accidentally
saw a case of Byzantine gold glass that held my attention
with potent hypnotic force. It occurred to me that here
was an art long dormant, that glass making, as a one-man
operation of art, belonged to the past. I recalled some of
the most exciting glass came from periods when glass
was handmade by the artist. I felt that the field was wide
open—no standards, no rules, no fashions, no cults."[6]

By 1954, after hundreds of experiments, Eckhardt
mastered the "lost art" of gold glass, which requires an
expert command of the differing rates of expansion and
contraction among the raw materials. To achieve this
control, she made her own glass—"from sand to the coloring oxide"—melting batches in an electric ceramics
kiln. Eckhardt thus became the first American studio
glass artist known to have formulated her own batch mixture rather than simply melt scrap glass.[7] Working in her
basement, rolling out paper-thin sheets of viscous glass
on a marble-topped table using a wet rolling pin, she
applied heated gold and silver leaves to the glass, followed
by staggered layers of colored sheet glass. She would
later develop special enamels for painting designs on the
panels. Protected by a huge asbestos apron and matching gloves, she then fused the layers of glass and gold
in her kiln, which was wrapped in asbestos to slow its
cooling time.

Eckhardt's facility with the ceramics technology she
adapted for glassmaking was established in the mid-1930s,
when she became supervisor of the Ceramics Division of

the Federal Arts Project in Cleveland. In the 1930s and '40s she created figurative ceramic sculpture, and her affinity for the figure carried over into her work in glass. In early gold-glass panels such as *Pharaoh's Horses* (1954; **FIG. 12.1**), the elongated anatomy is reminiscent of the flattened, simplified imagery of the Early Christian medallions she had studied in museums. In the mid-1950s, she began stretching body forms into streamlined columns and rendering the faces with geometrized simplicity.

After conquering gold glass, Eckhardt taught herself lost-wax casting. With the notable exception of Frederick Carder, few artists in the United States had successfully mastered this technique. Eckhardt did so with little outside technical help, wanting instead to "think independently, to understand the medium completely in light of a one-man operation with limited equipment."[8] To create cast forms such as the translucent *Archangel* (1956), she first coated hand-carved wax models with a strong ceramic shell. After heating, the wax ran out of the shell; the resulting space was then filled with powdered glass, which fused when refired. After the piece cooled, the ceramic shell was broken off, leaving a freestanding glass sculpture.[9]

In 1962, after receiving a Tiffany and two Guggenheim fellowships, Eckhardt was invited to teach and set up the art glass curriculum at the University of California at Berkeley. There she developed a special bronze alloy to combine with colored glass in her sculptures without shrinking. This was a technical feat thought to be almost impossible to achieve. In 1962 she also had her first one-person exhibition in New York, at the Museum of Contemporary Crafts.[10] Some fifty years later, although her affinity for religious or sentimentalized subject matter limited her audience, collectors and curators who value her subjects and period style as well as her technical virtuosity still form a strong regional network centered in the Midwest. As did Perrot, they find Eckhardt's work to be "more than the result of careful study and tenacity. It was also an expression of faith . . . reflected in many of the themes she chose."[11]

Sketching a collective portrait of "the American craftsman" in 1959, Rose Slivka pointed out that in the United States, craftsmen were everywhere and nowhere, "dispersed throughout the country with no real center, no market place where it is possible to gain a perspective on what is going on. In this respect they differ from all other areas of creative expression in the country."[12] The rise of artist-craftsmen in glass surprised the crafts

FIG. 12.1

Edris Eckhardt, *Pharoah's Horses*, 1954. Glass, enamel, gold leaf, and lead frame. 3¾ x 3¼ in. (9.6 x 8.3 cm). Corning Museum of Glass, Gift of Edris Eckhardt; 54.4.29.

establishment in part because the artists were geographically remote from one another and, like Eckhardt, were largely self-taught. Thus, while Eckhardt was developing her gold-glass and casting processes in Cleveland, John Burton was perfecting his lampworking techniques in Southern California. In Athens, Georgia, Earl McCutchen began molding and laminating glass at the same time Frances and Michael Higgins were turning out an astonishing range of fused and enameled glass in Chicago. In rural New York State, Maurice Heaton, already an established glass artist in the 1920s, was exploring a new method of laminating crushed enamel between layers of glass. Like Eckhardt, most of these artists were attracted to the medium because it represented a new, uncharted, "modern" category of individual studio production while also providing links to a venerable past.

Burton was inspired not only by the look of ancient Egyptian glass but also by the inverse relationship between the simple, preindustrial technology and the delicate refinement of the end product **(FIG. 12.2)**. Burton's own dedication to the "primitive" way of doing things was a form of protest against destructive technologies of late industrial capitalism. His studio setup was dictated by "what could be practiced in the average home" and was restricted to a propane torch resting on a brick, a glass blowpipe, brass shears, a carbon marver (graphite block used for rolling or shaping glass), forceps, a hot plate, and an asbestos-lined tin can for annealing (the slow cooling process that prevents glass from shattering).[13] He was interested in "forming glass, not making it from raw material."[14] Using traditional country-fair lampworking techniques—melting readymade glass rods with a gas torch—he created thousands of elegantly whimsical goblets, bottles, vases, and sculptures.

Burton had been born in England, where he trained as a metallurgist and worked for the British Admiralty before moving to California in 1927. He began working in glass in the late 1920s, slowly teaching himself lampworking techniques and technology as well as methods

FIG. 12.2

John Burton, from left (five vessels): *Blue Lace*, *Yellow Magic*, *The Emperor's Jewels*, *Soft Shoulders*, *Harlequin*, 1965–79. Flameworked glass. Tallest, height: 4½ in. (11.3 cm), diameter: 2¼ in. (5.7 cm). Corning Museum of Glass, Gift of Mrs. Elise Burton; 85.4.49, 85.4.51, 85.4.54, 85.4.59, 85.4.62.

for pigmenting readymade clear glass. By the late 1940s he had begun to produce a consistent body of work. Blue made from powdered cobalt became one of his stylistic signatures, although many of his compositions are decorated with multicolored hobnails or snaking threads of glass trailed over the surface to accentuate shape and volume. Photographs of Burton at work provide a marvelous burlesque of gender stereotypes. A burly unsmiling man is shown in his studio creating delicate, intimate little vessels. Burton also worked as a radio and television producer, lecturer, and teacher, in addition to publishing two books of poetry and a step-by-step guide to lampworking, *Glass: Philosophy and Method* (1967).

A favorite theme in Burton's lectures and writings was that the creativity and discipline of the artist-craftsman served as a model for an ideal world order. "Implicit in a society built on the worth of the individual, on law and justice, is the freedom of every man to live and work at his unique creative best," he once observed. "Freedom to function, each in his own way, within the laws that make for harmony in human society leads to what John Ruskin called 'the harmonious inequality of concurrent power.' I know of no six words that better describe the relatedness of men who would keep their individual and national orbits clear of chaos."[15]

Unlike Burton, most of the postwar studio glass artists had come to the field with a background in ceramics as Eckhardt had. Earl McCutchen was among those who began his career in ceramics, but in the mid-1940s he began working with glass, using his ceramics kiln to soften glass sheets until they slumped into clay molds. He also colored his platters and bowls with ceramic glazes. "Glass has been slow to come into its own," he observed in 1955. "Its tardiness can be explained partly by the expense and bulkiness of specialized equipment necessary for glassblowing, the most fruitful method for creative use of the material. But there are less costly ways of working with glass. . . . Just as different painting techniques offer their various and peculiar advantages to the painter, so the various ways of working with glass present their own unique qualities."[16]

McCutchen proposed scrounging materials for experimentation from junkyards or mirror shops, a suggestion that "demonstrated the limited resources and primitive state of prevailing technique," according to former Corning Museum of Glass curator Susanne Frantz.[17] Once he mastered a technique, however, McCutchen switched

FIG.12.3

Earl McCutchen in his studio, Mary McCutchen papers, Hargrett Library, University of Georgia. Photograph courtesy of Barbara Houze.

to high-quality blanks to create his molded bowls, trays, and plates, many of them decorated with glazes alternately applied in dry form or suspended in liquid. The suspended glaze was trailed or sprayed on the glass surfaces in bold patterns such as checkerboards, created with stenciling or overlaid color. Effects of depth and pattern were also highlighted by the addition of materials such as chicken wire, iron filings, metal foils, and glass yarns between layers of laminated glass. Large plates with geometric patterns illuminated from within by the soft glow of metal foils are typical of McCutchen's work. The round form of the plate is often repeated in what appear to be circles of color integrated into the geometric patterns. These circles are actually trapped air bubbles, carefully controlled to line up with the patterned forms.

"The advantages of the molding technique lie in its abundant possibilities for shape and ornament," McCutchen concluded in the mid-1950s,[18] and he continued to explore these options for the next two-and-a-half decades. In the early 1960s he wrote and produced a series of television programs for National Educational Television in which he demonstrated ceramics and glass techniques **(FIG. 12.3)**. Meanwhile, he installed a furnace at the University of Georgia, where he had long taught, and began blowing glass; by the mid-1960s, glassblowing classes had been integrated into the arts curriculum.[19] McCutchen blew bottles, bowls, and vases, restricting his color range primarily to smoky blue-grays, amber, and green. Although his blown glass was exhibited in Atlanta galleries, he is rarely acknowledged as a player in the hot-glass revolution of the 1960s.

Few studio glass artists were personally acquainted with one another in the early 1950s. An exception was McCutchen and Frances Stewart, a college roommate of McCutchen's wife, Mary, in Georgia. In 1942 Stewart began experimenting with heat-shaped glass at the University of Georgia, employing a variant of the glass-bending process used for curving automotive windshields.[20] She taught at the university from 1944 to 1948 before moving to Chicago to enroll in the MFA program at the Chicago Institute of Design. There she met Michael Higgins, head of the Department of Visual Design. In 1938 Higgins had come to the United States from England, where he had worked as a graphic designer for the Labour Party.[21] The couple married in 1948, left academia, and went into business producing fused and laminated glass. There was no retail market for their work or for crafts in general at the time. Frances Higgins recalled that even the most elite buyer "knew less about crafts than the average craft-fair customer today."[22] They first sold a line of bowls and plates through department stores and in 1959 were hired as designers for the Dearborn Glass Company. They also made small editions and one-of-a-kind compositions for art fairs and private buyers while working fourteen-hour days to fulfill their various commercial obligations.

Throughout their careers the Higginses used the same basic kiln-fired glass technology employed by most of their peers. Their work typically began with clear glass sheets coated with colored enamels. Shapes cut from the sheets were decorated with more enamel or cut pieces of variously colored glass. A second layer of colored glass was added and the stack placed on a mold in a kiln where it sagged into shape upon heating. The Higginses developed a staggering variety of decorative strategies, ranging from silkscreening to bas-relief "mother-of-pearl" lusters, which they applied primarily to utilitarian vessels, glass screens, mobiles, and wall plaques.[23]

Favored designs included graceful linear patterns radiating from the center of a plate or bowl and simplified landscapes that might illustrate a children's book. In the 1950s they produced biomorphic vessels and calligraphic surfaces that call to mind "automatic drawings" of the surrealists. From the beginning, their production included the unabashedly populist as well as the technically and formally sublime, but it has yet to be systematically reviewed by craft historians.

The Higginses' studio business was almost unprecedented among mid-twentieth-century glass artists. Certain parallels may be found, however, in the career of Maurice Heaton, the paterfamilias of postwar studio glass. By the mid-1940s, Heaton was already known for his glass murals, screens, lighting fixtures, and tablewares. In 1947 he invented a new method of applying designs to plates and bowls by fusing crushed enamel crystals to the underside of the glass. The powdered enamels, the same as those used by enamelists on metal surfaces, were sprinkled or dusted on glass to make drawings and create atmospheric effects, emulating the shadows he admired in the watercolors of Paul Klee. "I get a kick out of Klee's painting because he works inside and outside a line to get tonal effects," Heaton explained.[24] Unlike glazes, the enamels

FIG. 12.4
Robert Sowers, stained-glass facade, American Airlines Terminal 8, Idlewild Airport (now JFK International Airport), 1960 (dismantled 2008).

did not change color when fired, enabling an increase in brilliance, tonal contrast, and control in design. By the late 1950s Heaton had become a virtuoso of his new technique, executing subtle and intricate designs that combine linear pattern with delicately shaded color planes. In his Africa and bird plate series, for example, the softly graduated color in the background resembles airbrush painting. In the 1950s he also made new amoeba-shaped molds for his slumped bowls, reminiscent of Isamu Noguchi's famous furniture designs.

Heaton, Michael Higgins, and Eckhardt were called upon to represent studio glass at the First Annual Conference of the American Craftsmen's Council (ACC), held at Asilomar, California, in 1957. The first panel discussion devoted exclusively to glass, which was presented at the 1959 annual conference, was poorly attended. Panelists included Perrot, McCutchen, and Harvey Littleton, with comments by Heaton and Michael Higgins. (The low turnout "indicates the hollowness of the pretensions of interest in new materials," Higgins complained.

"Glass is the fastest-growing and most exciting medium in America.")[25] A statistical profile of the 1959 conference participants listed only three glass craftsmen, as opposed to ninety-three ceramists, sixty-one metalsmiths, eighty-three textile artists, and sixteen enamelists.[26] Higgins's claim notwithstanding, glass clearly remained an esoteric frontier for individual artists at the end of the 1950s, despite the support studio glass was beginning to receive from professional organizations such as the ACC and Midwest Designer-Craftsmen, the latter co-founded by the Higginses.

The range of activity in studio glass, however, was broader than the 1959 conference statistics suggest. Well-known ceramists such as Waylande De Santis Gregory and Glen Lukens worked extensively in glass during and after World War II. Lukens began producing small editions of slumped vessels in the mid- or late 1940s. Translating his luscious "ripe fruit" ceramics palette into glass, he favored simple bowls and plates with transparent pitted surfaces that fade softly into shades of delicate blue, rose, and yellow. He also experimented with rich combinations of color. Like most studio glass of the period, Lukens's work was kiln-fired in a mold. In contrast, Gregory devised bold patterns and figures painted and stenciled on readymade containers using crystal glazes. In the 1950s he explored sgraffito, incising the exterior surfaces to reveal different colors painted on the vessel's interior. In other examples, the figures are transparent and take on the colors of nearby environments. Much of his production is represented by small bowls and plates decorated with plants or animals, made for sale in upscale department stores.[27]

Enthusiasm for stained glass was revived in the 1950s, aided in part by the 1954 publication of Robert Sowers's history of stained glass, *The Lost Art*, followed by *Stained Glass: An Architectural Art* (1961).[28] The greatest increase in ecclesiastical building in the nation's history occurred in the 1950s; by 1955, churches, synagogues, cathedrals, and temples comprised the fourth largest category of privately funded construction.[29] In these new buildings, stained glass—an emblem of the traditional church—was fully integrated into a modern architectural setting. New materials and techniques for producing and installing stained glass popularized after the war attracted a number of contemporary architects and designers. Especially influential was the development of so-called Dallas glass by Gabriel Loire in his

FIG. 12.5

Adolph Gottlieb, designer; Heinigke & Smith, fabricators; stained glass windows (interior view), Milton Steinberg House (now in the school building), Park Avenue Synagogue, New York, 1954.

workshop near Chartres, France. This thick glass, which could be chipped and faceted to enhance its brilliance, made a spectacular debut in Fernand Léger's windows for Sacre Coeur Church in Audincourt, France. Among the first appearances of Loire's glass in the United States was a window created by the multimedia artist Gyorgy Kepes for Pietro Belluschi's Church of the Redeemer in Baltimore, begun in 1954. Like the windows at Audincourt, the glass was cast in concrete frames rather than being held in place with traditional leads. The patterns of the cement function as a decorative filigree that animates the church's interior even when no light is passing through the glass.[30]

Sowers himself was a glass artist who designed several stained-glass windows for ecclesiastical buildings in the 1950s. His most spectacular commission of the decade, however, was undoubtedly the 900-panel, 100-yard-long stained-glass window installed in the facade of Robert Jacobs's American Airlines terminal at Idlewild (now John F. Kennedy International) Airport in New York in 1960 (**FIG. 12.4** and **12.8–9** on page 264–65).[31] Another monumental stained-glass facade of the period was designed by New York painter Adolph Gottlieb (**FIG. 12.5**). The glass was commissioned for the Milton Steinberg House, a chapter building adjoining the Park Avenue Synagogue at 50 East 87th Street in Manhattan. The ensemble, completed in 1955, measured 1,300 square feet and included 91 individual panels—a monumental expansion of Gottlieb's pictographic paintings representing holidays and traditions of Jewish life.

Gottlieb's project inspired architectural critic Ada Louise Huxtable to ruminate on the contemporary relevance of stained glass as religious emblem. Sincere

FIG. 12.6
Harvey Littleton blowing glass,
Life **61 (July 29, 1966), 34.**

hybrids of illusionism and literal dimensionality in a series of geometric compositions combining clear and painted panes of glass positioned at different angles. Even Jackson Pollock painted on glass, as documented in Hans Namuth's famous 1950 film of the artist at work. Pollock was exhilarated by the experience, and concluded that glass painting seemed to offer a promising new method of architectural decoration.[34]

Despite this activity, individual artists working with glass remained invisible to many museums and art historians in the late 1940s and 1950s. New frontiers in glass were to be found instead, many believed, in the work represented in the Corning Museum of Glass's first major international survey exhibition, mounted in 1959. To Thomas Buechner, the first director of the museum, artists like Eckhardt who made objects with their own hands were "oddities so rare in those days as to defy categorizing. As I recall, we recognized them as adventurous exceptions, but saw them as insignificant compared with those determining the shape of production vessels with which our world was rapidly filling up. . . . [In retrospect] we had no idea what was coming or what was going."[35]

The exhibition *Glass '59* contained 292 objects from 22 countries. Most were functional, artist-designed forms manufactured by the glass industry. Included in the small American section were Freda Diamond's cocktail beakers produced by Libbey Glass, George Sakier's goblets manufactured by Fostoria, and a Higgins ashtray designed for Dearborn Glass. Also shown were three compositions by Eckhardt and single pieces by Burton, Heaton, McCutchen, and Priscilla Manning Porter, which were described in the accompanying catalogue as "types not previously known in the history of glass."[36]

A slender 16 percent of the participants in the *Glass '59* show actually designed and made their own work. When Corning repeated the format of the show in another major exhibition in 1979, nearly 90 percent of the work was designed and executed by individual artists.[37] Among the instigators of this major shift in studio glass practice was Harvey Littleton, who began his career as a ceramist. While teaching at the University of Wisconsin, Madison, he began research on contemporary glassmaking in Europe. Traveling to Paris in 1957, he met glass artist Jean Sala at his studio in Montparnasse. From the 1920s to the early 1950s, Sala blew glass in his own studio—perhaps the first in Europe built for use by an individual artist. Littleton also visited small, two-man furnaces in the

aesthetic standards inspired this country's best stained glass, she concluded, whatever the artist's religious feelings might be. In today's world, she wrote in 1955, "ecclesiastical art must stand less as a work of faith than as a work of art well suited to its religious and structural purposes."[32]

Other abstract painters worked in stained and colored glass on a smaller scale throughout the 1950s. The New York artist Joseph Meert, for example, created stained-glass reinterpretations of his canvases, spontaneously arranging pieces of colored glass, wire, and copper on flat glass panels. When the panel was fired to fuse the various materials, the result resembled a textured abstract expressionist painting.[33] I. Rice Pereira, a pioneering abstract painter whose career began in the 1930s, produced new

Murano glass factories outside Venice. "I realized then," he recalled, "that it was possible to have a small-scaled operation, to do everything as an artist would work in his own studio."[38]

Littleton returned to the United States determined to make and blow his own glass. His first hurdle was the development of a small, economical furnace. After several failures, he turned for help to Dominick Labino, then vice president and director of research for the Johns-Manville Fiberglass Corporation. Fortified by Labino's advice, Littleton organized a seminar on glass techniques to be held on the grounds of the Toledo Museum of Art in March 1962 (FIG. 12.6). The Higginses attended, along with six students and university faculty members.[39] After a disastrous first melt the first day, Labino came to the workshop and reconstructed the furnace. They began again, this time using low-melting glass marbles Labino had developed for fiberglass production. The marbles proved to be an ideal material, and blowing took place around the clock. On the last day of the seminar, Harvey Leafgreen, a then-retired glassblower from the Libbey Division of Owens-Illinois in Toledo, happened into the session and

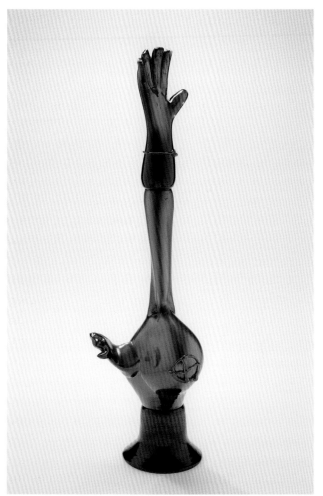

FIG. 12.7
Erwin Eisch, *Hand*, 1968. Glass. 26 9/16 x 7 3/4 x 6 1/2 in. (67.5 x 19.7 x 16.5 cm). Corning Museum of Glass; 98.3.11.

agreed to demonstrate basic techniques, thereby assuring the success of Littleton's venture.[40]

A second, more widely advertised workshop was held in June. "About 15 people from all over the country, most of them Harvey's friends, came to the workshop," recalled one participant, ceramist Howard Kottler. "They brought in [Leafgreen] and we learned from him how to use the blowpipe. It was all pretty disorganized and technically primitive—they didn't even have an annealing oven."[41] Like several members of this group, however, Kottler went on to develop a body of work in glass. In 1965 Labino retired from Johns-Manville and did the same, producing award-winning vessels by 1966. Hot glass had begun its liberation from the factory, and the studio glass movement entered a new and vigorous phase.

Later in the summer of 1962, Littleton traveled again to Europe, where he encountered the Bavarian sculptor Erwin Eisch. Eisch used glass as a sculptural material, treating it with "contempt and freedom," creating opaque surfaces often unrecognizable as glass (FIG. 12.7).[42] Eisch's work and attitude were a revelation to Littleton, who stopped producing ceramics after he returned to Madison in September. In 1963 he introduced a hot-glass undergraduate course into the arts curriculum at the University of Wisconsin and began a successful campaign for courses on glassblowing at other universities and colleges. These new classes were typically integrated into fine-arts curricula, and after 1964 many glass artists were educated in degree programs along with students in painting and sculpture. The campaign to position glass as a fine-arts medium in academia attracted not only artists and teachers, but ultimately dealers and collectors who would underwrite the success of the studio glass movement.[43]

In the next few years, Littleton's students and colleagues fanned out across the country. Marvin Lipofsky, the first to receive an MFA in glass, began a glassblowing program at the University of California, Berkeley, and the California College of Arts and Crafts in Oakland. Programs were established in many other locations: by Robert Fritz at San Jose State, Tom McGlauchlin at the University of Iowa in Iowa City, Fred Marcus at the University of Illinois, and Kent Ipsen at the University of Chicago. Norman Schulman, who assisted Littleton with the Toledo workshops, started a glass program at the Rhode Island School of Design in Providence in 1965, where he was joined by Littleton's graduate student Dale Chihuly in 1967.[44]

In addition to Littleton, other artists advanced the frontier of hot glass in the first half of the 1960s. Andre Billeci initiated an independent study of glassmaking at Alfred University in 1963. McCutchen and his students were blowing glass at the University of Georgia by 1964. That same year, Eisch visited the United States, offering the first of many workshops and seminars. The group effort typically required to build and equip a glass studio and the spirit of adventure generated by the new programs produced a wave of excitement, a sense of "movement" that would make glass one of the most popular craft mediums of the next decade.[45]

Within this group, however, differences in approach were apparent from the beginning. Influenced by Eisch, Littleton extolled experimentation and innovation over craftsmanship. In the mid-1960s, he created a series of smashed, remelted, and exploded vessel forms that recall Peter Voulkos's expressionistic ceramics of the later 1950s. Voulkos's focus on the physicality of clay is paralleled by Littleton's asymmetrical bottle forms from 1964, which emphasize visual traces of process, chance, and molten liquidity of the medium itself. Labino, in contrast, stressed technical control and mastery of glass chemistry.[46] If a student "really intends to use glass as an art medium and not merely as a vehicle for making shapes," he cautioned, he or she "should be able to control the entire creative process, beginning with the formation of a batch."[47] In the mid-1960s Labino concentrated on producing finely crafted functional objects with exotic colorings created by adding various metals to the glass formula and carefully regulating the furnace and the annealing process.

Along with college and university sponsorship, other forms of institutional support encouraged the burgeoning glass movement. Otto Wittmann, director of the Toledo Museum of Art, hosted Littleton's 1962 workshops at the museum and assisted Littleton in securing funding. With Wittmann's support, the museum subsequently initiated a series of competitive national exhibitions for glass artists, the Toledo Glass Nationals, in 1966, 1968, and 1970. A selection from the 1968 exhibition, which included the work of fifty-seven glassblowers, was circulated nationally, expanding the visibility of the field. Exhibitions featuring artists working in hot glass, however, did not entirely obscure the accomplishments of the postwar pioneers: Edris Eckhardt, for example, was honored with a retrospective exhibition at the Corning Museum of Glass in 1968.[48]

Work submitted to the Toledo Glass Nationals confirmed that glass was hot from coast to coast by the end of the 1960s. At the University of California, Berkeley, for example, Lipofsky's classes were attracting artists such as ceramist Richard Marquis, who became a convert to glass in 1966. In 1970 Marquis was hired to start a glass program at the University of Washington, where Howard Kottler and student Claire Colquitt had set up a furnace in 1968. Kottler's own project was prefaced by experiments in glass carried out by local artists Stephen Fuller and Russell Day, who had worked with kiln-forming techniques at the university as early as 1957.[49] Day reported on his progress at the Fourth National Conference of the ACC, held at the University of Washington in 1961, where he joined Michael Higgins, John Burton, and Eckhardt in a declaration that glassblowing by individual artists was now "a real possibility, rather than just a dream."[50]

Day attended one of Littleton's summer seminars in 1964 and encouraged Washington artists Bill Boysen and Dale Chihuly to join Littleton's program. Both followed this advice: Boysen built the first glass studio at North Carolina's Penland School of Crafts in 1965. After studying with Littleton, Chihuly completed his MFA at the Rhode Island School of Design in 1968 and began a ten-year appointment as chair of the school's glass department in 1969.[51] About the same time, he began to imagine a new school for glass art situated in an idyllic rural setting. In 1971 his vision started to materialize with a summer workshop held at an abandoned tree farm fifty miles north of Seattle. To the owners of the farm, John and Anne Hauberg, the property was known as Pilchuck, and the site became the Pilchuck Glass Center in 1974.[52]

Chihuly's education as a young glass artist coincided with a proliferation of international exchanges among glass artists and teachers from the United States and Europe. In the late 1960s both Chihuly and Marquis were awarded Fulbright-Hayes fellowships to study the traditional techniques used in Italian workshops, while Lipofsky was earning a reputation as a "glass ombudsman" for his work with small factories in Italy and Holland.[53] These exchanges laid the foundation for an international studio glass community whose success in the 1970s came to overshadow the self-taught instigators of the postwar studio glass movement—among them artists who anticipated Lipofsky's role as international mediator. Texas artist Robert Willson, for example, began working with glass in 1956 after receiving a scholarship from the Corning

Museum of Glass. He toured glass factories and museums in western Europe and studied with Venetian glass masters at Murano in 1957. Using solid masses of molten glass rather than blown glass, he was the first to create large-scale glass sculptures at Murano. His compositions were typically built from thick, heavy glass forms merged into colorful columnar stacks seventeen to twenty inches high. Reporting on Willson's achievements in 1969, Paul Perrot observed that "when we look at Willson's sculptures, we cannot say they are Venetian, for no one in Venice had though of handling form and color in this manner before, nor do we recognize them as products of American culture." When he began to conceive his sculptures, Perrot continued, Willson was "virtually alone" and could not have made his work anywhere but Venice.[54] Lacking established resources for technical training, Willson and the other instigators of the studio glass movement in the 1950s were resolute innovators. Supported primarily by ingenuity and tenacity, they can be credited with the production of remarkable objects that have now begun to find their place in panoramic histories of American studio glass.

1 Paul Perrot, "New Directions in Glassmaking," *CH* 20 (November/December 1960), 22.

2 Dominick Labino, *Visual Art in Glass* (Dubuque, IA: Wm. C. Brown, 1968), 106–8.

3 Ibid., 125.

4 Susanne K. Frantz confirms that "apart from glass-casting activities taking place in Czechoslovakia (generally unknown in the West), some lampworking in Germany and *pâte de verre* in France and Japan, there were no known equivalents" to the work of American studio glass artists active in the 1950s. See Frantz, *Contemporary Glass: A World Survey from the Corning Museum of Glass* (New York: Harry N. Abrams, 1989), 35. See also Martha Drexler Lynn, *American Studio Glass 1960–1990* (Manchester, VT: Hudson Hills Press, 2004), 35–47. She acknowledges the achievements of American independent glass artists of the 1950s.

5 Paul Perrot, "Introduction to Glass and Bronze," in *Edris Eckhardt: Fifty Year Retrospective* (Beachwood, OH: Beachwood Museum, 1982), n.p.

6 Edris Eckhardt, "Finding the Future in the Past," in ACC, *Research in the Crafts, Paper Delivered at the Fourth National Conference of the American Craftsmen's Council* (New York: ACC, 1965), 31. The early history of Eckhardt's work in glass is reviewed in Dido Smith, "Gold Glass: Ancient Technique Rediscovered," *CH* 16 (November/December 1956), 12–15.

7 Frantz, *Contemporary Glass*, 36. Ruth Kilby was also recognized for her technical innovations in the late 1950s and early 1960s. Kilby created her

compositions with a variety of industrial glasses fused into pictorial panels as thick as two inches. See Kenneth Wilson, "Contemporary American Studio Glassmaking," in *Annales du 4e Congres des Journées Internationales du Verre*, Ravenna and Venice, May 1967 (Liege: Association Internationale pour l'Histoire de Verre, [1967]), 215. Wilson was a curator at the Corning Museum of Glass, where Kilby's work was featured in a 1966 exhibition.

8 Eckhardt, "Finding a Future in the Past," 33. Eckhardt consulted with scientists at the Corning Glass Company when she designed her own glass furnace in 1956.

9 Lee Grover and Roy Grover, *Contemporary Art Glass* (New York: Crown Publishing, 1975), 14. Eckhardt's glass furnace is discussed in Ruth Dancygner, *Edris Eckhardt, Cleveland Sculptor* (Cleveland: John Carroll University, 1990), 49. For a recent overview of Eckhardt's life and career, see Eckhardt et al., *Edris Eckhardt: Visionary Innovator in American Studio Ceramics and Glass* (Lakewood, OH: Cleveland Artists Foundation, 2006).

10 Dancygner, *Edris Eckhardt*, 59–61. Eckhardt's technical achievements are reviewed in Paul Hollister, "Studio Glass Before 1962: Maurice Heaton, Francis and Michael Higgins, Edris Eckhardt," *Neues Glas* 4 (1985), 234–35.

11 Perrot, *Edris Eckhardt*, n.p. Dancygner's publication (*Edris Eckhardt*) lists the names and geographical locations of many private collectors of her work.

12 Rose Slivka, "U.S. Crafts in an Industrial Society," *CH* 19 (March/April 1959), 10.

13 Yoshiko Uchida, "John Burton: The Fluid Breath of Glass," *CH*

20 (November/December 1960), 26.

14 John Burton, *Glass: Philosophy and Method—Hand Blown, Sculptured, Colored* (Philadelphia: Chilton Book Company, 1967), 52.

15 Ibid., 11.

16 Earl McCutchen, "Glass Molding: Experimenting on a Low Budget," *CH* 15 (May/June 1955), 38–39; see also *Earl McCutchen: Craftsmanship in Ceramics and Glass*, exh. cat. (Athens, GA: Georgia Museum of Art, 2003).

17 Frantz, *Contemporary Glass*, 39.

18 McCutchen, "Glass Molding," 39.

19 Mary McCutchen (Earl McCutchen's wife), letter to the author, January 1996. The 1966 University of Georgia yearbook, *Pandora*, includes several illustrations of students blowing glass, but the university was unable to provide an exact date for the installation of the glassblowing equipment.

20 Harriette Anderson, *Kiln-fired Glass* (Philadelphia: Chilton Book Company, 1970), vii.

21 Grover and Grover, *Contemporary Art Glass*, 39.

22 Quoted in Deborah Farber-Isaacson, "Septuagenarians Francis and Michael Higgins Are Too Busy Making Glassware to Retire," *Crafts Report* 13 (December 1987), 17.

23 Pamphlet issued by the Higgins Glass Studio, Riverside, Illinois, c. 1990.

24 Quoted in Eleanor Bitterman, "Heaton's Wizardry with Glass," *CH* 14 (May/June 1954), 13.

25 Michael Higgins, "Media Discussion/Glass," in ACC, *The Craftsmen's World: Annual Conference, June 1959, Lake*

George, proceedings (New York: ACC, 1959), 176.

26 Ibid., 194.

27 Gregory's department store sales were confirmed by New York dealer Joel Rosencrantz (interview by the author, January 1996). Among the venues for Lukens's work was Bullocks on Wilshire Boulevard in Los Angeles. Lynn, *American Studio Glass*, 70.

28 Robert Sowers, *The Lost Art: A Survey of One Thousand Years of Stained Glass* (New York: G. Wittenborn, 1954); Sowers, *Stained Glass: An Architectural Art* (New York: Universe Books, 1961).

29 Meredith Clausen, *Spiritual Spaces: The Religious Architecture of Pietro Belluschi* (Seattle: University of Washington Press, 1992), 22.

30 Ibid., 98–99. See also Russell Day, "Glass in Architectural Decoration," in ACC, *Research in the Crafts*, papers delivered at the Fourth National Conference of the American Craftsmen's Council, University of Washington, Seattle, August 26–29, 1961 (New York: ACC, 1961), 34–35.

31 "Two-way" colored glass was used in the window, providing the exterior surface with brilliant color in the daylight. See Ada Louise Huxtable, "Art in Architecture 1959," *CH* 19 (January/February 1959), 24. Despite the efforts of preservationists, Sowers's window was dismantled and dismembered when the American Airlines terminal building was torn down in 2008. Ken Belson, "A Window That Reflected a Golden Age Comes Down at Kennedy Airport," *New York Times*, February 22, 2008.

32 Ada Louise Huxtable, "Gottlieb's Glass Wall," *Art Digest* 29 (January 15, 1955),

9. When the Park Avenue Synagogue was remodeled in the late 1970s, the panels were taken down and reinstalled in the main building.

33 Meert's work is illustrated in Herman Cherry, "Joseph Meert: Experiments in Stained Glass," *CH* 16 (March/April 1956), 14–17.

34 Ellen Landau, *Jackson Pollock* (New York: Harry N. Abrams, 1989), 197.

35 Thomas Buechner, foreword to Frantz, *Contemporary Glass*, 6–7. The Corning Museum of Glass opened in 1951 with Buechner as founding director.

36 Axel Von Saldern, introduction to Corning Museum of Glass, *Glass 1959: A Special Exhibition of International Contemporary Glass* (Corning, NY: Corning Glass Center, 1959), 32.

37 Frantz, *Contemporary Glass*, 159.

38 Harvey Littleton, "Littleton Remembers," *Glass Art* 4, no. 1 (1976), 22.

39 Those attending the March 1962 workshop, in addition to the Higginses, included Carl Martz of the University of Indiana; John Stevenson from the University of Michigan; Tom McGlauchlin, then teaching at Cornell College in Iowa; Dora Reynolds from Columbus, Ohio; and Littleton's students Clayton Bailey and Edith Franklin. Ibid.

40 Joan Byrd, *Harvey Littleton: A Retrospective Exhibition* (Atlanta: High Museum of Art, 1984), 11–12. Leafgreen was later called out of retirement by Owens-Illinois Glass to blow prototypes for the big-mouth beer bottle known as "Mickey." See Fritz Dreisbach, "An Anecdotal Description of the Debut of American Studio Glass Artists and the Family Tree" in Finn Lynggaard, ed.,

The Story of Studio Glass: The Early Years, a Historical Documentation Told by the Pioneers (Copenhagen: Rhodos, 1998), 29.

41 Quoted in Patricia Failing, *Howard Kottler: Face to Face* (Seattle: University of Washington Press, 1995), 48.

42 Frantz, *Contemporary Glass*, 55.

43 Lynn, *American Studio Glass*, 57. Prominent among the dealers who began to include studio glass in their exhibitions in the later 1960s was New Yorker Lee Nordness. Nordness began representing glass artists in 1969 and showed their work together with painting and sculpture. He and co-curator Paul Smith also included glass in the seminal exhibition *Objects: USA* (1969). Although glass art comprised only a small percentage of the work surveyed, this exhibition accelerated glass collecting in the United States. Ibid, 71, 78. For more on Nordness and his influence, see chap. 2 in this volume.

44 Tina Oldknow, *Pilchuck: A Glass School* (Seattle: University of Washington Press, 1996), 39.

45 Frantz, 55.

46 Ibid., 53–55.

47 Labino, *Visual Art in Glass*, 116–18.

48 Lynn, *American Studio Glass*, 79.

49 Bonnie Miller, *Out of the Fire: Contemporary Glass Artists and Their Work* (San Francisco: Chronicle Books, 1991), 8–9.

50 Oldknow, 43.

51 Ibid., 37–43.

52 See Patterson Sims, "A Founder's Perspective: Conversation with Dale Chihuly" in ibid., 19–25. The name was changed to the Pilchuck Glass School in

1986, in ibid., 127, 214-15.

53 Lynn, *American Studio Glass*, 57.

54 Paul Perrot, "Robert Willson: Sculptor in Glass, An Appreciation," *Art Journal* 29 (autumn 1969), 46–47. Willson's career is surveyed in Matthew Kangas, *Robert Willson: Image-Maker* (San Antonio: Pace-Willson Foundation and University of Washington Press, 2001).

192

ADOLPH GOTTLIEB, DESIGNER

HEINIGKE & SMITH, MANUFACTURER

Untitled (Stained Glass Window), c. 1954

STAINED GLASS

29 X 24½ IN. (73.7 X 62.2 CM)

COLLECTION OF THE ADOLPH AND

ESTHER GOTTLIEB FOUNDATION, NEW YORK, NY

193

HARVEY LITTLETON

Falling Blue, 1969

GLASS

21½ X 12½ X 6 IN. (54.6 X 31.8 X 15.2 CM)

MUSEUM OF ARTS AND DESIGN, GIFT OF
THE JOHNSON WAX COMPANY, THROUGH THE
AMERICAN CRAFT COUNCIL, 1977

194

EDRIS ECKHARDT

Archangel, 1956

GLASS

8¹¹⁄₁₆ X 3¹⁵⁄₁₆ IN. (22 X 10 CM)

CORNING MUSEUM OF GLASS, 61.4.64

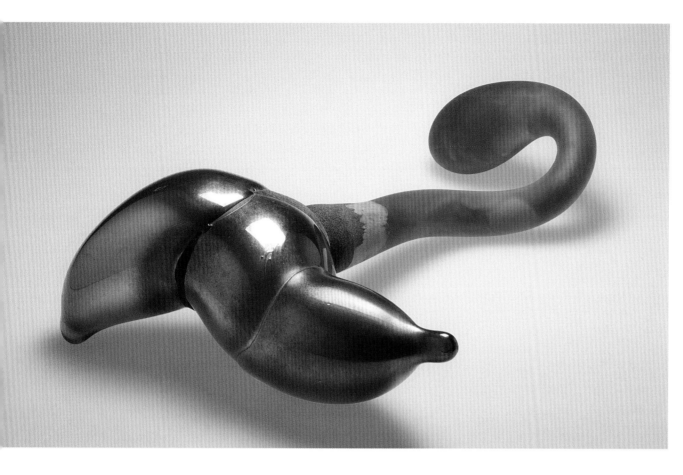

195
MARVIN LIPOFSKY
*California Loop
Series 1969 #29*, 1969
GLASS, RAYON FLOCKING, EPOXY
6 X 20 X 12 IN.
(15.2 X 50.8 X 30.5 CM)
CORNING MUSEUM OF GLASS,
2006.4.151

196
RICHARD MARQUIS
*American Acid
Capsule with
Cloth Container*,
1969–70
(CONTAINER BY NIRMAL
KAUER [BARBARA BRITTELL])
GLASS AND CLOTH
H. 4 IN. (10.2 CM),
DIAM. 1¼ IN. (3.2 CM)
COLLECTION OF PAM BIALLAS

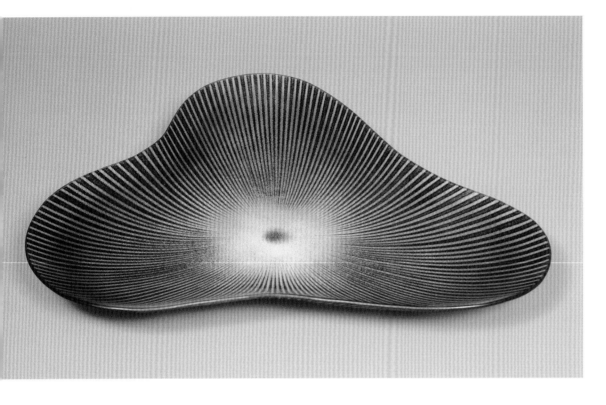

197

MAURICE HEATON

Amoeboid Plate, c. 1950

ENAMELED GLASS

2¼ X 20½ X 16 IN. (5.7 X 52.1 X 40.6 CM)

MUSEUM OF ARTS AND DESIGN,
GIFT OF SIMONA AND JEROME CHAZEN, 2003

198

EARL McCUTCHEN

Plate, c. 1960

SLUMPED AND LAMINATED GLASS, COPPER
SCREEN, PAPER, WIRE, AND GLAZE

DIAM. 11½ IN. (29.2 CM)

MUSEUM OF ARTS AND DESIGN, GIFT OF
THE ESTATE OF MRS. EARL McCUTCHEN, 2010

199

JOEL PHILIP MYERS

Form A, 1968

LEAD GLASS AND SILVER

H. 12½ IN. (31.8 CM),

DIAM. 8½ IN. (21.6 CM)

MUSEUM OF ARTS AND DESIGN,

GIFT OF THE JOHNSON WAX

COMPANY THROUGH THE

AMERICAN CRAFT COUNCIL, 1977

200

DALE CHIHULY

Wine Bottle, 1968

GLASS, WOOD, AND BRASS

8 X 23¾ X 7 IN. (20.3 X 60.3 X 17.8 CM)

MUSEUM OF ARTS AND DESIGN, GIFT OF

THE JOHNSON WAX COMPANY, THROUGH THE

AMERICAN CRAFT COUNCIL, 1977

201

DOMINICK LABINO

Gold-ruby Vase, 1969

GLASS

H. 4⁷/₁₆ IN. (11.2 CM), DIAM. 4½ IN. (11.4 CM)

CORNING MUSEUM OF GLASS, 70.4.24

202

GLEN LUKENS

Bowl, c. 1950

GLASS

H. 2½ IN. (6.4 CM), DIAM. 17⅞ IN. (45.4 CM)

FORREST L. MERRILL COLLECTION

FIG. 12.8–9
Robert Sowers, *Two sketches for stained-glass window, American Airlines, Terminal B, Idlewild Airport (now JFK International Airport), New York, NY*, c. 1959. Top: Pencil, acrylic, gouache. 2 x 20½ in. (5 x 52 cm); bottom: Pencil, construction paper, colored paper, painted paper. 3⅛ x 41⅓ in. (8 x 105 cm). Collection of the Rakow Research Library, the Corning Museum of Glass, Gift of Judi Sowers.

RESOURCE LIST

GUIDE TO THE READER

The Resource List is divided into six categories: Artists and Advocates; Schools and Workshops; Museums and Professional Associations; Conferences; Manufacturers and Design Firms; Galleries and Retailers. This list is intended to be as inclusive as earlier volumes in this series, but the exponential increase in artistic activities during the period under discussion, 1945 to 1969, and concomitant space limitations prevent publication of a truly comprehensive compilation. The entries that follow have been chiefly chosen for their relationship to works of art in the catalogue. The reader is directed to the bibliography for further research.

Every effort has been made to present accurate information in the Resource List.

KEY TO ABBREVIATIONS (used throughout this volume)

AAA, SI	Archives of American Art, Smithsonian Institution
AC	*American Craft*
ACC	American Craftsmen's Council (1955–69); or American Crafts Council (1969 onward), depending on the year
ACEC	American Craftsmen Educational Council
AFA	American Federation of the Arts
CH	*Craft Horizons*
Cranbrook	Cranbrook Academy of Arts, Bloomfield Hills, MI
MAD	Museum of Arts and Design
MCC	Museum of Contemporary Crafts
MoMA	Museum of Modern Art, NY
RIT	Rochester Institute of Technology
SITES	Smithsonian Institute Traveling Exhibition Service

U.S. Post Office abbreviations are used for state names (e.g., MA for Massachusetts).

REFERENCES CITED IN SHORTENED FORM

In addition to the titles listed below, sources of material quoted directly in the entries are given in short form in parentheses immediately following the quotation; the full reference is provided at the end of each entry.

Clark 1979
Garth Clark, *A Century of Ceramics in the United States, A Study of Its Development* (New York: E.P. Dutton in association with the Everson Museum of Art, 1979).

Craft in the Machine Age
Janet Kardon, ed., *Craft in the Machine Age, 1920–1945: The History of Twentieth-century American Craft* (New York: Harry N. Abrams in association with the American Craft Museum, 1995).

Cooke, Ward, and L'Ecuyer 2003
Edward S. Cooke, Jr., Gerald W. R. Ward, and Kelly H. L'Ecuyer, *The Maker's Hand: American Studio Furniture, 1940–1990*, exh. cat. (Boston: MFA Publications, a division of the Museum of Fine Arts, Boston, 2003).

Falino and Ward 2008
Jeannine Falino and Gerald W. R. Ward, eds., *Silver of the Americas, 1600–2000* (Boston: Museum of Fine Arts, Boston, 2008).

Frantz 1989
Suzanne K. Frantz, *Contemporary Glass: A World Survey from the Corning Museum of Glass* (New York: Harry N. Abrams, 1989).

Objects: USA
Lee Nordness, *Objects: USA,* exh. cat. (New York: Viking Press, 1970).

Strauss 2007
Cindy Strauss et al., *Ornament as Art: Avant-Garde Jewelry from the Helen Williams Drutt Collection*, exh. cat. (Houston: Museum of Fine Arts; Stuttgart: Arnoldsche Art Publishers, 2007).

CONTRIBUTORS (initials at end of each entry)

Natalie Balthrop	NB
Louisa Bann	LB
Nurit Einik	NE
Jeannine Falino	JF
Sarah Froelich	SF
Jeanne Gardner	JG
Carolyn Kelly	CK
Monique Long	ML
Bella Neyman	BN
Maile Pingel	MP
Jane Port	JP
Lindsey Rossi	LR
Michele Sala	MS
Jennifer Scanlan	JS
Tara Tappert	TT
Catherine Zusy	CZ

ARTISTS AND ADVOCATES

AKERS, ADELA
Born February 7, 1933, Santiago de Compostela, Spain
FIBER ARTIST, EDUCATOR

Known for her large-scale textiles, Akers weaves abstract designs inspired by her heritage and study of traditional technique. When she was four years old, her family fled Spain, which was in the throes of civil war, and moved to Havana, Cuba. In 1957 Akers moved to the U.S. and began her art studies at the School of the Art Institute in Chicago, where she was introduced to weaving. She transferred to Cranbrook in 1960 and studied there for two years. Akers was inspired not only by the abstract expressionist work of contemporary artists, but also by her travels abroad. In the middle of the 1960s, she visited Central and South America, where she worked with Mexican and Peruvian weavers. These experiences shaped her artistic career, and many of the colors, patterns, and zigzag lines of her designs are directly inspired by these travels. Akers was also greatly influenced by her Spanish roots, although she only lived in Spain for a short time. During visits to her ancestral home, she was captivated by the architecture of the churches, which then inspired her to create large, sturdy textiles, some of which are freestanding. Akers has also made important contributions to weaving and textile design as an instructor at the Tyler School of Art in Philadelphia, PA, where she taught for twenty-three years, serving as head of the department by the time of her retirement in 1995. —NB
Objects: USA, 319; Akiko Kotani and Bernard Freydberg, "Rich Surfaces for 'Pure Beholding,'" *Fiberarts* 28 (summer 2001), 46–48.

ALBERS, ANNI
(NÉE ANNELISE FLEISCHMANN; LATER MRS. JOSEF ALBERS)
Born June 12, 1899, Berlin, Germany; died May 9, 1994, Orange, CT
FIBER ARTIST, EDUCATOR

As a result of her innovative exploration of modern art and weaving, Anni Albers contributed to the breakdown of distinctions between art and craft and craft and industry. After she and her husband, Josef Albers, immigrated to the U.S. in 1933, the couple (the first of the Bauhaus faculty in Germany to move to America) assumed teaching positions at the newly founded experimental Black Mountain College, near Asheville, NC. As an assistant professor and head of the weaving workshop, Albers introduced her students to Bauhaus principles, as well as to pre-Columbian (Andean) textiles through the examples she amassed for the college's study collection. She also presented the artistic possibilities of using handweaving in the production process for industry. One of her major contributions was in helping to bring textiles to the forefront of art and design in industry, as in her 1949 commission for curtains, bedspreads, and room dividers in the dormitory of the Walter Gropius–designed Harvard Graduate Center in Cambridge. The fabrics followed the admonitions of her Bauhaus teacher, Paul Klee, who believed that textiles should be "serving objects" in which function is more important than aesthetics. That same year she became the first weaver to have a solo exhibition at MoMA.

Albers and her husband moved to New Haven, CT, in 1949, and thereafter she shifted her work to freelance commissions and writing. She began designing textiles for Knoll in 1958 and for Sunar in 1978, producing geometric designs and patterns that incorporated the weaving structure of the ancient Andean textiles she admired. Her books—*Anni Albers: Pictorial Weavings* (1959); *On Designing* (1959); and *On Weaving* (1965)—presented her theoretical approach to weaving, including the belief that if one worked within the "authority" and limitations of a given artistic discipline (such as weaving), one was then prepared to innovate and experiment within those limitations. In 1964 Albers accepted a fellowship at the Tamarind Lithography Workshop in Los Angeles, CA, and her work shifted almost exclusively to printmaking. In 1970 she gave away her loom. Albers's weaving and print work has been exhibited nationally and internationally, and she has been awarded numerous honorary doctoral degrees. —TT

"Handweaving for Modern Interiors," *CH* 9 (winter 1949), 23–25; Virginia Gardner Troy, *Anni Albers and Ancient American Textiles: From Bauhaus to Black Mountain* (Burlington, VT: Ashgate Publishing Company, 2002); Nicholas Fox Weber and Pandora Tabatabai Asbaghi, *Anni Albers* (New York: Guggenheim Museum Publications, distributed by Harry N. Abrams, 1999). For earlier history see *Craft in the Machine Age*, 227.

APODACA, JOE REYES JR.

Born March 18, 1942, Tucson, AZ
METALSMITH, JEWELER, GLASS ARTIST, EDUCATOR

Known for work that combines the delicacy of jewelry with the impact of sculpture, Apodaca began making jewelry when he was in high school, and in 1961 he attended a summer school session at the University of Arizona, where he concentrated on jewelry casting techniques. Shortly thereafter he moved to Rochester, NY, and matriculated at the School for American Craftsmen (SAC), RIT, studying silversmithing with Hans Christensen and earning an associates degree in 1964, a BFA in 1966, and an MFA in 1967.

Apodaca began his career assisting with commissions for Charles Clement, a well-known Arizona designer-craftsman in 1961–62. He was a self-employed jeweler fulfilling orders for galleries in Rochester, Tucson, and Washington, DC, from 1964 to 1967, while also designing limited production jewelry for I & E Associates of Tallahassee, FL, from 1965 to 1967. In 1967 Apodaca began his teaching career, first as an instructor of jewelry at George Brown Community College, Toronto, Canada (1967–68), and then teaching enameling, jewelry, and holloware at California State College at Los Angeles (1968–69). He has subsequently been influential as a teacher and prolific studio jeweler in the Pacific Northwest, establishing the jewelry program at the Oregon College of Art and Craft in Portland.

He eventually devoted himself full-time to studio work, in collaboration with his wife Linda, producing jewelry and sculpture made of precious metal, steel, and concrete. He won numerous awards throughout the 1960s, including the 1965 *Sterling Today Competition* sponsored by the Sterling Silversmiths Guild of America, for a wine decanter and candelabra, and the following year, a National Merit Award from the ACC. He regularly exhibited throughout the 1960s at a wide range of American venues, including: the Tucson Art Center (1961 and 1962), the Rochester Memorial Art Gallery (1964), the Delaware Art Center (1966), the New York State Craft Fair in Ithaca (1967), the California Institute of Technology in Pasadena (1968), and the University of Texas (1969). —TT

Objects: USA, 172, 213; Sharon Elaine Thompson, "Lively Complements," *Lapidary Journal* (November 1999), 52–55.

ARNESON, ROBERT CARSTON

Born September 4, 1930, Benicia, CA;
died November 2, 1992, Benicia, CA
CERAMIST, EDUCATOR

Robert Arneson was a recognized leader of the Funk art movement that flourished in northern California in the 1960s. His technically brilliant polychrome ceramic sculptures display a distinctive and powerful artistic perspective and a wide range of references including surrealism, pop art, the work of Joan Miró, historical portraiture, and glaze formulas developed in China during the ninth-century Song Dynasty. His work is full of humor, whimsy, even buffoonery, making rude political commentary and satire. It grapples with the conditions of artistic process and form in the wide gap that separated art from craft during the 1950s and '60s.

Initially interested in cartoon work as a high school student, Arneson later studied at the College of Marin, Kentfield, CA, from 1949 to 1951. He earned a BA in art education in 1954 from the California College of Arts and Crafts, Oakland, and an MFA in 1958 from Mills College, Oakland, where he studied under Alfred-trained ceramist Antonio Prieto, whose purist aesthetics are evident in Arneson's 1958 MFA exhibition.

It was while Arneson was teaching high school in the early 1950s that his interest in ceramics took hold, particularly during the summer of 1956, when he took courses with Herbert Sanders at San Jose State College and with Edith Heath at the California College of Arts and Crafts. From this training, along with *Ceramics Monthly* instructional articles by F. Carlton Ball and subsequent work at Mills College, Arneson became a competent functional potter, producing work that reflected the "clean pot ethic." While working as Prieto's assistant at Mills College (1960–62), Arneson followed the abstract expressionist work of Peter Voulkos, who had begun teaching at the University of California, Berkeley, in 1959. Arneson never studied with Voulkos but was nevertheless influenced by him and began producing work that denied functional purpose, which he described as "quasi-Voulkos." When he created *No Return* (1961), the capped ceramic bottle signaled his break

from the ceramic establishment. He left Mills College, and from 1962 until his retirement in 1991, he was head of the ceramics department at the University of California, Davis. Over the next few years such work as *Funk John* (1963), *The Artist Losing His Marbles* (1965), *Typewriter* (1965–66), and *Call Girl* (1966) established his reputation in the Funk movement, and as Garth Clark has noted, he "profoundly offended, dismayed, and delighted both the sculptural world and that of the ceramic arts" (Clark 1979). His work was included in such exhibitions as *Contemporary Craftsmen of the Far West* (1961), *Creative Casting* (1963), and *Monuments, Tombstones and Trophies* (1967). —TT

Clark 1979, 271; Neal Benezra, *Robert Arneson: A Retrospective,* exh. cat. (Des Moines, IA: Des Moines Art Center, 1985), 18.

ARTSCHWAGER, RICHARD ERNST

Born December 26, 1923, Washington, DC
SCULPTOR, WOODWORKER, FURNITURE MAKER

Most closely associated with the pop-minimalism and photorealism of the 1960s, Artschwager's work in fact resists categorization and is best understood as a fusion of abstraction and realism, as well as science and aesthetics. With Marcel Duchamp and the surrealists (especially René Magritte and Salvador Dalí) often cited as kindred spirits, he also presents a commentary on the utility of art and its ambiguous role in culture. Artschwager once noted in a *New York Times* article that the purpose of art making is "to explore the world of the subjective—of the viewer's ability to see and to know an object in several ways at once" (McGill 1998). A long apprenticeship in living informs his work. Raised in Washington, DC, and Las Cruces, NM, Artschwager spent his formative years attending various schools, including a year in Munich, where he learned German. He studied cell biology and chemistry at Cornell University, and following a three-year interruption for military service (in part with the Counterintelligence Corps in Vienna), he earned his undergraduate degree in science from Cornell in 1948. In 1949 he moved to New York City for a year of study with School of Paris artist Amédée Ozenfant. Following this training, he held a number of odd jobs, some of which (such as his work as a baby photographer) proved useful when he turned to making art. In 1953 Artschwager took up cabinetmaking, and by 1956 he had begun a small company that mass-produced simple, well-made furniture and was among the first major suppliers for the Workbench Furniture Company. A fire in his workshop in 1958 destroyed everything and left him deeply in debt. He put his shop back together and continued making furniture until 1970, but from 1958 onward he concentrated on art, starting with abstract paintings based upon his memories of the New Mexican landscape.

The staples of his oeuvre, however, derived in part from his work as a professional cabinetmaker. They include such "nonuse" objects as abstracted furniture forms that incorporate a variety of surfaces and textures—woodgrain Formica, abstracted grisaille images of architecture (some based on photographs), interiors, landscapes, still lifes, figures, and portraits drawn in graphite on Celotex (an inexpensive fiberboard used in ceilings). He is also known for his signature "blp" form—pronounced "blip" after the sound made by radar. These were small black, lozenge-shaped forms, made of Formica, wood, or rubberized hair. In the mid-1960s he placed blps on the sides of buildings, construction sites, and empty outdoor walls throughout Manhattan, as a kind of precursor to graffiti. In 1959 Artschwager showed his work for the first time at Manhattan's Art Directions Gallery and in 1963 began exhibiting regularly at the Leo Castelli Gallery. By the late 1960s he had solo exhibitions in such international venues as the Galerie Konrad, Düsseldorf, and Galerie Ricke, Cologne. In 1968 he was an artist-in-residence at the University of Wisconsin, and in 1969 he was given the Cassandra Award. —TT

Richard Artschwager—MATRIX 71, exh. brochure (Berkeley: University of California Berkeley, Art Museum, and Pacific Film Archives, 1984); Douglas C. McGill, "He Furnishes Objects to Fit a World Gone Awry," New York Times, January 17, 1998, 27, 31; Richard Artschwager, oral history interview by Paul Cummings, March 3 and 22, 1978, AAA, SI.

ASAWA, RUTH AIKO
(MRS. WILLIAM ALBERT LANIER)
Born January 24, 1926, Norwalk, CA
FIBER ARTIST, SCULPTOR, PRINTMAKER, EDUCATOR

Ruth Asawa is nationally recognized for her wire sculptures (crocheted and tied), her public art commissions, and her activism in education and the arts. Raised in a farming community in Southern California, Asawa's artistic journey began in 1942 as a sixteen-year-old in an internment camp during World War II. Among the internees at the Santa Anita Race Track in Arcadia, CA, were animators from the Walt Disney Studios (such as Tom Okamoto) who gave art lessons in the grandstands of the racetrack. Asawa spent most of her free time painting and drawing with them and continued making art when her family was later sent to the Relocation Center in Rohwer, AR. In 1943, with scholarship assistance from the Quaker Japanese American Student Relocation Council, Asawa traveled to Wisconsin to train as an art teacher at the Milwaukee State Teacher's College. When she was not allowed to graduate in 1946 because no school would hire a Japanese American for practice teaching, she left for Black Mountain College, where she spent three years studying design and drawing with Josef Albers, R. Buckminster Fuller, and Merce Cunningham. (In 1998 Asawa was awarded a BFA from the University of Wisconsin–Milwaukee.) At Black Mountain she also met her future husband, architecture and design student Albert Lanier; they married and settled in San Francisco in 1949. A Quaker-sponsored summer trip to Toluca, Mexico, in 1947 provided an opportunity for Asawa to learn techniques for crocheting egg baskets from galvanized wire. During the 1950s this training informed her free-hanging basket-globes that combined fiber techniques with metal. While initially labeled a weaver, or fiber artist,

Asawa became known as a sculptor after a review of her wire abstractions appeared in *Time* magazine in 1955. In 1962 she began experimenting with tied-wire and electroplating techniques; in 1965 she accepted a fellowship with the Tamarind Lithography Workshop and spent two months in Los Angeles making prints with master printmakers. An early public art commission was her mermaid fountain, *Andrea* (1966), for San Francisco's Ghirardelli Square. In the 1960s Asawa also became an arts activist, co-founding the Alvarado School Arts Workshop in 1968. With the purpose of providing young children with the opportunity to develop more fully as individuals, this innovative program involved parents, artists, musicians, and gardeners, and at its height was in fifty public schools throughout San Francisco. She has had solo exhibitions at the San Francisco Museum of Art (1973), the Fresno Art Center (1978 and 2001), the Oakland Museum (2002), and the de Young Museum (2006), among others. —TT

Ruth Asawa and Gerald Nordland, *Ruth Asawa: A Retrospective View*, exh. cat. (San Francisco: San Francisco Museum of Art, 1973); Daniell Cornell et al., *The Sculpture of Ruth Asawa: Contours in the Air,* exh. cat., (Berkeley: University of California Press and Fine Arts Museums of San Francisco, 2006); artist file, ACC library.

BAILEY, CLAYTON GEORGE
Born March 9, 1939, Antigo, WI
CERAMIST, EDUCATOR

Clayton Bailey's art is regarded by Garth Clark as "the most truly Funk of the Bay Area" (Clark 1979). This observation is borne out by his unconventional slab-constructed, hand-worked forms of the 1960s that include ceramic critters, *Nitepots*, urinals, first-aid boxes, burping bowls, burping busts, wall gargoyles, and dripping gargoyle fountains. He also produced lightweight latex rubber masks and four-foot-long inflatable rubber grubs that could be shipped easily and inexpensively to museums and galleries. In the late 1960s he created jumping and "shocking" machines with hardware-store items and using electricity for light and movement. While initially a prepharmacy student at the University of Wisconsin–Madison, in 1959 Bailey took a pottery class with Harvey Littleton and was "immediately hooked on clay." Bailey decided to major in ceramics, and between 1959 and 1961, when he earned his BS in art education, he attended workshops with Bernard Leach and Peter Voulkos and took pottery classes with Toshiko Takaezu and Clyde Burt. Bailey continued in the graduate program at Madison, working as Littleton's studio technician, teaching a beginning pottery class, and earning an MS in art and art education in 1962. For the next few years he held a variety of teaching positions throughout the Midwest, including a summer at the University of Iowa, where he had access to the school's large salt kilns. In 1963 he was awarded a Louis Comfort Tiffany grant and an ACC Research grant to support his work with salt glazes. He was also hired that year as an artist-in-residence at Wisconsin State University–Whitewater (now University of Wisconsin–Whitewater), where he taught ceramics until

1967. An opportunity to participate in the 1964 College Art Association conference—in a panel discussion titled "Whither the Pot?"—brought Bailey into contact with such California ceramists as Robert Arneson, Jim Melchert, and David Gilhooly. These connections led to his appointment as a visiting artist at the University of California, Davis, in 1967. After two semesters as a replacement for Arneson, in a department where he worked alongside painters Roy De Forest and Wayne Thiebaud, Bailey decided to settle permanently in California. He taught first at the University of California, Los Angeles, in the summer of 1968, and then moved to California State University, Hayward, in northern California, where he was on faculty from 1968 until his retirement in 1996. Bailey was given solo exhibitions during the 1960s at MCC (1964) and the Beloit Art Center (1966). He began showing his work at the Candy Store Gallery, Folsom, CA, in 1968—a popular gathering place for Funk artists from the San Francisco area—and he is one of the artists featured in the television special, *With These Hands: The American Craftsman* (1969), which was sponsored by the S. C. Johnson Company. —TT

Clark 1979, 275; "A Short Chronology of the Artist's Life," at www.claytonbailey.com; G. Joan DePaoli, *Clayton Bailey: Happenings in the Circus of Life* (Davis, CA: John Natsoulas Press, 2000).

BALL, FREDERICK CARLTON
Born April 2, 1911, Sutter Creek, CA;
died June 5, 1992, Tacoma, WA
CERAMIST, EDUCATOR, AUTHOR

A third-generation Californian, F. Carlton Ball helped popularize pottery making in the West, transforming the ceramics department at Mills College into one of the most active centers for clay in the 1940s. During his years at Mills he became the first ceramist in the San Francisco Bay Area to fire a kiln to pyrometric cone 10 (about 2,340°F) for art pottery. During World War II, under the auspices of the U.S. Army Occupational Therapy Emergency Program, he created a department at Mills that taught craft techniques. Shortly before he left the college in 1950, he brought Bernard Leach to campus to teach a workshop. He also helped found the Mills Ceramic Guild, as a support for the ceramics program and a venue for workshops and exhibitions, as well as the San Francisco Potters Association, which united the various pottery groups and individual ceramists within the San Francisco Bay Area. A West Coast pioneer on the potter's wheel, Ball was particularly interested in the throwing and assembly techniques required to make extremely large vessels—many of his pieces were up to 6 feet in height, requiring as much as 150 pounds of clay. During the 1950s his successful art/craft collaboration with painter Aaron Bohrod resulted in more than 200 wheel-thrown, low-fired stoneware forms made by Ball that were then hand-decorated by Bohrod. A Ford Foundation fellowship (1954–55) allowed Ball to work with Daniel Rhodes at Alfred University in New York and Katherine Choy at Sophie Newcomb Memorial College in Louisiana.

Ball's formidable teaching career included stints at California College of Arts and Crafts (1935–38), San Jose State College (1938), Sacramento High School (1938–39), Mills College, Oakland (1939–50), California School of Fine Arts, San Francisco (now the San Francisco Art Institute, 1943–44), University of Wisconsin–Madison (1950–51), Southern Illinois University, Carbondale (1951–56), University of Mississippi (1953), University of Southern California (1956–68), Whittier College (1959–61), and University of Puget Sound (1968–77). During his retirement years he continued to teach at the Tacoma Community College. In addition he designed and helped market at least six different pottery wheels, his work was shown in more than 500 national and international museum and gallery exhibitions, he was a first-place winner in fourteen shows, and he wrote four books and approximately 150 technical articles for *Ceramics Monthly, Ceramics Industry, Studio Potter,* and *American School and University Yearbook,* intended to supplement the meager educational literature of the day. —TT

F. Carlton Ball and Janice Lovoos, *Making Pottery Without a Wheel: Texture and Form in Clay* (NY: Reinhold, 1965); Ball, *Decorating Pottery with Clay, Slip and Glaze* (Columbus, OH: Professional Publications, 1967); Ball and Spencer L. David, *F. Carlton Ball: Ceramic Works, 1940–1990,* exh. cat. (Tacoma, WA: Tacoma Art Museum, 1990). For earlier history and publications see *Craft in the Machine Age,* 229.

BATES, KENNETH FRANCIS
Born May 24, 1904, North Scituate, MA;
died May 24, 1994, Euclid, OH
ENAMELIST, SILVERSMITH, EDUCATOR

In the mid-twentieth century, Cleveland, OH, became the foremost center for the study and production of enamel work, an archaic medium resurrected in part by the teaching, writing, and art of Kenneth Bates. Regarded as the dean of American enameling, Bates studied with enamelist Laurin Hovey Martin at the Massachusetts Normal Art School (now called the Massachusetts College of Art), graduating in 1927. He taught design and enameling at the Cleveland School of Art (later, the Cleveland Institute of Art) from 1927 to 1968, influencing generations of students, including John Paul Miller, Fred Miller, Ed Winter, Mary Ellen McDermott, and James M. Someroski. The study and production of enameling became Bates's lifework, and over the years he gained an extensive knowledge of enameling technique—from cloisonné to plique-à-jour. Bates experimented with a range of modernist styles. The jewel-like plant, flower, leaf, butterfly, and bird motifs are indicative of his passion for gardening and the natural world. He was also drawn to the medieval enamels and goldsmith's work in the Guelph Treasure, a collection of sumptuous medieval reliquaries and liturgical objects from the cathedral at Brunswick, Germany, some of which are in the Cleveland Museum of Art. Bates used the museum's collection as a teaching tool and encouraged his students to participate in the museum's annual May Show. He

himself exhibited in sixty-two consecutive shows (1928–90), winning more than forty awards and four silver medals. During the 1950s and '60s Bates published several books on enameling and design, including *Enameling: Principles and Practice* (1951) which went through seven printings in seven years.—TT

Kenneth F. Bates, *Enameling: Principles and Practice* (Cleveland, OH: World Publishing Company, 1951); Bates, *Basic Design: Principles and Practice,* foreword by William M. Milliken (Cleveland, OH: World Publishing Company, 1960); and Bates, *The Enamelist* (Cleveland, OH: World Publishing Company, 1967); Mark Baldridge, "Kenneth Bates, Dean of American Enameling," *Metalsmith* 8 (spring 1988), 25; artist file, ACC library.
For earlier history see *Craft in the Machine Age,* 229.

BAUER, FREDERICK
Born January 1937, Memphis, TN;
CERAMIST, EDUCATOR

According to Garth Clark, Bauer "achieved early notoriety as a ceramic artist in the Funk/Super-Object vein" (Clark 1979). He developed from a skilled functional potter, producing slab-built forms "that were a little bit of early American and a little bit of Japanese," to an imaginative sculptor, producing his most intriguing work—phallic cameras, plates with pyramids of lustered peas, and six-foot-high Funk stiletto-heeled shoes—in the latter part of the 1960s. Bauer earned a BA from the Memphis Academy of Arts in 1962 (now the Memphis College of Art), where he trained with Thorne Edwards, and an MFA in 1964 from the University of Washington, Seattle. In 1966 he was awarded a Louis Comfort Tiffany grant and worked at the Archie Bray Foundation, MT. His ceramics were also shown that year in the *First National Invitational Crafts Exhibition* at Illinois State University. Bauer taught at a number of art schools and universities throughout the country: University of Wisconsin–Madison (1964–65); Haystack Mountain School of Craft, Liberty, ME (1967); University of Michigan, Ann Arbor (1965–68); and University of Washington, Seattle (1968–71). He also offered numerous workshops until 1972. Wayne Higby was one of his students. While his sense of style and irreverence made him something of a "romantic hero" to young ceramists of the day, he eventually found the pressure of "artist-performer-guru" too damaging and left the field in 1972 to farm in seclusion in northern California. —TT

Objects: USA, 105; Clark 1979, 275–76; John Gill lecture, Schein-Joseph International Museum of Ceramic Art, http://ceramicsmuseum.alfred.edu/exhibitions/pondered/gill_lecture.html

BENNETT, GARRY KNOX
Born October 8, 1934, Alameda, CA
FURNITURE MAKER

A talented artist with a deep interest in self-expression and social responsibility, Garry Knox Bennett found inspiration in the cultural milieu of the San Francisco Bay Area of the early 1960s and a politicized lifestyle predicated on the

making of objects. Bennett attended the California College of Arts and Crafts (CCAC, now California College of the Arts) in Oakland from 1959 to 1961, studying painting and metal sculpture. The abstract sculptures of Constantin Brancusi and the organic shapes of Isamu Noguchi especially inspired his work. On leaving CCAC, Bennett moved to the rural setting of Lincoln, CA, where he built a house and tried to establish himself as a sculptor-artist living close to nature. In 1965 he moved back to the Bay Area and settled in Alameda, where he started a metalworking business named Squirkenworks, creating roach clips and peace pendants for necklaces but also making fine jewelry, clocks, and light fixtures for sale to galleries. By the late 1970s he began to think of himself as a furniture maker, consciously choosing this more neutral term over artist, sculptor, or craftsman. Bennett found craftspeople's attention to details and preciousness misplaced in a postindustrial world, and he remained interested in the expressive design, humor, and social commentary that marked the Bay Area's approach to woodworking. —MS

Ursula Ilse-Neuman, ed., *Made in Oakland: The Furniture of Garry Knox Bennett* (New York: American Craft Museum, 2001).

BERTOIA, ARIETO (HARRY)
Born March 10, 1915, San Lorenzo, Udine, Italy;
died November 6, 1978, Bally, PA
SCULPTOR, PRINTMAKER, JEWELER,
FURNITURE DESIGNER

The design legacy of Harry Bertoia stretches from modernism's beginnings in the U.S. to the first suggestions of postmodernism. Greatly influenced by organic forms in nature, Bertoia successfully explored nontraditional, interdisciplinary approaches to art and design in forms unrelated in function. His oeuvre includes graphic arts, hand-hammered brass jewelry, industrially produced steel-wire furniture, and kinetic sculpture. Immigrating with his father to Detroit, MI, in 1930, Bertoia first trained at the Detroit Society of Arts and Crafts and in 1937 received a scholarship to Cranbrook, where he studied under Eliel Saarinen. He taught jewelry and metalworking at Cranbrook until 1943, when he moved to California and began collaborating with Charles and Ray Eames at Evans Products in Venice. Bertoia worked on metal-grid seating, molded-plywood technology, and airplane and medical equipment for the war effort. He participated in Charles Eames's solo exhibition at MoMA in 1946, the year he received his U.S. citizenship. After his move to the East Coast, Bertoia's metal-rod basketwork technology for seating resulted in the production of such work as his *Diamond* chair (regarded as an iconic modern furniture design) by Knoll International in 1952–53.

From the mid-1950s Bertoia was active primarily as a sculptor and jewelry designer, creating abstractions that have been described as "suggestive of fields of grain, shooting stars, or plant forms . . . but always with multiple interpretations relative to scale, color, movement, and sound" (Montgomery 1987). Frequently commissioned by

Eero Saarinen, he worked on monumental public sculptures that are installed in a number of buildings throughout the country, including the General Motors Technical Center in Detroit. His awards included the Fine Arts Medal (1955), Craftsmanship Medal (1956), Graham Foundation Grant for European travel (1957), and the Fine Arts Medal, American Institute of Architects–Pennsylvania Chapter (1963). —TT

Susan J. Montgomery, "The Sound and the Surface: The Metalwork and Jewelry of Harry Bertoia," *Metalsmith* 7 (summer 1987), 33; Nancy N. Schiffer and Val O. Bertoia, *The World of Bertoia* (Atglen, PA: Schiffer Publishing Ltd., 2003); artist file, ACC library.

For earlier history see *Craft in the Machine Age*, 229.

BLASHFIELD, JAMES (JIM)
Born September 4, 1944, Seattle, WA
ARTIST, GRAPHIC DESIGNER, FILM/VIDEO DIRECTOR

When Portlander Jim Blashfield moved to San Francisco in the winter of 1967 at the age of twenty-two, the self-taught artist, cartoonist, and budding filmmaker was struck by the colorful and imaginative "psychedelic" posters seen on telephone poles nearly everywhere, promoting rock concerts at the Avalon Ballroom, the Fillmore Auditorium, and other venues. Blashfield was particularly interested in the poster designs of Wes Wilson, long the nearly exclusive graphic face of Bill Graham's Fillmore. Shortly after Wilson and Graham parted ways, Blashfield arrived at Graham's office with a bundle of drawings, urged on by his neighbor, Jack Casady, bass player for the band Jefferson Airplane, which was also managed by Graham.

Blashfield produced several posters for Graham's shows during 1967 and '68, as well as a few posters and record covers for others. Back in Portland in the early 1970s, he continued to design rock posters and began making animated, experimental, and documentary films. He taught filmmaking at Portland State University, and later became the art director and co-editor of Portland's graphically adventurous *Clinton Street Quarterly*.

In the mid-1980s Blashfield and producer/partner Melissa Marsland embarked on a series of innovative and award-winning animated and live action music videos for Talking Heads, Paul Simon, Peter Gabriel, Tears for Fears, and others, which Blashfield directed. His video for Michael Jackson received a Grammy for best video of the year in 1990. Blashfield, still in Portland, is currently creating multiple-screen video installations, as well as short narrative and experimental films and videos. —JF

Jim Blashfield, e-mail to Jeannine Falino, November 7, 2010; "Jim Blashfield Info," Blashfield Studio, www.blashfieldstudio.com.

BLUMENAU, LILI
Born November 28, 1912, Berlin, Germany;
died September 6, 1976, Bronx, NY
TEXTILE ARTIST, WRITER, CURATOR, EDUCATOR

Lili Blumenau was a leading textile designer in mid-twentieth-century America. Describing herself as a "designer-stylist and technician for the decorative and apparel textile industry," she further noted that she created "every type of fabric and floor covering," as well as "wall hangings and room dividers," for architects and interior designers. Blumenau studied fine and applied arts at the Academy of Fine Art, Berlin (1932–34), and at Academy Scandinave, Paris (1934–36). She also studied weaving and textile technology at the New York School of Textile Technology (1938–40) and at Black Mountain College (1950). Blumenau's multifaceted career included designing for industry, as well as teaching and writing. From 1944 to 1950 she was keeper of textiles at the Cooper Union Museum for the Art of Decoration (now the Cooper-Hewitt Museum). She also taught, lectured, and conducted workshops at colleges, art schools, textile trade associations, and craft councils, notably at the School of Education at New York University (1948–50); Teachers College, Columbia University, where she established a weaving workshop and taught (1948–53); and the Fashion Institute of Technology, NY, where she started a weaving department in 1952 and remained on its faculty until 1958. She wrote about the creative process for such journals as *Craft Horizons*, *Handweaver and Craftsman*, and *Upholstery Magazine,* and in 1955 she published her first book, *The Art and Craft of Hand Weaving Including Fabric Design,* a groundbreaking investigation of textile history. In 1950 she also established the Lili Blumenau Weaving Workshop, and Lili Blumenau Designs. The workshop offered classes in creative and technical weaving, while the design studio was a consulting service for industry, focused on upholstery, drapery, rugs, and tapestries, as well as women's wear fabrics, and shoe and handbag materials. Blumenau's work was included in numerous exhibitions in the 1950s and '60s, including *Designer Craftsmen U.S.A.* (1953), *Craftsmanship in a Changing World* (1956), and *Designed for Production* (1964). Blumenau was named an Honorary Fellow of the ACC in 1975. —TT

Lili Blumenau, *The Art and Craft of Hand Weaving Including Fabric Design* (New York: Crown Publishers, 1955); Blumenau, *Creative Design in Wall Hangings: Weaving Patterns Based on Primitive and Medieval Art* (New York: Crown Publishers, 1967); artist file, ACC library.

BLUNK, J. B. (JAMES BLAIN)
Born August 28, 1926, Ottawa, KS;
died June 15, 2002, Inverness, CA
WOODWORKER, SCULPTOR, CERAMIST, JEWELER

A master of the chain saw, Blunk became internationally known for monumental wood sculptures of sinuous, anthropomorphic forms. Using massive redwood trunks, buried stumps, and driftwood, Blunk created furniture, sculpture, and installations distinctive to the California counterculture of the 1960s and beyond. He also produced ceramics, jewelry, paintings, and large sculptures in bronze and stone.

In 1946, Blunk moved to California, where he trained under Laura Andreson at the University of California, Los Angeles, earning his BA in 1949. He worked in the West Indies for the next two years and enlisted in the army during the Korean War. Discharged in 1952, he visited Japan, where by chance he met Isamu Noguchi, who invited him to Kamakura to study with Japanese potter Rosanjin Kitaoji. Blunk also apprenticed with Toyo Kaneshige, one of Japan's living treasures, in Bizen. Blunk regarded his time with these two men as his great spiritual awakening, an experience that provided him with an altered perspective concerning natural elements such as earth and wood. In 1954, with funds from a show of his pottery and drawings in Noguchi's Chou-Koron Gallery in Tokyo, Blunk returned to the U.S., and through Noguchi, he met painter Gordon Onslow-Ford. Blunk helped the painter build a house, carving unconventional rafters for it, at Inverness, north of San Francisco. By 1959, on the same property, Blunk had built a home for his own family and for the rest of his life drew inspiration from this woodsy Marin County mountaintop. While his earliest training and involvement with ceramics were extensive—he was an artist-in-residence at Palo Verde College in 1954–55—he often supported himself by cutting wood and by carpentry. By 1962 wood sculpture had become his major focus. Edith Wylie included some of his work in the inaugural show at her Egg and the Eye Gallery in Los Angeles in 1965. His first public commission—outdoor seating on the campus plaza at the University of California, Santa Cruz—came in 1968, and in 1969 his sculptures were in *Objects: USA*. —TT

J. B. Blunk, oral history interview by Glenn Adamson, May 16, 2002, AAA, SI; Cooke, Ward, and L'Ecuyer 2003, 47.

BRAND, STEWART
Born December 14, 1938, Rockford, IL
EDITOR, PUBLISHER, ENVIRONMENTALIST

A committed environmentalist who believes that computer technology offers the best means to focus attention on this global issue, Stewart Brand has spent his life "floating upstream" and offering fresh insights on working and living together on earth (Stipp 1995). A graduate of Phillips Exeter Academy (1956) and Stanford University (1960), where he earned a degree in biology, Brand joined the U.S. Army in 1960, eventually working for the Pentagon as a photojournalist. He was among writer Ken Kesey's Merry Pranksters and by 1963 was producing multimedia events employing film, slides, video, lighting, and music, such as *America Needs Indians; War: God; Astronomia;* and *We Are All 1*. At about this time he organized countercultural gatherings called "Trips Festivals," which were said to attract 10,000 people.

When he realized that no photographic images of planet earth existed, Brand created and sold a button that asked why this was the case. His intent was to create awareness of the earth as a single entity. NASA's subsequent release of photos taken during the Apollo space program provided the central image around which Brand created *The Whole Earth Catalogue*, a compendium of environmental information, a sourcebook for helpful tools for self-sufficient living, and a collection of information on such topics as music, crafts, and spirituality. It was published between 1968 and 1972 and intermittently thereafter. By the early 1970s Brand had concluded that the nascent personal computer was fomenting an information revolution that would challenge the hierarchy of centralized authorities around the globe. The concepts of the browser and linked text are partly credited to Brand. The personal computer offered a paradigm shift that was originally embraced by a small coterie of hackers and ultimately came to typify activity on the Internet.

Brand has since continued to share his ideas about the future. He published *CoEvolution Quarterly* (1974–85; now called *Whole Earth* magazine) and *Space Colonies* (1976). He started the Whole Earth 'Lectronic Link (WELL) in about 1985, as an early online community forum, and in 1988 he co-founded the Global Business Network (GBN), an environmental consulting group sought by corporations including the administration of President Bill Clinton, the Pentagon, AT&T, Monsanto, and Xerox. In 1995, with Danny Hills, Brand co-founded the Long Now Foundation that offers thinking on long-term responsibility for planet earth. —JF

David Stipp, "Stewart Brand," *Fortune* 132 (October 15, 1995), 160–72; "Stewart Brand," in David Weill, ed., *Leaders of the Information Age* (New York: H. W. Wilson, 2003).

BRAY, ARCHIE C., SR.

Born October 10, 1886, Helena, MT;
died February 17, 1953, Helena, MT
INDUSTRIALIST, ARTS PATRON

After earning a degree in ceramic engineering from Ohio State University in 1911, Archie Bray joined his father's brick manufacturing business, the Kessler Brick and Sewer Pipe Works in Helena, MT. Within two years he had become foreman of the brickyard, then superintendent, ultimately assuming the position of manager and president in 1931 after the death of his father, Charles Henry Bray. The company was reorganized as Western Clay Manufacturing Company and expanded under Bray's administration, manufacturing some five thousand bricks or tiles an hour. The success of the brickyard afforded Bray the opportunity to indulge his other interests, including music, horticulture, theater, and the arts. His ambition to establish an art center on the grounds of his company—complete with a pottery, studio for artists, and theater building for drama groups—was partially realized with the establishment of the Archie Bray Foundation, a nonprofit educational organization devoted to the ceramic arts. Before his death in 1953, Bray saw his foundation developing into a renowned ceramics institution that attracted the field's cutting-edge ceramists, beginning with Peter Voulkos and Rudy Autio. —TT

Peter Held and Rick Newby, *A Ceramic Continuum: Fifty Years of the Archie Bray Influence* (Seattle, WA: University of Washington Press; Helena, MT: Holter Museum of Art, 2001).

BRYNNER, IRENA

Born December 1, 1917, Vladivostok, Russia;
died January 26, 2003, New York, NY
JEWELER, SCULPTOR, PAINTER

Irena Brynner is known for her sculptural approach to jewelry making, with a specialty in fusing and casting. Her distinctively modernist three-dimensional rings, necklaces, earrings, bracelets, collar pendants, and pins consistently relate to the scale of the human body. A notable characteristic of her work is an absence of clasps or fasteners. Her necklaces frequently wind around the neck rather than hang from it, much like Etruscan body ornament. Brynner's path to jewelry making was circuitous. Raised in Russia with her cousins Yul and Vera Brynner, Irena was eleven when her family moved to Manchuria. Her Swiss-Mongolian father was counsel for the Swiss and French governments at Dairen, China, and her Russian mother was a psychiatrist and musician. Brynner completed high school in Harbin, Manchuria, and then moved to Lausanne, Switzerland, where she received an art education and academic training at the École Cantonal de Dessin (1936–39). She returned to Manchuria to continue art studies in painting and sculpture with private tutors, a direction disrupted by World War II. Her father died in 1942, and she and her mother were forced out of Manchuria in 1944. They lived in Beijing until 1946, when they moved to San Francisco. For the next two years under the tutelage of sculptor and painter Ralph Stackpole, Brynner made sculpture in clay and stone. When her efforts at making a living as a sculptor did not come to fruition, she turned to craft. Impressed by a Claire Falkenstein ornament that looked sculptural, Brynner recognized the commercial and aesthetic possibilities of jewelry making. In 1949 she apprenticed with Bay Area jewelers Carolyn Rosine and Franz Bergman, and then took adult education classes to learn "the practical side of buying materials and tools." Brynner began working on her own in January 1950, and by March she was marketing her work in gift shops in San Francisco. Within a few years Georg Jensen featured her work. Brynner prided herself on her largely self-taught skills, having developed her own approaches to setting gems and stones. A founding member of the Metal Arts Guild in San Francisco in 1951, she met other local jewelers through the association such as merry renk and Margaret De Patta. Brynner's earliest work, much like De Patta's, was constructed, architectonic, geometric, and stark. She began teaching adult education classes in 1955, and when she and her mother moved to New York City in 1956, she continued to teach at the art center affiliated with MoMA until 1963. Brynner's first New York City exhibition was in the fall of 1956 at the Walker and Eberling Studio. She opened a shop of her own on Fifth Avenue in 1959 and wrote on her process in *Modern Jewelry Design and Technique* (1968). Brynner's style changed in New York. She began casting in the lost-wax method, creating jewelry that was more organic and reminiscent of the architecture of Antonio Gaudi, whose work she saw in an exhibition at MoMA 1958. During the 1950s and '60s she was included in solo and group exhibitions at the Philadelphia Art Alliance; Goldsmiths' Hall, London; and the Brussels World's Fair. —TT

Irena Brynner, *Modern Jewelry Design and Technique* (New York: Reinhold, 1968); artist file, ACC library; Brynner, oral history interview by Arline M. Fisch, April 26 and 27, 2001, AAA, SI.

BUECHNER, THOMAS SCHARMAN

Born September 25, 1926, New York, NY;
died June 13, 2010, Steuben, NY
MUSEUM DIRECTOR, WRITER, PAINTER

Corning Museum director Thomas Buechner attended Princeton University in 1945 and served as a cadet in the Naval Air Corps from 1945 to 1946. Following military service, he pursued art training at the Art Students League in New York and the École des Beaux-Arts, Fontainebleau, in 1946; the École des Beaux-Arts, Paris, and the Institute Voor Pictologie, Amsterdam, in 1947; and again at the Art Students League in 1948. One of his teachers was M. M. van Dantzig, from whom Buechner learned the painting techniques of the old masters, particularly seventeenth- and eighteenth-century methods for layering colors from a limited palette and for painting even the most important lines spontaneously. In 1949 Buechner was hired as an assistant manager in the display department at The Metropolitan Museum of Art, NY. Buechner greatly impressed Francis Henry Taylor, the museum's director, who recommended the twenty-four-year-old to the newly established Corning Museum of Glass, and Buechner was hired as its first director in 1951. During his tenure he wrote several books (see below) and organized numerous exhibitions, including *Glass 1959*, the most significant contemporary glass survey mounted in the 1950s. From 1958 to 1960 Buechner also headed the art department at Corning Community College. In 1960 he left Corning to become the director at the Brooklyn Museum, a position he held from 1960 to 1971, when he returned to Corning, NY, to work in the private sector from 1972 until his retirement in 1986—as president of Steuben Glass, president of the Corning Glass Works Foundation, director of Corning Glass Works International, and president of the Corning Museum of Glass. He also wrote on Norman Rockwell and founded both the *Journal of Glass Studies* and the *New Glass Review*. For most of his life Buechner painted still lifes, portraits, and landscapes. —TT

[Thomas S. Buechner], *Glass Vessels in Dutch Painting of the 17th Century*, exh. cat. (Corning: the Museum, 1952); Buechner, *Frederick Carder: His Life and Work* (the Museum, 1952); Buechner, *Glass from the Corning Museum of Glass: A Guide to the Collections* (Corning, NY: Corning Glass Center, 1955); Buechner, *Norman Rockwell: Artist and Illustrator* (New York: Harry N. Abrams, 1970); Thomas S. Buechner files: ACC library; Corning Museum of Glass archive.

CALDER, ALEXANDER

Born July 22, 1898, Lawnton, PA;
died November 11, 1976, New York, NY
SCULPTOR, JEWELER, METALSMITH,
DESIGNER, PAINTER

While a major artist of the mid-twentieth century and best known for his sculptural and kinetic mobiles and stabiles created for public spaces throughout the world, Calder also produced jewelry, toys, and kitchenware for personal use, as well as maquettes for rugs and cartoons for tapestries that were executed in limited productions in the 1950s and '60s by weavers in Aubusson, France. He created glass designs for art dealer Egidio Costantini in the mid-1950s, porcelain designs for Sèvres in 1969, and shortly thereafter he decorated planes owned by Braniff Airlines and racing cars in the Bavarian Motor Works fleet. He also made book illustrations as well as costume and set designs for various ballet and theatrical productions. Calder's work reflects a vigorous assimilation of diverse aspects of European modernism (particularly surrealism and constructivism). His signature motif is a bold, abstract form executed in primary colors.

In speaking of Calder's jewelry, the artist's wife, Louise, noted that he created "suitcases of it," and indeed some 1,800 pieces have been documented. As a boy, Calder made jewelry to adorn his sister's dolls, and over the years he fashioned rings, brooches, earrings, necklaces, bracelets, and hair ornaments for his wife, as well as for the wives of friends such as Marcel Duchamp, Joan Miró, and Marc Chagall. He also made cuff links for men and "unisex" pieces before the idea was popular. While contemporaries such as Salvador Dalí made jewelry as a sideline, Calder considered his jewelry designs as important to him as his other work. It was often oversized and theatrical, handcrafted from brass, silver, or steel wire. If he wished to add a bit of color he used shards of pottery and glass. Calder's sources were Celtic and pre-Columbian, and his repertoire of images included spirals (his most frequent design) and a menagerie of "beasties" (fish, birds, and insects) that recall his interest in Miró and Paul Klee's fantastic imagery of the 1920s. Each design was one-of-a-kind, being simply constructed by twisting wires and attaching them to each other. Many pieces were also meant to move. While Calder was unusually preoccupied with jewelry making around 1940—and jewelry was included in his 1943 MoMA retrospective, *Sculptures and Constructions*—the bulk of his oeuvre was made in the U.S. between 1935 and 1952. Calder rarely offered his jewelry for sale; documented exceptions are from shows at the New Orleans Arts and Crafts Club in 1941; the Willard Gallery, NY, in 1940 and 1941; and the Perls Gallery, NY, in 1966. Despite persistent interest, Calder refused to have his jewelry put into production, preferring instead to give it as gifts. Calder's utilitarian objects were the subject of an international traveling exhibition in 1989–90, and his jewelry was the subject of a major exhibition in 2009. —TT

"Calder's Kitchen Collection," *CH* 22 (September/October 1962), 18–23; Majorie Welsh, "Calder Tapestries," *CH* 31 (December 1971), 41; John Russell, "Alexander Calder, Leading U.S. Artist, Dies," *New York Times,* November 12, 1976, 42; Alexander S. C. Rower, ed., *Calder Jewelry* (New York: Calder Foundation; West Palm Beach: Norton Museum of Art; New Haven, CT: Yale University Press, 2007); Alexander Calder, oral history interview by Paul Cummings, October 26, 1971, AAA, SI.
For earlier history see *Craft in the Machine Age*, 231.

CAMPBELL, DAVID ROBERT
Born November 6, 1907, Boston, MA;
died March 24, 1963, New York, NY
ARCHITECT, ARTS ADMINISTRATOR
Campbell earned a BA from the University of New Hampshire, an MA in architecture from the school of design at Harvard University, and in 1959 the honorary Doctor of Humane Letters from the University of New Hampshire. Campbell's lifelong association with the emerging American crafts movement began in 1939 when he was appointed director of the New Hampshire League of Arts and Crafts. Through this position Campbell met philanthropist Aileen Osborn Webb, and in August 1939 she included him in a meeting of craft artists and advocates brought together to discuss the incorporation of a national crafts organization, which would be called the Handcraft Cooperative League of America. Their mission was to find urban markets for the sale of work by rural craftspeople. By the 1950s Campbell's multifaceted career had developed into a mix of architectural commissions for private clients and the administration of arts and crafts organizations. To meet the obligations of his various occupations, Campbell regularly commuted between Concord, NH—where he continued to serve as the director of the New Hampshire League of Arts and Crafts—and New York City, location of his thriving architectural practice. His architectural commissions included Webb's penthouse apartment on East 72nd Street and the remodeling of two Victorian brownstones that had been purchased by Webb for what would become the ACC. The first building, at 29 West 53rd Street, was converted in 1955–56 into a contemporary exhibition space for the newly established MCC, and the second structure, at 44 West 53rd Street, was redesigned in 1959 for America House and the ACC. In the 1950s Campbell participated in numerous activities associated with the ACC. He was a jury member for *Designer Craftsmen U.S.A.* (1953); assumed the presidency of the ACC in 1958; was a conference panelist for the council's third national conference at Silver Bay, Lake George, NY, in 1959; and regularly traveled to the council's regional conferences and exhibitions in 1960 and 1961. He was appointed director of MCC in 1960. Many exhibitions took place during his tenure: *Woven Forms* (March 22–May 12, 1963), opened two days before his untimely death at the age of fifty-five. —TT
Aileen Osborn Webb, "David R. Campbell, 1908–1963," *CH* 23 (May/June 1963), 8; Rose Slivka, "Aileen Osborn Webb, David Campbell—A Reminiscence," *CH* 53 (August/September 1994), 132–36; David R. Campbell files, ACC library.

CAROË, FRANCES WRIGHT
Born September 3, 1898, Chicago, IL;
died February 17, 1959, Washington, DC
ARTS ADMINISTRATOR
Frances Wright Caroë, the youngest daughter of the architect Frank Lloyd Wright from his first marriage, had her father's passion and intuition when it came to American crafts and interior design. Wright himself schooled his

daughter in architecture and interior decoration. From 1935 to 1941 she was the editor of "Counter Points," a shopping column featured in *Town & Country,* and in November of 1940 she became executive director of America House, a retail shop specializing in American crafts, a post she held until 1952. Her role was to scour the country for emerging craftspeople whose work could be sold through America House. Caroë published an advice column in *Craft Horizons* called "Prevailing Winds" (the first installment appeared in the August 1947 issue). While she tried to involve her father in her work, it is unclear if they actually did collaborate, but Wright may have purchased textiles through America House for some of his Usonian Housing Projects. Caroë taught courses on production and marketing at the School for American Craftsmen from about 1945 to 1951, at Dartmouth College, then at Alfred University and RIT. Caroë opened her own crafts shop called A Tisket and A Tasket at the Bird & Bottle Inn in Garrison, NY, which was in operation from about 1952 to 1955. —BN
Frances Wright Caroë, "Prevailing Winds," *CH* 8 (August 1941), 68; *Bulletin of the School for American Craftsmen of the Rochester Institute of Technology, 1950–1951,* archives, RIT; *School for American Craftsmen,* pamphlet (Alfred, NY: Alfred University Publication, 1948–49 and 1949 –50), archives, RIT; Aileen O. Webb, "Almost a Century," typescript, Aileen Osborn Webb papers, AAA, SI.

CARPENTER, ARTHUR ESPENET (ART)
Born January 20, 1920, New York, NY;
died May 25, 2006, Bolinas, CA
FURNITURE MAKER
Arthur Espenet Carpenter helped shape the American contemporary woodworking movement and was an important influence and mentor for craftspeople in the San Francisco Bay Area. Among the first generation of self-taught woodworkers creating experimental and organic work, by the 1960s Carpenter had developed a signature style that incorporated the curved lines and rounded edges later known as "California Roundover." After earning a BA in economics at Dartmouth College in 1942, Carpenter spent four years in the U.S. Navy, following which he entered his father's Asian art wholesale business in New York City. When he saw a turned-wood bowl by James Prestini in a group show at MoMA in 1947, his life took a new direction. Intrigued by the idea of making objects that were useful, beautiful, and also potentially profitable, Carpenter quit his job, took his savings and his $100 monthly stipend from the GI Bill and drove to San Francisco, where he purchased a lathe, set up shop in a condemned building on Mission Street, and taught himself about the inherent properties of wood by turning bowls. He chose the lathe as the simplest tool for making the simplest objects that he could imagine. Within a year he was selling in Los Angeles and Chicago, and from 1950 to 1954 his bowls were included in MoMA's Good Design exhibitions. Using his mother's maiden name, Espenet, as a business name, Carpenter established a small manufacturing firm and by the mid-1950s employed a staff of seven. In 1957,

when he found himself spending more time on book-keeping than working in the shop, he sold the business. With a small inheritance he bought a farm in Bolinas, CA, a rural town about twenty-five miles north of San Francisco, and turned to furniture-making full-time. Influenced by the work of Wharton Esherick, Sam Maloof, and Bob Stocksdale, as well as by Danish furniture, Carpenter soon became known for his spare but sensual designs that were both durable and practical. During the 1950s and '60s his work was included in various group exhibitions: *Designer Craftsmen U.S.A.* at the Brooklyn Museum (1953); *Craftsmanship in a Changing World*, held at MCC (1956); and *Contemporary Craftsmen of the Far West*, also at MCC (1961; his work received a merit award); and three of the California Design exhibitions at the Crocker Art Museum (1962, 1965, and 1968). —TT

Michael Stone, "The Espenet Style," *AC* 42 (June/July 1982), 6–9; "Arthur Espenet Carpenter," *AC* 67 (August/September 2007), 51; Arthur Espenet Carpenter, *Education of a Woodsmith* (Bolinas, CA: Bubinga Press, 2010); artist files, ACC library.

CASTLE, WENDELL KEITH
Born November 6, 1932, Emporia, KS
FURNITURE DESIGNER AND FURNITURE MAKER, EDUCATOR

At the forefront of today's American art furniture movement, Wendell Castle has challenged traditional concepts of furniture design, providing new and surprising inter-pretations of furniture forms—work that has inspired woodworkers since the 1960s. Through his keen awareness of current trends in industrial design and contemporary sculpture, Castle has created furniture that blurs the line between the fine and the applied arts. While studying painting in college, to satisfy his family's wishes that he pursue something employable, he took industrial design as his major, studying and traveling in Europe in 1955–56, and earning a BFA from the University of Kansas in Lawrence in 1958. Following a brief stint as a designer for an aerospace firm, Castle returned to the University of Kansas and received an MFA in sculpture in 1961. Self-taught as a woodworker, he began making furniture in 1958 after exposure to the work of Wharton Esherick, whose furniture he saw as a form of sculpture and as an expressive art. Castle's early work won prizes in juried craft exhibitions in the late 1950s and early 1960s—among them the Kansas Designer Craftsman shows (1959, 1960); the National Decorative Arts exhibitions, Wichita, KS (1959, 1960); and *Young Americans* at MCC (1962). He was also given solo shows at the Little Gallery in Kansas City (1960, 1961), and at the Hopkins Center, Dartmouth College (1962). Castle taught at the University of Kansas from 1959 to 1961; at the School for American Craftsmen, RIT, in 1963; and the State University of New York at Brockport from 1969 to 1980. At RIT he began devoting himself to nontraditional, organic, sculptural furniture forms, experimenting with stack lamination, a technique in which wood is glued together in multiple layers and then

shaped through carving. While both aesthetic and practical matters interested Castle, it was the aesthetic that most concerned him. His sinuous *Music Rack* of 1963 was docu-mented in a teaching film (Tom Muir Wilson Production) that showed raw wood being transformed by the hands of a maker. The music stand was selected for inclusion in the American section of the thirteenth Milan Triennale in 1964, and that year he produced multiples of the design that were sold at America House. Throughout the 1960s reviewers frequently aligned Castle's work with that of French surre-alist Odilon Redon and Catalan art nouveau architect Antonio Gaudi. Later in the decade Castle developed a line of furniture made of fiberglass-reinforced polyester for the manufacturer Stendig. His tooth-shaped chairs in the Molar series clearly relate to pop art. The broad scope of Castle's work ranges from fine jewelry boxes to spiral staircases and music stands to office suites, with commissions for schools, businesses, and ecclesiastical settings. Castle's furni-ture was included in exhibitions at MCC throughout the 1960s: *The American Craftsman* (1964), *Fantasy Furniture* (1966), and *Craftsmen USA* (1966), among others. He received a gold medal from the American Craft Council (1997) and the Modernism Lifetime Achievement Award from the Brooklyn Museum (2007). —TT

Helen Giambruini, "Wendell Castle," *CH* 28 (September/October 1968), 28–31, 50–51; Davira Spiro Taragin, *Furniture by Wendell Castle* (New York: Hudson Hills Press, in association with the Founders Society, Detroit Institute of Arts, 1989); Cooke, Ward, and L'Ecuyer 2003, 41–43, 114; artist files, ACC library.

CHATT, ORVILLE KEITH
Born December 12, 1924, Tekamah, NE; died July 25, 2007, Sedro Woolley, WA
JEWELER, EDUCATOR

Deeply influenced by trends in studio art jewelry of the 1950s and '60s, Orville Chatt's work references abstract styles from painting and sculpture, particularly surrealism, cubism, and abstract expressionism, and mixes everyday objects—shells, bits of pottery, and beads—with gemstones and precious metals. Chatt noted that "Jewelry to me is a song or a poem to be worn. It should enhance the person wearing it both inside and out. Sometime it's mood music, sometime a march" (Crichfield 2007). As a farm boy in Nebraska, Chatt's artistic interests were encouraged by an aunt who was a painter. Following military service in the U.S. Air Force in the Philippines, he enrolled at the Chicago Art Institute and earned a BFA in education in 1951, supplementing his studies with interior decorating assignments. Chatt moved to Eugene, OR, in 1951, but returned to the Midwest in 1956 for a teaching position at North High School in Des Moines, IA. He earned an MFA at Drake University in 1963. From 1961 to 1964 he was an instructor at Iowa State University in Ames, and from 1964 until his retirement twenty-five years later, he was head of the humanities department and professor of craft design at Skagit Valley Community College in the Puget Sound community of Mount Vernon, WA. An active member

of Northwest Designer Craftsmen, Chatt exhibited and sold jewelry at the annual Anacortes Arts and Crafts Fair, and at galleries and shops throughout the West. His book, *Design Is Where You Find It* (1972), explained his artistic process and use of natural forms in creating his designs. —TT

Orville K. Chatt, *Design Is Where You Find It* (Ames, IA: Iowa State University Press, 1972); Bev Crichfield, "Remembering a Man of Style" (August 2, 2007), www.goskagit.com/home/print/7657/.

CHIHULY, DALE PATRICK
Born September 20, 1941, Tacoma, WA
GLASS ARTIST, EDUCATOR

Perhaps the most renowned contemporary glass artist, Dale Chihuly has turned the craft of glassblowing into a modern art form, creating glass sculpture in multitudes of shapes and sizes and exploring the possibilities of color, line, and assemblage. His interest in the medium has resulted in significant technical advances—changes in scale, color, complexity, and strength—now regarded as unparalleled developments in the medium's more than two-thousand year history. Chihuly—who views his role as similar to that of a cinema director—has contributed to the studio glass movement's shift from a solitary artist working in a studio to a collaborative endeavor with divisions of labor within the creative process.

The foundations of Chihuly's groundbreaking contri-butions were set in the 1960s when he received his art training and began experimenting with glass, initiating his first collaborations. In 1959 Chihuly enrolled at the College of Puget Sound (now University of Puget Sound), where a term paper on Van Gogh and the remodeling of his mother's recreation room motivated him to transfer to the University of Washington in Seattle in 1960 to study interior design and architecture. He became disillusioned with academia and dropped out in 1962 to travel in Europe and the Middle East, but by then he had had his first experience with melting and fusing glass in a class with Steven Fuller in 1961. While working on a kibbutz in Israel in 1963, Chihuly met architect Robert Landsman, whose counsel helped Chihuly refocus and return to the University of Washington to complete his degree. He earned a BA in interior design in 1965, but his interest in glass manifested itself in his weaving class with Doris Brockway. He incor-porated glass shards into woven tapestries (and exhibited a panel at the Washington Art Fair in Bellevue in 1965). He continued to experiment with blowing bits of colored flat glass with a metal pipe in his basement studio. Chihuly later noted that when he blew his first glass bubble, he "was hooked completely." Abandoning a career as an interior designer, Chihuly received a full scholarship to the University of Wisconsin, where he studied glassblowing with Harvey Littleton and completed his first collaboration with fellow student Fritz Dreisbach. Chihuly blew long-necked organic forms that he grouped into simple installations. His work won awards in several state art competitions, and he earned his MS in fine art in 1967. That year he accepted a teaching assistantship at the Rhode Island

School of Design (RISD), teaching glass courses while matriculating in an MFA program in sculpture, earning his degree in 1968 and gaining recognition for his postminimalist, free-form, multimedia "glass room" installations. Awarded a Fulbright Fellowship and a Louis Comfort Tiffany Foundation Grant to study glass in 1968, Chihuly went to the Venini Fabrica factory in Murano, Italy, an island in the Venice lagoon, where he absorbed the collaborative master-and-team approach he would later make his own. Returning to RISD in 1969, Chihuly established their glass department, where he taught for fifteen years. He also began collaborating with his student Jamie Carpenter. The summers he spent at Haystack Mountain School of Crafts (1969–72) offered him the model and inspiration needed to develop plans for a glass school. Chihuly founded Pilchuck Glass Center outside Seattle in 1971. —TT

Dale Chihuly and Patterson Sims, *Dale Chihuly: Installations 1964–1992*, exh. cat. (Seattle, WA: Seattle Art Museum, 1992); Donald B. Kuspit, *Chihuly* (Seattle: Portland Press; New York: Harry N. Abrams, 1997).

CHOW, FONG

Born December 2, 1923, Tianjin, North China
CERAMIST, CURATOR, PHOTOGRAPHER

Equally fascinated with ceramics production and the care and scholarship of art from Asia, Fong Chow created award-winning designs, shapes, and glazes for the Glidden Pottery in Alfred, NY. Raised in Hong Kong, he attended Chinese schools, but his formal education was interrupted by the Japanese occupation in 1942. At sixteen he thus turned to painting in "Western styles," under the tutelage of Yu Been (who had been trained in Canada). After the war Chow traveled to mainland China, visiting Shiwan, a ceramic center dating to the twelfth century. There he saw wood-fired dragon kilns, as well as glazed vases, roof ornaments, and ancient ceramics, all of which served as inspiration. His grandfather Shouson Chow had been educated in the U.S. at Andover and Columbia University in the late nineteenth century, and Fong Chow followed suit. He traveled to Boston in 1947 and studied ceramics with Norman Arsenault at the Boston Museum School (now School of the Museum of Fine Arts, Boston) for the next four years. He began making thrown fruitlike globular shapes perforated with up to three openings and also began developing his own glazes based on the Chinese reduction glazes developed by Tang and Song dynasty potters. In 1951 he went to Alfred University, earning a BFA in ceramics in 1952 and an MFA in 1954. One of his teachers, Charles Harder, recommended that he learn production methods, and this proved to be useful when he began working for Glidden Parker, founder of Glidden Pottery, a ceramics company that created product lines in unusual shapes and colors. On staff from 1952 until the pottery closed in 1957, Chow collaborated with Parker, helping to develop some of the firm's most popular series, such as Charcoal and Rice, New Equations, Gulfstream Blue, Green Mesa, and Sandstone (patterns Chow refers to as his "Flower Line"). His glaze formulas include High Tide and Boston Spice. A bowl and

bottle in his Charcoal and Rice series shared the $100 prize (with another Glidden designer) at the seventeenth annual Ceramic National exhibition in 1952. A commission in 1956 from MCC for a dinner service for the members' lunchroom resulted in a square-shaped pattern called Snowdrop in glazes of blue and yellow, a pattern later made available through America House. In 1960 the museum mounted *The Pottery of Fong Chow*, a solo exhibition of his work.

Chow joined the curatorial staff of the Far Eastern Department at The Metropolitan Museum of Art in 1958. During his twenty-five years of service he was responsible for the care of Chinese, Japanese, and Thai ceramics, the development of the collection and installation of the Altman Collection of Chinese porcelain, management of the John D. Rockefeller bequest, and assistance in the redesign of the museum's ceramics spaces (including two major Chinese sculpture galleries). Chow retired from the museum in 1983, but continued to work as a ceramist in New York City until about 2000. —TT

The Pottery of Fong Chow, exh. brochure (New York: MCC, 1960); Margaret Carney, "The History of Glidden Pottery," *Studio Potter* 30 (December 2001), 80–86; Margaret Carney et al., *Glidden Pottery,* exh. cat. (Alfred, NY: Schein-Joseph International Museum of Ceramic Art, New York State College of Ceramics, Alfred University, 2001), 34–36; Fong Chow, oral history interview by Margaret Carney, February 6, 2002, AAA, SI.

CHOY, KATHERINE (CHOY-PO-YU)

(MRS. WEND-CHUNG CHOU)
Born August 17, 1927, Shanghai, China;
died February 23, 1958, Rye, NY
CERAMIST, EDUCATOR

An innovative ceramist whose work paid homage to Chinese and Japanese pottery (a key aesthetic influence in American studio ceramics of the 1940s and 1950s), as well as merging experimental and abstract forms, Katherine Choy drew from her own research into classical Asian pots with lush traditional glazes to create large sculptural vessels with irregular broken shapes and brushed glaze work. While such ceramists as Peter Voulkos and John Mason are remembered for their monumental abstract expressionist clay forms, Choy was among the first American potters, male or female, to make this artistic leap. Born to a wealthy mercantile family who fled from Shanghai, China, to Hong Kong after the communist takeover, Choy came to the U.S. when she was nineteen, attended Wesleyan College in Macon, GA, from 1946 to 1948, and transferred to Mills College in Oakland, CA, where she earned her BA and MA degrees, studying weaving, jewelry, enameling, metalwork, and also ceramics. Her clay studies were under the tutelage of F. Carlton Ball and Antonio Prieto, and in 1950 she attended a workshop led by Bernard Leach. In 1951 Choy spent a year at Cranbrook for postgraduate studies, where she worked with Maija Grotell. In 1952 Choy was hired as professor of ceramics at Sophie Newcomb Memorial College, part of

Tulane University, in New Orleans. While at Newcomb, she trained such artists as Viola Frey, and worked for industry, formulating a line of stoneware clay bodies for the Good Earth Pottery in Port Chester, NY, and making weave samples for Isabel Scott Fabrics in New York City, where she was on staff in 1956. She also participated in group and invitational exhibitions as well as solo shows at the Delgado Museum of Art, New Orleans (1953); Gallery 77, New Haven, CT (1954); and Mi Chou Gallery, NY (1955); among others. In the fall of 1957 she fulfilled a personal dream by purchasing the Good Earth Pottery with the help of her friend Henry Okamoto, whom she had met at Mills College. They reorganized it as the Clay Art Center, a cooperative studio space, whose mission was "to promote the art of clay—that is, ceramics and sculpture—as culture on an advanced level." Less than a year later, in the spring of 1958, at the age of twenty-nine, she died of undiagnosed pneumonia. Choy produced more than 200 pieces in that year in Port Chester. Her surviving work gives testimony to the promise of a great career unfulfilled. —TT

Faith Corrigan, "Fabric Houses Unfold Fall Collections for Home," *New York Times*, September 22, 1956, 18; Dido Smith, "Three Potters from China," *CH* 17 (March/April 1957), 23–25; *Katherine Choy: Ceramics*, exh. cat. (Newark, NJ: Newark Museum, 2000); Roberta Hershenson, "Footlights: Haven for Artisans in Port Chester," *New York Times*, April 15, 2001, WE8; artist file, ACC library.

CHRISTENSEN, HANS JORGEN THORVALD

Born January 21, 1924, Copenhagen, Denmark;
died January 16, 1983, Henrietta, NY
METALSMITH, JEWELER, EDUCATOR

Described as "a kind of Mies van der Rohe of silver," Hans Christensen created hollowware, jewelry, flatware, ecclesiastical silver, large presentation bowls, and trophies, in shapes that ranged from architectonic to free-form and that exquisitely demonstrated the principle of "less is more." The students who studied with him during his twenty-nine-year career at the School for American Craftsmen at RIT benefited from his own extensive training and his commitment to ideas of service and the importance of creating work with the recipient in mind. Christensen's classroom was his studio. He created his own work within an academic schedule, working on commissions that ranged from commemorative pieces for organizations and corporations (North American Figure Skating Association and Eastman Kodak, for example) to one-of-a-kind designs for public figures (the Nelson Rockefeller family, the royal families of England, Denmark, Norway, Iran, and Sweden, among others). Trained in Denmark through a journeyman apprenticeship in Copenhagen, Christensen began his education in 1939, when at the age of fifteen, he worked at the Georg Jensen Silversmithy during the day and studied at the Kunsthaandvaerkerskolen (School of Arts and Crafts) in the evening. His mentors and instructors were accomplished Scandinavian painters, sculptors, artists, and men of industry. In 1944 Christensen created his journeyman's piece, a teapot and warmer, for which he received two silver medallions—one for design and the other for execution—presented to him by King Frederick IX of Denmark. In March of that year he received his silversmith's certificate and later that spring earned the equivalent of a master's degree for his studies at the Kunsthaandvaerkerskolen. He continued at Jensen in various positions for the next ten years—jewelry (1944–45), holloware (1948–50), the model department (1950–52), and as head of the model department (1952–54). Meanwhile Christensen completed a course of study for teaching in the craft field at the Kunsthaandvaerkerskolen (1949–50). He also earned the equivalent of another master's degree concentrated in business management, technique, and design at the Teknologisk Institut (College of Technical Society for Advanced Silversmiths) in Copenhagen (1951–53) and completed a course sponsored by the Institute of Design in Chicago at the Statens Håndverks -og Kunstindustriskole (National College of Crafts and Industrial Design) in Oslo, Norway (1952). Christensen made about 80 percent of the work displayed in an exhibition of Georg Jensen silver in 1952 and traveled to New York to represent the factory. This was his introduction to the modern craft movement in America and his first meeting with the persuasive Aileen Osborn Webb, who invited him to teach at the School for American Craftsmen, an offer he accepted. In 1954 he immigrated to America and taught at RIT, where he was a major voice for the Danish modern aesthetic in metalsmithing until his death in a car accident in 1983. —TT

Harold J. Brennan, "Three Rochester Craftsmen," *American Artist* 22 (June–July–August 1958), 36–43, 87–89; Barry Targon, "The Achievements of Hans Christensen," *AC* 43 (February/March 1983), 25–29; Bernard Bernstein, "A Remembrance: Hans Christensen, 1924–1983," *Metalsmith* 3 (spring 1983), 6; "Hans Jorgen Thorvald Christensen," http://www.gold-silver-casting.com/HansChristensen-Life-Times-Work.htm; artist files, ACC library.

CLARK, WILLIAM L.

Born in August 15, 1942, St. Louis, MO;
died June 21, 2008, Berkeley, CA
JEWELER, METALSMITH

William Clark is celebrated for creating jewelry as sculptural extensions of the human form. Meticulously crafted, some were also used by the artist to make political and social commentary. During the height of the Vietnam War, Clark designed provocative protest pieces. He worked with recognizable symbols such as bombs, crucifixes, and the Star of David, while also experimenting with other forms and words to adorn his designs. Clark was introduced to metalsmithing as a teenager living in Saudi Arabia, where he met local artisans who taught him various styles and techniques. These early interactions molded Clark's career. In the early 1960s, after a stint in the U.S. Navy, he moved to California, where he began to work as a jewelry designer. Throughout his career, Clark worked with

a variety of materials (metals, aluminum, plastic tubing, plumbing hardware, wood, glass, organic material, stone) and explored the boundaries of contemporary jewelry design. —NB

Roberta Loach, "William Clark: Body Sculpture," *Art Week*, December 1, 1973; Jennifer Cross Gans, "William Clark: Jewelry and Sculpture, 1960–2005," *Metalsmith* 26 (summer 2006), 55.

COHEN, MICHAEL

Born March 7, 1936, Boston, MA
CERAMIST

Self-employed as a studio potter since 1961, Michael Cohen is known for his limited-production sponge-stamped functional stoneware—plates, mugs, bowls, pitchers, bread and berry baskets, vases, planters, wall tiles, and more—and for his ceramic sculpture. He regards himself as working in the same traditions as Bernard Leach and Shoji Hamada, producing beautiful and useful goods for everyday life. He views his dynamic approach to pottery-making as similar to that of Peter Voulkos and Eric Gronberg. Reared in Brighton, MA, in a self-described Jewish ghetto, in high school Cohen was awarded a scholarship to take art classes at the Boston Museum School (now School of the Museum of Fine Arts, Boston). He went on to study at the Massachusetts College of Art in Boston and was introduced to ceramics by teacher Charles Abbott, who became his mentor. During his senior year, Cohen spent weekends throwing mugs and ashtrays and making cast-porcelain decanters and porcelain mugs for Herring Run Pottery, the production studio founded by William Wyman in 1953. Cohen earned his BFA in 1957 and the summer after graduation was a pottery studio assistant at Haystack Mountain School of Crafts in Maine, working with founding director, Francis Merritt and learning how to make raku pottery with fellow students Toshiko Takaezu and Hal Riegger. Cohen joined the army, and during his two-and-a-half year stint in Germany (1957–59) he trained as a photographer. On weekends and leave, he traveled throughout Europe, going to museums and visiting potters at their studios. Cohen hoped for an apprenticeship with Harry Davis at Crowan Pottery or Bernard Leach at St. Ives Pottery, both in Cornwall, England, but neither studio took him on. When he returned to the U.S. he won a full scholarship to the MFA program at Cranbrook in 1960, but was unhappy with Maija Grotell, who did not value his interest in production work. He did not return for the second year but instead set up his first studio in the basement of his mother's home and returned to Haystack for the summer of 1960. Throughout the 1960s Cohen established himself as a production potter and crafts entrepreneur. He built a studio in New Hampshire, consigning work to America House and to other galleries in the Northeast, and fulfilling a wall-tile commission for a Puerto Rican bank designed by Raymond Loewy (1963). He participated in craft fairs in Mt. Snow, VT, and Rhinebeck, NY, and accepted short-term teaching and workshop assignments at various schools—Haystack (1963); Penland School of Crafts, NC

(1964); Wagner College, New York City (1964); Ohio State University (1965); and Colby Junior College, CT (1968). He also exhibited at the Everson Museum, Syracuse (1962), Victoria and Albert Museum, London (1963), New York World's Fair (1964), Smithsonian Institution (1965), and MCC (1966), and he had a solo show at Bonnier's store in NYC in 1967. —TT

Michael Cohen, oral history interview by Gerry Williams, August 11, 2001, AAA, SI; artist files: ACC library; MAD archives.

CONSTANTINE, MILDRED "CONNIE"

(MILDRED CONSTANTINE BETTELHEIM)
Born 1913, Brooklyn, NY;
died December 10, 2008, Nyack, NY
CURATOR, AUTHOR

Mildred Constantine spent most of her career at MoMA, where as a curator she advanced the work of innovative graphic and fiber artists. She was hired in 1948 as an assistant curator in the department of architecture and design, where she specialized in graphic art. From 1953 to 1970 she was an associate curator, and then finally served as a consultant to the department and special assistant to the director until her retirement in 1971. She earned a reputation for championing obscure aspects of design and applied arts with a diligence that made the exhibit *Wall Hangings* (1969), co-curated with textile designer Jack Lenor Larsen, a pioneering show and a hallmark of her career.

Her long investigation and advocacy of art made with fiber began in the late 1960s, when she traveled to Eastern Europe to do empirical research on fiber art in contemporary practice and became determined to provide the genre the same prominence as other works of fine art. Many of the artists she met were included in *Wall Hangings*, which toured eleven other cities before being installed in the special exhibition galleries at MoMA, a site that Constantine lobbied for to assure the work the scholarly examination and intellectual status she felt it warranted. The twenty-eight men and women artists in the show represented eight countries in the Americas and Europe. Their training and experience included Bauhaus, traditional weaving, and modern design taught in elite U.S. programs. Constantine and Larsen's thesis initiated an important debate about the place of works made with fiber within the realm of fine art, a subject still being considered today.

After she left MoMA, Constantine maintained a commitment to fiber art and went on to collaborate with Larsen and others on subsequent exhibitions and publications. At the time of her death in 2008, she was writing a history of the use of fiber as an art medium from the beginning of human existence to the present. —ML

Elissa Auther, "Fiber Art and the Hierarchy of Art and Craft, 1960–80," *Journal of Modern Craft* 1 (March 2008), 19; Stephen Heller, "Mildred Constantine, 95, MoMA Curator, Is Dead," *New York Times*, December 14, 2008, A42; Jenni Sorkin, "Way Beyond Craft: Thinking through the Work of Mildred Constantine," *Textile* 1 (2008), 32.

COOKE, BETTY

Born May 5, 1924, Baltimore, MD

JEWELER, METALSMITH, DESIGNER, EDUCATOR

Internationally recognized as a modernist jeweler and studio artist, Betty Cooke meticulously crafts forms that reflect her clear interest in simply blending mathematical, architectural, and sculptural design elements. Cooke describes her jewelry as "precision work done in freehand" (*Design–Jewelry–Betty Cooke* 1995), and she has been a limited production jeweler selling from her own shop since 1946. Cooke drew constantly as a child in Baltimore. Her decision to go to art school was "automatic," and during her college years she apprenticed with a local jeweler named Carothers, a woman who taught her how to solder. Cooke earned a BFA in art education from Johns Hopkins University and the Maryland Institute College of Art in 1946, intending to pursue a career as a sculptor. In order to make a living, however, she began teaching courses in jewelry, welding, and design and materials at the Maryland Institute, where she remained for twenty years. Her first students were returning World War II veterans. Cooke also started producing jewelry in a studio on the first floor of her Baltimore townhouse on Tyson Street, where she opened her first retail space, marketing not only her own jewelry and metalwork (bells, andirons, grates, and mobiles), but also pottery by Nancy Wickham, Robert Turner, and Karen Karnes, home furnishings by Isamu Noguchi, and Japanese folk art. In 1948 she took a cross-country camping trip, visiting museums and retail shops, and selling work from the "little box of jewelry" she had brought with her. In this way several of her pieces were selected for the Walker Art Center's Everyday Gallery exhibition, *Modern Jewelry Under Fifty Dollars,* in Minneapolis. Her jewelry was included in the 1951 *Alumni Exhibition: Textiles, Ceramics, Metalwork* at Cranbrook (where she had taken a summer course). She won prizes in the Young Americans competitions sponsored by the American Craftsmen's Educational Council in 1951 and 1953. She exhibited dinner bells at the fourth annual *Design for Christmas* exhibition at the Institute for Contemporary Arts in Boston in 1953 and showed an andiron (designed for the Harwin Company) in the Good Design exhibition at MoMA in 1954. The same year she exhibited with Gertrud and Otto Natzler in a show at the Ursell Gallery in the Georgetown neighborhood of Washington, DC. Her work was also sold at America House, Georg Jensen, and Tiffany's in New York City, as well as at MoMA and the Hirshhorn Museum in Washington, DC. In 1955 Cooke married designer William O. Steinmetz, and throughout the 1950s they collaborated on work for architects, for showrooms and offices, as well as exhibitions. In 1965 the couple moved to an old carriage house in Riderwood, MD, and opened The Store Ltd. in the Village of Cross Keys, a shopping center, selling household items and clothing, as well as Cooke's jewelry. The shop remains operational to this day. —TT

Design–Jewelry–Betty Cooke, exh. cat. (Baltimore, MD: Meyerhoff Gallery, Maryland Institute College of Art, 1995); *Messengers of Modernism*, exh. cat. (Montreal: Museum of Decorative Arts, in association with Flammarion, 1996), 122–23; Betty Cooke, oral history interview by Jan Yager, July 1 and 2, 2004, AAA, SI.

CORY, KENNETH

Born December 5, 1943, Kirkland, WA;

died January 16, 1994, Ellensburg, WA

METALSMITH, JEWELER, EDUCATOR

Kenneth Cory created intentionally provocative, small-scale sculptural jewelry that epitomized the 1960s Funk art movement. Cory was also one of the artistic forces who helped propel the Pacific Northwest to the forefront of contemporary jewelry making in the 1960s. An iconoclast and punster, he was influenced by beatnik poetry, sex, and drugs. His jewelry work, characterized by impeccable technique and intellectual content, was wickedly humorous and displayed a ribald irreverence. Emblematic of Funk's subversive, anti-establishment message, his diminutive pieces were also related to Dada and the theatrical Fluxus movement. Cory explored the use of nonprecious metals. He drew upon shapes from both man-made and natural environments and eschewed the preciousness of jewelry as body ornament. Instead his pieces were intended to be held and fondled like Japanese netsukes. Cory earned a BFA in metalsmithing from the California College of Arts and Crafts (CCAC, now California College of the Arts) in Oakland in 1966 and an MFA from Washington State University in 1969. He taught for two years at CCAC, and in 1972, when Don Tompkins left Central Washington University, Cory became the metalsmith professor, teaching there for twenty years. Among Cory's students were Merrily Tompkins, his predecessor's younger sister, and Nancy Worden, whose level of technique and precision were similar to her teacher. Worden later noted that Cory was "a true academician" with significant knowledge of archetypal imagery and symbols. —TT

Robin Updike, "Kenneth Cory, 50, Professor Renowned for his Art Jewelry," *Seattle Times*, January 29, 1994; Ben Mitchell, *The Jewelry of Ken Cory: Play Disguised*, exh. cat. (Seattle: University of Washington Press, 1997).

CRAVER, MARGRET

(MRS. CHARLES C. WITHERS)

Born October 11, 1907, Pratt, KS;

died November 22, 2010, Cambridge, MA

SILVERSMITH, METALSMITH, EDUCATOR

During the 1940s and '50s Margret Craver blazed a trail in the development of contemporary silversmithing and metalwork in the U.S. and revived the techniques and production of handmade silver hollowware. During World War II, on a visit to the New York offices of Handy & Harman, refiners of precious metals, Craver met the company's president, Gustav Niemeyer. She mentioned to him that metalsmithing was not included in occupational therapy rehabilitation programs at armed services hospitals, noting that metalworking skills helped improve hand, arm, and upper-body strength and coordination. Niemeyer hired Craver as a consulting silversmith in 1944, and for the next nine years she developed the company's newly established nonprofit division. Her first success was the Hospital Services Program, a prototypical rehabilitation therapy that brought metalsmithing to wounded soldiers in the hospitals of the thirteen commands in the U.S., and to Veterans Hospitals in the U.S., Canada, and Great Britain. In 1946 Handy & Harman's nonprofit division was renamed the Craft Services Department, and Craver's new mandate was to assemble a group of professional metalsmith designers and teachers. Her series of five national silversmithing workshop conferences held between 1947 and 1953 at the Rhode Island School of Design and RIT trained the nucleus of a nationwide teaching corps in the metals field. Twelve participants were selected for a month of training each summer; among those who attended were Alma Eikerman, Fred Miller, John Paul Miller, and Earl Pardon. In 1949 the efforts of workshop students were showcased in a didactic exhibition, *Form in Handwrought Silver*, organized by Craver at The Metropolitan Museum of Art, NY. During her years at the firm, Craver also wrote technical brochures on silversmithing and developed two instructional films on silver. She resigned in 1953 and began working independently, concentrating on jewelry and reviving a seventeenth-century French enamel technique known as *en résille*. —TT

Jeannine Falino and Yvonne Markowitz, "Margret Craver: Jeweler, Educator, Visionary," *Journal of the American Society of Jewelry Historians* 1 (spring 1997), 9–23; *Dodge City Daily Globe* [Kansas], Obituary, December 6, 2010. For earlier history see *Craft in the Machine Age*, 232.

CUMMINGS, FRANK E., III

Born November 6, 1938, Los Angeles, CA

WOODWORKER, EDUCATOR

Known for furniture and sculptural lathe-turned vessels, Frank Cummings creates work that is as much about ideas, events, and emotions as it is about his time-intensive work process, involving hand-carving, chiseling, and sawing, and the materials he chooses, namely, exotic woods, gems, and metals. His work is designed to generate reactions and cause change. It is a form of visual communication intended to leave the viewer speechless. He was inspired by the spiritual meaning of everyday objects in Africa as well as by the religious significance of simple, well-made Shaker furniture, which conveys truth to materials and the belief that to do a thing well is in itself an act of prayer. Cummings learned hand-carving techniques in the village of Kumasi in Ghana in 1973 and made extensive studies of West African sculpture. His objects are intended to enrich the soul and contribute to spiritual and emotional well-being. Critics have compared the exquisite detail in Cummings's vessels to the workshop of Peter Carl Fabergé. Born in the Watts section of Los Angeles and raised in Central L.A., Cummings suffered from asthma as a child and was dyslexic, graduating from high school a few years after his contemporaries. He earning a BA in art in 1968 from California State University, Long Beach, and an MA in design and craft in 1971 from California State University, Fullerton. His interest in pursuing a career in the arts had solidified by the time he finished college. As an asthmatic child, kept quiet and frequently out of elementary school, Cummings had focused his attention on model airplane building, due to his father's involvement in the field as a 1948 award-winning champion of the Academy of Model Aeronautics (a division of the National Aeronautic Association). From this hobby Cummings learned how to take raw materials—sticks, glue, and paper—and build them into something that functioned. In 1954 a model plane that the young artist built remained airborne for approximately twenty-five minutes and established an endurance record that was still standing as of 2007. Cummings regards this hobby as "the beginning of where I am now." The tenacity and perseverance Cummings maintained throughout his undergraduate years was recognized by two Long Beach faculty members—sculptor Raymond Hein and ceramist Tom Ferreira. Hein mentored him and was instrumental in his artistic development, and Ferreira helped launch his professional career. Ferreira recommended Cummings for a position in the experimental and short-lived Black Faculty Teaching Program. He began teaching beginning crafts and basic design in the art department at California State University, Long Beach, while at the same time working toward his master's degree. Teaching became a passion, and from 1969 to 2000 Cummings worked in various academic and administrative positions in the California State University system. —TT

Wood Turning Center, *Wood Turning in North America since 1930*, exh. cat. (Philadelphia: Wood Turning Center; New Haven, CT: Yale University Art Gallery, 2001), 52; Frank E. Cummings III, oral history interview by Jo Lauria, December 28, 2006, and January 5, 2007, AAA, SI.

D'AMICO, VICTOR

Born May 19, 1904, New York, NY;
died April 1, 1987, Southhampton, NY
EDUCATOR

Victor D'Amico, who studied in New York at Cooper Union, Pratt Institute, and Columbia University Teachers College, was a distinguished teacher and pioneer of arts education, serving as director of the department of education at MoMA for more than thirty years (1937–69). He brought art to children through workshops, classes, and innovative programming, favoring an interactive, hands-on art education over traditional classroom instruction and memorization. He believed that "the arts are a humanizing force and . . . their major function is to vitalize living; to make each child and man the richer for having taken part in them" (D'Amico 1966). In 1942 D'Amico initiated the Children's Art Carnival, a space filled with toys, worksta-tions, and art materials to encourage creative production of painting, sculpture, and collage. The event was held annually until 1969 and traveled to Milan, Barcelona, and New Delhi. It was also part of the U.S. Pavilion at the Brussels World's Fair in 1958, representing America's innovations in art education. D'Amico's aspirations for art education were not only limited to the expansion of interests of children. He instituted the War Veterans' Art

Center (1944–48), a MoMA program that provided studio art classes for returning veterans, and he began community outreach initiatives around New York, such as the Harlem Art Carnival and the Art Barge, a studio art space on Long Island. D'Amico was also a professor of art education at Columbia College, New York University, the University of Wisconsin, Columbia University Teachers College, and Southampton College. He taught at the Millbrook School for Boys and the Fieldston School. —NB

Victor D'Amico, "Art Education Today: Millennium or Mirage?," *Art Education* 19 (May 1966), 27; Douglas C. McGill, "Victor D'Amico, 82, A Pioneer in Art Education for Children," *New York Times*, April 3, 1987; Christopher Kohan, Victor D'Amico Institute, e-mail to Jeannine Falino, October 17, 2010.

DANIEL, GRETA

Born in 1905, Essen, Germany;
died June 9, 1962, New York, NY
CURATOR

An invaluable expert in modern craft and design and a tireless supporter of their cultural relevance, Greta Daniel worked for almost twenty years as associate curator in the design department at MoMA, where she played a major role in building the museum's collection of design objects. For many years a member of the editorial board of *Craft Horizons*, Daniel served on the advisory board at MCC in New York, where she was responsible for the *Fabrics International* exhibition (1961). At MoMA she organized such shows as *Thonet* (1953), *Textile USA* (1956), and *Art Nouveau* (1960). With fellow MoMA curator Arthur Drexler, she also curated *Twentieth Century Design From the Museum Collection* (1959), which constituted one of the most important attempts to define modern design in the early postwar decades.

Daniel started her career in Germany in the late 1920s, when she worked at Museum Folkwang, Essen. Soon after her move to the U.S. in 1945, she became a protagonist in the developing field of craft and design criticism. An "ency-clopedic" knowledge on everything produced in Europe and the U.S. and a humble personality made her a quiet arbiter of taste. —MS

"Greta's Era," *Interiors* 121 (July 1962), 51; "Miss Greta Daniel, Curator at Museum of Modern Art," *New York Times*, June 10, 1962, 86.

DANN, STAN

Born May 23, 1931, Vancouver, British Columbia, Canada
WOODCARVER, SCULPTOR

Originally trained as a graphic designer, Stan Dann worked as an art director for two Bay Area advertising agencies, but by the mid-1960s he was making carved signs for stores in the San Francisco Bay Area, creating caricatures and scenes in relief on wooden placards and doors. His lettering has distinctive rounded, sometimes bulging edges and asymmetrical shapes and is similar in spirit to 1960s poster art in its psychedelic subject matter and distorted forms. Dann graduated from the Art Center School (now Art

Center College of Design) and the Faulkner Smith Academy of Fine Art in Vancouver. —NB

Stan Dann, cover image, *San Francisco* 6 (August 1964); "With Mallet and Chisel," *San Francisco Chronicle* (May 9, 1965), n.p.; Victoria Dalky, "Sculptures Afoot at Himovitz, Big World Wear Thin," *Sacramento Bee*, March 7, 1999, EN.9; Stan Dann and Carl Worth, *Stan Dann* (Lafayette, CA, Design Farm 2003); Stan Dann website, www.standann.com.

DAVIS, WILLIS "BING"

Born July 30, 1937, Greer, SC
CERAMIST, EDUCATOR

Willis "Bing" Davis celebrates his life experiences and African heritage through his work. As an art educator he has also helped to shape these skills in students. Davis has lived most of his life in the Midwest. He was a scholarship athlete recruited to play basketball at DePauw University, IN, where he studied art education. Remaining committed to academics, he continued his studies at the School of Dayton Art Institute, Miami University, Ohio, and Indiana State University. In order to fund his art career, Davis began teaching at local high schools and soon progressed to the college level. He was a professor of art at DePauw University (1971–76) and Miami University, Ohio (1976–78). For twenty years, he was chair of the art department at Central State University in Wilberforce, OH (1978–98). Davis has helped young artists give form to their cultural, social, and political values, thereby building a connection between the past and present. As a ceramist, sculptor, painter, and photographer, he creates a modern expression of the spirit of Africa, embodying its culture, customs, and identity. His art expresses an African American experience that celebrates tradition in a modern aesthetic. Davis's work has been included in exhibitions at the Studio Museum of Harlem, Field Museum in Chicago, Indianapolis Museum of Art, and National Afro-American Museum. —NB

Willis "Bing" Davis, *Bridging the Gaps: African-American Art Conference,* Harvard University, 2004, www.news.harvard.edu/gazette/2004/10.28/10-bridge.html; Chris Garcia, "Willis 'Bing' Davis: A Community Artist," *Ceramics Monthly* 50 (September 2002), 86.

DeFEO, JAY

(NÉE MARY JOAN DeFEO)
Born March 31, 1929, Hanover, NH;
died November 11, 1989, Oakland, CA
PAINTER, JEWELER

A key figure in the avant-garde West Coast art scene during the 1950s and '60s, Jay DeFeo represented an indepen-dent and influential voice. She discovered art through a high school teacher in San Jose, CA, whom she credits as the most influential person in her development. DeFeo attended the University of California, Berkeley, where she studied under John Haley, Margaret Petterson O'Hagan, and Erle Loran, earning her BA in 1950, and her MA in 1951. After traveling and working abroad—visiting Europe and North Africa and working briefly in Paris and

Florence—DeFeo settled in the San Francisco Bay Area, where she became closely connected to the circle of Beat authors, poets, and artists who flourished there at the time. Throughout her career her work was experimental and employed a variety of media including graphite, plaster, collage, and photography, and it was generally executed in a monochromatic palette of black, white, and gray.

DeFeo had her first solo exhibition at The Place in San Francisco in 1954. At this time she also supported herself by making jewelry and collages. Her work was included in the important MoMA exhibition *Sixteen Americans* along with pieces by Ellsworth Kelly, Jasper Johns, Louise Nevelson, Robert Rauschenberg, and Frank Stella in 1959, soon after her jewelry was included in the *American Jewelry and Related Objects* exhibition (1955) sponsored by the Hickok Company of Rochester and toured by the Smithsonian. In 1958 she embarked on a journey of creativity that lasted nearly eight years: The result, *The Rose*, a 1-ton painting, is synonymous with DeFeo's life and career. She built and reworked layer upon layer of impasto, creating a radiant and otherworldly starburst, but in the process her health deteriorated, and she was not able to return to the painting for four years. While devoting much of her time during this period to *The Rose*, in 1962 she began to teach night courses at the San Francisco Art Institute, and through 1970 divided her time first between there and Pasadena and later between there and her new home in Marin County.

Signaling a resurgence in her career, in 1973 she was awarded an NEA fellowship, and she had a solo exhibition at the Wegner Gallery in San Francisco a year later. Although her work was critically well received, it was not commercially successful. In 1981 she joined the faculty of Mills College in Oakland, but with a cancer diagnosis in 1986, her teaching career was cut short. She died in 1989 at the age of sixty. A major retrospective of her work was organized by the Berkeley Museum of Art in 1990, and the Whitney's seminal 1995 exhibition, *Beat Culture in America: 1950–1965*, prominently featured *The Rose*. —CK

Jane Green and Leah Levy, eds., *Jay Defeo and the Rose* (Berkeley: University of California Press, 2003); Jay DeFeo, oral history interview with Paul Karlstrom, June 3, 1975 and January 23, 1976, AAA, SI.

De Patta, Margaret Strong

(MRS. SAMUEL DE PATTA;
LATER, MRS. EUGENE BIELAWSKI)
Born March 18, 1903, Tacoma, WA;
died March 19, 1964, Oakland, CA
JEWELER, METALSMITH, EDUCATOR

One of the foremost modernist jewelers of the mid-twentieth century, Margaret De Patta created architectonic and sculptural pieces based on the ideology of Bauhaus constructivism, biomorphism, and surrealism. Writing in the mid-1950s, De Patta stated that "contemporary jewelry must characterize our times with its emphasis on space and structure, strong light, open forms, cantilever, floating

structures, and movement" (Glass 1976), themes that were tenets of constructivism. The jewelry she designed—with an aesthetic rigor usually applied to painting and sculpture—consistently reflected her contemporary perspective. De Patta explored spatial dimension (planes and levels), movement (actual and contained), solids and voids, and light and shadow. She made use of new materials such as stainless-steel screens, plastics, and synthetic adhesives, using the latter to attach stones to metal. She collaborated with San Francisco lapidary Francis J. Sperisen Sr. in experimental cutting and faceting techniques on transparent stones—crystal, smoky quartz, and topaz, among others. Calling the process "opti-cuts," De Patta made innovative use of optical effects—reflection, refraction, illusion, and magnification—in stone settings for her jewelry. Almost all of her jewelry was made with white or yellow gold, usually wrought rather than cast, because of the strength of the hammered metal. From her studies with former Bauhaus teacher László Moholy-Nagy at Mills College (summer 1940) and at the School of Design in Chicago (1940–41), De Patta learned to make her stones seem to float in the air. She was able to create this illusion by mounting two stones in "invisible" support devices. From 1935 onward De Patta maintained a studio in San Francisco, where she worked full-time as a jeweler and was an important role model for other metalsmiths. De Patta was among the founders of the Metal Arts Guild of San Francisco in 1951. (After De Patta's death in 1964, the guild established a Margaret De Patta annual award in jewelry design and a scholarship fund.)

De Patta remained committed to Bauhaus ideals throughout her career. Between 1944 and 1947 she was chairman of the Basic Design Workshop at the California Labor School in San Francisco, teaching design and sculpture, and in 1951 she and her designer husband Eugene Bielawski attempted to start their own Bauhaus-style school. De Patta's meteoric success was such that by the mid-1940s she felt impelled to address her Bauhaus-inspired social belief that good design should be affordable to everyone—demand for her work having become such that only those who could pay luxury prices were able to own a piece of her jewelry. In 1946, in an attempt to deal with this dichotomy, De Patta and Bielawski established Designs Contemporary, a limited-production company through which she competed with the quality costume jewelry industry by altering her production methods—casting her metal—and by distributing nationally. By the mid-1950s her company was producing up to sixty-five handmade duplicates of a given design, and it delighted De Patta that "the handcraft-for-handcraft's-sakers" could not distinguish her one-of-a-kinds from her production pieces (Uchida 1964). In 1958, after nearly twelve years in production, De Patta felt the strain of repetition and refocused her energies on experimentation and the creation of unique items. —TT

Yoshiko Uchida, "Margaret De Patta, 1903–1964," *CH* 24 (August 1964), 10; Laurie Glass, "The Jewelry of Margaret De Patta," March 6, 1976, p. 9 [Oakland, California], artist file, ACC library; Robert Cardinale and Hazel Bray,

"Margaret De Patta—Structure Concepts and Design Sources," *Metalsmith* 3 (spring 1983), 11–15; Margaret De Patta, "Jewelry for an Ever Increasing Minority" [written in 1949], *Metalsmith* 9 (winter 1989), 8.
For earlier history see *Craft in the Machine Age*, 232.

DeRespinis, Lucia N.

(NÉE LUCIA NEUMANN; MRS. LOUIS E. DeRESPINIS)
Born May 28, 1927, Cleveland, OH
INDUSTRIAL DESIGNER, EDUCATOR

As New York City became the focus for cutting-edge contemporary design after World War II, Lucia DeRespinis built a wide-ranging and successful career as an industrial designer. She attended St. Lawrence University, Canton, NY, for three years, and transferred to Pratt Institute, Brooklyn, NY, where she received a Bachelor of Industrial Design in 1952, the first year this degree was granted.

In an era when women were rare in the field, DeRespinis was the first female industrial designer hired by George Nelson in his New York office. As a member of Nelson's design team from 1956 until 1963, DeRespinis designed and installed on-site in Moscow a section of the 1959 American exhibit—a complete apartment, appropriate for a Manhattan professional, such as a physician. The designer filled the rooms with a variety of contemporary American furniture from firms such as Herman Miller, Dunbar, and Knoll.

Further examples among DeRepinis's diverse projects were the iconic pink and orange logo design for Dunkin' Donuts, packaging for Shisedo Cosmetics, chinaware for the Hall China Co., clocks for Herman Miller, lighting for Nessen, designs for Pomona Tile, stainless steel flatware for airlines, and bar stools for the Tower Suite atop New York City's Time-Life Building. Her other accomplishments included the design and installation of showrooms and sets for television news programs, as well as interiors of tour buses. Along with consulting and design work for major American firms, since 1980 DeRespinis has taught in the Department of Industrial Design at Pratt Institute in Brooklyn, NY. —JP

"Iconic Workplaces 1947- 86," *Metropolis* (June 2009), www.metropolismag.com/story/20090617/nelson-company-iconic-workplace-1947-86; Lucia DeRespinis, e-mail to Jane Port, November 24, 2010.

De Swart, Jan

Born April 19, 1908, Breda, the Netherlands;
died April 15, 1987, Pasadena, CA
SCULPTOR, WOODWORKER, INVENTOR

The singular career of Jan de Swart is best described as a mid-twentieth-century "meditation on the interrelationships of art, science, and technology" (Weinberg 2009). He made lean and lyrical forms in materials ranging from wood and metal to cast concrete and plastic. They closely resembled industrial design products because machines (such as band saws and molds) were used with technical mastery. His metal sculptures, laminated wood furniture, plastic vases, and nonfunctional forms, along with aluminum wall panels and concrete play structures, were often compared to work by such modernists as Piet Mondrian, Paul Klee, Joan Miró, and Isamu Noguchi. As an inventor de Swart patented hundreds of items—seals that held ships together in turbulent seas, plastic lenses that breathed life into the animated "Mr. Magoo" character, fasteners for aircraft, appliance shelves and doors, plastic tops for medicine bottles and cans, and rivets and grommets used by the millions in the manufacture of electronic products. De Swart's ability "to visualize the unknown" proved to be an asset when his parents died, and at age eleven he was separated from his brothers and sisters. Enduring several years in cruel orphanages, he often visited an influential uncle who was a philosopher/artist/monk and headed a Trappist monastery. The monastery's collection of anthropological paintings of "types of men" was memorable for the young de Swart. At age fifteen he entered the S'Hertogenbosch atelier of liturgical carver Master Yonkers, learning self-discipline and skills in the shaping, cutting, fitting, and finishing of wood. From a German chemical company experimenting with plastic, he obtained plastic blocks, which he carved and turned on a lathe, discovering an interest he later pursued in the U.S. In 1929, at the age of twenty-one, he immigrated to the U.S., where he was employed in mining, homesteading, and working for an Italian furniture maker through the 1930s. By the 1940s he began to set his own agenda, functioning as an artist, scientist, and inventor who refused to live and work within fixed career categories. In solitude at Allegro, his Eagle Rock hilltop home and studio in northeastern Los Angeles, de Swart divided his time between projects for technical companies and architects as well as experiments and inventions for his own pleasure. He made aluminum sculptures and reliefs for the Kaiser Aluminum headquarters in Oakland, CA, conducted research on plastics for DuPont, Dow Chemical, and Monsanto, and collaborated with California architects on many innovative homes built in Los Angeles in the 1950s and '60s. De Swart paid little heed to the mainstream art world during his long and creative life, seldom exhibiting and becoming something of a legend among the artist-craftspeople who knew about him but had never seen his work. Solo exhibitions were held at Pasadena Art Museum (1945), Caltech (1959), Lang Gallery, Scripps College (1962), and elsewhere. *Metamorphosis*, a film about the process of his cast-aluminum work, was made at the Museum of Fine Arts, Boston, in 1969. —TT

Conrad Brown, "The Pure Research of Jan de Swart," *CH* 18 (January/February 1958), 12; Mike McGee, William G. Otton, *Jan de Swart*, exh. cat. (Laguna Beach, CA: Laguna Art Museum, 1986); Larry Weinberg, "Bio-Feedback: The Work of Jan De Swart," "Cindy's Salon," April 23, 2009, www.interiordesign.net/blog/1850000585/post/1120043712.html.

DI MARE, DOMINIC

Born January 11, 1932, San Francisco, CA
FIBER ARTIST, SCULPTOR, EDUCATOR

Dominic Di Mare began producing talismanic and autobiographical weavings and sculpture in the early 1960s. His initial inspiration came from illustrations of work by artists in *Craft Horizons*—especially the weaving of Kay Sekimachi, and largely self-taught, he created his precise and impeccably crafted objects that are both avant-garde and ancient, sacred and profane. His father was a Sicilian-born commercial fisherman; his mother a prolific crocheter. Intending to be an art teacher, he studied at the California College of Arts and Crafts (now California College of the Arts), Monterey Peninsula College, San Francisco State College (where he took a weaving class as a requirement for his teaching certificate), and the Rudolph Schaefer School of Design in San Francisco. Before establishing himself as a full-time studio artist, Di Mare taught art for fifteen years at Francisco Junior High School in San Francisco. His boyhood experiences helping his father in Monterey on his fishing boat—mending nets, making feathered lures, cutting bait, and setting up the *barangali* (Sicilian fishing basket)—not his art education were the foundations for his work. Purchasing a loom in the early 1960s and setting strict parameters as to materials and process—bones found on the beach in front of his house in Tiburon, wood from a single hawthorn tree on his property, feathers gathered near the emu cage at the Fleishhacker Zoo in San Francisco, horsehair, handmade paper and ceramics, and string to which he applied a simple double half-hitch knot—Di Mare created structures, boxes, altars, temples, shrines, and bundles that are directly connected to the work of his fisherman father. His first exhibition was in 1963 at the Yarn Depot in San Francisco. With the encouragement of one of the owners, Helen Pope, he continued to exhibit in the biennial *Fiber/Clay/Metal* (1964) in St. Paul, MN; the *Western Crafts Competition* (1964) in Seattle, WA; and the *Wichita National Decorative Art Exhibition* (1964). Through a request from Jack Lenor Larsen, he was also included in the U.S. section of the 1964 Milan Triennale. Pope traveled to New York to show samples of Di Mare's work to MCC director Paul Smith, and in 1965 a solo show titled *Dominic Di Mare—Woven Forms* was mounted there, followed by another solo show at Museum West in San Francisco in 1966. The artist was honored in 1997 with *Dominic Di Mare: A Retrospective*, at the Palo Alto Art Center. —TT

Jeremy Adamson, "Mnemonic Connections: The Transcendent Art of Dominic Di Mare," in Palo Alto Cultural Center, *Dominic Di Mare: A Retrospective*, exh. cat. (Palo Alto, CA: the Center, 1997), 26; Dominic Di Mare, oral history interview by Signe Mayfield, June 4 and 10, 2002, AAA, SI.

DRERUP, KARL

Born August 26, 1904, Borghorst, Westphalia, Germany; died November 22, 2000, Newton, MA
ENAMELIST, CERAMIST, PAINTER, EDUCATOR

Karl Drerup is credited with the revival of enameling in the 1940s—through the reinvention of fifteenth-century pictorial Limoges-style enamel painting on metal. The medium suited him on several levels: He had a love of color and storytelling, and enameling required little workshop space. Described as "the venerable enamelist of liquid transparent colors shaped into private fantasies" (review in *CH* 1962), Drerup depicted humans and animals at peace in serene natural surroundings, Christian iconography, and images from memory of times and places from his own life (such as the Canary Islands and New Hampshire). Drerup's technique and compositions reflect the influence of sixteenth-century Northern Renaissance artist Pieter Bruegel, nineteenth-century German painter Hans von Marées, as well as twentieth-century cubists, including Pablo Picasso. Drerup came to enamel work from a broad-based art background. Allowed to attend art school after studying at a Cistercian monastery school, he focused on the graphic arts, earning an undergraduate degree from the Kunstgewerbeschule in Münster in 1924. He continued his studies in Berlin in 1928 with graphic artist Hans Meid and earned a graduate degree in graphic art from the Vereinigte Staatschulen für Freie und Angewandte Kunst (United State Schools for Fine and Applied Arts) in 1929. The following year he went to Florence and in 1933 earned a second graduate degree in painting from the Academia di Belle Arti, where he concentrated on the figure and composition with painter Felice Carena. In Italy, Drerup also studied painting on ceramics, a useful skill when he immigrated to the U.S. in 1937. He earned his living producing "carloads" of decorated porcelain vases, lamp bases, and tiles for Georg Jensen, Inc., and for Rena Rosenthal's Austrian Workshop. In 1939 one of Drerup's ceramic paintings won a Purchase Award at the eighth Ceramic National exhibition in Syracuse. Enamels were considered a part of the ceramics field in the 1930s, so his interest in one medium developed from his work in the other. In 1937, when furniture designer Tommi Parzinger suggested that there was no fine enamel work being created in New York City, Drerup taught himself from textbooks and trained for a short time with William Frederick Stark, a German painter and enamelist. By 1940 Drerup's enamels were being sold by Hudson Walker on West Fifty-seventh Street, and that same year The Metropolitan Museum of Art acquired a piece for its permanent collection. Drerup taught drawing and painting at Adelphi College in Garden City, NY, from 1942 to 1944. He then relocated to Thornton, NH, where in 1948 he joined the faculty at Plymouth State Teacher's College (now University), founding their art department and teaching there until 1968. In the 1950s his work appeared in many important enamel exhibitions, such as a Cooper Union show that traced the medium's history (1954); *Enamels* (1959); and *Masters of Contemporary Crafts* at the Brooklyn Museum (1961). —TT

Oppi Untracht, "Karl Drerup: Enamelist," *CH* 17 (February 1957), 10–15; review of *New England Invitational Crafts Exhibition*, DeCordova Museum, *CH* 22 (September/October 1962), 33; Jane Port, "Karl Drerup: American Enamelist," *Metalsmith* 15 (spring, 1995), 30–35; Port, *Karl Drerup (1904–2000) Enchanted Garden: Enamels by an American Master*, exh. cat. (Plymouth, NH: Karl Drerup Art Gallery, Plymouth State University, 2007).

DUMAS, MARY ADRIENNE

Born January 31, 1912, Eau Claire, WI;
died May 11, 1971, Berkeley, CA
PAINTER, TEXTILE DESIGNER, EDUCATOR

Mary Adrienne Dumas was one of the first American artists to adapt modern dye technology to the ancient Javanese technique of batik. She received her MA in painting from the University of California, Berkeley, and this back-ground, especially her admiration of the work of Paul Klee, influenced her expressionistic use of color and intuitive approach to design. As with traditional batik, Dumas applied wax resist to cotton, linen, and silk to create a design, but she eschewed dye vats as a vehicle for applying color, preferring to brush or sponge her colors directly onto the fabric. Ed Rossbach compared her methods to watercolor painting, because Dumas also favored bright, transparent silkscreen dyes, which she could layer and blend, instead of the vegetable dyes (such as indigo) that were in vogue in the 1960s and '70s. She was also known for enriching her textiles with layers of silkscreen or block-printing, indicating an affinity for nineteenth-century design and ancient folk textiles. A teacher in the decorative art program at Berkeley for twenty-seven years, Dumas encouraged the study of textiles from an anthropo-logical and historical perspective, aided by a close working relationship between her department and the Robert H. Lowie Museum of Anthropology (now the Phoebe A. Hearst Museum). —JG

Ed Rossbach, "Contemporary Batiks," *CH* 13 (November/December 1953), 19–21; Alan Meisel, "Letter from San Francisco," *CH* 32 (August 1972), 49; Sandra Harner, "A Year of Cloth: Celebrating Textiles at the Phoebe A. Hearst Museum," *Fiberarts* 23 (January/February 1997), 54–58.

EAMES, CHARLES ORMOND, JR.

Born June 17, 1907, St. Louis, MO;
died August 21, 1978, St. Louis, MO
EAMES, RAY
(NÉE BERNICE ALEXANDRA KAISER)
Born December 15, 1913, Sacramento, CA;
died August 21, 1988, Pacific Palisades, CA
FURNITURE DESIGNERS, TEXTILE DESIGNERS,
ARCHITECTS, FILMMAKERS

Undoubtedly the most influential design team of the mid-twentieth century, Charles and Ray Eames led the charge to modernize postwar America through partner-ships with the federal government and the country's top corporate businesses. Aiming to improve the functional capability as well as the cultural and intellectual standing of American society, the Eameses created a plethora of design and educational products—furniture, textiles, toys, and buildings, as well as exhibitions, films, and books—for a diverse range of clients between the 1940s and '70s. Embracing the message of "better living through better design," the Eameses were in the forefront of American designers addressing the postwar demand for products that met the needs of a more casual lifestyle. Charles defined his and Ray's job as "the simple one of getting

most of the best to the greatest number of people for the least" ("Eames" 1965), and theirs was a partnership that balanced his "affinity for order" and hers for the "dynamics of space" (Albrecht 1997). The couple met at Cranbrook, married in 1941, and moved to Los Angeles, where they established a design studio. Charles was first employed in the art department at Metro-Goldwyn-Mayer and Ray initially designed covers for *Art & Architecture* magazine (1942–48). Charles designed a leg splint for the U.S. Navy in 1943, and he and Ray also began experimenting with molded compound-curved plywood for furniture and sculp-ture. After operating a research laboratory with California modernist John Entenza and others (1941–45) and having established the Plyformed Wood Company (1942) resulting in the Molded Plywood Division of Evans Products (1943), the Eameses began vigorously producing plywood furni-ture. In 1946 MoMA presented a solo exhibition of chairs, tables, screens, and storage units by Charles (Ray was not recognized then as his equal partner), and as a result the Eameses became consultant designers to the Herman Miller Co., a relationship that lasted until the end of their careers. The simple and functional pieces they designed for the company were almost entirely machine made and were considered revolutionary. They used fiberglass, a new material developed during the war, for their produc-tion furniture beginning in 1948. During the 1950s and '60s their prolific output included: *Eames Storage Units* (1950); a sofa that folded for easier shipment (1954); the iconic leather and rosewood-veneer *Lounge Chair* (1956); the *Aluminum Group* (1958); and the *Eames Chaise* (1968). In addition to furniture design, Ray worked on the company's advertisements (1948–53). She was also an independent fabric designer. Her *Cross Patch* textile was produced by Schiffer Prints in 1945. That same year she entered *Brown and Black Free Shapes on a White Ground* in a fabric design competition, and in 1946 the pattern was shown at MoMA. The Eameses participated in the *Art & Architecture* Case Study House Program, which had been established in 1945. It drew on Los Angeles's progres-sive architectural tradition to address the urgent housing needs of returning veterans. The Eameses steel and glass house was built using factory-produced windows, structural beams, and sliding doors—all of which could be ordered from commercial trade catalogues. Intended to serve as a model for low-cost, do-it-yourself modern design, the Eameses house, with its bright panels of color, expanses of glass, and interior assemblages of handmade objects and folk artifacts, became an architectural icon much publicized in popular magazines such as *Life* and *Look*. In addition to their design work, the Eameses also generated communication systems in the form of exhibitions, films, and books. Charles was responsible for exhibition instal-lations, including the first Good Design show at MoMA (1950) and *Textiles and Ornamental Arts of India* (1955). He designed *The India Report,* a publication documenting the emerging craft industries on the Indian subcontinent. The Eameses also collaborated on *Day of the Dead* (1957), a film featuring Mexican craft. —TT

"Charles Eames," in *Current Biography Yearbook* (New York: H. W. Wilson Co., 1965), 140; Pat Kirkham, *Charles and Ray Eames: Designers of the Twentieth Century* (Cambridge, MA: MIT Press, 1995); Donald Albrecht et al., The *Work of Charles and Ray Eames: A Legacy of Invention* (New York: Harry N. Abrams in association with the Library of Congress and the Vitra Design Museum, 1997), 56. For earlier history see *Craft in the Machine Age*, 233.

ECKHARDT, EDRIS

Born January 28, 1905, Cleveland, OH;
died April 27, 1998, Lakewood, OH
GLASS ARTIST, CERAMIST, EDUCATOR

Initially known for ceramic sculpture created for Cleveland-based WPA projects, Edris Eckhardt turned to glassmaking in the 1950s. Her revival of ancient Egyptian gold glass-making brought her international recognition as one of the earliest practitioners of studio glass production, along with Maurice Heaton and Frances and Michael Higgins. Eckhardt was tenacious in her pursuit of technical and artistic goals and was highly influential in the glassmaking programs that flourished in the late 1960s. Fascinated by the ancient Egyptian gold glass on display at The Metropolitan Museum of Art, in 1953 Eckhardt, working alone in her home studio and using only materials avail-able to the ancient Egyptians, produced a perfect piece of gold glass but had forgotten to note the formula. The technique involves engraving gold or silver foil with a stylus, laminating it between thin layers of glass that were rolled out on hot marble with a wet rolling pin. Starting over again she painstakingly recorded recipes, firing times, and temperatures, and after nearly one thousand tries was once again successful. Using her hard-earned technical knowl-edge, Eckhardt began producing gold glass in relatively large sizes for such Cleveland commissions as the memo-rial doors at Heights Temple; the cross in the sanctuary of Gethsemane Lutheran Church; and the head of Christ at Bethlehem Lutheran Church. With the aid of a Louis Comfort Tiffany fellowship (1959) and two John Simon Guggenheim awards (1956 and 1959), Eckhardt mastered an astonishing array of techniques, including "vertical laminations, [and] full sculptural casting by the *cire perdue* [lost-wax] process" (Hollister 1985). She also rediscovered ways of achieving the reds and blues found in stained glass in cathedrals such as the one at Chartres. She was among the first to prove that through careful handling glass and bronze could be combined and was among the first American artists to use glass in highly evocative abstract expressionist works. Eckhardt was inspired by religious and mythological subjects as well as by Emily Dickinson's nature-filled poetry and the whimsy of *Alice in Wonderland*. Her work has been shown in five world's fairs, including the Brussels Fair (1958), and she was given a rare, six-month-long solo exhibition at the Corning Museum of Glass in 1968. —TT

Paul Hollister, "Studio Glass before 1962, Maurice Heaton, Frances and Michael Higgins, Edris Eckhardt, Four Poineers and True Originals." *Neues Glass* 4 (1985):

232–40; "Edris Eckhardt, 1905–1998," *Ceramics Monthly* 46 (September 1998), 28; artist file, ACC library; artist file, Rakow Library, Corning Museum of Glass. For earlier history see *Craft in the Machine Age*, 233.

EDWARDS, JOEL E.

Born June 23, 1923, New York, NY

CERAMIST, EDITOR

Joel Edwards produces utilitarian vessels with strong tactile qualities. Inspired by abstract expressionism, he has experimented with various forms to create unexpected shapes and configurations. He studied at the City College of New York and the Brooklyn Museum School; he earned an MFA from the Los Angeles County Art Institute (now the Otis College of Art and Design), where he was taught by Peter Voulkos. Beyond his work as a ceramist, Edwards has been editorial coordinator for *Popular Ceramics* magazine and editor of *Creative Crafts* magazine (beginning in 1960). —NB

Janice Lovoos, "Three California Ceramists," *American Artist* 30 (December 1966), 50–4; Mary Davis MacNaughton et al., *Revolution in Clay: The Marer Collection of Contemporary Ceramics* (Seattle and London: University of Washington Press, 1994); artist statement, Long Beach Museum of Art, www.lbma.org.

ESHERICK, WHARTON

Born July 15, 1887, Philadelphia, PA;

died May 6, 1970, Paoli, PA

WOOD SCULPTOR, FURNITURE DESIGNER AND MAKER

Wharton Esherick spent the bulk of his life in Pennsylvania, surrounded by the woods he treasured for his work, becoming a founder and leader of the American studio craft movement. He began as a painter, studying at the School of Industrial Arts in Philadelphia and at the Pennsylvania Academy of Fine Arts. In a characteristic display of determination, he quit his formal art education six weeks before graduating. In 1913, at the age of twenty-six, Esherick and his wife purchased land in Paoli, PA, and moved into the 1839 farmhouse that was on the property. By 1926 he began to construct a home and studio, a project that became his life's work, culminating only posthumously in the Wharton Esherick Museum.

After giving up painting, Esherick became intrigued by theater design, woodcarving, woodblock prints for books, and sculpture. He began handcrafting wood frames for paintings but soon was making handcarved sculptures in the form of chairs, sofas, tables, and cabinets. By the late 1920s Esherick was creating one-of-a kind pieces of furniture for private clients and exploring many furniture styles, from Arts and Crafts to the asymmetry and prismatic effects of cubism.

Much like his contemporary Frank Lloyd Wright, Esherick worked on every aspect of his home studio, imbuing it with his personal style. The esoteric exterior of the structure featured a plum-colored front door and a stucco-covered silo in a subtle blend of autumn shades. The furniture and hardware, including wooden coat hooks carved with caricatures of the friends who had helped him build the house, captured Esherick's free-form style. He deplored waste and salvaged wood scraps from his supplier to use in his interiors. A crowning feature of the house was the red oak spiral staircase (1930), ingeniously built with steel supports that could be disassembled, allowing the staircase to be displayed at the 1939–40 New York World's Fair in a collaboration with architect George Howe in "Pennsylvania Hill House" and later in the Esherick retrospective at MCC in 1958.

From the 1920s to '50s Esherick hired assistants who were responsible for construction and joints, while he personally designed and shaped furniture. He worked primarily with native woods from southeastern Pennsylvania, including walnut, black cherry, cottonwood, and hickory. Esherick's furniture always presented the tree's natural lines, angles, and forms, allowing the piece to follow the wood's natural shape and grain.

The *Hammer Handle* chairs of the 1950s represent Esherick's industrious and whimsical nature. He bought an entire lot of hammer handles at auction and used them as chair legs, rails, and footrests in a series of thirty-six chairs for the local Hedgerow Theatre. —LB

Cooke, Ward, and L'Ecuyer 2003, 118–19; Todd Merrill, and Julie V. Iovine, eds., *Modern Americana: Studio Furniture from High Craft to High Glam* (New York: Rizzoli, 2008), 58–67.

EVANS, PAUL

Born May 20, 1931, Newtown, PA;

died March 7, 1987, Nantucket, MA

FURNITURE MAKER, DESIGNER, SCULPTOR, METALSMITH, ENTREPRENEUR

Paul Evans was known for his highly stylized work and a unique aesthetic that was guided by technological innovation and creativity. As a student at Cranbrook, Evans focused on silversmithing, but he quit school to work in New Hope, PA, with established furniture maker and designer Phillip Lloyd Powell. As the two men began to integrate their artistic ideas, the pieces they made grew in scale: chests, cabinets, decorative screens, and consoles. Evans's sculptural approach to working iron complemented Powell's organic woodwork. They collaborated and worked independently on one-off, handmade furniture, in a partnership that lasted from 1955 until 1964. Powell and Evans offered a full-service furniture atelier, making adjustments to the pieces they created according to their customers' needs.

With the arrival in 1959 of Dorsey Reading, a machinist, who became Evans's apprentice and eventually his assistant and foreman, details emerged that became his trademark: sunbursts, spider webs, pipes, buttons, loops and stalagmites, welded onto the facades of many of his pieces. He preferred that the natural texture of the metal be seen, and he opted for textured edges, gold leaf accents, and muted primary colors. He worked organically, never planning the design at the outset, but rather, making artistic decisions as the work progressed. In the early 1960s Powell and Evans held a two-man show at America House where their unorthodox blending of wood and patinated metal won accolades. In 1964 the partnership ended when Powell decided to focus more on his own artwork; meanwhile the upscale furniture firm Directional drafted Evans to design for them in a lengthy partnership that lasted until 1980. —JF and ML

"America House," *Interiors,* 121 (December 1961), 142; Todd Merrill and Julie V. Iovine, eds., *Modern Americana: Studio Furniture from High Craft to High Glam* (New York: Rizzoli, 2008), 90–111.

FALKENSTEIN, CLAIRE

Born 1908, Coos Bay, OR;

died October 23, 1997, Venice, CA

SCULPTOR, JEWELER, EDUCATOR

Claire Falkenstein followed her own artistic path for more than sixty years, studying and working in the U.S. and Europe. Disenchanted with the conservative ideas she was exposed to as an undergraduate art student at the University of California, Berkeley, in the late 1920s, Falkenstein blossomed under the tutelage of a substitute teacher from Paris, George Luss, who challenged her to look inward in her drawings and find her personal vision instead of merely copying the subject. In 1933 she became a student of Alexander Archipenko at Mills College and in the 1940s also encountered Bauhaus emigrés László Moholy-Nagy and Gyorgy Kepes who taught summer sessions at Mills, experiences that proved instructive to her artistic growth. Over the next two decades, she taught at various schools and summer sessions around California to earn a living, including the California College of Arts and Crafts (now California College of the Arts), but always continuing to focus on creating her own art. In the 1940s she taught at the California School of Fine Arts in San Francisco (now the San Francisco Art Institute), where she admired the work of colleagues Clyfford Still and Richard Diebenkorn.

For Falkenstein, Paris was the center of the contemporary art world, and in 1950 she traveled to Europe. In Paris she became loosely connected to the Art Autre circle of artists seeking alternative paths of expression and began sculpting in earnest, beginning with mahogany and moving on to metal. She remained in the city until 1963, developing a personal vocabulary of abstract forms using the screen, the lattice, and combinations thereof.

She worked in both nonfunctional and functional modes and in both small and large scale, producing works of engaging immediacy and drama. She exhibited widely in the U.S. and abroad, in addition to executing a number of commissions in Europe, including the bronze, steel, and glass gates for the Peggy Guggenheim Museum in Venice, which were installed in 1962. Over her career, Falkenstein designed furniture, fountains, screens, wallpaper, and jewelry. In 1963 she returned to the U.S, settling in Venice in Southern California. —JP

Maren Henderson, "Claire Falkenstein: Small Sculpture/ Large Jewelry," in *The Modernist Jewelry of Claire*

Falkenstein, exh. cat. (Long Beach: Long Beach Museum of Art, 2004); Claire Falkenstein, oral history interview by Paul Karlstrom, March 2–21, 1995, AAA, SI.

FERRINI, VINCENT

Born April 24, 1933, Brockton, MA

METALSMITH, JEWELER, EDUCATOR

Vincent Ferrini studied silversmithing under Joseph L. Sharrock at the School of the Museum of Fine Arts, Boston, and received his BFA with honors in 1955. A pair of candlesticks by Ferrini received third prize in the 1959 Sterling Today competition held by the Sterling Silversmiths Guild of America for original and imaginative design in hollowware (cat. 146). Ferrini continued his studies at Tufts University, where he earned a BS in education in 1956. He taught in his hometown's public schools until the early 1960s, while continuing his graduate studies in silversmithing and jewelry at the Boston Museum School. In 1963 he studied with silversmith Hans Christensen at the School for American Craftsmen at RIT, and in 1964 received his MFA degree.

In 1964 Ferrini began a two-decade teaching career at Boston University in the School for the Arts, serving with J. Fred Woell in the acclaimed Program in Artisanry, which was part of the school from 1974 to 1985. Both sleek polished surfaces that recall Christensen's modernist sensibility and a more traditional rich texture and ornament of earlier periods are found in Ferrini's hollowware and jewelry. Beginning in 1983 he became a founding partner, along with Robert Fairbank and John Reynolds, of Goldsmiths 3 in Concord, MA, a business he continued until his retirement in 1999. Ferrini is an Associate of the Worshipful Company of Goldsmiths in London. —JP

Vincent Ferrini, Designer, Goldsmith: A Retrospective, 1953–1983, exh. cat. (Brockton, MA: Brockton Art Museum / Fuller Memorial, 1983); Ferrini, "Preciousness," *Metalsmith* 5 (spring 1985), 30–35; Curtis LaFollette, "Vincent Ferrini," *Metalsmith* 5 (fall 1985), 36–37.

FISCH, ARLINE MARIE

Born August 21, 1931, Brooklyn, NY

JEWELER, METALSMITH, EDUCATOR

Arline Fisch made her reputation as a jeweler who employed woven wire at a time when few were practicing this method. She has had a long career as a metalsmith, with a focus not only on jewelry, but also on education and service to the field. Fisch attended Skidmore College, earning her BFA in 1952. She continued her education at the University of Illinois, Champaign-Urbana, studying metalwork with Arthur Pulos. In 1956–57 she received a Fulbright Grant to attend the Kunsthaandvaerkerskolen (School of Arts and Crafts) in Copenhagen, and she studied with Bernhard Hertz Guldvaerefabrik, a jewelry fabricator. She made a second trip to Denmark in 1966–67. In 1958 she visited Mexico to explore weaving and jewelry making. These early trips were just the start of Fisch's brilliant use of travel as a means of education for herself and others. She traveled regularly to learn and teach jewelry methods and to confer with colleagues in the field.

Her weaving experience at Haystack, under the direction of Ted Hallman and Jack Lenor Larsen, led to a focus on woven wire that would profoundly influence her career. She briefly returned to Skidmore to teach and in 1961 moved to San Diego State University to establish the jewelry and metalsmithing program, where she remained until her retirement in 1999. Her textbook, *Textile Techniques in Metal,* which was first published in 1975, has become a standard in the field of woven metalwork.

Fisch has had solo exhibitions at the Pasadena Museum of Art (1962); The Egg and the Eye Gallery, Los Angeles (1969); Goldsmiths' Hall, London (1971); and was included in *American Jewelry and Related Objects* (Huntington Museum of Art, WV, 1955), *Fulbright Designers* (ACC, 1958), *Art of Personal Adornment* (MCC 1965), and *Objects: USA* (MCC, 1969), among many others. The retrospective *Elegant Fantasy, The Jewelry of Arline Fisch* was held in 1999. She is a founding member of the Society of North American Goldsmiths (SNAG) and served on the boards for the American Crafs Council, World Crafts Council, and Haystack, among other institutions. —JF

David Revere McFadden et al., *Elegant Fantasy, The Jewelry of Arline Fisch* (San Diego, CA: San Diego Historical Society; Stuttgart: Arnoldsche Art Publishers, 1999).

FREUND, ELSA

(NÉE ELSIE MARIE BATES)

Born January 12, 1912, Taney County, MO;

died June 14, 2001, Little Rock, AR

PAINTER, JEWELER, TEXTILE ARTIST, EDUCATOR

Elsa Freund was raised on a 1,500-acre game preserve in the Ozarks, where her father, of Irish and Cherokee descent, was the gamekeeper. She attended a one-room schoolhouse until high school, and using materials she found in the woods, she declared herself to be an artist from a young age. After graduating from high school, she taught grade school under a special arrangement for rural teachers, saving enough money to attend the Kansas City Art Institute. Upon graduation, with the Depression underway, she moved to Arkansas, where she operated a gift shop, selling items she made from woodland materials, such as jewelry from walnut shells. Her husband, the muralist Louis Freund, taught at Hendrix College in Hendrix, AR, and when he was drafted during the war, Elsa took over his classes. The couple established a Summer Art School of the Ozarks (1940–51) in their home, teaching weaving, ceramics, and other media. During this period Freund experimented with jewelry, using ceramic "stones" that she shaped to resemble river rocks, and glazed with broken glass that she fired in her enameling kiln. Untrained as a jeweler, she hammered aluminum and copper wire (she later used silver) and set them into holes in the back of her "stones," covering the back with aluminum sheet. She began calling these unique, biomorphic forms "Elsaramics."

In 1949 the couple began a dual residency, teaching during the winter at Stetson University in DeLand, FL, and during the summer in Arkansas. Elsie taught watercolor, jewelry, and textiles. In 1951 they founded the Florida Craftsmen's Association. Freund's jewelry was carried in shops in Key West, Palm Beach, and Sarasota, as well as Aspen, CO; in 1957, America House became one of her biggest retailers, advertising in the *New York Times* and the *New Yorker.* Freund gave up making jewelry about 1964. —JF

Anne Allman, "Biography of Elsie Marie Bates-Freund," typescript, College of the Ozarks, 1991; *Elsa Freund, American Studio Jeweler,* exh. cat. (Little Rock, AR: Arkansas Arts Center Decorative Arts, Museum, 1991).

FRIMKESS, MICHAEL JOEL

Born January 8, 1937, Los Angeles, CA

CERAMIST, PAINTER

A product of the Voulkos ceramics scene, yet aesthetically on his own path, Michael Frimkess was born in the immigrant neighborhoods of East Los Angeles. He was the son of an art director at an advertising firm and was encouraged in the arts, especially sculpture, from an early age. He attended the Los Angeles County Art Institute (now Otis College of Art and Design), entering in 1955 at the age of seventeen. He studied with Peter Voulkos and also met Paul Soldner and John Mason, as well as Ken Price and Billy Al Bengstrom. Later, when Voulkos moved to Berkeley to teach and to work in bronze, Frimkess followed and learned to cast with him. Frimkess did not graduate from Otis, instead traveling to Italy, where he worked at a small ceramics factory while studying traditional production methods. When he returned to the U.S., Frimkess settled on the East Coast and in 1963 briefly worked at the Clay Art Center in Port Chester, NY. While there, he met his wife and future collaborator, the Venezuelan painter Magdalena Suarez. Frimkess also worked at a ceramics factory in Pennsylvania at this time, where he was taught by potter Clara Rosen to throw vessels using dense clay without water, a method he claims was used by the ancient Greeks. Visits to The Metropolitan Museum of Art in New York introduced Frimkess to ancient Greek and Asian ceramics, which inculcated in him a love of traditional vessel forms. Soon he was producing these shapes using his new throwing method and decorating them in sgraffito and rich colors, in an often humorous or satirical comic-book style. One volute crater, for example, is ornamented with a procession of modern cyclists rather than the usual gods and goddesses, while on a Chinese-style vase, the interactions of a modern ceramics class replaced scenes of domestic life. Frimkess has been affected by muscular dystrophy since about 1971, and his wife has taken over the application of surface decoration on his vessels. —JF

Suzanne Muchnic, "Their Lives Poured into Clay: A Husband-and-Wife Team's Wide-ranging Experiences—Including Illness—Are Reflected in their Noted Ceramics," *Los Angeles Times,* November 19, 2000; Michael Frimkess and Magdalena Suarez Frimkess, oral history interview by Paul J. Karlstrom, March 8, 22, 2001, and April 17, 2001, AAA, SI.

GIL, DAVID

(NÉ DAVID GOLDFARB)

Born May 29, 1922, Harlem, NY;

died March 18, 2002, Pownal, VT

CERAMIST, DESIGNER, CERAMIC MANUFACTURER

Inspired by the Bauhaus and Bernard Leach, David Gil embraced the machine to manufacture ceramics with a hand-crafted aesthetic. The son of Polish-Jewish immigrants, David Gil grew up in Harlem, New York, where his parents ran a hand laundry. His WPA art classes at the 92nd Street Y and ceramic classes at the Inwood Pottery Studio led him to the New York College of Ceramics at Alfred (1940–42, 1946–48). Gil's studies were interrupted by World War II, and when his duties took him to Swansea, Wales, he made a pilgrimage to Leach's studio. While Leach was strongly influenced by Japanese pottery, Gil returned home determined to create an industrial pottery that reflected the best of American culture.

In 1948 Gil bought a pottery studio in Bennington, VT, and established Cooperative Design, intent on bringing good design to the masses. He won awards for his work from the Syracuse Museum of Fine Art (1951, 1954), Akron Museum of Art (1953), MoMA (before 1961), Chicago Merchandise Mart, and the Académie Internationale de la Céramique in Cannes. Gil's now-classic "trigger" mug, developed in the 1950s and produced on a RAM press by the thousands, established the pottery commercially. Gil distinguished Bennington Potters (as it was renamed in 1965) by serving as both chief designer and general manager and by bucking the trend to move production overseas. The firm has produced more than 1,000 designs in three clay bodies and fourteen glazes in its Vermont location. Mostly designed by Gil himself, Bennington Potters' dinnerware, bakeware, artware, and terracotta has sold throughout the U.S., Asia, and Europe.

There have also been many collaborations, with Bennington Potters producing pieces for Richards Morganthau (Raymor), and Restaurant Associates, as well as reproductions for The Metropolitan Museum of Art, MoMA, and the Nelson Rockefeller Collection. Furthermore, the pottery has realized designs by other artists, including the *Classic* dinnerware developed by Japanese artist Yusuke Aida and a series of limited-edition artworks by Helen Frankenthaler, Alexander Lieberman, Leonard Baskin, and other prominent artists, illustrated in *Art in America* (December 1964). —CZ

N. Nelson, "David Gil's Bennington Potters," *CH* 24 (March 1964), 34–35; David Gil, oral history interview by Catherine Zusy, March 13, April 3, June 6, and September 21, 1999.

GILHOOLY, DAVID

Born April 15, 1943, Auburn, CA

CERAMIST

David Gilhooly, one of Robert Arneson's first students at the University of California, Davis, was an integral part of the Funk ceramics movement. His cartoonish, humorous, but often unsettling work frequently featured animals and food as vehicles for expressing his opinions about consumption and abundance. In 1963, a scant year after Gilhooly took his first ceramics class with Arneson, his work was included in *California Crafts III* at the E. B. Crocker Art Museum. Gilhooly received his undergraduate degree from UC Davis in 1965 and had his first solo exhibition at the Richmond Art Center in the same year. While pursuing his graduate degrees, Gilhooly switched from high-fire stoneware to low-fire white ware in order to widen his palette of glazes. He made full-sized animals, but also worked in mixed-media sculpture, such as ceramic footstools with Naugahyde and fake fur. His work was included in the seminal *Funk* show at the UC Berkeley Art Museum in 1967. The next year he began teaching regularly at UC Davis, which he continued to do at Arneson's invitation even after he moved to Canada to teach at the University of Saskatchewan in 1969. It was in that year the Gilhooly began to concentrate on one iconic animal—the frog—and to develop a "frog world" replete with classical and mythological allusions from the annals of art history. —JG

"Funky Figurines," *Time* 91 (April 26, 1968), 90; Ellen Paul Denker, "USA VII: Ceramics," Grove Art Online; John Natsoulas, *David Gilhooly* (Davis, CA: John Natsoulas Press, 1992).

GOTTLIEB, ADOLPH

Born March 14, 1903, New York, NY;

died March 4, 1974, East Hampton, NY

PAINTER, DESIGNER, WRITER, EDUCATOR

With a career that spanned more than five decades, Adolph Gottlieb is regarded as one of the leading American artists of the abstract expressionist movement. His work is generally classified in two distinct categories: the Pictograph series made during the 1940s and early 1950s, and the Bursts made in the later part of his career. In addition to the time he devoted to painting, Gottlieb also pursued his art through leadership roles in art associations, writing, and teaching.

Gottlieb studied art in high school, taking courses at Parsons School of Design and at the Cooper Union. In 1921 he took an illustration course with John Sloan at the Art Students League and attended lectures by Robert Henri, who influenced his ideas about art training and education. At the age of eighteen he went to Europe with a friend, staying in Paris for a year while taking sketching courses. In 1923, after returning to New York, he enrolled in a teaching program at Parsons and graduated the following year. During the same period he took painting classes from Sloan, maintained a studio, and began to exhibit his work around the city. In 1929 he met Milton Avery and Mark Rothko, and the three artists became good friends. (In 1943 Rothko and Gottlieb sent a joint letter to the *New York Times* outlining their relationship to abstract expressionism.) In 1930, at the age of twenty-six, Gottlieb had his first solo show at the Dudensing Gallery in New York City.

Gottlieb, who by this time had married Esther Dick, primarily lived and worked in Brooklyn between 1932 and 1956. In 1935 he became a founding member of The Ten, a group of New York-based artists including Rothko, Ilya Bolotowsky, and Louis Schanker. They argued against museum and gallery exhibitions promoting academic painting and exhibited their work together in nine exhibitions over five years. In 1936 Gottlieb joined the Artists' Union, and the same year he worked in the easel division of the Federal Art Project (FAP). He was also a founding member of the American Artists' Congress organized by Stuart Davis.

In the 1950s Gottlieb collaborated on a number of architectural projects, providing designs for stained glass for the Congregation Beth El Synagogue in Springfield, MA, and for the 1,300-square-foot facade of the Milton Steinberg Memorial Center at the Park Avenue Synagogue in New York City. Beginning around 1955 he began to move away from the dense visual vocabulary of the Pictograph series he had started in 1941 and to create the simpler, more abstract paintings with open areas of space that defined his later work and was first fully articulated in *Burst* (1957). In 1970 Gottlieb suffered a stroke; he continued to paint, however, with the aid of an assistant, until just before his death in 1974. —CK

James Fitzsimons, "Adolph Gottlieb," *Everyday Art Quarterly*, 25 (1953), 4; Lee Dembart, "Adolph Gottlieb, Abstractionist, Dies," *New York Times*, March 5, 1974, 36; Lawrence Alloway and Mary Davis MacNaughton, *Adolph Gottlieb: A Retrospective* (New York: Arts Publisher, Inc., in association with the Adolph and Esther Gottlieb Foundation, Inc., 1981), 19.

GRAVENITES, LINDA

(NÉE LINDA McCLEAN)

Born December 23, 1939, NY;

died February 11, 2002, Cazadero, CA

COSTUME DESIGNER

Linda Gravenites made signature clothing for marquee rock and folk stars of the early sixties including Jessica McClintock, Mimi Fariña, and Janis Joplin. Oftentimes mentioned by her iconoclastic friends and clients, she was responsible for creating many of the highly inventive costumes that helped to establish these performers' public personas. She was among the first to create pieces from unusual textiles and vintage clothing, while also referencing Native American and other ethnic styles; she once made a jumpsuit for Joplin out of an antique lace tablecloth.

Gravenites, who learned to sew as a child from her mother, made ballet costumes as a teenager and later designed costumes for an avant-garde theater group. Her trademarks were embroidery, fastidious workmanship, and combinations of couture pieces with thrift-store discoveries, a mainstream practice today, but considered subversive at the time. She moved to San Francisco in 1959 at the age of nineteen and became inspired by the counterculture that was emerging in the Haight-Ashbury area. There, young people were turning their backs on the tailored and prim silhouettes of 1950s clothing in favor of flamboyant costumes. Married to musician and singer Nick Gravenites, she quickly became immersed in the neighborhood overflowing with artists and bands that had begun to challenge social norms. By 1967 she was well established among counter-culture celebrities and superstars, especially after Joplin approached Gravenites to make a costume for an upcoming concert. —ML

Joel Lobenthal, *Radical Rags: Fashions of the Sixties* (New York: Cross River Press, 1990), 109–15; Marian Hall et al., *California Fashion* (New York: Harry N. Abrams, Inc., 2002), 128–33.

GUERMONPREZ, TRUDE

(NÉE GERTRUDE E. JALOWETZ;
LATER, MRS. PAUL GUERMONPREZ;
LATER, MRS. JOHN ELSESSER)

Born November 9, 1910, Danzig, Germany (now Gdansk, Poland); died May 8, 1976, San Francisco, CA

WEAVER, TEXTILE DESIGNER, EDUCATOR

Known for her custom-woven rugs, upholstery fabrics, tapestries, "space hangings," and "textile graphics," as well as her prototype designs for industry, Guermonprez embraced a Bauhaus approach to production and frequently collaborated with architects to create textiles for building interiors. A gifted teacher, Guermonprez found her ideas in the materials she used and discovered that teaching helped her define her own work. Raised in a family where art was an integral part of life, she received her formal education in the Bauhaus tradition in Germany at the School of Art, Cologne (1930–31) and the School of Fine and Applied Arts in Halle/Saale (1931–33), also known as the "little Bauhaus," where her affinity for weaving became apparent. She undertook graduate studies at the Textile Engineering School, Berlin (1933) and later studied weaving independently in Finland (1937) and Sweden (1946). Upon graduation Guermonprez accepted a position as head designer at the Dutch handweaving production studio, Het Paapje, creating rugs, upholstery fabrics, and other custom textiles from 1934 to 1939. She was a freelance designer for textile mills, architects, and Holland America from 1939 to 1945, and an artistic advisor and designer for De Ploeg, creating handwoven fabrics for interiors from 1945 to 1947. After the death of her first husband, she taught weaving at the Volkshogeschool, in the Adult Education Program of the Netherlands, from 1944 to 1946. Following the death of her father in 1947—her family had immigrated to the U.S. in 1933 and both parents taught at Black Mountain College—Guermonprez was invited by Josef and Anni Albers to teach at the college. Filling in initially for Anni Albers during a sabbatical leave (summer and fall 1947), Guermonprez stayed on as an assistant weaving instructor (through spring 1949). When she received an invitation from Marguerite Wildenhain, whom she had known in Germany, to join the Bauhaus-inspired Pond Farm Workshops, Guermonprez moved to Guerneville, CA, where she taught weaving from 1949 to 1952. Her marriage in 1951 to John Elsesser, a San Francisco builder-craftsman,

brought Guermonprez to San Francisco, and she began teaching in local art schools—California School of Fine Arts (now the San Francisco Art Institute, 1950–51) and California College of Arts and Crafts (now California College of the Arts), where she taught summer sessions from 1952 to 1954. She joined the faculty at CCAC full-time in 1954, was appointed chair of the department of crafts (1960–71), and chair of the department of weaving (1960–76). Among the students who benefited from her teaching were contemporary fiber artists Barbara Shawcroft and Kay Sekimachi. Guermonprez continued her own design work, completing commissions for Architects Associated in New York, Eric Mendelsohn in San Francisco, and Marcel Breuer in Asheville, as well as creating Ark curtains for synagogues in Ohio and California. Guermonprez was a charter member of Designer Craftsmen of California and a trustee in the Southwest Region, American Craftsmen's Council. In 1970 she was awarded the American Institute of Architects Craftsmanship Metal. —TT

"Maria Kipp, Trude Guermonprez and other California Weavers," *CH* 16 (September 1956), 24–25, 35–37; Ed Rossbach, Obituary, *CH* 36 (August 1976), 10; *The Tapestries of Trude Guermonprez*, exh. cat. (Oakland, CA: Oakland Museum, 1982); Hazel Bray, "Trude Guermonprez," *AC* 43 (June/July, 1983), 40–44; artist file, ACC library.

HALLMAN, HENRY THEODORE (TED) III

Born December 23, 1933, Bucks County, PA

FIBER ARTIST, EDUCATOR

Ted Hallman has been at the vanguard of American textile design since the late 1950s, when he began juxtaposing natural and synthetic fibers in his weavings. Acrylic was a relatively new material developed for military use during World War II, and few textile artists were using the combination when Hallman began. His breadth of technique—knitting, crochet, wrapping, needle lace, and such weaving processes as overshot, satin, brocade, and inventive twills—was applied to such materials as hand-dyed and discharged fabric, wool, linen, feathers, wire, gemstones, plastic, and steel. The finished work includes tapestries, prayer rugs, breastplates, room dividers, and sculpture.

The son of an accomplished Pennsylvania painter, illustrator, and teacher, Hallman got his first taste of fiber arts as a Boy Scout, when he created a weaving. On a Pew scholarship he earned a certificate in painting and pipe organ from the Fontainebleau Fine Arts and Music Schools in France in 1955; a BFA and BS in education on a Senatorial scholarship from Tyler School of Art, Temple University, in 1956; and separate MFAs in painting and in textile design on a Joy Griffin West scholarship from Cranbrook in 1958. At Cranbrook, Hallman came to understand weaving as an art form. A Louis Comfort Tiffany grant gave him the opportunity to learn commercial knitting at the Bundestextilschule in Dornbirn, Austria, in 1962, and he completed his formal schooling with a PhD in education from the University of California, Berkeley, in 1974. In the 1960s Hallman was well known for his dyed acrylic

plastic screens, which were made into tapestries and room dividers and used like stained glass in windows and as wall hangings in lobbies, offices, and apartments. He created patterned double weaves of great complexity, sculptural knitted trees, and seamless garments using intense color combinations. He also designed textiles commercially, with work produced by such firms as Jack Lenor Larsen, Inc., in New York. A double-woven cloth piece was included in Larsen's 1961 *Fabrics International* show at the MCC. Hallman also staged events, weaving textiles into the environment, beginning the "installations" that are now a major phenomenon in the art world. He taught summer sessions at Haystack in Maine, in 1958, 1960, and 1962, and at Penland in North Carolina from 1964 to 1968. He served as professor and head of the textile design department at Moore College of Art and Design, Philadelphia, from 1963 to 1969, where he established design studios for woven and printed textiles and developed and coordinated a work-study program with the New York textile industry. He was also a textile consultant for the International Labor Organization of the United Nations in Jamaica during the summer of 1967. Hallman exhibited widely both nationally and internationally, including the 1958 *Young Americans* exhibition at MCC, where he won a first prize in textiles for a screen woven entirely of plastics; a 1960 solo show of screens, paintings, textiles, and constructions at the Philadelphia Art Alliance; a 1962 *Wall Hangings* show at the Victoria and Albert Museum in London, where his piece was purchased for the collection; and as an invited exhibitor at the 1964 Milan Triennale. —TT

Ruth Sumners, "Weaving a Tale of Success," *Rocky Mountain News* (Denver, CO), June 5, 1973; *Sunrise Titles and Twills: Hangings by H. Theodore Hallman*, exh. cat. (Toronto: Royal Ontario Museum, 1978); Lisa Tremper Hanover, *Ted Hallman: Versatile Visionary* (Bethlehem, PA: ArtsQuest and Banana Factory, 2008); artist files, ACC library.

HARASZTY, ESZTER

Born September 28, 1920, Hungary; died November 30, 1994, Malibu, CA

TEXTILE DESIGNER

Eszter Haraszty arrived in the U.S. in 1946, after having received an art academy education in her native Budapest, where she also opened a screen printing shop. Originally Haraszty came to the U.S. to visit her sister and brother-in-law, but a Stalinist coup in Hungary made it difficult for her to return. Eventually Haraszty was able to take advantage of a connection to fellow Hungarian émigré, architect, and designer Marcel Breuer to secure a position at Knoll Associates, which produced some of Breuer's designs.

Haraszty's primary focus area at Knoll was textiles, and in 1949 she became director of the textile division, while also contributing to several other areas of the company including interiors and graphic design. She went on to win several Good Design Awards from MoMA for her work at Knoll. Haraszty worked for Knoll for ten years, during which time she also designed fashion for B. H. Wragge and Company, often based on the patterns of her upholstery textiles for Knoll. After leaving Knoll, Haraszty worked as a freelance designer on a number of projects including part of the interiors for the 1958 Brussels World's Fair Pavilion.

In 1960 Haraszty left New York for California after marrying television producer Bruce Colen. In California her lifestyle and aesthetic shifted dramatically, and she began to focus on handwork and embroidery, designing embroidery patterns for *McCall's* magazine and writing books on embroidery and the use of floral patterns, among other projects. —NE

Olga Gueft, "The Exhilarated World of Eszter Haraszty," *Interiors Magazine* 115 (May–July 1956), 94; Edith Ashbury, "Brussels Fair Restaurant Next Project for Designer," *New York Times*, October 7, 1957, 24; Peter Jost Blake, "Obituary," *Interior Design* 66 (February 1995), 29.

HARPER, IRVING
(NÉ IRVING HOFFZIMER)
Born July 14, 1916, New York, NY
DESIGNER, SCULPTOR

Through his activities with George Nelson and Herman Miller, Irving Harper has produced many iconic designs of the mid-twentieth century. The son of an Austrian-born bookbinder, Harper graduated from Brooklyn College and attended night school at Cooper Union, where he earned a certificate in architecture. He began his career in the 1930s as a draftsman in the Gilbert Rohde office, during which time he was engaged in designing the *Home Furnishings Focal* exhibit for the 1939 New York World's Fair. After the war he was hired by Raymond Loewy Associates, where he designed interiors for the department store division. Harper met George Nelson during the 1940s and was invited to join his firm in 1947, mostly working on trade advertising for the Herman Miller account. During his seventeen years with Nelson, however, he saw many of his ideas translated into production. The Herman Miller logo, first sketched in the late 1940s, was one of Harper's first creations for the company. The legendary Marshmallow Sofa manufactured by Herman Miller in 1956 was designed by Harper. His wide-ranging designs for sculptural and graphic clocks, which adorned countless American homes, were manufactured by the Howard Miller Clock Company beginning in 1949. Harper also created the Chronopak clock series for Howard Miller, as well as the playground of automotive parts for the Chrysler Pavilion at the 1964 World's Fair in New York. In the 1960s he also began to create what eventually became a large body of sculpture made from paper. These sculptures included abstract forms and fantastic animals, in addition to stylized masks and peoples inspired by South American, African, and Asian cultures. —MS

Martin Eidelberg, ed., *Design 1935–1965: What Modern Was—Selections from the Liliane and David M. Stewart Collection* (Montreal: Musée des arts décoratifs de Montreal; New York: Harry N. Abrams, 1991), 254–55, 308–9; Guy Trebay, "Undercover Icon," *New York Times Style Magazine*, May 2, 2010, 46L; Irving Harper, telephone conversation with Jeannine Falino, December 13, 2010.

HEATH, EDITH
(NÉE KIERTZNER)
Born May 25, 1911, Ida, IA;
died December 27, 2005, Tiburon, CA
CERAMIST, SCULPTOR, PAINTER, EDUCATOR

Devoted to ceramics as both functional ware and art, Edith Heath created distinctive dinnerware and architectural tiles for sixty years through Heath Ceramics, the small production company she and her husband established in 1948 in Sausalito, CA. She combined a craft-based heritage with clean and minimalist designs that satisfied the needs of a more relaxed, postwar American lifestyle where indoor/outdoor living had begun to take hold. Heath proved that quality need not be sacrificed to mass production and accessibility. Raised on a farm in Iowa, the second of seven children, she enrolled at the Chicago Normal School (later, Chicago Teachers College) in 1931 and found her direction as a teacher and artist through art education courses. In the late 1930s she studied sculpture and painting at the Art Institute of Chicago and worked at a Federal Art Project training school, where she was exposed to the ideas of Bauhaus émigré László Moholy-Nagy, then teaching in Chicago. In 1941, while working at an FAP children's camp, she met and married Brian Heath, and the two set out for San Francisco. On a stop in New Mexico they met Native American ceramist Maria Martinez, which inspired Heath to become a ceramist. In San Francisco, she taught art at the Presidio Hill School and audited ceramics classes at the California School of Fine Arts (later, San Francisco Art Institute). She began producing pieces on a potter's wheel converted by her husband from a treadle-powered sewing machine. Driven to understand the science of clay and glazes, Heath petitioned the University of California, Berkeley, extension program to host a year-long ceramic chemistry course. Working with a gas-fired kiln in the basement below her apartment, she became an expert on how different clay types affected the aesthetic qualities of her wares and she formulated a distinctive speckled glaze that would become a hallmark. Her solo exhibition at the California Palace of the Legion of Honor in 1944 brought her work to the attention of a buyer from Gump's department store in San Francisco. She was soon selling her dinnerware and accessories there and at Neiman Marcus, Marshall Field, Bullock's, and other venues. In 1946 Heath was one of ten artists invited to exhibit at the San Francisco Gift Show, where she met Nelson Gustin, who offered to represent her work and guaranteed to purchase a year's output. In 1948 Heath Ceramics was born and production was expanded to the small factory in Sausalito. In 1960, in addition to dinnerware, Heath began manufacturing architectural tiles. Heath Ceramics dinnerware patterns were used by Frank Lloyd Wright, Eero Saarinen, Alexander Girard, and other architects. The firm of Skidmore, Owings & Merrill applied her tiles on the exteriors of such commissions as the Norton Simon Museum. In 1950 curator Edgar Kaufmann Jr. included her work in MoMA's permanent collection. In 2003 the company was sold to Cathy Bailey and Robin Petravic, who are continuing the Heath Ceramics line. —TT

Steven Skov Holt, "Edith Heath (1911–2005)," *I.D.* 53 (2006), 90–91; Amos Klausner, *Heath Ceramics: The Complexity of Simplicity* (San Francisco: Chronicle Books, 2006); Marsha Ginsberg, "Edith Heath: Renowned Ceramist," *San Francisco Chronicle*, January 1, 2006, B-6.

HEATON, MAURICE
Born April 2, 1900, Neuchâtel, Switzerland;
died April 6, 1990, Rockland County, NY
GLASS ARTIST

A pioneer studio glass artist whose work reflects a Bauhaus perspective—simple, well-designed, everyday objects executed in easily reproducible forms—Heaton brought an appreciation of modern art and an understanding of engineering to the craft of glass design and production. Heaton was the first glass artist to create in a modernist idiom. He is best known for lighting fixtures, murals, plaques, and screens, and for fused and enameled tableware (plates and bowls) displaying abstract and spiraling patterns or whimsical figures in the spirit of Paul Klee and the cave paintings at Lascaux, France. The Heaton family moved to New York City in 1914, and from 1915 to 1919 Heaton was a scholarship student at the progressive Ethical Culture School. He credits that experience with teaching him the importance of experimentation, a quality later helpful as he developed his own glassmaking techniques. One of the science teachers suggested engineering as a profession, and from 1920 to 1921 Heaton attended the Stevens Institute of Technology in Hoboken, NJ. Although Heaton soon realized he was better suited for a life as an artist—he was a third-generation glassmaker who had learned the trade from his father—he frequently used his training as an engineer for the design and creation of kilns and tools unique to glassmaking. In the 1930s when the demand for stained glass in revivalist styles diminished, Heaton turned to modernism. As a result of his friendship with textile designer Ruth Reeves (who had boarded with the Heaton family while a student at Pratt Institute), his glass work was exhibited in the late 1920s at the American Designer Gallery, and Heaton began meeting such modernist designers as Henry Varnum Poor, Joseph Urban, and Donald Deskey. The sconces and ceiling lights he contributed to industrial art exhibitions at The Metropolitan Museum of Art in 1931 and 1934 brought him recognition, and for ten years he designed lighting fixtures for the Lightolier Company. During this same period he also began a fruitful association with Eugene Schoen, a prominent interior designer with whom he developed innovative glass murals and screens decorated with abstract geometric patterns or cubist motifs that were then incorporated into large architectural projects. His signature plates, bowls, and tableware began as a sideline to his mural and lamp work. Intended for everyday use, his tableware was initially sold in the New

York specialty shops of Eugene Schoen and Rena Rosenthal and later at America House. In the mid-1940s when his affiliation with the Lightolier Company ended, Heaton refocused his interests on the technical aspects of glass-making. In 1947 he invented a process of fusing crushed crystals of enamel to glass, later adapting the technique to lamination, which was especially successful for large plaques. Enamelist Karl Drerup assisted Heaton, and the process they devised resulted in glass with more luminous and brilliant effects than could be achieved with vitreous glazes. In the 1960s Heaton experimented with mobiles and multicolored fused glass wall sculptures. —TT

Eleanor Bittermann, "Heaton's Wizardry with Glass," *CH* 14 (May 1954), 10–14; Karen Davies, "Maurice Heaton: American Pioneer in Studio Glass," *AC* 44 (August/ September, 1984), 50–54; artist file, ACC library. For earlier history see *Craft in the Machine Age*, 236.

HERNMARCK, HELENA

Born April 22, 1941, Stockholm, Sweden

TAPESTRY ARTIST

Helena Hernmarck is a tapestry artist, a title she chose for herself since her Swedish job description—a *textilkonstnar* (artisan highly trained in the design and production of decorative and functional fabrics)—has no easy English translation. Hernmarck's weavings are innovative and picto-rial, highly textured and richly colored. She is known for her enlarged hyperrealistic images. Hernmarck began to weave in 1958 during a six-month program in Stockholm sponsored by the Association of Friends of the Textile Arts, and she entered the University College of Arts, Crafts, and Design in Stockholm the following year. She graduated in 1963, married engineer Jan Barynin, and in 1964 moved to Montreal. In 1965 Hernmarck participated in the first of three sequential Tapestry Biennials in Lausanne and also wove two tapestries for the 1967 World's Fair in Montreal. A savvy businesswoman, Hernmarck traveled across the U.S. in 1967 and 1972, presenting her portfolio to major archi-tectural firms. Her first trip resulted in a commission from the Weyerhauser Company in Seattle. The piece, *Rainforest*, was installed in 1971 in the company's corporate offices, the first of many monumental tapestries created by Hernmarck to enhance commercial architecture. —JG

Lawrence Knowles, "Found in Translation: The Life and Art of Helena Hernmarck," *Fiberarts* 26 (January–February 2000), 28–34; Edie Cohen, "A Weave for All Seasons," *Interior Design* (New York) 77 (March 2006), 120, 122.

HICKS, SHEILA

(MRS. ENRIQUE ZANARTU)

Born July 24, 1934, Hastings, NE

FIBER ARTIST

In the 1960s Sheila Hicks was among a select group of international artists whose highly original thread construc-tions were both widely used by modern architects and interior designers and embraced by artisans throughout the world as a point of reference for an aesthetic and economic revitalization of their countries' traditional handcrafts.

Hicks produces individual wall hangings, sculptures, bas reliefs, and installations from recycled material. Her pieces exhibit a fusion of archaic and modern weaving techniques—pre-Columbian, Persian, and Indian twining, knotting, netting, and wrapping, as well as the language of Bauhaus constructivism. Her work reveals a mastery of structural organization and complex design, and she intro-duced new forms intrinsic to soft sculpture. In one piece, for example, knotted and wrapped construction relates to methods of the indigenous Zapotec Indians; it was created with Rufino Reyes for Jack Lenor Larsen's *Fabrics International* exhibition at the MCC in 1961.

Hicks's family heritage includes a "long line of home-steaders" who made their own dish towels from linen flax, and she describes her youth as "migratory," with thread representing "continuity" as her family moved from city to city (Werther 1971a). She began her academic training at Syracuse University (1952–54), studying Greek mythology, engraving, and lithography. She then moved to Yale University, where she earned both a BFA (1957) and an MFA (1959) and studied painting with Josef Albers and Rico Lebrun. Her focus shifted when she discovered pre-Columbian textiles in a course on Andean art history offered by George Kubler. Her interest in architecture developed under the tutelage of architectural historian Vincent Scully. These professors, as well as weaver Anni Albers and curator Junius Bird, an expert in pre-Columbian textiles at the American Museum of Natural History, were Hicks's most influential mentors during the early years of her career. She was awarded a Fulbright Travel Grant for a trip to the Andes (1957–58). She also visited Chile and Peru, where she researched Andean weaving and produced "miniatures" on her portable frame loom. In 1959–60 she was given a Fribourg Society Scholarship for painting and weaving in France. She also studied and lived in Mexico (1960–63), establishing an experimental workshop in Taxco and working with Mexican weavers. She taught design in the architecture department of the Universidad de Mexico in Mexico City. During this period she collaborated with Claire Zeisler in the study of pre-Inca techniques; her *White Letter Series* was acquired by MoMA, and her work was shown at exhibitions in Milan, Italy (1962); Caracas, Venezuela (1963); and in New York (*Woven Forms* at MCC in 1963).

Hicks moved to Paris in 1963 and opened a tapestry studio, Atelier des Grands-Augustins. During the 1960s her career took on a two-pronged focus—she completed impor-tant architectural commissions for companies, foundations, and design centers, and brought a new awareness of textile art and design to museums and industry, using her talents to encourage the development of worldwide local craft initiatives. She also worked as the design director for the Commonwealth Trust, Ltd., at the handweaving workshop located in Calicut, Kerala, India, encouraging the weavers to remain loyal to their own weaving tradition. In a Chilean village menaced by famine and drought, she helped estab-lish a textile studio, Taller Artesanal Huaquen. Managed by twenty-five sheepherders and their families, it produced contemporary textile and tapestries sold in design centers

throughout the world. In Morocco she was invited to help revitalize part of that country's traditional rug industry and asked to serve as permanent consultant to the Moroccan National Crafts Council. —TT

Betty Werther, "Radical Rugs from Rabat," *Design* (London) *270* (June 1971a), 48–53; Betty Werther, "Sheila Hicks at Rabat," *CH* 31 (June 1971b): 30–33; Nina Stritzler-Levine, ed., *Sheila Hicks: Weaving as Metaphor* (New York: Bard Graduate Center for Studies in the Decorative Arts, Design, and Culture; London: Yale University Press, 2006).

HIGGINS, FRANCES

(NÉE STEWART)

Born December 24, 1912, Haddock, GA; died February 12, 2004, Riverside, IL

HIGGINS, MICHAEL

Born September 29, 1908, London, England; died February 13, 1999, Riverside, IL

GLASS ARTISTS

Frances and Michael Higgins are recognized as pioneers of the American studio glass movement. In 1948, in kilns behind the sofa in their Chicago apartment, the couple launched Higgins Glass Studio, a company that created technologically daring, laminated, fused, and enameled glass with bold textures, saturated colors, and in patterns inspired by the art of Joan Miró, Alexander Calder, and the surrealists. Over the next five decades, the work they fabricated ranged from mass-produced platters, dishes, bowls, and trays to jewelry, room dividers, mobiles, and church windows. By the late 1940s, when Frances came to the Institute of Design in Chicago to earn her MFA, she was an assistant professor at the University of Georgia teaching design and crafts. Earlier, she had earned a BS from Georgia State College for Women (now Georgia College & State University). In Chicago, Michael was one of her instructors. He had attended Eton as a King's Scholar and had then studied at Cambridge University and the London Central School of Arts and Crafts but had never earned a university degree. In 1938 he came to America working first in New Orleans as a graphic designer before moving to Chicago in 1947 to head the visual design department at the Institute of Design. When Michael and Frances married in 1948, they left their respective academic positions and set out to make their living producing and selling fused enameled glass. From 1949 to 1951 they worked out of their Oak Street apartment. Encouraged to develop a line of products to sell wholesale, they secured a $1,500 loan, moved to N. Wells Street, occupied rooms above their studio, and from 1951 to 1959 developed their business. Working fourteen-hour days, seven days a week, the Higginses, with a staff of eight, eventually marketed their work through a broker who placed their glass with boutiques and at such retailers as Marshall Field, Gump's, Bloomingdale's, Georg Jensen, and Bullock's Wilshire. They also sold at arts festivals and crafts fairs. From 1959 to 1965 they earned royalties from designs sold to the Dearborn Glass Company, a large industrial manufacturer of sheet glass. There they refined their skills, made mass-produced tableware, and an array of ashtrays. They marked their pieces with the distinctive gold "Higgins" stamp and took advantage of the opportunity to send their work to exhibitions, including the seminal *Glass 1959* at the Corning Museum of Glass, where their experimental techniques were praised by curator Alex von Saldern. The relationship with Dearborn ended in 1965 and the couple briefly became affiliated with Haeger Potteries, but by 1966 they had bought back their equipment, purchased a building in Riverside, IL, opened a studio and showroom, and moved into an upstairs apartment. The business continued as an independent entity for the rest of their lives. Michael also became involved in the professionalization of handcrafts. In 1953 he was a founding member of the Midwest-Designer Craftsmen, the first regional organization for craftspeople. In 1956 he attended a meeting called by Aileen Osborn Webb to discuss the reorganization of the American Craftsmen's Educational Council. He advocated for the inclusion of craftspeople on the board of trustees, and as a result became one of the first working craftsmen so elected. In 1961 he delivered an address at the fourth National Conference of the American Craftsmen's Council. —TT

Donald-Brian Johnson and Leslie Piña, *Higgins: Adventures in Glass* (Atglen, PA: Schiffer Publishing, 1997); Julie V. Iovine, "Michael Higgins, an Innovator in Glass Design, Is Dead," *New York Times,* March 7, 1999, 99; obituaries by Edward Lebow and Donald-Brian Johnson, *AC* 64 (June–July 2004), 21, 25l; artist files, ACC library.

HOPKINS, JACK ROGERS
Born December 28, 1920, Modesto, CA;
died March 30, 2006, Alpine, CA
WOOD SCULPTOR, FURNITURE DESIGNER

Jack Rogers Hopkins linked art, design, and furniture and contributed to the formation of the studio art movement on the West Coast. As a young boy he created wooden toys for his friends in his father's woodshop in a furniture factory. After high school, Hopkins enlisted in the U.S. Navy as a photographer and was stationed in Pearl Harbor. Following the war, he attended the California College of Arts and Crafts (now California College of the Arts) in Oakland, where he studied painting and drawing, and he earned an MFA from California's Claremont Colleges. Hopkins began teaching at Bakersfield High School and Modesto Junior College between 1950 and 1961 before moving to San Diego State University, where he was a faculty professor for the next thirty years, retiring in 1991. Hopkins's teaching career paralleled a concurrent career in art. His first interest was in becoming a watercolorist, but the medium was not physical enough, and he complained that a two-dimensional surface was too limiting. Hopkins next experimented with sculpture in wood, clay, and metal, creating unusual sensual shapes inspired by the potter's wheel. Working with wood evolved after a successful and established career in ceramics and jewelry. It was Hopkins's stack-laminated and elegantly swooping

furniture, influenced by Scandinavian modern furniture and the work of Wendell Castle, which brought him acclaim in the mid-1960s and established him in the vanguard of the California studio furniture movement.

Hopkins defined himself as a designer-craftsman who made limited edition works using the stack-lamination method. While laminated furniture—whereby thin layers of wood are stacked, glued, and set with clamps—had been made for generations, Hopkins's version employed an automated high-frequency wood welder, which accelerated the slow, labor-intensive process, curing the glue in minutes. Hopkins also employed ¾-inch wood stock (½-inch was the norm), which permitted sturdier arcs, resulting in organic, sculptural shapes made with vibrant wood grains and color combinations. Hopkins executed his designs in hardwoods—walnut, cherry, mahogany, maple, and rosewood—without assistants. He always carried a sketchbook that included planned works and philosophical thoughts inspired by forms in nature such as driftwood and dried bones. Hopkins was a frequent participant in the California Design exhibitions held at the Pasadena Museum of Art. Throughout the 1970s he experimented with combining furniture functions in a single piece, such as a table-chair-lamp. His monumental 1972 *Womb Room* was thirteen feet long, six feet deep, and seven feet tall, made with four interlocking parts: a radio, speaker, bookshelf, and footrest. After its initial exhibition at the Pasadena Museum of Art (where it did not sell), Hopkins burned it rather than store it, reiterating his philosophy that the creative process was more important than the final product. —LB

Cooke, Ward, and L'Ecuyer 2004, 123; Jo Lauria, Suzanne Baizerman et al., *California Design: The Legacy of West Coast Craft and Style* (San Francisco, CA: Chronicle Books, 2005); Todd Merrill and Julie V. Iovine, eds. *Modern Americana: Studio Furniture from High Craft to High Glam* (New York: Rizzoli, 2008).

HUI, KA-KWONG
Born August 16, 1922, Hong Kong, China;
died October 17, 2003, Caldwell, NJ
CERAMIST, EDUCATOR

The ceramics of Ka-Kwong Hui have a primitive quality both in surface decoration and the organic forms such as double gourd shapes, attenuated or bloated bottles, and squashed vases. His later, more linear work has been associated with pop art, though each has a distinctive playful quality. He experimented widely in his surface decoration, using loose brushwork, wax-resist techniques, photo transfer, and low-fire glazes. Hui found inspiration in sources ranging from Chinese bronze and jade sculpture to architectural elements.

Between 1940 and 1944, Hui studied painting and sculpture at the Shanghai School of Fine Arts and the Kwong Tung School of Art in Quangzhou (Canton). After working as an apprentice in China, he traveled to San Francisco in 1948 and studied ceramics under Marguerite and Frans Wildenhain at their Pond Farm Workshops. He then attended the State University of New York, College of

Ceramics at Alfred University, earning his MFA in 1952. After graduation he became head of the ceramics department at the Brooklyn Museum Art School. He also exhibited his own work widely. During the 1950s and '60s he lectured and taught summer courses at both the Haystack Mountain School of Crafts in Maine and the Brookfield Craft Center in Connecticut. In 1964 he joined the faculty of Douglass College at Rutgers University (later Mason Gross School of the Arts), where his teaching has been described as gentle and attuned to student exploration, being presented "by example. He never stood still with his own work" (Tsubota 2003).

In 1964–65, he collaborated on a series of ceramic works with pop artist Roy Lichtenstein, creating the molds, glazes, and overglazes for mannequin head and crockery sculptures. This experience led Hui to experiment with hard-edged glazes in his own work, resulting in bold, geometric, yet whimsical forms. In 1969 his work was included in *Objects: USA*. He won several distinguished prizes for ceramics, including an NEA grant in 1976. He retired from Rutgers in 1988 and continued to produce new work, including a series of large ceramic sculptures and lidded forms based on the phoenix and other birds. —CK

Ann Tsubota, "Ka Kwong Hui, 1922–2003," *Studio Potter* 32 (December 2003), 92; Margaret Carney, "Hui Ka Kwong," *Ceramics Monthly* 53 (May 2005), 42.

JENNINGS, CARL
Born April 10, 1910, Marion, IL;
died May 18, 2003, San Pablo, CA
METALWORKER, WOODWORKER

Carl Jennings's work as a blacksmith was an essential part of his life, from his youth until his death at age ninety-three. Jennings, whose mother died soon after he was born, was largely raised by his grandmother, but as a teenager he went to live with his blacksmith father and stepmother in Texas. The family moved to San Francisco, and in 1928 Jennings joined his father in the blacksmith shop of Pacific Gas and Electric. After being laid off in 1931, he registered as a student at the California College of Arts and Crafts (now California College of the Arts)—working as a janitor, cutting firewood, and assisting the grounds crew to support himself and pay for classes. One of the few blacksmithing students, Jennings studied with Harry Dixon, who had worked in Dirk Van Erp's studio, and earned his applied art certificate in 1934.

After graduation Jennings worked as a journeyman in several blacksmith shops in the San Francisco Bay Area, and in 1947 he opened his own studio, El Diablo Forge, in Lafayette, CA. The shop specialized in decorative metalwork—light fixtures, gates, and fireplace accessories—using steel, copper, and brass. Described as generous, spontaneous, and passionate, Jennings imbued his metalwork with elements of delight, surprise, and energy. In addition to his independent work habits, Jennings also made or modified special tools in order to execute his own hollow, raised, and other forms. After closing the El Diablo Forge in 1969, he and his wife, Elizabeth Gallagan, spent five years building the round stone house, fifty feet in diameter, in Sonoma County that was his masterpiece. It contained patterned and colored concrete lintels, as well as a chased and raised central copper stove. Throughout this period Jennings continued to experiment with his metal-work and in later years with a hydraulic press.

Jennings's work has been exhibited in the de Young Museum, San Francisco Museum of Art (now San Francisco Museum of Modern Art), and Oakland Museum, and he has had solo shows at the Richmond Art Center in Richmond, CA (1964) and the Anneberg Gallery in San Francisco (1967). In 1988 he was elected to the College of Fellows of the American Craft Council and honored with a lifetime achievement award from the Artist-Blacksmiths' Association of North America. In 1990 the National Ornamental Metal Museum had a solo exhibition of his work and named him that year's master metalsmith. —CK

F. Jack Hurley, "Benchmark: C. Carl Jennings," *Metalsmith* 11 (spring 1991), 34–37; "Anvil Interview: Carl Jennings," *Anvil Magazine* (June 1992), 12–16, 29–31.

KAGAN, VLADIMIR
Born 1927, Worms, Germany
FURNITURE DESIGNER

Vladimir Kagan created organic furniture forms, some with tapered legs, others with cantilevered seats floating on translucent Plexiglas legs. The omnibus sofa, barrel chair, and kidney-shaped couch are classic Kagan designs. Using walnut wood, stainless steel, polished aluminum, and Plexiglas, he combined innovative design with functionality, creating a variety of interior landscapes. Kagan's family fled Nazi Germany and immigrated to the U.S. in 1938 when he was eleven years old. The family consisted of three generations of furniture enthusiasts; his grandfather owned an avant-garde folk-art store in Dachau, and his father, Illi, was a Russian master cabinetmaker who set up a wood-working shop in New York City. Kagan studied architecture and design at Columbia University but soon joined his father in the family shop.

Kagan's furniture designs were inspired by scenes from his childhood, by the folk furniture he had seen in his grandfather's shop, as well as Danish modern furniture, and his own exploration of woodworking and fabrication technologies. A zeppelin he saw in Germany as a young boy led to his first celebrated design, a curvaceous barrel chair of 1947 in which form follows function. The chair was not dependent on springs and cushions for comfort, but rather employed innovative materials, including rubber strapping and foam rubber. In 1948 Kagan opened a retail store on East Fifty-sixth Street in New York that sold avant-garde ceramics, textiles, and fine art, as well as furniture, and within two years he partnered with Hugo Dreyfuss, a lace manufacturer and artisan. The business moved to Madison Avenue supported by an eminent clientele, largely from the realm of arts and entertainment. In 1950 Kagan introduced the serpentine sofa. In addition to private commissions, Kagan designed furniture for public spaces, including hotels and offices, where sophisticated informality was his

signature, and ergonomics and new shapes defined his style. His three-legged tables were inspired by tree roots and had a dual function: turned upside down they could be used as three-point supports for wider surfaces. By 1958 Kagan's powder-coated stainless steel for both indoor and outdoor furniture was widely used in contemporary American furniture design. —LB

Vladimir Kagan et al., *The Complete Kagan: Vladimir Kagan, A Lifetime of Avant-Garde Design* (New York: Pointed Leaf, 2004); Todd Merrill and Julie V. Iovine, eds., *Modern Americana: Studio Furniture from High Craft to High Glam* (New York: Rizzoli, 2008), 113–14.

KANEKO, JUN
Born July 13, 1942, Nagoya, Japan
CERAMIST

Jun Kaneko began his artistic career as a painter in Japan, studying with Satoshi Ogawa. When Kaneko decided to pursue graduate studies in the U.S., Ogawa introduced him to California ceramic artist Jerry Rothman. Upon arriving in Los Angeles in August 1963, Kaneko stayed with the collectors Fred and Mary Marer, who at the time had already acquired hundreds of pieces of contempo-rary ceramic art. The Marers introduced Kaneko to the many of the key artists who were revolutionizing ceramic art in California. Kaneko made his first ceramic works in Rothman's studio in the summer of 1964. A flat, painted piece was included in a national show at the Everson Museum of Art in Syracuse, NY, the same year. Kaneko began to study informally with Ralph Bacerra at Chouinard Art Institute in Los Angeles (now the California Institute of the Arts) in 1964, before going on to work with Peter Voulkos at the University of California, Berkeley, in 1966. In 1967 Kaneko was one of the first artists-in-residence at the Archie Bray Foundation in Montana. He graduated with an MFA from Scripps College in Claremont, CA, in 1971 after studying with Paul Soldner. His background as a painter and his fascination with patterns is evident in the striped and polka-dot surface decoration on his work, as well as his careful placement of objects in space. This concern, along with his studies with Voulkos, with whom he had a two-person show in 1968, encouraged Kaneko to work on a large scale. Today he is perhaps best known as a maker of monumental sculptures and installations. —JG

Robert Silberman, "Jun Kaneko," *AC* 60 (October/November 2000), 84–89, 112; Jun Kaneko, oral history interview by Mary Drach McInnes, May 23 and 24, 2005, AAA, SI.

KAPEL, JOHN
Born June 17, 1922, Cleveland, OH
FURNITURE MAKER AND DESIGNER

A leader of the modern California crafts movement, John Kapel effortlessly blended studio furniture making with industrial design. After earning a bachelor's degree at the Ohio Wesleyan University (1947), he trained for two years in Prague, then-capital of Czechoslovakia, and returned to the U.S. to earn an MFA in industrial design

at Cranbrook (1950). Kapel joined the George Nelson Design Office in New York in 1952, but inspired by the work of furniture designer and woodworker Sam Maloof, he moved to California two years later with his wife, sculptor Priscilla Kapel. The couple built a house in Woodside, thirty-five miles south of San Francisco, which included a woodworking and cabinetmaking studio. Kapel began to produce prototypes for local furniture manufacturers while taking studio commissions for handmade chairs, cabinets, and tables, primarily of wood but with other materials as well, such as Formica, cane, and leather. He worked for more than twenty years for the firm Glenn of California and with the Japanese company Kosuda Furniture, which manufactured Kapel's work internationally. Kapel also created custom furniture, cabinets, doors, and wall pieces for private clients, often in collaboration with his wife, and participated to numerous exhibitions in California. —MS

"Cabinet Maker's Dream House," *Interiors* 121 (November 1961), 132–35; *California Design 9* (Pasadena, CA: Pasadena Art Museum, 1965), 13, 91–2, 110; *Fine Woodworking Design Book 2* (Newtown, CT: Taunton Press, 1979), 85.

KARNES, KAREN
(FORMERLY MRS. DAVID WEINRIB)
Born November 17, 1925, New York, NY
CERAMIST

Karen Karnes is a self-supporting, independent studio potter who has produced traditional and sculptural ceramic vessels since the 1950s. Her output encompasses func-tional ware for the home—plates, bowls, mugs, lidded jars, and casseroles—as well as such larger coil-built pieces as garden seats and fountains, fireplaces and ovens, and basins set into bathroom counters or on pedestals. The daughter of Russian immigrants who worked in the New York garment industry, Karnes was independent-minded from an early age. Without her parents' knowledge, she applied to and was accepted by the High School of Music and Art in Manhattan when she was just eleven years old. After high school graduation Karnes earned a BA at Brooklyn College (1946), studying with British architect and educator Serge Chermayeff. From him she learned the Bauhaus approach to the arts, which she described as an imaginative and skillful use of materials. Yet it was not until she met David Weinrib (whom she married, had a son with, and later divorced) that she had her first experience with clay. In 1947 Weinrib went to work at the Design Techniques factory, in Stroudsburg, PA, where he made clay lamp bases, vases, and dinnerware. Karnes joined him there in 1949 and became a production sprayer. When Weinrib brought her a lump of clay, Karnes found her medium. Rather than work on the potter's wheel, she began to carve and hand-build the clay. In 1950 the couple went to Italy, spending a year and a half at Sesto Fiorentino, a pottery village outside Florence, where Karnes learned to throw on the wheel. Back in the U.S. and on a fellowship, she studied with Charles Harder at Alfred University (1951–52). But the following year, rather than completing a master's degree, Karnes managed the pottery at Black Mountain College with Weinrib, in a studio designed and built by Robert Turner. After a semester they were invited to stay on as resident potters. Karnes's high-fire kiln was one of the first in the region, and income from work sold through the Southern Highland Handicraft Guild covered pottery expenses. From 1952 to 1954 the couple benefited from the college's remarkable creative energy. They met a wide range of avant-garde artists, and in 1952 they organized an important workshop with Bernard Leach, Shoji Hamada, and Soetsu Yanagi that was moderated by Marguerite Wildenhain. Strongly influenced by Hamada's approach to pottery-making, Karnes regards him as her most important mentor, and she follows his example of daily contact with materials and tools. In 1954, with an invitation to become founding members of an artists' housing cooperative at Stony Point, NY, Karnes and Weinrib returned to the Northeast, joining poet and potter M. C. Richards, her husband David Tudor, musician John Cage, architect Paul Williams, and his wife Vera, in a venture called The Land. The first workshop built at Stony Point was the pottery shared by Karnes, Richards, and Weinrib. The work Karnes made there established her reputation, and in 1958 she was awarded a Tiffany Fellowship. Karnes and Richards developed a flame-proof clay that enabled them to make ceramic cookware, and the pots Karnes produced spoke strongly of form, function, and process. In 1966 while teaching at Penland, Karnes fired a salt kiln. For the next ten years she produced salt-glazed pottery that sold well in such New York venues as Bonnier's, Georg Jensen, and America House. Throughout the 1950s and '60s, Karnes also sent her work to such exhibitions as the Ceramic Nationals in Syracuse (1950, 1958), *Fiber-Clay-Metal* (1953), the Milan Triennale (1964), and *Objects: USA* (1969). —TT

Karen Karnes, oral history interview by Mark Shapiro, August 9 and 10, 2005, AAA, SI; Karnes and Mark Shapiro, *A Chosen Path: The Ceramic Art of Karen Karnes* (Chapel Hill, NC: University of North Carolina Press, 2010).

KAUFMANN, EDGAR JR.

Born April 9, 1910, Pittsburgh, PA;
died July 31, 1989, New York, NY
CURATOR, ART HISTORIAN

Edgar Kaufmann Jr. was born to a wealthy Pittsburgh family. His father, Edgar J. Kaufmann Sr., ran a successful department store business, and the family wealth allowed the younger Kaufmann to travel widely to Italy, Austria, and England, in pursuit of an art education. When he returned to the U.S. in 1933, he apprenticed himself to Frank Lloyd Wright as part of Wright's Taliesin Fellowship. It was this connection that led his father to commission Wright to build the family a country house in Pennsylvania, and today Fallingwater is acknowledged as one of Wright's most accomplished and iconic works.

In 1935, he returned to Pittsburgh to work for the family business as a merchandise manager in home furnishings. Meanwhile, Fallingwater had attracted the interest of John McAndrew, MoMA's curator of architecture and industrial

design, and an exhibition on the house took place in 1938. For his part, Kaufmann proposed and became deeply involved with the museum's *Organic Design* exhibition, and the experience convinced him of the need to change careers. He moved to New York City in 1940 and became head of MoMA's influential industrial design department. Between 1950 and 1955 Kaufmann instituted and oversaw the series of Good Design exhibitions put on as a partnership between MoMA and the Chicago Merchandise Mart. The series focused on educating the public in what was considered good home design, and it also represented an unusual partnership between business and the museum world.

Kaufmann was a longtime adjunct professor of architectural history at Columbia University, as well as the founder of the Architectural History Foundation, and the author of several books on Frank Lloyd Wright. —NE

Paul Goldberger, "Edgar Kaufmann Jr., 79, Architecture Historian," *New York Times,* August 1, 1989, A17.

KELLEY, ALTON

Born June 17, 1940, Houldon, ME;
died June 1, 2008, Petaluma, CA
GRAPHIC ARTIST

MILLER, STANLEY GEORGE

[A.K.A. STANLEY MOUSE]
Born October 10, 1940, Fresno, CA
GRAPHIC ARTIST

A motorcycle racer who painted pinstripes on biker gas tanks before his move in 1964 to the Haight-Ashbury district of San Francisco, Alton Kelley became famous, with his collaborator, Detroit native Stanley "Mouse" Miller, for creating some of the most memorable posters of the psychedelic era. Miller, raised in Detroit, was a precocious artist and also a painter of hot rod art. Between 1966 and about 1968, the duo designed numerous posters for many emerging names in rock music, including Big Brother & The Holding Company, Quicksilver Messenger Service, Bo Diddley, and the Grateful Dead. An early poster by Kelley and Miller drew its inspiration from the logo of Zig-Zag cigarette rolling paper—with its proverbial Zouave soldier (who, when his pipe was broken, rolled a cigarette using paper torn from his bag of gunpowder) and eccentric typeface. This format became a leitmotif for many posters of the era, with the head of a figure, or an object either drawn or extracted from an old photograph or film still, surrounded by imaginative lettering based on sources as varied as old "Wanted" posters and art nouveau. The duo found much of their visual material in the public library; catholic in their taste, they surveyed Native American, Chinese, art nouveau, art deco, modern, Bauhaus, and any other visual material that took their fancy. Their signature "skull and roses" poster for the Grateful Dead, for instance, is a close copy of an illustration by Edmund J. Sullivan in *The Rubáiyát of Omar Khayyám* (1859).

Kelley, Stanley Mouse, Wes Wilson, Rick Griffin, and Victor Moscoso, known as the San Francisco Five, formed Family Dog Productions with promoter Chet Helms to mount rock music dances. Kelley and Mouse produced

posters through the late sixties and early seventies to publicize local bands and light shows that mostly appeared at the Avalon Ballroom and the Longshoreman's Hall in San Francisco. Later, they worked in the same capacity for Bill Graham and his shows at the Fillmore Auditorium. All employed intense colors combinations with exaggerated lettering that en masse, possessed a nervous energy. The group was featured in a *Life* magazine article of September 1, 1967, that described their work as a "phantasmagoria of best-selling avant-garde" (Selvin 2008).

By 1968 Helms and Graham were seeking out other graphic artists to produce their posters, but in the early 1970s both Kelley and Mouse found a burgeoning market in designing album covers, particularly for the Grateful Dead and Journey. —JF

Joel Selvin, "Alton Kelley, Psychedelic Poster Creator, Dies," *San Francisco Chronicle*, June 3, 2008, B-5; "Stanley Mouse," Wikipedia, Wikipedia.org/wiki/Stanley_Mouse.

KING, ROBERT J.

Born January 17, 1917, Madison, WI
SILVERSMITH, ENAMELIST, INDUSTRIAL DESIGNER

Robert J. King earned his BA from the University of Wisconsin in 1940, studying metalwork with John Van Koert, in whose commercial jewelry and novelty firm he worked during and after his undergraduate training. After serving in the U.S. Air Force (1943–46), King enrolled at the School for American Craftsmen (1947–49), where his teachers included John Prip, Laurits Christian Eichner, and Mitzi Otten. King worked mainly in industrial design, first with Towle Silversmiths in Massachusetts and, beginning in 1962, with the International Silver Company in Connecticut. His sleek, simple *Contour* pattern (1951) made Towle the industry leader in innovative modern design for sterling silver flatware. Later, King produced the *Celestial Centerpiece*, a six-light silver and sapphire-studded candelabrum for International Silver's *Moon Room* exhibit at the 1964 New York World's Fair.

King also worked independently in flatware, hollow-ware, jewelry, and enamels. His pieces were exhibited in numerous nationally juried exhibitions. In 1953 a silver decanter by King was included in *Designer Craftsmen U.S.A.,* and his work was included in the 1958 Brussels World's Fair. Responding to the popularity of enameling on metal in the 1950s, the Museum of Contemporary Crafts (now the Museum of Art and Design) commissioned ten artists to produce pieces that demonstrated various enameling techniques. The results were exhibited in *Enamels* in 1959. King's covered silver box illustrated the champlevé technique. One of his six-piece silver and enamel flatware place settings was also included in the landmark exhibition *Objects: USA.* —JP

Enamels, exh. cat. (New York: American Craftsman's Council, 1959), 13, 23; *Objects: USA,* 178; Jewel Stern, *Modernism in American Silver* (New Haven: Yale University Press, 2005), 197–99, 336.

KINGTON, L. BRENT

Born July 26, 1934, Topeka, KS
METALSMITH, EDUCATOR

L. Brent Kington introduced the ancient craft of black-smithing to higher education over a long career at Southern Illinois University, Carbondale. After graduating from Topeka High School, which had a thriving art program, he spent his college years at the University of Kansas at Lawrence, under Carlyle Smith. Kington went on to Cranbook, and while studying for his MFA, he began to accept outside projects, for a time considering a career in industrial design. After earning his degree in 1961, he interviewed with Oneida Silver and with Raymond Loewy Associates, but his Cranbrook metals professor Richard Thomas intervened, urging him to take a teaching position at Carbondale instead, which he did; he remained there until his retirement in 1997.

Kington's early career was spent working with the lost-wax process. He began by emulating Ashanti gold weights that he had admired while at Cranbrook. He fashioned small birds, fish, and other creatures, each one animated with piercing eyes and curious stances. When his children were born in the early 1960s, Kington began to fashion silver toys using the same technique. These pieces first took the forms of bells, soldiers, and cannon that gradually grew in size and complexity to become tricycles, dragsters, and charming air machines, peopled with an assortment of amusing, often bird-beaked figures that he likened to himself.

The blacksmithing phase of his career began in 1964 when he traveled to New York to attend the First World Craft Council. While in the city, he saw the ferrous metal-work then on view in The Metropolitan Museum of Art and was catapulted into a personal odyssey that led him to seek out books, tools, artifacts, and the dwindling number of smithies that still practiced this once common trade. In 1970 he held the first modern conference on black-smithing, a landmark event attended by students from around the country. From 1972 onward Kington shared his discoveries in a classroom setting, while in the studio he pursued a gestural, linear expression in iron. A founding member of the Society of North American Goldsmiths (SNAG) and the Artist Blacksmith's Association of North America (ABANA), he received the Gold Medal from the American Craft Council (2000), the Award of Distinction from SNAG (1983), and the Bealer Award of Distinction from ABANA (1983). —JF

L. Brent Kington, oral history interview by Mary Douglas, May 3–4, 2001, AAA, SI; Jeannine Falino, "The Lyrical Gesture in Iron," in *L. Brent Kington, Mythic Metalsmith* (Springfield, IL: Illinois State Museum Society, 2008), 24–35.

KOTTLER, HOWARD

Born March 5, 1930, Cleveland, OH;
died January 21, 1989, Seattle, WA
CERAMIST, EDUCATOR

The enormous body of work created by Howard Kottler relates art historically to surrealism, pop art, Funk, and conceptual art, and takes aim at "fine" art, politics, sexual mores, and religious dogma. While reality, illusion, and humor were Kottler's chief concerns, he was also interested in the history of styles, readymade materials, and recycled art conventions. During the 1960s his two series—art deco and decal china plates—demonstrated his awareness of the psychological value of outrageous theatrics and his ability to challenge, undermine, and deviate from the traditional foundations of fine and decorative arts. With such Funk-inspired pieces as *Gilt Feeler* (1966) and *Bunny Hop Pot* (1970), Kottler introduced fur, bright colors, and glaring metallic and hobby-shop glazes still considered taboo then. He played with sexual innuendo and eroticism, carrying the vessel tradition to dizzying, hallucinogenic heights. He went on to create sets of dinnerware from store-bought blank plates that he decorated with altered, collaged commercial glaze decals. The plates spoofed the American flag and the Founding Fathers, focused on political violence, and reinterpreted icons of art, transforming Leonardo's *Last Supper* into *Da Vinci's Revenge* (1967–71) and Grant Wood's *American Gothic* into *American Gothicware Look Alikes* (1972). Kottler's plates sparked controversy and debate in the crafts arena, not only because he was assembling rather than making the object, but also because of his use of cultural icons in assigning new meaning related to social concerns of the sixties. Kottler stretched the limits of ceramics and art in his time.

As an undergraduate at Ohio State University, Kottler was working toward a degree in optometry when he switched to ceramics. The university offered one of the country's oldest ceramics programs, and Kottler earned a BA in 1952 and an MA in 1956, training with such production potters and ceramics engineers as Carlton Atherton, Edgar Littlefield, and Paul Bogatay (who had run his own Columbus-based limited-production ceramics company in the 1930s). On an Ellen Scripps Booth Memorial Scholarship, Kottler attended Cranbrook, working with Maija Grotell (whose influence he considered negligible). He earned an MFA in 1957 and secured a Fulbright to study in Finland. Shortly before his departure, Kottler saw a display of work by Peter Voulkos at the Art Institute of Chicago. It was a seminal moment, and while in Helsinki, he began breaking loose from his conservative training, spending time at the Central School of Arts and Crafts and the renowned Arabia Factory, where he studied the creation and application of ceramic decals. His experience at Arabia greatly affected his future development; Arabia's director told him that he was the first visiting American to create work that looked nothing like the firm's traditional tableware. Returning to Columbus, Kottler went back to Ohio State, which had one of the few PhD programs then available in ceramic arts, earning his degree in 1964. His dissertation exhibition featured both thrown and hand-built pots that recalled Japanese Bizen ware and was influenced by abstract expressionism. Kottler taught at Ohio State University (1961–64) and at the University of Washington as a visiting assistant professor (1964–65) and was hired on faculty the following year by department chair, Robert Sperry. Although the new professor was once described as closer to "Dr. Demento" (Kangas 1989) than other educators, Kottler was a consummate professional, known as a generous and encouraging teacher. His work was included in more than 300 exhibitions around the world, and he developed extensive collections of things that interested him—Tiffany glass, tramp art, and Noritake interwar Japanese export wares—which he used in his teaching and as inspiration for his own work. —TT

Judith S. Schwartz, "Obituaries—Howard Kottler," *AC* 49 (April/May, 1989), 69; Matthew Kangas, "Howard Kottler," *American Ceramics* 7 (1989), 6; artist files, ACC library.

KRAMER, SAM

Born November 22, 1913, Pittsburgh, PA;
died June 9, 1964, New York, NY
JEWELER

The origin of contemporary jewelry is said to trace to 1936, when Sam Kramer began creating surrealistic ornaments for the human body. Kramer drew upon those aspects of modernism most concerned with fantasy, the absurd, the unconscious, chance, and parody. His was a journey through a cultural underworld teeming with creatures, complexes, and primordial ooze. Meant to shock and provoke, his exquisitely crafted creations included a silver pendant suggesting an embryo; a brooch inspired by spirochete, a bacterial organism; a ring set with an artificial eye; a golden bracelet studded with moose teeth; and platinum cuff links set with old buttons from subway motormen's uniforms. Kramer frequently combined precious metals, crystals, and stones with a variety of materials such as fossils, corroded shells, animal tusks and bones, meteorites, ancient coins, Victorian shoe buttons, and the eggs of antediluvian reptiles. In addition to his constructed jewelry, Kramer perfected three art-inspired techniques: a kind of lost-wax casting to achieve sculptural forms; a method of rapidly heating and fusing dripping granules of metal using flame as the tool; and a type of sand casting that produced unique results.

Raised in Pittsburgh, where his happier moments as a youth were in the jewelry-making and machine shop classes he took in high school, Kramer completed two years in the journalism department at the University of Pittsburgh (1930–32) before moving to California with his mother and siblings and transferring to the University of Southern California. A colorful figure on the USC campus, Kramer lived in a shack, wore dock hand's clothing, and spent hours poring over modernist paintings and avant-garde books. He took a jewelry-making class with Glen Lukens, the innovative chairman of the ceramics department, but his primary studies were in English literature, psychology, and art. He planned to be a writer. After earning a BA in 1936, he worked briefly for the *Santa Monica Topic* covering women's club meetings. When his family moved back to Pittsburgh in 1937, Kramer followed but detoured to study Navajo and other Indian jewelry and to spend a few months in Florida reading extensively about stones. Back in Pittsburgh he spent three months in a manufacturing jeweler's shop gaining technical knowledge, and he opened a tiny shop of his own but closed it after only a few weeks. By 1938 he had moved to New York City, taken a course in gemology at New York University, and begun building his life as a craftsman. In Greenwich Village he was at home among the neighborhood's free-spirited bohemians. By 1940 he had settled into a second-floor walk-up apartment at 29 West 8th Street, where he remained for the rest of his life. Kramer developed a global interest in art and crafts, making four trips to Mexico to study art, archaeology, and jewelry (1942, 1943, 1945, and 1946). In 1952 he toured Italy and France to examine historical examples of craft, jewelry, and art.

His work referenced abstraction and cubism, action painting, and a fascination with primitivism as well as surrealism. Kramer also maintained a vigorous gem trade, accumulating some 500,000 stones, and occasionally writing technical articles. Dubbed "the Surrealistic jeweler," by the *New Yorker* in 1942, Kramer's advertising and promotional stunts—pamphlets announcing "Fantastic Jewelry for People Who Are Slightly Mad," and "Space Girls" dressed in tights and with green-painted faces roaming the Village to publicize his shop—made Kramer and his Greenwich Village studio on Eighth Street a landmark. —TT

"Surrealistic Jeweler," *New Yorker* (January 3, 1942), 11–12; Richard Gehman, "The Doodads Women Wear," *Saturday Evening Post* (June 18, 1955), 112–14; Mark Foley, "Sam Kramer—Fantastic Jewelry for People Who Are Slightly Mad," *Metalsmith* 6 (winter 1986), 11–17; Toni Lesser Wolf, "Sam Kramer," in Martin Eidelberg, ed., *Design 1935–1965, What Modern Was* (Montreal: Musée des arts décoratifs de Montréal; New York: Harry N. Abrams, Inc., NY, 1991), 380–81.

KRASNER, LEE
Born October 27, 1908, Brooklyn, NY;
died June 19, 1984, East Hampton, NY
PAINTER, MOSAICIST
Lee Krasner's body of work was long overshadowed by the career of her husband, Jackson Pollock. It was only after his death that she was "rediscovered" as an artistic talent in her own right. Krasner studied art at Cooper Union and the National Academy of Design, both in New York City, and was later employed by the WPA Federal Art Project (1935–43). Beginning in 1940 she showed her work with the American Abstract Artists group and, in 1945, married Pollock and moved to Springs, NY, on the South Fork of Long Island.

The move to Long Island profoundly influenced Krasner's artistic output as she became a purely abstract painter in this period, producing her Little Image series, which was shown in 1948 at the Bertha Schaefer Gallery as part of *The Modern House Comes Alive 1948–49*, an exhibition in which Schaefer combined furniture and fine art. Krasner also created a mosaic table for this show, with a top decorated in an aesthetic that closely mirrored the style and feel of her paintings in this period. Krasner's work on mosaics

continued through the 1950s, when she, painter and mosaicist Ronald Stein, created a 1,100 square foot mosaic wall for Two Broadway, a building designed by Emery Roth & Sons in 1957.

Krasner's work has experienced a resurgence of interest since the 1970s, as galleries, museums, and audiences have reexamined her career. A retrospective was held at MoMA in 1984, the year she died. —NE

"House That 'Lives' Theme of Exhibit," *New York Times*, September 20, 1948, 22; B. H. Friedman, "Manhattan Mosaic," *CH* 9 (January/February 1959), 26–29; Grace Glueck, "Lee Krasner Finds Her Place in Retrospective at Modern," *New York Times*, December 21, 1984, C31; Gail Levin, "Lee Krasner's Little Images," *Lee Krasner: Little Image Paintings 1946–1950*, exh. cat. (Stony Brook, NY: Stony Brook Foundation, Inc., 2008).

LABINO, DOMINICK
Born December 4, 1910, Fairmount City, PA;
died January 10, 1987, Grand Rapids, OH
ENGINEER, INVENTOR, GLASS ARTIST
In a career that spanned more than fifty years, Labino was a glass industry inventor and specialist who made a key contribution at the first studio glass sessions in the U.S. and then became one of the field's earliest and most productive artists. Trained as an engineer at the Carnegie Institute of Technology, he worked in Pennsylvania for Owens-Illinois, Inc., before moving to Johns-Manville of Toledo, OH, where by the time he retired in 1965, he was vice president and director of research. Labino held more than fifty patents. Among his best-known technical contributions was the use of pure silica fibers to make insulating tiles that covered the space shuttle *Columbia*.

Labino was a key participant in the seminal glassblowing workshops conducted in March 1962 by Harvey Littleton at the University of Wisconsin–Madison and at the Toledo Museum of Art. Labino supplied the workshops with #475 glass marbles, which he had developed for the production of fiberglass, and these proved to be of a sufficiently low melting temperature to enable glassblowing to take place. By 1963 he had set up his own studio on his farm near Grand Rapids, OH, demonstrating that studio glassmaking could take place outside of an industrial setting. With his impressive technical knowledge, he created a body of richly colored hand-blown glass vessels and sculpture. Labino built a portable furnace and annealing oven for a demonstration at the first World Crafts Conference at Columbia University in New York, after which the equipment was shipped to Haystack Mountain School on Deer Isle, ME, so that glassmaking could be introduced into their curriculum. His book *Visual Art in Glass* (1967) was the first primer on the field for the modern glassblower. Labino exhibited widely: at Toledo Museum of Art's May exhibitions (beginning in 1964); *Art in the Embassies* (1966); and the first three Toledo Glass National Exhibitions (Toledo Museum of Art, 1966, 1968, 1970), among others. He was included in *New Glass*, an internationally traveling exhibition (Corning Museum of Glass, 1979–82), and

his solo exhibition, *Dominick Labino: A Decade of Glass Craftsmanship, 1964–1974* (Toledo Museum of Art, 1974), traveled internationally. —JF

Suzanne K. Frantz, "Dominick Labino 1910–1987, *AC* 47 (April / May 1987), 40–41; http://dominicklabino.com/.

LARSEN, JACK LENOR
Born August 5, 1927, Seattle, WA
TEXTILE DESIGNER, EDUCATOR, ENTREPRENEUR
The son of Danish-Norwegian immigrants from Canada, Larsen entered Washington University in Seattle in 1945 and in 1950 began his advanced studies at Cranbrook. He then worked as a freelance designer in Seattle (1949–50) and New York City (1952–53). His first commission was from architects Skidmore, Owings & Merrill for Lever House draperies (1952) in New York. At this early time he was machine-weaving goods that looked as if they were handwoven, a technique many others began to imitate. In 1953 he founded Jack Lenor Larsen, Inc. for experimentation in and fabrication of ambitious architectural assignments. In the late 1950s he was a consultant to the U.S. State Department for grass-weaving projects in Taiwan and Vietnam; in the early 1960s he co-directed the fabric design department of the Philadelphia College of Art and was both design director and commissioner for the U.S. exhibition at the thirteenth Milan Triennale (1964), where he also won a gold medal. A dominant force in international fabric design, he has been an innovator in fabric techniques, usage, and structure. His inventions included several firsts: stretch upholstery fabric (1961), printed-velvet upholstery fabric, and warp-knit Saran-monofilament casement fabrics. Larsen's knowledge of textile history has allowed him to go far beyond the ordinary, and his far-reaching travels have provided him with inspiration from a range of cultural traditions, exemplified by his collections: The Andean (1966), The African (1963), and The Irish (1969). His work has been included numerous exhibitions, beginning with the Good Design series at MoMA (1951–55). Working with MoMA curator Mildred Constantine, he collaborated on *Wall Hangings* (MoMA 1969), which placed fiber arts in a fine arts context. —TT

Jack Lenor Larsen, *Jack Lenor Larsen: A Weaver's Memoir* (New York: H. N. Abrams, 1988); David Revere McFadden, ed., *Jack Lenor Larsen: Creator and Collector* (London: Merrell Publishers; New York: Museum of Arts & Design, 2004).

LASSAW, IBRAM
Born May 4, 1913, Alexandria, Egypt;
died December 30, 2003, East Hampton, NY
METALSMITH, SCULPTOR, EDUCATOR
Known for his welded, three-dimensional open space sculptures of intersecting lines, Lassaw was an early and influential nonobjective artist. Of Russian-Jewish origin, Lassaw arrived in Brooklyn, NY, with his family in 1921. Artistically inclined from an early age, he attended classes at the Brooklyn Children's Museum for five years beginning in 1927, learning to model and cast. He continued his

education at the Beaux Arts Institute of Design, New York, and City College of New York. His plaster and wire sculptures made in the 1930s evolved into works constructed in sheet metal and forged steel. As he moved from the figure to abstraction, he organized the American Abstract Artists group, which promoted this art form through cooperative exhibitions. Following a stint in the army, he developed "projection paintings" that were handpainted on 2-by-2-inch slides and could be viewed in as many as eight possible directions. About this time he also experimented with plastics and colored dyes.

In the early 1950s he purchased oxyacetylene welding equipment, which enabled him to fashion molten drip sculptures on an architectonic armature. The rather spontaneous results aligned him with work by jeweler Sam Kramer as well as the action painters of abstract expressionism, although he was also influenced by constructivism and surrealism. A number of large-scale commissions followed, for synagogues, hotels, and other public settings. His success with these sculptures led to further experiments on a smaller scale with jewelry, which he ornamented with patination and gemstones.

During the 1960s and '70s Lassaw taught at Southampton College, Mount Holyoke College, University of California, Berkeley, and Duke University. He was included in *Abstract Painting and Sculpture* (MoMA, 1950) and *Nature in Abstraction* (Whitney Museum of American Art, 1959). —JF
Ibram Lassaw, Arthur Frederick Jones, and Denise Lassaw, *Ibram Lassaw: Deep Space and Beyond, A Retrospective Exhibition of Works and Photographic Documents From the Artist's Studio in Springs, East Hampton, New York* (Radford, VA: Radford University Foundation Press, 2002); Campbell Robertson, "Ibram Lassaw, 90, A Sculptor Devoted to Abstract Forms," *New York Times*, January 2, 2004.

LECHTZIN, STANLEY
Born June 9, 1936, Detroit, MI
METALSMITH, JEWELER, EDUCATOR

Trained in traditional methods of metalsmithing, Stanley Lechtzin broadened the field by applying industrial techniques to jewelry, specifically by adapting electroforming for this purpose, and by adopting computer-aided design and manufacture (CAD/CAM) in his work. He studied under Philip Fike at Wayne State University and received his BFA in 1960. He earned his MFA in 1962 under Richard Thomas at Cranbrook. In the same year, Lechtzin established the metals program at Tyler School of Art, Temple University.

In 1963 Lechtzin began his experiments with electroforming in creating sculptural jewelry forms. In this process metal is deposited around a matrix or core that is then removed, allowing for lighter and larger-scale forms than possible through casting. Lechtzin's organic designs for brooches and neckpieces also incorporated a wide variety of materials, from precious stones to plastic. Cast acrylic formed the body of the artist's Torque series of neckpieces that were embellished with elaborate gold forms at each

end. In the late 1970s his innovations in jewelry design and manufacture continued with CAD/CAM applications.

In the 1960s Lechtzin's jewelry appeared in national and international venues, including a solo show at the Museum of Contemporary Crafts (1965), and exhibitions in Germany, England, and Japan. In 1967 he received a Louis Comfort Tiffany Foundation Grant. In 1969 he was one of nine founding members of the Society of North American Goldsmiths (SNAG). He has also exhibited at London's Goldsmiths' Hall (1973) and had a retrospective in 2009 at the Philadelphia Art Alliance. —JP
Objects: USA, 225; C. E. Licka, "Technique and the Organic Paradigm," *Metalsmith* 2 (summer 1982), 8–13; Daniella Kerner, *Stanley Lechtzin: Selections from Five Decades, 1959–2009, Jewelry and Objects* (Philadelphia, PA: Philadelphia Art Alliance, 2009).

LEEDY, JAMES A.
Born November 6, 1930, McRoberts, KY
CERAMIST, PAINTER, EDUCATOR

Celebrated for his progressive and expressive work, James Leedy experimented with forms and technique, revolutionizing modern ceramics in the process. Influenced by abstract expressionists in his youth, he was one of the first artists to give structural form to the movement and pay homage to them by his use of primary colors. To expose the natural and raw state of clay, Leedy worked with various kilns and firing techniques and used technologies such a handheld blowtorch, merging the industrial and traditional and building pieces with extensive texture and detail that were unique to the medium.

Leedy encountered abstract expressionism when he worked as a painter in Manhattan in the 1950s. His pieces on canvas and paper combine the expressiveness and gestural brushstrokes indicative of the period. As the decade progressed, his paintings became three-dimensional, with thick paint providing relief interest to the canvas. At times, he worked on unconventional canvas shapes such as triangles and trapezoids. As he transitioned to ceramics, Leedy again tested new forms, creating many large and sculptural vessels, favoring structure and creativity over function. As he explained, "Most of my pots are sculpture, using the suggestion of a pot only as a point of departure to a purely aesthetic, personal, and sculptural statement. Other than aesthetic, my pots have no function" (quoted in *Objects: USA*). Leedy considers his sculptures to be sacred, oftentimes referencing ritual figures, as well as social and personal symbols. In some pieces, he layers and combines molded, abstract figures and shapes to create a finished, anthropomorphic piece.

Leedy received his BFA from Richmond Professional Institute, College of William and Mary (1957); his MFA at Southern Illinois University (1958); an MA at Michigan State University (1959); and began his PhD studies at Ohio State University (1958, 1959). In addition to his own work, Leedy has taught several generations of young artists. Since 1966 he has been at the Kansas City Art Institute, where his teachings center on the idea that students should learn

by example. Following this philosophy, he has encouraged an interactive educational experience. —BN
Matthew Kangas, *Jim Leedy: Artist Across Boundaries* (Kansas City: Kansas City Art Institute, 2000); *Objects: USA,* 137.

LIEBES, DOROTHY KATHERINE WRIGHT (MRS. LEON LIEBES; LATER, MRS. REHLMAN MORIN)
Born October 14, 1899, Santa Rosa, CA;
died September 20, 1972, New York, NY
WEAVER, TEXTILE DESIGNER, ENTREPRENEUR, ARTS ADMINISTRATOR

An American weaver and textile designer renowned for innovative, custom-designed modern fabrics for architects and interior designers, Dorothy Liebes also became the dominant aesthetic influence in the textile industry's conversion to man-made fibers and new technologies in dyes and finishes in the post–World War II era. Viewing weaving as an art with unlimited creative possibilities without sacrificing beauty to mass production, Liebes created richly textured fabrics with transformative concepts of what was suitable for the warp and weft of the loom. Her repertoire of weaving elements included such exotic materials as strings of beads, strips of bamboo, grass, tickertape, cellophane, feathers, and leather, which she used in experiments on her handloom, creating adaptations for open mesh (leno) and dobby weavings. Known for a bold and unconventional use of color—lacquer red, chartreuse, fuchsia, tangerine, and turquoise—often in unorthodox combinations, and for a love of glitz—she regularly used metallic threads—Liebes achieved a wide reputation as a colorist aligned with the latest trends and as a decorator devoted to the creation of colorful modern interiors. In a career that transitioned from handcraft artisan to industrial designer, she completed one-of-a-kind commissions for ocean liners, hotels, theaters, and private homes, and served as a home-furnishings consultant to textile mills, architects, designers, and interior decorators. Her "idea fabrics" showed how to use new synthetic fibers in draperies, upholstery, and carpets. She also built commercial markets through public appearances and on television, where she functioned as a spokeswoman for new synthetic textile products and their makers. Liebes opened her first studio—Dorothy Liebes Designs, Inc.—in San Francisco in 1934, and in response to a growing clientele of East Coast–based textile manufacturers, she moved her design studio to New York City in 1948 and her production studio in 1952. She stopped taking on custom work in 1958 to concentrate on industrial consulting and designing for mass production. Her first industrial project was for Goodall Fabrics, Inc., in Sanford, ME, in 1940. Hired to design twelve fabrics for mass production but with the look and feel of handweaving, Liebes not only experimented with new yarns, colors, and weaves, but also assisted in the development of machinery that could replicate the aesthetic irregularities and uneven tensions of handloomed fabrics. Consultancies with other companies soon followed: design and color use for Lurex metallic yarns for Dobeckmun Co. (1946–62); product development for acrylics, polyesters, synthetic straw, and nylon rug yarns for E. I. du Pont de Nemours & Company (1955–71); designs for area rugs and home carpets for Bigelow-Sanford, Inc. (1957–71); and development of colorful fabrics widely marketed by Sears, Roebuck Co. (1969–72). Liebes's designs were used for everything from mattress ticking and sound-filter screens for radios to wallpaper and airplane upholstery, blinds, clothing, and home furnishings. Clients ranged from architects Frank Lloyd Wright and Edward Durell Stone to King Ibn Saud of Saudi Arabia, for whom she designed gold and silk fabrics for his traveling throne room. Her commissions included curtains for the Paramount Theatre in Oakland, California, the Persian Room of the Plaza Hotel in New York City, and the main lounge of the S.S. *Constitution,* an ocean liner. In addition to her design work and consultancies, Liebes was the director of arts and skills for the American Red Cross during World War II, instituting therapeutic craft programs for war veterans in hospitals throughout the country. She served on the board of many organizations, including the San Francisco Art Institute, MoMA Advisory Council, and America House. She was awarded the American Institute of Architects Craftsmanship Medal for outstanding contribution in textile design (1947); an LLD degree by Mills College (1948); and the American Interior Decorators Recognition Award for international influence as a colorist and an innovator with man-made fibers (1969). —TT

Nell Znamierowski, *Dorothy Liebes: Retrospective Exhibition,* exh. cat. (New York: MCC, 1970); "Dorothy Katherine Wright Liebes," in Barbara Sicherman and Carol Green, eds., *Notable American Women: The Modern Period—A Biographical Dictionary,* vol. 4 (Cambridge: Harvard University Press, 1980), 420–21; Rebecca Mary Trussell, "Dorothy Wright Liebes, American Designer—Weaving for Art, Craft and Industry 1920–1970," MA thesis, Masters Program in the History of Decorative Arts, Cooper-Hewitt, National Design Museum and Parsons School of Design, 2004.

For earlier history see *Craft in the Machine Age,* 239.

LIPOFSKY, MARVIN
Born September 1, 1939, Barrington, IL
GLASS ARTIST, EDUCATOR

Marvin Lipofsky studied industrial design and then worked as a sculptor before realizing his calling and aptitude as a technical master in glassmaking, becoming known as the Roving Ambassador of Glass. Lipofsky's formal education began in 1962 with a BFA in industrial design at the University of Illinois, followed by MS and MFA degrees in sculpture at the University of Wisconsin in 1964. In Madison, WI, Lipofsky was among the first students to participate in Harvey Littleton's groundbreaking studio glass program. Lipofsky adopted the "technique is cheap" philosophy of Littleton, alluding to his lifelong dedication to education, communication, and experimentation. The year he graduated, Lipofsky initiated a glass program at the University of California, Berkeley, resulting in a

student following and unrivaled attention to glass as a fine art.

While maintaining a glass studio in Berkeley, Lipofsky also founded a glass department at California College of Arts and Crafts (now California College of the Arts) in Oakland, where he taught from 1967 to 1987. The idea of a glass designer/professor teaching glassblowing as a fine art was still novel. On sabbatical in 1970, Lipofsky's first factory experience was in Leerdam in the western Netherlands, followed by stops in Finland, Yugoslavia, Milan, Venice, and Japan. Thrilled with the opportunity to work under master craftsmen, Lipofsky insisted on producing both the design and the glass object to the bemusement and confusion of factory workers. This interest in collaborating with students, colleagues, and mentors resulted in a life of travel to fifteen countries and more than twenty-five factories and schools throughout Europe, Asia, and North America, to research and exchange information with glassblowers and designers. Through the course of his career, he has pursued diverse techniques including mold-blowing, cutting, etching, sandblasting, and electroplating. —LB

E. M. Treib, "Marvin Lipofsky: Just Doing his Glass Thing," *CH* 28 (September 1968), 16–19; *Marvin Lipofsky-Glass,* exh. cat. (New York: MCC, 1969), 2; Cheryl White, "Marvin Lipofsky: Roving Ambassador of Glass," *AC* 51 (October/November, 1991), 47–50.

LITTLETON, HARVEY K.
Born June 14, 1924, Corning, NY
CERAMIST, GLASS ARTIST, EDUCATOR

Harvey Littleton was among the first glass artists to demonstrate that the medium could be melted and blown outside of industrial settings. His commitment to this belief established him as the founder of the American studio glass movement. Littleton had an almost predetermined affinity for glass. His fascination began with summer jobs in the 1940s at the Corning Glass factory where his father, J. T. Littleton, headed the department of research and development and was the inventor of Pyrex cookware. Littleton studied industrial design at the University of Michigan in Ann Arbor (1939–42), and while in the armed forces, he took ceramics classes at the Brighton School of Art in England in 1945. Upon returning to the U.S., Littleton earned a BA in design at the University of Michigan in 1947, and an MFA at Cranbrook in 1951.

When the Corning Glass management rejected his 1947 proposal for an experimental glass workshop, Littleton turned his attention to pottery and began to teach ceramics at the University of Wisconsin (1951–77). In 1957 he traveled to Murano, Italy, to study the Venetian glass industry and began glassblowing experiments back in his pottery studio in Wisconsin. In 1961 he presented a paper titled, "A Potter's Experience with Glass," at the ACC conference. A year later he conducted a groundbreaking series of glassblowing workshops at Ohio's Toledo Museum of Art and soon established the first American college-affiliated glass program at the

University of Wisconsin. Over the next twenty years, approximately one hundred educational institutions came to offer glassmaking instruction as an accredited part of the curriculum.

Littleton's experimental glassblowing in the early 1960s illustrated that form and structure could combine with complex textures into impressive mouth-blown glass sculptures, employing a mastery of both hot- and cold-work processes. Museum recognition and acclaim came early: one-man shows at the Chicago Art Institute (1963), the Museum of Contemporary Crafts, New York (1964), and Boston's Society of Arts and Crafts (1965). In the 1970s Littleton pioneered a glassmaking style of rainbow-colored loops, twists, tubes, and geometric forms, for which he is best known. Color was always a primary concern in Littleton's glass works, and he used fiberglass marbles and metallic sulphates to achieve deep combinations of overlaying colors. He developed an intimate working knowledge of the material and maintained an ongoing fascination with obtaining brilliant color and optical effects through the studio process. —LB

W. W. Colescott, "Harvey Littleton," *CH* 19 (November 1959), 20–23; D. Smith, "Offhand Glass Blowing: Harvey Littleton's Course at Wisconsin University," *CH* 24 (January 1964), 22–23; Barbara Jepson, "Harvey Littleton and his Rainbows," *Wall Street Journal,* May 29, 1984.

LOLOMA, CHARLES
Born January 7, 1921, Hotevilla, AZ; died 1991, Phoenix, AZ
JEWELER, POTTER, PAINTER, EDUCATOR

Innovative artist and teacher, Charles Loloma elevated Hopi Indian jewelry to the height of critical acclaim with nontraditional forms, spectacular gemstones, and colors. As a high school student in the 1930s, Loloma studied with Hopi painter Fred Kabotie and became an accomplished muralist. In 1939, at the age of nineteen, he assisted in painting murals at the 1939 San Francisco Golden Gate International Exposition. Two years later he worked alongside Kabotie on authentic Hopi murals reproduced for the MoMA exhibition, *Indian Art of the United States* (1941). Curator René d'Harnoncourt, who was among the first to exhibit Native American art as a fine art, played an instrumental role in Loloma's development as designer, connecting him with European designers, painters, and future exhibitions. After serving in the U.S. Army in World War II, Loloma studied ceramics at the School for American Craftsmen (SAC) at Alfred University, NY, from 1947 to 1949. While at SAC, Loloma won a Whitney Foundation Fellowship to research ceramics on the Hopi Reservation of his youth. Throughout the 1950s he met with Native American artists who were experimenting and developing jewelry and textiles in Scottsdale, AZ. These included Cherokee artist Lloyd Kiva New, Navajo jeweler Kenneth Begay, and Begay's cousins Allen and George Kee.

By 1954 Loloma and his wife, Otellie, had opened a pottery shop in Scottsdale, producing innovative, wheel-thrown ceramics marketed as Lolomaware. Throughout this period, Loloma taught ceramics at the University of

Arizona and Arizona State University. Despite the demands of teaching, by 1955 Loloma's attention had also turned to jewelry-making, and by 1963 he had a successful exhibition in Paris. His lifelong struggle to reconcile his Hopi culture with modernism meant that he was often ridiculed within his own tribe for producing good work that was not considered truly Native American. The Gallup Inter-Tribal Ceremonial, which held an annual wholesale fair in Scottsdale, rejected Loloma's works three times in the 1950s. Paradoxically, within a decade, he was criticized for winning the prize too often at the Scottsdale National. Loloma persevered and succeeded in creating one-of-a-kind jewelry that evoked both architecture and the Hopi landscape by blending surface contrasts with unusual combinations of gemstones and materials in pieces that are often considered miniature sculptures. He was the first Native American jewelry designer to forego silver in lieu of gold and to use diamonds and other gemstones unconnected with his culture. He was interested in the spatial relationships of gemstones and inlay in jewelry while embracing the formal rules of painting, his original passion. He also embedded gems in the interior of bracelets and rings, his nod to inner beauty both in humans and objects. In 1966 he returned to the Hopi Reservation where he was raised, establishing a studio and art gallery in Hotevilla. He was a Hopi spiritual leader (snake priest) and member of the Badger Clan, and the clan's symbol recurred in his art throughout his thirty-year career. —LB

Indian Art of the United States, MoMA exh. no. 123, January 22–April 27, 1941; Martha Hopkins Struever, *Loloma: Beauty Is His Name* (Santa Fe, NM: Wheelwright Museum of the American Indian, 2005); Ellen Berkovitch, "Charles Loloma: Hopi Modernist," *Metalsmith* 26 (summer 2006), 42–49; Diana F. Pardue with the Heard Museum, *Southwestern Jewelry* (Salt Lake City, UT: Gibbs Smith, Publisher, 2007), 11–12.

LUKENS, GLEN
Born January 15, 1887, Cowgill, MO;
died December 10, 1967, Los Angeles, CA
CERAMIST, GLASS ARTIST, EDUCATOR

A pioneer of the studio pottery movement, Glen Lukens produced ceramic pieces lush in color and expressive in form. He frequently used a press molding technique that allowed him to create thick vessels, rich with texture and imperfections. Lukens experimented with glazes and clays, embracing the natural elements of the medium—the cracks and unexpected superficial changes that can occur during a kiln firing. In the 1950s he became an innovator in a warm glass technique in which he created glass forms from the molds of his ceramic pieces. This unique combination of media produced "slumped" glass forms poured on top of his molds, then sprayed with color, which he called "desert glass."

Lukens was also a celebrated teacher of midcentury ceramists. About 1936 he began teaching at the University of Southern California, where he helped develop modern kilns and bring the technology of the potter's wheel to the West Coast. During that time, he promoted art education in area high schools. Not only did Lukens instruct prominent midcentury ceramists, he also trained teachers in the field, including F. Carlton Ball, Viveka Heino, Laura Andreson, and Richard Petterson. Beginning in 1945 he traveled to Haiti under the sponsorship of the Inter-American Educational Council and taught clay techniques to teachers and novices in Port-au-Prince, employing native clay and primitive kilns, and providing a sanitary alternative to the gourds that were commonly used as tableware but also spread disease. This effort was so successful that the Centre de Céramique, as it became known, fielded requests for pottery from the hotels of the city. In 1951, under the aegis of UNESCO, Lukens set up a ceramic center in Marbial, Haiti, to which he traveled until 1955.

In his own creations, Lukens was spontaneous, yet true to his materials. He experimented with the wide range of California's natural resources, using clays from the various ecosystems in the state, exploring different combinations of rich minerals to produce entirely new clays. Lukens developed unique ways of combining color and the clay surface and the textured surfaces of glass. Lukens's work preceded the expressionist ceramists working in the 1950s and '60s, but his lively and expressive forms helped to pave the way for their experimentation. —NB

"Desert Glass Exhibit at SC," *Los Angeles Times*, March 4, 1954, D6; Susan Peterson, "Glen Lukens: 1887–1967," *CH* 28 (March/April 1968), 22–25; *Glen Lukens: Pioneer of the Vessel Aesthetic* (Los Angeles: Fine Arts Gallery, California State University, 1982).

LYNN, THOMAS PENDLETON
Born October 27, 1939, Pasadena, CA;
died September 9, 2008, CA
SCULPTOR

Thomas Lynn studied at San Jose State College in California, where there was a growing interest in foundry work and students could experiment with several privately operated foundries in the area. In the mid-1960s Lynn used cast-aluminum to construct a series of chairs primarily intended as sculpture. In 1968, in *California Design Ten,* he exhibited one of these chairs along with a large aluminum and glass table (four by seven feet in size), with a candelabrum rising through the glass from the base of the table. Highly sculptural and expressionistic, Lynn's furniture hovers between function and surrealism. —JP

California Design Ten (Pasadena, CA: Pasadena Art Museum, 1968), 34; *Objects: USA*, 186; David Hampton, *Pouring Metal in the South Bay: The 1960s California Artist-Foundry Movement* (San Francisco: Blurb, 2009).

MacKENZIE, WARREN
Born February 16, 1924, Kansas City, MO
MacKENZIE, ALIXANDRA
(NÉE ETHEL KOLESKY)
Born July 10, 1922, Chicago, IL;
died January 25, 1962, Minneapolis, MN
CERAMISTS, EDUCATORS

The traditional, wheel-thrown vessels of Warren and Alix MacKenzie embody an Anglo-Oriental influence from potters Bernard Leach and Shoji Hamada, as well as philosopher Soetsu Yanagi, founder of the *mingei* folk craft movement in early twentieth-century Japan. Through the creation of utilitarian pots fired in a reduction kiln—mugs, cups, dishes, bowls, and vases, executed in stoneware and porcelain—the MacKenzies embraced an existence where art and life were one, and where the presence of the potter's hand was felt in the production of affordable pottery intended for use in everyday life. Beginning in the 1950s, through workshops and lectures—at Black Mountain College, Penland, Haystack, Archie Bray, and Anderson Ranch—the couple became major proponents of functional pottery in the U.S.

Warren and Alix initially studied painting at the Art Institute of Chicago. Warren began his training in 1941, but when he returned to the school in 1946 following three years of military service, the painting classes were full, so he registered for ceramics and drawing instead. Alix also switched to ceramics, but for an entirely different reason. She was teaching in a Mexican settlement house in Chicago and felt her students would be more receptive to clay than to paint. The two were introduced to the work of Bernard Leach when a classmate brought in a copy of *A Potter's Book* (1940). Their decision to create utilitarian pots developed from visits to the Field Museum of Natural History, where they viewed collections of ancient pottery. Upon graduation—Alix in 1946 and Warren in 1947—they married and moved to St. Paul, MN, where they took jobs in 1948 at the crafts-focused St. Paul Gallery and School of Art.

They soon discovered they were ill equipped to teach or to run a pottery and decided to pursue further training. During the summer of 1948, they visited St. Ives, in England, and arranged to apprentice with Leach at the Leach Pottery. For two and a half years (1949–52), the MacKenzies lived in Leach's home and worked six days a week at his pottery. Such an all-encompassing exposure focused their skills and gave them direction. They met many of Leach's friends, including Ben Nicholson, Barbara Hepworth, and Lucie Rie, and they fully explored Leach's extensive collection of pottery, which included their first introduction to the work of Shoji Hamada. Before their return to the U.S. in 1952, Leach asked the MacKenzies to attend the International Potters and Weavers Conference at Dartington Hall, where they met Hamada and Yanagi. When Leach decided to return to Japan with his friends, an idea was born to travel in the direction of America and for the three to give workshops as they crossed the country. Alix MacKenzie arranged their 1952–53 tour—which included Black Mountain College, in North Carolina; St. Paul Gallery and School of Art, in Minnesota; the Archie Bray Foundation, in Montana; and the Chouinard Art Institute (now the California Institute of the Arts), in California. Additionally, for the stop in St. Paul, the MacKenzies mounted the first American exhibition of Hamada's work.

After touring, the MacKenzies purchased an old farm in Stillwater, MN, set up their pottery in the barn, built an oil-fired kiln similar to the one at Leach Pottery, and used potter's wheels brought back from England. (In 1968, the pottery burned to the ground and was rebuilt.) Warren and Alix worked together—he threw the forms and fired the pots, and she focused on decoration. They exhibited and sold through the Walker Art Center in Minneapolis, but eventually opened their own showroom and sold directly to clients. Warren continued at the St. Paul Gallery and School of Art until 1953, when he began teaching part-time at the University of Minnesota. There his students were known as the "Mingeisota" (an amusing but respectful term amalgamating Minnesota and *mingei*), and he continued teaching at the university for the rest of his career. Alix died of cancer in 1962; toward the end of her life, when she was no longer able to pot, she returned to painting. —TT

David Lewis, *Warren MacKenzie: An American Potter* (Tokyo: Kodansha, 1991); Catherine Futter and Robert B. Silberman, *Warren MacKenzie: The Legacy of an American Potter*, exh. cat. (Rochester, MN: Rochester Art Center, 2007); Warren MacKenzie, oral history interview by Robert Silberman, October 29, 2002, AAA, SI; Kristin Makholm e-mail to Jeannine Falino, November 2, 2010.

MacLEAN, BONNIE

(MRS. BILL GRAHAM;
LATER, MRS. JACQUES FABERT)

Born December 28, 1939, Philadelphia, PA

GRAPHIC ARTIST, PAINTER

Bonnie MacLean grew up in the Philadelphia area and attended Pennsylvania State University, State College, PA, where in 1961 she received a BA in French. Shortly afterward, she moved to San Francisco, where she found work as a secretary for a heavy-machinery company. She soon married her boss, Bill Graham, who was starting a new career as a promoter of rock bands in the city, poised to become one of the most powerful impresarios in his field. MacLean became Graham's bookkeeper for his entertainment business and occasionally designed some of the concert posters.

MacLean continued her studies at the San Francisco Art Institute, the San Francisco Academy of Art, and the California College of Arts and Crafts, Mexican Extension. In 1972, she returned to the East Coast and settled in Bucks County, PA, where she has worked as a painter. —JF

Lauren Eckstein, "Rock On," *Bucks County Woman* 3 (June 8, 2010), 21.

MALOOF, SAMUEL SOLOMON

Born January 24, 1916, Chino, CA;

died May 21, 2009, Alta Loma, CA

WOODWORKER, FURNITURE DESIGNER,

FURNITURE MAKER

Known for elegant, yet simple and practical furniture—primarily chairs, but also pedestal desks, trestle tables, print stands, music racks, cradle hutches, and hi-fi cabinets—Sam Maloof was the quintessential mid-twentieth century self-taught designer-craftsman. He focused on the production of handcrafted pieces that unified the maker, object, and owner. Maloof's signature style—often compared to Shaker and Scandinavian modern—was based on variations of elemental designs he developed in the 1950s. Shorn of unnecessary adornment, nearly all the furniture was executed in hardwood, often black walnut. Simple, rounded pieces flowed together, reflecting a concern for and involvement with every detail of the design. Precisely created wooden joinery was incorporated, not hidden—nails and metal hardware were never used. The finished objects were sanded and polished to a sensuous luster. Initially catering to a Southern California clientele, Maloof developed personal relationships with his clients and, when possible, visited them in their homes. With the help of an assistant and an apprentice, Maloof produced between fifty and one hundred pieces of furniture annually, and his clients were willing to wait years for delivery.

Maloof was the seventh of nine children born to Lebanese immigrants. As a child he carved and made things, and at Chino High School he took courses in mechanical drawing and simple carpentry. After graduation in 1934 he designed for VORTOX, a company that made air filters for heavy-duty internal combustion engines (1934–39). He also did printing and poster work for the Padua Hills Theater in Claremont and was later employed by industrial designer Harold Graham, whose company built displays for the Bullock's department stores (1940–41). Following military service (1941–45), Maloof worked as a commercial artist for a decal firm in Los Angeles, and he outfitted his first apartment with furniture built in a night school class, where he had enrolled simply to use the machinery. Next, as an assistant to Millard Sheets, a well-known painter, designer, and head of the art department at Scripps College in Claremont (1946–48), he was introduced to a variety of media including sculpture, painting, murals, mosaics, and pottery.

In 1947 Maloof met Alfreda Louise Ward, a UCLA arts graduate, former Navy WAVE, and director of an arts and crafts program at the Indian School in Santa Fe, NM, from 1938 to 1941. The two married in 1948, as Maloof began to develop a successful crafts career, and Alfreda managed the books and business correspondence. Propelled by the interest of friends who wanted copies of the no-frills furniture Maloof designed for his and Alfreda's first home in Ontario, CA, in 1949 he went into business for himself, but continued freelancing as a graphic designer. Maloof's home was featured in a 1951 *Better Homes and Gardens* article as an example of how to economically furnish a tract-house. This work and the furniture Maloof made for a ranch house in nearby West Covina came to the attention of the *Los Angeles Times*. The publicity made it possible for Maloof—at age thirty-two—to become a full-time woodworker. His first important client was industrial designer Henry Dreyfuss, for whom Maloof made twenty-five pieces of furniture for his home and office in Pasadena (Maloof was paid $1,800). Maloof's chairs and bar stools were also installed in Case Study Houses—modernist, experimental homes in the Los Angeles area that were built between 1945 and 1966 by Richard Neutra, Charles and Ray Eames, Eero Saarinen, and other progressive architects.

The Maloofs purchased land in 1953, in a lemon grove in Alta Loma, near the San Gabriel Mountains. The home and studio that Maloof built there were a tribute to his love of wood. In the mid-1950s he helped establish the Southern Designer-Craftsmen organization. In 1957 he participated in and met for the first time other studio woodworkers (Wharton Esherick, Art Carpenter, and Tage Frid) at the ACC's first conference held at Asilomar, CA. In 1957, he participated in the first group furniture show to be mounted at the MCC. In 1959 he traveled to Iran and Lebanon as a design consultant for a State Department project to encourage the growth of craft industries in developing nations, and four years later he participated in a similar project in El Salvador. He received an American Institute of Architects award in 1967 from the Pasadena chapter for Outstanding Excellence of Craftsmanship and in 1969 was the first recipient of the Louis Comfort Tiffany Grant for the Craftsman Apprentice Program. —TT

Sam Maloof, *Sam Maloof, Woodworker* (Tokyo: Kodansha International, 1983); Jeremy Elwell Adamson, *The Furniture of Sam Maloof* (New York: W.W. Norton & Company; Washington, D.C.: Smithsonian American Art Museum, 2001); Janet Eastman, "Sam Maloof dies at 93," *Los Angeles Times*, May 23, 2009, A1.

MARER, FRED

Born September 24, 1908, CA;

died June 6, 2002, West Los Angeles, CA

COLLECTOR

Fred Marer was an early and avid collector of avant-garde California ceramics. Working as a math professor at Los Angeles City College, Marer amassed more than fifteen hundred ceramic pieces over a period of nearly forty years. Beginning in 1954, he formed a close relationship with Peter Voulkos and his pupils at the Los Angeles County Art Institute (Otis Art Institute, now Otis College of Art and Design). Of modest means, Marer made frequent visits to the classroom, becoming a patron and friend to Voulkos and his students. Many of these young artists were new to the field, and Marer's patronage provided much-needed encouragement. Marer and his wife, Mary, displayed their growing collection in their home, which included a spare bedroom for the occasional artist who needed a place to stay. One such artist was Japanese ceramist Jun Kaneko, who stayed with Marer soon after his arrival in the U.S. in 1963. In 1993 Marer donated most of his collection to the Ruth Chandler Williamson Gallery of Scripps College. —NB

Jim Melchert and Paul Soldner, "Fred Marer and the Clay People," *CH* 24 (June 1974), 38–47; Mary Davis MacNaughton et al., *Revolution in Clay: The Marer Collection of Contemporary Ceramics* (Claremont, CA: Ruth Chandler Williamson Gallery, Scripps College; Seattle, WA: University of Washington Press, 1994); Suzanne Muchnic, "Obituaries: Fred Marer, 93, Ceramics Collector, Math Professor," *Los Angeles Times*, June 20, 2002, B12.

MARQUIS, RICHARD

Born September 17, 1945, Bumblebee, AZ

GLASS ARTIST, EDUCATOR

The glass sculptures of Richard Marquis are notable for vibrant bursts of color, innovative glass forms, the blending of materials, and subtle humor. He was introduced to glassmaking and glassblowing in the summer of 1967, when, at the age of twenty-two, he worked as a teaching assistant to his friend and colleague, Marvin Lipofsky, at the Haystack Mountain School of Crafts in Maine. Shortly afterward, Marquis moved to Berkeley, CA, to study ceramics and glass at the University of California; he received a BA in 1968 and an MA in 1969. He went to Venice and Murano, Italy, on a Fulbright Scholarship to study glassmaking, and trained at the Venini Glass factory.

Marquis became adept at working with *murrine,* small, patterned glass disks that are created by bunching colored glass rods together so that they form a design in cross section. These are then fused by heating and stretched into a thin glass rod, which can be cut crosswise to produce multiples of the design. The *murrine* allowed Marquis to create works that were colorful and used small, repeated patterns, like the stars in *American Acid Capsule* (cat. 196).

When he returned to the U.S., Marquis disseminated his knowledge of Italian glassmaking techniques in academic and workshop settings. Studio glass artists in America at that time were largely self-taught, learning through experimentation. Marquis's expertise broadened the technical skills of these pioneering artists and forged connections between Italian tradition and American innovation.

Marquis has received four National Endowment for the Arts Fellowships and much recognition for his achievements from the studio glass community, including two Lifetime Achievement Awards from the Glass Art Society. —LB

Richard Marquis, "The Making of *Canne* and *Murrini* and Their Use in Glass Blown Forms," M.A. thesis, University of California, Berkeley, September 1972; *Who's Who in Contemporary Glass Art: A Comprehensive World Guide to Glass Artists – Craftsmen – Designers* (Munich: J. Waldrich Verlag, 1993), 351; Tina Oldknow, "2005 Honorary Lifetime Achievement Award: Richard Marquis— An Appreciation," *Journal* (Glass Art Society) (2005), 8.

MARSHALL, JOHN

Born February 25, 1936, Pittsburgh, PA

SILVERSMITH, EDUCATOR

Good mentors gave John Marshall an excellent start in the field of metalsmithing. He first studied the subject as a student in a 1948 Handy & Harman silversmithing workshop at the Rhode Island School of Design, where, under the tutelage of Baron Erik Fleming, he learned to stretch silver. After military service, he attended the Cleveland Institute of Art (CIA) in 1960 on the GI Bill. He studied design in his sophomore year with John Paul Miller, who encouraged his talent. An evening class with silversmithing professor Frederick Miller and his free-form vessels gave

Marshall a grasp of what it meant to be a consummate craftsman who was completely devoted to his material. These experiences gave him the confidence and drive to pursue a career in the field.

A fifth-year scholarship to CIA enabled Marshall to obtain his BFA in 1965. During that year he came to the attention of the dean of Syracuse University, who hired him to teach metalsmithing while pursuing his MFA, which he earned at Syracuse in 1967. He joined the University of Washington, Seattle, in 1970, where he remained for the rest of his teaching career.

Marshall's early years at Syracuse were spent strengthening his command of processes to become a better teacher, and he worked intensely with jewelry, enamel, granulation, and holloware. He became a superb manipulator of form and by the late 1960s was exploring the sculptural dimensions of the vessel. After the move to Seattle and over the next four decades, his experiments with a hydraulic press and the integration of magnificent geological specimens propelled him toward new abstract horizons. Marshall was a founding member of the Society of North American Goldsmiths and was made a Fellow of the American Craft Council (1994). —JF

Laurence Eli Schmeckebier, *John Marshall: An Exhibition of Recent Work in Gold and Silver* (Syracuse, NY: Syracuse University School of Art, 1967); Patterson Sims, "John Marshall, A Conversation with Patterson Sims," *Metalsmith* 11(summer 1991); Patricia Kane, introduction to *John Marshall, Metalsmith, Selected Work from 1991–1997* (Seattle, WA: Henry Art Gallery, 1997), 2–3; John Marshall, oral history interview by Lloyd E. Herman, April 5, 2001, AAA, SI.

MARTINEZ, MARIA

(NÉE MONTOYA)

Born in 1881, San Ildefonso Pueblo, NM;

died July 20, 1980, San Ildefonso Pueblo, NM

CERAMIST

Native American potter Maria Martinez was renowned for her rediscovery and mastery of the ancient technique of burnishing and dung-firing clay to create black pottery, thus reviving an old tradition of Pueblo pottery of the Southwest. Her home, San Ildefonso Pueblo, a Tewa-speaking village, is in an area with more than five hundred years of tradition in pottery making.

Martinez learned to make pottery helping her aunt and by watching contemporaries who worked clay in the ancient manner, without a potter's wheel, using long coils of clay, circling them around the base of the pot and blending them together to create the walls of the vessel. Maria and her husband, Julian, who later decorated the objects shaped by Maria, started producing polychrome pottery at a very young age, using ancient symbols as ornamentation, though in new combinations. They were invited to demonstrate their craft at several expositions, including the 1904 St. Louis World's Fair, the 1914 Panama-California Exposition in San Diego, and the 1934 Chicago World's Fair. In the early 1910s they were asked to replicate for museum purposes

some prehistoric pottery styles that had been discovered in an archaeological excavation near San Ildefonso, among which were the black-on-black wares. Maria and Julian invented a technique that would allow both matte and glossy black finishes, eventually achieving pots of a much finer, higher polish than the prototypes. After Julian's death in 1943, Maria began working with her daughter-in-law Santana and her son Popovi Da. —MS

Susan Peterson, *The Living Tradition of Maria Martinez* (New York: Kodansha International Ltd., 1981). For earlier history, see *Craft in the Machine Age*, 240.

MASON, JOHN

Born March 30, 1927, Madrid, NE

CERAMIST, SCULPTOR, EDUCATOR

Ceramist John Mason emerged in the California craft explosion of the 1950s. He moved from his boyhood home in Nebraska to Los Angeles in 1949 and studied drawing and painting at the Los Angeles County Art Institute (now Otis College of Art and Design). Mason briefly enrolled in a career-oriented program with ceramist Susan Peterson at the Chouinard Art Institute (now the California Institue of the Arts). Attracted to clay and to Peterson's deep practical and technical knowledge of the medium, he acquired the skill and knowledge to drive his work in a radically new direction from the vessel.

In 1954 ceramist Peter Voulkos visited Chouinard during a tour of area schools in preparation for starting a new MFA degree program at the Otis Art Institute. In January 1955, ready for a challenge and engaged by the charismatic Voulkos, Mason started graduate work at Otis, where he entered the circle of young ceramists who would soon revolutionize the clay vessel. Though still technically vessels, Mason's work in the late 1950s was characterized by flat, sculpted plains and bold color, more like "a three-dimensional abstract painting or sculpture" (Dietz 2003). In 1957 Voulkos and Mason built a studio together in an old building on Glendale Boulevard, adding space for a large kiln. Mason designed dinnerware during the day for Vernon Kilns in Los Angeles and labored in the new studio at night. Ferus Gallery began showing Mason's studio work and, at this point, he dropped his degree work at Otis.

By the 1960s, the last remnant of interior space disappeared in Mason's work, such as the monolithic tower *Spear Form* (1963) and *Red X* (1966). Both were five feet in height, nearly reaching the six-foot limit of his studio kiln and demonstrating his mastery of the technical aspects of firing large objects. During this period Mason began to produce large wall forms. Working on the floor of his studio or on an easel he applied slabs to a wall of clay in abstract compositions, often with colored glazes. The works were as large as fifty by nine feet, fired in sections, and after an outdoor exhibition at Ferus Gallery, he received numerous architectural commissions.

In the 1960s Mason's teaching credits include stints at the University of California, Berkeley, and Pomona College in Claremont, CA. In 1967 he lobbied for a position at the University of California's new branch at Irvine, where he was instrumental in setting up the ceramics program. In 1974 Mason moved to New York to teach at Hunter College in a new ceramics program started by Susan Peterson, where he remained until his retirement in 1985. —JP

Ulysses Grant Dietz, *Great Pots: Contemporary Ceramics from Function to Fantasy* (Madison, WI: Guild Publishing, 2003), 178–79; John Mason, oral history interview by Paul Smith, August 28, 2006, AAA, SI.

MASON, REX BERNARD
Born June 7, 1921, Madison, WI
CERAMIST

A student of classical and Native American ceramic cultures, Rex Mason developed a strong interest in wheel-thrown pottery in the early 1940s. Working with various decorating techniques, including sgraffito and porcelain inlay, he found inspiration in Northwest Coast, especially Haida symbols, adapting them to his own purposes. Mason studied at the Layton School of Art in Milwaukee and at the California School of Fine Arts of San Francisco (now the San Francisco Art Institute) with F. Carlton Ball. In the early 1950s, Mason set up a studio in San Francisco, where he worked while taking on short-term teaching positions in the San Francisco Bay Area, the western states, and Canada. He taught ceramics at Montana State College in Bozeman (where Peter Voulkos served as his teaching assistant in 1950), at the University of British Columbia in Vancouver (with the recommendation of Edith Heath), and at Mills College and the California College of Arts and Crafts (now California College of the Arts) in Oakland in the 1960s.

Mason was involved with the Association of San Francisco Potters, as president and a participant and designer for some of the group's annual shows held at the de Young Museum in San Francisco. He exhibited at the Oregon Ceramic Studio (1948–64; now Museum of Contemporary Craft, Portland); the fourteenth Ceramic National exhibition (1950); the International Exhibition of Ceramics at the Palais Miramar, Cannes (1955); *Designer-Craftsmen of the West* (1957, de Young Museum), the International Ceramic Museum of Faenza, Italy; and the California Biennial in Oakland (1963). In 1960 the Oakland Museum held a solo exhibition of his work. —JF

Design Magazine 49 (October 1947), 12, illus.; "Show at Oakland Art Museum," *CH* 20 (July 1960), 44; "Bray Foundation Wing to be Dedicated on Thursday Night," *Independent Record* [Helena, MT], May 3, 1964, 10; *3934 Corbett, Fifty Years at Contemporary Crafts* (Portland, OR: The Contemporary Crafts Association, 1987), 14.

McCUTCHEN, EARL STUART
Born January 13, 1918, Ida Grove, IA;
died October 24, 1985, Athens, GA
CERAMIST, GLASS ARTIST, EDUCATOR

First interested in the science of working with clay, Earl McCutchen studied ceramics engineering at Iowa State University from 1936 to 1939, and received his BFA from Ohio State University in 1941. In 1941–42 he established

the first university ceramics program in the southeast at the University of Georgia before returning to Ohio, where he spent three years as Research Engineer for the Ohio State University Research Foundation and received his MA in ceramic art in 1949. During the summer of that year, McCutchen taught ceramic glazing at the American School for Craftsmen at Alfred University in New York. His teaching career was at the University of Georgia (1941–83). In 1952–53 the university gave him a fellowship to study ceramics at the Istituto d'Arte Statale in Florence, Italy.

McCutchen made technical innovations in both ceramics and glass. In the 1950s he became fascinated with fusing, slumping, and laminating glass and produced a variety of round and square-shaped plates with abstract patterns and often interesting textures of transparent and opaque glass. He also experimented with incorporating a variety of metals into the mix. In the 1960s, as studio glass technology advanced, he extended his work to blown glass. —JP

G. Foster, "Earl McCutchen—Frances and Michael Higgins, the Signature shop, Atlanta, Ga." *CH* 27 (May 1967), 66; *Objects: USA*, 146; *Earl McCutchen: Craftsmanship in Ceramics and Glass*, exh. cat. (Athens, GA: Georgia Museum of Art, 2003); Ashley Callahan, "Earl McCutchen," the New Georgia Encyclopedia [search "McCutchen"], www.georgiaencyclopedia.org/.

McVEY, LEZA MARIE
(NÉE SULLIVAN; LATER, MRS. WILLIAM M. McVEY)
Born May 1, 1907, Cleveland, OH;
died September 24, 1984, Cleveland, OH
CERAMIST, FIBER ARTIST, EDUCATOR

With her asymmetrical, organic forms—often bottle-shaped with an elaborately styled stopper in the opening—Leza McVey was arguably the first mid-twentieth-century American ceramist to grasp the full potential of surrealist biomorphic forms. She was also one of the first to hand-build from clay coils and slabs (rejecting wheel-thrown symmetry), to work monumentally at the scale of sculpture, and to distance herself from utilitarian work by labeling her finished pieces as "Ceramic Forms." She drew upon the amorphous shapes in the work of Paul Klee and Jean Arp, using porcelain and stoneware and finishing her sculptural forms with neutral-colored matte glazes. McVey's work marks a turning point in the evolution of modern studio ceramics, an accomplishment made even more remarkable by the recurring bouts of blindness she endured from a viral infection called brucellosis.

She trained as a ceramic artist at the Cleveland Institute of Art (1927–31). Her early work gave little indication of a unique artistic perspective, and in 1932, when she married successful portrait sculptor William Mozart McVey, her artistic life fell much in the shadow of his—for years she was his technical advisor, mixing clay and supervising kiln firings for his commissions. The McVeys lived in Texas (1935–1947), and Leza taught ceramics in museums in Houston (1935–37) and San Antonio (1943–44). While William served in the military during World War II, Leza took art classes at the Colorado Springs Fine Arts Center (1943–44). In 1947 the

couple moved to Michigan for William's new teaching position at Cranbrook. There, in that extraordinary artistic environment, Leza began to blossom. Eero Saarinen purchased one of her asymmetrical vessels at the first faculty meeting the couple attended. She studied with Finnish ceramist Maija Grotell, who nurtured her technical development, and she developed a friendship with Japanese American artist Toshiko Takaezu, who also trained at Cranbrook (1951–54). In 1948 Leza McVey taught a summer course for Grotell, and then continued to teach at the school until 1953, when she and her husband moved to Cleveland and she established her own studio in nearby Pepper Pike. McVey was an advocate for contemporary craft in articles for *House Beautiful*, *Ceramics Monthly* (1953), and *Everyday Art Quarterly* (1953). She also taught at the Akron Art Institute (1955) and participated in such annual exhibitions as the Ceramic Nationals (1948–64), the Kiln Club of Washington exhibitions at the Smithsonian Institution (1951–61), and the May Shows of the Cleveland Museum of Art (1951–69). The Cleveland Institute of Art mounted a major retrospective of her work in 1965, and that same year her pottery was included in the American exhibition that won the Grand Prix de Nations at the Congress of Contemporary Ceramics in Ostend, Belgium. In the later 1950s McVey produced openwork receptacles in semitraditional shapes decorated with vertical bands; she also created stylized and whimsical figures, particularly cats. As her eyesight diminished and she was no longer able to work in clay, she turned to weaving and hooked a series of rugs in simple geometric patterns and bright colors. —TT

Martin P. Eidelberg, ed., *The Ceramic Forms of Leza McVey* (Hudson, NY: Philmark Publishers, 2002); "Obituaries: Leza Sullivan McVey '31," *Cleveland Institute of Art Magazine* 18 (winter, 1984/85), 15; Gregory Cerio, "American Studio Ceramics at Mid-Century," *Antiques* 175 (March 2009), 44–49.

MELCHERT, JAMES FREDERICK
Born December 2, 1930, New Bremen, OH
CERAMIST, PAINTER, EDUCATOR

Probably the only American ceramist in the 1960s creating idea- and text-based conceptual sculpture in clay, James Melchert experimented widely throughout the decade, producing art-, film-, and literary-influenced pieces. He worked in series, notably Ghostwares, a cluster of masks with blind, skeletal faces on boxes or plates surrounded by fragmented visual codes. His inspiration had been a single line spoken by one of the sisters in Ingmar Bergman's film, *The Silence* (1963): "Tread carefully among the ghosts of the past." Melchert's Games series consists of molded and at times identifiable objects placed on a grid or on a rectangular base, with the expressive qualities of clay suppressed in favor of a more intensely intellectual statement—these pieces are reminiscent of Alberto Giacometti's assemblages of the 1930s. In his "a" series—inspired by Raymond Queneau's *Exercises in Style* (1958), a book that retold an inconsequential story in one hundred literary styles—sculptural pieces were made from various materials, with the title providing the key to content: *Precious a* is a lustrous glazed piece mounted on a plinth; *Pre-a* is twenty pounds of unfired clay; and *a Made Forty Pounds Lighter* is a form from which handfuls of clay were roughly gouged from the surface before firing. Melchert's series additionally manifested a fascination with chance and accident. In the 1960s, he was also interested in the music of John Cage, whose compositions were based on throwing the coins of the I Ching to determine pitch and to decide how long a note would be held.

At Princeton, Melchert studied art history, earning a BA in 1952, and then went abroad for four years. When he returned from Japan, he studied painting at the University of Chicago, earning an MFA in 1957 and becoming aware of nonobjective, nonrepresentational art. In 1958 he participated in a summer pottery workshop taught by Peter Voulkos in Missoula, MT. The experience changed his life, and a year later he went to California to train with Voulkos, serving as a studio assistant (mixing clay, sweeping the floor, and firing the kilns), and earning a master's degree from the University of California, Berkeley, in 1961. From Voulkos, Melchert learned to work at a larger scale than he had previously and gained an awareness of the benefits of intense physical involvement with clay. His early work was inspired by abstract expressionism. Melchert taught ceramics at the San Francisco Art Institute from 1961 to 1965, and while there, he came under the influence of colleagues William Wiley, William Geis, and Richard Hudson, in whose work content took precedence over form. Melchert began moving beyond the expressionist approach of Voulkos and toward the use of low-fire, brightly colored glazes on white ware. He began treating the surfaces of his work with painted and relief images, fragments of words, and motifs that challenged the traditional relationships of surface and volume. In the Ghostware series, for example, he pushed boundaries by using hobbyist decals and china paint and by developing a conceptual theme that took the work beyond that of his mentor. Awarded a Louis Comfort Tiffany fellowship in 1964 and the Adeline Kent Award from the San Francisco Art Institute in 1970, Melchert also began exhibiting his work. He had solo shows in Los Angeles (1968) and San Francisco and Boston (1970), and he participated in important group exhibitions such as *Abstract Expressionist Ceramics* at University of California, Irvine (1966). Melchert joined the faculty of the University of California, Berkeley, in 1965, and taught sculpture. In the 1970s he set aside ceramics to focus on photographic "rubbings," and then moved into arts administration, serving as director of the National Endowment for the Arts (1977–81) and director of the American Academy in Rome (1985–1988). In recent years he has returned to ceramics, using randomly broken and reconfigured commercial tiles to create conceptual works. —TT

J. Pugliese, "James Melchert at the Art Center of Richmond. California," *CH* 21(May 1961), 41; Marsha Miro, "Jim Melchert: Mister In-Between," *American Ceramics* 12, no. 2 (1996), 30–35; James Melchert, oral history interview by Renny Pritkin, September 18 and October 19, 2002, AAA, SI.

MERRITT, FRANCIS SUMNER
Born April 8, 1913, Danvers, MA;
died December 27, 2000, Belfast, ME

MERRITT, PRISCILLA HARDWICK
Born April 26, 1913, Malden, MA;
died September 1, 2006, Deer Isle, ME

EDUCATORS, ADMINISTRATORS
Known for his innovative approach to art education, Francis Merritt, and his wife, Priscilla, ran Haystack Mountain School of Crafts in Deer Isle, ME, from its establishment in 1951 to his retirement in 1977. They altered postwar craft education when they introduced summer courses at Haystack based upon the master/student traditions of Cranbrook. Merritt studied art at the Vesper George Art School, Boston; San Diego Academy of Fine Arts; Massachusetts College of Art; and Yale University School of Art. He apprenticed to Boston stained-glass artist Charles J. Connick. During the late 1930s and '40s, while working as a printmaker, he taught printing and drawing at Abbott Academy in Andover, MA, Colby Junior College in Maine, and the Cranbrook Summer Institute. He also headed the art department at Bradford Junior College in Massachusetts and was director of the Flint (MI) Institute of Arts; state director of the Artists Equity Association of Michigan; and chairman of the Michigan Academy of Science, Arts, and Letters. He was a trustee and a fellow of the American Craft Council as well as a fellow of the Royal Society of Art.

Early in her career, Priscilla was a fashion illustrator for Boston retailer Filene's. Much later she became the owner of Centennial House, a Deer Isle craft gallery. At Haystack, she assumed numerous roles, from business manager to weaving instructor to chief cook. —MS

"Francis Merritt, 87, Whose School Broadened the Study of Crafts," *New York Times*, January 8, 2001, B7; "Francis Sumner Merritt, 1913–2000," *Studio Potter* 29 (June 2001), 100; "Remembrances," *Penobscot Bay Press*, September 7, 2006, 6.

MILLER, FREDERICK A.
Born February 6, 1913, Akron, OH;
died January 8, 2000, Cleveland, OH

SILVERSMITH, JEWELER, DESIGNER, EDUCATOR
Frederick Miller studied design at the Cleveland School of Art (later, Cleveland Institute of Art 1936–40). Though he had discovered an interest in working with metal in high school, only jewelry-making and enameling courses were offered at the Institute, and he experimented with enameling under Kenneth Bates. In 1946, after serving in World War II, Miller joined the Cleveland firm of Potter and Mellen as a designer. The following year he began his teaching career at the Cleveland Institute of Art, where he remained until 1975.

Miller worked as a silversmith along with teaching and design work. In the summer of 1948, he participated in the second of five National Silversmithing Workshop Conferences, sponsored by the Handy & Harman metal refining company. It was led that year by Swedish silversmith Baron Erik Fleming who focused the class on the stretching method of raising silver, a technique that allows for free-form as well as asymetrical designs. Photographs of Fred Miller making a bowl by this method appeared in an article in *Craft Horizons* the following winter.

Miller produced sleek modernist pitchers, coffee and tea sets, vases, and candlesticks. The stretching method he had learned proved to be seminal to Miller's inventive series of free-form bottles and bowls whose elegantly simple organic shapes elude the confines of modernism. —JP

Margret Craver, "An Ancient Method Goes Modern," *CH* 9 (winter 1949), 15–17; "Fred Miller Makes a Silver Bowl: The Stretching Method," *CH* 16 (December 1956), 37–39; *Objects: USA*, 90; William Baran-Mickle, "Frederick A. Miller: A Precarious Balance," *Metalsmith* 13 (spring 1993), 34–39.

MILLER, JOHN PAUL
Born April 23, 1918, Huntingdon, PA

METALSMITH, JEWELER, EDUCATOR
One of America's foremost goldsmiths, John Paul Miller brought the ancient technique of gold granulation to the attention of modern jewelers. In this process, the artist embellishes a gold surface with infinitesimal spheres of gold, some as tiny as one-two-hundredth of an inch in diameter, and without the use of solder. Perfected by the Etruscans, granulation was virtually lost for more than a millennium until it was rediscovered by the Castellani firm in Rome in the late nineteenth century. By Miller's day, the technique had largely fallen into disuse, and when he came across photos of granulation work by German jeweler Elizabeth Treskow in a 1940 issue of *Die Kunst*, he was fascinated. In his research, Miller found a treatise by an archaeologist at the American Academy in Rome that explored the subject. The author speculated that certain alloys could form a eutectic bond (at the lowest possible temperature of solidification) when heated in a reducing atmosphere, thus permitting a small and precise fusion of tiny spheres of metal onto a surface.

Miller's first success was with 14-karat gold. He then began exploring a range of variables, including different alloys, flames, fluxes, and adhesives, and as his skill increased, he discovered how to join larger components and to fuse long seams so an entire piece could be made using only one alloy. By the 1950s Miller was creating elegant and contemporary work in three distinctive series: Fragments, where large floating shapes were held together at hidden points; Black and Gold, where fragments of 18-karat and 24-karat gold were blackened for dramatic effect; and his most widely known—a menagerie of animals and crustaceans, each no more than 2¼ to 2½ inches at the longest dimension—where delicately enameled surfaces and granulation were combined. For much of his career, Miller typically made between four and eight pieces of jewelry a year.

Miller's precocious interest in the arts had been encouraged by his parents, who introduced him to the Cleveland Museum of Art when he was just five years old. He took Saturday classes and explored the museum (small objects in the decorative arts collections intrigued him), and as a high school student he learned enameling at the museum school from Kenneth Bates. In 1936 Miller entered the industrial design program at the Cleveland School of Art (later, Cleveland Institute of Art), where he met fellow student and silversmith, Frederick Miller, who taught him the fundamentals of working with a mouth blowtorch and an alcohol lamp. (Later, the two of them shared a studio.) With the torch equipment and a small brick kiln he built in his parents' basement, Miller began making rings and brooches, some of which he enameled. At the School of Art, Miller completed a broad range of classes—painting, watercolor, and design. He was influenced by a number of teachers, including Kay Dorn Cass, Paul Travis, and Viktor Schreckengost, and he graduated in 1940 having been hired onto the faculty during his senior year. In 1946, after five years of military service Miller took up his teaching post and remained there until his retirement nearly forty years later. Miller taught drawing, painting, watercolor, three-dimensional design, color, jewelry, silversmithing, and film animation. In the 1950s he began designing and installing all the gallery exhibitions. Miller augmented his metalsmithing skills in 1951 by participating in one of the Handy & Harman silversmithing workshops organized by Margret Craver and taught by Swedish silversmith Baron Erik Fleming. Among Miller's many accomplishments was filmmaking, and in 1951 he and Frederick Miller produced a film on the stretching process in silversmithing that was released by Handy & Harman. In 1953, again with Frederick Miller's assistance, he made two teaching films on technique. In the first he demonstrated the processes of gold granulation and enameling, and in the second Frederick Miller created a free-form silver bottle. Miller first exhibited his work in 1949 at the Cleveland Museum of Art's May Show. He was given a one-man exhibition at the Art Institute of Chicago in 1957, and his work was included in the prestigious Brussels international exposition of 1958. —TT

Conrad Brown, "Gold Granulation; J. P. Miller's Modern Technology Brings an Ancient Art Back to Life," *CH* 17 (March 1957), 10–15; Frances Taft, "John Paul Miller: Infusing Form with Feeling," *Metalsmith* 26 (fall 2006), 44–51; John Paul Miller, oral history interview by Jan Yager, August 22 and 23, 2004, AAA, SI.

MOORE, EUDORAH
(NÉE EUDORAH GOODELL MORSE; LATER MRS. ANSON C. MOORE)
Born June 15, 1918, Denver, CO
CURATOR

Eudorah Moore promoted the experimental design innovations of the California postwar period as director and curator of the California Design exhibitions from 1962 until 1978. These triennial exhibitions, held primarily at the Pasadena Art Museum, began in 1955 and focused on California designers in Los Angeles County. Moore graduated from Smith College in 1940, and immediately moved to California, where she soon became a volunteer at the

Pasadena Art Museum; in time she became president of the board. Meanwhile, with a small group, she founded and later became first president of the Pasadena Art Alliance, a volunteer and support organization for the museum. When the County of Los Angeles offered the museum a grant of ten thousand dollars to promote the city (under the State Fair Fund), Moore proposed to use the funds to widen the scope of the California Design exhibitions; she was appointed director of the show in 1962. She broadened submissions to include California artists, designers, and manufacturers working in furniture, jewelry, fiber, ceramics, glass, metal, and wood. Moore established a jury to select submissions and encouraged designers to submit prototypes. This not only resulted in exhibitions that showcased the most current designs, but also created a forum for designers and manufacturers.

Moore became Crafts Coordinator of the Visual Arts Program at the National Endowment for the Arts (1978–81), and Project Director of the National Crafts Planning Project (1980–81); a national congress for the latter was held in Denver in 1981. For her contributions to the field, Moore received a medal from Smith College (1973) and an honorary doctorate from the California College of Arts and Crafts (now the California College of the Arts) (1979). —NB

Joy Deweese-Wehen, "Eudorah M. Moore: Crafts Program Director, Crusader, Enthusiast," *Design for Arts in Education* 81 (October 1979), 9–12; Jo Lauria and Suzanne Baizerman, *California Design: The Legacy of West Coast Craft and Style* (San Francisco: Chronicle Books, LLC., 2005); Eudorah Moore, telephone conversation with Jeannine Falino, November 3 and December 15, 2010.

MORAN, LOIS
Born October 26, 1933, Elizabeth, NJ
ADMINISTRATOR, AUTHOR, EDITOR

As editor-in-chief of *American Craft* from 1980 to 2006, Lois Moran helped to define the complex world of craft and its ever-changing relationship with the modern world, while also serving in a range of overlapping positions during her many years at the American Craft Council.

Educated at Rutgers University and the New York School of Interior Design, Moran studied tapestry weaving with Alice Adams and Paula Adler. She joined the ACC in 1963 as director of regional programming, with the goal of bringing greater attention to craft-based activities throughout the country. In 1966 she became responsible for the newsletter *ACC Outlook* and soon after, was appointed director of the research and education department at the ACC. Over forty-three years she worked in many capacities, including director of national programming (1977–78), vice president of operations (1979), acting executive director (1979–80), and executive director (1988–90), the latter positions held during her tenure as editor.

Moran oversaw numerous ACC publications from the 1970s onward and has held numerous advisory positions, including on the World Craft Council executive committee (2003–7) and the National Endowment for the Arts (1980–81). She has been a frequent exhibition juror and

conference panelist. In 1993 she received the Lifetime Achievement Award at the Women in the Craft Arts conference at the National Museum of Women in the Arts and was elected an Honorary Fellow of the ACC in 2008. —MS

Andrew Wagner, "Lois Moran: Labor of Love," *AC* 67 (April–May 2007), 6.

MORGAN, ANNE TRACY
Born July 25, 1873, Highland Falls, NY; died January 29, 1952, Mt. Kisco, NY
PHILANTHROPIST

Anne Morgan, the youngest daughter of financier J. P. Morgan, worked for humanitarian causes throughout her life. Her earliest interests revolved around women's issues, and with Florence J. Harriman and Elisabeth Marbury, she founded the Colony Club in New York City (1903), which was the first women's social club and residence in New York City. She also helped found the American Woman's Association, serving as president (1928–43). Some of her greatest contributions, however, took place during the two world wars, when, with Isabel Lathrop, she established the American Fund for French Wounded in 1915 (the same year she published *The American Girl: Her Education, Her Responsibility, Her Recreation, Her Future*). In 1917 she formed the American Committee for Devastated France, with its headquarters at the Château de Blérancourt, which she purchased and later donated for this cause. In addition to providing financial support, she worked with volunteers and directed relief efforts. France recognized her contributions by awarding her the Croix de Guerre in 1918 and the Legion of Honor in 1924, elevated to the rank of commander in 1932, the first American woman to receive this honor. Lastly, in 1939 she founded the American Friends of France. Upon her return to America in 1940, she headed the American Handicraft Council (established a year earlier), which merged with Aileen Osborn Webb's organization, the Handcraft Cooperative League of America to form the American Craftsmen's Cooperative Council in 1942. In September 2010, the Morgan Library in New York City organized *Anne Morgan's War: Rebuilding Devastated France, 1917–1924,* chronicling her volunteer efforts in France. —BN

Aileen O. Webb, "Almost A Century," typescript, Aileen Osborn Webb papers, AAA Art; "Anne Morgan Dies in Mt. Kisco Home," *New York Times*, January 30, 1952, 25.

MYERS, JOEL PHILIP
Born January 29, 1934, Paterson, NJ
GLASS ARTIST, DESIGNER, EDUCATOR, AND CERAMIST

Joel Philip Myers developed a passion for blown glass that culminated in a lifelong studio craft career, designing, creating, teaching and mentoring glass artists. Trained in advertising design at the Parsons School of Design, Myers graduated in 1954. He first worked as a designer for Donald Deskey Association, New York, before attending a ceramics program in Copenhagen, Denmark, between 1957 and 1958. He returned to the U.S., and by 1963 had completed his BFA and MFA in ceramics from Alfred

University. Within the year, Myers accepted a position as director of design at Blenko Glass Company in Milton, WV (1964–70), where he designed glass in vibrant, rainbow hues, a career change that piqued his interest in setting up a glass studio. With his design credentials and raw glass material at his disposal, Myers began to teach himself glassblowing. After leaving Blenko, he pursued studio glass full-time and also taught at Illinois State University at Normal, IL, where he initiated a glassblowing program that allowed him the freedom to experiment and to mentor new generations of glass artists. He retired in 1997.

The period at Blenko illustrates Myers's interest in form and color. The glass he designed for the company was typically functional, long, lean, and tapered. Color fascinated Myers both for its vibrancy in glass and its opaque qualities. By contrast, Myers's independent studio work has often been nonfunctional, though usually of a recognizable form: hand, globe, vase, goblet. The pieces often encompass technical experimentation with glass shards and cut and engraved glass, embedded into the forms. —LB

J. H. Kay, "Exhibition at Craft Center, Worcester, Massachusetts," *CH* 28 (May 1968), 54; William V. Ganis, "Joel Philip Myers & Steven I. Weinberg," *Glass* [New York] 111 (summer 2008), 73; Joel Philip Myers, oral history interview with Dan Klein, May 1, 2007, AAA, SI.

NAKASHIMA, GEORGE KATSUTOSHI

Born May 24, 1905, Spokane, WA;
died June, 15, 1990, New Hope, PA
FURNITURE DESIGNER, FURNITURE MAKER

Described by his daughter Mira as an artisan in the *mingei* tradition (a folk craft movement in early twentieth-century Japan), George Nakashima produced one-of-a-kind, often site-specific furniture that embodies a rich blend of Eastern and Western traditions. They reflect a reverence for the trees that supplied the wood and an aesthetic awareness of designs adaptable to contemporary life. Elements of Japanese folk traditions, the simplicity of Shaker motifs, and the linear elegance of American spindle-backed Windsor chairs converged in Nakashima's settees, stools, chairs, and benches. His flamboyant free-edged creations—often with dovetail joinery and his trademark butterfly joint in rosewood—speak to a love of nature and organic form. In tabletops, armrests, lamp bases, and music stands, he often retained the cavities, cracks, and dynamic outlines of the trunks or roots from which they were cut. Specializing in black walnut, cherry, and redwood acquired from local sources, Nakashima often purchased wood while a tree was still standing. With the assistance of his many apprentices, he used power lathes and machinery to shape the furniture, finishing it by hand with Japanese chisels and saws, and then waxing and oiling the wood to a fine sheen. Nakashima believed wood had a spirit of its own and through its "second life" as furniture the essence of the wood emerged.

Born of samurai lineage to parents who had emigrated from Japan, Nakashima studied architecture and received a diploma from the École Americaine des Beaux Arts in Paris in 1928. He earned an undergraduate degree in architecture from the University of Washington in 1929 and a master's degree in architecture from MIT in 1931. Nakashima then set out on a spiritual quest and by 1934 had landed in Tokyo, where he was employed by American architect Antonin Raymond, a collaborator with Frank Lloyd Wright on the Imperial Hotel. Nakashima toured Japan to study carpentry techniques, design, and architecture. As the primary construction consultant for Raymond's firm, Nakashima supervised the building of a dormitory for the Sri Aurobindo ashram in Pondicherry, India (1937–39). In India he lived as a monk, experienced a transformation of consciousness, and was given the Sanskrit name "Sundrananda" (one who delights in beauty). He also made his first pieces of furniture.

Nakashima returned to the U.S. and was in Seattle by 1940, setting up his first studio and making Shaker-inspired furniture by 1941. During the war he was interned for a time in 1941 in the Camp Minidoka Relocation Center, Hunt, ID, where he met Japanese carpenter Gentaro Hikogawa, who helped him to master traditional Japanese hand tools and joinery techniques. In 1943 Raymond sponsored Nakashima's release from internment and invited him to his farm in New Hope, PA.

In 1944 Nakashima set up a studio and workshop on a parcel of land he purchased just outside of New Hope, and working on his own, he absorbed the area's vernacular furniture styles, particularly eighteenth-century Windsor chairs. By 1946 Knoll Associates was carrying a line of Nakashima furniture, and he was gaining a clientele. By the early 1950s he was garnering commissions from individuals and institutions. His work was included in the MoMA's Good Design exhibitions, and he was awarded the craftsmanship medal from the American Institute of Architects in 1952. His designs became part of the mass-production furniture line marketed by Widdicomb-Mueller in 1958. Nakashima began teaching integrated woodworking methods by designing and consulting for two workshops in India and Japan in 1960. Today, his work is seen within an international modernist context, and through a lens that reexamines the notion that modernism is an exclusively industrial form. —TT

George Nakashima, *The Soul of a Tree: A Woodworker's Reflections* (Tokyo: Kodansha International, 1981); Wolfgang Saxon, "George Nakashima is Dead at 85; Designer and Master Woodworker," *New York Times*, June 18, 1990, B11; Stephen Beyer, *George Nakashima and the Modernist Moment*, exh. cat. (Doylestown, PA: James Michener Art Museum, 2001); Mira Nakashima, *Nature, Form and Spirit: The Life and Legacy of George Nakashima* (New York: Harry N. Abrams, 2003).

NATZLER, GERTRUD (NÉE AMON)

Born July 7, 1908, Vienna, Austria;
died June 3, 1971, Los Angeles, CA
NATZLER, OTTO
Born January 31, 1908, Vienna, Austria;
died April 7, 2007, Los Angeles, CA
CERAMISTS

During their nearly forty years as artistic collaborators, Gertrud and Otto Natzler created work now regarded as a perfect harmony of form and glaze. Gertrud was considered one of the most sensitive and refined throwers of her era, forming clay into graceful, thin-walled vessels. Otto was one of the most experimental glazers of his time, using unpredictable firing techniques to achieve colorful and textured surfaces that ranged from smooth and glassy to blistered and fissured. Between 1939 and 1971 the Natzlers produced twenty-five thousand vessels for which more than two thousand glazes were developed. These objects were intended primarily for display rather than daily use. Through an approach steeped in modernism that also mediated various craft traditions—Bauhaus and Scandinavian in particular, with passing glances at British studio pottery and Chinese ceramics—the Natzlers translated vernacular European theories and practices of industrial design and decoration into American ceramic, arriving at a synthesized aesthetic that was quintessentially American.

The Natzlers' artistic partnership began as a love story. The two met in Vienna in 1933 when Gertrud was employed as a secretary and Otto was an unemployed textile designer. Gertrud had graduated from the Handelsakademie in 1926 and Otto from the Lehranstalt für Textilindustrie in 1927. The year before they met, Gertrud had taken courses in drawing, painting, and ceramics, and the following year when their friendship developed, Gertrud introduced Otto to clay. Together they established a studio in 1935. Two years later, they won a silver medal for work exhibited in the Austrian pavilion at the Paris Exposition Internationale des Arts et Techniques dans la Vie Moderne. Nevertheless, their careers in their native country had come to an end, as both Gertrud and Otto were Jewish, and Hitler's troops marched into Vienna in March 1938. By the fall of that year they had immigrated to the U.S. and settled in Los Angeles. There they discovered an existing tradition of studio pottery and a wide and varied awareness of the tenets of modernism. While establishing a market for their work, they taught ceramics intermittently from 1939 to 1942 to such students as Laura Andreson and Beatrice Wood. For a time, Gertrud was the only potter in Southern California producing vessels entirely on the wheel. A first prize at the eighth Ceramic National exhibition in Syracuse in 1939 brought them American recognition, and for the next twenty-five years the Natzlers participated in virtually every Ceramic National. They also strategically placed their work in exhibitions throughout the country and in Europe, with their first solo show in the Fine Arts Gallery of San Diego in 1940. By the early 1940s they had created an important gallery relationship with Los Angeles dealer Dalzell Hatfield, who marketed their work from 1940 to 1967. —TT

R. Henderson, "Natzler Ceramics," *Studio* 153 (January 1957), 18–21; *Form and Fire: Natzler Ceramics, 1939–1972* (Washington, DC: Renwick Gallery of the National Collection of Fine Arts by the Smithsonian Institution Press, 1973); "Otto Natzler 1908–2007," *AC* 67 (August/September 2007), 18, 20.

NELSON, GEORGE HAROLD

Born May 29, 1908, Hartford, CT;
died March 5, 1986, New York, NY
ARCHITECT, WRITER, DESIGNER, EDUCATOR

One of the most articulate and eloquent voices on design and architecture in America in the mid-twentieth century, George Nelson is associated with the postwar glory years at Herman Miller, Inc. (beginning in 1947). He helped legitimize and stimulate the field of industrial design with the creation of *Industrial Design* magazine (1953). His corporate office, George Nelson Associates, Inc. (founded in 1955), employed the best and the brightest in the emerging design field, completing a wide range of projects—furniture, industrial products, exhibitions, and urban planning—for a host of Fortune 500 clients. In addition to his design work, Nelson taught at Columbia, Harvard, and Pratt. He was also an editor and the author of numerous articles and books, such as *Chairs* (1952) and *Problems of Design* (1957), which were regarded as seminal in the field. He was a creator of exhibitions—as conceptual catalyst for the American National Exhibition pavilion in Moscow (1959, with Charles Eames and William Katavalos) and the Chrysler and Irish pavilions at the New York World's Fair (1964)—and he was a conference organizer, spearheading the legendary Aspen design gatherings.

Trained as an architect at Yale, Nelson has been described as a part of the generation of architects who had too few projects but found success in related fields. He won a Prix de Rome while studying architecture at Catholic University of America and spent a year in Europe (1932) meeting a number of the pioneer modernists—Walter Gropius, Mies van der Rohe, Le Corbusier, and Gio Ponti. He then introduced these men and their work to Americans through articles for the magazine *Pencil Points,* and this helped land him an editorial position at *Architectural Forum.* His idea for the Storagewall, presented in *Tomorrow's House* (1945, co-authored with Henry Wright), inspired D. J. De Pree, chairman of Herman Miller, Inc., to collaborate with Nelson, helping to launch his career as a designer. Nelson's affiliation with Herman Miller began in 1947 and lasted forty years, keeping the company at the cutting edge of design thinking.

Nelson applied design to everything—furniture collections, corporate logos, catalogues, letterhead, truck signage, advertising, literature, and invitations. He also cultivated a stable of designers—among them Charles and Ray Eames, Alexander Girard, Harry Bertoia, Richard Schultz, Irving Harper, Lucia DeRespinis, and Isamu Noguchi. While the Herman Miller contract was one of Nelson's earliest and most important, by the time he established George Nelson Associates, Inc., his clientele had expanded internationally, and his staff of designers were generating some of the most important designs of the era: William Renwick (*Bubble* lamp, 1953), John Svezia (*Sling* sofa, 1963), Irving Harper (*Marshmallow* sofa, 1956), John Pile (Steelframe Storage System, 1954), and Don Ervin and George Tscherny (graphics and advertising). Nelson helped people understand that design had universality, and that the natural

world provided a kind of basic model that could be used by designers to create the manufactured world. —TT

Stanley Abercombie, *George Nelson: The Design of Modern Design* (Cambridge, MA: MIT Press, 1995); Jochen Eisenbrand, *George Nelson* (Weil am Rhein, Germany: Vitra Design Museum, 2008).

NEW, LLOYD KIVA

Born February 18, 1916, Fairland, OK;
died February 8, 2002, Santa Fe, NM
FABRIC DESIGNER, PAINTER, EDUCATOR,
ADMINISTRATOR, DIRECTOR

Often considered the father of Native American contemporary art, Lloyd Kiva New was not only an artist and designer, but also a prominent leader and proponent of Native American culture. New was committed to establishing organizations and institutions that offered opportunity to Native American artists to work in nontraditional sectors of the arts.

Born the tenth child to a Cherokee mother and Scotch-Irish father, New was raised on a farm in northeastern Oklahoma. He graduated from the Art Institute of Chicago in 1938 and held a post in the U.S. Navy during World War II. In 1946 he launched an apparel business in Scottsdale, AZ, where he sold Cherokee-based designs to Neiman Marcus and other stores. In 1954 he organized a landmark exhibition, *Past with Present*, at the Heard Museum in Phoenix, which attracted national media attention by challenging modern haute couture with traditional Native American clothing and crafts. Indian craftspeople, including potters, silversmiths, and rug makers, worked on their crafts in the gallery while dressed in Native attire. He is also credited with shaping the contemporary fine arts program at the Heard.

In the late 1950s New focused on progressive educational projects, including the Southwest Indian Arts Project (1958) and the Phoenix Indian School, intended to heighten awareness of Native American culture while providing a larger platform for education. For a short period in the 1960s he collaborated with Native American jeweler Charles Loloma—New designed handbags and Loloma executed the silver clasps. In 1962 he and Dr. George Boyce founded the Institute of American Indian Arts (IAIA), which was financed by the Bureau of Indian Affairs, Department of the Interior. New served as its first art director and longtime president, assembling a predominantly Native American faculty that could provide an intertribal visual and performing arts experience for students who hailed from around the country. —LB

Lloyd Kiva New, "Feathers or Freedom: An Essay on the Dynamics of American Indian Arts," *Craft International* 6 (July–September, 1987), 12–13; Gary Avey, "A Tribute to Lloyd Kiva New," *Native Peoples Magazine* 15 (July/August 2002), 84–86; Hollis Walker, "Collections: Aysen and Lloyd Kiva New," *Native Peoples Magazine* 19 (September/October 2006), 86.

NG, WIN

Born April 13, 1936, San Francisco, CA;
died September 6, 1991, San Francisco, CA
CERAMIST, DESIGNER, ENTREPRENEUR

Chinese American and native San Franciscan Win Ng was among a group of West Coast studio artists who launched the abstract expressionist movement in ceramics in the 1960s. Ng studied at City College of San Francisco and San Francisco State University, and after serving in the U.S. Army during World War II, he continued his education at the San Francisco Art Institute, receiving a BFA degree in 1959. The Art Institute was at the center of artistic experimentation, where the concept of fine art was being challenged and expanded to include performance arts, graphic art, conceptual art, and personal and social commentary.

Ng's early abstract work was enriched with earth tones and natural textures and shapes. He won a purchase prize in 1961 at the twenty-first Syracuse Ceramic Nationals competition with clay slab stoneware forms, decorated with incised lines and polychrome glazes. He focused on shapes, circles, or squares, consistently exploring the elemental concepts of positives and negatives in nature. Rectangular shapes represented the form in space, while curvilinear forms represented fluid movement. His work was exhibited in *Forms from the Earth: 1,000 Years of Pottery in America* at the MCC in 1962, and at the prestigious Third International Ceramics Exhibition in Prague the same year.

A pivotal year for Ng was 1965, when he met Spaulding Taylor. The two artists founded Environmental Ceramics in San Francisco, featuring handcrafted functional pieces and studio pottery. The firm was soon renamed Taylor & Ng, and the focus changed to large-scale production and retailing of housewares designed by Ng. Their signature style popularized Asian culture and cuisine and provided Ng the opportunity to expand into such areas as cookbooks and linens. —LB

Yoshiko Uchida, "Win Ng," *CH* 20 (January 1960), 32–35; Kenneth B. Sawyer, "U.S. Ceramics at the Third International Exhibition of Contemporary Ceramics in Prague," *CH* 22 (May 1962), 58; Allen R. Hicks, *The Art of Win Ng: A Retrospective* (San Francisco, CA: Chinese Historical Society of America, 2004).

NOGUCHI, ISAMU

Born November 17, 1904, Los Angeles, CA;
died December 30, 1988, New York, NY
SCULPTOR, DESIGNER, CERAMIST, WOODWORKER

During the course of a sixty-year career, Isamu Noguchi created an extraordinary range of work, from sculptures—for which he was best known—to public gardens, environmental art installations, fountains, plazas, playgrounds, portrait busts, paintings, interior designs, and architecture. His reach extended to craft and design, creating ceramics for exhibitions, numerous stage sets for dance, and furniture and lamps for industry. At the heart of Noguchi's work is the duality of his own history. The son of a Japanese father and an American mother, he spent his life in search of cultural unity between East and West, living at various times in both Japan and the U.S. He often pursued contradictory directions in his work—it was both organic and geometric, and it expressed European modernism (surrealism and abstraction) as well as Japanese traditionalism. There was a tension of conflicting impulses—it was spiritual and scientific, as well as utopian and pragmatic.

Believing all the arts to be interlinked, Noguchi was constantly searching for ways to bring them together. He collaborated with artists and manufacturers from East and West, among them Japanese potter Kitaoji Rosanjin, American choreographer Martha Graham, Ozeki & Company in Gifu, Japan, and Herman Miller, Inc. in Zeeland, MI. Noguchi's craft and design work spanned the 1930s to the 1960s. He immersed himself in ceramics on only three occasions. Each experience was charged with emotion and artistic energy. In 1931, reuniting with his estranged father, he met and worked with Kyoto master potter, Uno Jinmatsu, an expert in celadon glazes. In 1950 he and his half-brother, Micho Noguchi, traveled to Seto in Aichi Prefecture, where the potter Hajime Kato provided materials and facilities for the vessels and sculptures that Noguchi created for an exhibition in the Mitsukoshi Department Store in Tokyo that year. His last foray into ceramics was in 1952, the year he married Japanese actress Shirley Yamaguchi. They set up a studio in Kita Kamakura in a valley belonging to potter Kitaoji Rosanjin, and Noguchi used Rosanjin's kilns to fire the traditional forms and sculptures he produced for an exhibition at the Museum of Modern Art in Kamakura. Noguchi later noted that "the attractions of ceramics lie partly in its contradictions. It is both difficult and easy, with an element beyond our control" (Noguchi 1968). The first U.S. exhibition of the ceramic work he made in Japan was at the Stable Gallery, in New York City, in 1954.

An interest in theater set design also began in the 1930s, resulting in a long association between Noguchi and choreographer Martha Graham. He created the first stage set for her dance production, *Frontier,* in 1935, and continued designing for her until 1967, when he completed the set for *Cortege of Eagles.* Today, he is recognized as the leading set designer for twentieth-century modern dance.

Noguchi's furniture, which he also began making in the 1930s, was biomorphic in character, revealing a love of simple construction and natural materials typically seen in Asian art and architecture, but also with the streamlined look of a modern industrial design product. His first piece, made in 1939, was a one-off table in rosewood and plate glass for A. Conger Goodyear, the president of MoMA. That same year he designed a three-legged coffee table for Terrence Harold Robsjohn-Gibbings, executing a small model in plastic. According to Noguchi, Robsjohn-Gibbings stole the design, claiming anyone could design a three-legged table. In retaliation, Noguchi created a glass-topped variant that was illustrated in an article by George Nelson ("How to Make a Table") and this version was popularized by the Herman Miller Co. From the mid-1940s Knoll

Associates produced Noguchi's table lamps, forms that took on something of the qualities of Japanese lanterns with translucent shades wrapped around simple geometric frames. Knoll also manufactured his rocking stool (1955) and a Formica-topped dining table using cast iron and steel rods to support its top (1953). When Noguchi was in Japan in the early 1950s, he also created for export to the modern design market a chair whose backrest and seat were fabricated by traditional basket-weaving techniques using bamboo strips.

It was also in Japan, following a visit to Gifu in 1951, that Noguchi first designed the *Akari* lamp—a light sculpture that had its roots in the traditional spiral paper lanterns of Japan, but was transformed by Noguchi into an art object. The *Akari* lamp became an important international product and was initially manufactured by Ozeki & Company, Gifu, Japan. It was exhibited in New York City in April 1955 and was available at the Bonnier's store by the 1960s. —TT

"Noguchi's Akari," *Interiors* 114 (April 1955), 118–21; Isamu Noguchi, *A Sculptor's World* (New York: Harper Row, 1968); Bruce Altshuler, *Isamu Noguchi* (New York: Abbeville Press, 1994); Bruce Altshuler, "The Ceramic Sculpture of Isamu Noguchi," in *Isamu Noguchi, Kitaoji Rosanjin*, exh. cat. (Tokyo: Sezon Museum of Art, 1996). For earlier history see *Craft in the Machine Age*, 241.

OLDENBURG, CLAES
Born January 28, 1929, Stockholm, Sweden
SCULPTOR

A fresh spirit in contemporary American sculpture, Claes Oldenburg was born into a Swedish diplomat family that moved to Chicago in 1936. He studied literature and art history at Yale University (1946–50) and earned an art degree at the Art Institute of Chicago. By 1956, Oldenburg had moved to New York, where he joined a group of artists who challenged the approach of abstract expressionism by exploring performance art, termed Happenings, first at the Judson Memorial Church and Gallery in Greenwich Village and later converting his "store" at 107 East 2nd Street, the Ray Gun Mfg. Co., into a live unscripted theater. At the Judson Gallery, Oldenburg had complete artistic freedom and consistently conveyed emotional or expressive subjects. His 1959 exhibition reflected his interest in figurative paintings and papier-mâché sculptures, while in 1960, his installation titled *The Street* depicted urban squalor, combining scraps and objects from the street with paint into a three-dimensional 'mural.'

The three-dimensional, theatrical props Oldenburg had created for the gallery evolved into another art form—painted plaster versions of everyday commodities, such as *White Shirt and Blue Tie* and *Danish Pastry*, both made in 1961. These works put him on the front lines of the American pop art movement of the 1960s. He went on to enlarge the scale of these mundane objects, working in canvas and other textiles to create malleable, colossal sculptures that changed shape as air moved inside or around them. Parody and humor were mainstays of

Oldenburg's "soft" works, some of which he replicated in hard materials, such as wood and aluminum.

In 1977 Oldenburg married Dutch/American pop sculptor, Coosje van Bruggen, and they began to collaborate on oversize outdoor sculptures such as *Spoonbridge and Cherry* (Walker Art Center, Minneapolis, 1988). —LB
S. Tillim, "Claes Oldenburg's 'The Store,'" *Arts Magazine* 36 (February 1962), 35–37; Barbara Rose, *Claes Oldenburg* (New York: Museum of Modern Art; Greenwich, CT: New York Graphic Society, 1970); F. R. Schwartz, "Exhibition at Museum of Modern Art," *CH* 29 (November 1969), 57.

OSOLNIK, RUDE
Born March 4, 1915, Dawson, NM;
died November 18, 2001, Berea, KY
WOODWORKER

An accomplished woodturner, Rude Osolnik was known for his remarkable output of bowls, vases, pots, and hourglass candleholders crafted from found sources, such as tree stumps, fallen trees, logs with deformities, burls, and spurs—the wood near tree roots that has a wild and disordered grain and is richly colored by minerals in the soil. Freely yielding to accidents of nature, Osolnik turned pieces to twist and meander according to the original wood form. The artist believed in letting wood speak for itself, and he regarded form as the objective, with color, texture, balance, and proportion in supporting roles. In the 1960s he developed a process for laminating sheets of Baltic birch plywood to form large blocks that he then turned on a lathe to create powerful graphic forms that revealed stacked-layer edges.

The son of Slovenian immigrants who settled in Johnson City, IL, Osolnik was introduced to woodturning in high school. At Bradley University in Peoria, IL, he tried his hand at such other media as leather, metalwork, enameling, lost-wax casting, and woodcarving, but under the tutelage of Harry Huff, he devoted himself to production woodturning, acquiring proficiency and speed. He earned a BFA in 1937 and an MFA in 1950, both in industrial arts. Hired as an instructor in the Industrial Arts Program at Berea College in Kentucky in 1937, Osolnik began a forty-year teaching career (with time out for service in the U.S. Navy during World War II). He helped establish the industrial arts program as a department in the college in 1968, serving as its first chairman, and he directed the Berea College Woodcraft Industry (which manufactures custom furniture and other items as a source of income for the college and as employment for its students) from 1975 to 1977, when he retired. He and his wife Daphne established Osolnik Originals, a studio that produced turned-wood objects to be marketed through the college's Log House Sales Room, the Southern Highland Handicraft Guild, and America House in New York City. Osolnik won the National Award for Contemporary Design from International Wood Manufacturers in 1950, the Best Utilization of Waste Wood award from Chicago's Museum of Sciences and Industry in 1955, and the Award of Good Design from the Furniture Association of America for his distinctive candleholders in 1955. A birchwood bowl made from laminated sheets received national exposure in *Craft Multiples*, a 1965 competition sponsored by the Smithsonian's Renwick Gallery. From 1958 to 1968 Osolnik was on the board of directors of the Southern Highland Handicraft Guild and served as president from 1961 to 1962. In 1960 he was also a founder (and lifetime member) of the Kentucky Guild of Artisans and Craftsmen. In 1994, he was elected to the American Craft Council College of Fellows. —TT

Rude Osolnik: A Retrospective, exh. cat. (Asheville, NC: Southern Highland Handicraft Guild, 1989); Jane Kessler, "Rude Osolnik: By Nature Defined," *AC*, 50 (February/March, 1990), 54–56; Ernie Conover, "Rude Osolnik 1915–2001," *Fine Woodworking* 155 (March/April 2002), 24.

PALEY, ALBERT
Born March 28, 1944, Philadelphia, PA
METALSMITH, JEWELER, EDUCATOR

Albert Paley earned undergraduate (1966) and graduate (1969) degrees from Temple University's Tyler School of Art in Philadelphia, studying jewelry-making with Stanley Lechtzin. He then joined the faculty of the School for American Craftsmen at the Rochester Institute of Technology (1969–72; since 1984 as Artist-in-Residence), with a stint at the State University of New York at Brockport (1972–84).

At Tyler, Paley majored in sculpture as an undergraduate but was more in tune with Lechtzin's jewelry-making, with his three-dimensional approach to jewelry and the challenging program well-suited to Paley. He also became acquainted with the international world of contemporary jewelry-making through exhibitions and by meeting metalsmiths such as Olaf Skoogfors, who was then teaching at the Philadelphia Museum School of Art. Skoogfors's Scandinavian aesthetic with its respect for materials and rigorous technical standards was another influence, but Paley sought to define his own path.

Paley preferred silver and gold for jewelry, and he sometimes cast and chased pieces but came to favor forging with its direct experience of moving the metal. Forging allowed for an expressive style that would accommodate the drama of art nouveau's curving "whiplash" line, which he modified for his own artistic purposes. His jewelry is often of larger than traditional scale, intended to relate to the movement of the body, rather than to function as static decoration. The dynamic jewelry forms Paley developed provided the groundwork for his later monumental iron sculpture. He is the recipient of a Lifetime Achievement Award from the American Institute of Architects. —JP

Strauss 2007, 240–43, 492.

PAPPAS, MARILYN R.
Born January 1, 1931, Brockton, MA
FIBER ARTIST, EDUCATOR

Marilyn Pappas is an artist and teacher best known for her innovative work with textiles. Originally interested in fashion design, she emerged as an artist in the early 1960s, having been influenced by the abstract expressionist movement, as well as Henri Matisse, Mariska Karasz, and Robert Rauschenberg. Pappas has primarily been concerned with corporeality, clothing, and the feminine form through figurative representations using various textiles and stitchery. Pappas earned a BS in education from the Massachusetts College of Art in Boston (1952) and an MA in education from Pennsylvania State University (1960), respectively, and spent much of her professional life teaching art at the college level—nearly twenty years of which was spent at the Massachusetts College of Art. In 1994 she retired as professor and chair of the three-dimensional fine arts department and became professor emerita.

Pappas has said that the time it takes for her to complete a work is an essential part of her creative production. She makes aesthetic decisions organically, revising the stitchery as she goes along. She has embraced the association of her work with the (feminine) virtue of patience, particularly in the labor-intensive sewing she practices for her art, sewing itself being culturally considered as "women's work." By using women's traditional tools, materials, and techniques, Pappas identifies with generations of women who have patiently and laboriously constructed the fabric of their lives. —ML

Objects: USA, 320–21; Beth Frankl, "Marilyn Pappas," *American Craft* 61 (August/September 2001), 64–66; Marilyn Pappas, *Muses,* exh. cat. (Worcester, MA: Fletcher/Priest Gallery, 1999), 7.

PARDON, EARL
Born September 6, 1926, Memphis, TN;
died May 1, 1991, Boston, MA
ENAMELIST, JEWELER, METALSMITH, EDUCATOR

Earl Pardon played a principal role in the early art jewelry movement, particularly in the revival of the art of enameling. Trained as a painter, he received his BFA from the Memphis Academy of Arts (now Memphis College of Art) in 1951 and his MFA from Syracuse University in 1959. He joined Skidmore College in Saragota Springs, NY, as an art professor in 1951, and from 1968 through 1977 he served as chairman of the art department.

Pardon was first drawn to jewelry when he took a required craft course at the Memphis Academy of Art. He studied with Dorothy Sturm, who was noted for concurrently exploring painting, collage, and enameling, all of which would come to characterize Pardon's jewelry. He also attended the metalsmithing workshops sponsored by the Handy & Harman metal refinery, and through this experience he met metalsmiths and jewelers from around the country. Pardon formed a friendship with workshop coordinator Margret Craver, who had recently married Charles Withers, president of Towle Silversmiths, in Newburyport, MA. Through Craver he was made designer-in-residence at Towle in 1954, and was responsible for designs including the *Contempra House* flatware line, and a Revere-style enameled punch bowl with matching cups, as well as smaller enameled dishes. He also collaborated with Craver on a plique-à-jour bowl for Queen Elizabeth II and an enameled cigar box for Sir Winston Churchill, for the Ancient and Honorable Artillery Company of Massachusetts's visit to London.

After his Towle experience, Pardon returned to Skidmore, where he applied his ongoing fascination with primitive art and its elemental shapes to his jewelry. Pardon worked in a variety of natural materials in combinations of gold, silver, ivory, ebony, colored gemstones, copper, enamel, wood, and abalone. His technical range was nearly as diverse, but he is most frequently noted for his painterly skill with an array of enameling techniques. Although he had no formal training in jewelry, his work has been widely praised for its sophisticated composition and construction.

Pardon's career was marked by numerous awards and commendations. His jewelry has been featured in solo and group exhibitions throughout the U.S., including early shows with notable contemporaries such as Max Ernst and Charles Eames. In 1980 Skidmore College held a retrospective that featured ninety paintings, drawings, and sculptures in addition to 219 pieces of jewelry. —LR

JoAnn Goldberg, "Earl Pardon: Master American Jeweler," *Ornament* 10 (autumn 1986), 42–49; Sharon Church, "Color, Construction and Change, The Inventive Jewelry of Earl Pardon," *Metalsmith* 10 (winter 1990), 18–19; Falino and Ward 2008, 455–56, 59, cat. no. 369.

PARRY, WILLIAM
Born May 5, 1918, Lehighton, PA;
died February 16, 2005, Alfred Station, NY
CERAMIST, EDUCATOR

William Parry considered himself equal parts teacher and artist. He was especially fond of imparting to his young students the notion that creativity is really a dialogue between the artist and him- or herself. His beginnings were inauspicious; by the time he was eleven, both parents had died, and he had entered Girard College in Philadelphia, which functioned as an orphanage and school. An early start in banking, and a banker friend who graduated from Alfred University, led to a discussion of ceramics. Intrigued by the transformational quality of the medium, he applied and was accepted into the New York State College of Ceramics, in Alfred, NY, to study ceramic engineering and ceramic industrial design. Wartime service interrupted his education, but he returned under the GI Bill and received his BFA degree in 1947.

He taught at the Philadelphia College of Art (now the University of the Arts) from 1949 to 1963, and later in 1963 he returned to Alfred, where he remained until his retirement in 1989. Parry participated in founding the National Council on Education for the Ceramic Arts (NCECA) and served as its first president. He was also involved with Alfred's nascent museum (today's Schein-Joseph International Museum of Ceramic Art). Little interested in the gallery scene, Parry was devoted to teaching and developing his craft on his own terms. Ceramic sculpture became a focus of his work at an early stage of his career. He often played with scale to create large reductive shapes based upon ordinary objects, achieving a sober, almost platonic classicism. —LR

Richard Zakin, "William Parry: The Medium is Insistent," *Ceramics Monthly* 46 (March 1998), 63–66; Barbara Perry, ed., *American Ceramics, The Collection of the Everson Museum of Art* (NY: Rizzoli; Syracuse, NY: Everson Museum of Art, 1989), 314; Edward Lebow and Donald-Brian Johnson, "Obituaries," *AC* 64 (June/July 2004), 21, 25.

PATCH, MARGARET MERWIN

Born January 24, 1894, New York, NY;
died March 19, 1987, FL
ECONOMIST, ARTS ADMINISTRATOR

Margaret Patch was dedicated to establishing an international craft community. Trained as an economist, she worked with the Hoover Relief Commission after World War I. She first became involved with the arts at Cranbrook, where her husband was a faculty member in the secondary school. After moving to Massachusetts in the 1940s, she led the state's Association of Handicraft Groups, which sponsored exhibitions on folk art, craft, and their industrial applications. Beginning in 1952 she met Aileen Osborn Webb and soon began to work with the American Craftsmen's Council (now the American Craft Council).

As Patch's involvement with the ACC grew, she traveled the world to study international crafts. Her 1960 trips throughout Africa, Asia, and Latin America led to the development of the World Crafts Council (WCC) with Webb and Kamaladevi Chattopadhyay just four years later. In its first year, the WCC became of member of the art division of UNESCO, the global government body that assists in establishing conversations between cultures. With this assistance, the WCC was able to increase collaborations, bringing funding and programs to international craft cultures. The WCC held its first international conference at Columbia University in New York City in 1964. Patch's legacy lives on as the WCC continues to improve lives of craftspeople around the world. —NB

"World Crafts to be Aided by UNESCO," *New York Times,* March 17, 1965, 40; Rose Slivka, Margaret M. Patch, and Aileen Webb, *The Crafts of the Modern World* (New York: Horizon Press: 1968); Margaret M. Patch, "Africa: Travelogue: Three-month Trip through Seventeen Countries," *CH* 29 (May 1969), 32–39; James S. Plaut, "Obituary: Margaret Merwin Patch 1894–1987," *AC* 47 (June/July 1987), 68–69.

PEARSON, LORNA BELLE

(MRS. DAVID WATSON)
Born December 23, 1925, East Orange, NJ
SILVERSMITH, JEWELER, EDUCATOR

Lorna Pearson is the sister of silversmith Ronald Pearson. She began her education at Black Mountain College in 1944 but after two years transferred to the School for American Craftsmen in Alfred, NY. She studied with jeweler Philip Morton and silversmiths Alden Wood, Lauritz Eichner, Charles Reese, and John Prip. Pearson graduated in 1948 with a certificate of Master Craftsmanship in Metal. In 1951 she was appointed crafts director for the U.S. Army Special Services Program in Japan and spent two years there.

Pearson was an accomplished jeweler and metalsmith, and entered early juried craft exhibitions, including the Wichita Nationals (1949) and the landmark traveling exhibition *Designer Craftsmen U.S.A. 1953*. Her silver pitcher in this volume won the highest prize in the metals division for the 1953 exhibition. She taught at the University of New Hampshire at Durham (1952–54), but, like many of her generation, she left her career behind shortly after she married. —JP and LR

American Craftsman Educational Council, *Designer Craftsman U.S.A. 1953* (New York: American Federation of the Arts, 1953), 5, 20, 71; L. B. Pearson, "Japanese Household Crafts," *CH* 13 (March 1953), 27–29; Falino and Ward 2008, 432–33.

PEARSON, RONALD HAYES

Born September 22, 1924, New York, NY;
died August 25, 1996, Deer Isle, ME
JEWELER, METALSMITH

A successful craftsman-entrepreneur, Pearson had a fifty-year career as a jeweler, metalsmith, and sculptor, producing simple, elegant, organic pieces that consistently emphasized form over surface decoration. Hayes created jewelry, bowls, candlesticks, and flatware, as well as sculptural pieces on commission for ecclesiastical settings, using a broad range of techniques (enameling, casting, forging, hammering, spinning, and mass production). His products were made available to customers and clients through craft galleries starting in the late 1940s.

Pearson's father, Ralph M. Pearson, was an etcher and educator who had his own art school in New York City. Ronald Pearson made his first object in metal—a copper and pewter letter opener—when he was twelve years old, at a pewter-smithing workshop taught by his father in Gloucester, MA. In 1943, after one semester at the University of Wisconsin studying political science, Pearson left to join the U.S. Merchant Marines, where he remained until 1947. He spent a year at the School for American Craftsmen, then in Alfred, NY, also attended by his sister, Lorna. Pearson became a student of jeweler Philip Morton, but when Morton was not rehired the following year and a scholarship did not materialize for Pearson, he left to become an independent jeweler. After a month in Morton's studio learning a few jewelry techniques, Pearson established his own studio in a former chicken coop, where he worked alone for a year developing approximately twenty spun-bronze forms—bowls, ashtrays, candleholders, and desk accessories—that were retailed throughout the country. Marketing of Pearson's work was helped through exhibitions. His bowls were included in MoMA's Good Design exhibitions (1950–54), and he had solo exhibitions at the St. Paul Gallery and School of Art (1950) and the Museum of Contemporary Crafts (1963). He also sold through America House.

In the early 1950s Pearson moved to Rochester, NY (where the School for American Craftsmen had moved to join the Rochester Institute of Technology), and in 1952, with Frans Wildenhain, Tage Frid, and John Prip, all faculty members at the School for American Craftsmen, Pearson co-founded Shop One. Building on the shop's concept of connecting object, maker, and customer, Pearson and Prip set up a jewelry studio in the same building as Shop One, allowing their clients greater accessibility and gaining artistic independence for themselves. At the same time, Pearson designed jewelry for Hickok Jewelry Manufacturing Co. of Rochester and fulfilled architectural/sculptural commissions for the Kresge Chapel at the Massachusetts Institute of Technology (MIT), Cambridge (1954/55), and for Church of the Redeemer, Baltimore (1959). His award-winning entry, *Vision*, in the 1960 International Design Competition for Sterling Silver Flatware, co-sponsored by the Museum of Contemporary Crafts and the International Silver Company, presented an elegant solution for a three-dimensional form in space and is regarded as among his most significant work. Pearson taught part-time at the School for American Craftsmen (1959–61), and in 1971 he moved to Deer Isle, ME, where he maintained an independent studio, retailing his work nationwide. —TT

Arline M. Fisch, "Ronald Hayes Pearson American Classic," *AC* 52 (June/July 1992), 30–35, 40; Arline Fisch, "Obituary," *Metalsmith* 16 (fall 1996), 7; W. Scott Braznell, "The Early Career of Ronald Hayes Pearson and the Post–World War II Revival of American Silversmithing and Jewelrymaking," *Winterthur Portfolio* 34 (winter 1999), 185–213.

PETERSON, SUSAN HARNLY

Born July 21, 1925, McPherson, KS;
died March 26, 2009, Scottsdale, AZ
CERAMIST, EDUCATOR, AUTHOR

The indefatigable and peripatetic Susan Peterson spent a lifetime as a passionate advocate for ceramics. She earned a BA under F. Carlton Ball in 1946 at Mills College, Oakland, CA, and an MFA in ceramics in 1950 at the New York State College of Ceramics at Alfred University. In the early 1950s, Peterson moved to Los Angeles, where she was pivotal in reestablishing knowledge of wheel-thrown pottery and high-fire glazes. From 1952 to 1955 she taught at the Chouinard Art Institute (now the California Institute of the Arts), and in that first year she hosted Bernard Leach, whom she had met at Alfred, for an intensive workshop with Japanese ceramists Shoji Hamada and philosopher Soetsu Yanagi. In 1955 she took over and developed the undergraduate and graduate ceramics programs at the University of Southern California, where Kenneth Price and John Mason were her students. Meanwhile, summers were spent teaching at the Idyllwild School of Music and the Arts, and in the late 1960s Peterson promoted studio pottery to the general public in fifty-four half-hour live television programs, *Wheels, Kiln and Clay,* for CBS-KNXT. In 1972 Peterson moved to New York City to develop a ceramics program at Hunter College of the City University of New York, where she remained until 1994, when she retired from teaching.

Peterson began to write in 1955, starting with reviews of West Coast exhibitions for *Craft Horizons*. Her first book, a monograph on Shoji Hamada, appeared in 1974, and she published more than ten books on ceramics during her lifetime. Her biographies of Maria Martinez and Lucy Lewis raised awareness of women in Native American pottery. She was a central figure in the advancement of ceramics through her worldwide travels for workshops, lectures, and curatorial endeavors. —JP

Gerry Williams, "Susan Peterson, The Craft and Art of Writing Books," *Ceramics: Art and Perception* 61 (2005), 100–105; "Susan Harnly Peterson: A Legend—A Legacy, 1925–2009," *Ceramics* (Sydney, Australia) 76 (2009), 110–11; Margaret Carney, "Susan Peterson, 1925–2009," *Ceramics Monthly* 57 (June/July 2009), 55.

POPOVI DA

(RED FOX; BORN ANTONIO JOSE MARTINEZ)

Born April 10, 1922, San Ildefonso Pueblo, NM;
died 1971, San Ildefonso Pueblo, NM

POTTER, JEWELER, WATERCOLORIST

The son of the famous Pueblo potters Maria and Julian Martinez, Popovi Da studied art at the Indian School in Santa Fe in the early 1930s and, after serving in the army during World War II, began helping his mother to dig clay and fire pots. In 1948, with an increasing awareness of his Tewa heritage, he changed his name from Antonio Martinez to Popovi Da (Red Fox). That same year he and his wife, Anita, opened the Popovi Da Studio of Indian Art at San Ildefonso Pueblo, marketing and promoting their pueblo's pottery. Although beginning in 1950 he helped to decorate and paint his mother's pottery, at first he made few pieces of his own. A great experimenter, however, in 1956 he started working with polychrome ware and is credited with having revitalized it at San Ildefonso Pueblo. One of his polychrome vessels was awarded best in class at the Gallup Inter-Tribal Ceremonial in 1957. Popovi Da experimented with firing techniques in the early 1960s, developing a new sienna color and a way to achieve two colors on the same vessel. He served as a member of the New Mexico Arts Commission. In 1967 the Institute of American Indian Art organized an exhibition of the Martinez family pottery, which traveled to the U.S. Department of the Interior in Washington, DC, representing three generations of Martinez family potters: Maria, Popovi Da, and his son Tony Da, also a potter. —MS

Louann Faris Culley, "Popovi Da," in Harvey Markowitz and Adams McCrea, *American Indian Biography* (Pasadena, CA: Salem Press, 1999), 237.

POUSETTE-DART, RICHARD WARREN

Born June 8, 1916, St. Paul, MN;
died October 25, 1992, New York, NY

PAINTER, METALSMITH

Richard Pousette-Dart was an abstract expressionist and visionary artist who helped found the New York School.

Despite a close association with members of the group—Robert Motherwell, Mark Rothko, Willem de Kooning, among others—and while he was among the fifteen portrayed in the now-famous "Irascibles" photograph published in *Life* magazine in January 1951, the fiercely independent Pousette-Dart distanced himself from the freewheeling and angst-ridden group. In 1951 he moved to Rockland County, where he remained for the rest of his life, finding the isolation he needed to determine his own direction as a symbolist and solitary spiritual seer. Pousette-Dart delved into every possible aspect of his own life's journey, recording his aesthetic and philosophical ideas in journal notebooks and then translating those ideas into paintings, prints, and small brass sculptures that reference his interests in cubism, biomorphic surrealism, Jungian and Freudian theories of the unconscious, and African and Native American art. Central to Pousette-Dart's work was his internal dialogue with the natural world that resulted in a self-made cosmology of powerful dualities—circles and squares, man and the cosmos, spirit and body, light and substance. Recognizable shapes, symbols, and grids seen in his early work of the 1940s and '50s gave way in the 1960s to diffuse "implosions" of pointillist color and overtly tactile versions of op art, minimalism, and color-field painting.

The son of a painter-writer and poet-musician, Pousette-Dart was raised in the culturally vibrant community of Valhalla, NY, where he was encouraged by his parents to pursue his interests in art, philosophy, music, and literature. In 1936, after a few months at Bard College, Annandale-on-Hudson, NY, Pousette-Dart set out to paint, sculpt, and draw, and by 1939 he was a full-time artist. MoMA acquired its first Pousette-Dart painting in 1940, and he had his first solo exhibition at the Artist Gallery in 1941. While his reputation as a painter continued to develop throughout the 1940s, his metalwork also drew critical interest through such exhibitions in New York City as *Forms in Brass* (1943) and *Forms in Brass and Watercolors* (1946), both shows held at the Willard Gallery, and *Brasses and Photographs* (1948) at the Betty Parsons Gallery. Throughout the 1940s Pousette-Dart participated in discussions about abstraction at the legendary Studio 35, involved himself in the activities of the Eighth Street Club, and socialized with other abstract expressionist artists at the Cedar Tavern on University Place and the Automat on Fifty-ninth Street. By the late 1950s and throughout the 1960s, he was winning awards and honorary degrees in recognition of his work. Among them were a Ford Foundation Grant (1959), the M. V. Kohnstamm Prize from the Art Institute of Chicago (1961), an Honorary Doctorate of Humane Letters from Bard College (1965), and the National Endowment for the Arts Award for Individual Artists (1967). He also taught at various New York colleges: New School for Social Research (1959–61), School of Visual Arts (1964), Bard College (1965), and Columbia University (1968). —TT

Lowery Stokes Sims, *Richard Pousette-Dart (1916–1992)*, exh. cat. (New York: Metropolitan Museum of Art, 1997);

Robert Carleton Hobbs, *Richard Pousette-Dart*, exh. cat. (Indianapolis: Indianapolis Museum of Art, 1990).

POWELL, PHILLIP LLOYD

Born August 26, 1919, Germantown, PA;
died March 9, 2008, Langehorne, PA

FURNITURE MAKER

Powell was drawn to furniture-making as a high school student in the mid-1930s and made pieces for his friends and family. He studied engineering at Philadelphia's Drexel Institute of Technology (now Drexel University). After serving in the Army Air Corps in Great Britain during World War II, he returned to Pennsylvania and purchased land in New Hope, a town that is home to many artists, galleries, and antique shops. He opened a shop himself and sold Herman Miller furniture and lamps by Isamu Noguchi. Encouraged by neighbor and master furniture maker, George Nakashima, Powell began to design his own furniture, and in 1953 he presented his first pieces, a group of walnut lamp bases.

Beginning in the mid-1950s, Powell collaborated with metalsmith and designer Paul Evans on furniture and accessories—sofas, lounges, chairs and ottomans, screens, tea carts, lamp bases, end tables, and more. Although inspired by Scandinavian modernism, they integrated naturalistic lines and imagery into their designs. In 1961 their work was featured at America House, and sales increased. The partnership lasted more than a decade, after which Powell continued on his own, working in a sculptural style of modernist furniture often incorporating surprises such as a lining of silver leaf or exotic textiles, or found objects that he discovered on his myriad travels. —JP

"America House Abets its Collections of Accessories with New Creative Furniture Created by P. L. Powell and P. Evans," *Interiors* 121 (December 1961), 142; Margalit Fox, "Phillip Lloyd Powell, a Designer of Sculptural Furniture, Dies at 88," *New York Times*, March 16, 2008, A39.

PRESTINI, JAMES LIBERO

Born January 13, 1908, Waterford, CT;
died July 26, 1993, Berkeley, CA

WOODWORKER, SCULPTOR, EDUCATOR

An internationally known woodturner and sculptor, James Prestini created thin-walled symmetrical wooden bowls and, in his later career, mirror-surfaced geometrical stainless steel sculpture. Unlike many of his contemporaries, Prestini accepted the reality of machine-based art, the nature of materials, and the technologies of his time, and used them to find higher orders of structure. As a craftsman, Prestini saw the significance of contemporary crafts as a standard-setter and model-maker for industry. Regarded as a superb teacher, he believed that the key artists of the machine age were industrial designers. Prestini was trained in the Bauhaus tradition at the Institute of Design in Chicago by László Moholy-Nagy (1939), and his approach to teaching was that of a militant propagandist for the cause of sober, honest design, especially in quantity production. Prestini taught his students to consider intellectual rigor and practical training as inseparable from creative design. He taught for seven years at the Institute of Design (1939–46) and completed one-year stints at Mills College (1940), North Texas State University (1942), and Black Mountain College (1944). He was in Italy studying sculpture (1953–56) when architect William Wurster invited him to join the faculty at University of California, Berkeley. There Prestini taught generations of architecture and city planning students from 1956 until his retirement in 1975.

According to a colleague, the modern movement for Prestini "was a revolutionary way of getting back to basics, not a new style but a new way of thinking. He tended to tell his students that the thinking was most important; that he would provide them with no solutions, only an approach to problems of design" (Claude Stoller, quoted in Krogh 1994). He and Jesse Reichek set up a program at Berkeley for beginning students that became one of the best of its kind in American architectural education. In addition to his teaching and artistic production, Prestini also undertook materials studies in Latin America for the U.S. State Department (1951). He conducted a survey of the Italian furniture industry for Knoll International (1954), directed an analysis and evaluation of design school education for West Germany (1962), and participated in developing a postgraduate design school for India that included building design, curricula planning, and design programming for native industry (1963). Edgar Kaufmann Jr. of MoMA commented on Prestini's contributions to modernism when his work was exhibited at the museum in 1950: "This feat has been Prestini's, to suggest within the limits of simple craft the human pathos of art and the clean, bold certainties of science. He has made grand things that are not overwhelming, beautiful things that are not personal unveilings, and simple things that do not urge usefulness to excuse their simplicity. . . . Art or not, craft or not, bowls or plain shapes, they speak directly and amply of our days to our days" (*Prestini's Art* 1950). —TT

Prestini's Art in Wood, exh. cat. (Lake Forest, IL: Pocahontas Press; New York: Pantheon Books, 1950), n.p.; Richard Peters et al., "James L. Prestini, Architecture, Berkeley," in David Krogh, ed., *University of California: In Memoriam, 1994,* [search "Prestini"] at www.calisphere .universityofcalifornia.edu/; artist file, ACC library. For earlier history see *Craft in the Machine Age*, 242.

PRIP, JOHN AXEL (JACK)
Born July 2, 1922, Yonkers, NY;
died April 8, 2009, Cranston, RI
METALSMITH, JEWELER, EDUCATOR

The imaginative and talented silversmith John (Jack) Prip was born in the U.S. to a Danish father and an American mother. In 1933 the family sailed to Copenhagen, and his father, a third generation silversmith, returned to the family's silver flatware firm. In 1937 Prip began a five-year apprenticeship with master silversmith Evald Nielsen

while attending the Copenhagen Technical College. In spite of the German occupation that began in 1940, the school functioned through 1942, the year Prip graduated with the school's silver medal and began three years of service on a minesweeper in the Danish Navy. After the war, Prip worked for several Scandinavian firms and in the family business but found the environment stifling. In 1948 he returned to the U.S. to accept a position as head of the department of jewelry and silversmithing at the School for American Craftsmen, which was then at the State University of New York, College of Ceramics at Alfred University, in Alfred, NY. Two years later Prip moved with the school to the Rochester Institute of Technology (RIT) in Rochester, NY.

In 1952 Prip founded Shop One (1952–75) in Rochester with his former student, Ronald Hayes Pearson and two faculty members—woodworker Tage Frid and ceramist Frans Wildenhain—to provide a sales venue for the group's work. Prip showed his work extensively in the craft exhibitions springing up across the country in the postwar years. His technical virtuosity and elegant silver hollowware designs won immediate acclaim. In the first juried show he entered, the 1949 Wichita National, he won first prize. At the same time, Prip continued to produce wares for sale in Shop One, sometimes collaborating with Pearson.

In 1954, having established his American reputation and the school's thriving metalworking department, he departed to begin work as resident designer-craftsman for silversmithing manufacturer Reed & Barton, in Taunton, MA. In this position he fashioned sterling prototypes for a number of patterns including *Diamond* and *Dimension*. After three years of full-time work, he continued to consult for the firm while also teaching at the School of the Museum of the Fine Arts in Boston (1960–63) and the Rhode Island School of Design in Providence (1963–80). During his RISD years, Prip produced a brilliant series of small and larger sculptures, many of them in pewter, in a humorous and surrealistic vein, which pointed the way for the next generation of metalsmiths. —JP

Falino and Ward 2008, 436–37, 458, cat. no. 354; Bill Van Siclen, "'Jack' Prip, Noted RISD Silversmith, Dies at 86," *Providence Journal*, April 10, 2009; Jeannine Falino, "Restless Dane: The Evolving Metalwork of John Prip," *Metalsmith* 30, no. 1 (2010), 44–51.

PULOS, ARTHUR JON
Born 1917, North Vandergrift, PA;
died 1993, Colorado Springs, CO
METALSMITH, DESIGNER, EDUCATOR, AUTHOR

Trained as a silversmith and designer, Arthur Pulos eventually pursued a career as a professor and practitioner of industrial design, and used his vast knowledge to write two books on the history of this field—*American Design Ethic* (1983) and *American Design Adventure* (1988)—among other publications. He graduated from Carnegie Institute of Technology in Pittsburgh in 1939 with a BA in art education. He first became excited about metal in a materials

class under Fred Clayter, an English-trained goldsmith who taught Pulos the basics of jewelry and who gave him a small set of metalworking tools at graduation. As a third-year student, Pulos studied industrial design under German-trained silversmith Peter Müller-Munk. In the fall of 1939 Pulos accepted an assistantship in the School of Art and Architecture, University of Oregon, Eugene, where he taught a design course and a metals course, putting together his own graduate program focusing on ecclesiastical silver. He received his MFA in silversmithing in 1941 on the eve of the country's entry into World War II. As a civilian he taught metalwork to servicemen in the U.S. Air Force, who were training for aircraft production and maintenance. In 1943 he joined the service and spent three additional years teaching in the U.S. and in Europe.

Pulos served as associate professor of design at the University of Illinois from 1946 to 1955. During that time he also produced his own studio work and exhibited extensively. In the summer of 1948 he participated in the Handy & Harman workshop held at the Rhode Island School of Design under Swedish silversmith Baron Eric Fleming. There Pulos met others in the field, notably Alma Eikerman and Frederick Miller. In 1953 Pulos entered silver flatware and a cocktail pitcher executed in the sleek Scandinavian modernist style in *Designer Craftsmen U.S.A.*; in 1958 a beverage server was displayed in the U.S. Pavilion at the Brussels World's Fair. Pulos directed the industrial design program at Syracuse University in New York from 1955 to 1982. He founded Pulos Design Associates in 1958 and remained in active practice until 1988. —JP

Arthur J. Pulos, oral history interview by Robert Brown, July 31, 1982 and December 5, 1982, AAA, SI; Suzanne M. Jackson, "Arthur Jon Pulos, 79; silversmith, design expert," *Syracuse Herald-Journal*, February 4, 1997.

RADAKOVICH, RUTH
(NÉE CLARK)
Born April 25, 1920, Winnetka, IL;
died January 6, 1975, San Diego, CA
JEWELER, SCULPTOR, EDUCATOR

Ruth Radakovich earned her BA in painting at Sarah Lawrence College in New York and her MA in anthropology and art from the University of Michigan, Ann Arbor. Her humanitarian impulses took her to Belgrade, Yugoslavia, in 1946 to work as a secretary for the United Nations Relief and Rehabilitation Administration, after which she spent a summer studying ceramics and metalwork under F. Carlton Ball at Mills College in California. At the School for American Craftsmen at the Rochester Institute of Technology (RIT), she studied metalwork under John Prip. She traveled to Europe in 1952 to join Svetozar (Tozar) Radakovich, a painter and art editor whom she had met in Belgrade years earlier. They studied casting with metalsmith Mogens Bjorn-Andersen in Copenhagen, Denmark, where they also met Hans Christensen, the Danish silversmith who was then foreman of the Jensen model-making shop. The couple married in Paris in 1955 and sailed for New York.

They settled in Rochester, where both taught metalwork at the Memorial Art Gallery of the University of Rochester; Tozar also taught painting at the School for American Craftsmen. In 1959 the Radakovichs moved to Southern California to concentrate on studio work. Although the couple worked side by side, they did not collaborate. Ruth made rough drawings before making either a wax or metal model to be sent out for casting in gold or other precious metals. She finished the cast pieces by forging and often set them with one or two semiprecious stones.

Ruth Radakovich made jewelry and sculpture in an organic, abstract style. She exhibited extensively throughout the U.S. and Europe and won numerous awards. Her gold and turquoise brooch won first prize in the precious metals category in 1956 at the Second National Exhibition of American Jewelry at the Rochester Memorial Art Gallery and was featured on the cover of *Craft Horizons* in February 1957. Both she and her husband were represented in the U.S. Pavilion at the Brussels World's Fair of 1958. They began to explore new media in the 1960s, and they both began to create doors made of fiberglass, plastic, and wood, developed in consultation with master surfboard maker, Carl Eckburg, an indication of their Southern California culture. One of Ruth's doors was included in *Objects: USA*. (cat. 19) —JP

Bernice Stevens Decker, "Couple Link Skills," *Christian Science Monitor*, August 28, 1958, 12; Toni Greenbaum, "Svetozar and Ruth Radakovich: Love in Three Dimensions," *Metalsmith* 27, no. 3 (2007), 34–41.

RAUSCHENBERG, ROBERT

(NÉ MILTON ERNEST RAUSCHENBERG)

Born October 22, 1925, Port Arthur, TX;

died May 12, 2008, Captiva Island, FL

PAINTER, SCULPTOR, PRINTMAKER, CHOREOGRAPHER, PERFORMER

A brilliant catalyst who reshaped the meaning of art in the twentieth century, Rauschenberg worked in a range of media and was one of the first to blur the lines between them. He was also influential in moving the focus from abstract expressionism to new expressions in pop art, happenings, process art, and conceptualism. Taking a page from Marcel Duchamp, Rauschenberg saw beauty in ordinary and castoff objects, frequently incorporating them into his own work.

In Rauschenberg's frugal Texas family, his mother made all his clothes from scraps. While this distressed him as a youth, his later assemblages are probably indebted to these youthful experiences, for throughout his life, Rauschenberg found pleasure in making something from nothing. After seeing his first painting in San Diego as a young man serving in the U.S. Navy, he became determined to become an artist. Rauschenberg studied fashion design at the Kansas City Art Institute in 1947–48 on the GI Bill and continued his education at the Académie Julian in Paris, and later at Black Mountain College, where Josef Albers made a deep impression upon him.

Indebted to the abstract expressionists, he nevertheless rebelled against them from an early date, preferring to explore the random nature of objects around him. He created set designs and costumes in the 1950s for Merce Cunningham, Paul Taylor, and Trisha Brown. He also created his own performances, mixing art and other technologies, which culminated in Experiments in Art and Technology, a nonprofit organization that encouraged joint projects by scientists and artists. By the mid-1950s Rauschenberg was including an array of objects, such as shirts, parasols, cardboard, and printed matter, into the surfaces of his paintings, which he called Combines. Current events began to influence his work by the early 1970s, and he created a series of silkscreens based upon newspaper headlines and magazine images. His career was marked by solo exhibitions, beginning in 1963 at the Jewish Museum and a later retrospective in 1997 at the Solomon R. Guggenheim Museum in New York. Awards include the first prize for painting at the Venice Biennale (1964) and the National Medal of the Arts (1993). —JF

Walter Hopps et al., *Robert Rauschenberg: A Retrospective*, exh. cat. (New York: Guggenheim Museum, 1997); Thomas Crow et al., *Robert Rauschenberg: Combines,* exh. cat. (New York: Metropolitan Museum of Art; Los Angeles: Museum of Contemporary Art, 2005).

RENK, MERRY

(NÉE MARY RUTH GIBBS;

LATER MRS. STANLEY RENK;

LATER MRS. EARLE CURTIS)

Born July 8, 1921, Trenton, NJ

JEWELER

In 1946 merry renk (as she prefers her name to be styled) went to Chicago, where she studied design at the Bauhaus-oriented Institute of Design for three semesters. Inspired by the workshops at the school, renk and two friends founded 750 Gallery and Studio (so named for its address at 750 Dearborn Street). They sold their own work and that of other artists: ceramics by Polia Pillin, who helped renk construct an enameling kiln in the studio, Eugene Deutsch, and Warren and Alix MacKenzie; enamels by Doris Hall, whose work inspired renk to learn to enamel; and textiles by Lenore Tawney and others. As renk became successful as a studio artist making silver and enamel jewelry, she decided to leave the Institute of Design with its emphasis on industrial design. In 1948, with her two friends deciding to get out of the business, she sold the shop and relocated to San Francisco. There, renk helped establish the Metal Arts Guild and found a new circle of artist friends. She also spent eighteen months in Paris, where her friend and colleague Lenore Tawney was then living, and the pair traveled together to Spain and North Africa.

Through the 1950s and '60s renk continued to create jewelry in her studio, learning as she progressed. She used various enameling techniques but worked mainly with forging silver and gold objects. She often incorporated cultured pearls or other precious or semiprecious stones in the design. Her nonobjective forms are characterized by rich, rhythmically interlocking patterns. Her wedding crowns made in the late 1960s epitomize renk's originality and technical virtuosity. Her jewelry was included in *Design Quarterly's* double issue of American jewelry published in 1959 and in *Objects: USA*. —JP

Walker Art Center, "American Jewelry," *Design Quarterly* 45/46 (1959), 36; *Objects: USA,* 210–11; merry renk, oral history interview by Mia Riedel, January 18–19, 2001, AAA, SI.

RHODES, DANIEL

Born 1911, Fort Dodge, IA;

died July, 23, 1989, Reno, NV

CERAMIST, EDUCATOR, AUTHOR

Through his long teaching career, exploration of sculptural clay, and authoritative publications on pottery techniques, Daniel Rhodes made important contributions to the field of studio pottery. After graduating in 1933 from the University of Chicago, Rhodes spent the next seven years working as a painter, studying with regionalists Grant Wood and John Steuart Curry. Under the Works Projects Administration (WPA) he worked on several murals and won prizes for his paintings at the Iowa State Fair.

Rhodes's wife, Lillyan Jacobs, whom he married in 1940, was a potter, and she inspired him to take up ceramics. He studied at the Colorado Springs Fine Arts Center, and then at the New York State College of Ceramics at Alfred University, NY, where he received his MFA. He spent about six years on the West Coast developing high-heat ceramics for the Henry J. Kaiser Corporation, as well as creating both cast and thrown wares for the luxury retailer, Gump's of San Francisco. He then returned to Alfred and taught and inspired generations of ceramists from 1947 to 1973. He dug deeply into the technical aspects of the medium and published three seminal books, among others: *Clay and Glazes for the Potter* (1957), *Stoneware & Porcelain: The Art of High Fired Pottery* (1959); and *Kilns: Design, Construction, and Operation* (1968). A Fulbright Fellowship enabled him to travel to Japan in 1962, where he studied both the ancient and contemporary history of the medium. Some of his own works from this period reflect his examination of Noguchi ceramics as well. In the same period, he began to explore the potential of ceramic sculpture, and in 1973 he moved to Davenport, CA, where he focused on head and torso sculptures created without preliminary drawings. These reflected his interest in nature and natural materials. From 1977 to 1980 Rhodes taught ceramics at the University of California, Santa Cruz. —LR

Daniel Rhodes, "A Clay Life," *Ceramics Monthly* 35 (September 1987), 38–31; "Daniel Rhodes, 78, Ceramic Sculptor, Dies," *New York Times*, July 28, 1989, A10; William Parry, "Obituary," *AC* 49 (October/November 1989), 74.

RISOM, JENS

Born May 8, 1916, Copenhagen, Denmark

DESIGNER

Jens Risom was among a wave of Scandinavian designers who brought their aesthetic to the U.S. before World War II. Risom studied design at the Copenhagen School of Industrial Arts and Design, where Hans Wegner was a classmate, and he arrived in New York in 1939 expressly to experience American design. His designs were included in *Collier's* "House of Ideas" designed by Edward Durell Stone and displayed on a terrace at Rockefeller Center during the 1939 New York World's Fair. By 1941 Risom had joined entrepreneur Hans Knoll in producing furniture. Risom's *600 line* chair was the first chair produced by what eventually became the Knoll furniture company. Their partnership continued successfully until 1943, when he was drafted into the U.S. Army. After the war, Risom split with Knoll and in 1946 began his own company, Jens Risom Design Inc. (JRD). For the next twenty-five years JRD produced furniture in a Scandinavian-inflected style, similar to his designs for Knoll (for which he was not credited by name until the 1990s). When Risom sold JRD to the Dictaphone Corporation in 1970, he had 300 workers and showrooms throughout the U.S. and in numerous countries abroad.

Risom received considerable press coverage throughout his career and participated in both commercial and museum installations, including a living room designed for Georg Jensen (New York) in 1942 and a room devoted to his furniture designs, alongside others by George Nelson, Charles Eames, Florence Knoll, and Alvar Aalto in *For Modern Living* (1949) held at the Detroit Institute of Art.—NE

Amber Bravo, "Fascinating Risom," *Dwell* 9 (September 2009), 62–67.

ROSSBACH, CHARLES EDMUND (ED)

Born January 2, 1914, Edison Park, IL;
died October 7, 2002, Berkeley, CA

FIBER ARTIST, TEXTILE DESIGNER, CERAMIST, EDUCATOR, WRITER

Charles Edmund (Ed) Rossbach has been regarded as the dean of American fiber arts and father of the contemporary fiber movement. He earned his BA in painting and design from the University of Washington, Seattle, in 1940, and his MA in art education from Teachers College, Columbia University, in 1941. After a year teaching seventh grade in a Washington farm community, he joined the Army Signal Corps and was sent to the Aleutian Islands, where the indigenous grasses intrigued him, stimulating an interest in basket-weaving. From 1945 to 1947, Rossbach studied on the GI Bill at Cranbrook, where he earned an MFA in ceramics and weaving. He subsequently taught weaving at the University of Washington, where his assistant was future textile designer Jack Lenor Larsen. It was also there that he met his future wife, fiber art professor Katherine Westphal. The couple moved to the University of California, Berkeley, when Rossbach joined the faculty in 1950; he remained there until his retirement in 1979.

As a researcher and active artist, Rossbach helped to transform the faculty into a dynamic force in which the instructors engaged with their students not only as professors, but as advocates of craft experimentation and free thinking.

Throughout his career, Rossbach studied the materials and techniques used by older civilizations in their basketry and textiles. He was particularly interested in creating off-loom textiles as well as baskets and other sculptural forms that incorporated basketry techniques and materials not traditionally associated with basket-weaving. From 1950 onward his work was seen in major exhibitions in the U.S. and abroad, including *Designer Craftsmen U.S.A.* (1953) at the MCC; the Brussels World's Fair (1958); *Objects: USA* (1969) at the MCC; *Wall Hangings* (1969) at MoMA; and *Structures in Textiles* (1976) at the Stedlijk Museum in Amsterdam. He became a fellow of the ACC in 1975. —TT

Charles Edmund Rossbach, "Artist, Mentor, Professor, Writer," oral history interview by Harriet Nathan, April 1 and 8, 1983, typescript, Regional Oral History Office, The Bancroft Library, University of California, Berkeley; Pat Hickman, "Charles Edmund (Ed) Rossbach (1914–2002)," *Fiberarts* 29 (March/April 2003), 24–26.

ROTHMAN, JERRY

Born 1933, Brooklyn, NY

CERAMIST, SCULPTOR, EDUCATOR

Jerry Rothman earned his BA from Art Center College of Design in Los Angeles in 1956. He remained in Los Angeles and studied under Peter Voulkos at the Otis Art Institute (1956–58; 1960–61), where he earned an MFA. Between his stints at Otis he worked in Japan designing for ceramics manufacturer Sango. After graduation he briefly taught ceramics at the University of Iowa in Iowa City, moving to California State University in Fullerton, where he taught for more than twenty-five years.

Freedom, individuality, and experimentation reigned at Otis, and Rothman's independent attitude and drive to innovate served him well. He developed shrink-free clay that enabled him to create sculptures up to twenty feet in height. He constructed armatures with high-fire metal rods for armlike extensions of large ceramic sculptures that kept them from collapsing in the kiln. In 1957 he exhibited these sculptures at the Ferus Gallery in Los Angeles.

Rothman's free-form sand-glazed stoneware Sky Pots of the late 1950s and early 1960s were constructed from thrown and slab parts. Colorful paintings with biomorphic forms appeared on a flattened area of each pot, like an ancient image on a stone wall or a fragment from that wall preserved in a frame. In the mid-1960s he created a series of large sculptures resembling ancient totems or deities that featured monochromatic glazes and sensuous, organic forms. —JP

J. Bennet Olson, "Soldner-Mason-Rothman," *CH* 17 (October 1957), 41; Garth Clark, *American Potters: The Work of Twenty Modern Masters* (New York: Watson-Guptill Publications, 1981), 47; Susan Peterson et al., *Feat of Clay:*

Five Decades of Jerry Rothman (Laguna Beach: Laguna Art Museum; Santa Ana, CA: Grand Central Press, 2003).

SAMARAS, LUCAS

Born September 14, 1936, Kastoria, Greece

MULTIMEDIA ARTIST

Widely recognized for his inventive use of different media including drawing, painting, sculpture, furniture, and jewelry, Lucas Samaras has spent his career exploring the nature of the self, creating works from such diverse materials as clay, steel, fabric, pastel, oil, pins, and nails. Samaras left Greece and immigrated to the U.S. in 1948. At Rutgers University his teachers included Allan Kaprow and George Segal. After graduating in 1959 with a degree in art, he studied art history with Meyer Shapiro at Columbia University.

Always self-referential, Samaras has created thousands of works, ranging from nonfunctional chairs made out of wire hangers to color photographs of his own apartment. He had his first exhibition in 1961 at the Green Gallery, where a few years later he showed his seminal work *Room 1*, a gallery installation that duplicated his childhood bedroom down to the bedstead and mattress. Samaras's work has been exhibited throughout the U.S., Europe, and Asia. His first retrospective was organized in 1971 by the Museum of Contemporary Art of Chicago, and in 1988 the Denver Art Museum organized another major exhibition of the works produced between 1969 and 1986. —MS

Roberta Smith, "A Playful Narcissist's Song of Himself," *New York Times*, November 14, 2003, E31; Thomas McEvilley, Donald B. Kuspit, and Roberta Smith, *Lucas Samaras: Objects and Subjects, 1969–1986* (New York: Abbeville Press, 1988).

SCHEIER, MARY

(NÉE GOLDSMITH)

Born May 9, 1908, Salem, VA;
died May 14, 2007, Green Valley, AZ

CERAMIST

SCHEIER, EDWIN

Born November 11, 1910, Bronx, NY;
died April 20, 2008, Green Valley, AZ

CERAMIST, EDUCATOR

Like the Natzlers, Mary and Edwin Scheier were collaborative potters. Mary threw vessels on the wheel, and Edwin applied the surface decoration. Mary experimented with the balance between thick and thin, creating forms that were both utilitarian and elegant. On the surface, Edwin worked with Mary's designs, exploring the possibilities of positive and negative space, etching narratives that represented mythological stories, birth and regeneration, Adam and Eve, while also moving the form from its utilitarian roots into sculpture. The couple met in 1937, during the Great Depression, while working for the Works Progress Administration (WPA). They were married the same year and began traveling the U.S., experimenting with various art forms, primarily puppetry, before focusing on ceramics. In 1940 they were invited by David Campbell, then director of the League of New Hampshire Craftsmen, to join the University of New Hampshire in Durham—Edwin as an instructor, Mary as an artist-in-residence—where they remained until 1968. As part of the postwar Operation Bootstrap (1945), they traveled to Puerto Rico to foster an island-based pottery industry that would mean employment to many islanders. The couple exhibited their work in the traveling exhibition *Contemporary New England Handicrafts* (1943), won a grand prize in *Designer Craftsmen U.S.A.* (1953), and the Medaille d'Argent at the Cannes (France) International Exposition of Ceramics (1955). From 1968 to 1978 the Scheiers lived in Oaxaca, Mexico, where they studied the designs of the Zapotec people, translating their traditions into pottery. Upon returning to the U.S., they settled in Green Valley, Arizona. —BN

Edward Lebow, "A Sense of Line," *AC* 46 (February/March 1988), 25–31; Michael K. Komanecky, *American Potters: Mary and Edwin Scheier* (Manchester, NH: Currier Gallery of Art, 1993).
For earlier history see *Craft in the Machine Age*, 245–46.

SCHILDKNECHT, MARY ANN

Born January 28, 1947, Los Angeles, CA
EDUCATOR, FASHION DESIGNER

A second-generation Californian who grew up in Los Angeles, Mary Ann Schildknecht was fascinated from an early age with painting and other art forms. In high school, she was voted commissioner of fine arts, supervising decorations for dances, helping to design the school mascot's costume, and creating posters for various school events. At San Diego State College, she majored in fine arts.

When traveling in Europe in the late 1960s, Schildknecht visited museums, but was also involved in the counterculture of that period. She and a friend found themselves in an Italian prison convicted of smuggling hashish. She used the time to embroider a blouse and skirt in satin stitch. Her various careers since the 1960s have included fashion design, advertising, painting, and teaching. —JF
Suzy Menkes, "Hippie Flower Power as Wearable Art," *International Herald Tribune*, June 16, 2005, 9; Mary Ann Schildknecht, e-mail to Jeannine Falino, September 6, 2010.

SCHMIDT, CHRISTIAN F.

Born August 28, 1928, Minneapolis, MN;
died April 22, 1974, Minneapolis, MN
JEWELER, EDUCATOR

Christian Schmidt received his BS in art education at the University of Minnesota, Minneapolis, in 1956, studying under Philip Morton, who had established the jewelry program in 1948. Schmidt then taught crafts at the university for a year while continuing to work on his own jewelry. He worked as a precious-metal caster for a ring manufacturing firm in Minneapolis for five years and taught art in the city's public schools as well as jewelry making at the St. Paul Gallery and School of Art.

Believing that the U.S. lacked a traditional or national style of jewelry, Schmidt felt free to experiment. In his own studio he constructed forms inspired by natural objects such as seedpods, plants, marine life, and insects. Some pieces joined disparate materials—silver or gold inlays in ebony panels combined to create a bracelet, or a polished stone or pearl set into a silver or gold pod for a pendant. Schmidt used fusing and lost-wax casting, occasionally working directly with the metal, to achieve his expressive goals.

Schmidt's pendants, bracelets, and cuff links were included in national exhibitions in the 1950s and '60s. He won awards at the *Fiber, Clay, and Metal* competitions (1953, 1955, 1959) in St. Paul, MN; at *American Jewelry and Related Arts* (1956) in Rochester, NY; and the Midwest Craftsmen competitions (1957, 1959), the latter included in an internationally traveling exhibition in 1960, organized by the U.S. Information Agency. In 1968 Schmidt wrote about design and his working methods in a textbook (co-authored with W. Reid Hastie) titled *Encounter with Art* (1969). —JP
David Campbell, "National Jewelry Show," *CH* 17 (February 1957), 33–36; Lair Felt, "Jewelry by Christian Schmidt," *CH* 20 (May/June 1960), 25–27; Janet Schmidt, "Christian Schmidt, The New Naturalism," *Metalsmith* 9 (spring 1989), 34–37.

SCHULTZ, RICHARD

Born September 26, 1926, Lafayette, IN
FURNITURE DESIGNER

Richard Schultz studied to be a mechanical engineer and industrial designer at Iowa State University and the Design Institute of the Illinois Institute of Technology. He started working at Knoll Associates in New York in 1951, assisting Harry Bertoia in the design of the *Diamond* chair. When Florence Knoll discovered that the *Diamond* chair rusted when left outdoors, Schultz offered to find a solution. The resulting *Leisure* collection (later renamed the *1966 Collection*) launched Schultz as a designer of outdoor furniture. The 1966 seating forms—wheel-based chaise longues and dining chairs—included a mesh seat, woven from vinyl-coated polyester yarn, and a metal frame. With their matching tables, the suite became desirable outdoor furnishings in the well-appointed suburban home. Schultz's *Petal* table, made with redwood and inspired by the wildflower Queen Anne's lace, was originally conceived to accompany the *Diamond* chair. Schultz became a freelance designer in 1972, and with his son, Peter, founded his eponymous furniture company in 1992. —MS
Mel Byars, *The Design Encyclopedia* (London: Laurence King Publishing; New York: MoMA, 2004), 670–71; Paul Makovsky, "The Outdoorsman," *Metropolis* 29 (May 2010), 108–13.

SCHWARCZ, JUNE THERESA

(NÉE MORRIS; MRS. LEROY SCHWARCZ)
Born June 10, 1918, Denver, CO
DESIGNER, ENAMELIST

June Schwarcz studied literature at the University of Colorado (1936–38) and the University of Chicago (1938–39). Not interested in a career teaching English, however, she transferred to the Pratt Institute in Brooklyn, NY, to study design (1939–41) and then worked as a commercial designer. In the early 1950s during a visit home, she attended an enameling workshop at the Denver Art Museum, and, being greatly engaged by what she had learned, she closely studied Kenneth Bates's *Enameling: Principles and Practice* (1951).

Having worked in graphic design, Schwarcz favored the *basse taille* technique of etching a design into the metal and firing enamel over it. From the beginning, Schwarcz approached her work from an experimental and searching viewpoint; her designs were derived first from nature and, later, from such disparate sources as handwriting, technical drawings, and abstraction. She began with premade metal forms as foundations for enameling but soon raised or constructed her own vessels, ultimately employing lightweight copper sheets that she cut, stitched, and otherwise altered and electroformed as the substrate for her enamels. Many firings of both opaque and transparent enamels created depth and texture on the etched and hammered surfaces of her pieces.

Schwarcz's work was included in *Craftsmanship in a Changing World* (MCC, 1956); *Enamels* (MCC, 1959); several Everson Ceramic Nationals (1957, 1958, 1960); and *Objects: USA* (1969). Her *basse taille* pieces were published in Oppi Untracht's textbook *Enameling on Metal* (1957). In 1959 she participated in the enamels panel for the third National Craft Conference of the ACC, held in Lake George, NY. She received the Gold Medal from the ACC in 1997, and a traveling retrospective exhibition of her work was held in 1998. —JP
Oppi Untracht, *Enameling on Metal* (New York: Chilton Company, 1957), 63, 65; *Enamels* (New York: MCC, 1959) 13, 28; Carole Austin, *June Schwarcz, Forty Years, Forty Pieces*, exh. cat. (San Francisco: San Francisco Craft & Folk Art Museum, 1998); June Schwarcz, oral history interview by Arline M. Fisch, January 21, 2001, AAA, SI.

SEEGER, DICK

Born August 11, 1929, Cedar Rapids, IA
PLASTIC ARTIST, WOODWORKER, GALLERY OWNER

Recognized for his experimentation with plastics in the late 1950s, Dick Seeger has worked in various media throughout his career. After studying at Coe College in Iowa under Marvin Cone, Seeger traveled the U.S. in search of an artist community, eventually settling in Scottsdale, AZ. Trained in woodcarving, Seeger began experimenting with plastics in the 1950s. Mesmerized by the translucence and pliable nature of the medium, he began to create large-scale plastic sculptures. He tested various chemicals to create texture in the plastic as well as mold the medium into shapes, adding colors to his plastic forms and stringing pieces together to act as room dividers in architectural space. Through this manipulation, Seeger was able to create lamps, tabletops, window decorations, and room dividers for the domestic market. He also designed plastic panel dividers for Raymond Loewy Associates that were installed in United Airlines Boeing 720 jets. In 1957 he opened the Seeger Studio, which featured his own work as well as that of local artists and craftspeople in wood sculpture, plastic decorations, and ceramics. When the studio closed in 1962, Seeger opened the Dick Seeger Gallery in Lloyd Kiva New's Craft Center on Fifth Avenue in Scottsdale, where he was able to display a wider range of work by southwestern artists. —NB

Donald Key, "The Arts in Eastern Iowa," *Cedar Rapids Gazette*, September 28, 1958, 12; "Scottsdale Arts and Crafts Displayed Today," [Phoenix] *Arizona Republic,* January 24, 1960, 10, sect. 5; "Maker of Decorative Screens Captures Light in Plastic," [Phoenix] *Arizona Republic*, April 2, 1961; David Hampton, *The Seeger Studio 1957–1962: Desert Modern in Scottsdale, Arizona* (San Francisco: Blurb, 2008).

SEKIMACHI, KAY (KEIKO)
(MRS. ROBERT STOCKSDALE)
Born September 30, 1926, San Francisco, CA
WEAVER, TEXTILE ARTIST, EDUCATOR

Kay Sekimachi is widely credited with helping to revive contemporary fiber and weaving arts and renew their legitimacy as forms of artistic expression. Her parents were Japanese immigrants, and throughout her Berkeley childhood, Sekimachi admired the Japanese and American textiles that her mother kept as mementos. During World War II, the Sekimachi family was sent to the Tanforan Assembly Center internment camp for three months before being moved to Topaz, UT, where Sekimachi graduated from high school in 1944. When her family returned to Berkeley in 1946, she began classes at the California College of Arts and Crafts in Oakland (CCAC, now California College of the Arts). In 1949 she bought her first loom and dropped out of the program, although she later resumed classes. Sekimachi apprenticed with Dorothy Ahrens, who owned a weaving studio in Berkeley and taught the fundamentals of the craft. In 1956 Sekimachi and her sister went to the Haystack Mountain School of Crafts, then in Liberty, ME, where she was taught by Jack Lenor Larsen, who became an enthusiastic advocate of her work. Larsen's assistant, Win Anderson, invited her to work in their New York studio, but she declined, returning to California, where she began classes at the Berkeley Adult School. Sekimachi studied weaving there under Trude Guermonprez, whom she credits with instilling in her a strong desire to explore artistically.

Throughout the 1950s and '60s Sekimachi created small tapestries. In 1963 she began off-loom weaving experiments resulting in multiple layers, which eventually became her nylon monofilament hangings. When Guermonprez took a teaching assignment at Haystack in 1964, Sekimachi filled in for her at the Berkeley Adult School, and she continued teaching there until 1972. She was also on the faculty of the adult division of the San Francisco Community College from 1965 to 1986.

By the late 1950s Sekimachi's work was gaining public recognition. It was featured in *Craftsman in a Changing World* (MCC, 1956), *Modern American Wall Hangings* (the Victoria & Albert Museum, London, 1962–63), and *Wall Hangings* (MoMA, 1969). Sekimachi was made a Fellow of the American Craft Council in 1985; in 1993 she and her husband, woodturner Bob Stocksdale, were honored with a joint retrospective exhibition. —LR

Yoshiko Uchida, "Kay Sekimachi," *CH* (May/June), 1959, 22–25; Virginia Nagle, "American Weaving," *Design Quarterly* 48–49 (1960), 45; Signe Mayfield, *Marriage in Form: Kay Sekimachi & Bob Stocksdale*, exh. cat. (Palo Alto, CA: Palo Alto Cultural Center, 1993); Kay Sekimachi, oral history interview by Suzanne Baizerman, July 26, 2001, AAA, SI.

SENUNGETUK, RONALD W.
Born 1933, Wales, AK
JEWELER, EDUCATOR

An Inupiat artist, Ron Senungetuk has spent most of his life in Alaska, and his work reveals a mixture of Native Alaskan, European, and American influences. In 1953 he became one of the first Alaskans to enter a college-level craft-based program when he enrolled in the School for American Craftsmen at RIT in Rochester, NY. He studied metalwork under Hans Christensen and woodworking under Tage Frid, and after a brief interruption due to service in the U.S. Army, earned a BFA in 1960. That year Senungetuk traveled to Oslo, Norway, for a Fulbright Fellowship at the Statens Håndverks og Kunstindustriskole (National College of Crafts and Industrial Design). He returned to Alaska in 1961 as a Visiting Carnegie Professor of Design at the University of Alaska at Fairbanks, where he founded the metals department. In 1966 he established the Native Arts Center at the university, and from 1977 to 1986, he was head of the art department. —JP

Objects: USA, 220; artist statement, in *Alaska Native Land Claims Part II*, Hearings before the Subcommittee on Indian Affairs of the Committee on Interior and Insular Affairs, House of Representatives, Ninety-first Congress, First Session on H.R. 13142, H.R. 10193, and H.R. 14212, Bills to Provide for the Settlement of Certain Land Claims of Alaska Natives, and for Other Purposes, U.S. Government Printing Office, 1970; Glen Simpson, *Ronald Senungetuk* (Anchorage, AK: Anchorage Museum of History and Art, 1991).

SHAW, RICHARD
Born September 12, 1941, Hollywood, CA
CERAMIST, EDUCATOR

The son of an artist and a Disney cartoonist, Richard Shaw earned his BFA in 1965 from the San Francisco Art Institute under ceramists Ron Nagle and Jim Melchert. He received his MFA in 1968 from the University of California, Davis, as a student of Robert Arneson. His work first appeared publicly in the *New Ceramic Forms* exhibition mounted by the MCC (1965).

Shaw's 1960s series of miniature ceramic sofas painted with romantic landscapes—a winter forest or dairy cows in a pasture—reflected the new direction of the Funk art movement on the West Coast. In 1966 he and six other Davis students exhibited along with Arneson at Museum West, the San Francisco outpost of ACC, in one of the early public displays of this style. These humorous representations of ordinary objects led in time to his *trompe l'oeil* work, aided by a National Endowment for the Arts grant in 1975 that allowed him to master a photo silkscreen method of reproducing decals and perfecting ceramic transfers, which remains a focus of his work.

In 1966, Shaw began teaching at the San Francisco Art Institute, and since 1987, he has been at the University of California, Berkeley, where he teaches ceramics and drawing. Shaw has been a resident artist at Shigaraki Ceramic Cultural Park in Japan and the Manufacture National de Sèvres in Paris; in 1998 he was elected a Fellow of the American Crafts Council. —JP

Joseph Pugliese, "At Museum West, Ceramics from Davis," *CH* 26 (November/December 1966), 26–29; *Objects: USA*, 108; Garth Clark, *American Ceramics: 1876 to the Present* (New York: Abbeville Press, 1987), 121; Glen R. Brown, "Richard Shaw, Illusion and Absence," *Ceramics* (Sydney, Australia) 58 (December 2004), 3–6.

SIMPSON, THOMAS (TOMMY)
Born 1939 Elgin, IL
FURNITURE MAKER, EDUCATOR

Tommy Simpson earned his undergraduate degree in painting at Northern Illinois University, DeKalb, in 1962. He continued his studies at the University of Iowa and the University of London. He received his MFA in 1964 from Cranbrook, where he began to focus on furniture as sculpture and as a three-dimensional ground for painting. The pine bodies of his chests were put together with glue and dowels and then gessoed to provide a white ground for paint. Forms were often whimsical or curvy with characteristic anatomical references. His work was featured in MCC exhibitions in the 1960s—*Amusements IS* (1965), *The Bed* (1966), and *Fantasy Furniture* (1966).

Simpson followed an independent artistic path, creating sculptural works that do not emphasize wood grain and visible joinery as in the output of the first generation of furniture makers, nor do they follow the reductive formulas drawn from the world of industrial design. His imaginative chests, tables, and chairs, with their bright colors, humorous shapes, and sensuous carving, are decorative, engagingly human, while always functional. Throughout his career, Simpson has taught in formal academic settings—Cranbrook (1965), the Program in Artisanry at Boston University (1979), and Rhode Island School of Design (1979–90)—as well as at workshops and conferences. —JP

Thomas Simpson, *Fantasy Furniture, Design and Decoration* (New York: Reinhold Book Corp., 1968); *Objects: USA*, 269; Edward S. Cooke Jr., *New American Furniture: The Second Generation of Studio Furnituremakers* (Boston: Museum of Fine Arts, 1989), 112–13.

SKOOGFORS, OLAF

(NÉ GUSTAV OLAF JANSSON,
LATER GUSTAV OLAF JOHNSON)
**Born June 27, 1930, Bredsjo, Sweden;
died December 20, 1975, Philadelphia, PA**
SILVERSMITH, JEWELER, EDUCATOR

Olaf Skoogfors immigrated to Wilmington, DE, with his family in 1934. He returned briefly to Sweden to work as a draftsman, but in 1949 he entered the Philadelphia Museum School of Art (now the University of the Arts), where he studied under silversmiths Virginia Wireman Cute and Richard Reinhardt, graduating in 1953. In 1955 Skoogfors continued his education at the School for American Craftsmen at RIT, where he learned from Hans Christensen. He graduated in 1957 and returned to Philadelphia to do studio work and to teach at his alma mater.

Skoogfors's holloware reflected the clean aesthetic and rigorous craftsmanship of his teachers' Scandinavian modernism. In the 1960s, as the market for holloware faded and jewelry took center stage, Skoogfors created pendants and brooches influenced by abstract expressionist painting and the new interest in strongly textured surfaces. He worked with various metals, singly and in combination: bronze, silver, brass, and gold, sometimes adding ivory or a semiprecious or precious stone. Brooch designs were organically textured, with abstract compositions often contained in a framelike structure more like a painting than sculpture. Pendants descended from simple circles and adhered to designs composed of geometric forms.

Skoogfors began to exhibit his work in the early 1950s at the National Decorative Arts Ceramics shows in Wichita, KS, and in *Young Americans* shows held at America House in New York. In 1968 a solo exhibition, *Jewelry by Olaf Skoogfors,* was mounted at MCC in New York, and one of his pendants was included in the landmark exhibition *Objects: USA.* —JP
Objects: USA, 221; *Olaf Skoogfors, 20th Century Goldsmith 1930–1975,* exh. cat. (Washington, D.C.: Renwick Gallery of the National Collection of Fine Arts, Smithsonian Institution, 1979); Strauss 2007, 292–93; Falino and Ward 2008, 445–48.

SLIVKA, ROSE

**Born January 9, 1919, New York, NY;
died September 2, 2004, Southampton, NY**
ART CRITIC, WRITER

Rose Slivka documented the progression of the American studio craft movement through her work, first as associate editor of *Craft Horizons* in 1955 and then as editor from 1959 to 1979, giving voice and recognition to artists who broke with tradition by exploring the boundaries of their craft. Slivka studied English at Hunter College, receiving her BA in 1941, and worked as a writer for various publications before joining *Craft Horizons.* She is best remembered for her progressive articles championing the avant-garde in craft media. With the publication of "The New Ceramic Presence" in *Craft Horizons* (July/August 1961) and "The

American Craftsman" (May/June 1964), she became one of the definitive shapers of studio craft discourse in America. She wrote the first monograph on Peter Voulkos, her long-time friend—*Peter Voulkos, A Dialogue with Clay* (1978). Slivka was also a poet, and she organized an exhibition, *The Object as Poet,* exploring the relationship between word and object at the Renwick Gallery in Washington in 1977. Slivka was named an honorary fellow of the ACC in 1979 and received honorary degrees from the Rhode Island School of Design and the Massachusetts College of Art. —NB
Ken Johnson, "Rose Slivka, 85, Writer and Champion of Crafts as Fine Art," *New York Times,* September 4, 2004, B7; Stephanie Cash and David Ebony, "Obituaries: Rose Slivka," *Art in America* 92 (October 2004), 188; "Rose Slivka, 1919–2004," *AC* 65 (February/March 2005), 20–21.

SMITH, ART

**Born October 28, 1917, Cuba;
died February 20, 1982, Brooklyn, NY**
JEWELER

Art Smith's Jamaican parents emigrated with him from Cuba to Brooklyn around 1920. His artistic talent was recognized at an early age, and he received a scholarship to attend Cooper Union for the Advancement of Science and Art. He graduated in 1940 with commercial art skills and a concentration in sculpture. He learned basic jewelry from a colleague while working part-time as a craft supervisor at the Children's Aid Society in Harlem during his years at Cooper Union and acquired additional bench skills from a night course at New York University. After graduation he worked for the National Youth Administration (a division of the Works Progress Administration) and Junior Achievement. Winifred Mason, a black jewelry designer with a small store in Greenwich Village, hired him as a full-time assistant and was a formative influence on his artistic path. He opened his own shop in 1946. Two years later his work was included in a pioneering exhibition of studio jewelry, *Modern Jewelry Under Fifty Dollars* (1948) at the Walker Art Center in Minneapolis, MN. This set his career in motion.

Smith fashioned large-scale necklaces, bracelets, earrings, rings, and brooches with fluid organic forms intended to meld with the shape and movement of the body. He worked with brass, copper, and silver, and, occasionally included colorful cabochons. He used patination to affect dramatic color contrasts in neckpieces and bracelets. Through dancer Talley Beatty, Smith became part of a circle of African American artists—dancers, musicians, singers, and painters. Smith designed large-scale jewelry for Beatty's dance company as well as that of Pearl Primus and Claude Marchant, and it may have been this experience that informed his sense of scale and drama.

In 1956 three of Smith's silver pieces—a cuff bracelet, neckpiece, and bracelet entitled *Crown of Thorns*—were included in *Craftsmanship in a Changing World* (1956) at MCC, which also gave him a solo exhibition in 1969 and

included his work in *Objects: USA* (1969). —JP
Objects: USA, 208; Toni Greenbaum, *Messengers of Modernism: American Studio Jewelry, 1940–1960* (Montreal: Montreal Museum of Decorative Arts; Paris and New York: Flammarion, 1996), 86–95; Barry R. Harwood, *From the Village to Vogue: The Modernist Jewelry of Art Smith* (Brooklyn: Brooklyn Museum, 2008).

SMITH, PAUL J.

Born September 8, 1931, Batavia, NY
CURATOR, DIRECTOR

Paul Smith introduced contemporary craft to American and international museum-going audiences as the chief proponent behind most of the shows mounted by the Museum of Contemporary Crafts between 1963 and 1984. Now MCC's director emeritus, Smith joined the staff of ACC in 1957 as assistant to director David Campbell; he was appointed assistant director at MCC in 1962, and director in 1963, and he remained there until his retirement in 1987.

Smith attended the Art Institute of Buffalo and the School for American Craftsmen in Rochester and pursued painting, metalwork, woodwork, and other media. He was associated with the York State Craftsmen exhibitions and the group's annual fair and was a featured craftsman in wood in 1958. It was in this manner that Smith came to Campbell's attention at ACC. An earlier stint as a display director of Flint & Kent, a luxury department store in Buffalo, served Smith well at MCC, as he soon began to conceive, develop, and install exhibitions.

Smith was an innovative curator with a willingness to explore current trends in American culture as manifested in craft media. Many of the 200 or so exhibitions he mounted were reflective of their times, featuring materials or techniques that had never before received attention in a museum setting. Exhibitions such as *Cookies and Breads: The Baker's Art* (1960), *Body Covering* (1965), *The Door* (1968), *Objects for Preparing Food* (1973), and *The Great American Foot* (1978) only hint at the range of subjects tackled by Smith during his long tenure. Blessed with an insatiable appetite for visiting artists around the country and seeing new developments in their studios, Smith integrated their work into *Designed for Production: The Craftsmen's Approach* (1964), *The Teapot* (1966), and other shows, while also mounting important regional and solo exhibitions. As curatorial advisor for *Objects: USA* (1969) with Lee Nordness, Smith drew upon his considerable knowledge to illuminate craft in all media at a high-water mark in its development.

Smith has received numerous awards for his exceptional efforts to advance the field of American craft. These include an Honorary Doctorate of Fine Arts from the New School University–Parsons School of Design, an Honorary Fellowship from ACC, and the Aileen Osborn Webb Award for philanthropy. —JF
"York State Craft Fair," *Cross-Country Craftsman* 9 (mid-June 1959), n.p.; Paul Smith, "Reflections on the Past and Current Observations," *Studio Potter* 32 (December 2003), 3–16; Suzanne Ramljak, "Interview Paul J.

Smith," *Metalsmith* 27 (2007), 20–23; Robert Kehlmann, "Consummate Connoisseur," *AC* 47 (October/November 1987), 52–55.

SODERGREN, EVERT

Born July 19, 1920, Seattle, WA

FURNITURE DESIGNER, FURNITURE MAKER, EDUCATOR

The son of a Swedish furniture maker who had settled in the Pacific Northwest, Sodergren first became interested in woodworking in 1935, when he began assisting his father and learning about the family business. After spending World War II making test-model aircraft at Boeing and two years in the Army Air Corps, Sodergren joined his father's business in Seattle as a fourth-generation woodworker. The elder Sodergren was a traditionalist, while Evert preferred to create his own sculpted designs, citing the influence of Hans Wegner, Finn Juhl, and George Nelson. In 1947, when his father returned to Sweden, Evert took over the family workshop. Sodergren and eight others (Russell Day, Hella Skoronski, Coralynn Pence, Lisel Salzer, Henry Lin, Irene McGowen, Robert Sperry, and Ruth Penington) founded Northwest Designer Craftsmen in 1954 to promote their work and to affirm excellence in craftsmanship and business practices.

Sodergren taught furniture design and construction at the University of Washington in Seattle (1951–78). Over the years he has also taken on more than 150 apprentices, providing them with a close look at the complexities of the art and business of studio furniture. When the Northwest Designer Craftsmen initiated a Living Treasures project in 1997 to honor pioneers in the studio craft movement in the region, among the first to be named was Evert Sodergren. —LR

Robert Silberman, "Virginia Harvey: A Legacy in Fiber Arts/Evert Sodergren: Master Woodworker" *AC* 63 (October/November 2003), 47; Cooke, Ward, and L'Ecuyer 2003, 138.

SOLBERG, RAMONA

Born May 10, 1921, Watertown, SD;

died June 13, 2005, Seattle, WA

JEWELER, EDUCATOR

Ramona Solberg earned her BA in 1951 and MFA in 1957 under Ruth Penington at the University of Washington, Seattle. Inspired by patriotism and an older brother who had traveled the world, in 1943 she interrupted her fourth year of college to enlist in the Women's Army Corps. She spent two years in Georgia and Texas and reenlisted in 1945 for the opportunity to work in Germany as an information and education officer. When she returned to civilian life in 1948, she studied weaving and jewelry in Mexico on the GI Bill before returning to Seattle to finish her undergraduate degree.

Although Solberg's mentor Penington pursued a formal Scandinavian modernism and had a serious demeanor, she recognized and encouraged the exuberant, fun-loving Solberg. After graduation Solberg taught in the public schools for two years and then in 1953 used the GI Bill to continue her education in Oslo, Norway, where she learned to enamel. She was especially drawn to the Celtic and Viking jewelry of the Iron Age. In her thesis work, Solberg combined the metal-based discipline of Penington's approach with a variety of enameling techniques and her own delight in the varied materials she had begun to collect for inclusion in her designs. Her book *Inventive Jewelry-making* (1972) advanced the use of nonprecious and found materials and influenced countless artists who followed in her wake.

After her thesis work, she gradually abandoned enameling, choosing instead to use precious metals, bone, ivory, coral, ebony, glass, and man-made and natural found objects for color, composition, and texture; all were grist for the mill of Solberg's imagination. An enthusiastic and tireless traveler, Solberg collected wherever she went. At her bench, she created neckpieces characterized by strong formal designs. The works suggest a mysterious and important history, but Solberg's primary goal was beautiful design, not content. Solberg taught at Central Washington University in Ellensburg from 1956 to 1967 and served as professor of metal design and art education at the University of Washington School of Art from 1967 to 1983. —JP

Vicki Halper, *Findings: The Jewelry of Ramona Solberg* (Seattle: University of Washington Press; London: Bank of America Gallery, 2001); "Obituary: Ramona Solberg 1921–2005, *AC* 65 (December 2005/January 2006), 15.

SOLDNER, PAUL EDMOND

Born April 24, 1921, Summerfield, IL;

died January 3, 2011, Claremont, CA

CERAMIST, EDUCATOR

Potter and inventor Paul Soldner earned a BA in arts education in 1946 from Bluffton College (now University) in Bluffton, OH, and an MA in arts administration in 1954 from the University of Colorado, Boulder, where he became interested in ceramics. He was Peter Voulkos's first student at the Los Angeles County Art Institute (the Otis Art Institute), where he earned an MFA in 1956.

The majority of students around Voulkos discarded the idea of utility in their work, but Soldner continued to make functional pots, although experimentation drove his creations. He devised a technique for constructing slender vessels that soared to eight feet. After graduation Soldner was a visiting assistant professor at Scripps College in Claremont near Los Angeles (1957–64). He spent a year at the University of Colorado, Boulder, and in 1969 returned to Scripps, where he remained until 1991. He has also lectured and exhibited widely and conducted workshops around the U.S.

In 1960 he began exploring the Japanese technique of raku by following the directions in *A Potter's Book* by Bernard Leach. As he experimented, Soldner became intrigued by the unpredictable nature of reduction firing, which introduced uncertainty into the final appearance of the surface texture and color of the piece. Spontaneity and personal expression were paramount in the late 1950s and '60s. When Soldner made plaques using raku techniques, he manipulated the clay by folding, incising, stamping, and texturing the surface with whatever object or material was around him before firing. His expressionistic version of raku pottery appealed to American artists who created their own interpretations of the technique.

In 1955, he established his own company to produce and sell pottery equipment, patenting eponymous kick wheels, electric potters' wheels, and clay mixers. In 1966, Soldner was one of the founders of the National Council on Education for the Ceramic Arts (NCECA). That same year he was invited to develop a ceramics cooperative that became the Anderson Ranch Arts Center, in Snowmass, CO; later he was influential in bringing Fred Marer's collection of ceramics to Scripps College. —JP

Garth Clark, *American Potters: The Work of Twenty Modern Masters* (New York: Watson-Guptill Publications, 1981), 48; Mary Davis MacNaughton et al., *Paul Soldner: A Retrospective* (Claremont, CA: Lang Gallery, Scripps College; Seattle: University of Washington Press, 1991).

SPERRY, ROBERT

Born March 12, 1927, Bushnell, IL;

died April 12, 1998, Seattle, WA

CERAMIST, EDUCATOR

Robert Sperry was originally a painter and in 1950 earned his BA at the University of Saskatchewan, Saskatoon. After taking a ceramics course at the School of the Art Institute of Chicago, he became enamored of the art form and the many possibilities for combining it with painting. By 1953 Sperry had earned his BFA from the Art Institute of Chicago, and in 1954 he became an artist-in-residence at the Archie Bray Foundation in Montana, where he encountered the work of ceramists Peter Voulkos and Rudy Autio. Their large-scale work and painted surfaces profoundly influenced his own by demonstrating the virtually limitless possibilities clay offered the artist. In 1954, while still a graduate student, he was among the founders of the Northwest Designer Craftsmen organization. A year later he earned his MFA from the University of Washington and was awarded a teaching fellowship there. He remained on the faculty until his retirement in 1982, and continued on for many years as an emeritus professor. As a teacher, he was less likely to lecture and more likely to encourage experimentation through trial and error. He believed that more was to be gained by finding one's artistic voice from within an art-minded community than by heavy-handed instruction.

Sperry's ceramics were featured in several solo and group exhibitions between 1949 and 1958, including the 1955 *Young Americans* exhibition held at America House, where he won first prize. In 1959 his ceramics were exhibited alongside the work of international artists at the *International Exhibition of Ceramics* at the Smithsonian Institution in Washington, DC, as well as in a touring European exhibition, *La Céramique Contemporaine* organized by the Musée des Beaux-Arts in Ostend, Belgium. Sperry's work was featured at MCC for the first time in 1961 and subsequently in 1966. In 1963 his creations toured South America as part of the *American Potters* exhibition organized by the United States Information Agency. That same year he received his first grant from the Center for Asian Studies at the University of Washington to film potters in the village of Onda in Japan. In 1965 Sperry's ceramics were featured in *Three Men from the U.S.A.* at the Nihonbashi Gallery in Tokyo. He received an additional grant in 1966 to complete his film, *Village Potters of Onda*, which became a prizewinning documentary. In 1968 his ceramics were featured in the Victoria and Albert Museum's *American Studio Pottery* exhibition. —LR

Matthew Kangas, *Robert Sperry: Bright Abyss* (Pomona, CA: American Museum of Ceramic Art, 2008).

STAFFEL, RUDOLF (RUDY)

Born June 15, 1911, San Antonio, TX;
died January 20, 2002, Alfred, NY
CERAMIST, EDUCATOR

Rudy Staffel experimented with porcelain to create delicate yet distorted translucent pieces. Most of his works are asymmetrical vessels that he called "light gatherers," each being small in scale with various layers of thickness. When illuminated from the interior, the light exposes many layers, revealing Staffel's intimate shaping of each form. As a teenager in San Antonio, he was enthralled with Chinese and Japanese brushwork, and in 1931 he moved to Chicago and enrolled in painting classes at the School of the Art Institute. He frequented the city's museums and became enamored of the translucent quality of glass. Staffel moved to Mexico City to study glass, but upon seeing the collection of the National Archeological Museum, he became passionate about ceramics. When he returned to San Antonio, he continued his experiments with clay, adding color and combining hand-building and wheel-thrown techniques to create unique pieces. His first experience of porcelain came in the 1950s, and he found it to be an ideal medium to bring light to clay. Spirituality was at the core of Staffel's artistic career, and the shapes and surfaces he created reflect a Zen influence. In 1936 he taught ceramics at the Arts and Crafts Club in New Orleans, and in 1940 he was invited to develop a ceramics program at the Tyler School of Art at Temple University in Elkins Park, PA. Staffel taught at Tyler until 1978, encouraging students to find their own artistic voice and to translate his teachings to their own practice. —NB

Rob Barnard, "Rudolf Staffel/Temple Gallery," *AC* 49 (December 1989/January 1990), 72–73; "Seeing the Light: Rudolf Staffel at 80," *AC* 51 (June/July 1991), 14, 64; Paula and Robert Winokur, "Obituary," *AC* 62 (April/May 2002), 38.

STEPHENSON, JOHN

Born October 27, 1929, Waterloo, IA
CERAMIST, EDUCATOR

John Stephenson studied under ceramist William Daley at the University of Northern Iowa, receiving his BFA in

1952. After four years in the U.S. Air Force, he enrolled at Cranbrook and studied under Maija Grotell, earning his MFA in 1958. He taught at the Maryland Institute of Baltimore along with Alfred Jensen and at the Cleveland Institute of Art before moving in 1959 to the University of Michigan, Ann Arbor, where he remained for more than thirty-five years.

Stephenson's emergence as an artist occurred in the midst of the clay revolution of the 1960s when Peter Voulkos and other clay artists were breaking free of the age-old orthodoxy of functional ceramics, reinventing the definition of clay as an art medium with its own expressive potential. During the 1960s Stephenson's ceramics assumed an increasingly sculptural form. He experimented with mixed media, incorporating metal, glass, and paper in his creations, often addressing contemporary social issues. His works have been exhibited in Europe and Asia. He participated at several early Michigan Artist-Craftsmen exhibitions and in 1965 was awarded the gold medal of the City of Faenza, Italy. In 1969 he was included in *Objects: USA*, and in 2010 he and his wife, potter Susanne Stephenson, were made Fellows of the ACC. —MS

Objects: USA, 135; Paul Kotula, "About the Work," in *John Stephenson: After the Fire. A Retrospective*, exh. cat. (Ann Arbor, MI: University of Michigan, 1994); John C. Cantú, "John Stephenson," *American Ceramics*, 12 (1995), 56; "Three Cheers! [Aileen Osborn Webb Awards]" *AC 70* (October/November 2010), 41.

STOCKSDALE, ROBERT

Born May 25, 1913, Warren, IN;
died January 6, 2003, Berkeley, CA
WOODTURNER

Robert Stocksdale is credited with reviving the craft of woodturning and raising it to a true art form. He grew up on the family farm, where he repaired and built furniture using a homemade lathe (driven by a gasoline-powered Maytag washing machine engine) and other simple tools available to him there. As a conscientious objector during World War II, he spent four years at a civilian public service camp, and it was there that he produced his first turned bowl. In 1946, Stocksdale was released and settled in Berkeley, CA, where he set himself up as a woodturner, producing bowls, platters, and other forms. Entirely self-taught, Stocksdale did not restrict himself to the kinds of wood commonly used in turning. He actively collected samples of rare and exotic wood from all over the world, which provided interesting grain patterns and colors. Stocksdale preferred to work freehand with green, or wet, wood because of its ease of use. He utilized only the most basic tools, which often surprised fellow turners and admirers. Although he had a profound affinity for his craft, he regarded it as a profession instead of an art and treated it as such by producing multiple pieces each day of more common wood to sell at reasonable prices. Several upscale retailers, including Gump's in San Francisco, Fraser's in Berkeley, as well as Neiman Marcus, Georg Jensen, and Bonnier's, found that his more sculptural objects, evocative of ceramics, made

with rare and expensive woods, sold exceedingly well. In 1957 Stocksdale attended the first ACC conference at Asilomar, CA. There he made the acquaintance of several woodworkers including Walker Weed, head of the wood shop at Dartmouth College, who invited Stocksdale to demonstrate and speak about his craft for the first time.

Stocksdale gave numerous workshops throughout the country and taught at the Berkeley Adult School (1964–72) and San Francisco Community College (1965–86). He was a member of the Baulines Craft Guild. Stocksdale's woodwork has been shown in exhibitions throughout the U.S. and abroad, including MoMA's Good Design series (1950); *Designer Craftsmen U.S.A.* (1953); the 1958 World's Fair in Brussels; and the Milan Triennale (1960). In 1959 the Long Beach Museum of Art in California mounted his first solo exhibition, and in 1965 he had a one-man show at MCC in New York. Stocksdale and his wife, weaver Kay Sekimachi, shared a retrospective exhibition with catalogue, entitled *Marriage in Form: Kay Sekimachi and Bob Stocksdale* (Palo Alto Art Center, 1992). He was named a California Living Treasure in 1986 and received the Gold Medal from the ACC in 1995. —LR

"Bob Stocksdale Turns a Bowl," *CH* 16 (September 1956), 38–39; *Woodturning in North American Since 1930,* exh. cat. (New Haven: Woodturning Center and Yale University Art Gallery, 2001), 177; Signe Mayfield, "Bob Stocksdale 1913–2003," *AC* 63 (April/May 2003), 62.

STRENGELL, MARIANNE

(MRS. CHARLES DUSENBURY;
LATER, MRS. OLAV HAMMARSTROM)
Born May 24, 1909, Helsinki, Finland;
died May 9, 1998, Wellfleet, MA
WEAVER, TEXTILE DESIGNER, EDUCATOR

Marianne Strengell studied design at the Central School of Industrial Design in her native Finland. After graduation she participated in a number of international design fairs and competitions, won several international prizes, and worked as the artistic director for a major department store in Helsinki. In 1936 Strengell immigrated to the U.S. at the invitation of fellow Finns Eliel and Loja Saarinen, then teaching at Cranbrook. Strengell also taught there from 1937 on and was head of the department of weaving and textile design from 1942. Beginning in the 1940s she was active in the design of industrial textiles for a number of clients, including upholstery for the United Airlines fleet, as well as acting as an advisor for a number of major companies and government organizations.

In 1957 Strengell's wall hangings and rugs were the subject of a solo exhibition at MCC in New York City. Strengell retired from Cranbrook in 1961 the same year that a traveling retrospective of her work was organized by MCC, Philadelphia Museum of Art, and others. She continued to produce commercial designs and win awards through the 1970s until she retired to Cape Cod with her husband, architect Olav Hammarstrom. —NE

Robert Judson Clark et al., *Design in America: The Cranbrook Vision, 1925–1950* (New York: Abrams, in association with the Detroit Institute of Arts and The Metropolitan Museum of Art, 1983); Christine Cipriani, "Fruits of the Loom," *Dwell* 10 (July/August 2009), 104–6.

STURM, DOROTHY MAY
Born August 2, 1910, Memphis, TN;
died March 29, 1988, Shelby, TN
ENAMELIST, EDUCATOR, DRAFTSMAN, COLLAGE ARTIST

Memphis-born Dorothy Sturm showed artistic promise at an early age. She moved to New York to study at the Grand Central School of Art and the Art Students League from 1929 to 1934. In 1938 she began her long teaching career at the Memphis Academy of Arts (now the Memphis College of Art). Interested in medical illustration, she provided the drawings for *Morphology of Human Blood Cells* (1956) by L. W. Diggs. At midcentury, photomicrography was not advanced enough to show the detail needed in medical textbooks, but Sturm's draftsmanship was equal to the task. She continued with this work through the 1960s.

Sturm's early studio work was on paper and centered on social issues. Around 1950 she experimented with paper and textile collage, and her style became more abstract. She discovered enameling when she designed and made stained-glass windows. Subsequently, her unique enamels on metal included chunks of glass and pieces of stained glass that she fired at a high temperature to induce the enamel to crack.

Sturm's collages and enamels were shown at the Betty Parson's Gallery in New York from 1954 to 1970; in 1954, and the following year, her enamels appeared in *Nine Craftsmen in Contemporary Enamels* at America House. In 1957 Oppi Untracht included one of her enamels in his textbook *Enameling on Metal*, and in 1959 six of her plaques were shown in *Enamels,* an exhibition held at MCC. —JP

S.P., "About Art and Artists," *New York Times*, December 24, 1954; Oppi Untracht, *Enameling on Metal* (New York: Chilton Company, 1957), 109; *Enamels,* exh. cat. (New York: ACC and MCC, 1959), 42; Karen Blockman Carrier and Donna Leatherman, *Cobalt: The Art of Dorothy Sturm* (Memphis, TN: Cobalt Publications, 1988).

TAKAEZU, TOSHIKO
Born June 17, 1922, Pepeeko, HI;
died March 8, 2011, Honolulu, HI
CERAMIST, WEAVER, EDUCATOR

Born to Japanese immigrant parents, Toshiko Takaezu first studied pottery at the Hawaiian Potters Guild. In 1948 she enrolled in the University of Hawaii to study under Claude Horan, head of the ceramics program, while also learning weaving and design. From 1951 to 1954 Takaezu was at Cranbrook, then as now a breeding ground for progressive artists. She earned an MFA in ceramics, having studied with Maija Grotell, who had a profound influence on Takaezu's creativity. Takaezu also began her teaching career at Cranbrook as an instructor of summer classes. She moved to the art department at University of Wisconsin, Madison (1954–55), to teach during Harvey Littleton's sabbatical. In 1955 she traveled for

eight months to Japan, where she studied Buddhism and traditional Japanese pottery-making, visiting the studios of Kitaoji Rosanjin, Shoji Hamada, and Kaneshige Toyo. Upon her return, Takaezu accepted a teaching position as head of the ceramics department at the Cleveland Institute of Art in Ohio, where she remained for a decade. It was during this period that she began to close the mouths of her vessels as a way of transforming their utilitarian origins into sculpture. She moved to Clifton, NJ, and in 1967 began to teach ceramics in the program in visual arts at nearby Princeton University, where she remained for about twenty-five years.

Takaezu's earliest ceramic designs are predominately wheel-thrown, but after years of clay exploration, she began to make oversized, hand-built vertical forms, eliminating the restrictions of the circular potter's wheel as her early attraction to functional vessels shifted to abstract, sculptural forms. Her explorations of the closed vessel came to symbolize her work. She also created expressive, painterly surface decorations. Her use of glaze was improvisational and innovative. She would circle the object, spontaneously pouring and painting with glaze, as if to intentionally balance the disciplined forms she built in clay. Throughout her career, Takaezu has merged a love of the natural world with Eastern and Western techniques and aesthetics.

Takaezu's work was first exhibited in the late 1950s. She was included in "Eighty-two American Ceramists and their Work," in *Design Quarterly* (1958), and participated in many of the May Shows presented by the Cleveland Museum of Art. She also exhibited with the Arts and Craftsmen of the Western Reserve, had a solo exhibition at MCC in 1961–62, and was included in *Objects: USA* (1969). —LB

Conrad Brown, "Toshiko Takaezu" *CH* 19 (March 1959), 22–26; Cary C. Liu, "Presence and Remembrance: The Art of Toshiko Takaezu," *Record of the* [Princeton] *Art Museum* 68 (2009), 46–59.

TAKEMOTO, HENRY
Born 1930, Honolulu, HI
CERAMIST, DESIGNER, EDUCATOR

Henry Takemoto earned a BFA at the University of Hawaii in 1957 and joined the circle of ceramists around Peter Voulkos at Otis Art Institute in Los Angeles, earning an MFA there in 1959. At Otis, Takemoto produced large-scale organically shaped vessels and wall murals. His hand-built stoneware pieces with their exuberant overall calligraphic decoration of dark inky blue slip over a light surface were distinctive and influential for other ceramists.

Takemoto's artistry was recognized with reviews in *Art in America* and by his participation in the Third International Exhibition of Contemporary Ceramics in Prague in 1962; he was also included in *Objects: USA* (1969). By then, however, he had turned away from studio ceramics to teach and to design for the Interpace Corporation and Wedgwood Pottery. He has taught at the San Francisco Art Institute, Montana State University at Missoula, Scripps College in Claremont, CA, and the Claremont Graduate School. —LB

"New Talent 1959, Sculpture," *Art in America* 47 (spring

1959), 36–37; K. B. Sawyer, "U.S. Ceramics at the Third International Exhibition of Contemporary Ceramics in Prague," *CH* 22 (May 1962), 58.

TAWNEY, LENORE
(NÉE LEONORA AGNES GALLAGHER;
LATER MRS. GEORGE TAWNEY)
Born May 10, 1907, Lorain, OH;
died September 24, 2007, New York, NY
WEAVER

Lenore Tawney was a leader in fiber art; her woven sculptures redefined weaving in the second half of the twentieth century from household craft to a respected art medium. In 1943 Tawney attended the University of Illinois, Champaign–Urbana, followed by the Chicago Institute of Design, studying with such avant-garde artistic luminaries as the school's founder, László Moholy-Nagy, who taught drawing. Cubist sculptor Alexander Archipenko and abstract expressionist painter Emerson Woelffer were among her other teachers. Tawney's earliest training in weaving was at the institute under the tutelage of leading industrial and textile designer, Marli Ehrman, but it was not until she took a six-week tapestry workshop with Finnish weaver Martta Taipale in 1954 at Penland School of Crafts that an interest in the medium was stirred.

From 1949 to 1951, Tawney lived in Paris and traveled to various weaving centers in Europe, South America, India, North Africa, and the Middle East. Her earliest weaving designs in the 1950s were predominately traditional but revealed glimpses of unconventional and innovative methods, such as exposed warp threads for spatial effect and expressive commentary. In 1957, Tawney relocated again, this time to New York City and a loft on Coenties Slip, which was then a celebrated haven for artists in an unlikely place—the financial district of lower Manhattan. Her neighbors included several painters: pop artist Robert Indiana, modernist Ellsworth Kelly, and minimalist Agnes Martin. James Rosenquist, Jack Youngerman, Robert Rauschenberg, and others also had studios there at various times.

Tawney's weavings were deeply influenced by her travels. She pursued a diverse array of techniques including binding, twining, and knotting in plain and gauze weaves. Tawney studied meditation and considered knotmaking, a hallmark of her work, to be an extension of this practice. The mystical symbols of the circle within the square (a metaphor for inner life) were often utilized by Tawney as a conduit for expressing spirit and soul. In addition to weaving, in the 1960s she produced low-relief collages as "postcards," which she mailed to friends. She used found objects, including eggs, bones, thread, and feathers; each collage was not considered "finished" until it had journeyed from one location to the next. The ACC awarded Tawney a gold medal in 1987. —LB

Holland Cotter, "Lenore Tawney, an Innovator in Weaving, Dies at 100," *New York Times,* September 28, 2007; Kathleen Nugent Mangan, "In Memoriam: Lenore Tawney," *Fiberarts* 34 (January/February 2008), 8.

THIEBAUD, WAYNE

Born November 15, 1920, Mesa, AZ
PAINTER, ILLUSTRATOR, EDUCATOR

Wayne Thiebaud is famous for the mimetic quality of his work and for his deep commitment to landscape, portrait, and still-life painting. He exalted the iconography of postwar Americana by painting a taxonomy of cakes, pies, and other quotidian objects of American life. Although initially labeled a pop artist and satirist commenting on American consumerism and industry, Thiebaud investigated the formal aspects of composition to further his interest in traditional academic painting. He painted each subject without context or narrative, from memory, releasing the nostalgia he felt for his childhood in the American West and documenting a way of life that he saw disappearing from the culture.

Raised in Southern California, Thiebaud worked for a time at the Walt Disney Studios and during World War II drew comic strips for his army base newspaper. In the late 1950s, when many of his contemporaries turned to abstract painting, Thiebaud sought to deepen his technical skills by focusing on the shapes of things he saw every day. Pies, hot dogs, typical roadside fruit stands, and pinball machines all became subjects of his compositions. He has cited Pieter Bruegel and Jean Chardin as influences, especially the way Chardin used paint to mimic form. Thiebaud coined the term *object transference* to define, for example, his use of impasto made to look like actual swirls of cake frosting, a technique he employed to stimulate the viewer's senses. He exhibited his first cake and pie paintings in 1962 at the Allan Stone Gallery in New York to critical acclaim. The following year, his monumental *Cakes*, a five-by-six-foot painting of thirteen cakes, is not only emblematic of this phase of his career but also memorializes a particular place and time in American history. Thiebaud has taught periodically at the University of California, Davis, and has illustrated various monographs, including two about food: *Meditations on Transcendental Gastronomy* (1995) and *Chez Panisse Desserts* (1985). —ML

Regina Schrambling, "The Painter Knows the Real Thing, Too," *New York Times,* June 27, 2001, F4; Adam Gopnik, "Window Gazing," *The New Yorker* (April 29, 1991), 78; A. LeGrace Benson, "An Interview with Wayne Thiebaud," *Leonardo* 2 (January 1969), 65–72.

TOMPKINS, DONALD PAUL

Born November 1, 1933, Everett, WA;
died March 23, 1982, Seattle, WA
JEWELER, EDUCATOR

Donald Tompkins left his mark on studio crafts jewelry by creating imaginative, satiric, one-of-a-kind silver compositions using found objects and other nontraditional materials, while exploring experimental techniques. His work frequently commemorated the events and people who mattered to him.

Tompkins's interest in jewelry began in high school when he had an opportunity to study with Russell Day, an influential Northwest artist and teacher who taught him at Everett

High School and later at Everett Community College. Tompkins submitted three pieces of jewelry to the 1954 *Northwest Craftsmen's Exhibition* at the Henry Art Gallery of the University of Washington in Seattle. It was the first juried exhibition Tompkins entered, and one of his designs was chosen for the cover for the exhibition catalogue. The same year Tompkins transferred from Everett Junior College to the University of Washington to study with Ruth Penington. In 1956 he received a BA in art education, specializing in metalwork, jewelry, and sculpture, followed by a master's degree in engineering in 1958. Tompkins returned to Everett Junior College and joined Russell Day in the art department, where they taught together for five years. During the 1950s and '60s Tompkins exhibited his jewelry regionally in such venues as the Pacific Northwest Arts and Crafts Fairs, held in Bellevue, WA, and won numerous design awards in the Northwest Craftsmen's exhibitions (1955–63).

Tompkins's signature work includes the commemorative medal designs he produced between 1965 and 1976, in which precious gemstones and materials were replaced by treasured subjects evocative of American society. The medals expressed Tompkins's personal and political views, often illustrating his humor and his satirical opinions, which became inseparable from his creative personality. In 1963 Tompkins received a teaching fellowship at Syracuse University, and in 1966 he returned to the Northwest to teach design, jewelry, and metalsmithing at Central Washington University in Ellensburg, with the encouragement of his colleague Ramona Solberg. By 1972 Tompkins had moved to New York City, where he completed a PhD in education at Columbia University Teachers College and taught jewelry courses at New York University. During this period he exhibited frequently, both in New York City and elsewhere. Of particular note are two solo exhibitions that were mounted at the Teachers College Gallery: *Jewelry and Other Old Stuff* (October 1970) and *The Late Late Show* (January 1972). In 1975 personal setbacks forced him to leave New York for Washington, where he taught goldsmithing at Northwest Technical School until his death in 1982. —LB

Celia Ben Mitchell, "Heart and Head, The Life and Work of Don Tompkins," *Metalsmith* 23 (summer 2003), 28–37; Merrily Tompkins, e-mail to Jeannine Falino, November 11, 2010.

TURNER, WARWICK A. (RICK)

Born July 30, 1943, Washington, DC
LUTHIER

A music lover and amateur musician, Rick Turner designs and builds guitars that blend advanced technology with traditional craftsmanship. Raised in Marblehead, MA, Turner grew up among artists, his father being a painter and his mother a poet. He studied briefly at Boston University in the early 1960s but soon left to join the local folk music scene, playing in various groups while apprenticing as a guitar repairman at the Stringed Instrument Workshop in Boston. In 1966 he moved from Cambridge to New York,

where he experimented with new electronics for the guitars he was creating. In the late 1960s he and his wife, Amber, moved to Pt. Reyes Station in Marin County, CA, where Turner worked as a studio musician while building electric guitars and basses in a home workshop. In 1970 Turner co-founded Alembic Guitars and developed the acoustic/electric Renaissance Ampli-Coustic line of instruments. He also designed Turner Model 1, which is still in production. In the late 1980s, after a brief experience in the Gibson Lab's research and development department, where he worked with Les Paul, he resumed his focus on building his own line of instruments and founded Rick Turner Renaissance Guitars, which he continues to operate. He worked on the Grateful Dead's legendary Wall of Sound in the 1970s and has built, repaired, and customized instruments for an impressive list of clients including The Who, Led Zeppelin, Jefferson Airplane, Santana, Jackson Browne, Ry Cooder, and Crosby, Stills, and Nash. —MS

Jonathan Peterson, "An Interview with Rick Turner," *American Lutherie* 64 (winter 2000), 20–36; January 2011 *Premier Guitar* web-exclusive Builder Profile, Max Mobley, "Rick Turner: The Father of Boutique Guitars" [search Builder Profile: Rick Turner] at www.premierguitar.com.

TURNER, ROBERT CHAPMAN

Born July 22, 1913, Port Washington, NY;
died July 26, 2005, Sandy Spring, MD
CERAMIST, EDUCATOR

An early and influential leader in the studio pottery movement, Robert Turner built a career on wheel-thrown improvisational stoneware intended to inspire spirituality and human awareness. Turner attended Swarthmore College, earning an economics degree in 1936. He studied painting at the Pennsylvania Academy of Fine Arts, completing his studies in 1941 as the U.S. was entering World War II. As a Quaker and a conscientious objector with pacifist views, Turner was assigned to public service work camps during the war. In 1944 he questioned his direction as a fine art painter and enrolled in the New York State College of Ceramics in Alfred, New York (now the New York State College of Ceramics at Alfred University), earning his MFA in 1949. Turner established the first ceramics studio at Black Mountain College, NC, between 1949 and 1951, and in 1958 he returned to Alfred, where he taught until 1979.

Turner's substantial clay objects, washed in monochromatic glaze, rely on the dynamic interplay of forms characterized by unexpected contours, bumps, and occasional incisions, and are influenced by African ceramics and Nigerian stonework carvings. Turner made the transition from functional vessels (seemingly intended for ancient rituals) to more abstract, sculptural forms. He consistently reexamined the fundamental act of creating art as social commentary, reflective of his personal view that the artist serves to transmit life through his work.

Turner exhibited widely throughout his career. Early highlights include the 1946 and 1947 Ceramic National exhibitions in Syracuse and a solo exhibition at American House in 1953. He received a silver medal at the International Exposition of Ceramics at the Palais Miramar, Cannes, France (1955). —LB

Marsha Miro and Tony Hepburn, *Robert Turner: Shaping Silence, A Life in Clay* (Tokyo: Kodansha International, 2003); "Robert Turner 1913–2005," 66 *AC* (February/March 2006), 16–17.

VOULKOS, PETER
(NÉ PANAGIOTIS HARRY VOULKOPOULOS)
Born January 29, 1924, Bozeman, MT;
died February 16, 2002, Bowling Green, OH
CERAMIST, EDUCATOR

A legendary artist who was both celebrated and reviled for his rule-breaking art and unorthodox teaching, Peter Voulkos revolutionized American studio pottery in the 1950s and '60s with intellectually and visually challenging work on a grand scale. His spontaneously created objects became known as abstract expressionist ceramics. He influenced an entire generation of ceramists through his teaching—among them Paul Soldner, John Mason, Ken Price, and Jim Melchert—encouraging experimentation and the rejection of traditional ceramic concerns, and engaging them in a no-theory, all-action competition that resulted in a burst of new clay forms. Voulkos shaped the way ceramics were regarded in the art world and forced critics to think differently about the medium.

In the early 1940s he worked in Portland, OR, as a welder on navy ships and later served in the U.S. Air Force. He subsequently earned a bachelor's degree in 1950 at Montana State University, where he studied on the GI Bill and turned to clay and sculpture after taking a ceramics course under Frances Senska. He earned a master's degree in sculpture in 1952 at the California College of Arts and Crafts in Oakland (now California College of the Arts), where he created simple ceramic vessels with small spouts or spooled lids, to which he frequently added sgraffitoed figures like those in the art of Joan Miró and Pablo Picasso. Upon graduation Voulkos returned to Montana to the Archie Bray Foundation, where the previous summer he had helped construct the newly established educational facility's first pottery building. There, he and Rudy Autio shared the directorship and in December 1952 helped organize a weeklong workshop with British ceramist and author Bernard Leach, Japanese ceramist Shoji Hamada, and Soetsu Yanagi, director of the Museum of Folk-Crafts in Tokyo. Teaching at Black Mountain College in North Carolina during the summer of 1953 and during his later visit to New York City, Voulkos gained new contacts with influential avant-garde artists including prominent abstract expressionists. The experience altered his trajectory at the ceramics department at the Otis Art Institute in Los Angeles, where he began teaching in 1954; he started to create large forms with free glaze drippings and brutal slash strokes. In 1959 Voulkos established the art ceramics department at the University of California, Berkeley, and he taught there until 1985. Voulkos was awarded numerous prizes in his career; early ones include a gold medal at the

International Exposition of Ceramics at the Palais Miramar, Cannes, France (1955) and the Musée Rodin prize at the first Paris Biennial (1959); in 1986 he received a gold medal from the ACC. MoMA held a solo exhibition of his ceramic sculpture and paintings in 1960. He turned to bronze casting in the 1960s but returned to ceramics by the end of the decade, producing simple, monumental forms, including large plates, which were often glazed black. —TT

Rose Slivka, *Peter Voulkos: A Dialogue with Clay* (Boston: New York Graphic Society, 1978); Jim Leedy, "Voulkos by Leedy," *Studio Potter* 21 (June 1993 supp.), 24–55.

WATSON, LYNDA
(FORMERLY WATSON-ABBOTT)
Born May 24, 1940 Orange, CA
JEWELER, METALSMITH, EDUCATOR

Lynda Watson studied at California State University at Long Beach, earning her BA in drawing and general crafts with an emphasis on metals (1966) and her MA (1969) and MFA (1977) in jewelry/metals. Watson came to the attention of Lee Nordness, who was traveling the country searching for young artists to include in *Objects: USA*, and Nordness selected two of her ornaments for that exhibition. Watson was head of the jewelry/small metals workshop at Cabrillo College in California (1970–95) and participated in the CabrilloARTS Workshop (2005–8). In 1995 a retrospective exhibition of her work, *The Beautiful Object,* was held at the Art Museum of Santa Cruz County, California. —BN

Objects: USA, 329; Charlotte Moser, *Beautiful Objects: The Work of Lynda Watson-Abbott,* exh. cat. (Santa Cruz, CA: Museum of Art and History, 1995); Dorothy Spencer, "The Visual Dairies of Lynda Watson-Abbott," *Metalsmith* 12 (fall 1992), 14–19.

WEBB, AILEEN CLINTON HOADLEY
(NÉE OSBORN; LATER, MRS. VANDERBILT WEBB)
Born June 25, 1892, Garrison, NY;
died August 15, 1979, Garrison, NY
PHILANTHROPIST

Aileen Osborn Webb is widely regarded as the most influential advocate of the burgeoning mid-twentieth-century studio craft movement in America. A substantial inheritance from her maternal aunt, Mary Melissa Hoadley (an heiress to a copper fortune)—and the expectation that the money be used for a good cause—fueled the crafts empire Webb systematically developed, beginning in the Depression when she founded Putnam County Products, to sell homegrown and handmade goods. At the core of her commitment was a desire to elevate the status of crafts and of craft artisans, an aspiration that craft work could generate enough income for a moderate living, and a belief that in an industrial society craft production could transform the everyday life of its maker. Webb helped put in place institutional and educational entities that promoted crafts through retail marketing, advocacy, educational outreach (publications, exhibitions, conferences,

and workshops), as well as through international diplomacy—American Craftsmen's Cooperative Council (now the American Craft Council; 1939), America House (1940), *Craft Horizons* (now *American Craft*; 1941), the School for American Craftsmen (now at RIT; 1944), the Museum of Contemporary Crafts (MCC, now the Museum of Arts and Design; 1956), and the World Craft Council (a UNESCO affiliate; 1964).

Webb was able to accomplish such an ambitious agenda in part because her network of contacts included several gifted people who shared her dreams. Frank Lloyd Wright's daughter Frances Caroë helped launch America House, developing markets for the work of American craftspeople and shaping the retail outlet's displays and exhibitions. Architect David Campbell, on the board of the ACC, helped design and build the world's first modern craft museum and then served as its director. Paul Smith joined the museum in the late 1950s and assumed the directorship in 1963, remaining there until his retirement in the mid-1980s. Mark Ellingson, president of RIT, proposed bringing the School for American Craftsmen to his campus in 1950, and Harold Brennan, who led the school during its brief period at Alfred, joined Ellingson in creating a leading educational institution in the crafts field. Rose Slivka became the editor of *Craft Horizons* in 1959, helping define the philosophy of crafts and the terms in which they were discussed at a time when the field was experiencing fast-growing popularity and professionalism. Lois Moran joined ACC in 1963 as director of regional programming, but held many positions in her lengthy career, including twenty-six years as editor of *American Craft* magazine. And Margaret Patch traveled the world to determine interest in a world craft organization, identifying 250 organizations that embraced the possibility of a global craft network, and aiding Webb in establishing the World Craft Council.

Webb had her hand in the work of all these entities. She purchased the brownstone at 44 West 53rd Street that was to become America House. She also bought a second building across the street at 29 West 53rd Street that became the first home for MCC. In deeding both structures to ACC, she established the financial base upon which the museum has grown. She herself was the first editor of *Craft Horizons*, when it was just a mimeographed sheet distributed to America House consignors. She served as chairman of ACC and held that position until her retirement in 1976. She assured the success of the World Crafts Conference at Columbia University in 1964 by paying all expenses for the attendance of no less than forty-five craftspeople from some twenty-seven countries. —TT

Aileen Osborn Webb, "Almost a Century," typescript, 71–76, 88–91, 94–101, 110–22, Aileen Osborn Webb papers, AAA, SI; Ellen Paul Denker, "Aileen Osborn Webb and the Infrastructure of Contemporary Craft," *The Journal of Modern Craft* (in preparation for publication).
For earlier history see *Craft in the Machine Age*, 249.

WELLS, GEORGE JEWETT
Born November 23, 1905 Brooklyn, NY; died July 1988
FIBER ARTIST

George Wells was educated at Rutgers University in New Jersey. In 1955 he took over a small studio in Glen Head, Long Island, called the Ruggery, founded decades earlier by Percy and Ellen Porter to fill the demand for hooked rugs in the colonial revival style. Wells experimented with abstract geometric designs using various materials in his hooked rugs. He worked with a small group of assistants, doing all of the designing and dying, and some of the hooking. In his commissioned work he used only wool yarn to control quality, color, and texture. Gradually, working mainly on commission, he expanded his repertoire of imagery to fill his customer's desires for personal designs illustrating family history, homes, gardens, special occasions, and pets.

In 1953 his abstract hooked wool rug *Pastorale* won an award in *Designer Craftsmen U.S.A.*; two rugs were included in *Craftsmanship in a Changing World* (1956), and the same year his rugs were used to furnish the conference room and office of the new MCC. A decade later, Wells's work also appeared in *Objects: USA*.

In 1989 the Sea Cliff Village Museum on Long Island mounted a retrospective exhibition to honor Wells that included early and later rugs as well as the watercolor patterns he created and a sampling of his yarns and tools. —JP
Craftsmanship in a Changing World (New York: MCC, 1956), cat. nos. 273–74; Helene von Rosenstiel, *American Rugs and Carpets from the Seventh Century to Modern Times* (New York: William Morrow and Company, 1978), 163–64; *Objects: USA*, 130.

WESTERMANN, HORACE CLIFFORD (H. C.)
Born December 11, 1922, Los Angeles, CA;
died November 3, 1981, Brookfield Center, CT
SCULPTOR, PRINTMAKER

After service in the U.S. Marine Corps, H. C. Westerman performed as an acrobat and toured with the USO during 1946, as quotas for education on the GI Bill were filled for that year. In 1947 he entered the Art Institute of Chicago, where he earned a BFA in 1954, having interrupted his schooling for a year to serve in the Korean War. His sculpture began to gain recognition in the late 1950s in Chicago.

Westermann's abstract wood and metal constructions drew from surrealism and from the ideas of Freudian psychoanalysis that interested many artists in Chicago, the location of the first Institute of Psychoanalysis founded in the U.S. in 1932. In 1959 Westermann was one of three Chicagoans to be invited to participate in *New Images of Man* at MoMA. Alternatively witty and troubling, but always of idiosyncratic design and made with impeccable craftsmanship, Westermann's creations influenced the Hairy Who, a sixties-era avant-garde group in Chicago. In 1968 a solo exhibition of his work was mounted at the Los Angeles County Museum of Art. —JP
Michael Rooks, *H.C. Westermann: Exhibition Catalogue*
and Catalogue Raisonné of Objects (Chicago: Museum of Contemporary Art; New York: Harry N. Abrams, 2001).

WESTPHAL, KATHERINE
Born January 2, 1919, Los Angeles, CA
TEXTILE ARTIST, EDUCATOR

Katherine Westphal is widely considered to be one of the most prolific contemporary textile artists and a leading exponent of the wearable art movement. In her work, which is defined by process and interest in surface rather than three-dimensional form, she continually introduces new materials and methods of construction.

Westphal was drawn to art at an early age and as a teenager took night classes in drawing at Los Angeles City College with Alan Workman, a former student of Hans Hofmann. She studied painting at the University of California, Berkeley, receiving a BA in 1941 and an MA in 1943. After graduation she traveled to Mexico on a grant to study art. While teaching at the University of Washington, she met fellow artist Ed Rossbach, and in 1950 they married. That same year Rossbach accepted a teaching post at University of California, Berkeley, and Westphal began to study textile design there with Mary Dumas. Both Westphal and Rossbach, working with agent Frederick Károly, began to design textiles for industry—a partnership that lasted eight years until Károly's retirement. In 1966 Westphal began to teach design at the University of California, Davis, and, using unsold pieces from her production work, began cutting and resewing textiles to make her own art.

As with her teaching, Westphal has always allowed for experimentation in her work, making imagery—often inspired by her extensive world travels—a central component of her art, especially by using photocopying techniques and the heat transfer of photographic images. Likewise, she uses hand-dying techniques and spontaneously assembles materials without preliminary drawings. Westphal also cites the influence of the impressionists in her preference for bright colors without sharp tonal contrasts. In addition to textiles, she has created artist's books, drawings, paper jewelry, mixed media constructions, and baskets.

In 1968 Westphal had a solo exhibition at MCC, and the following year was included in *Objects: USA*. She taught at University of California, Davis, until 1979—the same year that she was appointed to ACC's College of Fellows—after which time she was named professor emerita. —CK
Jan Janiero, "Piece Work: The World of Katherine Westphal," *AC* 48 (August/September 1988), 33–38; Paul J. Smith, "Katherine Westphal and Ed Rossbach: Reflections on Life and Work," in *Ties that Bind: Fiber Art by Ed Rossbach and Katherine Westphal from the Daphne Farago Collection* (Providence, RI: Museum of Art, Rhode Island School of Design, 1997).

WIENER, EDWARD
Born 1918, New York, NY; died July 21, 1991, New York, NY
JEWELER

The midcentury jeweler Ed Wiener was the son of a butcher and worked in his father's shop until World War II, when he
developed an aptitude for manual skills while working on radio assembly lines. He considered a career in jewelry and in 1944, with his wife, Doris Levin, enrolled in a general craft class offered at Columbia University. He made wire monogram jewelry at home using plumber's and carpenter's tools and by 1946 was emboldened to open a shop in the seaside village of Provincetown, MA, at the tip of Cape Cod. The area had become a magnet for midcentury bohemians and artists, and the shop attracted Hans Hofmann, Adolph Gottlieb, and Chaim Gross, among others. The Wieners opened a New York gallery in the fall of 1946, and maintained it at several locations, the last one at Fifty-seventh Street and Madison Avenue, until 1981. The Provincetown shop remained in existence until 1965. In the opinion of one admirer, Wiener's defiantly noncommercial jewelry was for the "aesthetically aware, intellectually inclined, and politically progressive. . . . [It] was our badge, and we wore it proudly. Diamonds were the badge of the philistine" (quoted in *Jewelry by Ed Wiener*).

Wiener had a natural talent for design and composition that was based in abstract expressionism, surrealism, and nonobjective imagery; however he claimed that the improvisational nature of jazz had the most influence upon his approach to making jewelry. During the 1950s he fashioned spirals, flora, and fish, mainly in heavy gauge silver, which were textured and occasionally ornamented with a pearl or garnet. He began to use gold, opals, and other gemstones after a trip to the Musée National du Moyen Age, Thermes de Cluny, Paris, and a visit to Jaipur, India, where the gem industry impressed him. As a result of these experiences, the jewelry of this period is richly encrusted with gemstones and is medieval in feeling. In the latter part of Wiener's career, he returned to his early primitive shapes, this time casting them in gold. —JP
Objects: USA, 209; Dr. Blanche Brown, "Ed Wiener to Me," in *Jewelry by Ed Wiener* (New York: Fifty/50 Gallery, 1988), 13; Toni Lesser Wolf, "Ed Wiener, 1918–1991," *Metalsmith* 12 (winter 1992), 10.

WILDENHAIN, MARGUERITE
(NÉE FRIEDLANDER; MRS. FRANS WILDENHAIN)
Born October 11, 1896, Lyons, France;
died February 24, 1985, Guerneville, CA
CERAMIST, EDUCATOR, AUTHOR

French-born ceramist and visionary Marguerite Wildenhain developed an art colony and school, known as Pond Farm, overlooking Armstrong Redwoods State Park outside of Guerneville, CA. Wildenhain integrated life and work, and she found meaning in the creation of pottery. She followed this craft philosophy throughout her life. In her view, Pond Farm was the preeminent environment for students to explore their craft beyond technique, learning to relate to clay and to produce an organic whole, to develop a critical eye and to make vessels with an emotional and intellectual content that was nothing less than an expression of humanity.

Wildenhain's family moved from France to Germany while she was still a child. She began formal art training in 1914, studying sculpture at the School of Fine and Applied Arts in Berlin. She attended the famed Bauhaus School in Weimar, Germany, from 1919 to 1925, working with sculptor Gerhard Marcks, who became a lifelong friend, and master potter Max Krehan. In 1926 Wildenhain was appointed head of the ceramics program at the School of Fine and Applied Arts in Halle/Saale, Germany, where she designed prototypes for elegant, mass-produced dinnerware. In 1933 her Jewish identity forced her out of Germany, and she and her husband, Frans Wildenhain, moved to Putten, Holland, where they founded a pottery studio. In 1940, just prior to the Nazi occupation of Holland, Wildenhain immigrated to the U.S., settling in northern California and working as a ceramics teacher at the California College of Arts and Crafts. Two years later she moved permanently to Pond Farm, which had been founded by San Francisco architect Gordon Herr. After becoming a U.S. citizen in 1945, Wildenhain sponsored her husband Frans's emigration from Holland. The Wildenhains and their artist colleagues—textile artist Trude (Jalowetz) Guermonprez and metalworker and jeweler Victor Ries—taught classes at the Pond Farm summer school until 1952. When the Wildenhains divorced, Marguerite became the sole manager of the Pond Farm workshops. Her earliest vessels from Pond Farm range from modest, functional forms to detailed, figurative narratives arranged over openwork, relief tiles.

Wildenhain favored painted or incised geometric patterns and organic abstractions based on nature. By the late 1960s the forms of her vessels remained simple, but the subject matter of the decoration became more narrative, based on her experiences at home and in her travels, with such motifs as fishermen, children, and kites. Her teaching focused on process, not product; for this reason, students were not allowed to keep their work. In 1952 she briefly took a teaching position at Black Mountain College, and another at Alfred University in New York. In 1962 she wrote *Pottery: Form and Expression* (1962), followed by *The Invisible Core: A Potter's Life and Thoughts* (1973), among other publications. —JP

Billie Sessions, Elaine Levin, and Richard Johnston, *Ripples: Marguerite Wildenhain and her Pond Farm Students* (San Bernardino, CA: California State University, 2002).

WILSON, BYRON AUGUST

Born July 6, 1918, Alameda, CA;
died June 15, 1992, Sonoma, CA
JEWELER, EDUCATOR

Byron Wilson taught at the California College of Arts and Crafts (now California College of Arts) beginning in 1956, in all likelihood assuming Bob Winston's post when he left the college that same year. He remained on the faculty until about 1982. Active in etching, painting, and sculpture, he constructed jewelry mainly in silver, ivory, and ebony. Practically self-taught, he learned casting from a dental technician and was schooled in soldering and the

use of specific metalsmithing tools by commercial jewelers in Oakland.

Wilson, who participated in the Metal Arts Guild of California and Designer Craftsmen of California, exhibited his jewelry nationally. In 1955 a silver and black jade pendant was shown in *84 Contemporary Jewelers* at the Walker Art Center in Minneapolis. In 1957 he won two prizes for his silver, ebony, and ivory necklace in the second national *American Jewelry and Related Objects* exhibition in Rochester (cat. 171), and two years later the Walker Art Center displayed a cuff bracelet of silver and alloy and a pendant constructed of silver, ebony, and ivory. These pieces are composed of rows of simple abstract silver shapes within a linear metal framework. The varied materials in the pendant create a dramatic color contrast, as do the applied silver forms laid on the dark patinated metal band that forms the cuff bracelet. —JP

"84 Contemporary Jewelers: American Jewelry Designers and Their Work," *Design Quarterly* 33 (1955), 31, no. 83; *American Jewelry and Related Objects,* exh. cat. (Rochester: Memorial Art Gallery, 1957), n.p., no. 195; "American Jewelry," *Design Quarterly* 45/46 (1959), 44, 63; Toni Lesser Wolf, "Byron Wilson, The Gadget Man," *Metalsmith* 12 (winter 1992), 34–37.

WILSON, ROBERT WESLEY (WES)

Born July 15, 1937, Sacramento, CA
GRAPHIC DESIGNER

Wes Wilson was one of the first graphic designers to produce posters for the legendary rock dances held in San Francisco at the height of the hippie movement. Primarily self-taught, he had taken night classes in painting and life drawing at the San Francisco Academy of Art in 1964. In that year, Wilson was also working as a printer at Contact Printing Company with Bob Carr, an early proponent of LSD, and well-connected with the beatnik and psychedelic underground activity in the area. Wilson quickly learned the basics of the business and began producing work for Carr's contacts in the counterculture. These included San Francisco Mime Troupe events, the Merry Prankster Acid Tests, and the Trips Festival in January 1966, promoted by Stewart Brand, who established the *Whole Earth Catalogue* in 1968. Wilson also produced an antiwar poster in 1965 entitled *Are We Next?*, featuring a swastika within an American flag and bringing him some notoriety. As these events were entwined with an emerging dance-hall concert scene, Wilson's designs came to the attention of Chet Helms, then promoter of the weekly dance concerts produced under the name Family Dog at the Avalon Ballroom, and Bill Graham, whose programs took place at the Fillmore Auditorium. In 1966 Wilson produced two posters per week for both men until friction with Helms over artistic decisions led to a split later that year; he continued to work for Graham until May 1967.

Wilson's greatest legacy was perhaps his graphic style, in which he fit the lettering around central figures or elements to the extent that all interstices of the page were filled

with his molten, moving, ballooning text; in addition, his use of photographic imagery, begun under Helms, and his preference for the female form were powerful influences for the artists who produced graphic arts for the rock-and-roll scene through the end of the decade. —JF

Michael Erlewine, "A Brief Biography," www.wes-wilson .com/?page_id=488; Walter Medeiros, "Robert Wesley Wilson," www.wes-wilson.com/?page_id=519.

WINSTON, CHARLES ROBERT (BOB)

Born April 15, 1915, Long Beach, CA;
died April 9, 2003, Pleasant Hill, CA
JEWELER, EDUCATOR

As a youngster, Bob Winston made furniture and jewelry, concocted glues for his model airplanes, and rigged machines for his many inventions. His ingenuity and intelligence enabled him to compensate for an undiagnosed dyslexia. He earned a BA at the University of California, Berkeley, in 1940 and an MA in 1944 and taught at the California College of Arts and Crafts (now California College of the Arts) from 1942 to 1956.

After moving to Arizona in 1959 to do studio work, he continued to teach in the extension programs at Arizona State. With the help of his wife, he also established his own school in a rented building near Phoenix. In the early 1960s he developed a superior oxidizer for jewelers that he marketed as WinOx (Winston Oxidizer). The profits from sales supported him as he continued his studio work on his own terms.

While others, such as Arthur Vierthaler, taught lost-cast waxing to jewelry students, Winston popularized its use among studio artists in this country, and by 1944 he was introducing his techniques around the nation in workshop demonstrations. He exhibited in numerous California fairs and shows, participated in landmark jewelry shows in the late 1940s and 1950s at the Walker Art Center in Minneapolis. Winston's organic sculptural pieces were always unique, never made in multiples. He worked in both silver and gold, and though he made modernist abstract jewelry from silver sheet and wire early in his career, he eventually focused on casting, which he believed offered him more complexity for his organic design than forging or other techniques. He later wrote a textbook on the technique, *Cast Away* (1970). —JP

N. Krevitsky, "Jewelry of Bob Winston," *CH* 22 (January 1962), 10–13; Bob Winston, oral history interview by Suzanne Baizerman, July 31 and October 10, 2002, AAA, SI; "Obituaries," *AC* 63 (August/September 2003), 21, 23.

WOELL, JAMES FREDERICK (FRED)

Born February 4, 1934, Evergreen Park, IL
JEWELER, EDUCATOR

Fred Woell, a transplanted Midwesterner who settled in Maine in the 1960s, has been described as an "anti-jeweler," creating offbeat "collaged jewelry sculptures" (Gold 1999). Woell's wearable art encapsulates segments of America's popular culture. Formed of cast silver, the compositions combine unrelated found objects, such as plastic toys, coins, photographs, miniature dolls, and pebbles. His thought-provoking designs reflect a somewhat cynical, serendipitous ideology. Woell prefers designing by happenstance, not by planning or drafting, and uses satire, which, in his opinion, makes life bearable. For Woell, the value of an object lies in its content and fabrication, not the intrinsic value of the gemstones and precious metals he has consistently avoided. By reusing discarded junk, he also declares his allegiance to recycling.

Though he graduated with a degree in economics from the University of Illinois, Champaign-Urbana, Woell enrolled in ceramics courses with Don Frith, who became his first important mentor. Frith encouraged his protégé to take a metallurgy class with Robert Von Neumann, the resident expert metalsmith and jeweler. Working on the bench with Von Neumann was the start of a lifelong passion. In the mid-1950s and early 1960s, Woell pursued an MFA in metalwork at University of Wisconsin–Madison, under jeweler Arthur Vierthaler, who became a friend and guide. By 1969 he had earned an MFA in sculpture at Cranbrook.

Woell found inspiration in the music of John Cage, which he often plays in his classes or during exhibitions of his work. His heroes are neither deified nor glorified but subjected to the metaphorical breakdown of society, much like the discarded junk he gathers for his art. Political commentary is another favorite form of expression; as an Illinois native, Abraham Lincoln is Woell's choice personality whose visage prominently peers from coins melded into designs, objectified in subtle, sociopolitical messages. Woell has taught crafts and design at the State University of New York, New Paltz; Haystack Mountain School of Crafts, Deer Isle, ME; the Program in Artisanry at Boston University; and the Swain School of Design (now University of Massachusetts, Dartmouth). —LB

N. J. Loftis, "Jewelry of J. Fred Woell," *CH* 28 (March 1968), 36–37; Donna Gold, "The Unpredictable Precisions of J. Fred Woell," *Metalsmith* 19 (Winter 1999), 34–41.

WOLPERT, LUDWIG YEHUDA

Born October 7, 1900, Heidelberg, Germany;
died November 6, 1981, New York, NY
DESIGNER

Ludwig Yehuda Wolpert trained first as a sculptor, then a few years later as a metalworker at the School for Arts and Crafts in Frankfurt-am-Main, Germany. His teachers included Bauhaus artist Christian Dell and silversmith and sculptor Leo Horovitz. Wolpert challenged the traditional designs of Jewish ceremonial objects, applying the forms and principles of the Bauhaus school to his work. He introduced new forms, new materials, and unusual colors. He also modernized the Hebrew alphabet, achieving a successful synthesis of tradition and modernity.

Before immigrating to Palestine in 1933, he showed his work in *Cult and Form* in Berlin and in an exhibition of ceremonial art at the Berlin Jewish Museum. From 1935 he taught metalwork at the New Bezalel Academy for Arts and Crafts in Jerusalem, stressing the principles of simplicity and functionality. In 1956 he was invited to New York to establish and direct the Tobe Pascher Workshop, which created Jewish ceremonial objects at the Jewish Museum, a position he held until his death in 1981. In the U.S., Wolpert participated in the design of several synagogue interiors and their furnishings, eventually realizing the modernist principle of integrating a building and its content. —MS

Ludwig Yehuda Wolpert: A Retrospective, exh. cat. (New York: Jewish Museum, 1976).

WORMLEY, EDWARD

Born in December 31, 1907, Rochelle, IL;
died in November 3, 1996, Weston, CT
DESIGNER

A modernist with a strong admiration for traditional and historical design, Edward Wormley worked as chief designer and director of design for the Dunbar Furniture Company of Berne, IN, from 1931 to 1970. He studied for two years at the Art Institute of Chicago in the mid-1920s and was on the design staff of the Marshall Field department store and of Berkey and Gay in Grand Rapids, MI. At Dunbar he helped move the firm's designs toward a more contemporary Scandinavian idiom. During World War II, Wormley headed the Furniture Unit of the Office of Price Administration in Washington. In 1945 he set up shop in New York City, designing modern home products—furniture, fabrics, lamps, glassware, decorative serving accessories—as well as interiors for private and corporate clients. His *Janus* line of occasional tables and dressers, designed in 1957 for Dunbar, combined a modernist design aesthetic with a handmade sensibility, incorporating glass tiles from Tiffany Studios and ceramic tiles by Gertrud and Otto Natzler.

Always convinced that a designer should cultivate a sense of the market, losing neither moral integrity nor the respect for human values, Wormley often denounced and challenged the dogmas of 1920s European avant-garde design. His vernacular modern designs were very successful in the 1950s and '60s, and he participated in MoMA's Good Design exhibitions (1950–55) and the Milan Triennale of 1964. —MS

"Contemporary Furniture Designers and Their Work: Edward J. Wormley," *Everyday Art Quarterly* 28 (1953), 8–12; Judith Gura, Chris Kennedy, and Larry Weinberg, *Edward Wormley: The Other Face of Modernism* (Northampton, MA: Designbase/Lin-Weinberg Gallery, 1997).

WRIGHT, RUSSEL

Born April 3, 1904, Lebanon, OH;
died December 21, 1976, New York, NY
DESIGNER

Russel Wright began designing modestly priced, simple utilitarian objects for American homes in the late 1920s, embarking on a forty-year career promoting stylish contemporary living, based on principles later extolled in *Guide to Easier Living* (1950). In a business partnership with his wife, Mary Small Einstein, who was responsible for public relations and marketing, Wright promoted mass-produced china and plastic derivatives in subtle, pastel colors, and furniture in bleached maple—dubbed "blonde" by Mary—and spun aluminum. The designs melded utility with a sleek, modern aesthetic, while embracing American practicality and simplicity, and ultimately advancing the nation's taste for the modern.

In the 1920s Wright studied at the Arts Students League in New York and at Princeton University. He became active in theater set design, apprenticing to Norman Bel Geddes and Aline Bernstein and working with regional theater companies. Wright's work was neither streamlined nor Bauhaus-inspired, distinguishing it from the work of other designers in Europe and the U.S. The multihued *American Modern* dinnerware, which was manufactured between 1939 and 1959 by Steubenville Pottery in Steubenville, PA, became the most widely sold American ceramic dinnerware in history. Other designs in this line included *American Modern* table linen (1946–48), which was designed by Marianne Strengell under Wright's name and produced by Leecock & Company, and *American Modern* colored and shaped drinking glasses made by the Morgantown Glass Guild (1951). In the 1940s Wright also designed tabletop accessories and plastic dinnerware (1945) in the new Melamine plastic for mass-production by American Cyanamid. He created a *Casual China* ceramic line (1946) for Iroquois China Company. The Statton Furniture Company produced his *Easier Living* furniture line (1950), while Paden City Pottery in West Virginia made his *Highlight* ceramics.

Wright was a founder and president of the Society of Industrial Designers (1952–53). His vision for "American-Way" products, promoted in 1940, was composed of machine-made and handcrafted products from a stable assembled by Wright himself. He also consulted on developing native handicrafts in Cambodia, Taiwan, and Vietnam (1959–60) through a U.S. government commission, and was a craft consultant and advisor in Japan (1957–58). As a result, crafts goods from these countries flooded the U.S. market in the late 1950s. His work was included in the Good Design exhibitions (1950, 1952, 1953) held at MoMA. From 1946 to the end of his life, Wright lived in New York City and at Dragon Rock, the country house he built near Garrison, NY. —LB and TT

Donald Albrecht et al., *Russel Wright: Creating American Lifestyle,* exh. cat. (New York: Harry N. Abrams, Inc.; Washington, DC: Cooper-Hewitt, National Design Museum, Smithsonian Institution, 2001); Dianne Pierce, "Design, Craft, and American Identity: Russel Wright's 'American-Way' Project, 1940–42," master's thesis, MA Program in the History of Decorative Arts and Design, Cooper-Hewitt, National Design Museum and Parsons the New School for Design, December 2010.

WYMAN, WILLIAM

Born June 13, 1922, North Scituate, MA;
died April 1, 1980, North Scituate, MA
CERAMIST, EDUCATOR

William Wyman studied at the Massachusetts College of Art, Boston, and Columbia University. From 1953 he was a potter and sculptor in his Herring Run Pottery, East

Weymouth, MA. He taught at Drake University, Des Moines, IA; University of Maryland, College Park; Massachusetts College of Art; De Cordova and Dana Museum and Park, Lincoln, MA; and Haystack Mountain School of Crafts, Deer Isle, ME.

Wyman produced functional work, expressive slab-built nonfunctional vessels, and sculpture. Imagery derived from American poetry, popular culture, and, later in his career, political and spiritual topics, were combined with abstract compositions. In creating the slab-built stoneware vessel, *Before You Know There is Love* (1962), Wyman used the flat surface like a painter's canvas. The imagery features the incised words of its title and other phrases within an abstract composition of richly colored glazes. In the late 1960s he produced sculpture that focused on representations of the Christian cross. The works remained expressive and abstract but somber in color and feeling. In 1965 he worked in Honduras for the U.S. Agency for International Development. Some years later he visited the ruined city of Copán, Honduras, an event that had a profound effect on him, resulting in his Temple series and other works from 1977–79. —JP and TT

Objects: USA, 78; Marcia Manhart and Tom Manhart, eds., *The Eloquent Object: The Evolution of American Art in Craft Media Since 1945* (Tulsa, OK: Philbrook Museum of Art, 1987), 284; Garth Clark, *American Ceramics: 1876 to the Present* (New York: Abbeville Press, 1987), 310.

YOORS, JAN
Born April 12, 1922, Antwerp, Belgium;
died November 27, 1977, New York, NY
TAPESTRY DESIGNER, AUTHOR, PHOTOGRAPHER

An innovator of twentieth-century tapestry design, Jan Yoors combined medieval tradition with a modern aesthetic. The son of a stained-glass artist, he drew from this tradition in his early designs, which include dark outlines and large, bold sections of color. His life experiences directly influenced his unorthodox artistic career and creative life. When he was twelve, he ran away (with his parent's permission) to join a nomadic tribe of gypsies and traveled with them throughout Europe. Six years later, when war broke out, he worked with the Allies to establish an underground resistance strategy with his gypsy friends, whose unique survival skills were useful in devising escape routes for victims of Nazi persecution. Yoors was captured, tortured, and condemned to death, but managed to escape.

In 1944 Yoors moved to London, enrolling in classes at the School of African and Oriental Studies at London University. Here he encountered medieval French tapestries for the first time and was instantly captivated by the medium. Completely committed to the practice, he and wife Annabert van Wettum, and their friend Marianne Citroen (whom he later married), built a large-scale loom and became self-taught weavers. Yoors was meticulous about his designs, hand-drawing each cartoon and collaborating with the wool dealer to ensure that each shade of yarn matched his vision. He used strong, bright colors, dramatically contrasted with swaths of black to create his signature, abstract designs. Annabert and Marianne translated his cartoons into woven tapestries. He continued this practice when he moved to New York in 1950, creating large-scale tapestries that embody a modern spirit as well as his heritage. Beyond his work as an artist, Yoors was a prolific writer who recorded his life experiences in *The Gypsies* (1967), *Crossing* (1971), and *The Gypsies of Spain* (1974). —NB

Beatrice V. Thornton, "Bohemian Rhapsody," *Modern Magazine* 2 (summer 2010), 104–13.

ZABARI, MOSHE
Born 1935, Jerusalem, Israel
SILVERSMITH

From 1955 to 1958, Moshe Zabari was educated at the Bauhaus-oriented Bezalel Academy of Art and Design in Jerusalem, where he studied with German-trained David Gumbel and Ludwig Yehuda Wolpert. Zabari also taught at the school from 1956 to 1957. In 1961 he immigrated to the U.S. and was artist-in-residence at the Tobe Pascher Workshop at the Jewish Museum in New York, which was directed by Wolpert. The workshop had been founded in 1956 by friends of the museum and admirers of Wolpert's work after its exhibition in the Palestine Pavilion at the 1939 World's Fair in New York. Zabari assumed Wolpert's post as director, serving from 1981 to 1988.

Zabari's work in 1950s and '60s reflects the influence of Bauhaus functionalism. At the Jewish Museum he had access to one of the world's largest collections of ceremonial art, and he focused on creating ritual silver suitable for the twentieth-century Jewish community. His design solutions are contemporary but retain a connection with tradition, preserving and honoring that past by employing a visual quotation or other element that carries a sense of history.

Zabari has exhibited internationally and has received numerous commissions and awards for his work. He participated in *Young Americans* at MCA (1962) and in the *Sixth Biennial National Religious Art Exhibition* at Cranbrook (1969), where he won first prize. —JP

Ronald Hayes Pearson, "Young Americans 1962: Jewelry," *CH* 22 (July 1962), 13; Nancy Berman, *Moshe Zabari: A Twenty-Five Year Retrospective* (New York: Jewish Museum; Los Angeles: Hebrew Union College Skirball Museum, 1986).

ZEISLER, CLAIRE
(NÉE BLOCK;
MRS. HAROLD FLORSHEIM;
LATER MRS. ERNEST ZEISLER)
Born April 18, 1903, Cincinnati, OH;
died September 30, 1991, Chicago, IL
FIBER ARTIST

At eighteen years of age, Claire Block married Harold Florsheim, an heir to the shoe manufacturer, and during the 1930s she acquired a collection of European modernist paintings and tribal arts from around the world, including Native American baskets. She divorced Florsheim in 1943 and married Dr. Ernest Zeisler in 1946. She studied at the Chicago Institute of Design (formerly New Bauhaus) in the 1940s with Eugene Dana and at the Illinois Institute of Technology, where she was taught by sculptor Alexander Archipenko and designer László Moholy-Nagy, but her interest in baskets and textiles led her to change focus and to study with local weaver Bea Swartchild.

Throughout the 1950s Zeisler produced functional, loomed weavings, but in the early 1960s she began to experiment with three-dimensional fiber sculptures. The works were nonobjective and nonfunctional; they emphasized knotting, wrapping, and orderly cascades of unwoven strands of fiber. By the end of the decade, she was working on sculptural forms of increasing scale and complexity. Zeisler's work was included in *Woven Forms* at MCC (1963). Along with the unconventional work of Sheila Hicks and Lenore Tawney, Zeisler's free-form sculpture pointed to new directions for the fiber arts. —JP

Paul J. Smith, and Edward Lucie-Smith, *Craft Today: Poetry of the Physical* (New York: American Craft Museum and Weidenfeld & Nicolson, 1986), 315; Roberta Smith, "Claire Zeisler, An Artist, Collector and Fiber-Art Innovator, 88," *New York Times*, October 1, 1991, D-23.

ZIEGFELD, ERNEST
Born September 13, 1912, Ohio;
died October 26, 2004, Taos, NM
JEWELER, EDUCATOR

Ernest Ziegfeld graduated in 1935 from the Columbus Art School in Ohio. In 1938 he earned a BS in education from Ohio State University and an MA in Educational Psychology from the University of Minnesota in 1942. He went on to earn an Ed.D. in art education in 1951 from Teachers College, Columbia University. His early teaching history includes the Owatonna Public Schools in Minnesota (1938–40) and the University of Minnesota (1940–42). He served in the U.S. Army during the war, after which he continued his teaching career, this time at Stanford University (1946–48), Long Beach State College (1950–52), and State University Teachers College in New Paltz, NY, where he was director of art education until 1956. He published his theories of art education in an influential textbook, *Art in the College Program of General Education* (1953). In 1959 Ziegfeld became professor of art at the Jersey City State College.

In his own studio, Ziegfeld worked in silver and gold with precious and semiprecious stones. He created his designs in metal, usually without sketches, and noted that he was "continually aware of striving to achieve a kind of organic quality in my forms—what, for lack of better words, I must call a quality of warmth and human-ness" ("Ernest Ziegfeld" 1960). His work has a graphic linear quality and is characterized by playful repetition of forms—from spiderlike shapes scattered over a web of gold wire for a hair ornament to a row of forged-silver fringe that swings from a wire frame. He exhibited his jewelry in the late 1950s at the Brussels World's Fair and in a one-man show at the Long Beach Museum of Art (1958). In 1959 two forged-silver hair ornaments and a necklace were included in *American Jewelry* at the Walker Art Center (1959). He placed his jewelry for sale at America House in New York, Bordelon North in Chicago, Little Gallery in Birmingham, MI, and Nanny's in San Francisco. —JP

"American Jewelry," *Design Quarterly* 45/46 (1959), 50, 63; "Ernest Ziegfeld . . . Artist-Teacher," *Art Education* 13 (April 1960), 13–15.

203

WILLIAM PARRY

Flower Form, 1966

STONEWARE

25 X 15½ X 13½ IN. (63.5 X 39.4 X 34.3 CM)

COLLECTION EVERSON MUSEUM OF ART,

MUSEUM PURCHASE, 66.30

SCHOOLS AND WORKSHOPS

ARCHIE BRAY FOUNDATION
Founded 1951, Helena, MT

In the early 1940s Montana lawyer and occasional ceramist Peter Meloy approached Archie C. Bray Sr., cultural patron and owner of the Western Clay Manufacturing Company in Helena, MT, with a request to fire his ceramic pots on top of the brick firings in the company's round beehive kilns. The experience convinced Bray to establish an art center in his company's brickyard. With the support of Meloy and Branson Stevenson, a district executive of the Socony-Mobile Oil Company who was also interested in ceramics, the Archie Bray Foundation was incorporated as a nonprofit educational institution in 1951. Meloy, Stevenson, and Peter Voulkos and Rudy Autio, two Montana State University art students, built the first building featuring a showroom, studio, clay-mixing and kiln room, glaze room, and the first gas-fired kiln in the state. The facility provided northwest ceramists the opportunity to work for the first time in the very high stoneware range. Voulkos and Autio earned their graduate degrees in 1952 and returned to the foundation as resident artists, sharing the directorship until 1954, when Voulkos left to head the ceramics department at the Otis Art Institute in Los Angeles. In 1952 foundation members were invited to send a selection of their pottery for an exhibition at America House, and that December the foundation sponsored a groundbreaking weeklong workshop conducted by British ceramist and author Bernard Leach, who was accompanied by Japanese ceramist Shoji Hamada, and Soetsu Yanagi, director of the Museum of Folk-Crafts in Tokyo. The workshop introduced the raku-firing technique, and the participants cast craftsmanship as a spiritually humbling effort to converge art with nature. The presentations profoundly influenced the ceramics community. When the foundation offered its second workshop, with Marguerite Wildenhain in May 1954, some forty-seven craftspeople came to train with her. A new structure added that year provided space for sculptors to design and produce architectural walls and other large pieces. Autio continued at the foundation until 1956 and was assisted by Seattle ceramists Nan and James McKinnell, who taught classes there until 1957 in exchange for the use of the facilities. Other workshops in the late fifties and early sixties were conducted by Antonio Prieto, Val Cushing, Warren MacKenzie, and Daniel Rhodes, all of whom represented a level of training which contributed to the inclusion of work by five Archie Bray Foundation potters in a 1962 international ceramics exhibition in Prague, Czechoslovakia. During its earliest years the foundation attracted such ceramists as Robert Sperry, Frances Senska, Manuel Neri, Doris Strachan, and F. Carlton Ball. In 1955 Ball used part of a Fulbright grant to spend several weeks at the Bray experimenting with glazes and throwing. The informality of the foundation during this time gave way to a more organized structure under the leadership of such later resident directors as Kenneth R. Ferguson

(1957–1963) and (George) David Shaner (1964–1970). Both men helped to get the foundation on sound financial footing after the assistance of Western Clay Manufacturing Company was phased out. —TT

Peter Held and Rick Newby, *A Ceramic Continuum: Fifty Years of the Archie Bray Influence* (Helena, MT: Holter Museum of Art, 2001).

ARROWMONT SCHOOL OF ARTS AND CRAFTS
Founded 1968, Gatlinburg, TN

The Pi Beta Phi women's fraternity started a settlement school in 1912, offering home industries including weaving and woodworking classes, as a means to improve the social and economic conditions of the community. For several decades the local artisans trained at the school were given not only the knowledge and equipment to produce woven textiles, baskets, chairs, brooms, and a host of other handcrafted items, but also a venue in which they could sell their works. When the local government assumed control of primary and secondary education in 1943, the fraternity redirected its efforts away from the production of traditional handcrafts and toward the promotion of general arts and crafts literacy. The resulting Summer Workshop of Crafts and Community Recreation Program, first organized by the fraternity in 1945 in conjunction with the University of Tennessee, paved the way for the founding of the Arrowmont School of Arts and Crafts in 1968, with Marian Heard, professor of craft design at the University of Tennessee, as its first director. Ray Pierotti succeeded her in 1977. Two years later Sandra Blain became director and guided Arrowmont into the modern era. Today, under the direction of David Willard, the school organizes conferences and exhibitions, while also sponsoring a highly selective artist-in-residence program. —MS

"The Founding of Arrowmont," www.lib.utk.edu/arrowmont/history_arts.htm.

BLACK MOUNTAIN COLLEGE
1933–56, Asheville, NC

A progressive co-educational liberal arts school, Black Mountain College developed a curriculum that strongly emphasized community and recognized the arts as central to individual development. The college presented a threefold approach to life and learning: studio arts, intellectual disciplines, and community work. The structure made it a haven for the intellectual and spiritually curious, attracting a diverse constituency that included painters, writers, architects, musicians, and dancers, as well as an unprecedented number of foreign refugees. Less than a month after the Bauhaus closed in Germany in 1933, the college offered teaching positions to Josef and Anni Albers via MoMA curator Philip Johnson. Under their leadership, Black Mountain became a center for the transmission of Bauhaus ideas and a hub for experimental art in America. In 1949 a ceramics course was added to the curriculum, and the faculty included Robert Turner, Karen Karnes, and David Weinrib. Among the teachers who passed through

Black Mountain College were Peter Voulkos, Robert Motherwell, Robert Rauschenberg, Franz Kline, Ben Shahn, Buckminster Fuller, Willem de Kooning, Jack Tworkov, Walter Gropius, Bernard Rudofsky, the dancer Merce Cunningham, and the composer John Cage. —JF

Mary Emma Harris, *The Arts at Black Mountain College* (Cambridge, MA: MIT Press, 1987).

See also *Craft in the Machine Age*, 263.

CALIFORNIA COLLEGE OF THE ARTS (CCA)
Founded 1907, Berkeley and Oakland, CA
School of the California Guild of Arts and Crafts (1907–8);
California School of Arts and Crafts (1908–36);
Califoria College of Arts and Crafts (1936–2003);
California College of the Arts (2003–)

Started during the Arts and Crafts era, from the beginning the school emphasized an integrated study of fine, applied, and industrial arts. In the postwar era, studio crafts dominated, and a steady influx of faculty members brought excitement to the program. Ceramics were taught in the 1930s by F. Carlton Ball, followed by Antonio Prieto, Marguerite Wildenhain, Edith Heath, and alumna Viola Frey. Graduates Robert Arneson and Peter Voulkos stoked the fires of the ceramic revolution in both form and content. In metalsmithing, Bob Winston, followed by Byron Wilson, Margaret De Patta, Victor Ries, and Ken Cory taught jewelry, casting, and some hollowware techniques. In weaving, Trude Guermonprez oversaw the transformation of fiber arts from weaving for yardage and interior design to sculptural form; Kay Sekimachi and Lillian Elliot were also on faculty. Marvin Lipofsky, then teaching at the University of California, Berkeley, brought hot glass to the school in the late 1960s, first creating a glass studio for the school on Fourth Street in Berkeley. Lipofsky served as a link between the two schools and fostered CCA's growth in this seminal period with glassblowing competitions and symposia. —JF

Nine Decades: The Northern California Craft Movement 1907 to the Present (San Francisco: San Francisco Craft & Folk Art Museum; Oakland, CA: Oliver Center/California College of Arts and Crafts; San Francisco, CA: California Crafts Museum, 1993), 11–19; *Glance, Centennial Issue,* special issue of *California College of the Arts* 15 (winter 2007), 20–31; Marvin Lipofsky, "Roots Revisited," *Glass: The Urban Glass Art Quarterly* 110 (2008), 52–61.

See also *The Ideal Home*, 272; *Craft in the Machine Age*, 264.

CALIFORNIA INSTITUTE OF THE ARTS
Founded 1921, Los Angeles, CA
Chouinard Art School (1921–35);
Chouinard Art Institute (1935–61);
merged with Los Angeles Conservatory of Music (1883–1961) to form California Institute of the Arts (1961–)

In 1918, widow and Pratt Institute–trained painter Nelbert Chouinard left New York for the sunshine, fresh air, and blossoming arts community of Pasadena. She became part of what was dubbed the Eucalyptus School, a group of

California plein air painters, but she felt a greater calling as a teacher and began working at several local schools, primarily the Los Angeles County Art Institute (now Otis). Because the classrooms were crowded, in 1921 she opened her own teaching space in a two-story house in the Westlake area of downtown Los Angeles. Success was immediate, and by 1929 the school had moved into a nearby 17,000-square-foot building, changing its name in 1935 to the Chouinard Art Institute. A major shift in direction occurred when Walt Disney, who had dreamed of creating an arts institution that incorporated visual and performing arts, organized the 1961 merger of the Chouinard Art Institute and the Los Angeles Conservatory of Music (although Chouinard continued to operate as a separate entity until 1972, when the original campus closed). It was not an entirely easy transition—Disney died in 1966—and much of the dream was never realized, but the newly created California Institute of the Arts, commonly known as CalArts, would ultimately become one of Southern California's most influential and progressive arts schools. In 1969, the year of Chouinard's death, the school broke ground on a new campus located in Valencia, about thirty miles outside the city, where it remains today. Under Chouinard's tutelage, students of all media focused on the fundamentals of drawing, painting, and design. In Disney's vision, students received the same classical arts training but with a greater degree of creative exchange due to an expanded curriculum of music, dance, theater, and film. A brief list of faculty and alumni (both pre- and postmerger) reads like a film credit of celebrities: Millard Sheets, David Alfaro Siqueiros, Tony Duquette, Vivika and Otto Heino, Edith Head, Anthony Heinsbergen, Herbert Jepson, Bob Mackie, Henry Mancini, Milo Baughman, Susan Peterson, John Mason, Peter Shire, Ed Ruscha, Richard Serra, Ken Price, Laddie John Dill, Jun Kaneko, Ralph Bacerra, Kazuko Matthews, and Adrian Saxe. —MP

"History," at Chouinard Foundation, www.chouinard foundation.org; "History [1964–2006]," at "About CalArts," California Institute of the Arts at www.calarts. edu; Ceramics artists research courtesy of Billie Sessions, California State University, San Bernardino.

CALIFORNIA STATE UNIVERSITY, LONG BEACH

Founded 1949, Long Beach, CA
Los Angeles–Orange County State College (1949–50);
Long Beach State College (1950–64);
California State College at Long Beach (1964–68);
California State College, Long Beach (1968–72);
California State University, Long Beach (CSULB) (1972–)
Established after a 1947 study by the State Board of Education and the Regents of the University of California—and essentially to meet postwar demand—Los Angeles–Orange County State College opened its doors in 1949 at an apartment complex converted to classrooms. The focus was teacher training and business education, as well as liberal arts. By 1950 city residents approved the purchase of a 320-acre property for the school's expansion, and in

1962 the college hired University of Southern California–trained architect Edward Killingsworth to develop the site's master plan. Killingsworth consulted the students in order to assess their needs, and the resulting campus offered a sense of intimacy (despite its large scale) and had beautifully landscaped grounds. In 1965 the architect, along with art professor Kenneth Glenn and artist Kosso Eloul, coordinated the International Sculpture Symposium, which brought eight artists (including Claire Falkenstein, Gabriel Kohn, Robert Murray, and André Bloc) to Long Beach to create sculptures for the school over a six-week summer program. This early emphasis on art and cultural exchange, which kick-started the university's expansive outdoor sculpture museum, is still felt today. CSULB, the first California university to offer an MFA degree, boasts a long list of distinguished arts professors (many of whom were also alumni), including John Olsen, Ernst Ziegfeld, Ray Hein, Alvin Pine, Ward Youry, Mary Jane Leland, Thomas Ferreira, Robert Ramsey, and Frank E. Cummings III. The roster of acclaimed students includes Lynda Watson, Marcia Lewis, Gary Griffin, John Cederquist, Joe Soldate, Michael Arntz, Ferne Jacobs, and Gilbert Luján. —MP

"A Brief History," under "About CSULB," www.csulb .edu; Toni Greenbaum, "California Dreamin': Modernist Jewelers in Los Angeles, 1940–1970," *Metalsmith* 22 (winter 2002), 38–47; Ceramics artists research courtesy of Professor Billie Sessions, California State University, San Bernardino.

CLEVELAND INSTITUTE OF ART

Founded 1882, Cleveland, OH
Western Reserve School of Design for Women (1882–91);
Cleveland School of Art (1891–1949);
Cleveland Institute of Art (1949–)
Inspired by the ideas of William Morris and the Arts and Crafts movement, and believing in vocational education for women in the arts, Sarah M. Kimball established a design school, initially for women only but soon including male students as well. After World War II, the GI Bill and a renewed interest in ceramics, metalsmithing, and industrial design brought increased numbers of students to art schools. The renamed Cleveland Institute of Art responded with an enlarged educational program that embraced the growing design and studio craft movement. Viktor Schreckengost headed the department of industrial design; Claude Conover and Toshiko Takaezu, the ceramics department; and in metalworking and enameling, Kenneth Bates, John Paul Miller, and Fred Miller led the field at midcentury. John Marshall and William Harper were notable graduates in metal and enamel, respectively, during this period. Many teachers, students, and alumni were active participants in the Cleveland Museum of Art's *Annual Exhibition of Work by Cleveland Artists and Craftsmen*, known as the May Show, which was held from 1919 to 1990. Following a two-year hiatus, the May Show held its last exhibition in 1993. —MS

Evan Turner, *Object Lessons: Cleveland Creates an Art Museum* (Cleveland: Cleveland Museum of Art, 1991); Carol Boram-Hays, *Bringing Modernism Home: Ohio*

Decorative Arts, 1890–1960 (Athens, OH: Ohio University Press in association with the Columbus Museum of Art, 2005); Louis V. Adrean, Senior Librarian for Research & Public Programs, Cleveland Museum of Art, to Jeannine Falino, January 14, 2011.

CRANBROOK ACADEMY OF ART

Founded 1932, Bloomfield Hills, MI
The Cranbrook Academy of Art produced many of the postwar period's finest designer-craftspeople. Both Ellen and George Booth, founders of the school, had been among the leading proponents of the Arts and Crafts movement in America. Their idea of forming a community where artists could live and work became reality in 1927 when they set up the Cranbrook Foundation as the governing body of an educational and cultural center to be established near Detroit, MI. Cranbrook officially opened in 1932, accompanied by a decorative and applied arts museum to support, broaden, and extend the didactic program of the school.

The fundamental courses in metalwork, textiles, and ceramics given by such forward-thinking professors as Harry Bertoia, Richard Thomas, Marianne Strengell, and Maija Grotell yielded talented graduates in the world of design including Charles and Ray Eames, Florence Knoll (Florence Schust Knoll Bassett), and Ralph Rapson. Faculty and graduates offered inspiration to rising young artists with diverse artistic viewpoints—Jack Lenor Larsen, Ed Rossbach, Ted Hallman, Toshiko Takaezu, Harvey Littleton, Brent Kington, and Fred Woehl, among others. The expressive and humanistic design vision of the school and its informal educational approach account for much of Cranbrook's success. —MS

Robert Judson Clark et al., *Design in America: The Cranbrook Vision, 1925–1950* (New York: Harry N. Abrams, in association with the Detroit Institute of Arts and The Metropolitan Museum of Art, 1983), 268–77.
See also *Craft in the Machine Age*, 263.

HANDY & HARMAN

National Silversmithing Workshop Conferences for Teachers
Each August, 1947–51
Rhode Island School of Design, Providence (1947–49);
School for American Craftsmen, Rochester Institute of Technology, Rochester, NY (1950–51)
Margret Craver, a silversmith in charge of the Craft Service Department of Handy & Harman, a New York City metal refining company, was the only American invited to attend a silversmithing workshop in London at the Worshipful Company of Goldsmiths in 1946. Her experience there, studying under such leading contemporary craftsmen as Baron Erik Fleming, silversmith to King Gustav of Sweden, inspired her to organize a similar program for American craftsmen. For the next five years, under the auspices of her employer, Handy & Harman, Craver coordinated a four-week workshop for twelve carefully selected teachers and craftsmen. The purpose of the conference was to provide experiences with various silversmithing techniques, to stimulate experimentation in design and creative thinking,

and to increase knowledge of current industry research in precious metals. Craver's hope was that by training silversmiths in the U.S., eventually their work would equal that of their European contemporaries. Under the guidance of a master silversmith—William Bennett, on faculty at the Sheffield College of Arts and Crafts in England (1947); Baron Erik Fleming, founder of the Atelier Borgila in Sweden (1948, 1949, and 1951); and Reginald Hill, an English silversmith (1950)—the students spent six to seven hours each day in the actual work of raising and forging a hollowware object. The idea was to develop a design based on an understanding of the medium, which was accomplished by mastering a specific smithing technique. The art of raising a silver bowl with a thickened edge was the focus of the first year, while the second year, the workshop concentrated on stretching, a process of hammering inside a thick plate of silver to create a bowl with a very thick edge. For many of the students, who were chosen for their background in the arts and design rather than in metals, it was their first attempt at smithing. Coupled with their workshop experiences, the students were also given demonstrations and lectures. During the five years that this highly competitive workshop was held, its participants included such aspiring silversmiths as Ruth Penington, Alma Eikerman, Earl Pardon, Frederick A. Miller, Arthur J. Pulos, Robert Von Neumann, and John Paul Miller, all of whom taught the postwar generation of academically-trained metalsmiths. —TT

[Craft Services Department, Handy & Harman], "The Technique of a Thickened Edge," *AC* 8 (November 1947), 22–23; Margret Craver, "An Ancient Method Goes Modern," *CH* 9 (Winter 1949), 15–17; Jeannine Falino and Yvonne Markowitz, "Margret Craver, Jeweler, Educator, Visionary," *Journal of the American Society of Jewelry Historians* 1 (spring 1997), 9–23.

HAYSTACK MOUNTAIN SCHOOL OF CRAFTS

Founded 1950, Liberty, ME

Liberty, ME (1950–61); Deer Isle, ME (1961–)

The concept for Haystack evolved in discussions between Maine craftspeople and Mary Beasom Bishop of Flint, MI, who owned a summer home in Maine. Her deep interest in ceramics, painting, and sculpture, and her fascination for the liberal and progressive values rooted in arts and crafts education, inspired her to lend several hundreds of acres of farmland, lakeshore, and woods to the opening of a school of crafts. The school was founded on a farm and named after a neighboring mountain. Francis Sumner Merritt and his wife, Priscilla, who also taught weaving, organized summer courses and school management beginning in 1951. In 1961 architect Edward Larrabee Barnes designed the floating pavilions of workshops that link the rocky landscape with the ocean. In 2006 the campus was added to the National Historic Register. In 1955, the summer faculty consisted of Jack Lenor Larsen, Anni Albers, Lili Blumenau, and Mariska Karasz (weaving); Svea Kline and Phil Ward (ceramics); John Ward (woodworking);

Estelle Shevis and William Shevis (block printing); William J. Brown (design); and Francis Merritt (painting). Over time, the school has hired teachers to conduct workshops in virtually all media. Thomas Gentille and Timothy Lloyd taught the first jewelry workshops in 1964; Arline Fisch, who in 1959 attended the weaving course team-taught by Larsen and Ted Hallman, returned in later years to teach jewelry. A strong sense of nature and humanity interwoven with craftsmanship and the absence of orthodoxy characterize the school, where empirical teaching methods are preferred and each discipline is promoted as a medium of expression rather than taught as a handicraft. —MS

Jack Lenor Larsen, "Summer School with a Difference: Haystack Mountain School of Crafts in Maine, *CH* 13 (May 1953), 31–33; advertisement, *CH* 15 (May/June 1955), 45; Carl Little, "Haystack Mountain School of Crafts: Craft on the Coast of Maine," *Ornament* 31 (December 2007), 65–70.

INSTITUTE OF AMERICAN INDIAN ARTS (IAIA)

Founded 1962, Santa Fe, NM

Institute of American Indian Arts (1962–1986);

Institute of American Indian and Alaska Native Arts Development (1986–)

An outgrowth of two Rockefeller-funded initiatives—the Southwest Indian Arts Project (1958–61), held at the University of Arizona, and the 1959 conference "Directions in Indian Art"—the founding of the Institute of American Indian Arts represents a turning point in the modern history of Native American art. Earlier attempts to encourage artistic activities, such as the Santa Fe Indian School established in 1932 by Dorothy Dunn, had focused on the teaching of traditional imagery and styles, excluding advancements in the field of modern art. The protagonist and true visionary of the new school was Lloyd Kiva New, a charismatic figure who had directed the Southwest Indian Arts Project and was responsible for varied developments in the arts of the Southwest. New advocated for a school that was open to all American tribes, that championed artistic expression in all media, and was grounded in Native as well as contemporary topics. A high school was created under the Bureau of Indian Affairs (BIA), Department of the Interior, by executive order of President John F. Kennedy in 1962. George A. Boyce was the first head of the school, and New served as artistic director. In the first year, 69 tribes were represented in a class of 130, and the distinguished faculty included Alan Houser (sculpture), Fritz Scholder (painting), Otellie Loloma (ceramics), and Azalea Stuart Thorpe (fiber). Works of art produced by students of IAIA and the Alaska Designer-Craftsman Training project, the latter held in Nome, AK, from September 1964 to June 1965, were featured in a special exhibition at MCC in July 1965. In 1975 IAIA became a college offering two-year associate degrees, and today the school offers a four-year fine arts degree. In 1986 the school was removed from BIA management and made a congressionally chartered institution of higher learning, one of only three in the country. Although the school name was officially changed at

that time, it is still known as the Institute of American Indian Arts. —JF

Azalea Stuart Thorpe, "Institute of American Indian Arts, Santa Fe," *CH* 25 (July 1965), 12–16, 40; Robert M. Coates, "Our Far-Flung Correspondents: Indian Affairs, New Style," *New Yorker* (June 17, 1967), 102–11; John Richard Grimes, "The I.A.I.A. and the New Frontier," in David Revere McFadden and Ellen Napiura Taubman, *Changing Hands: Art Without Reservation*, vol. 2, *Contemporary Native North American Art from the West, Northwest & Pacific* (New York: Museum of Arts and Design, 2005), 180–81; Ryan Flahive, IAIA archives, to Jeannine Falino January 14, 2011.

INSTITUTE OF DESIGN, ILLINOIS INSTITUTE OF TECHNOLOGY

Founded 1937, Chicago, IL

New Bauhaus (1937–38); Chicago School of Design (1939–44);

Institute of Design, Chicago (1944–48);

Institute of Design, Illinois Institute of Technology (1949–)

One of the clearest attempts to re-create the spirit of the legendary Bauhaus, the German school that gave birth to modern design, the New Bauhaus was conceived by the Chicago Association of Art and Industry and was founded by the former Bauhaus teacher László Moholy-Nagy. As at the original Bauhaus, the school's ideological objective of stimulating students' artistic creativity as a way to educate industrial designers was difficult to carry out, and the school closed the year after its opening due to financial problems. In 1939, however, it reopened as the independent Chicago School of Design funded by Walter Paepcke, who was president of the Container Corporation of America. Such prestigious figures as Alfred Barr, director of MoMA, and the progressive educator John Dewey, along with the Carnegie Foundation and the Rockefeller Foundation, sponsored the school. At first, the new school structure included disciplines beyond the industrial arts, such as music and poetry. In 1944, however, the departments were reduced to four: industrial design, advertising arts, textile design, and photography, and the school was renamed the Institute of Design. Moholy-Nagy, who remained its director until his death in 1946, was succeeded by Serge Chermayeff and in 1955 by Jay Doblin. In 1949 the school was incorporated into the Illinois Institute of Technology (IIT) but retained a separate identity. IIT was then headed by the former Bauhaus director Ludwig Mies van der Rohe. Among the craftspeople who attended the school are James Prestini, merry renk, Lenore Tawney, Margaret De Patta, and designers Edgar Bartolucci, Angelo Testa, and Jack Waldheim. —MS

Alan Findeli and Charlotte Benton, "Design Education and Industry: The Laborious Beginnings of the Institute of Design in Chicago in 1944," *Journal of Design History* 4, no. 2 (1991), 97–113; "IIT History: The Sermon and the Institute," Illinois Institute of Technology, www.iit.edu/about/history/index.shtml; "Our History," under "Who We Are," Institute of Design, Illinois Institute of Technology, www.id.iit.edu/149.

See also *Craft in the Machine Age*, 264.

MILLS COLLEGE

Founded 1852, Benicia, CA

Young Ladies' Seminary (1852–65);

Mills College (1865–)

Benicia, CA (1852–71); Oakland, CA (1871–)

This small, liberal arts college for women flourished as a women's seminary under the early leadership of Mary Atkins. In 1865 Susan and Cyrus Mills purchased the school, changed its name, and six years later moved it to its present location in Oakland. By the 1940s the impressive faculty included Igor Stravinsky, Imogen Cunningham, Roi Partridge, and Claire Falkenstein. F. Carlton Ball taught ceramics and jewelry from about 1936 through the 1940s; Antonio Prieto, a Spanish-born potter, arrived in 1957. Susan Peterson, Katherine Choy, Win Ng, and Ruth Clark Radakovich were among their best-known students. —JF

Miriam Duncan Cross, "Gaw Retires; Prieto Gets Post," *Oakland Tribune*, June 2, 1957, 10-C; Susan Peterson, oral history interview by Paul J. Smith, March 1, 2004, AAA, SI.

MONTANA STATE UNIVERSITY

Founded 1920, Bozeman, MT

Montana State University, a land grant institution, is the largest of six universities and colleges that make up the state's system of higher education. Frances Senska, a ceramist brought on faculty in 1946, was responsible for developing the ceramics curriculum. In 1950, her class included undergraduate art majors Rudy Autio and Peter Voulkos, then in their senior year. Senska taught all aspects of the ceramic process: how to dig and process clay and glazes, how to throw, and how to balance form and decoration. Senska had first studied pottery with Edith Heath at the California Labor School in San Francisco, with Hal Riegger at the San Francisco Art Institute, and with Maija Grotell at Cranbrook. In about 1952, Jayne Van Alstyne joined the design faculty, bringing her knowledge of high-fired stoneware from Alfred University. This was the beginning of a long line of Alfred–Montana connections. During the late '40s and early '50s, only electric kilns were available at the school, which limited the students to lower-fired earthenware in oxidation firings. Henry Takemoto, a Voulkos student at the Otis Art Institute in the mid-1950s, briefly joined the art department in the 1960s. —TT

Frances Senska, oral history interview by Donna Forbes, April 16, 2001, AAA, SI.

NEW YORK STATE COLLEGE OF CERAMICS AT ALFRED UNIVERSITY

Founded 1900, Alfred, NY

New York State School of Clay-Working and Ceramics (1900–32);

New York State College of Ceramics (1932–50);

State University of New York, College of Ceramics at Alfred University (1951–72);

New York State College of Ceramics at Alfred University (1972–)

Established in 1836 by Seventh Day Baptists, Alfred University is the oldest co-educational institution in New York and the second oldest in the nation. The ceramics division, founded in 1901 under Charles F. Binns of Worcester, England, offered the first college-level ceramics engineering curriculum in the U.S. with a parallel art program. From the beginning each successive art director of the college—Charles Harder, Ted Randall, Val Cushing, Bob Turner, and Tony Hepburn—sought to create an influential curriculum that would incorporate ceramic art and manufacture, design and commerce, research and development, museum exhibits and trade magazines, and expositions and fairs. The faculty wrote textbooks of enduring value, while developing a body of work that is strongly based upon the vessel and yet embraces the sculptural potential of ceramics. Many influential ceramists graduated from Alfred, including Edward S. Eberle, Kenneth Ferguson, Chris Gustin, Karen Karnes, Judy Moonelis, and Betty Woodman. Graduates who became professors at Alfred include Val Cushing, Andrea Gill, John Gill, and Robert Turner. —TT

Melvin Herbert Bernstein, *Art and Design at Alfred: A Chronicle of a Ceramics College* (Philadelphia: Art Alliance Press, 1986); Anna E. McHale, *Fusion: A Centennial History of the New York State College of Ceramics, 1900–2000* (Virginia Beach, VA: Donning Company Publishers, 2003).

OTIS COLLEGE OF ART AND DESIGN

Founded 1918, Los Angeles, CA

Otis Art Institute of the Los Angeles Museum of History, Science & Art (1918–39);

Otis Art Institute (1939–54);

Los Angeles County Art Institute (1954–61);

Otis Art Institute of Los Angeles County (1961–78);

Otis Art Institute of Parsons School of Design (1978–91);

Otis School of Art and Design (1991–93);

Otis College of Art and Design (1993–)

Civil War general and *Los Angeles Times* publisher Harrison Gray Otis bequeathed his downtown Los Angeles mansion, The Bivouac, and its contents to the city, intending it to form the nucleus of an arts institution that could grow with future generations. By the 1920s the institute was the largest art school west of Chicago. By 1939 it had acquired additional property and built fifteen large studios, and had initiated an annual art show for cash prizes, collaborating with what is now the Los Angeles County Museum of Art. With the outbreak World War II, thirty Otis students were drafted in a single month, and many others of Japanese descent were interned. The boom of the postwar era, however, brought new energy to the school's programming, due in large part to painter Millard Sheets, who became director in 1954, and Peter Voulkos, whom Sheets hired that year to head the new ceramics department. With the assistance of his first student, Paul Soldner, Voulkos spent a semester building studio equipment and pottery wheels. The two were soon joined by John Mason, Jerry Rothman, Ken Price, Billy Al Bengston, Henry Takemoto, and Michael Frimkess, students who collectively produced unconventional ceramic objects over the next several years, challenging traditional notions of pottery as a utilitarian form. Working in one large room side by side with his students—often late into the night—Voulkos motivated them by example rather than by formal classes, critiques, or discussions of their work. This process helped establish what would become a defining trait of Los Angeles–area art schools: cross-pollination. Just as leading faculty moved between the schools, they encouraged their students to experience working with other local artists and teachers. Vivika Heino, for example, sent her Chouinard students to Peter Voulkos at Otis, and Richard Pettersen recommended his Scripps students to Marguerite Wildenhain's Pond Farm. In 1968 Otis director Andreas S. Anderson was awarded an NEA grant to research European art schools with pivotal programs in the design arts, particularly those institutions pushing new materials and advanced technologies, a marker of Otis's continued expansion and development on an international level. Among the faculty members who helped shape the institution are Arthur Ames, Leonard Edmonson, Renzo Fenci, Harrison McIntosh, Wayne Long, Helen Watson, and Ward Youry. Notable graduates include Dorothy Jeakins, John Altoon, Edith Head, Robert Irwin, Joel Edwards, Tom Van Sant, Dean Tavoularis, Barry Le Va, Kayla Selzer, Martha Longenecker, Janice Roosevelt, and Carol Radcliffe. —MP

"History/Mission [with many links to online archives and collection]," under "About," Otis College of Art and Design, www.otis.edu; Mary Davis MacNaughton, "Innovations in Clay: The Otis Era 1954–1960," in *Revolution in Clay, The Marer Collection of Contemporary Ceramics* (Claremont, CA: Scripps College; Seattle and London: University of Washington Press, 1994), 47–68.
See also *The Ideal Home*, 273; *Craft in the Machine Age*, 264.

PENLAND SCHOOL OF CRAFTS

Founded 1938, Penland, NC

Penland School of Handicrafts (1938–84);

Penland School of Crafts (1984–)

Penland's founder, Lucy Morgan, believed that handcrafts could provide spiritual inspiration and a good business sense. The school's early curriculum included basketry, weaving, jewelry, metalwork, lapidary, and shoemaking, and it attracted international students. Occupational crafts for rehabilitation were stressed after World War II. Bill Brown, Morgan's chosen successor, became the director in 1962 when the school's focus was shifted to the education of college-trained craftspeople. Brown modernized the school's programs along with its goals: minor crafts courses were canceled, classes were extended through the fall, and the faculty became a mix of university teachers and full-time studio craftspeople. In 1965 Brown organized a glass workshop with the help of Bill Boysen: since then, Penland has remained identified with the development of contemporary glass. —MS

Jean McLaughin, ed., *The Nature of Craft and the Penland Experience* (New York: Lark Books, 2004); Jo Lauria et al., *Craft in America: Celebrating Two Centuries of Artists and Objects* (New York: Clarkson Potter, 2007), 200–205.

POND FARM COMMUNITY
1949–53, Guerneville, CA

In 1939 architect Gordon Herr went to Europe to seek participants for an artists' community that he and his wife, writer Jane Herr, wanted to establish in California. Ceramist Marguerite Wildenhain responded to Herr's invitation, and in 1942 she arrived at their 400-acre property, where she assisted in creating a garden and building what became her pottery workshop. In 1949 the Herrs constructed Hexagon House as housing for students. Wildenhain's husband, Frans, was in Europe through World War II and arrived at Pond Farm in 1947 to teach sculpture but left soon afterward to teach at the School for American Craftsmen.

In 1949 Pond Farm held its first summer session, with teachers including Trude Guermonprez (weaving), Victor Ries and Harry Dixon (metalsmithing), Gordon Herr (architecture), Claire Falkenstein (painting), and Lucienne Bloch and Stephen Dimitroff (fresco). Jane Herr served as the business manager. The school was short-lived, a victim of the strong personalities involved, and it closed in 1953. Marguerite Wildenhain took it over and ran her own school and workshop, called Pond Farm Pottery, where she remained until her death in 1985. —MS

Tim Tivoli Steele, "School of the Pond Farm Workshops: An Artist's Refuge," in *A Report, The San Francisco Craft and Folk Art Museum Journal* 10, no. 2 (1992); Dean Schwarz and Geraldine Schwarz, eds., *Marguerite Wildenhain and the Bauhaus: An Eyewitness Anthology* (Decorah, IA: South Bear Press, 2007).

RHODE ISLAND SCHOOL OF DESIGN
Founded 1877, Providence, RI

The founders of the Rhode Island School of Design (RISD) wished to prepare students for the manufacturing world, and in its first years, classes focused on drawing, painting, modeling, and designing. The curriculum expanded soon afterward to include textiles and jewelry, a result of the region's dependence on these two industries. By midcentury, the school had added ceramics (1947) under Alfred graduates Lyle Perkins and his wife Dorothy Wilson Perkins. Norman Schulman arrived in 1965 and introduced a sculptural dimension to clay reflecting national developments. In 1962, Danish furniture maker Tage Frid began teaching in the department of industrial design, until a separate furniture-making department was created in 1969. Like Frid, Jack Prip had trained in Denmark and taught at the School for American Craftsmen. Prip came to RISD 1963 and not only shared his knowledge of silversmithing, which he had learned as a journeyman in a Danish silversmithing firm, but also encouraged his students to expand the traditional utilitarian aspects of the craft toward more expressive ends. Dale Chihuly obtained his MFA in ceramics from RISD in 1968, but when he returned from studying the creative potential of glass in Murano, Italy, he was instrumental in establishing a glass program within the ceramics department, which he led in its early years. An MFA program in glass was launched in 1972, and a separate glass department was established in 1990. The school had developed a museum beginning in its early years, and students benefited from examining ancient and historic examples of work in all media. —NB

Jo Lauria et al., *Craft in America: Celebrating Two Centuries of Artists and Objects* (New York: Clarkson Potter, 2007), 145–51.

See also *The Ideal Home*, 274; *Craft in the Machine Age*, 264.

SCHOOL FOR AMERICAN CRAFTSMEN
Founded 1944, Hanover, NH
Locations: Dartmouth College, Hanover, NH (1944–46);
Alfred University, Alfred, NY (1946–50);
Rochester Institute of Technology, Rochester, NY (1950–)

When Aileen Osborn Webb established this modern school of craft education, her first vision was of a facility exclusively for returning veterans. The program soon expanded to include all students interested in developing skills in a craft discipline. The school was founded jointly by the American Craftsmen's Educational Council and Dartmouth College Student Workshop in October 1944. Its first director, Virgil Poling, had been head of the Dartmouth College Student Work Shop, which was itself an outgrowth of the manual-training movement and was intended to balance the mental efforts of college students with hands-on learning experiences. Poling's successor in 1948 was Harold J. Brennan.

Early faculty and special instructors included, by department: Lynn Phelan, Hobart Cowles, Marianne de Trey (Haile), Fred Meyer, Olin Russum, and Earl McCutchen (pottery); Frank Ernest Brace, Michael Marmes, and Tage Frid (wood); Laurits Eichner, Larry Copeland, Charles Reese, Philip Morton, John (Jack) Prip, Hans Christensen, and Mitzi Otten (metal); Joy Lind, Karl Laurell, and Marie von Stockenstrom (weaving). The school held an exhibit at America House in October 1951, and many faculty members and young graduates were included in the American display of crafts at the Brussels World's Fair in 1958. —JF

Aileen O. Webb, "School for American Craftsmen 25th Anniversary," *CH* 26 (February 1976), 40–43, 71–72; Andrew Phelan, "50 Years at the School for American Craftsmen," *Ceramics Monthly* 43 (February 1995), 51–56; Jo Lauria et al., *Craft in America: Celebrating Two Centuries of Artists and Objects* (New York: Clarkson Potter, 2007), 183–87.

See also *Craft in the Machine Age*, 265.

SCRIPPS COLLEGE
Founded 1926, Claremont, CA

Scripps College, founded by Ellen Browning Scripps, is the women's college at the Claremont Colleges, an institution comprised of six colleges and two graduate schools, based upon the English collegiate system of Oxford University. The campus, designed by Gordon Kaufmann (and added to the National Register of Historic Places in 1984), opened with fifty students and a broad-based curriculum developed by educator Hartley Burr Alexander with studies in ethics, philosophy, literature, and art history. Alexander lured painter Millard Sheets away from Chouinard in 1932 to head the art department by convincing him that an artist's education must involve a wider range of education beyond the studio. Sheets—by that time a nationally recognized painter—hired acclaimed faculty and fostered the local arts community. He taught at Scripps throughout the 1930s, became director of art at Claremont Graduate University, and returned in 1944, after the war, remaining on staff until 1955 when he left for the Los Angeles County Art Institute (now Otis.) The arts at Claremont continued to flourish under a dynamic faculty that included William Manker (who founded the Scripps Ceramic Annual exhibitions and brought in guest artists including Bernard Leach, Shoji Hamada, and Antonio Prieto), Richard Petterson (who, like so many Southern California arts teachers, encouraged his students to collaborate with each other and with professors, and to study with artists like Marguerite Wildenhain at Pond Farm), ceramist Paul Soldner (whose temporary teaching position turned into a thirty-year career), Paul Darrow and James Fuller (who taught mixed media, printmaking, and drawing), weaver Marion Stewart and husband Albert Stewart (who headed the sculpture department), sculptor Aldo Casanova, painter and enamelist Jean Goodwin Ames, and printmaker Samella Lewis. Graduates from Scripps have included weaver Maria Kipp and ceramist Betty Davenport Ford, but it was the Claremont Graduate University (est. 1925), which was largely staffed by the same arts faculty but open to students of both genders, that produced the longer line of successful students, particularly in ceramics: Helen Watson (a Scripps graduate), Martha Longenecker, Ward Youry, Harrison McIntosh, Rupert Deese, Joe Soldate, Philip Cornelius, John Mason, Mac McClain, and Henry Takemoto. —MP

Jo Lauria, interviewed by Maile Pingel, November 16, 2010; Ceramic artist research courtesy of Professor Billie Sessions, California State University, San Bernardino; see "Facts & Figures," under "About Scripps," Scripps College, www.scrippscollege.edu and www.claremont.edu.

TOLEDO MUSEUM OF ART
The Toledo Workshops
March 23–April 1, 1962, and June 18–30, 1962, Toledo, OH

Otto Wittmann, director of the Toledo Museum of Art, suggested that Harvey K. Littleton, who was searching for a site to conduct glass experiments, consider the resources of the museum and the city of Toledo. The first of two glass-blowing workshops, held on the grounds of the museum in 1962, was organized by Littleton and Wittmann, with the assistance of the museum's School of Design ceramics instructor Norman Schulman and art education supervisor Charles Gunther. The program encompassed instruction in kiln construction, glass composition, glass melting, casting, lampworking, and finishing techniques, with afternoons spent in the practice of glassblowing. There were also presentations on the history of glass conducted by museum staff members, as well as a tour of the Toledo-based Libbey Glass facility. At the March workshop neither Littleton nor any of the seven students were skilled in the craft of glass-making and glassblowing. Participants included Clayton

Bailey, Karl Martz, and Tom McGlauchlin. Over the course of a week, with the technical assistance of two industrial glass workers—Dominick Labino of Johns-Manville Fiber Glass, who provided raw ingredients for the glass batch recipe and advice on the use of the furnace that Littleton had constructed, and Harvey Greenleaf, a retired glassblower from the Libbey Division of Owens-Illinois, who demonstrated blowing techniques—the students progressed in the handling of molten glass and the creation of experimental bubbles and solid forms. The success of the March session motivated Wittmann and Littleton to organize a second more ambitious conference for June. With funding from Georg Jensen, Inc., and the University of Wisconsin Research Committee, they were able to offer a two-week workshop that included additional lectures on the history of glass, a visit to Dominick Labino's laboratory/workshop, and instruction on furnace and annealing oven technology by Larry Gagan of Johns-Manville Fiber Glass. There were also demonstrations in glassblowing by Harvey Leafgreen and James Nelson, another retired glassblower, and by Nils Carlson of Detroit, who showcased lampworking. The twelve students, among whom was Howard Kottler, explored graphite and wood mold-making, investment casting, grinding and polishing, and color staining. Instruction on glass composition and melting points were also covered. The main objective was to gain experience in glassblowing, which was accomplished by assigning each student the task of copying a simple object from the museum's glass collection. A *Glass Workshop Report* later documented the achievements of the June seminar and further elucidated its purpose: "to introduce the basic material (glass) . . . to the artists and craftsmen—to design and test equipment which they might construct for themselves—to investigate techniques for the artist working alone—to look with this knowledge at the glass of the past and present—to look at education possibilities within the secondary, college, and university systems." These workshops were responsible for generating a new relationship between artists and the glass medium. —TT

"Toledo Glass Workshop," *American Artist* 26 (October 1962), 6; "Glass Workshop Report, June 1962, The Toledo Museum of Art," booklet, Harvey K. Littleton papers, 1946–1975. AAA, SI.

UNIVERSITY OF CALIFORNIA, BERKELEY

Founded 1868, Berkeley, CA

In the 1950s and early '60s Berkeley's Department of Decorative Art, located in the university's College of Letters and Science, offered a diverse program of study. Matriculating art and design students earned BFA and MFA degrees with concentrations in the mediums of ceramics, glass, metal, textiles, and wood. With tenured faculty and adjunct professors, who were themselves renowned designers and master craftspeople, students were given dynamic studio experiences as well as rigorous academic training. In the 1950s the textile program—which drew upon such collections as the university's anthropology laboratory—was at the vanguard in the study of non-European traditions. Under the tutelage of department chair Lila O'Neale, and other faculty such as Lea Van Puymbroeck Miller, Charles Edmund Rossbach, Mary Adrienne Dumas, Ragnhild Langlet, and Winfield Scott Wellington, students were exposed to a myriad of fiber designs created by craftspeople from Peru, Africa, Japan, and preindustrial America—including native Californians. Woodworker James Prestini joined the faculty in 1956, and Peter Voulkos arrived in 1959 to teach in the ceramics department. Voulkos worked in bronze casting during his earliest years at Berkeley and did not return to the clay medium until 1968, but he quickly established a circle of students and other area artists who benefited from his inspiring method of peer teaching. Several of his students, including James Melchert and Michael Frimkess, focused on ceramics. Marvin Lipofsky, who joined the faculty in 1961, was responsible for developing the department's glassblowing program. Other faculty during the 1950s and early '60s included merry renk Anna Gayton, Imogene Geiling, Alan Meisel, Ron Nagle (as an assistant to Voulkos), Lucretia Nelson, Joseph Pugliese, Herwin Schaefer, and Virginia Schoener. —TT

UNIVERSITY OF CALIFORNIA, LOS ANGELES (UCLA)

Founded 1919, Los Angeles, CA
Southern Branch of the University of California (1919–27);
University of California at Los Angeles (1927–58);
University of California, Los Angeles (1958–)

What began as a teachers college became a small university campus between Hollywood and downtown Los Angeles in 1919. In 1925 the campus moved to a new 400-acre site on the city's west side, and by 1939 the College of Applied Arts and its art department had been established with courses in design, art history, and the studio arts. Legendary teachers Olive Newcomb and Laura Andreson (whose involvement with the university lasted from 1933 to 1970) generated a group of graduates who contributed to the practice of ceramics in Southern California: Richard Petterson, Minnie Negoro, Barbara Willis, Martha Longenecker, David Cressey, Robert Maxwell, and Neil Moss. Other successful programs were initiated in jewelry and textiles. Warren Carter taught metalwork and jewelry to Marcia Chamberlain, while Bernard Kester, on the ceramics faculty, also headed the textile department and trained students Raul Coronel, Ed Traynor, Jim Bassler (who would go on to teach at UCLA for nearly twenty-five years), Kris Dey, Neda Al-Hilali, Françoise Grossen, and Gerhardt Knodel. In 1960 the College of Applied Arts merged with the music, theater arts, and dance departments, creating the College of Fine Arts, a structure that would remain in place until the departments of design and art were established in 1988. —MP

"Timeline of UCLA History," under "About UCLA," University of California, Los Angeles, www.ucla.edu/about .html; "UCLA Arts History," under "About UCLA Arts," UCLA School of the Arts and Architecture, www.arts.ucla

.edu; Jane Fassett Brite, "Fiber Art Gathers Momentum," in *Contemporary Crafts and the Saxe Collection* (Toledo, OH: Toledo Museum of Art; New York: Hudson Hills Press, 1993), 134; Kay Koeninger, "The Studio Pottery Tradition, 1940–1970," in *Revolution in Clay: The Marer Collection of Contemporary Ceramics*, (Claremont, CA: Scripps College; Seattle and London: University of Washington Press, 1994), 19; Toni Greenbaum, "California Dreamin': Modernist Jewelers in Los Angeles, 1940–1970," *Metalsmith* 22 (Winter 2002), 40–47.

UNIVERSITY OF SOUTHERN CALIFORNIA

Founded 1879, Los Angeles, CA

The University of Southern California was established by Judge Robert Widney and a small group of prominent local figures who donated a large property just south of downtown Los Angeles for the school's campus. The university's School of Fine Arts, which was located in Pasadena from 1887, joined the main campus in 1937 with the opening of the May Ormerod Harris Hall for the School of Architecture and Fine Arts, which included an arts library and an art gallery. A 1940 university newsletter, *The Archi*, boasted the new school's state-of-the-art offerings: "two drafting rooms, a painting studio, a freehand studio, two lecture rooms, a seminar, and an auditorium. A well-equipped ceramics studio with an especially built kiln is an outstanding unit. There is a studio with tools and equipment for the production of the finest jewelry. Another studio provides for any type of sculpture and modeling work. Photographic darkrooms are provided and a studio and shops for work in industrial design are included." It was during this time that Glen Lukens accepted a teaching post; he later became head of the ceramics department. His ceramics students included F. Carlton Ball (who became a professor of art at the university), Jane Bennison, Myrton Purkiss, Laura Andreson, Beatrice Wood, Jean Goodwin, Arthur Ames, and Harrison McIntosh; his most acclaimed jewelry student was Sam Kramer. Other ceramics teachers included Vivika and Otto Heino, whose students included Ken Price and Dora De Larios. Susan Peterson later became head of the ceramics department and taught the university's summer ceramics program at the Idyllwild School of Music and the Arts. Other notable students include Houston Conwill, Raul Coronel, Fred Olsen, and Frank Matranga. Proving the value of a varied course of study, prominent graduates include textile artist Jack Lenor Larson, who studied architecture, and architect Frank Gehry, who studied ceramics. —MP

Toni Greenbaum, "California Dreamin': Modernist Jewelers in Los Angeles, 1940–1970," *Metalsmith* 22 (Winter 2002), 40–47; "History Timeline," under "About USC," University of Southern California, www.usc.edu; Ceramic artist research courtesy of Professor Billie Sessions, California State University, San Bernardino; Jack Lenor Larsen oral history interview by Arline M. Fisch, February 6–8, 2004, AAA, SI.

UNIVERSITY OF THE ARTS

Founded 1876, Philadelphia, PA

Pennsylvania Museum and School of Industrial Art (1876–48);

Philadelphia Museum School of Art (1948–64);

Philadelphia College of Art (1964–85);

Philadelphia Colleges of the Arts (1985–87);

University of the Arts (1987–)

Heavily influenced by the Centennial Exposition that was held in Philadelphia the year of its founding, the school offered early classes addressing some aspects of industrial arts, such as textile design and manufacture, chemistry and dyeing, while others were designed to prepare students for work in providing architectural finishing details such as woodcarving, decorative paint, mural decoration, decorative sculpture, and architectural design. By the mid-twentieth century, studio crafts had emerged as a popular postwar interest, and in 1966 the craft department was established. Ceramists Harold (Hal) Reigger and William Parry set the tone for explorations of vessel and sculptural forms. Parry directed the ceramics department from 1948 to 1963 and was succeeded by World War II veteran William P. Daley, who joined the faculty in 1957 and taught until his retirement 1990. Louis Mendez taught ceramics from 1963 to 1965. Roland Jahn, who studied with Harvey Littleton, began the glass program. In metals, Samuel Yellin led the department beginning in the 1920s, followed in the 1930s by Douglas Gilchrist, who in turn was succeeded in the 1940s by Virginia Wireman Cute, a jewelry and metalsmithing teacher. Richard Reinhardt studied with Gilchrist and Cute and joined the faculty himself in 1947, while Olaf Skoogfors, who studied at RIT, arrived in 1959. Reinhardt and Cute both attended the Handy & Harman workshops run by Margret Craver. RIT graduate and Tage Frid student Daniel Jackson began teaching at the school in the mid-1960s where he established the woodworking and furniture-design department, before illness forced his retirement in 1976. Jack Lenor Larsen was director of the fabric design department from 1960 to 1962. He was succeeded by Ruben Eshkanian, who had previously worked as a designer for Larsen. Eshkanian led the department until 1978. —JF

Daniel Jackson: Dovetailing History (Philadelphia: University of the Arts, 2003); Jeannine Falino, "'I Am a Craftsman, Except Sometimes I Think I Have Been an Artist,'" in *Richard H. Reinhardt: Full Circle, A Legacy of Metalwork* (Philadelphia: University of the Arts, 1998), 4–9; Falino and Ward 2008, 416–17; Warren Seelig, e-mail to Jeannine Falino, January 11, 2011.

UNIVERSITY OF WASHINGTON, DEPARTMENT OF ART

Founded 1916, Seattle, WA

The art school at the University of Washington had its beginnings in 1916, offering courses in jewelry, silver-smithing, ceramics, textile printing, and printmaking along with painting and sculpture.

Swiss-born Paul Bonifas was hired to establish the ceramics department at the University of Washington, and arrived in 1946. He had worked in Paris as a ceramics designer and had been associated with the Purism movement of Amédée Ozenfant and Le Corbusier; Nan McKinnell was his assistant when he first arrived. Robert Sperry, who was an MFA student at the university, arrived in 1954 and became an acting instructor, graduating in 1955. Sperry remained on faculty when Bonifas retired in 1956, retiring in 1982 as professor emeritus. Other ceramics professors included Louis Hafermahl (1958–59) and Harold Myers (1961–63). Howard Kottler took Myers's position and taught until 1989, while Fred Bauer taught here only briefly, from 1968–70 before leaving to join the faculty at Mills College.

Virginia Isham Harvey was a major force in the Northwest and in fiber circles for her work with textiles. She was curator of the costume and textile study collection in the School of Home Economics, which was later moved to the Henry Art Gallery at the university. Her books on macramé and basketry were well-known, and she received a solo exhibition at MCC in 1968. After her retirement, Harvey became a consultant with Nike, designing mesh tops for athletic shoes and a Kevlar tether for towing satellites behind the NASA space shuttle.

Ruth Penington had studied at the university in the 1920s and also attended Columbia Teachers College as well as the Handy & Harman workshop. She began teaching at the school before her graduation in 1930 and remained until 1970. While Penington began as a general teacher of crafts, over time she focused on metalwork. Ramona Solberg arrived about 1965, first in Art Education and soon assisting in metalwork; she retired about 1982. John Marshall was hired to replace Penington, and about 1980, when the school decided to offer an MFA degree, Mary Lee Hu was added to the faculty. Marshall retired in 2001, Hu retired in 2008, and the department was closed down shortly thereafter. —JF

Nan McKinnell, oral history interview by Kathy Holt, June 12–13, 2005, AAA, SI; Ruth Penington, oral history interview by LaMar Harrington, February 10–11, 1983, AAA, SI; Jill Nordfors Clark, "In Memoriam [Virginia I. Harvey]" *Fiberarts* 28 (September/October 2001), 24–25; Mary Lee Hu, e-mail to Jeannine Falino, January 13, 2011; Patty Warashina, e-mail to Jeannine Falino via Mary Lee Hu, January 13, 2011. Harvey's books include *Macramé: The Art of Creative Knotting* (1967), *Color and Design in Macramé* (1967), and *The Techniques of Basketry* (1974), one of them also printed in French and Dutch, and all published by Van Nostrand Reinhold.

UNIVERSITY OF WISCONSIN

Founded 1848, Madison, WI

The instruction of art on the campus of the University of Wisconsin–Madison began in 1911 with the creation of a course for the teaching of manual arts. First called the department of industrial education and applied arts, then the department of art and art education, the current department of art emerged in the 1960s. During the 1940s, the weaving department at the University of Wisconsin–Madison supported Bauhaus tenets. Faculty promoted the practical applications of handweaving for use as prototypes for mass production, encouraging students to approach their craft like designers for industry. Helen Louise Allen was a professor at the university from 1927 until her death in 1968, teaching interiors, textiles, and embroidery as well as weaving; she was followed by Ruth Ketterer Harris, who taught until 1977. In 1963 ceramist Harvey Littleton introduced hot glass into the university's arts curriculum, and Madison graduates influenced by Littleton had a significant impact on the development of studio glass in the U.S. Several of them established glass-blowing programs at schools throughout the country. Arthur Vierthaler taught drawing, design, and metalwork (primarily jewelry) beginning in 1946, and among his students were J. Fred Woell and Robert von Neumann. A Summer Institute was initiated in the 1950s, which brought working artists and designers to campus for residencies and inter-action with students. Ben Shahn, Josef Albers, Charles Eames, Buckminster Fuller, and Victor D'Amico, educator at MoMA, were early teachers for the series. Cranbrook graduate Fred Fenster arrived in 1961 to teach metalwork, woodworking, and textile design; Eleanor Moty began teaching metalsmithing and jewelry in 1972. Fenster and Moty both retired in 2001. Skip Johnson, a graduate of the School for American Craftsmen, taught woodworking from 1965 to 1990, retiring as professor emeritus. —TT

Arthur Hove, "Exploring Artistic Potential: An Informal History of the University of Wisconsin–Madison Department of Art," typescript, ca. 1999; Jody Clowes, *Metalsmiths and Mentors: Fred Fenster and Eleanor Moty at the University of Wisconsin–Madison*, (Madison, WI: Chazen Museum of Art, University of Wisconsin–Madison, 2006); "Memorial Resolution: Clifford 'Skip' Johnson, University of Wisconsin–Madison," presented by Tom Loeser, November 1, 2009, UW–Madison Faculty Senate.

See also *The Ideal Home*, 274; *Craft in the Machine Age*, 266.

MUSEUMS AND PROFESSIONAL ASSOCIATIONS

ALLIED CRAFTSMEN OF SAN DIEGO
Founded 1946, San Diego, CA

The architect Lloyd Ruocco and his wife, Ilse Ruocco, a San Diego State College professor of ceramics and interior design, were influential postwar modernists who formed the Allied Arts Council for arts professionals, out of which Ilse organized the craft division, called the Allied Craftsmen of San Diego. The group's first exhibition was a survey of contemporary objects for domestic use and was held in 1947 at the Art Department of San Diego State College. Nature was the subject of the 1952 exhibition, in which beach rocks, tree bark, and plants were employed as the setting for works of art, while *Roots of the Past* (1959) juxtaposed contemporary works with antiques. Members included sculptor, jeweler, and furniture designer Harry Bertoia; enamelists Ellamarie Woolley, Jackson Woolley, and Kay Whitcomb; ceramists Martha Longnecker and Rhoda Lopez; sculptor-architect James Hubbell; jewelers Arline Fisch, Ruth Clark Radakovich, and Svetozar Radakovich; and furniture makers John Dirks, Larry Hunter, and Jack Rogers Hopkins. The furniture makers, along with Fisch, also taught at San Diego State University. —JF
Toni Greenbaum, "Tea and Jewelry: Modernist Metal-smithing in San Diego, 1940–1970," *Metalsmith*, 22 (summer 2002), 26–33; David Hampton, *Rediscovering San Diego's Mid-Century Artists* (Julian, CA: Hubbell Press, 2007); David Hampton, e-mail to Jeannine Falino, January 2, 2011.

AMERICAN CRAFT COUNCIL
Founded 1939, New York, NY
American Handcraft Council (1939–42); merged with Handcraft Cooperative League of America (founded 1939) to form American Craftsmen's Cooperative Council, Inc. (1942–43); American Craftsmen's Educational Council (1943–55); American Craftsmen's Council (1955–69); American Crafts Council (1969–79); American Craft Council (1979–)
New York, NY (1939–2010); Minneapolis, MN (2010–)

The ACC (also called the Council below) was the brain-child of Aileen Osborn Webb (Mrs. Vanderbilt Webb), whose visionary efforts in securing a national platform for contemporary craftspeople began in 1939 when she convened a group of independent craft organizations as the Handcraft Cooperative League (affiliates listed at the end of this entry) for the purpose of developing retail markets for rural craftspeople. America House opened the following year in Manhattan as the retail outlet for these groups. In 1941 the first newsletter was published. In 1942 the Handcraft Cooperative League merged with the American Handcraft Council, a sister organization formed by Webb's neighbor, Anne Morgan, with officers Horace F. Jayne, Holger Cahill, Laura Smith, Alfred Auerbach, Mary Vail Andress, and Humphrey J. Emery. They named their new group the American Craftsmen's Cooperative Council and soon afterward published the first issue of *Craft Horizons* (called *American Craft* beginning in 1979), which replaced the newsletter. Webb opened the School for American Craftsmen (SAC) in 1944, in partnership with Dartmouth College. In 1949 the ground-work for a museum was laid in the founding of a small gallery in America House; the first exhibition, *The Modern Embroideries of Mariska Karasz*, coincided with the publication of the artist's book *Adventures in Stitches* (1949). At the request of the U.S. State Department, the council organized *Craftsmanship in the United States 1952*, an exhibition that traveled to Europe and South America, and portions of which were shown at The Metropolitan Museum of Art (New York) and the State Department building lobby (Washington, DC). *Designer Craftsmen U.S.A. 1953* opened at the Brooklyn Museum as a joint venture between the museum and the council.

In 1955 Webb purchased a brownstone at 29 West 53rd Street that became the first location for the American Craft Council and the Museum of Contemporary Crafts (MCC). The museum opened on September 20, 1956, with an inaugural exhibition, *Craftsmanship in a Changing World*. Herwin Schaefer was the first director; after his early departure that same year, he was succeeded by Thomas S. Tibbs. Webb purchased a second building in 1957 at 44 West 53rd Street for America House. The council also initiated a series of annual national conferences in 1957, the first one taking place in Asilomar, CA. A year later the council organized the entries for American crafts (130 objects by 75 makers) shown at the U.S. Pavilion at the Brussels World's Fair. Branches of America House opened in Sun Valley, ID (1959), Birmingham, MI (1963), and Seattle, WA (1964–65). To strengthen its national scope, in 1960 the council established a regional structure having six sections (North West, North East, South West, North Central, South Central, South East) with two craftsmen-trustees for each, and called for regional assemblies and meetings linked to ACC, a practice that was mostly dismantled by the mid-1980s. Council president David Campbell succeeded Tibbs as director of the museum in 1960. With Campbell's sudden death in 1963, Paul J. Smith, who had been hired in 1957 to develop educational programs, was made director, a position he held until 1987, after which he became director emeritus. For the 1964 New York World's Fair, the council contributed a photographic essay on studio-craftspeople including ceramist John Mason, fiber artist Alice Parrott, metalsmith John Prip, enamelist Paul Hultberg, and furniture maker Sam Maloof. That same year ACC sponsored the First World Congress of Craftsmen, resulting in the formation of the World Crafts Council (WCC), and its affiliation with UNESCO on a consultative basis. At the 1966 "Confrontation" regional conference in Stowe, VT, the council's first craft fair took place. This became an annual event leading to the establishment of wholesale and retail venues managed by American Craft Enterprises, Inc. The council restructured itself in 1990, establishing the museum as an independent organization, and the subsidiary American Craft Enterprises merged with the council. In 2010 the American Craft Council moved its headquarters to Minneapolis, MN. —JF

Affiliates of Handcraft Cooperative League: Agricultural Extension Service, University of Puerto Rico (Rio Piedras, Puerto Rico); Associated Handweavers (Media, PA); Association of Maine Craftsmen (Blue Hill, ME); Catskill Arts & Crafts League (Catskill, NY); Columbia County League for Arts & Handicrafts (Stuyvesant Falls, NY); Connecticut Society of Craftsmen (Hartford, CT); Detroit Handweavers' Guild (Detroit, MI); Greenwich House Potters (New York, NY); Hampshire Hills Handicraft Association (Northampton, MA); Handicraft League Craftsmen/America House (New York, NY); The Journeymen (Alfred, NY); League of New Hampshire Arts & Crafts (Concord, NH); Marli Weavers (Chicago, IL); Middle Tennessee Craft Guild (Nashville, TN); Minute Man Crafts (Melrose, MA); New York Society of Craftsmen (New York, NY); Opportunity, Inc. (Palm Beach, FL); Oregon Ceramic Studio (Seattle, WA); Pennsylvania Guild of Craftsmen (Highland Park, Camp Hill, PA); Putnam County Products (Garrison, NY); Rowantrees Kiln (Blue Hill, ME); Saranac Lake Study & Craft Guild (Saranac Lake, NY); Society of Designer-Craftsmen (New York, NY); Southern Highlanders, Inc., (New York, NY); Southern Highland Handicraft Guild (Ashville, NC); Vermont Arts & Crafts Service (Montpelier, VT); Vermont Craftsmen (Thetford, VT); Vermont Guild (Weston, VT); Villa Handicrafts (Providence, RI); Women's National Farm & Garden Association; Woodstock Guild of Craftsmen (Woodstock, NY).
"American Craft Council 1943–1993: A Chronology," *AC* 52 (August/September 1993), 137–44.

ARIZONA DESIGNER-CRAFTSMEN
Founded 1959, Tucson and Phoenix, AZ

Scottsdale artist Lloyd Kiva New led the formation of the Arizona Designer-Craftsmen at a meeting held in Sedona, AZ. Some of the craftsmen in attendance were Ben Goo, Maurice Grossman, Charles Loloma, Mary Pendleton, Berta Wright, Don Schaumburg, Adrian Shaw, Elsie Graves, Ray Graves, Margaret Graves, and Bertha Wunderlich. Aileen Osborn Webb lent her assistance at the beginning. The group began holding juried exhibitions that same year at the Heard Museum in Phoenix, AZ. Otellie Loloma gave pottery demonstrations during the second exhibition, held at the museum in the following year. The criteria for membership in the early years are unknown, but by 1971, a separate "juried membership" involved approval by a review board, "on the basis of excellence in craftsmanship and design." By that year, of 188 members, 109 were juried. —JF
"State's Artists Hold Meeting at Sedona Lodge," [Flagstaff] *Daily Sun*, June 15, 1959, 10; "Tasteful Show at Heard Museum Presented by Designer-Craftsmen," [Phoenix] *Arizona Republic*, November 20, 1959, 2; "Local craftsmen to sell wares," [Phoenix] *Arizona Republic*, March 7, 1971, 12-K; www.azdesignercraftsmen.org.

ARTIST-CRAFTSMEN OF NEW YORK

Founded 1892, New York, NY

The New York Society of Ceramic Arts (founded 1892) merged with New York Society of Craftsmen (founded 1920; formerly the National Society of Craftsmen, 1906–20) to form Artist-Craftsmen of New York, Inc. (1958–)

Artist-Craftsmen of New York, was created when several venerable organizations united to encourage and support new works of fine quality in a variety of creative disciplines. Along with the artist-craftspeople members, several individuals important in the craft movement in New York and in the nation gave their support, including Aileen Osborn Webb, David Campbell, and Richard F. Bach. Just Lunning, president of New York's Georg Jensen retail firm, was elected the new president of the combined group.

The Artist-Craftsmen of New York initiated annual juried exhibitions in 1959. The third annual exhibition (1961) was held at the Cooper Union Museum for the Arts of Decoration in New York City. The exhibition catalogue listed three hundred members; among those exhibiting were enamelists Kaethe Berl, Harold Tishler, and Oppi Untracht; jewelers Adda-Husted Andersen, Irena Brynner, Paul Lobel, and Kurt J. Matzdorf; glass artist Maurice Heaton; ceramists Vivika Heino, Otto Heino, and Polia Pillin; rug maker George J. Wells; and silversmith Ludwig Wolpert. Though smaller today, the group retains its goals of fine craftsmanship in diverse arts and showing members' work in regional exhibitions. —JP

Current Craft Perspectives, Third Annual Exhibition of Artist-Craftsmen of New York (New York: Cooper Union Museum for the Arts of Decoration, 1961); Artist-Craftsmen of New York, Inc., at www.artistcraftsmenofnewyork.com.

CORNING MUSEUM OF GLASS (CMOG)

Founded 1950, Corning, NY

Corning Glass Works (now Corning Incorporated) founded the museum as a non-profit institution to collect and preserve examples of glass from around the world. When the museum opened to the public in 1951, two thousand objects were in the collection, and a research library had been established. The museum's collection and library grew under founding director Thomas S. Buechner, who served from 1951 to 1960, and later from 1973 to 1980, and Paul Perrot (1960–1972) who was instrumental in advancing Buechner's aims of collecting contemporary glass and editing the museum's *Journal of Glass Studies*, which began in 1959. —JF

www.cmog.org [search history].

THE CREATIVE ARTS LEAGUE OF SACRAMENTO (CALS)

Founded 1952, Sacramento, CA

This league was formed by ten women—Cary Bauer, Joy Cain, Dorothy Gordoy, Gertrude Mihsfeldt, Maude Pook, Betty Carney Pope, Increase Robinson, Marjorie Vasey, Charlotte Walker, and Margaret Winter—with the purpose of bringing outstanding work by contemporary artists to the community of Sacramento. By the late 1950s the

group had begun to focus on crafts, organizing statewide craft shows that were held biennially at the Crocker Art Museum between 1959 and the 1990s. As these shows increased in size and complexity, the league's other exhibitions were phased out. California artists whose works have been shown in league exhibitions include Laura Andreson, Robert Arneson, Fred Uhl Ball, Robert Else, Arline Fisch, Lee Kavaljian, Ruth Rippon, June Schwarcz, Lois Franke Warren, and Robert Winston. —TT

"Music and Art," *Oakland* [CA] *Tribune*, January 2, 1961, C-3; founding members identified by Lesli Pletcher, e-mail to Jeannine Falino, December 29, 2010; "History," under "About CALS," Creative Arts League of Sacramento, www.creativeartsleague.com/About/History.html.

DESIGN GALLERY, WALKER ART CENTER

1946–1962, Minneapolis, MN

Everyday Art Gallery, Walker Art Center (1946–54); Design Gallery, Walker Art Center (1954–62)

Under the premise "that many modern objects have captured the essence of our time as a Greek vase did in its time," the Walker Art Center opened the Everyday Art Gallery as a permanent addition to the museum in January 1946 (all quotations in this entry are from *Everyday Art Quarterly* 1946). The gallery was devoted to the selection and display of "the best ideas concerning the home and the many articles that go into it, from factory-made coffee pots to hand-woven fabrics." Initially, the exhibition schedule included six shows a year, assembled from objects loaned to the museum by Twin City retailers as well as national manufacturers and designers. The purpose of these early shows was to provide the public with "practical information about design, materials, costs and sources of supply." The museum maintained a comfortable reading lounge within the gallery, which was well-stocked with current magazines on architecture, interior design, home planning, and industrial design. There was also a small library containing books, clipping files, pamphlets, and catalogues. Early exhibitions included *Hand-Made and Machine-Made Art* and *Contemporary Ceramics*, a July 1946 display that featured the Coor's Porcelain Company's chemical dishes, which were described as "typical useful objects whose form and finish are not intended to be 'artistic' . . . [but are, nevertheless,] works of art." Works designed by Russel Wright and Eva Zeisel were also shown, along with thrown vessels by the Scheiers, the Natzlers, and Marguerite Wildenhain. The Walker also published the *Everyday Art Quarterly*, the first design magazine to be issued by a museum, which included descriptions of the exhibitions as well as articles by design luminaries such as Edgar Kaufmann Jr., the director of MoMA's department of industrial design, Don Wallance, and Ed Wormley. In 1954 the gallery's name was changed and the magazine was renamed *Design Quarterly*, but until it closed in 1962, the Design Gallery continued to present the work of contemporary craftspeople. —TT

Preface, *Everyday Art Quarterly* 1 (summer 1946), 2.

FLORIDA CRAFTSMEN

Founded 1951

St. Petersburg, FL (1986–)

Organized by Louis and Elsa Freund, professors at Stetson University in Deland, FL, the Florida Craftsmen had no fixed base until 1986 when they acquired offices in St. Petersburg. From the beginning, the group focused their efforts on developing annual exhibitions held in a different location around the state each year. The first was held at Florida State University, Tallahassee. —JF

Michele Tuegel, "Short History of Florida Craftsmen," typescript, courtesy of Diane Shelly, director of Florida Craftsmen, e-mail to Jeannine Falino, December 24, 2010; mission statement, Florida Craftsmen, www.floridacraftsmen.net/about.

THE KILN CLUB

Founded 1946, Washington, DC

Begun by the students in the advanced ceramics class taught by Ollie Palmer Long at Friendship Settlement House in Southeast DC, the Kiln Club had an educational objective—to create opportunities for the exchange of knowledge and to sponsor exhibitions and talks introducing the larger public to quality ceramic work. Among the group's members were Alexander Giampietro, George Higgs, Florence Higgs, and George Beishlag. Although it was made up of artists working primarily in clay, it also had members who worked in kiln-fired glass and enamel.

In 1950 Paul Gardiner asked the Kiln Club to prepare a juried international exhibit to be held in the Constitution Avenue foyer at the Smithsonian's National Museum of Natural History. Gardiner was a former designer in the art department of the Corning Glass Works and had worked at Alfred University. He was also head of the Smithsonian Institution's Collection of Fine Arts and became acting curator of the Division of Glass and Ceramics at the Smithsonian Institution. The 1950 show led to the organization of annual exhibitions of ceramic arts at the Smithsonian from 1950 to 1965. These international exhibitions eventually became biennial events with the alternating years devoted to All-Creative Craft exhibitions organized in collaboration with other local craft groups and presenting works produced in the District of Columbia, Maryland, and Virginia. For the international exhibitions, the group worked closely with the foreign embassies in Washington. Each show featured a workshop given by professional potters and displayed work by regional and national U.S. artists alongside international craftspeople. This introduced many people to the work of ceramists from outside the Washington area. In addition to these exhibitions, every year the Kiln Club also organized a members-only exhibition. —MS

Kiln Club, archival files, National Museum of American History, Washington, DC; The Kiln Club, www.kilnclubwdc.com/Kiln_Club/Welcome.html.

LEAGUE OF NEW HAMPSHIRE CRAFTSMEN

Founded 1932, Concord, NH

League of New Hampshire Arts and Crafts (1932); League of New Hampshire Craftsmen (1968–)

The League of New Hampshire Arts and Crafts was formed in 1932 to help support crafts workers through the Depression and to educate the younger generation. In the mid-1920s philanthropist Mary Hamilton Hill Coolidge (Mrs. Randolph J. Coolidge) had founded a crafts shop in the small town of Center Sandwich, NH, and art educator A. Cooper Ballentine led a craft education enterprise in nearby Wolfeboro. Together they envisioned a statewide educational program along with a network of shops that would market New Hampshire crafts, and this led to the founding of the league. Governor John Winant supported their efforts and in 1931 established and funded the concurrent New Hampshire Commission of Arts and Crafts, the first such state fund in the nation. A number of shops, all known as Home Industries, were set up in the first two years of the league's life, including those in Concord, the Conways, Meredith, and Wolfeboro. By 1935 forty-seven local craft groups had spread around the state, twenty-three of them operating small shops.

The league's first director, Frank Staples, a graduate of the Massachusetts School of Art (now Massachusetts College of Art and Design), traveled the state to promote the organization. In 1938 the league engaged as director architect David Campbell, who pursued top-level instructors in his support for the craftspeople of New Hampshire. Campbell was also on the board of New York's Handcraft Cooperative League of America (now ACC) and became its executive director in 1955, dividing his time between New Hampshire and New York. Although determined to preserve the best of the past, Campbell brought contemporary craft to New Hampshire as well. In the 1940s and '50s, he persuaded potters Edwin and Mary Scheier to relocate from Virginia to New Hampshire to teach at the University in Durham. At Campbell's suggestion, Karl Drerup, a European-trained artist and craftsman working in New York, also moved to New Hampshire, where he founded the art department at Plymouth Normal School (now Plymouth State University). Drerup in turn was instrumental in bringing ceramists Vivika and Otto Heino to the state to teach for the league, while Campbell invited many nationally known artists, such as ceramists Frans Wildenhain and Toshiko Takaezu, textile designer Dorothy Liebes, and metalsmith Adda Husted-Andersen, to visit New Hampshire and give workshops for league members. Young craftspeople continued to migrate to New Hampshire throughout the 1960s and '70s.

The league's annual juried Craftsman's Fair began in the summer of 1934 in a barn in Crawford Notch in the White Mountains. Successful from the start, the fair moved from town to town each year, until it settled in Gilford for many years (and at present in Sunapee State Park). As the league grew, its roster of regional retail shops expanded from single showrooms in craftspeople's homes to regular retail galleries (at present in Sandwich Center, Concord, Hanover, Littleton, Meredith, Nashua, North Conway, and Wolfeboro). For many years, America House in New York offered an important out-of-state outlet for league members to market their goods. —JP

Betty Steele, *The League of New Hampshire Craftsmen's First Fifty Years* (Concord: The League of NH Craftsmen, 1981); "The League's History: Rich with Tradition and Innovation," under "About Us," League of New Hampshire Craftsmen, www.nhcrafts.org/about_us/aboutus.html.

MIDWEST DESIGNER-CRAFTSMEN

1952–63, Chicago, IL

Founded on the notion of supporting avocational as well as professional craftspeople, the Midwest Designer-Craftsmen (MDC) maintained two levels of membership—associate and professional. As a true regional organization, its members were drawn from Indiana, Iowa, Michigan, Missouri, Nebraska, Ohio, and Wisconsin, as well as Illinois, with its center of activity being Chicago.

With the assistance of Art Institute of Chicago curator Meyric Rogers (who was also a trustee of ACC), the group mounted an eponymous show in 1953 at the Art Institute and shown alongside the first *Designer Craftsmen U.S.A.* exhibition mounted by ACC. MDC produced regularly juried exhibitions in concert with the Art Institute, an arrangement that lasted until 1963. At least two of these exhibitions were circulated by the Smithsonian Traveling Exhibition Service in 1957 and 1959. Working to access the marketplace for its constituency, MDC operated Street Art Fairs, including one held on the back terrace of the Art Institute, with a portion of sales donated to the museum's design fund.

MDC voted to dissolve in 1963 in the belief that it had achieved its goal of stimulating the nascent regional craft scene. The organization encouraged its membership to support ACC as a national organization. —JF

Michael Higgins, "The Happy Life and Dutiful Death of the Midwest Designer-Craftsmen," *CH* 23 (March/April 1963), 52–53.

THE MUSEUM OF MODERN ART (MoMA)

1929–present, New York, NY

Under the leadership of Alfred H. Barr Jr., the Museum of Modern Art's first director, MoMA developed the world's finest modern art collection, set aesthetic standards for architecture, cinematography, industrial design, and photography, and expanded the mission of contemporary art museums. In addition to acquiring a fine arts collection, Barr envisioned the museum as the arbiter of good design. With the arrival in 1944 of René d'Harnoncourt, the museum created a department of manual industry, the purpose of which was to assure the survival of indigenous craft traditions in the face of rapid industrialization; it was also intended to "parallel" MoMA's department of industrial design, which had been established in 1940 (MoMA press release no. 44131-4, 1944). D'Harnoncourt became director of MoMA in 1949, by which time the department of manual industries had been dissolved.

In 1946 Edgar Kaufmann Jr. assumed the directorship of the department of industrial design, a position he held until 1955. One of his most significant contributions during his tenure was the organization of the *Good Design* exhibitions. Held annually from 1950 through 1955, these exhibits were jointly sponsored by the museum and the Chicago Merchandise Mart. In organizing them, Kaufmann secured the services of the era's most important designers—such as ceramist Eva Zeisel, who participated in roundtable seminars, and architect Alexander Girard who helped select the objects for the 1953 and 1954 exhibits. Represented in the shows were such artists as Arthur Espenet Carpenter, Charles and Ray Eames, Eszter Haraszty, Florence and Hans Knoll (who received thirteen awards in 1953), Jack Lenor Larsen, Erwine and Estelle Laverne, Ronald Hayes Pearson, Robert Stocksdale, and Russel Wright. Assisting Kaufmann in the design department in the early 1950s were curators Greta Daniels and Arthur Drexler. Drexler succeeded Kaufmann as department head, and from 1956 until his retirement in 1985, he was the museum's interpreter of modern architecture and good design. —TT

"The Museum of Modern Art Appoints René D'Harnoncourt Director of New Department," January 31, 1944, MoMA press release no. 44131-4, online press release archive, www.moma.org

MUSEUM OF ARTS AND DESIGN

Founded 1956, New York, NY

Museum of Contemporary Crafts (1956–79); American Craft Museum (1979–2002); Museum of Arts and Design (2002–)

The museum's first location was 29 West 53rd Street, a brownstone purchased by Aileen Osborn Webb at the suggestion of René d'Harnoncourt, director of MoMA and an ACC trustee. With the assistance of another ACC trustee, architect David Campbell, the building was radically transformed into an open, modern space. Herwin Schaefer was appointed the first director, and when he resigned within a few months, Thomas S. Tibbs, former director of the Huntington Gallery, WV, took his place. On September 20, 1956, the museum opened its inaugural exhibition, the invitational *Craftsmanship in a Changing World*. Webb purchased a second brownstone across the street, at 44 West 53rd Street, to accommodate America House and the ACC offices. In 1969 she deeded the building to ACC, and as with the first building, Campbell designed an acclaimed renovation of the space. In 1960 Campbell, who was then president of ACC, was named the museum's third director when Tibbs resigned to become director of the Des Moines Art Center. With Campbell's death in 1963, Paul J. Smith, who was assistant to Campbell in his role as president of ACC, was appointed director. A western outpost of MCC, called Museum West, opened in Ghirardelli Square, San Francisco (1965–68). *Objects: USA* was a major survey of 300 contemporary craft objects assembled by Lee Nordness for S. C. Johnson with the curatorial assistance of Paul J. Smith, and funded by S. C. Johnson as a traveling exhibition. It opened at the National Collection of Fine Arts,

Smithsonian Institution, in 1969, and traveled extensively, both nationally and internationally; many of the objects were later made a gift to the museum and other participating institutions by S. C. Johnson.

MoMA's 1977 expansion plans included the purchase of the museum's first brownstone (for $1,475,000) and the provision of temporary office space at 22 West 55th Street until ACC's second building could be renovated. A satellite gallery at 77 West 45th Street, sponsored by International Paper and called Museum II, operated from 1982 to 1985. With later corporate interest in the museum's location at 44 West 53rd Street, a plan was developed for a new office tower incorporating the museum's galleries at the street and basement levels. The building and three-level museum space opened in 1986. *Craft Today: Poetry of the Physical,* curated by Paul J. Smith, inaugurated the galleries and then traveled to five venues in the U.S.; an adapted version of the exhibition, called *Craft Today USA,* traveled internationally to fifteen cities under the auspices of USIA. Smith retired in 1987, after twenty-four years of service, and Lois Moran became acting director until 1989 when Janet Kardon, former director of the Institute of Contemporary Art in Philadelphia, was appointed director. She initiated the centenary series of exhibitions documenting craft in the twentieth century, of which *Crafting Modernism: Midcentury American Art and Design* is the fourth installment. The museum and ACC became separate entities in 1990. Kardon resigned in 1995, and in 1996 Holly Hotchner was appointed the sixth director. In 2002 the museum changed its name to the Museum of Arts and Design (MAD), and in 2008, it moved to 2 Columbus Circle. —JF

"American Craft Council 1943–1993: A Chronology," *AC* 52 (August/September 1993), 137–44; Paul J. Smith, "Museum chronology," typescript, 2009, Departmental files, Museum of Arts and Design; "Museum History," under "Info," Museum of Arts and Design, www.madmuseum.org.

NATIONAL COUNCIL ON EDUCATION FOR THE CERAMIC ARTS (NCECA)
Founded 1966

NCECA became an independent organization in 1966, after several years of affiliation with the Ceramics Education Council of the American Ceramic Society. William Parry was the founding president. The first national meeting of the council took place in 1961, and was attended by twenty-two ceramic art educators from seventeen colleges. The second conference was held in 1968 at the Rhode Island School of Design, and the third (1970) in Kansas City. —JF

Donna Rozman, "History, Influence and Evolution," *Ceramics Monthly* 52 (September 2004); "About Us: History," NCECA, http://nceca.net/static/about.php.

NORTHWEST DESIGNER CRAFTSMEN
Founded 1955, Seattle, WA

This organization of professional craftsmen was established as a regional answer to the national ACC. There were nine founding artists—jewelers Ruth Penington and Coralynn Pence, ceramists Robert Sperry and Henry Lin, enamelist and painter Lisel Salzer, furniture maker Evert Sodergren, weaver Hella Skowronski, lighting designer Irene McGowan, and sculptor Russell Day. The group was led in its early years by Penington, a professor of metalsmithing at the University of Washington. In 1956, the Northwest Designer Craftsmen held its first annual exhibition, at the Emma Frye Public Art Museum; many others followed, mostly at the Henry Art Gallery of the University of Washington. Planning for Century 21, the 1962 Seattle World's Fair, prompted the group to lobby for participation, and they were included in the Pavilion of Interiors within the Domestic Commerce and Industry Building. The success of their display led to the creation in 1963 of the independently operated, nonprofit Northwest Center and Gallery directed by Ruth Nomura in the former Swedish pavilion of the fair. —JF

"New Group Organized," *Seattle Times,* November 10, 1955, 42; "Craft Exhibition Opens at Frye Museum Today," *Seattle Times,* October 14, 1956, 42; J.L "Northwest Designer Craftsmen at 80," *AC* 66 (October/November 2004), 6.

PHILADELPHIA COUNCIL OF PROFESSONAL CRAFTSMEN (PCPC)
1967–74, Philadelphia, PA

Led by Helen Drutt, the council emphasized a "professional" commitment to craft and rejected the kind of open membership practiced by the Pennsylvania Guild of Craftsmen. The only artists admitted were those who had attained an MFA in their field, made a living by working in their chosen medium, or were otherwise deemed to be making a significant contribution to the field. Early members included William Daley, Naomi Davis, Ted Hallman, Daniel Jackson, Richard Koga, Stanley Lechtzin, Alan Mitosky, and Olaf Skoogfors, many of whom were educators. Mitosky, then a curator at the Museum of the Philadelphia Civic Center, mounted *Craftsman '67* which was largely composed of PCPC members. Albert Paley, then in his first year of graduate school, received first prize in jewelry and soon became a member. —JF

Matthew Drutt, "A Sense of History: Albert Paley and Philadelphia in the 1960s," in *Albert Paley: Sculptural Adornment* (Washington, DC: Renwick Gallery of the National Museum of American Art; Seattle: University of Washington Press, 1991), 57–71.

SOCIETY OF NORTH AMERICAN GOLDSMITHS (SNAG)
Founded 1969, Chicago, IL

In November 1968 jeweler Philip Morton gathered fellow metalsmiths Robert Ebendorf, Phillip Fike, Hero Kielman, Brent Kington, Stanley Lechtzin, Kurt Matzdorf, Ronald Pearson, and Olaf Skoogfors to discuss the formation of an international guild of designer-craftsmen working in metal. The following year a larger group met, named the organization, and outlined its primary goals; Brent Kington was elected the first president. Membership to the society was not initially limited to proven professionals and based on both creative achievement and broader contributions to the field. Today SNAG has open membership. The society's inaugural annual conference took place in 1970 at the Minnesota Museum of Art in St. Paul. Their first newsletter, *SNAG News,* appeared in 1975, followed in quick succession by *Golddust* (1976), *Goldsmiths Journal* (1977) and, finally, *Metalsmith* (1980 to present). —JP

Philip Morton, *Contemporary Jewelry* (New York: Holt, Rinehart and Winston, 1976); "Mission & History of SNAG," under "Info," Society of North American Goldsmiths, www.snagmetalsmith.org.

SOUTHERN CALIFORNIA DESIGNER CRAFTS
Founded 1957, Los Angeles, CA
Southern California Designer Craftsmen (1957–c. 1973); Southern California Designer Crafts (c. 1974–)

Originally formed as an elite group of craftsmen, chosen by jury, the Southern California Designer Craftsmen began mounting exhibitions at prominent museums in the Los Angeles area soon after being founded. Chairman Brooke Morris and designer Dextra Frankel (later gallery director and professor of art at California State University, Fullerton) were chiefly involved in mounting *Craftsmanship,* a 1958 exhibition held at the Los Angeles County Museum. Architectural ceramist David Cressy and ceramists Joel Edwards and Betty Davenport Ford were among the artists whose works were included in this show. A second exhibition held at the Pasadena Museum, *Crafts Related to Architecture,* was praised for the high quality of the work shown. It provided "an encouraging glimpse at the possibilities of greater integration of art and architecture" (Seldis 1959). Ceramists Henry Takemoto, Raul Coronel, Paul Soldner, and David Cressey were represented, along with Bernard Rosenthal (metal wall sculptures) and Roger Daricarrere (stained glass). The group eventually opened membership to all and developed programs to aid the professionalization of the field, including teaching, exhibiting, and selling. —JF

Craftsmanship: February 5 through 23, 1958, Los Angeles County Museum, Exposition Park, Los Angeles (Los Angeles, CA: Los Angeles County Museum, 1958); "Crafts in Architectural Scale," *Los Angeles Times,* September 20, 1959; Henry J. Seldis, "Once-Roving Show Improved," *Los Angeles Times,* October 4, 1959, E-10; Southern California Designer Crafts records, 1957–1982, UCLA Library, Department of Special Collections, Manuscripts Division, Los Angeles, CA.

SOUTHERN HIGHLAND CRAFT GUILD
Founded 1930, Asheville, NC
Southern Mountain Handcraft Guild (1930–33); Southern Highland Handicraft Guild (1933–91); Southern Highland Craft Guild (1991–)

Around 1900 railroads and new roads encouraged travel into mountainous areas of the southeastern United States. Visitors like Frances Goodrich, a Christian missionary and social worker who had studied art at Yale University, recognized the beauty and value of the traditional hand skills that survived among the people of the Southern Highlands.

In 1897 she founded Allanstand Cottage Industries in North Carolina to assist women weavers of wool and cotton coverlets. During the same period, schools such as John C. Campbell School and Biltmore Industries in North Carolina were founded to encourage traditional skills and to teach woodworking, woodcarving, pottery, textiles, and metalworking. In 1930 Goodrich joined with others in the craft movement to found the Southern Mountain Handcraft Guild.

Starting in western North Carolina, eastern Tennessee, and Kentucky, the guild continued to grow over the years. In the mid-1950s it partnered with the National Park Service to operate the Blue Ridge Parkway's Folk Art Center in Asheville, NC. Since 1948, craft fairs have been held in July and October each year. Today the guild includes around nine hundred juried members in several hundred counties within the Appalachian Mountains in nine states (the Carolinas, Tennessee, Kentucky, the Virginias, Maryland, Georgia, and Alabama). —JP

Mary Daley, "Crafts of the Southern Highlands," *New York Times*, July 9, 1967, 381; "Guild History," Southern Highland Craft Guild, www.southernhighlandguild.org/pages/resources/guild-history.php.

STERLING STYLE COUNCIL

Founded 1916, New York, NY

Sterling Silver Manufacturers Association (1916–26); Sterling Silversmiths Guild of America (1926–90); reorganized as Sterling Style Council (2004–)

The Sterling Silver Manufacturers Association was formed to promote the domestic silverware industry. In 1956 it supported annual competitions for young silversmiths to aid the industry's efforts to bring modern design to the silverware market and to discover talented designers. The same year they announced their Sterling Today Student Design Competition. Early prizewinners included Robert King (1958), who designed for Towle and International Silver, educator Vincent Ferrini (1959), and Burr Sebring (1959), who worked for Gorham. In June 1969 the Museum of Contemporary Crafts mounted an exhibition of the Sterling Silversmiths Design Competition.

The stylish new stainless steel silverware patterns of the 1960s and '70s, two-career families, and informal dining gradually eroded silver's pride of place in the home, and silver manufacturers suffered accordingly. When the guild disbanded in 1990, its remaining members were Kirk-Steiff, Lunt, Oneida, Reed & Barton, Towle, and Wallace-International, all descendants of the original members. It was reorganized in 2004 as the Sterling Style Council. —JP

Jewel Stern, *Modernism in American Silver, 20th Century Design* (Dallas: Dallas Museum of Art; New Haven: Yale University Press, 2005), 266, 339; Press release, "Weber Shandwick Appointed Agency of Record for Sterling Style Council," Tuesday, July 06, 2004, www.webershandwick.com.

WICHITA CENTER FOR THE ARTS

Founded 1920, Wichita, KS

Wichita Art Association (1920–90); Wichita Center for the Arts (1990–)

Formed by a group of twenty-four civic-minded Wichita citizens, the Wichita Art Association began as a way to promote the arts in their community. An art school was added in 1922, and a building constructed by 1925. Early crafts teachers included silversmith and Kansas native Margret Craver. With the election of interior designer Maude Gwen Schollenberger (1881–1963) as president in 1933, the organization began to expand from its original fine arts focus to a broader-based crafts perspective. In 1945 Schollenberger launched the National Decorative Arts and Ceramic Show, a national juried exhibition that was the first annual show to include works in all craft media. Prominent craftsmen of the day served as judges, including Bernard Leach, Kenneth Bates, Maija Grotell, designer John van Koert, and William Milliken, director of the Cleveland Museum of Art, who initiated the popular May shows of Ohio craftsmanship. The Art Association produced an annual exhibition catalogue in which the names of virtually all the pioneering craftsmen in the field of American craft can be found. The exhibition continued as an annual event until 1968, after which it became a largely biennial event. From the start, the association purchased objects from each exhibition for their permanent collection, which today is maintained by the Wichita Center for the Arts. —JF

Commemorative Issue: Wichita Art Association, 1920–1965 (Wichita, KS: Wichita Art Association, 1965), 2–5; "80 Years of Celebrating the Arts, 1920 to 2000," *The Wichita Center for the Arts Center News* (December 2000), 3–6.

WISCONSIN DESIGNER CRAFTS COUNCIL

Founded 1916, Milwaukee, WI

Wisconsin Society of Applied Arts (1916–36); Wisconsin Designer-Craftsmen (1937–82); Wisconsin Designer Crafts Council (1982–)

The society was founded in 1916 by Dudley Crafts Watson, a former director of the Milwaukee Art Institute, and first managed by Elsa Ulbricht, a former staff member of the Wisconsin State Teachers College at Milwaukee. In 1921 they began sponsoring annual craft exhibitions, which by the mid-1950s featured such artists as Harvey K. Littleton, Helen and Karl Peters, and Aaron Bohrod. The society had close ties to the Milwaukee Art Institute where they held their annual shows until 1957, when a move was made to the Milwaukee Art Center, an arrangement that lasted until 1974. In 1961 the annual exhibit *Wisconsin Designer-Craftsmen* was selected by the Smithsonian Institution as a touring exhibition. In 1962 David Campbell, president of ACC and director of MCC, juried the annual show. —TT

"A Rich History," under "About Us," Wisconsin Designer Crafts Council, Inc., www.wdcc.org/about_us/history.cfm; early papers of the WDCC, AAA, SI.

WORLD CRAFTS COUNCIL (WCC)

Founded 1964, New York, NY

New York, NY (1964–84); various locations until Chennai, India (2010–)

The World Crafts Council, which aids craftsmen around the globe by fostering a wider recognition of their work through programming, conferences, and communication among craft organizations, was conceived and founded by Aileen Osborn Webb, who first investigated the possibilities of forming such a council around 1960 by sending Margaret Merwin Patch on an information-gathering trip to meet craftspeople around the world. Webb convened the First International Congress of Craftsmen in New York in New York at Columbia University (June 8–19, 1964). Webb paid for forty-five craftspeople to attend the conference and offered others free room and board for the session, but travel expenses still prevented many from attending. Even so, forty-seven countries were represented with foreign visitors arriving primarily from Canada, Italy, Mexico, and India. In all there were 942 conferees, 692 of them being American. Membership and activities were organized into five regions (Africa, Asia Pacific, Europe, Latin America, and North America). The first board of directors for the WCC consisted of president Aileen Osborn Webb; vice president Kamaladevi Chattopadhyay, chairman of the All-India Handicrafts Board, New Delhi; second vice president Dr. Daniel F. Rubin de la Borbolla, director of the National Museum of Popular Arts and Industries in Mexico City; secretary Sam Ntiro, high commissioner, Tanganyika High Commission, London; and treasurer Cyril Wood, director of the Crafts Centre of Great Britain, London. Speakers at the conference included Dr. D'Arcy Hayman of UNESCO, critic Harold Rosenberg, MoMA director René d'Harnoncourt, poet Stanley Kunitz, novelist Ralph Ellison, architect Paolo Soleri, and architect Louis Kann. In addition to the lectures, participants saw a glassblowing demonstration by Harvey Littleton, a presentation of new applications for electroforming given by Stanley Lechtzin and others, and a viewing of "The Music Stand," an award-winning film by Tom Muir Wilson's featuring Wendell Castle. In 1965 the WCC was named an international nongovernmental organization affiliated with UNESCO. Successive conferences in the decade were held in Montreux, Switzerland (1966), and Lima, Peru (1968). The 1974 conference, held in Toronto, Canada, saw increased participation with 1,500 craftspeople attending from more than seventy countries. For this occasion, the WCC held a competition that resulted in what was termed the first World Craft Council exhibition, shown at the Ontario Science Center during the Toronto conference. A companion volume was entitled *In Praise of Hands;* a related film was produced by the Canadian Film Board. The WCC continues to work on behalf of global crafts, giving dignity to craftspeople around the world, providing support, communication, and resources for traditional modes of fabrication and encouragement for new art forms. —JF

"First World Congress of Craftsmen," *CH* (July/August 1964), 8–15, 55; *The First World Congress of Craftsmen*, (New York, NY: American Craftsmen's Council, 1965); "World Crafts Council: accepted as a member of UNESCO's division on art and community development," *Interiors* 124 (April 1965), 12.

CONFERENCES

INTERNATIONAL DESIGN CONFERENCE IN ASPEN (IDCA)

1953–, Aspen, CO

Walter Paepcke, head of Container Corporation and his wife, Elizabeth, fostered a number of musical, cultural, and sports-related activities in Aspen, CO, beginning in the late 1940s. At that time, Aspen was a quiet former mining town set in a spectacular natural environment that the Paepckes believed would become an attractive gathering place. Paepcke had become involved with design at his firm, and in the process become interested in the benefits of design when applied to business, Egbert Jacobsen, design director for Container Corporation, and Bauhaus typographer and graphic designer Herbert Bayer, a consultant to the firm, developed the idea for IDCA with Paepcke. They believed that Aspen's dazzling mountain setting would inspire fresh thinking, and that the conferences would be of mutual benefit to the worlds of business and design.

The first conference, attended by some two hundred people, was held in the summer of 1953. From the start, participants included a mix of influential business leaders, designers, architects, artists, and cultural leaders. A sampling of them include Stanley Marcus, Charles Eames, Josef Albers, George Nelson (1951); R. Buckminster Fuller (1952); Gyorgy Kepes, Nikolaus Pevsner (1953); Harry Bertoia (1955), Claire Falkenstein (1958); Edith Heath (1961); Mildred Constantine, Richard Lippold (1962); Ralph Caplan, Paul Rudolph (1964); Leo Lionni, Edgar Kaufmann (1966); Victor Papaneck (1971). —JF

Reyner Banham, ed., *The Aspen Papers, Twenty Years of Design Theory from the International Design Conference in Aspen*, (New York and Washington: Praeger Publishers, 1974).

AMERICAN CRAFTSMEN'S COUNCIL

National Conferences of American Craftsmen, 1957–61

CRAFTSMEN TODAY

First National Conference of American Craftsmen

June 12–14, 1957, Asilomar, CA

Conference organizer Aileen Osborn Webb opened the ACC's first conference by stating that the aim was "to afford participants . . . the chance to meet, communicate and cooperate in solving problems; [and] to formulate . . . a basic understanding of the place of the craftsman in our contemporary society—the philosophical and sociological role of the crafts, the need of a creative and experimental approach to design, and the craftsman's practical problems of production, marketing, and industrial affiliation" (*Asilomar* 1957). More than 450 people, from the U.S., Mexico, Canada, Finland, Sweden, Denmark, Japan, and Afghanistan attended, including Alan Adler, Anni Albers, F. Carlton Ball, Margaret De Patta, Charles Eames, Edris Eckhardt, Wharton Esherick, Tage Frid, Edith Heath, Michael Higgins, Jack Lenor Larsen, Sam Maloof, Frederick

Miller, John Paul Miller, John Prip, Daniel Rhodes, Victor Ries, Harold Sitterle, Toshiko Takaezu, Peter Voulkos, and Lenore Tawney, among others. Each day was devoted to a different theme. On the first day ("The Socio-Economic Outlook"), following a keynote address by Dr. Karl With, a professor from the University of California, Los Angeles, there were five media-based panel discussions—on ceramics, enamel, metal, textile, and wood—with an emphasis on the craftsperson's relationship to society in economic, social, and aesthetic terms. The second day ("Design: Its Importance and Its Relation to Techniques") began with a lecture by Illinois Institute of Technology industrial designer Jay Doblin. This was followed by "Forum on Design," a discussion moderated by Daniel Defenbacher, former president of the California College of Arts and Crafts. The afternoon panels—enamels and glass, metals, textiles, wood, and ceramics—considered the practical application of design theories to the various craft fields, while an evening session was devoted to the concerns of jurying. The final day ("Professional Practices") opened with a presentation by Dr. Asger Fischer, director of Den Permanente, a Danish design cooperative. The ensuing "Forum on The Small Business Man" was moderated by textile designer Henry Kluck. The day concluded with another series of media-oriented sessions focused on the day's topic. Augmenting the conference was the exhibition *Designer-Craftsmen of the West* at the M. H. de Young Memorial Museum, San Francisco, organized by conference participant Elizabeth Moses, the museum's curator of decorative arts. —TT

Asilomar, First Annual Conference of American Craftsmen Sponsored by the American Craftsmen's Council, June, 1957 (New York: ACC, 1957).

DIMENSION OF DESIGN

Second National Conference of American Craftsmen

June 23–25, 1958, George Williams College, Lake Geneva, WI

The second national conference of the American Craftsmen's Council drew more than four hundred conferees from thirty-three states and Canada (with one visitor from Europe). All of the crafts were represented by such participants as Marguerite and Frans Wildenhain, Lili Blumenau, Irena Brynner, Hans Christensen, D. Lee Du Sell, Trude Guermonprez, Mariska Karasz, Earl Pardon, Ronald Hayes Pearson, Arthur J. Pulos, Daniel Rhodes, Robert Sperry, Robert Von Neumann, and Edward Wormley, among others. There were also teachers, museum directors, industrial designers, and architects. The three-day program began with broad-based presentations on design by the conference's four keynote speakers—George Culler (director of the San Francisco Museum of Art), Josef Albers (chairman of the department of design, Yale University), David Chapman (industrial designer and president of Chapman Industrial Design Office, and Design Research, Inc., Chicago), and William Kolodney (educational director at YM-YWHA, New York City). The conferees were then split into three groups, and the remaining two days were devoted to morning and afternoon sessions on topics concerning

the craftsperson as creative designer. Rotating from group to group, three panels of seven craftspeople, representing various media, discussed "Discipline and Freedom," "Vision and Industrial Response," and "External Pressure on Creativity." The sessions began with two of the artisans delivering prepared statements, followed by open discussions and audience participation. A fourth session, held on the afternoon of the final day, allowed the participants to break up into media groups—ceramics, enamels, jewelry, metals, printed textiles, weaving, and wood—for design conversations appropriate to the issues of each field. At an evening session on the second day, ACC president Aileen Osborn Webb reviewed the council's increased emphasis on marketing, ACC vice president David Campbell discussed industrial design and the crafts, and MCC director Thomas S. Tibbs explained the relationship between the museum and the craftsperson. The evening ended with a comedic parody of the jurying process, written by Michael Higgins and performed by members of the Midwest-Designer Craftsmen, the conference's host organization. There was also an exhibition curated by David Laughlin of work by members as well as of craftsperson panelists and speakers. Following the conference, the National Advisory Board held a meeting attended by representatives from twenty-one affiliate groups throughout the country. They drafted a resolution asking ACC to petition "those agencies of the U.S. Government who are concerned with international cultural relations throughout the world to include in their program the work of craftsmen." —TT

Dimension of Design: Second Annual Conference, American Craftsmen's Council, June 1958, Lake Geneva (New York: ACC, 1958).

EXPLORING THE CRAFTSMAN'S WORLD

Third National Conference of American Craftsmen

June 19–21, 1959, Silver Bay, Lake George, NY

More than five hundred participants from a variety of professional backgrounds attended— craftspeople, architects, designers, decorators, manufacturers, teachers, writers, art directors, museum personnel, retailers, and students. Some forty states were represented, as well as Canada and Mexico. Thirteen craft program directors with the U.S. Army Special Services came from places as far away as the Philippines and Japan. Among the craftspeople participating in the conference were Adda Husted-Andersen, Edgar Anderson, Irena Brynner, Karl Drerup, Karl Laurell, Dorothy Liebes, Harvey K. Littleton, Earl McCutchen, Peter Ostuni, Antonio Prieto, June Schwarcz, Robert Sowers, George Wells, and Robert Stocksdale. The conference focused on three topics relevant to craftspeople—"His Expanding Educational Needs," "The Purpose of His Product," and "The Challenge of Society." Presented sequentially each session began with a keynote address—the first by University of Michigan Museum of Art director Charles Sawyer, the second by furniture designer and manufacturer Jens Risom, and the third by Barnard College, Columbia University English professor John Kouwenhoven. Each day the conferees chose to attend one of the three panels devoted to the daily topic. Papers were presented by, among others, Harold Brennan (director of the School for American Craftsmen), silversmith-designer Arthur J. Pulos, and art critic Dorothy Adlow. The panels included lively discussions with conferees. There was also an industry-oriented session ("Fields of Product Use") as well as media-specific gatherings focused on bookbinding, ceramics, enamels, glass, hollowware and flatware, jewelry, mosaics, leather, rugs, printed fabrics, wall hangings, weaving, and wood. A report of the proceedings noted that the conferees grappled with the main topics as well as "the place of the craftsman in industry, architecture, interior design, and the problems of quantity production." They also raised basic questions regarding craftspeople, handcrafted objects, and industrial mass-production. The accompanying three-part exhibition presented more than two hundred craft objects by 180 craftspeople working in the East, a grouping of works by forty craftspeople who were speakers or panelists, and a traveling exhibition (organized by the ACC's Education and Extension Department) comprising wood design, color slides of craft objects and techniques, and craft and design books available from the ACC library. —TT

The Craftsman's World (New York: ACC, 1959).

CREATIVE RESEARCH IN THE CRAFTS
Fourth National Conference of American Craftsmen
August 26–29, 1961, University of Washington, Seattle, WA
Traveling from thirty-two states and from Canada, 440 conferees—craftspeople, designers, architects, museum professionals, teachers, writers, and U.S. Army Special Services craft program directors—were present for the fourth national ACC conference. A thought-provoking keynote address, "The Form We Seek," by noted psychologist Dr. Rudolf Arnheim, author of *Art and Visual Perception: A Psychology of the Creative Eye*, and professor of psychology at Sarah Lawrence College, opened the conference. Arnheim questioned the validity of abstract and nonuseful art, a position that was quickly challenged by abstract sculptors Robert Mallary and David Weinrib. This set the tone for three days of lively debate. The panel meeting on the first day was "The Use of Research," and lectures on the topic were delivered by Skidmore, Owings & Merrill architect David Pugh, Pratt Institute professor Robert Mallary, and Corning Museum of Glass director Paul Perrot. The second day's panel came to grips with "Art in Public Building, U.S.A.," with ACC president David R. Campbell moderating a discussion among potter Rudy Autio, sculptors Tom Hardy, Glen Alps, and David Weinrib, architect David Pugh, and mosaicist Joseph Young. "The Art of Contemporary Craftsmen," a debate on the final morning, specifically revolved around the touchy question of the difference between an artist and a craftsperson. The discussion was moderated by Arnheim, with panelists David R. Campbell, Robert Mallary, Paul Perrot, David Pugh, Joseph Young, and jeweler John Frase. Media panels also met each afternoon of the conference, focusing on the day's topic as it applied to specific media. There were

also three major exhibitions installed on the University of Washington campus. The first, an assemblage of work by twenty-six artists who were speakers or panelists, was mounted in the Henry Art Gallery by assistant director T. Gervais Reed. The second presented craftwork by eighty-three artisans of the Southwest Region, representing Arizona, California, and Nevada. The third displayed the work of eighty-two craftspeople from the Northwest Region, including Washington, Oregon, Montana, and Idaho. In addition, small exhibits of craft work from the Oregon Ceramic Studio and the Washington Arts and Crafts Association were on view, as was an installation of work by students from the university's art department. —TT
Research in the Crafts: Papers delivered at the Fourth National Conference of the American Craftsmen's Council, August 26–29, 1961, held at the University of Washington, Seattle, Washington (New York: ACC, 1961).

AMERICAN CRAFTSMEN'S COUNCIL
Regional Conferences 1960
North East Region: State University College of Education, New Paltz, New York, June 10–12, 1960; North West Region: University of Washington, San Juan Island, Puget Sound, Washington, June 12–15, 1960; North Central Region: Cranbrook Academy of Art, Bloomfield Hills, Michigan, June 24–25, 1960; South West Region: University of California, Goleta campus, Santa Barbara, California, August 30–September 1, 1960; South East Region: Pi Beta Phi Craft Workshop, Gatlinburg, Tennessee, October 21–23, 1960; and South Central Region: Witte Memorial Museum, San Antonio, Texas, November 5–6, 1960
At the third national conference the ACC resolved to change the national conference cycle to a biennial schedule and to begin sponsoring regional conferences in alternate years. Continuing as an ACC activity until the late 1970s these regional events took various forms—conferences, workshops, and exhibitions. The first year (1960) there were six regional conferences. Marketed as an opportunity "to provide an informal social setting for craftsmen to exchange views on their techniques, their philosophies, and the business of earning a living by their craft," the conferences attracted large numbers of participants and were considered quite successful. Reports on the first three gatherings—in New Paltz, NY, San Juan Island, WA, and Bloomfield Hills, MI—were published in the September/October issue of the *ACC Forum*. With a focus on design, production, and the marketing of crafts, the North East conference in New Paltz drew some 220 craftsmen. A keynote speaker, Virginia Cute of the Philadelphia Art Alliance, opened the weekend with a lecture on basic principles for the marketing of craft objects, a presentation which was followed by panel discussions on such topics as "Guides for Costing, Pricing, and Sales Promotion." An exhibition organized by two instructors from New York State University, the host institution, showcased the crafts, paintings, drawings, graphics, photographs, and sculptures produced by students. A smaller contingent of thirty craftspeople assembled at Friday Harbor,

in San Juan Island, WA, for the North West conference. While no formal program had been planned, an agenda for the conference focused on forming the Northwest Regional Assembly of the American Craftsmen's Council. Among those elected to positions for the region were Ruth Penington, Frances Senska, and George Federoff. In Michigan, some 250 conferees gathered at Cranbrook Academy of Art for a weekend devoted to the theme of "The Craftsman and His Public." Alfred Auerbach, president of an advertising-public relations firm in New York City, and an ACC trustee, directed his keynote address to craftspeople who wanted to gain wider recognition of their work in the marketplace, emphasizing the importance of promotion. A series of lectures further developed the theme. Jack Denst, wall covering designer and manufacturer, stressed the importance of having a well-planned public relations and advertising program that included, among other things, a clearly-defined public identity and the promotion of a newsworthy design. Kay Sherwood, a columnist with the Newspaper Enterprise Association, observed that craftspeople needed to broaden their outlooks regarding press reviews, to consider not only articles in the Sunday art section, but also coverage on the women's page, in home furnishings, and in the fashion and beauty sections. Readers could then picture crafts within their homes, rather than in art galleries. In the media panels—moderated by such craftspeople as Philip Fike and Russel Dunbar—conferees considered the importance of making greater contact with consumers. The conference ended with the election of Harvey K. Littleton as the chairman for the newly organized North Central Regional Assembly of the American Craftsmen's Council. There was also a professional advisory committee established to set standards for professional status at the state level.—TT
"Regional Conference Reports 1960," *ACC Forum* (September/October 1960), 51–53; "ACC Regional Conferences," *CH* 23 (March/April 1962).

AMERICAN CRAFTSMEN'S COUNCIL
THE FIRST WORLD CONGRESS OF CRAFTSMEN
International Conference
June 8–19, 1964, Columbia University, New York, NY
Organized by Aileen Osborn Webb and Margaret Patch, this gathering drew delegates from fifteen geographical areas throughout the world. It also attracted many observers, official representatives, and individual craftspeople. The agenda for the conference was a discussion of the most feasible approach to establishing an international association of craftspeople. The conference's main achievement was the formation of the World Crafts Council, with delegates voting on a working constitution for the new organization. —TT
"First World Congress of Craftsmen; Report of Proceedings and Media Panel Discussions," *CH* 24 (September 1964), 8–19, 55; Rose Slivka, "First World Congress of Craftsmen," *CH* 24 (January 1964), 11.

THE ART INSTITUTE OF CHICAGO
CRAFTSMEN AND MUSEUM RELATIONS
National Conference
May 20–21, 1954, Chicago, IL

As reported in *Craft Horizons* in July/August 1954, this conference was "the first concerted effort to coordinate on a national basis the activities and interests of craftsmen, craft groups, and museums," and it was thought to have served as "an important milestone in the fostering of crafts in this country." The conference speakers were Helen Foote of the Cleveland Museum of Art, lecturing on "What the Museum Can Do for the Craftsman"; David R. Campbell, director of the New Hampshire League of Arts and Crafts, presenting the views of the craft groups; Arthur J. Pulos, silversmith, offering the craftsperson's perspective, and Louisa Dresser of the Worcester Museum, discussing the problems associated with craft exhibitions. A committee began to delineate the long-range goals required to achieve increased cooperation between craftspeople and institutions. The mission was to define the needs of the designer-craftsperson, to recommend action on exhibitions, and to determine sources for the dissemination of information. On the committee were Meyric R. Rogers, Elizabeth Moses, Aileen Osborn Webb, David R. Campbell, Michael Higgins, and Arthur J. Pulos. —TT

"Museum Conference," *CH* 14 (July/August 1954), 42.

204
LINDA GRAVENITES
Handbag (made for Janis Joplin), c. 1965
CLOTH, GOAT SKIN, GLASS BEADS
COLLECTION OF ROSLYN LISA KOT ROSEN

MANUFACTURERS AND DESIGN FIRMS

BENNINGTON POTTERS
SEE GIL, DAVID

BLENKO GLASS COMPANY
Founded 1890, London, England

Blenko Glass Company (in business intermittently, 1893–1921); Kokomo, IN (1893–1905); Point Marion, PA (1910); Clarksburg, WV (1911–13); Eureka Art Glass (1921–30), Milton, WV; Blenko Glass Company (1930–)

The firm began as a maker of mouth-blown sheet glass for use in stained glass. Its London-born founder, William John Blenko (1854–1930), started out as an apprentice in a bottle factory. About three years after establishing his own company, he moved to the U.S., where he produced ecclesiastical stained glass for such buildings as St. John the Divine and St. Patrick's Cathedral, both in New York City, as well as for Liverpool Cathedral in England. By the early 1930s, the firm had begun producing inexpensive, mold-blown, brightly colored decorative and utilitarian wares and became the exclusive manufacturer of reproductions for Colonial Williamsburg. In the 1940s, the hiring of design directors made Blenko Glass a popular name in contemporary domestic glass. They were inspired in their choice of design directors: Winslow Anderson (1946–52), Wayne Husted (1952–62), and Joel Philip Myers (1963–70). These efforts at modernization paid off, with Blenko glass being included in a 1945 exhibit at America House, where the work was favorably grouped with Steuben. Other exhibitions included MoMA's *Useful Objects* (1946) and Good Design exhibitions (1950) and Macy's exhibit of 1955, where their glass was featured with Corning and international makers including Venini, Leerdam, and Lobmeyr. By 1987 there were five designers on staff. The family-run company continues to make blown-glass tableware, jewelry, and accessories. —NB

Mary Roche, "Modern Glass—And Victorian," *New York Times*, June 3, 1945, SM15; Mary Roche, "'Useful Objects' Exhibit is Opened," *New York Times*, November 27, 1946, 18; "Show Views Glassmaking as Living Art," *New York Times*, October 26, 1955, 35; Mel Byars, *The Design Encyclopedia* (London: Laurence King Publishing, Ltd.; New York: MoMA, 2004), 85; "Blenko Glass Company—110 Years of Success and Four Generations of Leadership, 1893–2003," courtesy Blenko Glass.

DIRECTIONAL INDUSTRIES, INC.
Founded 1950, New York, NY

Bernard G. "Bud" Mesberg founded and led Directional Industries, Inc., one of the longest-operating makers of designer furniture in America, from a showroom in New York City which was tied to manufacturing in High Point, NC. Over the years, Directional specialized in original, custom, and high-quality designs. These were often based on specifications provided by architects and interior designers who flocked to the showroom at 979 Third Avenue in the 1950s and '60s. Directional sold the work of several key designers of the period: Paul McCobb's uncluttered modular designs; Milo Baughman's nonmatching pieces, such as op-art tabletops, tufted tub chairs, and Bauhaus pieces; Kipp Stewart's bedroom furniture; and Paul Evans's intricate and nature-inspired pieces. Mesberg was known for his avant-garde tastes and ability to discover new talent—qualities that brought success to the firm and allowed it to open showrooms in Los Angeles, Miami, and Chicago. In the 1960s Directional exhibited and sold pieces with concealed details, ranging from a hidden foldaway bed to a built-in ice bucket for the cocktail hour. The materials and forms were often sensuous but also practical for modern living. Baughman's suede-covered chairs, for example, folded perfectly to fit under a walnut buffet, edged in rosewood and laurel. Some styles brought about a 1930s renaissance, with sausage-armed sofas and tufted upholstery, while others referenced fictional characters such as James Bond with colorful biomorphic shapes that concealed small drawers and electrical outlets. Directional's most celebrated designs include Baughman's Parsons Table (1963), named for Parsons School of Design in New York City, George Mulhauser's rosewood molded tub-shaped chairs (1968), the ABS modular system called UMBO (1972), and modernized versions of Vladimir Kagan's chairs and sofas (1990s). Three generations of Mesbergs managed the firm before selling it to a former Baker Furniture executive in 1994. It was sold again in 2001 to Tomlinson/Erwin Lambeth, Thomasville, NC, to serve as their contemporary division. —SF

"New Furniture Shown in Store," *New York Times*, September 18, 1963; Rita Reif, "Variations on Some Familiar Themes," *New York Times*, June 20, 1968; "Bernard Mesberg; Founded and Ran Furniture Concern," *New York Times*, March 27, 1977; "History," Directional Inc., www.directionalinc.com/history.

DUNBAR FURNITURE LLC
Founded 1910, Linn Grove, IN

Dunbar Furniture Company, Linn Grove, IN (1916–19); Berne, IN (1919–93); reopened as Dunbar Furniture LLC (2004–)

Established by L. L. Dunbar and Homer Niederhauser in 1910 as a maker of buggies and horse-drawn carriages, Dunbar changed direction along with advancements in transportation. They began making upholstered seating for carriages before focusing solely on furniture by 1916. In 1931 Edward Wormley was hired by Dunbar to upgrade their product line, and his success led them to specialize in modern designs by 1944. The firm published Wormley's booklet titled *What Is Modern?* in 1951 to promote the concept of modern furniture to mainstream America. It included the work of such seminal designers as Marcel Breuer, Alvar Aalto, Ludwig Mies van der Rohe, Bruno Mathsson, Charles Eames, Dan Cooper, Russel Wright, Eva Ziesel, John Hedu, T. H. Robsjohn-Gibbings, and Walter von Nessen, among others. Wormley's own furniture designs were a distillation of a modern design tempered by knowledge of historical precedent and the realization that consumers required a measure of practicality and comfort. In 1954 Dunbar engaged Hockaday Associates to create an advertising campaign using unconventional, outdoor locations with an aspirational message, which helped to catapult the firm into greater national prominence. Hockaday's first advertisement captured the postwar desire for new homes and furnishings. In it, a *4907A* Wormley sofa lies in a verdant field, a woman stands nearby with a roll of house plans, and above them float the words "the long green hill of our desire." His 150-piece Janus Collection of 1957, the most ambitious line ever launched by Dunbar, proved to be their most successful. By the 1950s, the firm was internationally recognized for high-end furniture with commissions from the queen's palace in Jordan and the U.S. federal government offices in Washington, DC. Thanks to Wormley's designs, examples of Dunbar furniture were included in MoMA's Good Design exhibitions of 1951, 1952, and 1953. The firm closed in 1993, but the newly formed Dunbar firm reissued some forty-five examples of Wormley's designs in 2004, continuing their commitment to midcentury modern furnishings. —JF

Edward J. Wormley, *What Is Modern?* (Berne, IN: Dunbar Furniture Corporation of America, 1951); Roxanne Lucchesi and Jennifer M. Tiernan, "From Function to Fantasy, Dunbar's Legendary Ad Campaign," *Modernism* 9 (fall 2006), 72–81; Judith Gura, "Rediscovering Wormley: The Late Dunbar Designer is Gaining a New Following," *Interior Design* 68 (February 1997), 22, 25; Rita F. Catinella, "Return of a Modern Classic," *Architectural Record* 192 (June 2004), 364.

GEORGE NELSON & CO., DESIGNERS AND PLANNERS
1947–79, New York, NY

George Nelson & Co. (1947–49); George Nelson & Associates (1949–56); George Nelson & Co., Industrial Design (1956–62); George Nelson & Co., Designers and Planners (1962–79)

The Yale-trained architect George Nelson, a proselytizer of modernist design, hired many talented artists whose credits for specific works made for the company are only recently coming to public attention. These individuals produced a quantity of work for Herman Miller, Nelson's primary client, but for many other firms as well, including clock manufacturer Howard Miller, General Electric, Aluminum Extrusions, Olivetti, and plastics manufacturer Prolon. The designers also collaborated with Nelson on major exhibition designs and installations, including the 1959 American National Exhibition, Moscow, and the Chrysler and Irish pavilions at the 1964 New York World's Fair. Irving Harper, Nelson's first and most versatile designer, developed the Herman Miller logo, created a lively series of Howard Miller clocks, and designed the marshmallow sofa. Others in the group included John Pile (Steelframe group, 1954), Lucia DeRespinis (Interiors, American National Exhibition in Moscow, 1959), Lance Wyman (Graphics, *Industrial Design U.S.A.*, U.S. Industrial Design pavilion, USSR, 1967), Ernest Farmer (*Platform* bench, 1947), William Renwick

(*Bubble* lamps, 1947), John Svezia (*Sling* sofa, 1963), Robert Propst (*Action* office, 1964), and George Mulhauser (*Coconut* chair, 1956). Other designers were involved in graphics and packaging: George Tscherny, Chris Pullman, Tomoko Miho, Nicholas Fasciano, Don Ervin, Fred Witzig, Herbert Lee, Tobias O'Mara, Philip George, and Anthony Zamora. Ettore Sottsass and Michael Graves worked briefly for Nelson before going on to major careers in architecture and design. —JF

Olga Gueft, George Nelson, *Design Quarterly* 98/99 (1975), 10–19; Stanley Abercrombie, *George Nelson: The Design of Modern Design* (Cambridge, MA: MIT Press, 1995); Mel Byars, *The Design Encyclopedia* (London: Laurence King Publishing Ltd; New York: MoMA, 2004), 526; Paul Makovsky, Belinda Lanks, "Nelson & Company: Iconic Workplace, 1947–1986," *Metropolis* 28 (June 2009), 90–97.

GLIDDEN POTTERY

1940–57, Alfred, NY

Glidden Pottery was a commercially successful firm that produced innovative, high-quality stoneware pottery during the 1940s and '50s. Its retail outlet in Alfred was known as Glidden Galleries. The company founder, ceramist Glidden McLellan Parker Jr. (1913–1980) had earned his undergraduate degree from Bates College in Maine and studied philosophy and the history of film at the University of Vienna before entering the New York State College of Ceramics at Alfred University in 1937. There he trained under Charles Harder, Marion Fosdick, Forrest Burnham, and Katherine Nelson.

After completing the program at Alfred, Parker and his wife Harriet Hamill Parker began producing their own line of pottery in Fosdick's studio, based on a few samples. Thanks to product placement in advertisements, Glidden Pottery grew in popularity. Several midcentury television shows used pieces made by Glidden as props, as in a 1951 episode of *I Love Lucy* in which an egg server was featured as an ashtray. The affordable price of the Glidden line (a plain sixteen-piece set of tableware could be purchased for just under $15) was possible because their manufacturing methods relied on slip casting and RAM pressing, which sped production. Each object, however, was individually glazed and decorated. At its peak in 1953, Glidden's output was six thousand pieces per week. The firm had fifty-five employees, shipped all over the world, and produced more than four hundred different pottery forms. Parker, who was also a sculptor and painter, designed for the company while also employing a number of talented artists: Fong Chow, known for celebrated designs and glazes; Sergio Dello Strologo, who often collaborated with Parker; Katherine Nelson, who designed pottery in series as well as one-of-a-kind pieces; and Marion Fosdick, who developed the firm's popular sgraffito design. The company was featured in *For Modern Living*, an exhibition at the Detroit Institute of Arts (1949); George Jensen (1950), the eighteenth Ceramic National (1954), and five consecutive Good Design exhibitions (1950–54) jointly organized by MoMA and the Merchandise Mart of Chicago. The pottery ceased production in 1957 because of labor costs and a changing market. —ML

Margaret Carney, *Glidden Pottery* (Alfred, NY: Schein-Joseph International Museum of Ceramic Art, New York State College of Ceramics at Alfred University, 2001).

HEATH CERAMICS

SEE HEATH, EDITH

HERMAN MILLER FURNITURE COMPANY

Founded 1923, Zeeland, MI

This preeminent American manufacturer of modern furniture was originally founded by Dirk Jan (D.J.) DePree, as a producer of traditional, historically based furniture. DePree named the company after his father-in-law, and in 1932 hired Gilbert Rohde as its design director. Rohde was responsible for the firm's move toward modernism. After his death in 1944, DePree hired George Nelson, whose New York office of designers developed quantities of furnishings for Herman Miller. Nelson also secured a brilliant roster of talented artists and designers for the firm, from Isamu Noguchi and Charles and Ray Eames to Alexander Girard. The plywood-molded designs of the Eameses, including their *Lounge Chair and Ottoman* of 1956, were produced by Herman Miller, as was the adjustable *CSS Storage System* (Comprehensive Storage System) (1959). Herman Miller was a leader in the development of flexible office furniture systems having interchangeable elements, and the *Action Office 2* system, developed in 1962 by Robert Probst in the Nelson office, was perhaps the earliest and most commercially successful of these efforts. Nelson's impact on Herman Miller was considerable; sales rose from $500,000 to $3 million within seven years after he was hired. —JF

Mel Byars, *The Design Encyclopedia* (London: Laurence King Publishing; New York: MoMA, 2004), 320–32; John R. Berry, *Herman Miller: The Purpose of Design* (NY: Universe Publishing, 2004), 58–100.

HIGGINS GLASS STUDIO

SEE HIGGINS, MICHAEL; HIGGINS, FRANCES

JACK LENOR LARSEN INC.

Founded 1952, New York, NY

Larsen Design Studio a.k.a. Larsen Design Corporation (1958), New York, NY; Larsen International (1963), Zurich, Switzerland; Jack Lenor Larsen Inc. (1963–)

After an invitation to weave Edward Wormley's first collection of window treatments for Thaibok, Ltd., and a commission to weave the lobby draperies for Lever House in 1951, Jack Lenor Larsen and his Cranbrook classmate Win Anderson launched a business for the weaving, importing, and manufacturing of textiles from their New York office (1952) and a showroom at Park Avenue and Fifty-eighth Street (1954). Known for machine-weaving textiles that resembled handweaving, Larsen not only created the designs, but also developed production techniques and improved fiber technology and dyes in collaboration with textile artisans from Haiti, Morocco, Japan, Ireland, Burma, Nigeria, India, Afghanistan, and elsewhere. The Larsen firm brought color and texture to the clean and monotonous surfaces of modern office spaces and homes. Its work appeared in many exhibitions, including the Good Design series at MoMA (1951–55). A few years later, Larsen and Anderson opened the Larsen Design Studio as consultants to architecture, interior decorating, and institutional industries and to develop and promote new varieties of yarns, fibers, and colors for mass-manufactured textiles. They secured many commissions from the airline industry: for Pan American's 707 jet fleet (1958), Varig Airlines (1958), Pan American's 747 jet airliners (1969), and Braniff (1969). Larsen Design Studio initiated what is believed to be the first diagonal-stripe weave (1958), the first American hand-screened velvet (1958), the first stretch upholstery fabrics (1961), and the first designer collection for the bed-and-bath market (1965). Larsen International opened in Zurich for the purpose of distributing to the global market and later relocated to Stuttgart, Germany. In 1997 Larsen merged with Cowtan & Tout, Inc., the U.S. subsidiary of the London-based Colefax and Fowler Group, which later donated the Larsen archive to the Minneapolis Institute of Arts and Northwest Architectural Archives, University of Minnesota. —SF

Jack Lenor Larsen, *Jack Lenor Larsen: A Weaver's Memoir* (New York: Harry N. Abrams, 1998), 153–54; David Revere McFadden, *Jack Lenor Larsen: Creator and Collector*, exh. cat. (New York: Museum of Arts and Design, 2004); Mel Byars, *The Design Encyclopedia* (London: Laurence King Publishing, Ltd; New York: Museum of Modern Art, 2004), 415.

KNOLL, INC.

Founded 1938, New York, NY

Hans G. Knoll Furniture (1938–43); H. G. Knoll Associates (1943–46); Knoll Associates (1946–c. 1970); Knoll International (c. 1970–91); The Knoll Group, Inc. (1991–94); Knoll, Inc. (1994–)

Hans G. Knoll (1914–55), the son of Walter C. Knoll, grew up in a prominent modern furniture-making family in Stuttgart, Germany. After a few years in England working for his father's firm, Knoll moved to New York City and opened a modern furniture showroom on East Seventy-second Street. His first catalogue (1942) featured twenty-five items, fifteen of which were designed by Jens Risom, with whom Knoll collaborated on many projects, including the press lounge for the GM exhibit at the New York World's Fair in 1939. In 1943 Hans met Florence Schust, a gifted and well-connected architect and interior designer who sought furniture appropriate for the interiors of modern structures. Florence, nicknamed "Shu," worked for Hans until 1946, when the two married and formed a partnership as Knoll Associates. Florence Knoll led the Planning Unit and was in charge of interior design, while Hans Knoll led sales strategies and operations. The Knolls' decision to work with well-known designers—including

Harry Bertoia, Ludwig Mies van der Rohe, Eero Saarinen, George Nakashima, Isamu Noguchi, and many others—resulted in some of the icons of modern furniture, using new materials and production methods. Dissatisfied with available upholstery fabrics, Florence opened a textiles showroom on East Sixty-fifth Street in 1947, which would later sell directly to the trade. Focused on color, fabric, and furniture, Knoll Associates moved to the fourteenth floor of 575 Madison Avenue, where Shu designed the showroom (1951). By 1955 Knoll had expanded to showrooms in Los Angeles, Stuttgart, Dallas, Milan, Chicago, Detroit, Miami, Boston, Brussels, Stockholm, Zurich, and Toronto. They had completed prestigious commissions for Alcoa, the Rockefeller family, and U.S. embassies in Copenhagen, Stockholm, and Havana, to name a few. When Hans died in a car accident in Cuba in 1955, Florence (later Florence Knoll Bassett) became president of the firm. In 1959 she sold the company to Art Metal, Inc., but stayed on as president and design consultant until 1965—especially to complete the interiors of Eero Saarinen's CBS Headquarters in New York. After her retirement, the Knoll companies were purchased by Walter E. Heller, International, of Chicago and consolidated under the name Knoll International. Knoll was sold three more times and operates today as Knoll, Inc. —SF

William M. Freeman, "News of the Advertising and Marketing Fields," *New York Times*, June 19, 1955; Mel Byars, *The Design Encyclopedia* (London: Laurence King Publishing, Ltd.; New York: The Museum of Modern Art, 2004), 386–87; Nurit Einik, *Knoll Textiles: 60 Years of Modern Design* (New York: Knoll, Inc., 2007), 7–25; David Bright, Knoll, Inc., e-mail to Nurit Einik, January 10, 2011.

PUTMAN COUNTY PRODUCTS
SEE WEBB, AILEEN OSBORN

REED & BARTON
Founded 1824, Taunton, MA
Babbitt & Crossman (1824–27); Babbitt, Crossman & Company (1827–29); Crossman, West & Leonard (1829–30); Taunton Britannia Manufacturing Company (1830–37); Leonard, Reed & Barton (1837–40); Reed & Barton (1840–)

A nineteenth-century maker of jewelry and Britannia ware, Reed & Barton had grown into a significant manufacturer of domestic silver flatware and hollowware by the early decades of the twentieth century, joining other American firms in New York and New England, such as Gorham Manufacturing Co. and Tiffany & Co., in the great age of American silver production. Wishing to capture the post–World War II market for silver among returning GIs and their brides, Reed & Barton cast about for new designers to inject a modern profile and update their appeal to this new generation of consumers. In 1957 Roger Hallowell, then president of Reed & Barton, hired Danish-trained Jack Prip to interpret sketches provided by Italian designer Gio Ponti for a flatware line called *Diamond*. The resulting flatware was offered to the public along with a *Diamond* hollowware service designed by Prip. After working for Reed & Barton

as designer-in-residence until 1960, Prip continued his association with the firm on a part-time basis until 1970. Over the course of his career with the firm, Prip developed a number of designs, including *Denmark* (1958), *Dimension* (1961), and *Tapestry* (1964). —JF

John Prip, Master Metalsmith (Providence, RI: Museum of Art, Rhode Island School of Design, 1987).

TOWLE SILVERSMITHS
Founded 1857, Newburyport, MA
Towle & Jones (1857–73); A. F. Towle & Son (1873–82); Towle Manufacturing Company (1882–); later Towle Silversmiths

As with many silversmithing firms of the mid-twentieth century, Towle Silversmiths sought to add contemporary designs to its repertoire in order to entice purchases by young postwar consumers. In 1950 Charles Withers, then president of the firm, married silversmith Margret Craver, who was a forceful advocate for contemporary metal. Her previous work in the craft division of precious metals refiner Handy & Harman brought her into contact with many talented designers, and because of these connections, Towle engaged several of them, the most prominent including Earl Pardon, Robert J. King, John Van Koert, and William DeHart. Pardon's interest in enamel was the source of his turquoise green enamel-tipped *Contempra House* flatware, while King and Van Koert gave *Contour* flatware and hollowware a smooth organic shape that was increasingly popular across all media. —JF

Falino and Ward, 452–56, cat. nos. 367–68.

WIDDICOMB FURNITURE CORPORATION
1873–1971, Grand Rapids, MI
Widdicomb Furniture Company (1873–57); Widdicomb-Mueller Corporation (1957–62); Widdicomb Furniture Corporation (1962–71)

The Widdicomb family of Grand Rapids, MI, spawned several furniture companies, each of which had various names and one of which (John Widdicomb) remains in business. After opening a cabinetmaking shop in 1858, English-born George Widdicomb and his four sons produced traditional European furniture in Grand Rapids, MI, for an American audience. There followed decades of changes in leadership and company divisions. In 1943 the Widdicomb Furniture Company engaged English architect and designer T. H. (Terrance Harold) "Gibby" Robsjohn-Gibbings to design a collection of classically modern furniture. More a functionalist than a modernist, Robsjohn-Gibbings faulted the early modern period for not reflecting the individuality, comfort, and warmth he considered appropriate for living. His designs for Widdicomb were made of hardwoods, such as walnut, birch, and mahogany, and featured curved or intersecting table legs, built-in drawer pulls, hidden hardware behind smooth buffet doors, and sometimes biomorphic shapes, like those in his free-form glass and walnut coffee table (late 1940s) and Mesa Table (1951). Many of his pieces were visually uncomplicated and well-proportioned. Robsjohn-Gibbings left the firm in

1956, and a year later the Widdicomb Furniture Company merged with the Mueller Furniture Company to become the Widdicomb-Mueller Corporation. After contemplating at least thirty-five designers, Widdicomb-Mueller approached George Nakashima to design their Origins line, which made the designer-craftsman's work available to wider audiences. Nakashima's precisely hand-hewn tables with tapered legs, his spindle-back armchairs, benches, and room dividers established a new "American look" and were produced by Widdicomb through 1961. After Nakashima, Widdicomb produced the work of other designers such as Paul McCobb. The firm was purchased by the Grand Rapids Store Equipment Company in 1970. That same year, another Grand Rapids company descending from the Widdicomb family—John Widdicomb—known for manufacturing historical European-style furniture, purchased the Widdicomb name, bringing the company's history to a close.—SF

Albert Baxter, *History of the City of Grand Rapids, Michigan* (New York and Grand Rapids: Munsell & Company, Publishers, 1891), 465–66; Cynthia Kellogg, "A New 'American Look' in Furniture Is Unveiled," *New York Times*, June 14, 1958; for a complete company chronology, see "Genealogy of Widdicomb Furniture Companies," Grand Rapids History: Grand Rapids Historical Commission Online Archive, www.historygrandrapids.org/learn.php?id=38.

GALLERIES AND RETAILERS

AMERICA HOUSE
1940–71, New York, NY

America House was one of the first midcentury retail shops to specialize in American crafts of all media. Founded by Aileen Osborn Webb, it first operated under the auspices of the Handcraft Cooperative League of America. Its original mission was to bring the work of rural craftspeople to an urban-based retail outlet, but soon it included designs by artists from around the country. The early School for American Craftsmen professor, metal-smith Laurits Christian Eichner, named the shop America House since its objective was to create a market for American crafts, which had not existed prior to this time. Initially run as a cooperative in which everyone involved owned a two-dollar share of stock, America House became a private corporation in 1951. The shop's original location was at 7 East 54th Street, but mounting expenses forced it to move in 1943 to 485 Madison Avenue, where it remained until 1949 when it relocated around the corner to 32 East 52nd Street, its home until 1959, when it moved to 44 West 53rd Street, to a building purchased by Webb in 1957. The shop's first director, Frances Wright Caroë, who served until 1952, was largely responsible for establishing its reputation as the premier venue for American crafts in this country. Upon Caroë's departure, Florence Eastmead took over as shop director. The red, white, and blue design of each shop reflected its patriotic goals. While America House was predominantly a retail operation, on occasion the shop hosted non-selling exhibitions curated by Helen Watkins, the earliest of which was held in 1945. Their original purpose was to draw visitors to the shop rather than to educate the public in American craft, but their popularity laid the foundation for the Museum of Contemporary Crafts (now the Museum of Arts and Design).

During the 1960s America House underwent significant changes. David R. Campbell designed the shop's award-winning new home at 44 West 53rd Street, with decorative elements and furnishings made by craftsmen associated with the store. Soon after the appointment of Robert Hodges as the new director in 1964, a selection board was set up to establish standards for the work sold in the shop, and the mail-order catalogue was enhanced. A wider selection of home furnishings was introduced and an Architectural and Interior Design Consultation Service established to pair clients with craftspeople associated with America House. Its success in New York prompted the opening of branches in Sun Valley, ID, in the Frederick and Nelson's department store in Seattle, WA, and in Birmingham, MI.

More than fifteen hundred craftspeople were represented over the thirty-year history of America House. Exposure there helped launch the careers of Paul Evans, Wendell Castle, Michael Cohen, Elsa Freund, Michael Coffey, Wharton Esherick, Jere Osgood, Ronald Pearson, Earl Pardon, and Tage Frid, among others. When America House closed in 1971, it was no longer unique. Competitive galleries in Manhattan and elsewhere had been established, and Webb's goal of making handmade pieces by master craftspeople available to the general public had largely been achieved. —BN

Frances Wright Caroë, "Prevailing Winds," *CH* 8 (August 1941), 68; Charles Burwell, "The New America House and its Policies," *CH* 20 (September/ October 1960), 50–51; Cynthia Kellog, "America House a Tribute to Craftsman's Heroine," *New York Times*, September 6, 1960, 43; Charles Burwell, "The New America House and its Policies —Part II," *CH* 20 (November/ December 1960), 56–57; "Interior Design Data: Crafts Store," *P/A* (February 1961), 154–57; "America House Closes," *Outlook: American Craftsmen's Council Newsletter* 12 (February 1971); Aileen O. Webb, "America House 1940–1971," *CH* 31 (April 1971), 11.

ANNEBERG GALLERY
1964–81, San Francisco, CA
The Jewelry Shop (1964–66); Anneberg Gallery (1966–81)

The Anneberg Gallery, founded by jeweler Margery Anneberg (1921–2003) as The Jewelry Shop, showed ancient, ethnographic, and folk art, and was the first in the Bay Area to include art in craft media. With the help of her artist friend Gordon Holler, Anneberg turned the front room of a rented apartment on Hyde Street, San Francisco, into a gallery space. The earliest exhibitions included a show of Coptic textiles, *Ancient Textiles from Egypt*, which Holler had acquired in Cairo. Anneberg's was the first West Coast gallery to show contemporary glass: a 1966 exhibition of work by Marvin Lipofsky and his students in the department of design at the University of California, Berkeley. Anneberg featured other regional artists, such as Lillian Elliot, Imogene Gieling, Carl Jennings, Barbara Shawcroft, Bob Stocksdale, and merry renk. Later artists included Dominic Di Mare, Kay Sekimachi, June Schwarcz, Trude Guermonprez, and Katherine Westphal, along with displays of ethnographic materials from around the world that helped to demonstrate the kinship between these art forms. Anneberg closed her gallery in 1981 and by 1983 had helped to found the San Francisco Museum of Craft and Folk Art, where she served as curator until 1986. —JF

Margery Anneberg, "Anneberg Gallery 1966–1981, and Craft and Folk Art in the San Francisco Bay Area," interviewed by Suzanne B. Reiss, 1995, California Craft Artists Oral History Series, Regional Oral History Office, University of California, Berkeley; "Obituaries," *AC* 63 (August/ September 2003), 21.

ARIZONA CRAFTSMEN
1946–47, Scottsdale, AZ

Opened by businessman Tom Darlington at the corner of Brown Avenue and Main Street, the shop was visited twice by Eleanor Roosevelt, who described it as having a central patio around which artist workshops were open for visitors. Potter Mathilde Schaefer, leather craftsman Lloyd Kiva New, and woodworker-designer Philip Sanderson were the artists. A gift shop offering Indian and Mexican wares was run by Peggy and Horace White. At the time of Roosevelt's first visit in 1946, she reported, "New has decided to create an outlet for the young workers who have trained in the arts and crafts during their school years." After the site burned down about 1948, New took the opportunity to create his own craft center. —JF

Eleanor Roosevelt, "My Day," [Reno] *Nevada State Journal* March 26, 1946," 4; Roosevelt, "My Day," [Reno] *Nevada State Journal*, March 23, 1947, 4.

ARTS AND ENDS
1947–ca. 1981, New York, NY

Ed Wiener's Arts and Ends gallery opened in a small, street-level shop on West Fifty-fifth Street where his rings, necklaces, pins, pendants, and earrings were displayed on walls and low benches, as well as in glass cases. Behind a small partition was Wiener's workbench, laden with jewelry-making tools and instruments. From here Wiener, the jeweler-craftsman, worked and sold his modern silver-and-gemstone jewelry. Over the years, the shop moved around Manhattan: from Fifty-fifth to Fifty-third Street near MoMA (1953–65) and to Madison Avenue at Fifty-seventh Street (1965). He also maintained a second outlet in Greenwich Village until 1958, and a store in Provincetown, MA (1946–65). —SF

"Arts and Ends," *CH* 10 (spring 1950), 22–23; Toni Wolf, "Ed Weiner 1918–1991," *Metalsmith* 12 (winter 1992), 10.

BONNIERS
1948–74, New York, NY

Bonniers department store, located first on Madison Avenue and later on Fifth Avenue, was started in 1948 by the Swedish publishing empire of the same name. A New York store had been established in 1910 to sell Scandinavian books to immigrant communities. When demand for books in Swedish, Danish, and Norwegian fell after World War II, the firm introduced Scandinavian furnishings. The store became an important showcase for contemporary Scandinavian design, with exhibitions of works by artists Stig Lindberg, Astrid Sampe-Hultberg, Sven Pamquist, Tapio Wirkkala, and Hans Wegner, as well as companies such as Orrefors and Rorstrand. The store occasionally featured exhibitions of works from other countries, including Italy and Japan, and solo exhibitions, for example, of vessels by British ceramist Lucie Rie and California ceramists Peter Voulkos and Otto and Gertrud Natzler. They were particularly noted for introducing the *Akari* lamps designed by Isamu Noguchi. —JS

Murray Schumach, "Famed Publisher to Sell Furniture," *New York Times*, February 7, 1949, 7; "Bonniers, Furnishings Pioneer, Expected to Close Next Month," *New York Times*, September 28, 1974, 18.

BRAUNSTEIN/QUAY GALLERY

Founded 1961, Tiburon, CA

32 Main Street Gallery (1961); Quay Gallery (1961–65); Quay Gallery, San Francisco (1965–76); Ruth Braunstein's Quay Gallery (1976–78); Braunstein Gallery (1979); Quay Ceramics Gallery (separate entity, 1975–79); Quay Gallery (1979); absorbed into Braunstein/Quay Gallery (1980s)

In 1961, with five hundred dollars, Ruth Braunstein and her first partner, Verna Aré, established a gallery in Tiburon, CA, as The 32 Main Street Gallery, but changed its name that same year to Quay Gallery, as Tiburon township resembled the shape of a wharf or quay. In 1965 the gallery moved to San Francisco and also established short-lived satellite galleries in Santa Rosa (1966–67) and New York (1975–78). From the beginning, Braunstein exhibited some of the Bay Area's most adventurous artists in all media: clay by Win Ng, Peter Voulkos, and Richard Shaw; sculpture by Manual Neri and Bruce Connor; glass by Dale Chihuly; paintings by Richard Diebenkorn and Nathan Oliveira; and installations by Edward Keinholz. This trend continued, although with a greater focus on ceramics beginning in 1975, when Braunstein opened Quay Ceramics Gallery with partners Rena Bransten and Sylvia Brown. —JF

Braunstein Gallery Twentieth Anniversary (San Francisco: Braunstein Gallery, 1981); Ruth Braunstein, "How I Opened my Gallery," typescript (July 2010); Braunstein, "Dancer + Dancer = Art Gallery," typescript, both courtesy of Braunstein/Quay Gallery with thanks to Shannon Trimble.

CRAFTSMAN COURT

1947–1970s, Scottsdale, AZ

Craftsman Court was an innovative community space in which artists could create, display, and sell their work directly to the public. When the Arizona Craftsman building, owned by businessman Tom Darlington, was destroyed by fire in 1948, the artists decided to rebuild under the leadership of Lloyd Kiva New and the assistance of arts patron Anne McCormick. They relocated to a new, previously undeveloped site called Fifth Avenue because of the fashionable nature of the wares produced by these artists. By 1955 a building designed by T. S. Montgomery, and named Craftsman Court, was erected at 7121–7141 East Fifth Avenue, with seven separate workshops around a central patio with a pond and shade trees. To appeal to tourists, the workshop spaces were arranged as an inviting pedestrian area with open studios for visitors to see the artists at work and engage with them. Craftsman Court also served as a community center for the craftspeople. They could work together to develop new ideas, techniques, and styles with the occasional opportunity to collaborate and organize group exhibitions. The structure of the artist community provided many with an opportunity to fund their creative work and to gain exposure to their craft. Craftsman Court's success relied on the effectiveness and contributions of the community. —BN

"Scottsdale: Where Craftsmen Are Their Own Retailers,"

CH 17 (July/August 1957), 14–16; Joan Fudala, *Scottsdale* (Mount Pleasant, SC: Arcadia Publishing, 2010), 68; Douglas B. Sydnor, *Scottsdale Architecture* (Mount Pleasant, SC: Arcadia Publishing, 2010), 37; "Scottsdale History: Key Events in the History of Scottsdale," Scottsdale Historical Museum, www.scottsdalemuseum.com.

DALZELL HATFIELD GALLERY

1925–63, Los Angeles, CA

After World War I, Dalzell H. Hatfield (1893–1963), whose first gallery was in Chicago, moved to Los Angeles and by 1925 had opened another gallery. In 1939 he moved the gallery into the Ambassador Hotel at 3400 Wilshire Boulevard, where it remained until his death. Hatfield and his wife Ruth dealt in paintings by local artists such as Millard Sheets, as well as twentieth-century Europeans including Chaim Soutine, Max Pechstein, and Pablo Picasso. Hatfield also favored Southern California crafts and carried ceramics by Gertrud and Otto Natzler, Glen Lukens, and Betty Davenport Ford; enamels by Jean and Arthur Ames; and metalwork by Philip Paval. —JF

"Art Events," *Los Angeles Times*, November 16, 1952, D6; "Gift Offers Exciting at Galleries," *Los Angeles Times*, December 13, 1959, E10; "D. H. Hatfield, L.A. Art Gallery Operator, Dies," *Los Angeles Times*, July 14, 1963, 12.

DESIGN RESEARCH (D/R)

1953–78, Cambridge, MA

Hyannis, MA, branch (1960 [summer]; New York branch, two locations (1959–64; 1963–78); San Francisco branch (1965–78)

Credited as being one of the first retail stores focused on modern design, Design Research introduced an American audience to innovative European and American designs, primarily home furnishings and clothing. The Cambridge store itself was a glass-fronted model of modernist architecture designed by founder Ben Thompson. Prior to opening the shop, Thompson had studied with Walter Gropius in the Architect's Collaborative. He brought many of those modern ideals to Design Research (nicknamed D/R). D/R featured work by such influential designers as Marcel Breuer, Hans Wegner, and Joe Colombo and attracted an avant-garde clientele that included Jackie Kennedy and Julia Child. It became one of the first retail stores to carry modern Scandinavian design, introducing Marimekko fabrics and designs to a U.S. market. D/R also initiated new approaches to the sale and presentation of merchandise. The staff aspired to a modern display philosophy, experimenting with the public space to create an interior aesthetic that still resonates in contemporary showrooms. The store became a meeting place for young, innovative designers, providing a venue for creative minds to share new ideas and designs. Branches were opened in Hyannis, MA; New York City; and San Francisco in the 1960s and in the 1970s expanded to Easthampton, NY; Westport, CT; Beverly Hills, CA; and Philadelphia, as well as additional stores in San Francisco and Massachusetts. Though D/R closed in 1978, its impact on modern design in the U.S. was unprecedented and is carried on today by companies

such as Crate & Barrel and Design Within Reach, whose founders Gordon Segal and Robert Forbes, respectively, were influenced by D/R. —NB

Jane Thompson, Alexandra Lange, Rob Forbes, *Design Research: The Store That Brought Modern Living to American Homes* (San Francisco: Chronicle Books, LLC, 2010); Rachel Travers, "Through a Glass, Brightly: Design Research is Back—As an Installation—in its Old Home," *Boston Globe*, October 29, 2009; Andrew Wagner, "Partners in Design," *Dwell* 6 (October/November 2005), 148–55.

THE EGG AND THE EYE

1965–73, Los Angeles, CA

Described as a "feast . . . for oeuvres and omelets" (Seidenbaum 1965), The Egg and The Eye was located on Wilshire Boulevard, a short distance from the Los Angeles Museum of Art. Established by Edith Wyle and Bette Chase, with support from twenty-five local families in the area, the establishment included a gallery at the entrance and a café serving egg-based dishes at the rear. The name of the gallery was a pun on Betty McDonald's book *The Egg and I* (1945), combined with Wyle's belief that great culture includes both food and art. Like the Anneberg Gallery in San Francisco, The Egg and The Eye offered a mixture of international folk and ethnographic art along with art in craft media by California artists. In their inaugural year, the gallery offered Eskimo sculptures and prints, Native American crafts from New Mexico, Paolo Soleri wind chimes, pottery by Harrison McIntosh and Beatrice Wood, and furniture by Sam Maloof and J. B. Blunk. In 1973 the gallery was reorganized as the nonprofit Los Angeles Craft and Folk Art Museum; since 1999 it has been run by Los Angeles Cultural Affairs Department. —JF

Art Seidenbaum, "Where to Feast on Oeuvres, Omelets," *Los Angeles Times*, December 15, 1965, E1; "History," Craft and Folk Art Museum, www.cafam.org/history.html.

GUMP'S

Founded 1861, San Francisco, CA

Gump's was established in 1861 by brothers Solomon and Gustav Gump as a mirror and frame shop. Solomon's son Alfred Livingston took over the store shortly before the San Francisco earthquake of 1906, which gave him the opportunity to restock the store with elegant furnishings from Japan and China. By the 1920s, the store's offerings included upscale European and Asian objects. Richard Gump, Alfred Livingston's son, took over in 1947 and capitalized on the post–World War II economic boom, expanding the store's offerings to include contemporary Californian designers and craftspeople. His adherence to the "Good Design" philosophy espoused by institutions like MoMA was outlined in his book *Good Taste Costs No More* (1951). During this period, Gump's had a gallery called the Discovery Shop that featured the work of craftspeople such as Win Ng, Edith Heath, and Gertrud and Otto Natzler. —JS

"A.L. Gump, 77, Dies: Authority on Jade," *New York Times*, August 31, 1947, 36; Beatrice Sherman, "Objects of Beauty," *New York Times,* June 5, 1949, BR26; Kevin

Starr, *Golden Dreams: California in an Age of Abundance, 1950–1963* (Oxford; New York: Oxford University Press, 2009); about.gumps.com/history.

KIVA CRAFT CENTER
1956–present, Scottsdale, AZ

In October 1956, Lloyd Kiva New advertised a new building that he had built on Fifth Avenue in Scottsdale, near Craftsman Court in which he maintained a shop. He posed the question, "Have you dreamed of having a Scottsdale location on the most exclusive street in town where Arts, Crafts, Fashions, and Gift Shops cater to a select clientele? We are pleased to invite your inquiry about space in a charming new building on Scottsdale's Fifth Avenue." His building, called the Kiva Craft Center, increased the concentration of artists in the area, which had been growing for some time. Charles and Otellie Loloma and Dick Seeger were among his tenants. By the mid-1950s New was creating fashionable garments, and at this location he also sold a "Kiva blouse kit" for $4.95 containing handscreened textiles and "silver finish" buttons made by Charles Loloma. By 1960, the Center contained twenty-three arts and crafts studios and specialty shops. —JF

Advertisement, [Flagstaff] *Arizona Daily Sun*, October 19, 1956, 6; Advertisement [Phoenix] *Arizona Republic,* June 10, 1959, 62; Marion Eleanor Gridley, *Indians of Today,* (Chicago, Indian Council Fire, 1960), 65.

LEE NORDNESS GALLERY
1958–85, New York, NY

When Lee Nordness (1922–1995) first opened his gallery, he represented contemporary American painters and sculptors, but from the start he aspired to widen the scope to include lesser known American artists working in fine art and craft media. He organized large exhibitions to this end: *Art: USA:'58* held in the exposition hall at Madison Square Garden, and *Art: USA:'59*, mounted in the New York Coliseum at Columbus Circle. For the 1959 event, he invited Paul J. Smith (later the director of MCC) to add thirty craft pieces to the exhibition. In the 1960s, after the success of his exhibitions, he began integrating craft into his gallery. He exhibited contemporary ceramics, glass, and furniture, representing artists such as Sam Maloof, Lenore Tawney, Peter Voulkos, Harvey Littleton, Toshiko Takaezu, and Wendell Castle. The gallery also proved to be an important venue for Nordness to partner with other collectors. In 1962 he collaborated with S. C. Johnson Wax to mount *Art: USA: Now,* an exhibition that presented 102 American works and toured internationally. Six years later, he worked again with Smith and the Johnson Collection to curate the seminal *Objects: USA: The Johnson Collection of Contemporary Crafts,* which showcased more than three hundred pieces from the collection and also traveled throughout the U.S. and abroad. In 1994 Nordness was named an Honorary Fellow of ACC. The Lee Nordness Gallery was one of seven art-based businesses that he operated in New York City; the others were Lee Nordness Galleries Exhibition Section; Forms and Objects; The Little Studio; Lee Nordness Art Advisory Section; American Art Expositions; and the Talent Discovery Company. —NB

Lee Nordness, *Objects: USA* (New York: Viking Press, 1970); Rita Reif, "Lee Nordness, 72, Art Dealer who Promoted Crafts, Dies," *New York Times,* May 23, 1995, B1; "Lee Nordness 1922–1995," *AC* 55 (August 1995), 19; Lee Nordness papers, AAA, SI.

MERCHANDISE MART PROPERTIES
Founded 1930, Chicago, IL
The Merchandise Mart (1930–45); Merchandise Mart Properties, Inc. (1945–)

The art deco, landmark building Merchandise Mart was built by Marshall Field & Co. in 1930 as the largest commercial building in the world offering wholesale goods under one roof. The structure was acquired in 1945 by the prominent Massachusetts businessman and political figure Joseph P. Kennedy and renamed Merchandise Mart Properties, Inc. The sale coincided with a prosperous era for "The Mart," as it was known, during which the boom in postwar home purchases drove unprecedented consumer interest in home furnishings. By 1948 The Mart housed a pedestrian-level department store and eighteen stories of warehouse space. In 1950, through connections between Kennedy and Nelson A. Rockefeller, The Mart began a collaboration with MoMA in New York to produce and present the renowned series of Good Design exhibitions. The Mart continues to operate as a locus of the evolving design market, especially with the inception of the National Exposition of Contract Furnishings (NeoCon), which began in 1969. Since 1998, Merchandise Mart Properties, Inc. has been owned and operated by Vornado Realty. —SF

"Big 'Mart' Is Bought by Joseph Kennedy", *New York Times*, July 22, 1945; "Home Furnishings To Go On Display," *New York Times*, November 10, 1949; "Homemakers Tastes Like Those of Buyers," *New York Times*, May 27, 1953; Rita Reif, "Modern Is the Message in Chicago," *New York Times*, January 10, 1967.

MUSEUM OF CONTEMPORARY CRAFT
Founded 1936, Portland, OR
Oregon Ceramic Studio (1936–65); Contemporary Crafts Gallery (1965–2002); Contemporary Crafts Museum & Gallery (2002–7); Museum of Contemporary Craft (2007)

Led by Mrs. Lydia Herrick Hodge (d. 1960), the Oregon Ceramic Studio was conceived as a nonprofit, community-based organization that focused on education in the ceramic arts. Under the influence of Peter Voulkos, who had ties to the area and was given a show in 1953, a strong interest in sculptural clay developed. Hodge herself explored a range of craft media and in 1950 gave weaver Jack Lenor Larsen his first solo exhibition, one indication of widening scope of the organization. Ceramist Kenneth Shores began his association as a studio technician in 1957 and succeeded Hodge as director in 1964. Shores further expanded the studio's organizational embrace of a wider craft aesthetic that included architecture and design, as well as a stronger association with ACC. —JF

3934 Corbett, *Fifty Years at Contemporary Crafts* (Portland, OR: Contemporary Crafts Association, 1987); "History," Museum of Contemporary Craft, www.museumofcontemporarycraft.org/about/c/history.

NANNY'S DESIGN IN JEWELRY
1957–before 1971, San Francisco, CA

Known for showcasing beautifully crafted, handmade jewelry, German-born Nanny Benderson (1896–1971) operated a modern furniture gallery in San Francisco before becoming a leading retailer of contemporary design through her small gallery at 251 Grant Street. Despite its limited size, the gallery was influential in the region, "representing the finest contemporary jewelry by leading artists of two continents" according to her advertisements in *Craft Horizons*. Benderson showed the work of Bay Area artists merry renk, Margaret De Patta, and Bob Winston, among others. —NB

Yoshiko Uchida. "A San Francisco Jewelry Shop," *CH* 17 (July/August 1957), 12–13; advertisement, *CH* 18 (September/October 1958), 2; Kay Sekimachi, e-mail to Jeannine Falino, December 22, 2010; merry renk, e-mail to Jeannine Falino, January 4, 2011.

NEW BERTHA SCHAEFER GALLERY
1944–75, New York, NY
Bertha Schaefer Gallery (1944–1971); New Bertha Schaefer Gallery (1972–75)

Interior and furniture designer Bertha Schaefer (1895–1971), who opened a design business in New York City in 1924, established her reputation when she decided to start a gallery representing American painters and sculptors, thus bringing together the worlds of applied and fine arts. A designer and graduate of Parsons School of Design, Schaefer was responsible for the first domestic installation of fluorescent lighting. She was recognized for her achievements in 1952 when she received a Good Design award from MoMA. While Schaefer's gallery represented such painters, printmakers, and sculptors as Will Barnet, Alfred H. Maurer, David Smith, and Hale Woodruff, it also showed the work of craftspeople, including Alice Adams, Mariska Karasz, Trude Guermonprez, and Sue Fuller. Schaefer's interest in the crafts prompted her to help sponsor the 1957 MCC exhibition, *Wall Hangings and Rugs.* She also participated the third annual ACC conference in 1959. The gallery continued to operate for a few years after her death. —NB

Mary Roche, "Decoration Shown in Room Exhibit," *New York Times*, March 7, 1947, 22; "Bertha Schaefer, An Art Dealer and Interior Designer, 76, Dies," *New York Times*, May 26, 1971, 46; Bertha Schaefer papers and gallery records, 1914–1975, AAA, SI.

NORTHWEST CRAFT CENTER AND GALLERY
Founded 1963, Seattle, WA

The successful exhibition of the Northwest Designer Craftsmen at the 1962 Seattle World's Fair, called the

Century 21 Exposition, led to the creation of the Northwest Craft Center and Gallery in mid-1963. It was set up in the former Swedish Pavilion on the fairgrounds, renamed the Seattle Center. Craft demonstrations were held for a time in the former Danish Pavilion. Founders of the organization were largely drawn from the Northwest Designer Craftsmen group and included ceramists Robert Sperry, Lorene Spencer, sculptor Norman Warsinske, and weaver Jean Johansen. Also on the board was Donald Foster, the fair's director of exhibits, who later opened Foster/White Gallery. Works in craft media by artists from the northwestern U.S. were featured, with Seattle artists such as Evert Sodergren and Ruth Penington predominating. Ruth Nomura was hired in 1963 as director, a position she retained until 2005. —JF

"Seattle Center Plans for New Additions," *Seattle Times*, May 5, 1963, 19; "Craft Center Gets Exhibit for Display," *Seattle Times*, May 26, 1963, 10; "Visiting Seattle's Northwest Craft Center," *Seattle Times*, August 11, 1963, 20; Leslie Campbell, Northwest Craft Center trustee, e-mail to Jeannine Falino, January 3, 2011.

RABUN STUDIOS
1937–57, New York, NY

Founded by weaver Mary Hambidge (née Crovatt; 1885–1973), Rabun Studios brought the intricate, handweavings of artists from the Rabun Gap area of Georgia, along with work in a variety of media by other contemporary craftspeople, to New York City. Born in Georgia, Hambidge went to finishing school in Cambridge, MA, before moving to New York City where she met and married Canadian-born artist Jay Hambidge. She became passionate about weaving on a trip to Greece, and when her husband died in 1924 and she returned to Georgia, she saw Appalachian handweaving with fresh eyes. By the 1930s, Hambidge had established the Weavers of Rabun along Betty's Creek in Rabun Gap. Based on the production of the Weavers of Rabun, she opened Rabun Studios at 810 Madison Avenue in New York in 1937 to showcase the innovative, handmade designs. Rabun Studios sold draperies, bedding materials, and clothing to such notable clients as Georgia O'Keeffe, Greta Garbo, and President Harry Truman. The gallery also featured the work of contemporary craftsmen such as glass artist Harvey Littleton and potters Robert Turner, Gerry Williams, and William Wyman. Metalsmith Ron Pearson was represented by Rabun in MoMA's Good Design exhibition of 1951. Despite these activities, the store struggled to turn a profit, and it closed in 1957 when Hambidge was in her seventies. The Weavers of Rabun were featured in major museum exhibitions, including *Textiles USA* at MoMA in 1956, and *Weavers of Rabun* held at the Smithsonian Institution in 1958. —NB

Philis Alvic, *Weavers of the Southern Highlands* (Kentucky: University Press of Kentucky, 2003), 96–104; "Hambidge Center for Creative Arts and Sciences," New Georgia Encyclopedia, www.georgiaencyclopedia.org/nge/Article.jsp?id=h-2579.

RAYMOR/
RICHARDS MORGENTHAU & CO.
1941–early 1980s, New York, NY
Raymor (1941–early 1980s); Richards Morgenthau & Co. division (1947–early 1980s)

In the 1920s Irving Richards (1907–2003) owned a West Side bookstore from which he also sold desk accessories. He eventually closed his shop to work for Lightolier. By 1935 he was collaborating with designer Russel Wright to sell Wright's *American Modern* dinnerware. This very successful collaboration led Richards to establish Raymor as a wholesale distributor of contemporary home furnishings and accessories, promoting the work of emerging designers in the U.S. and abroad—Gilbert Rohde, Paul Frankl, Donald Deskey, Walter Dorwin Teague, Charles and Ray Eames, Walter van Nessen, Henry Dreyfuss, Peter Müller-Munk, Ben Seibel, George Nelson, Michael Lax, Eva Zeisel, Arne Jacobsen, Tapio Wirkkala, Hans Wegner, Finn Juhl, Ettore Sotsass, John Mascheroni, Aldo Londi, Paolo Venini, and Marchello Fantoni. In 1947 Richards established the Richards Morgenthau & Co. division, which functioned primarily as the sales and marketing arm for the company. Its showrooms were at 225 Fifth Avenue in New York and in The Merchandise Mart in Chicago. The Raymor part of the firm continued to focus on imports and also manufactured lighting, ceramics, and glass from their Union City, New Jersey factory, with Richards designing many of the pieces himself after 1947. Raymor/Richards Morgenthau & Co. was one of the first American companies to import Scandinavian goods for sale in the U.S., and Richards attributed his firm's success to the accurate targeting of the upper middle class, rather than more affluent clients and customers. Some of the company's most famous goods include Arredoluce's Model No. 12128 *Triennale* floor lamp (1951), the Howard Miller Clock line (1954), and the Scandinavian *Omnibus* wall unit (1962). Raymor/Richards Morgenthau & Co. disbanded in the early 1980s. —SF

Martin Eidelberg, ed., *Design 1935–1965: What Modern Was* (New York: Harry N. Abrams, 2001), 395; Nora Krug, "Irving Richards, 96, Distributor of Modern Design," *New York Times*, November 15, 2003; Charlotte Fiell and Peter Fiell, *1,000 Lights: 1878–1959* (New York: Taschen, 2005), 472.

750 STUDIO
1947–48, Chicago, IL

The short-lived but lively 750 Gallery (750 North Dearborn Street, Chicago) opened September 1947 in the front room of the ground-level apartment of merry renk, Mary Jo Slick (Godfrey), and Olive Oliver (Gilman). The women were students at the Institute of Design. They built their own displays and created a hand-and-eye design as their emblem for the gallery. They mounted a wide array of exhibitions in its brief existence, most of which highlighted artistic activities in the Chicago area: photographs by Institute of Design faculty member Harry Callahan; a posthumous retrospective of work by László Moholy-Nagy,

who had directed the institute; jewelry by Bay Area artist Margaret De Patta, who had been a Moholy-Nagy summer student; watercolors, manuscripts, and books by Henry Miller; enamels by Doris Hall; drawings, paintings, sculptures, and textiles by Warren and Alix MacKenzie, then graduate students at the Art Institute of Chicago; textiles by Julia McVicker and Elsa Regensteiner; and designs by Greenwich Village jeweler Winifred Mason. —JF

Alice Nelson, "Seven Fifty Studio, Imagination and Hard Work Build Studio and Crafts Shop," *Chicago Sun*, October 30, 1947; merry renk papers, AAA, SI.

SHOP ONE
1952–76, Rochester, NY

Shop One was located in a remodeled carriage house at 77 Troup Street, integrating the features of an elegant apartment into a gallery setting, with the purpose of establishing a connection between object, maker, and customer. The shop's environment helped clients to visualize craft objects in their own homes. Established by Tage Frid, Frans Wildenhain, and Jack Prip, all faculty members at the School of American Craftsmen, RIT, with Ron Pearson as manager, Shop One showcased jewelry, raised silver, ceramics, and modern cabinetmaking. Being the only local retail outlet devoted to craft objects, the shop served as an important cultural center for the community. Prip and Pearson also set up a jewelry studio in the Shop One building, allowing their clients greater accessibility while providing themselves with artistic and economic independence. —TT

"Shop One: A Retail Outlet," *CH* 16 (March 1956), 18–23.

THE STORE
SEE COOKE, BETTY

TEXTILES & OBJECTS
1961–63, New York, NY

When Alexander Girard was asked to design a wholesale showroom for Herman Miller, Inc., it had to be different from other showrooms. A year after the Girard-designed restaurant La Fonda Del Sol opened in the Time & Life Building, Textiles & Objects (T&O) opened its doors at 8 East 53rd Street, with Girard-designed textiles, draperies, toys, art, and found objects which Girard designed himself or collected from around the world. T&O was open to the general public and to the trade, and critics said the space resembled a museum exhibition more than textile showroom. Girard's fabrics hung in panels from ceiling to floor, upholstered cabinets, and framed mirrors. One hundred different textile designs, from nongeometric handprints to earthy wool upholsteries, were available for sale at almost any yardage. The store also sold museum-quality folk art gleaned by Girard from his travels, sofa pillows with Girard's distinctive sun motif, cloth dolls designed by Marilyn Neuhart, and stools with reversible cushions, among other works. The combinations of materials, furniture, and lighting coordinated well with modern interiors and inspired showroom visitors with new decorating ideas. It has been suggested that because Herman Miller did not devote enough to marketing the shop, T&O was a financial failure; it closed after a few years. Today the company máXimo, the official agent of the estate of Alexander Girard, continues to sell some of the items that were carried by T&O. —SF

"Shop Is Latest Venture for Designer," *New York Times*, May 22, 1961; "Colorful Textiles Set Off Store's Unusual Objects," ibid.; Laura Forde and Takaya Goto, "Interview with Marilyn and John Neuhart," *Petit Glam No. 7, Modern Crafts Issue* (2003); Sam Grawe, "Archive: Alexander the Great," *Dwell* 8 (February 2008), 90–99.

WILLARD GALLERY
1936–87, New York, NY

The Willard Gallery, founded by Marian Willard Johnson (1904–1985), was among the first in New York to embrace and showcase modern art. While other galleries were driven by market trends and popularity, Johnson chose artists based on her personal connection with their work: Paul Klee, Lyonel Feininger, David Smith, and Mark Tobey, among others. Johnson also recognized the sculptural qualities of modern craft and exhibited the work of fiber artist Lenore Tawney as well as jewelry by Alexander Calder. Johnson saw her gallery as a space for creative energy, not just commercial exchange. This philosophy allowed her to establish long-term relationships with her artists. Johnson also served as a trustee at MoMA, Asia House Gallery, and the Museum of American Folk Art. In 1974 when Johnson was seventy years old, her daughter, Miani Johnson Wirtz, became gallery director, a position she held until the gallery's closing. —NB

Grace Glueck, "Marian Willard Johnson, 81, Dealer in Contemporary Art," *New York Times,* November 7, 1985, D27; Dorothy Dehner, "Obituary," *Art in America* 74 (January 1986), 166; Douglas C. McGill, "Art People: Willard Gallery to Close after Half a Century" *New York Times*, February 6, 1987, C29.

205
MICHAEL COHEN
Heart/Flag, 1964
STONEWARE, GLAZES, SLIP, COLORED CLAY
23½ X 10⅝ X 10⅛ IN. (59.7 X 27 X 25.7 CM)
MUSEUM OF ARTS AND DESIGN, GIFT OF
G. F. HOLMQUIST THROUGH THE AMERICAN
CRAFT COUNCIL, 1967

SELECTED BIBLIOGRAPHY

This bibliography includes source lists—periodicals, archives, and exhibitions—and useful secondary sources, including books and journal articles as well as selected monographs, unpublished writings (primarily PhD dissertations), and later exhibition catalogues. It duplicates some references found in source notes elsewhere in this volume.

ARCHIVES

Many have searchable websites.

Adolph and Esther Gottlieb Foundation, New York, Archives: Adolph Gottlieb papers.

American Craft Council Archive, Minneapolis: Aileen Osborn Webb papers; artist files.

Archives of American Arts, Smithsonian Institution, Washington, DC: American Handicraft Council papers; Boston Society of Arts and Crafts papers; David C. Campbell papers; Wendell Castle papers, 1965–75; Paul Lobel papers; Nanette L. Laitman Documentation Project for Craft and Decorative Arts in America (oral history interviews); Lee Nordness papers; Margaret Merwin Patch papers.

Brooklyn Museum Archives: Art Smith papers.

Harvard University Art Museums, Fogg Art Museum: Stuart Davis papers.

Museum of Modern Art, New York, Archive: Good Design exhibition files, clipping files.

New York State College of Ceramics Archives, Alfred, NY: Charles M. Harder papers.

University of California, Berkeley, Bancroft Library, Regional Oral History Office: Fiber Arts Oral History Series.

University of California, Los Angeles, UCLA Library, Center for Oral History Research.

PERIODICALS

American Ceramics (New York, 1982–2010)

American Fabrics (title varies, New York, 1935–)

Architectural Digest (Los Angeles, 1924–)

Art Digest (New York, 1926–54)

Art in America (New York, 1939–)

Art International (Lugano, Switzerland, 1958–84)

Art International New Edition (Paris, 1987–91)

ARTnews (New York, 1902–)

Arts Magazine (New York, 1926–92)

California Arts and Architecture (Los Angeles, 1929–44); continues as *Arts & Architecture* (1944–85)

Ceramics Monthly (Columbus, OH, 1953–)

Craft Horizons (New York, 1941–79; continues as *American Craft,* 1979–)

Cross-Country Craftsman (Washington, DC, c. 1952–c. 1965)

Ebony (Chicago, 1945–)

Everyday Art Quarterly (Minneapolis, 1946–53; continues as *Design Quarterly* (Minneapolis, 1954–96)

Fiberarts (Asheville, NC, 1976–)

Fine Woodworking (Taunton, MA, 1975–)

Golddust (1976), continues as *Goldsmiths Journal* (1977–80); continues as *Metalsmith* (1980–)

Handweaver & Craftsman (New York, 1950–75)

House Beautiful (New York, 1896–)

Interior Design (New York, 1950–)

Interiors (title varies, New York, 1888–2001)

Journal of Design History (Oxford, 1988–)

Journal of Glass Studies (Corning, NY, 1959–)

Journal of Modern Craft (Oxford, UK, 2008–)

New Glass Review (Corning, NY, 1980–)

School Arts (title varies, Worcester, MA, 1901–)

Shuttle, Spindle & Dyepot (West Hartford, CT, 1969–)

Studies in the Decorative Arts (New York, 1993–2009; continues as *West 86th: A Journal of Decorative Arts, Design History and Material Culture* (2011–)

The Studio Potter (Goffstown, NH, 1973–)

Surface Design Journal (Halsey, OR, 1978–)

SELECTED EXHIBITIONS, 1945–70

Listed chronologically and then alphabetically within years; ongoing exhibitions appear under the first year they were held, at the end of the listings for that year. Most of the exhibitions below were accompanied by catalogues, pamphlets, or brochures. For a complete listing of exhibitions mounted during this period by the Museum of Contemporary Crafts (later, the American Craft Museum and today, Museum of Arts and Design), see Lorna Price, ed. *Forty Years, American Craft Museum* (New York: American Craft Museum, 1996), 42–45. Some early MCC exhibitions were published as articles in *Craft Horizons.*

BEFORE 1945

Wisconsin Designer-Craftsmen Exhibition. Annual. Milwaukee Art Institute (later Milwaukee Art Center), WI, 1916–74.

Exhibition of Work by Artists and Craftsmen of the Western Reserve—"The May Show." Annual, Cleveland, OH, 1919–90; 1993.

National Robineau Memorial Ceramic Exhibitions (later, *Ceramic National Exhibitions; Ceramic Nationals.* Annual, biennial, irregular. Syracuse Museum of Fine Arts (later, Everson Museum of Art), NY, 1932–87.

An Exhibition of Contemporary American Crafts. Baltimore Museum of Art, MD, 1944.

1945–49

Modern Handmade Jewelry. MoMA, 1946.

New Furniture Designed by Charles Eames. MoMA, 1946.

Exhibition for Michigan Artist-Craftsmen. Annual and biannual. Detroit Institute of Arts, 1946–71.

Wichita National Decorative Art Exhibition (later, *Wichita National All Media Crafts Exhibit).* Annual and biennial. Wichita, KS, 1946–72; 1985–present.

Good Design is Your Business; A Guide to Well-Designed Household Objects Made in the U.S.A. Albright-Knox Art Gallery, Buffalo, NY, 1947.

Modern Jewelry for Under Fifty Dollars. Walker Art Center, Everyday Art Gallery, Minneapolis, MN, 1948.

An Exhibition for Modern Living. Detroit Institute of Arts, 1949.

Form in Handwrought Silver. The Metropolitan Museum of Art, New York, 1949–50.

Texas Crafts Exhibition. Annual. Dallas Museum of Fine Arts with Craft Guild of Dallas, 1949–63 and intermittently until 1978.

1950S

Prize Designs for Modern Furniture from the International Competition for Low-Cost Furniture Design. MoMA, 1950.

Good Design: An Exhibition of Home Furnishings. Five installments. MoMA and Merchandise Mart, Chicago, 1950–55.

International Exhibition of Ceramic Art. Annual and biennial. Smithsonian Institution, Museum of History and Technology; Kiln Club, Washington, DC, 1950–63.

Young Americans—Competitive Exhibition. Annual and intermittent. America House (later MCC and ACC), New York, 1950–88.

Knife, Fork, Spoon: The Story of Our Primary Eating Implements and the Development of their Form. Walker Art Center, Minneapolis, MN, 1951.

Los Angeles County Fair, 1921–ongoing. Crafts and design were included from 1951 to 1969.

Craftsmanship in the United States 1952. ACC for the U.S. State Department, 1952.

Fiber-Clay-Metal, U.S.A. Biennial. St. Paul Gallery and School of Art, Minneapolis, MN, 1952–64. Circulated by USIA to Latin America and Asia, 1964.

Northwest Craftsmen's Exhibition. Annual and biennial. Henry Art Gallery, University of Washington, Seattle, 1953–77.

Designer-Craftsmen U.S.A. 1953. Brooklyn Museum; ACEC, New York, 1954. Circulated by AFA.

Design in Scandinavia: An Exhibition of Objects for the Home, from Denmark, Finland, Norway [and] Sweden. National Gallery of Canada, Ottawa, ON, 1954. Circulated in the U.S. by AFA.

Enamel, An Historic Survey to the Present Day. Cooper Union Museum for the Arts of Decoration, New York, 1954.

National Design Exhibition of Jewelry, Ceramics, Silversmithing, Enameling Presented by the Art Department of Texas Western College. Texas Western College Art Department, El Paso, 1954.

California Design. Annual and triennial. Pasadena Art Museum, CA, 1954–61; 1962–71.

Creative Crafts. Biennial. National Collection of Fine Arts, Smithsonian; Kiln Club; Potomac Craftsmen, Washington, DC, 1954–64.

Kansas Designer-Craftsman Exhibition. Annual and intermittent. Various venues, 1954–present.

American Craftsmen 1955. Festival of Contemporary Arts, University of Illinois, Urbana, Illini Union, 1955. Circulated by SITES.

American Jewelry and Related Objects, 1955, First National Exhibition. Huntington Galleries (later, Huntington Art Museum), WV, 1955.

California Designed. Municipal Art Center, Long Beach, CA, in collaboration with the Oakland Museum of Art, 1955.

The Enjoyment of Ceramic Art. Scripps College, Claremont, CA, 1955.

Fifty Years of Danish Silver—In the Georg Jensen Tradition. Corcoran Gallery of Art, Washington, DC, 1955.

International Exhibition of Ceramics. Palais Miramar, Cannes, France, 1955.

New England Craft Exhibition 1955. Worcester Art Museum; Junior League of Worcester, Inc.; Craft Center, Worcester, MA, 1955.

Textiles and Ornamental Arts of India. MoMA, 1955.

American Jewelry and Related Objects: The Second National Exhibition Sponsored by the Hickock Company of Rochester, New York. Memorial Art Gallery of the University of Rochester, NY, 1956. Circulated by SITES.

Craftsmanship in a Changing World. MCC, 1956. Circulated by AFA.

Textiles U.S.A.: A Selection of Contemporary American Textiles Produced by Industry and Craftsmen. MoMA and *American Fabrics* Magazine, 1956.

Designer-Craftsmen of the West, 1957. M. H. De Young Memorial Museum, San Francisco, CA, 1957.

Furniture by Craftsmen. MCC, 1957.

MDC: Exhibition of Works by Designer-Craftsmen of the Mississippi Basin. Chicago: Art Institute of Chicago and Midwest Designer-Craftsmen, 1957. Circulated by SITES.

The Patron Church. MCC, 1957.

Wall Hangings and Rugs. MCC, 1957.

Mid-States Craft Exhibition. Annual and intermittent. Evansville Museum of Arts and Sciences, IN, 1957–present.

Craftsmanship. Los Angeles County Museum, Exposition Park, co-sponsored by the Southern California Designer-Craftsmen, 1958.

Fulbright Designers: An Exhibition Developed in Cooperation with the Institute of International Education, First Shown at the Museum of Contemporary Crafts of the American Craftsmen's Council. MCC, 1958. Circulated by SITES.

International Congress of Contemporary Ceramics–First Exhibition. Brussels, Belgium, 1958.

Art USA 59: A Force, A Language, A Frontier. New York Coliseum, 1959.

Enamels. MCC, 1959. Circulated by SITES.

Glass 1959: A Special Exhibition of International Contemporary Glass. Corning Glass Center, Corning, NY, 1959.

International Congress of Contemporary Ceramics–Second Exhibition. Ostend, Belgium, 1959.

California Crafts. Biennial. E. B. Crocker Art Gallery (later, Crocker Art Museum, and Creative Arts League), Sacramento, CA, 1959–89.

1960S

The Arts of Denmark: An Exhibition Organized by the Danish Society of Arts and Crafts and Industrial Design. The Metropolitan Museum of Art, New York, 1960.

Arts of Southern California VI: Ceramics, A Survey Exhibition Originated by the Long Beach Museum of Art. Long Beach Museum of Art, CA, 1960.

Designed for Silver: An Exhibition of Twenty-Two Award-winning Designs from the International Design Competition for Sterling Silver Flatware. MCC, co-sponsored by ACC and International Silver Company, 1960.

Artist-Craftsmen of Western Europe: Contemporary Crafts from Austria, Belgium, France, the Federal Republic of Germany, Italy, the Netherlands, Spain, Switzerland. MCC and AFA, 1961. Circulated by AFA.

Contemporary Craftsmen of the Far West. MCC, 1961.

International Exhibition of Modern Jewellery, 1890–1961. Worshipful Company of Goldsmiths in association with the Victoria and Albert Museum, London, 1961.

Fabrics International. MCC and Philadelphia Museum College of Art, 1961–62. Circulated by AFA.

Adventures in Art, Century 21 Exposition. Seattle World's Fair, 1962.

Collaboration: Arts and Architect. MCC, 1962.

Creative Craft in Denmark Today: An Exhibition of Contemporary Work. Danish Handcraft Guild and Cooper-Hewitt Museum, New York, 1962.

Craftsmen of the Central States. MCC, 1962–63.

International Tapestry Biennale. Biennial. Centre international de la tapisserie ancienne et moderne, Lausanne, Switzerland, 1962–96.

Craftsmen of the Northeastern States. Worcester Art Museum, MA, sponsored by the ACC, 1963.

Woven Forms. MCC and ACC, 1963.

Piedmont Craft Exhibition. Annual and biennial. Mint Museum of Art and Piedmont Craftsmen, Charlotte, NC, 1963–present.

The American Craftsman. MCC, 1964.

Craftsmen of the Southeastern States. Atlanta Art Association, GA, sponsored by the ACC, 1964.

Craftsmanship Defined. Philadelphia Museum College of Art, 1964.

Designed for Production: The Craftsman's Approach. MCC and ACC, 1964.

Photomural installation [John Mason, Alice Kagawa Parrott, John Prip, Paul Eric Hultberg, and Sam Maloof], Pavilion of American Interiors. New York World's Fair, Flushing Meadows, 1964.

United States of America Section at the Thirteenth Annual of Milan 1964 (Sezione degli Stati Uniti d'America a tredicesima Triennale di Milano). Palazzo dell'arte Parco Sempione Milano, 1964.

Cookies and Breads: The Baker's Art. MCC, 1965.

Oklahoma Designer Craftsmen. Annual, Philbrook Art Center, Tulsa, OK; and University of Oklahoma, Norman, OK, 1965–79.

Abstract Expressionist Ceramics. Art Gallery, University of California, Irvine, 1966.

The Bed. MCC, 1966.

Fantasy Furniture. MCC, 1966.

National Invitational Glass Exhibition. San Jose State College, CA, 1966.

The Object Transformed. MoMA, 1966.

The Toledo Glass National, I–III. Toledo Museum of Art, OH, 1966, 1969, 1970. Selection circulated by SITES, 1970.

Craftsmen '67. Museum of the Philadelphia Civic Center, 1967.

Funk. University of California, University Art Museum, Berkeley, CA, 1967.

Architectural Glass. MCC, 1968.

Body Covering. MCC, 1968.

Directions 1968. Philadelphia College of Art, 1968.

Experimental Metalsmithing: Carnegie Grant Project. Indiana University, Bloomington, 1968.

Southwest Craftsmen 1968. Dallas Museum of Fine Arts and the Craft Guild of Dallas, TX, 1968.

Plastic As Plastic. MCC and Hooker Chemical Corporation, 1968–69.

Regional Craft Biennial. Louisville Art Center Association, KY, 1968–73.

Fibers, Fabrics 69. John Michael Kohler Arts Center, Sheboygan, WI, 1969.

Fiber Structure 69. University of Wisconsin, Milwaukee School of Art, 1969.

Objects: USA: The Johnson Collection of Contemporary Crafts. National Gallery, Washington, DC, 1969. Circulated nationally and internationally by the American Craft Museum.

ODC: Ohio Designer Craftsmen Invitational Exhibition. Kent State University School of Art, 1969.

Survey 1969: An Invitational Exhibition of California Artist-Craftsmen. Fine Arts Gallery of San Diego (today's San Diego Museum of Art), 1969.

Wall Hangings, MoMA, 1969.

1970
Contemplation Environments. MCC, 1970.

Craftsmen '70. Museum of the Philadelphia Civic Center, 1970.

Goldsmith '70. Minnesota Museum of Art, St. Paul, and MCC, 1970.

National Council on Education for the Ceramic Arts Glass Invitational. California College of Arts and Crafts, Oakland, 1970.

SECONDARY SOURCES

Abercrombie, Stanley. George Nelson: The Design of Modern Design. Cambridge, MA: MIT Press, 1995.

Abstract Expressionism: Further Evidence, Painting & Sculpture. Exh. cat. New York: Michael Rosenfeld Gallery, LLC, 2009.

Adams, Henry, et al. Edris Eckhardt: Visionary and Innovator in American Studio Ceramics and Glass. Lakewood, OH: Cleveland Artists Foundation, 2006.

Adamson, Glenn. The Craft Reader. Oxford: Berg Publishers, 2010.

———. Thinking Through Craft. Oxford and New York: Berg, 2007.

Adamson, Jeremy. The Furniture of Sam Maloof. Washington, DC: Smithsonian American Art Museum; New York: W. W. Norton & Company, 2001.

Aerni, April Laskey. "The Economics of the Crafts Industry." PhD diss., University of Cincinnati, 1987.

Albers, Anni. On Designing. New Haven, CT: Pellango Press, 1959.

———. On Weaving. Middletown, CT: Wesleyan University Press, 1965.

Albrecht, Donald, Robert Schonfeld, and Lindsay Stamm Shapiro. Russel Wright: Creating American Lifestyle. New York: Harry N. Abrams, 2001.

Albrecht, Donald, et al. The Work of Charles and Ray Eames: A Legacy of Invention. New York: Harry N. Abrams in association with the Library of Congress and Vitra Design Museum, 1997.

Alfoldy, Sandra. Crafting Identity: The Development of Professional Fine Craft in Canada. Toronto: McGill/Queen's University Press, 2005.

American Craftsmen's Council. Asilomar, First Annual Conference of American Craftsmen, Sponsored by the American Craftsmen's Council, June 1957. New York: ACC, 1957.

———. The Craftsman's World, Third Annual Conference, Lake George, New York. New York: American Craftsmen's Council, 1959.

———. Craftsmen of the Southwest. San Francisco: ACC Southwest Region, 1965.

———. Dimension of Design, Second Annual Conference, American Craftsmen's Council, June 1958, Lake Geneva, Wisconsin. New York: American Craftsmen's Council, 1958.

———. Research in the Crafts, Fourth Annual Conference, American Craftsmen's Council, Seattle, Washington. New York: American Craftsmen's Council, 1961.

American Craftsmen's Council and Brooklyn Museum. Designer-Craftsmen U.S.A. 1953. New York: Blanchard Press, 1953.

"American Jewelry Designers and Their Work." Design Quarterly, no. 33 (1955): 3–13.

Armstrong, Elizabeth. Birth of the Cool: California Art, Design, and Culture at Midcentury. Newport Beach, CA: Orange County Museum of Art and Prestel Publishing, 2007.

Ashton, Dore. Noguchi: East and West. New York: Alfred A. Knopf, 1992.

Austin, Carole. June Schwarcz: Forty Years/Forty Pieces. San Francisco: San Francisco Craft & Folk Art Museum, 1998.

Auther, Elissa. "The Decorative, Abstraction, and the Hierarchy of Art and Craft in the Art Criticism of Clement Greenberg." Oxford Art Journal 27 no. 3 (2004): 295–320.

———. "Fiber Art and the Hierarchy of Art and Craft, 1960–1980." *The Journal of Modern Craft* 1 (March 2008): 13–34.

———. *String Felt Thread, The Hierarchy of Art and Craft in American Art*. Minneapolis and London: University of Minnesota Press, 2010.

Baizerman, Suzanne, ed. *Marvin Lipofsky: A Glass Odyssey*. Oakland, CA: Oakland Museum of California; distributed by the University of Washington Press, 2003.

Ball, Frederick Carlton. *Decorating Pottery with Clay, Slip and Glaze*. Columbus, OH: Professional Publications, 1967.

Ball, Frederick Carlton, and Janice Penney Lovoos. *Making Pottery without a Wheel: Texture and Form in Clay*. New York: Reinhold, 1965.

Banham, Reyner, ed. *The Aspen Papers: Twenty Years of Design Theory from the International Design Conference in Aspen*. New York and Washington: Praeger Publishers, 1974.

Bates, Kenneth Francis. *Enameling: Principles and Practice*. Cleveland: World Publishing Co., 1951.

———. *The Enamelist*. 1967. Reprint, Middlebourne, WV: Wooden Porch Books, 1991.

Belgrad, Daniel. *The Culture of Spontaneity, Improvisation and the Arts in Postwar America*. Chicago and London: University of Chicago Press, 1998.

Bell, Robert, Arline Fisch, et al. *Elegant Fantasy: The Jewelry of Arline Fisch*. San Diego: San Diego Historical Society; Stuttgart, Germany: Arnoldsche Art Publishers, 1999.

Bernstein, Melvin Herbert. *Art and Design at Alfred: A Chronicle of a Ceramics College*. Philadelphia: Art Alliance Press; London and Cranbury, NJ: Associated University Presses, 1986.

Beyer, Steven, and Matilda McQuaid. *George Nakashima and the Modernist Moment*. Doylestown, PA: James A. Michener Art Museum, 2001.

Bovin, Murray. *Jewelry Making, For Schools, Tradesmen, [and] Craftsmen*. Forest Hills, NY: n.p., 1952.

Bray, Hazel V. *The Potter's Art in California, 1885 to 1955*. Oakland, CA: Oakland Museum, 1980.

———. *The Tapestries of Trude Guermonprez: The Oakland Museum*. Oakland, CA: Oakland Museum, 1982.

Braznell, W. Scott. "The Early Career of Ronald Hayes Pearson and the Post–World War II Revival of American Silversmithing and Jewelrymaking." *Winterthur Portfolio* 34 (winter 1999): 189.

Brown, Milton W., and Blanche R. Brown. *Jewelry by Ed Wiener: A Retrospective Exhibition*. Exh. cat. New York: Fifty/50 Gallery, 1988.

Bruce, Gordon. *Eliot Noyes: A Pioneer of Design and Architecture in the Age of American Modernism*. London and New York: Phaidon, 2006.

Brynner, Irena. *Jewelry as an Art Form*. New York: Van Nostrand Reinhold, 1979.

———. *Modern Jewelry, Design and Technique*. New York: Reinhold Book Corp., 1968.

Burton, John. *Glass: Philosophy and Method, Hand-blown, Sculptured, Colored*. Philadelphia: Chilton, 1967.

Byars, Mel. *The Design Encyclopedia*. London: Laurence King Publishing; New York: MoMA, 1994.

Byrd, Joan Falconer. *Harvey Littleton: A Retrospective Exhibition*. Exh. cat. Atlanta: High Museum of Art, 1984.

Caplan, Ralph. *Connections: The Work of Charles and Ray Eames*. Los Angeles: UCLA Art Council, 1976.

Carney, Margaret, Ron Kransler, and Wallace Higgins. *Glidden Pottery*. Alfred, NY: Schein-Joseph International Museum of Ceramic Art, 2001.

Claire Zeisler: A Retrospective. Exh. cat. Chicago: Art Institute of Chicago, 1979.

Clark, Garth. *American Ceramics 1876 to the Present*. New York: Abbeville Press, 1987.

———. *The Lustrous Art and Life of Beatrice Wood: Gilded Vessel*. Madison, WI: Guild Publishing; Cincinnati, OH: Distributed by North Light Books, 2001.

Clark, Garth, and Margie Hughto. *A Century of Ceramics in the United States 1878–1978*. New York: E. P. Dutton and Everson Museum of Art, 1979.

Clark, Robert Judson, et al. *Design in America: The Cranbrook Vision, 1925–1950*. New York: Harry N. Abrams, in association with the Detroit Institute of Arts and The Metropolitan Museum of Art, 1983.

Commager, Henry Steele. *The American Mind: An Interpretation of American Thought and Character Since the 1880s*. New Haven, CT: Yale University Press, 1950.

Constantine, Mildred, and Jack Lenor Larsen. *Beyond Craft: The Art Fabric*. New York: Van Nostrand Reinhold Company, 1972.

Contemporary Silversmithing . . . The Stretching Method. New York: Handy & Harman, 1952.

Cooke Jr., Edward S., Gerald W. R. Ward, and Kelly H. L'Ecuyer. *The Maker's Hand: American Studio Furniture, 1940–1990*. Boston: MFA Publications, 2003.

Cooper, Emmanuel. *Bernard Leach: Life and Work*. New Haven, CT: Published for the Paul Mellon Centre for Studies in British Art by Yale University Press, 2003.

Cornell, Daniell, et al. *The Sculpture of Ruth Asawa: Contours in the Air*. Exh. cat. San Francisco: Fine Arts Museums of San Francisco; Berkeley: University of California Press, 2006.

Cotter, Holland, George Emerl, and Lenore Tawney. *Lenore Tawney: Signs on the Wind, Postcard Collages*. Exh. cat. Petaluma, CA: Pomegranate Communications, 2002.

Craver, Margret. *Handwrought Silver*. New York: Handy & Harman, 1947.

Creech, Jane K., Aric Chen, and Anne Hellman, eds. *Vladimir Kagan: A Lifetime of Avant-Garde Design*. New York, NY: Pointed Leaf Press, LLC, 2004.

Crowley, David, and Jane Pavitt, eds. *Cold War Modern: Design 1945–1970*. London: V&A Publishing, 2008.

D'Amico, Victor, Moreen Maser, and Frances Wilson. *Art for the Family*. New York: MoMA, 1954.

Dancygner, Ruth. *Edris Eckhardt, Cleveland Sculptor*. Cleveland: John Carroll University, 1990.

de Beauvoir, Simone. *America Day by Day*. New York: Grove Press, 1953.

Drexler, Arthur. *Furniture from the Design Collection, The Museum of Modern Art*. New York: MoMA, 1973.

Drexler, Arthur, and Greta Daniel. *Introduction to Twentieth Century Design: From the Collection of The Museum of Modern Art*. New York: MoMA and Doubleday, 1959.

Drutt, Helen Williams, and Peter Dormer. *Jewelry of Our Time: Art, Ornament, and Obsession*. New York: Rizzoli International Publications, 1995.

Earl McCutchen: Craftsmanship in Ceramics and Glass. Exh. cat. Athens, GA: Georgia Museum of Art, 2003.

Eaton, Allen H. *Handicrafts of New England*. New York: Harper and Brothers, 1949.

Eidelberg, Martin, ed. *Design 1935–1955: What Modern Was: Selections from the Liliane and David M. Stewart Collection*. Exh. cat. New York: Harry N. Abrams in association with Musée des Arts Décoratifs de Montréal, 1991.

Eisenbrand, Jochen, ed. *George Nelson, Architect, Writer, Designer, Teacher*. Exh. cat. Weil-am-Rhein, Germany: Vitra Design Museum, 2008.

Emery, Olivia H. *Craftsman Lifestyle: The Gentle Revolution*. Pasadena: California Design Publications, 1977.

Faberman, Hilarie. *Fired at Davis: Figurative Ceramic Sculpture by Robert Arneson, Visiting Professors, and Students at the University of California at Davis, the*

Paula and Ross Turk Collection. Exh. cat. Stanford, CA: Iris & B. Gerald Cantor Center for Visual Arts at Stanford University, 2005.

Failing, Patricia. Howard Kottler: Face to Face. Seattle: University of Washington Press, 1995.

Falino, Jeannine. "Metalsmithing at Midcentury." In Sculptural Concerns: Contemporary American Metal Working, 10–27. Exh. cat. Cincinnati, OH: Contemporary Arts Center; Fort Wayne, IN: Fort Wayne Museum of Art, 1993.

Falino, Jeannine, and Yvonne Markowitz. "Margret Craver, Jeweler, Educator, Visionary." Journal of the American Society of Jewelry Historians 1 (spring 1997): 9–23.

Falino, Jeannine, and Gerald W. R. Ward, eds. Silver of the Americas, 1600–2000: American Silver in the Museum of Fine Arts, Boston. Boston: MFA Publications, 2008.

Fehrman, Cherie. Postwar Interior Design, 1945–1960. New York: Van Nostrand Reinhold Co., 1987.

Fitzgerald, Oscar P. Studio Furniture of the Renwick Gallery, Smithsonian American Art Museum. Washington, DC: Smithsonian American Art Museum, 2008.

Franke, Lois E. Handwrought Jewelry. Bloomington, IL: McKnight & McKnight, 1962.

Frantz, Susanne K. Contemporary Glass: A World Survey from the Corning Museum of Glass. New York: Harry N. Abrams, 1989.

Friedman, Mildred, et al. Jack Lenor Larsen: Creator and Collector. Exh. cat. New York: Museum of Arts & Design and Merrell Publishers Limited, 2004.

Fuller, Buckminster. Operating Manual for Spaceship Earth. Carbondale, IL: Southern Illinois University Press, 1969.

Galbraith, John Kenneth. The Affluent Society. Boston: Houghton Mifflin, 1958.

Greenbaum, Toni. "California Dreamin': Modernist Jewelers in Los Angeles, 1940–1970." Metalsmith 22 (winter 2002): 40–47.

———. Messengers of Modernism: American Studio Jewelry 1940–1960. Exh. cat. New York: Montreal Museum of Decorative Arts; Paris: Flammarion, 1996.

Grover, Lee, and Roy Grover. Contemporary Art Glass. New York: Crown Publishing, 1975.

Haddow, Robert H., Pavilions of Plenty: Exhibiting American Culture Abroad in the 1950s. Washington, DC: Smithsonian Institution Press, 1997.

Hall, Julie. Tradition and Change: The New American Craftsman. New York: E. P. Dutton, 1977.

Halper, Vicki, and Diane Douglas, eds. Choosing Craft: The Artist's Viewpoint. Chapel Hill: University of North Carolina Press, 2009.

Halsey, Elizabeth Tower. Ladies' Home Journal Book of Interior Decoration. Philadelphia: Curtis Publishing Company, 1954.

Hannah, Caroline. "Henry Varnum Poor: Crow House, Craft, and Design." PhD diss., Bard College, forthcoming.

Harrington, LaMar. Ceramics in the Pacific Northwest: A History. Seattle: Henry Art Gallery and University of Washington Press, 1979.

Harris, Mary Emma. The Arts at Black Mountain College. Cambridge, MA: MIT Press, 2002.

Harwood, Barry R. From the Village to Vogue: Modernist Jewelry of Art Smith. Exh. cat. Brooklyn: Brooklyn Museum, 2009.

Haskell, Barbara. H. C. Westermann. New York: Whitney Museum of American Art, 1978.

Held, Peter. A Ceramic Continuum: Fifty Years of the Archie Bray Influence. Exh. cat. Helena, MT: Holter Museum of Art, in association with the University of Washington Press, Seattle, 2001.

Helfrich, Kurt G. F., and William Whitaker, eds. Crafting a Modern World: The Architecture and Design of Antonin and Noémi Raymond. New York: Princeton Architectural Press, 2006.

Hennessey, William J. Russel Wright: American Designer. Hamilton, NY: Gallery Association of New York State, 1983.

Herman, Lloyd E., Looking Forward, Glancing Back: Northwest Designer Craftsmen at 50. Bellingham, WA: Whatcom Museum of History & Art; Seattle: Distributed by the University of Washington Press, 2004.

Hiesinger, Kathryn B., and George H. Marcus. Landmark of Twentieth-Century Design: An Illustrated Handbook. New York: Abbeville Press Publishers, 1993.

Hughes, Graham. Modern Jewelry: An International Survey, 1890–1967. London: Studio Vista, 1968.

———. Modern Silver Throughout the World, 1880–1967. New York: Crown Publishers, 1967.

Hughto, Margie. New Works in Clay by Contemporary Painters and Sculptors. Exh. cat. Syracuse: Everson Museum of Art, 1976.

Jackson, Lesley. The New Look: Design in the Fifties. New York: Thames and Hudson, 1991.

Jazzar, Bernard N., and Harold B. Nelson. Painting with Fire. Exh. cat. Long Beach, CA: Long Beach Museum of Art, 2007.

The Jewelry of Margaret De Patta: A Retrospective Exhibition. Exh. cat. Oakland: Oakland Museum, 1976.

John Prip: Master Metalsmith. Exh. cat. Providence, RI: Museum of Art, Rhode Island School of Design; New York: American Craft Museum, 1987.

Johnson, Donald-Brian. Higgins: Adventures In Glass. Atglen, PA: Schiffer Publishing Ltd., 1997.

Kangas, Matthew. Jim Leedy: Artist Across Boundaries. Exh. cat. Kansas City, MO: Kansas City Art Institute, 2000.

———. Robert Sperry: Bright Abyss. Exh. cat. Pomona, CA: American Museum of Ceramic Art, 2008.

———. Robert Willson: Image-Maker. San Antonio, TX: Pace-Willson Foundation; Seattle: University of Washington Press, 2001.

Karasz, Mariska. Adventures in Stitches: A New Art of Embroidery. New York: Funk & Wagnalls, 1949.

Kardon, Janet, ed. Craft in the Machine Age 1920–1945. Vol. 3 of The History of Twentieth-Century American Craft. Exh. cat. New York: Harry N. Abrams in association with the American Craft Museum, 1995.

———. The Ideal Home, 1900–1920. Vol. 1 of The History of Twentieth-Century American Craft. Exh. cat. New York: Harry N. Abrams in association with the American Craft Museum, 1993.

———. Revivals! Diverse Traditions, 1920–1945. Vol. 2 of The History of Twentieth-Century American Craft. Exh. cat. New York: Harry N. Abrams in association with the American Craft Museum, 1994.

Kaufmann, Edgar, Jr. Prestini's Art in Wood. Lake Forest, IL: Pocahontas Press; distributed by Pantheon Books, 1950.

———. What is Modern Design? Vol. 3 of Introductory Series to the Modern Arts. New York: MoMA, 1950.

———. What is Modern Interior Design? Vol. 4 of Introductory Series to the Modern Arts. New York: MoMA, 1953.

Kelly, Barbara M. Expanding the American Dream: Building and Rebuilding Levittown. Albany: State University of New York Press, 1993.

Kepes, Gyorgy. The Language of Vision. Chicago: P. Theobald, 1951.

Kessler, Jane, and Dick Burrows. Rude Osolnik: A Life Turning Wood. Louisville, KY: Crescent Hill Books, 1997.

Kinney, Kay. Glass Craft: Designing, Forming, Decorating. Philadelphia: Chilton, 1962.

Kirkham, Pat. *Charles and Ray Eames: Designers of the Twentieth Century*. Cambridge, MA: MIT Press, 1995.

———. "Humanizing Modernism: The Crafts, 'Functioning Decoration' and the Eameses." *Journal of Design History* 11, no. 1 (1998): 15–29.

———. ed. *Women Designers in the USA, 1900–2000: Diversity and Difference*. Exh. cat. New York: Bard Graduate Center for Studies in the Decorative Arts; London: Yale University Press, 2000.

Komanecky, Michael. *American Potters: Mary and Edwin Scheier*. Manchester, NH: Currier Gallery of Art, 1993.

Koplos, Janet, and Bruce Metcalf. *Makers: A History of American Studio Craft*. Chapel Hill, NC: University of North Carolina Press, 2010.

Labino, Dominick. *Visual Art in Glass*. Dubuque, IA: W. C. Brown Co., 1967.

Larsen, Jack Lenor. *Jack Lenor Larsen: A Weaver's Memoir*. New York: Harry N. Abrams, Inc., 1998.

Lauria, Jo, and Gretchen Adkins. *Color and Fire: Defining Moments in Studio Ceramics, 1950–2000: Selections from the Smits Collection and Related Works at the Los Angeles County Museum of Art*. Exh. cat. Los Angeles: LACMA in association with Rizzoli International Publications, 2000.

Lauria, Jo, and Suzanne Baizerman. *California Design: The Legacy of West Coast Craft and Style*. San Francisco: Chronicle Books, 2005.

Lauria, Jo, and Stephen Fenton. *Craft in America: Celebrating Two Centuries of Artists and Objects*. New York: Clarkson Potter, 2007.

Leach, Bernard. *A Potter's Book*. 1940. Reprint, Levittown, NY: Transatlantic Arts, 1976.

Lebow, Edward. *Ken Ferguson*. Exh. cat. Kansas City, MO: Nelson-Atkins Museum of Art, 1995.

Lesley, Jackson. *Twentieth Century Pattern Design: Textile & Wallpaper Pioneers*. Princeton, NJ: Princeton Architectural Press, 2007.

Levin, Elaine. *Glen Lukens: Pioneer of the Vessel Aesthetic*. Exh. cat. Los Angeles: Fine Arts Gallery, California State University, 1982.

———. *The History of American Ceramics, 1607 to the Present: From Pipkins and Bean Pots to Contemporary Forms*. New York: Harry N. Abrams, Inc., 1988.

Littleton, Harvey Kline. *Glassblowing: A Search for Form*. New York: Van Nostrand Reinhold, 1971.

Lovenheim, Barbara. *Breaking Ground: A Century of Craft in Western New York*. Rochester, NY: Institute of Technology, 2010.

Lynggaard, Finn, ed. *The Story of Studio Glass: The Early Years, A Historical Documentation Told by the Pioneers*. Copenhagen: Rhodos, 1998.

Lynn, Martha Drexler. *American Studio Glass, 1960–1990*. Manchester, VT: Hudson Hills Press, 2004.

———. *Clay Today—Contemporary Ceramicists and Their Work: A Catalogue of the Howard and Gwen Laurie Smits Collection at the Los Angeles County Museum of Art*. Exh. cat. Los Angeles: Los Angeles County Museum of Art; San Francisco: Chronicle Books, 1990.

MacNaughton, Mary Davis, Kay Koeninger, and Martha Drexler Lynn. *Revolution in Clay: The Marer Collection of Contemporary Ceramics*. Claremont, CA: Ruth Chandler Williamson Gallery, Scripps College; Seattle: University of Washington Press, 1994.

Mangan, Kathleen Nugent, ed. *Lenore Tawney: A Retrospective*. Exh. cat. New York: Rizzoli and American Craft Museum, 1990.

Manhart, Marcia, and Tom Manhart, eds. *The Eloquent Object: The Evolution of American Art in Craft Media Since 1945*. Exh. cat. Tulsa, OK: Philbrook Museum of Art, 1987.

Marling, Karal Ann. *As Seen on TV: The Visual Culture of Everyday Life in the 1950s*. Cambridge, MA: Harvard University Press, 1994.

Martin, Charles James, and Victor D'Amico. *How to Make Modern Jewelry*. New York: MoMA, 1949.

Martin, Richard Harrison. *Design—Jewelry—Betty Cooke*. Exh. cat. Baltimore: Maryland Institute, College of Art, 1995.

Martindale, Don. "Timidity, Conformity, and the Search for Personal Identity." *Annals of the American Academy of Political and Social Science* 378 (July 1968): 83–86.

Masterworks of Contemporary American Jewelry: Sources and Concepts. Exh. cat. London: Victoria and Albert Museum, 1985.

Maybee, Spice. "Forming the Studio Craft Movement: *Craft Horizons*, 1941–1959." MA thesis, Bard Graduate Center for Studies in the Decorative Arts, Design, and Culture, 2009.

McCutchen, Earl. "Glass Molding: Experimenting on a Low Budget." *CH* 15 (May/June 1955): 38–39.

McFadden, David Revere, ed. *Scandinavian Modern Design, 1880–1980*. New York: Harry N. Abrams, 1982.

McLaughlin, Jean W., ed. *The Nature of Craft and the Penland Experience*. Exh. cat. New York: Lark Books, 2004.

Meikle, Jeffrey L. *Design in the USA*. Oxford: Oxford University Press, 2005.

Meilach, Dona Z. *Contemporary Art with Wood: Creative Techniques and Appreciation*. New York: Crown Publishers, 1968.

Merrill, Todd, and Julie Iovine, eds. *Modern Americana: Studio Furniture from High Craft to High Glam*. New York: Rizzoli, 2007.

Miller, R. Craig. *Modern Design in the Metropolitan Museum of Art, 1890–1990*. New York: Metropolitan Museum of Art and Harry N. Abrams, 1990.

The Modernist Jewelry of Claire Falkenstein. Exh. cat. Long Beach, CA: Long Beach Museum of Art, 2004.

Moffett, Kenneth, and Jonathan Fairbanks. *Directions in Contemporary American Ceramics*. Boston: Museum of Fine Arts, Boston, 1984.

Morris, William. *News from Nowhere*. Boston: Roberts Brothers, 1890.

Morse, Edgar W., ed. *Silver in the Golden State: Images and Essays Celebrating the History and Art of Silver in California*. Oakland, CA: Oakland Museum History Department, 1986.

Morton, Philip. *Contemporary Jewelry: A Studio Handbook*. New York: Holt, Rinehart and Winston, 1970.

Munroe, Alexandra. *The Third Mind: American Artists Contemplate Asia, 1860–1989*. Exh. cat. New York: Guggenheim Museum, 2009.

Nagle, Virginia. "American Weaving." *Design Quarterly* 48/49 (1960): 1, 3–53.

Nakashima, George. *The Soul of a Tree: A Woodworker's Reflections*. Tokyo, New York, and San Francisco: Kodansha International, 1981.

Neuhart, John, Marilyn Neuhart, and Ray Eames. *Eames Design: The Work of the Office of Charles and Ray Eames*. New York: Harry N. Abrams, 1989.

Noguchi, Isamu. *A Sculptor's World*. Foreword by R. Buckminster Fuller. New York: Harper & Row, 1968.

Oldknow, Tina. *Richard Marquis Objects*. Seattle: University of Washington Press, 1997.

Ostergard, Derek. *George Nakashima: Full Circle*. New York: American Craft Museum, 1989.

Paul Soldner: A Retrospective. Exh. cat. Claremont, CA: Scripps College; Seattle: University of Washington Press, 1991.

Paz, Octavio. *In Praise of Hands: Contemporary Crafts of the World*. Foreword by James S. Plaut. Greenwich, CT: New York Graphic Society, 1974.

Perrot, Paul. "New Directions in Glassmaking." *CH* 20 (November/December 1960): 22.

Perry, Barbara, ed. *American Ceramics: The Collection of the Everson Museum of Art.* New York: Rizzoli, 1989.

Peterson, Susan. *The Living Tradition of Maria Martinez.* Tokyo: Kodansha International; New York: Harper and Row, 1977.

———. *Shoji Hamada: A Potter's Way and Work.* Tokyo: Kodansha International, 1974.

Phillips, Lisa, and David A. Hanks. *High Styles: Twentieth-Century American Design.* New York: Whitney Museum of American Art in association with Summit Books, 1985.

Plagens, Peter. *Sunshine Muse: Art on the West Coast, 1945–1970.* Berkeley, Los Angeles, and London: University of California Press, 1999.

Poor, Henry Varnum. *The Book of Pottery: From Mud to Immortality.* Englewood Cliffs, NJ: Prentice-Hall, 1958.

Port, Jane L. *Karl Drerup (1904–2000) Enchanted Gardens: Enamels by an American Master.* Plymouth, NH: Karl Drerup Gallery, Plymouth State University, 2007.

Potter, David. *People of Plenty: Economic Abundance and the American Character.* Chicago: University of Chicago Press, 1954.

Price, Lorna, ed. *Forty Years, American Craft Museum.* New York: American Craft Museum, 1996.

Pulos, Arthur Jon. *The American Design Adventure, 1940–1975.* Cambridge, MA: MIT Press, 1988.

———. *American Design Ethic: A History of Industrial Design to 1940.* Cambridge, MA: MIT Press, 1983.

Pye, David. *The Nature of Design.* London: Studio Vista/Van Nostrand Reinhold Company, 1964.

Rappaport, Brooke Kamin, and Kevin L. Stayton, eds. *Vital Forms: American Art and Design in the Atomic Age, 1940–1960.* Exh. cat. New York: Brooklyn Museum of Art and Harry N. Abrams, 2001.

Reich, Charles. *The Greening of America.* New York: Random House, 1970.

Rhodes, Daniel. *Clay and Glazes for the Potter.* New York: Greenberg, 1957.

———. *Kilns: Design, Construction, and Operation.* Philadelphia, Chilton Book Co., 1968.

———. *Stoneware and Porcelain: The Art of High Fired Pottery.* Philadelphia: Chilton Co., Book Division, 1959.

Riesman, David A. *Individualism Reconsidered, and Other Essays.* Glencoe, IL: Free Press, 1954.

Riesman, David, Nathan Glazer, and Reuel Denny. *The Lonely Crowd: A Study of the Changing American Character.* New Haven, CT: Yale University Press, 1950.

Robledo, Maria, A. S. C. Rower, and Holton Rower. *Calder Jewelry.* Exh. cat. New York: Calder Foundation; West Palm Beach: Norton Museum of Art; New Haven, CT: Yale University Press, 2007.

Robsjohn-Gibbings, Terrence Harold. *Good-bye Mr. Chippendale.* New York: Alfred A. Knopf, 1944.

———. *Homes of the Brave.* New York: Alfred A. Knopf, 1954.

Rogers, Kate Ellen. *The Modern House U.S.A.: Its Design and Decoration.* New York and Evanston, IL: Harper and Row, 1962.

Rosenberg, Alan. "Modern American Silver." *Modernism* 4 (fall 2001): 24–31.

Rossbach, Ed. "Fiber in the Forties." *AC* 42 (October/November 1982): 18.

Roszak, Theodore. *The Making of a Counterculture: Reflections on the Technocratic Society and its Youthful Opposition.* New York: Doubleday & Company, Inc., 1969.

Rowe, Ann Pollard, and Rebecca A. T. Stevens. *Ed Rossbach: 40 Years of Exploration and Innovation in Fiber Art.* Asheville, NC: Lark Books; Washington, DC: Textile Museum, 1990.

Schmidt, Kenneth E. "Conflict and Consonance: A Study of Two Traditions in the History of Modern Craft, Arts and Crafts, Craft History." PhD diss., Pennsylvania State University, 1991.

Schon, Marbeth. *Form and Function: American Modernist Jewelry, 1940–1970.* Atglen, PA: Schiffer Publishing, 2008.

Schuler, Frederic. *Flameworking: Glassmaking for the Craftsman.* Philadelphia: Chilton, 1968.

Schwartz, Judith. *Confrontational Ceramics: The Artist as Social Critic.* London: A&C Black; Philadelphia: University of Pennsylvania Press, 2008.

Selz, Peter. *Art of Engagement, Visual Politics in California and Beyond.* Exh. cat. Berkeley and Los Angeles: University of California Press; San Jose: San Jose Museum of Art, 2006.

A Short Guide to World Crafts. New York: American Craftsmen's Council, 1964.

Simpson, Tommy. *Two Looks to Home: The Art of Tommy Simpson.* Boston: Little, Brown and Company, 1999.

Sims, Lowery Stokes, and Stephen Polcari. *Richard Pousette-Dart (1916–1992).* Exh. cat. New York: Metropolitan Museum of Art, 1997.

Slivka, Rose. *Peter Voulkos, A Dialogue with Clay.* New York: New York Graphic Society, 1978.

———. "Hard String." *CH* 32 (April 1972): 17.

———. "The New Ceramic Presence." *CH* 21 (July/August 1961): 30–37.

———. "U.S. Crafts in an Industrial Society." *CH* 19 (March/April 1959): 10.

Slivka, Rose, ed., with Aileen O. Webb and Margaret Merwin Patch (essays). *The Crafts of the Modern World.* New York: Horizon Press, 1968.

Smith, Dido. "Gold Glass: Ancient Technique Rediscovered." *CH* 16 (November/December 1956): 12–15.

Smith, Elizabeth A. T., and Esther McCoy. *Blueprints For Modern Living: History and Legacy of the Case Study Houses.* Los Angeles: Museum of Contemporary Art; Cambridge, MA: MIT Press, 1989.

Smith, Paul J., and Edward Lucie-Smith. *Craft Today: Poetry of the Physical.* New York: American Craft Museum and Weidenfeld and Nicolson, 1986.

Solberg, Ramona. *Inventive Jewelry-making.* New York: Van Nostrand Reinhold, 1972.

Sowers, Robert. *The Lost Art: A Survey of One Thousand Years of Stained Glass.* New York: G. Wittenborn, 1954.

———. *Stained Glass: An Architectural Art.* New York: Universe Books, 1961.

Stern, Jewel, Kevin W. Tucker, and Charles L. Venable. *Modernism in American Silver: 20th-Century Design.* Dallas: Dallas Museum of Art, 2005.

Stone, Michael A. *Contemporary American Woodworkers.* Salt Lake City: Gibbs Smith, 1986.

Structure and Ornament: American Modernist Jewelry 1940–1960. Exh. cat. New York: Fifty-50 Gallery, 1984.

Struever, Martha Hopkins. *Loloma: Beauty Is His Name.* Santa Fe, NM: Wheelwright Museum of the American Indian, 2005.

Szarkowski, John, et al. *The Museum of Modern Art at Mid-century.* New York: MoMA, 1994.

Taragin, Davira, Jane Fassett Brite, and Terry Ann R. Neff. *Contemporary Crafts and the Saxe Collection.* New York: Hudson Hills, 1993.

Taragin, Davira S., Edward S. Cooke Jr., and Joseph Giovannini. *Furniture by Wendell Castle.* New York: Hudson Hills Press, 1989.

Taylor, Dianne. "The First Through the Tenth Biennales Internationales des la Tapisserie." PhD diss., Ohio State University, 1983.

Thompson, Jane, and Amanda Lange. *Design Research: The Store that Brought Modern Living to American Homes.* San Francisco: Chronicle Books, 2010.

Thomson, Irene Taviss, "From Conflict to Embedment: The Individual-Society Relationship, 1920–1991." *Sociological Forum* 12 (December 1997): 631–58.

Torbert, Meg, ed. *Design Quarterly,* nos. 45/46, *American Jewelry* (1959): 3–63.

Toshiko Takaezu Retrospective. Exh. cat. New York: American Craft Museum, 1997.

A Tribute to Alma Eikerman Master Craftsman: A Retrospective Exhibition of the Jewelry and Metalsmithing of Alma Eikerman and Forty Indiana University Alumni Metal-Arts. Bloomington, IN: Indiana University Art Museum, 1985.

Troy, Virginia Gardner. *Anni Albers and Ancient American Textiles: From Bauhaus to Black Mountain.* Burlington, VT: Ashgate, 2002.

Turner, Fred. *From Counterculture to Cyberculture: Stewart Brand, The Whole Earth Network, and the Rise of Digital Utopianism.* Chicago: University of Chicago Press, 2006.

Turner, Ralph. *Contemporary Jewelry: A Critical Assessment, 1945–75.* New York: Van Nostrand Reinhold, 1976.

Turner, Robert. *Robert Turner: A Potter's Retrospective.* Milwaukee: Milwaukee Art Museum, 1985.

Untracht, Oppi. *Enameling on Metal.* New York: Greenberg, 1957.

Varney, Carleton. *The Draper Touch.* New York: Simon and Schuster, 1988.

von Neumann, Robert. *The Design and Creation of Jewelry.* 1961. 3rd ed., Radnor, PA: Chilton, 1982.

Wallance, Don. *Shaping America's Products.* New York: Reinhold, 1956.

The Wharton Esherick Museum: Studio and Collection. Paoli, PA: Wharton Esherick Museum, 1977.

Whitaker, Irwin. *Crafts and Craftsmen.* Dubuque, IA: William C. Brown Co., 1967.

Whiting, Cécile. *A Taste for Pop: Pop Art, Gender, and Consumer Culture.* Cambridge, UK, New York, and Melbourne: Cambridge University Press, 1997.

Whyte, William H. Jr. *The Organization Man.* New York: Simon and Schuster, 1956.

Wight, Frederick Stallknecht. *Hans Hofmann.* Berkeley: University of California Press, 1957.

Wildenhain, Marguerite. *The Invisible Core: A Potter's Life and Thoughts.* Palo Alto, CA: Pacific Books, 1973.

———. *Pottery: Form and Expression.* New York: ACC and Reinhold, 1962.

Wilson, Kenneth. "Contemporary American Studio Glassmaking." In *Annales du 4e Congres des Journées Internationales du Verre, Ravenna and Venice, May 1967.* Liege, Belgium: Association Internationale pour l'Histoire de Verre, 1967.

Winebrenner, D. Kenneth. *Jewelry Making as an Art Expression.* Scranton, PA: International Textbook Company, 1953.

Winston, Bob, and Gina Winston. *Cast Away: A Treatise on the Technical Processes and the Aesthetic Development of "Lost Wax" Casting.* Scottsdale, AZ: Shelfhouse Publications, 1970.

Winter, Edward. *Enameling Art on Metals.* New York: Watson-Guptill, 1958.

Woodenworks: Furniture Objects by Five Contemporary Craftsmen—George Nakashima, Sam Maloof, Wharton Esherick, Arthur Espenet Carpenter, Wendell Castle. Washington, DC: Renwick Gallery, National Collection of Fine Arts; St. Paul, MN: Minnesota Museum of Art, 1972.

Wood Turning in North America since 1930. Philadelphia: Wood Turning Center; New Haven, CT: Yale University Art Gallery, 2001.

Wright, Mary Einstein. *Mary and Russel Wright's Guide to Easier Living.* New York: Simon and Schuster, 1951.

Yanagi, Soetsu. *The Unknown Craftsman, A Japanese Insight into Beauty.* 1972. Rev. ed., Tokyo: Kodansha International, Ltd., 1989.

Yoshitake, Mosuke. "The Work of Sculptor Isamu Noguchi." *Industrial Art News* 18 (October 1950): 24–25. Reprint, Bonnie Rychlak et al. *Design: Isamu Noguchi and Isamu Kenmochi,* 134–35. Exh. cat. New York: Five Ties Publishing, Inc., and Isamu Noguchi Foundation and Garden Museum, 2007.

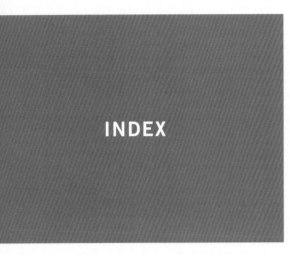

INDEX

NOTE: Exhibition objects are listed in **boldface**; a page number set in *italics* indicates an image; the *n and a number* following a page number indicate an endnote.

* Most individuals listed by profession are in the exhibition and are the subject of biographical entries in the Resource List.

PHOTOGRAPHY CREDITS

ACC: figs. 2.1, 2.4, 2.5, 2.6, 6.2, 6.3, 6.4, 6.5, 6.6, 6.10, 6.21

© Adolph and Esther Gottlieb Foundation/Licensed by VAGA, New York, NY: cat. 192

Anita Shapolsky Gallery, New York: fig. 3.4

Ryusei Arita: fig. 2.5

Art Institute of Chicago: fig. 1.3

© Artists Rights Society (ARS), New York/Pro Litteris, Zurich: cat. 119

© Richard Artschwager/Artists Rights Society (ARS), New York/Photo: Steven Sloman: cat. 41

Peter Basch/Estate of Peter Basch: fig. 6.1

David Behl: cats. 43, 79, 80, 81

Sylvia Bennett: cat. 13

© Bettmann/CORBIS: fig. 3.2

Jon C. Bolton: cat. 19

Braunstein/Quay Gallery: fig. 6.9

Brooklyn Museum/Archives: figs. 2.2, 6.1, 9.5

Robert Bucknam: fig. 8.4

Eduardo Calderon: cat. 180

Karen Block Carrier/Photo: Robert Carrier: cat. 139

Cleveland Museum of Art: cat. 165

Sheldan Comfort Collins: cat. 113

Betty Cooke: fig. 6.11

Corning Museum of Glass: figs. 12.1, 12.2, 12.8; cats. 194, 195, 201, 264

Matthew Cox: cat. 33

Dallas Museum of Art: fig. 9.2; cat. 86

Willis "Bing" Davis: fig. 6.12

© Estate of Alexander Calder/Artists Rights Society, New York: cats. 4, 43, 161, 162

© Estate of Harry Bertoia/Artist Rights Society (ARS), New York: cats. 14, 66, 71

© Estate of Isamu Noguchi/Artists Rights Society (ARS), New York: fig. 11.8; cats. 54, 75

© Estate of Jay DeFeo/Artist Rights Society, New York/Photo: Ben Blackwell: cats. 45, 46

Estate of J.B. Blunk: figs. 11.7, 179

© Estate of Richard Pousette-Dart/Artists Rights Society (ARS), New York: fig. 3.8; cats. 57, 61

© Estate of Robert Arneson/Licensed by VAGA, New York, NY: fig. 8.5, cat. 22

© Estate of Robert Rauschenberg/Licensed by VAGA, New York, NY: fig. 3.3, cat. 58

Everson Museum of Art: cats. 38, 124, 129, 136, 171, 203

M. Lee Fatherree: cats. 37, 47, 53, 91, 94, 95, 123, 202

John Ferrari: cat. 185

Vincent Ferrini: cat. 146

Fine Arts Museums of San Francisco: cats. 109, 138

Paulette T. Frankl: fig. 4.1

George Nakashima Woodworker, S.A: figs. 11.2, 11.6

Laura Gilpin: fig. 8.1

Richard Goodbody: fig. 3.7

Gottlieb Foundation: fig. 12.5, cat. 192

Ted Hallman: cat. 107

Heard Museum: cat. 9

Carolyn A. Hecker: fig. 6.8

Eva Heyd: cats. 29, 72, 100, 101, 102, 105, 111, 114, 128, 135, 137, 145, 147, 174, 177, 184, 200, 205

Barbara Houze/Photo: Wiley Sanderson, University of Georgia: fig. 12.3

© Imogen Cunningham Trust: fig. 7.1

© The Isamu Noguchi Foundation and Garden Museum, New York/Artists Rights Society (ARS), New York: cat. 5

Jewish Museum, New York/Art Resource, NY: fig. 3.7; cats. 108, 143

Yale Joel/Time & Life Pictures/Getty Images: fig. 4.4

© The Josef and Anni Albers Foundation/Artist Rights Society (ARS), New York: cat. 100

Clemens Kalischer: fig. 6.7

Pernille Klemp: figs. 11.4

Laguna Pottery: cat. 85

Patricia Riveron Lee: fig. 10.3

Nina Leen/Time & Life Pictures/Getty Images: figs. 6.10, 12.6

© Lester Beall, Jr. Trust/Licensed by VAGA, New York: cat. 40

Thomas Little: cat. 188

Larry Long: fig. 9.7

Long Beach Museum of Art: figs. 9.8, 9.9; cats. 42, 48, 82, 163

LongHouse Reserve/Photo: Dorothy Levitt Beskind: fig. 6.13

Avery Marriott: cat. 66

Memorial Art Gallery, University of Rochester: cat. 44

Richard Merritt: fig. 8.2

© The Metropolitan Museum of Art/Art Resource, NY: fig. 9.1; cat. 1

Michael Rosenfeld Gallery: cat. 52

Herman Miller: fig. 4.3

John Paul Miller: fig. 9.4

Minnesota Museum of American Art: cats. 12, 125, 126, 150, 151, 152, 158, 167

Monsanto Company: fig. 1.1

Montreal Museum of Fine Arts/Photo: Giles Rivest: fig. 10.6

© Museum Associates/LACMA/Art Resource, NY: fig. 8.8

Museum of Fine Arts, Boston: figs. 2.3, 9.3; cats. 115, 118, 10.1

Museum of Fine Arts, Houston: cat. 30

© The Museum of Modern Art/Licensed by SCALA / Art Resource, New York: figs. 3.3, 7.3, 7.4, 11.5; cat. 58

Joel Philip Myers/Photo: Bent Tilsted: fig. 6.15

Newark Museum of Art: cat. 168

Oakland Museum of California: fig. 11.7; cats. 112, 156

Ohio State Historical Society/Photo: David Barker: cat. 97

Olaf Starorypinski: cat. 107

© Claes Oldenburg, Courtesy PaceWildenstein/Photo: Ellen Page Wilson: cat. 59

Palo Alto Art Center: cat. 47

Todd Partridge: cat. 182

Philadelphia Museum of Art: fig. 7.2; cats. 69, 74, 142

Photographer unknown: figs. 5.2, 6.16, 8.3

Playboy Enterprises: fig. 5.1

© Pollock-Krasner Foundation/Artist Rights Society (ARS), New York: cat. 49

Rago Arts: cats. 10, 189

Louis Reens: fig.6.5

© Renate, Hans & Maria Hofmann Trust: figs. 3.5, 3.6

Richard Marquis Studio: cat. 196

Ruth Chandler Williamson Gallery, Scripps College: cats. 132, 134

S. C. Johnson & Son, Inc.: fig. 11.1; cat. 148

Marianne Schildknecht: cat. 117

Bill Schwob: fig. 6.14

Seagull Portrait Studios: fig.5.3

Seattle Art Museum/Photo: Paul Macapia: fig. 8.5

Kay Sekimachi: fig. 6.17

Paul Smith: figs. 6.18, 6.19

Smithsonian American Art Museum, Washington, DC/ Art Resource, NY: cats. 141, 170

Smithsonian Institution Archives: fig. 8.7

Peter Stackpole/Time & Life Pictures/Getty Images: fig. 4.2

Faith Stern: fig. 1.2

© Ezra Stoller/Esto Photographics: figs. 4.5, 12.4

© Arden Sugarman/Licensed by VAGA, New York, NY: fig. 11.9

Tacoma Art Museum: fig. 10.7; cats. 17, 36, 169, 176

Tate, London/Art Resource, NY: fig. 3.1

John Bigelow Taylor: figs. 10.4, 10.5; cats. 2, 3, 6, 7, 8, 11, 14, 16, 21, 23, 24, 25, 26, 27, 28, 31, 51, 61, 62, 67, 68, 71, 77, 83, 87, 88, 90, 93, 96, 98, 103, 157, 159, 160, 161, 162, 164, 166, 172, 175, 186, 198, 199, 204

© Wayne Thiebaud/Licensed by VAGA, New York, NY: cat. 44

Jerry L. Thompson: cat. 4

Jordan Tinker: fig. 3.5

Glenn Turner: cat. 149

Bastiaan van de Berg: fig. 7.7

Velvet Da Vinci Gallery: cat. 32

Alice von Neuman: fig. 10.2

Walker Art Center: fig. 11.9

Ed Watkins: figs. 7.5, 7.6, 8.6; cats. 15, 18, 22, 34, 35,
39, 50, 55, 56, 63, 64, 65, 70, 76, 78, 84, 89, 92,
104, 106, 110, 116, 120, 122, 127, 130, 131, 133,
154, 173, 178, 181, 183, 190, 193, 197

Wendell Castle Studio: cat. 99

Dylan Western: cat. 20

Whitney Museum of American Art, New York/The Pace
Gallery/Photo: Jerry L. Thompson: cat. 60

Leslie Williamson: cat. 179

Charles Withers: fig. 2.7

Jill A. Wittse and H. Kirk Brown III: cat. 73

Wood Turning Center Research Library/Photo: John Carlano:
cat. 191

Lynette Mager Wynn: cats. 10, 189

Yale University Art Gallery: fig. 11.3; cats. 140, 144,
155, 187

Yale University Library, Manuscripts and Archives:
figs. 4.6, 4.7

Jack Zilker: fig. 9.6

FOR THE MUSEUM OF ARTS AND DESIGN

GENERAL EDITOR AND CURATOR: Jeannine Falino

FOR ABRAMS, NEW YORK

EDITOR: Andrea Danese

DESIGNER: Sarah Gifford

PRODUCTION MANAGER: Jules Thomson

LIBRARY OF CONGRESS CATALOGING-IN-PUBLICATION DATA
Crafting modernism : midcentury American art and design / Jeannine Falino,
general editor ; Jeannine Falino & Jennifer Scanlan, curators ; with essays
by Glenn Adamson ... [et al.].
   p. cm.
 Includes bibliographical references and index.
 ISBN 978-0-8109-8480-6
1. Decorative arts—United States—History—20th century. 2. Modernism (Aesthetics)—United
States—History—20th century. I. Falino, Jeannine J. II. Scanlan, Jennifer. III. Adamson, Glenn.
IV. Title: Midcentury American art and design.
 NK808.C72 2011
745.0973'09045—dc22
                         2011009558

Paperback ISBN: 978-1-4197-0099-6

Printed and bound in China
10 9 8 7 6 5 4 3 2 1

Abrams books are available at special discounts when purchased in quantity for premiums
and promotions as well as fundraising or educational use. Special editions can also be created
to specification. For details, contact specialsales@abramsbooks.com or the address below.

ABRAMS
THE ART OF BOOKS SINCE 1949

115 West 18th Street
New York, NY 10011
www.abramsbooks.com

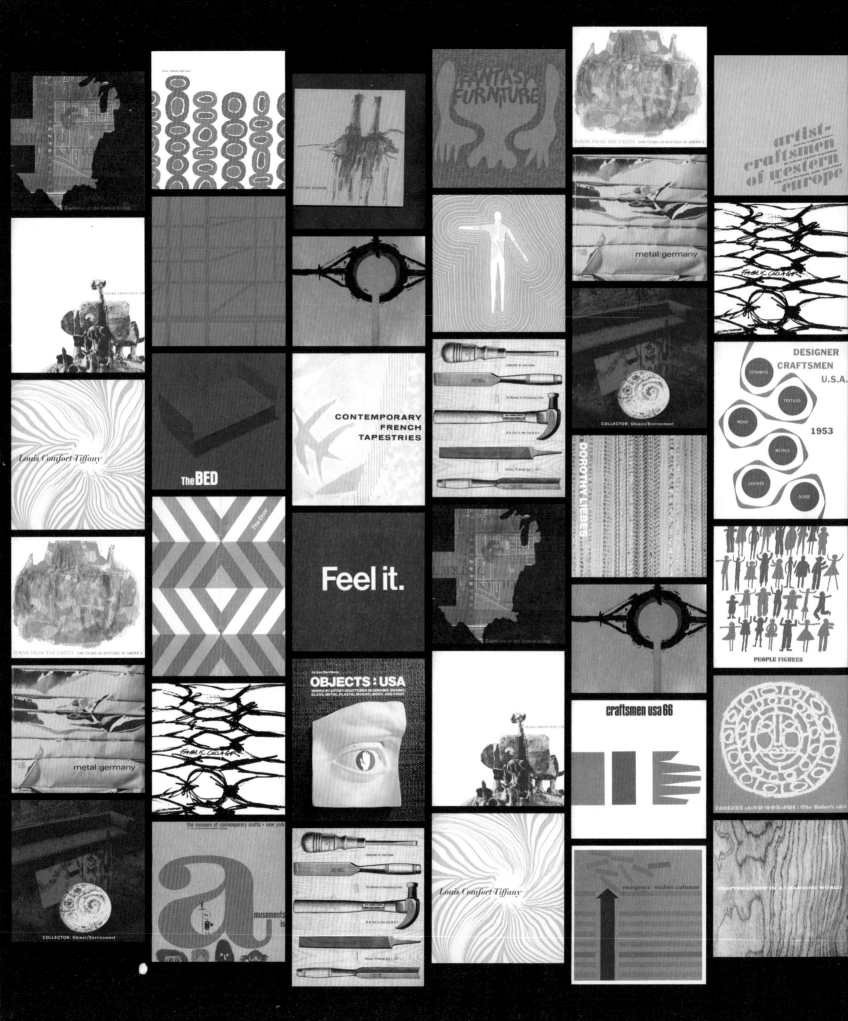